About the Author

Mark Lee Levine is a member of the Denver, Colorado and American Bar Associations. He has been admitted to practice in the Colorado, Federal District, Circuit, Tax and United States Supreme Courts. He is a graduate of New York University Tax Law School (LLM); University of Denver Law School (JD); Northwestern University, Graduate Division, Graduate School of Management (P.A.P.), University of Colorado, G.R.I.; Colorado State University with a BS degree in Business and Economics, *Magna cum laude*. He is presently in private law practice as President and Chairman of Levine and Pitler, P.C.

Dr. Levine is a Professor at the University of Denver. He is a frequent lecturer for the American Institute of CPAs, Realtors®, Realtors® National Marketing Institute, Real Estate Securities and Syndications Institute, and other groups on topics in real estate, law, investment, appraisal and tax, throughout the United States.

He has had numerous articles published in *Legal Economics News, Journal of Taxation, The Practical Lawyer,* and *Real Estate Securities and Syndications Institute Review*. He has eight books published in the areas of real estate, tax, business and law. Dr. Levine is certified in numerous areas, *e.g.,* Certified Commercial Investment Member and Certified Real Estate Securities Sponsor.

Real Estate Tax Shelter Desk Book

SECOND EDITION

*Adapted from the first edition
by the IBP Research and Editorial Staff.
Revised second edition by*
DR. MARK LEE LEVINE

*Institute for Business Planning, Inc.
IBP Plaza, Englewood Cliffs, N.J. 07632*

This publication is designed to provide accurate and authoritative information in regard to the subject matter covered. It is sold with the understanding that the publisher is not engaged in rendering legal, accounting, or other professional service. If legal advice or other expert assistance is required, the services of a competent professional person should be sought.

— From a Declaration of Principles jointly adopted by a Committee of the American Bar Association and a Committee of Publishers and Associations.

Library of Congress
Catalog Card No. 77-90141

Printed in the United States of America

ISBN 0-87624-502-5

What This Desk Book Will Do For You

It is no secret that real estate offers a unique package of tax benefits. It is also no secret that the Tax Reform Act of 1976 (TRA 1976) and the 1977 Tax Reduction and Simplification Act (TRSA) have made dramatic changes in our real estate tax laws. If you are going to make substantial earnings in real estate, you have got to keep up with those changes so that you know how they open new avenues for investment benefits or limit such benefits. You must have a thorough, up-to-date working knowledge of our tax laws to maximize your after-tax real estate profits. This Desk Book shows you how to do it.

To this end, this Desk Book brings together a full range of tax techniques used by the most sophisticated real estate people operating today. By using the concepts discussed in this book, you can increase your current income and build future real estate income and capital.

Whether you are a real estate investor, dealer, broker, salesperson, developer, builder or mortgage lender, one thing is certain: A thorough understanding of the tax angles is a major key to big money in real estate. No matter what your connection with real estate — as a professional advisor, attorney, Realtor or accountant — this Desk Book provides you with a handy guide to all the moves open to increase your after-tax profits from real estate. By using it, you have access to tested tax-saving techniques used by individuals who have built fortunes in real estate — techniques successfully used in the real estate world of the 1970s and under the present tax laws.

The reader will find this new second edition invaluable in spelling out the complex provisions in the law, as well as identifying specific areas which need to be closely examined.

Keep this handy book on your desk so that you have quick and easy access to it as a checklist of avenues to explore, as an idea tickler and as a quick refresher. Remember that you are operating in a rapidly changing world and that the latest developments should be checked before you make any final decisions.

Preface

Following the concepts established in the first edition, this second edition has been updated and expanded to allow for substantial changes that occurred in the Real Estate Tax Field. I have covered new legislation, the most important of which are the Tax Reform Act of 1976 and the 1977 Tax Reduction and Simplification Act (TRSA), along with new cases and other materials.

For example, the new Law includes a provision that should be a great boon to the real estate industry. It generally provides that investors in certain shelters are limited to deducting no more than their actual ("At risk") investment. Although certain kinds of farming shelters, movies, oil and gas and others come within the ambit of this provision, real estate investments do not. The result should be a shifting of investments from other tax shelters to real estate.

Accordingly, this edition has been expanded to provide new planning concepts which may be helpful for many users of this book, including real estate practitioners, investors, students and of course such professionals as attorneys and accountants. It is also hoped that the nature and organization of this book allows both the beginner and the advanced real estate tax planner to employ the attributes of this book.

Many attorneys, and most businessmen have not formally studied the Internal Revenue Code and therefore, may find it difficult to apply its provisions. Hopefully, use of this book will put the Code into perspective and allow the busy attorney and businessman to relate its provisions, quickly and easily, to any given case.

The nature of this subject is such that it often invites discussion and disagreement by many users. This proves helpful for new additions. With this in mind, I welcome comments and suggestions of the reader and encourage you to let me know what changes we might make in the future to enhance the application and use of this book.

This text has been updated for the TRSA of 1977, but it does not include all 1977 Cases, Rulings and Procedures pertinent to real estate tax.

Acknowledgments

Having written a number of other books, it becomes more and more evident that no book, at least by me, could be published without the strong support of so many people.

In this instance, as mentioned earlier, the book was issued in 1975 through the Institute for Business Planning research and editorial staff. I am grateful for the foundation for this book from this staff and the authors who work with the Institute for Business Planning staff.

Along with the support of the Institute for Business Planning, especially that of Ms. Olivia Goldenberg, I acknowledge and extend my warmest thanks to those who supported the work. They include, but are certainly not limited to, my law partners, my associates and colleagues at the University of Denver, College of Business Administration, and many secretaries in our office, and our law clerk, Mark Rubin. One of our tax lawyers, Mike Scena, deserves particular thanks for the tedious job of citation work and of backup.

As has been true in the past, the greatest support for this book, and all others I have written, has come from my wife Ellen. She has become accustomed to spending many days and nights with me, reviewing, proofing, typing, and reorganizing this material. Many possible fun weekends of travel and relaxation were relinquished in favor of this work. Her help, aid and support are clearly the reason for this book. Many thanks.

To those whom I have not listed by name, I have certainly not forgotten. So many people aid the production of any book; it is only fair to at least acknowledge that it would not be in existence without their help.

MARK LEE LEVINE

Denver, Colorado

Highlights of the 1977 Tax Reduction and Simplification Act

The 1977 Tax Reduction and Simplification Act (TRSA) was executed by the President on May 23, 1977. It is known as Public Law 95-30. The intent herein is to highlight some of the items under the TRSA that affect the real estate tax field. Keep in mind that is merely an overview or highlight of this Act. The Act, itself, should be reviewed.

STANDARD DEDUCTION

The standard deduction has been a very important item with regard to the determination by taxpayers as to whether it makes sense to itemize, that is, list specifically, each non-business expense item or whether it makes sense to merely take a standard amount allowed by statute. There have been a great number of problems by the IRS in policing itemized deductions. For example, there is the problem of determining the use of an office in the home and whether it qualifies as a business use. There have been problems with regard to calculating and overseeing sales tax, charitable deductions, medical expenses, interest and taxes on the personal home, sales tax on other items of a special nature, and many other factors which are important in the calculation of itemized deductions. The thought was that many of these items are justifiably deductible. This is the reason for the itemized deductions and the allowance of these items under various Code Sections as explained in the text. However, this also leads to additional policing problems, as mentioned. The employment of the standard deduction can alleviate some of this burden. The practical problem in the past has been that the standard deduction in many instances has been too low, thereby encouraging taxpayers to itemize their deductions as opposed to using minimum standard level deduction.

The 1977 TRSA attempts to rectify this problem by providing for a higher standard deduction and a minimum-level standard deduction. That is, before this change by the TRSA, the standard deduction was 16 percent of adjusted gross income, having a minimum standard deduction of $1,700.00 for a single person or $2,100.00 for a joint return.

Under the TRSA, the standard deduction will allow a *flat* standard deduction of $2,200.00 for a single person and for a person who is the head of a household. Thirty-two hundred ($3,200.00) is allowed for married persons filing joint returns and $1,600.00 is allowed for a married person who files a separate return. The important point is that the flat standard deduction is allowed no matter what the adjusted gross income might be. That is, rather than taking a percentage, such as 16 percent of the adjusted gross income, and treating this as the standard deduction amount, with also a minimum allowance being provided, the new position under the TRSA provides for the flat standard deduction as mentioned. A taxpayer will receive these amounts in any event, under most circumstances. Therefore, taxpayers need not be concerned with attempting to work out a percentage calculation against adjusted gross income. In summary, it would not be an advantage for a taxpayer who could show more itemized deductions, but by raising the minimum or a flat standard deduction amount, building the same into the tax tables, many taxpayers will find it advantageous to avoid the calculation of the itemized deduction amount. Obviously each taxpayer must judge his own circumstances to determine if the itemized deductions will exceed the flat standard deduction which is built into the tables.

As a practical matter, since the flat standard deduction is now built into the tables, the new concept will result in taking the total itemized deductions, such as $5,000.00, and subtracting the flat itemized deduction allowed by law, such as $3,200.00 for a married couple filing jointly. Thus, it would be the $1,800.00, which is the excess of the itemized deductions over the flat standard deduction which would be deducted. This new method of calculation is necessary because, once again, the tables build in the calculation of the $3,200.00 amount in the example given.

WITHHOLDING ADJUSTMENTS AND THE STANDARD DEDUCTION

As a result of the changes under the standard deduction, the Government has changed the withholding rates to reflect the minimum or flat standard deduction for wages.

Filing of tax returns will also be changed as result of the standard deduction. That is, a tax return will be due when income reaches $2,950.00 for a single person. A head of household also follows the same filing rule as a single person. With regard to a married couple filing a joint return, they will be required to file if their income is $4,700.00 or more. (Keep in mind that although the filing requirements mentioned indicated a dollar level, these are subject to some variance with regard to the nature of the income and also of course unusual circumstances, such as filing a return to obtain a refund of taxes that have been withheld from the income of the taxpayer). These new tax reporting requirements will be applicable for 1977.

CORPORATE TAX RATES

Under the 1977 TRSA, the corporate tax rates which were in effect for the last few years will be extended. That is, the 1975 Tax Reduction Act provided for a surtax exemption with regard to the first $50,000.00 of income. The first $25,000.00 is taxed at 20 percent and the next $25,000.00 of corporate income is taxed at 22 percent, with all the excess over $50,000.00 being taxed at 48 percent. These rates were extended and have been re-extended by the TRSA of 1977.

JOB TAX CREDIT

One of the more important changes by the TRSA of 1977 is the creation of a new job tax credit. Under this new rule employers can claim an income tax credit almost equal to what amounts to 50 percent of the Federal Unemployment Tax Act wage base, which is $4,200.00. This credit deals with that base, times 50 percent, with regard to additional employees who are added in 1977 and 1978. Technically, the credit is 50 percent of the increase in the employer's wage base under the Federal Unemployment Tax Act amount, over 102 percent of the FUTA wage base for the previous year.

However, the credit is somewhat reduced in importance because the employer's *deduction* under Code Section 162 for salary expense is reduced by the amount of the *credit*. This is true even if the credit is not used. Therefore, the maximum effective credit for each new employee results in $2,100.00 if we assume that 50 percent of $4,200.00 is the applicable amount, and then adjust it as noted. That is, $2,100.00 would be the maximum. This benefit from the credit is reduced by the effective tax rate of the employer in question. If the maximum tax rate in effect was 48 percent, then the loss of the deduction of $2,100.00 times 48 percent indicates the effective loss in the benefit of the *deduction*.

The credit is restricted by the number of other items, such as a limitation with regard to rapidly expanding businesses and overall limitations. The overall limitation provides that the credit cannot exceed 50 percent of the increase in total wages paid by the employer for the year in question over 105 percent of total wages paid by the employer in the prior year.

There is also a limitation with regard to a maximum credit of $100,000.00, exclusive of carrybacks and carryovers for the given year in question. The credit is also limited to a maximum of the taxpayer's tax liability for the year in question.

The credit applies to tax years beginning in 1977 and 1978. There are certain excluded employees, such as those who do not perform a majority part of their work in the United States. Employees in certain government organizations are also excluded.

Credit which is available but which cannot be used because of the taxpayer's position, that is, having no additional tax liability, can be carried back three years and forward seven.

WORK CREDIT FOR HANDICAPPED EMPLOYEES

In addition to the general credit for new employees, the TRSA also allows for a credit of 10 percent of the first $4,200.00 of Federal Unemployment Tax Act wages paid where the wages are incurred with regard to hiring new handicapped employees who are under certain vocational rehabilitation programs.

The credit only affects a *one*-year period and it is based on $4,200.00 of FUTA wage base for 1977 *or* 1978.

There are maximum amounts of credit. For example, the credit cannot exceed one-fifth of the regular 50 percent new job credit, as discussed earlier.

SICK PAY

Under the 1976 Tax Reform Act, the sick pay exclusion provided for in the Code was repealed for years beginning in 1976. However, the TRSA of 1977 delayed the effective date of the sick pay exclusion repeal until tax years beginning in 1977.

CHARITABLE CONTRIBUTIONS WITH REGARD
TO CONSERVATION EASEMENTS

Under the 1977 TRSA, the previous rule of allowing deductions for charitable contributions of remainder interests in real property has been extended through June 13, 1981. However, the deductions which are allowed for the charitable contributions are only allowed with regard to contributions that result in an exclusive use for conservation purposes of leases, options, and easements with respect to real property. Further, this rule only applies if the lease in question, the option, or the easement is perpetual in nature.

Contents

(Referenced by Paragraph Number)

CHAPTER 3

Tax Benefits for Homeowners, Condominium Unit Owners, and Cooperative Tenant-Stockholders

CHAPTER 4

Tax Benefits of Real Estate Depreciation

CHAPTER **5**

Casualty Loss Tax Deduction

CHAPTER 6
How Real Estate Sales are Taxed

CHAPTER 7
Taking Real Estate Profits
at Favorable Capital Gains Tax Rates

CHAPTER 8
Tax Credits

CHAPTER **9**
Involuntary Conversions

CHAPTER **10**
Tax-Free Real Estate Exchanges of Business or Investment Real Estate

CHAPTER **11**
Deferring Tax on Sales

CHAPTER **12**

Tax Consequences of Individual, Joint, and Partnership Ownership of Real Estate

CHAPTER **13**

Tax Treatment of
Real Estate Investment Trusts

CHAPTER **14**

Corporations

CHAPTER **15**

Subchapter S Corporations

CHAPTER **16**

Collapsible Corporations

CHAPTER **17**

Tax Angles in Leasing

CHAPTER **18**
Tax and Economic
Benefits of Sale-Leasebacks

CHAPTER **19**
Tax Considerations
in Foreclosing Mortgages

CHAPTER **20**

Tax, Financing, and Leverage in Real Estate

CHAPTER **21**

Tax Techniques for Owners of Undeveloped Land and Land Developers

CHAPTER **22**
Tax-Shelter in
Farms and Farmland

Appendix

(Referenced by Paragraph Number)

**For a further and more detailed treatment of specific items in which you may be interested, and forms which can be utilized to implement the ideas contained in the desk book, you may wish to refer to the following IBP Services:
>
> Real Estate Investment Planning, Volume I and II
> Tax Planning, Volume I and II
> Tax Sheltered Investments

CHAPTER 1

Tax Know-How — A Principal Key to Big Profits in Real Estate

[¶101]   **TAX BENEFITS FROM REAL ESTATE**

Tax matters have been very important in the real estate field, as in many other fields. Decisions to buy, sell, lease, transfer, or otherwise deal with property are often controlled by the tax ramifications.

The ramifications can easily be seen in the figures by the Chamber of Commerce. It stated that the average American would seem to have earned enough money by May 10 of a given year to pay Federal income taxes for that year! He or she works through May of every calender year simply to pay taxes. Thus, a taxpayer works 2 hours and 51 minutes of each day simply to pay Federal income taxes.

In many instances it would not be wise to invest, especially in the real estate field, when looking simply to straight dollar-and-cent considerations. When the dollar-and-cent considerations, economically, are modified by income tax considerations which can save taxes, the investment may look more favorable. (A real estate investment should not be made *simply* for tax considerations).

If $4,000 worth of tax loss can be generated by a property, and the taxpayer would otherwise have to pay tax at a marginal rate of 25%, meaning 25¢ of each dollar goes to taxes, the taxpayer would save $1,000 worth of tax. Tax savings might exist even though there is no *economic* loss; this may result from depreciation. For example, if a property grossed $20,000 and expenses constitutes $20,000, it may appear that there is a break-even. However, if the expense figure does not include depreciation and depreciation is $3,000, the $3,000 produces a tax loss. But, it did not cause a *cash* loss. It is a bookkeeping entry to adjust for the apparent decline in value of the property. It is treated as an expense for tax purposes. The $3,000 worth of depreciation can offset other income, such as dividends earned by the taxpayer.

You must also consider *cash generated* from the property. *Cash flow* would mean the excess of the cash-in over the cash-out. Tax benefits may be substantial, but there may not be sufficient cash flow from the property! Principal payments are not deductible for tax purposes; therefore, monies which are used to reduce amounts owing on a loan (excluding interest) would not be deductible.

The term "tax shelter" is often used to depict a case where there may be an additional amount of deduction in excess of that which caused a cash drain. For example, if property generates $20,000 worth of gross income, and the expense deductions are $22,000, $20,000 caused by "actual" expenses, and $2,000 more caused by depreciation, this $2,000 would cause an additional deduction on the return.

If the taxpayer was in the marginal 25 percent bracket, meaning that 25ᶜ on each new dollar of income is paid for Federal taxes, this would produce $500 worth of tax savings. Effectively, the $2,000 "sheltered" or protected $2,000 worth of other income. This sheltering caused the $500 to be saved which would otherwise be paid in taxes. This $500 might only be saved temporarily, or it may produce a permanent saving. This point is discussed later in the book.

"INVESTMENTS IN REAL ESTATE AS OPPOSED TO OTHER INVESTMENTS

Investments have their own advantages and disadvantages. It is clear that the benefits from real estate, assuming the real estate in question is a reasonable investment, can far outweigh, at least from the tax standpoint, most other types of investments.

One may utilize real estate to postpone the payment of taxes and therefore have the use of the money today, which saves and produces a time value (use) of benefit of money. Real estate may eliminate taxation altogether, such as income on certain types of property which may be excludable. An example of this is the sale of a home by a person who is 65 years of age or older and otherwise qualifies under the Internal Revenue Code (see ¶ 305). Under this rule, part or all of the gain from the sale of a principal residence may not be subject to tax.

Tax rates are progressive in the sense that the more income that is taxable the more tax that is paid, not proportionately, but a greater percentage or rate. Real estate can allow some ease to smooth the tax bracket so that the income reported may be spread over many years.

The *character* of gain or loss is very important. If you can produce long-term capital gain it may be taxed on only half of the amount. A sale of real estate with a $40,000 gain, assuming it is a long-term capital gain, will normally produce a tax on only half the amount.

Real estate results in the potential of producing many *deductions,* such as depreciation, management fee, interest, expense, taxes, insurance and other items with regard to investment property used in the trade or business.

Real estate also has the advantage of producing tax *credits,* such as investment credits. This is where an investor may receive a credit against tax for investments in tangible personal property for investments or use in business.

This comparison does not mean that other investments do not also have some of the benefits noted, but real estate normally will produce a greater amount of these benefits with a lesser amount of risk. Real estate offers an opportunity for the *average* person to enter the field.

There can also be other ways of postponing taxes, such as the use of *tax-free exchanges,* where the tax law allows investment property of like-kind property (normally real estate for real estate or personal property for personal property) to be exchanged tax-free for other "like-type" property. One might exchange an apartment house for another apartment house, or an apartment house for an unimproved parking lot.

The following illustrates the main benefits of investing in real estate:

☐ (1) *Depreciation Deductions.* A real estate investor shelters income by depreciation deductions. These deductions can produce a tax-free cash flow (Sec. 167 of the Code) by the tax savings. For example, a $2,000 depreciation deduction saves a 30 percent marginal tax rate taxpayer $600 (30 percent × $2,000 = $600).

☐ (2) *Tax-Free Exchanges.* A real estate investor can change-exchange property by way of tax-free exchanges of properties. In this way, he benefits from the appreciation in value of his property without creating an immediate tax liability [Sec. 1031 of the Code].

☐ (3) *Tax-Deductible Carrying Charges.* You can get the tax benefits of deducting or capitalizing qualified carrying charges. [Sec. 266 of the Code].

☐ (4) *Tax-Free Improvements.* A real estate investor benefits from the improvements made by his tenants, but he generally pays no income tax on these additions to the value of his properties at the time they are made. They add to his taxable gain when he finally sells the property if it produces more gain.

☐ (5) *Flexibility.* Real Estate can be purchased or rented, sold or leased, with different tax results. Real estate can be divided into different types of fees, leasehold and mortgage investments, each tailored to the tax position of its owner.

☐ (6) *Deductibility of Losses.* When property used in the trade or business is sold at a loss, the loss *may* be fully deductible [Sec. 1231 and 165 of the Code].

☐ (7) *Capital Gain Opportunities*. When property used in the trade or business is sold at a profit, part or all of the gain may qualify for a favorable capital gain treatment.

☐ (8) *Rent Deductions*. When business property is leased, the cost of occupancy can be charged off fully.

☐ (9) *Favorable Tax Treatment of Security Deposit*. A properly arranged security deposit is not taxed.

☐ (10) *Tax Advantages of Highly Leveraged Situations*. Ownership can be financed in a way that gives the owner depreciation on the mortgagee's investment, thus increasing the owner's equity with tax-free funds [Sec. 167 of the Code].

☐ (11) *Tax Advantages of Sale-Leasebacks*. The cost of the land can be made tax deductible by a sale followed by a leaseback for a long period. The investment in the building is recovered tax free through depreciation deductions [Sec. 167 of the Code].

☐ (12) *Interest and Tax Deductions*. The owner can elect to deduct or capitalize interest and taxes paid to carry unimproved property [Sec. 266 of the Code].

☐ (13) *Tax Deductible Repairs*. The owner can sometimes build up the value of his holdings by tax-deductible repair expenditures [Sec. 162 of the Code].

☐ (14) *Tax Savings from Choosing Best Form of Ownership*. Ownership can be held in whatever entity — partnership, corporation, trust, or personal ownership — will best protect the income from tax. When held in corporate ownership, income can accumulate at lower tax rates than might apply if personally owned. The tax savings can be applied to build up equity and future capital gain by improving the property and paying off mortgages.

☐ (15) *Opportunities for Postponing Taxable Gain*. Tax on the sale of real estate may be postponed by electing the installment method of sale, a deferred-payment sale, or by using option agreements, executory contracts, conditional contracts, lease with purchase options, escrow arrangements, and contingent price arrangements. When selling a portion of the land, retaining some rights (i.e., oil and mineral rights) may convert a sale into an easement so that the proceeds will go to reduce your basis rather than be a gain [Sec. 453, etc. of the Code].

☐ (16) *Flexibility as to Taxable Gain*. Even after an installment sale, we may be able to change our minds and have the gain taxed earlier, if that should prove to be desirable, by disposing of the installment obligations [Sec. 453(d) of the Code].

☐ (17) *Tax-Free Cash*. On the sale of real estate, there are methods of getting cash in advance, yet deferring the taxability of gain. One way is by borrowing on the installment obligations obtained on an installment sale of real estate, giving the installment notes as collateral.

☐ (18) *Opportunities to Avoid Personal Holding Company Penalty*. Rental income may be used to take a company out of the personal holding company category and thus avoid penalty tax.

☐ (19) *Capital Gain Opportunities from Leases:*. Leases can be cancelled for money which is taxed at capital gain rates.

☐ (20) *Tax-Free Treatment of Condemnation Awards*. Condemnation awards can be received without tax if reinvested in real estate.

☐ (21) *Tax-Free Sale of Home*. A residence can be sold without capital gain tax if the proceeds are used to buy or build a new residence.

[¶102]   REAL ESTATE INVESTMENTS CAN PRODUCE GREATER RETURNS THAN OTHER INVESTMENTS

Real estate is the greatest money maker of all forms of investments. Possibly no other form of investment offers greater opportunities for profit, capital growth, and tax shelter:

A sound real estate investment aids the investor in weathering economic cycles. An investment in good real estate that is well located provides a hedge against inflation. Real estate can be arguably a liquid investment, since good improved real estate is acceptable security for a mortgage loan. The management required need not be burdensome; the skills of certified property managers may be available, and their cost can be deducted against income.

Real estate is unique in its ability to compensate for decreases in the purchasing power of the dollar. Tax escalator clauses in leases keep investors on top of fluctuating dollar values. Despite depreciation, increased costs of construction add new dollar values. Improvements and increased land values also help. These values, coupled with increased personal and business incomes, can justify almost immediate adjustments in new cash flow commensurate with changing money markets and the general economy.

[¶103] REAL ESTATE VALUES, SALE PRICES, AND TAX FACTORS

How are values and sales prices modified by tax planning or by considerations arising out of the impact of taxes on buyer and seller? Writing in the *Appraisal Journal* some time ago, accountants Charles Considine and John O'Bryan analyzed what they called the appraiser's dilemma, which is the appraiser's problem in determining whether he is dealing with fair market value or a controlled income tax value in considering comparative sales prices.

Here are some examples of why you cannot always judge whether the price of real estate is "high" or "low" until you take into account certain tax considerations:

☐ (1) *Sale at Loss to Offset High Income.* An individual's earnings for the year would be $190,000. However, he had reinvested most of these earnings in his business and did not have the cash with which to pay his income taxes. He personally owned the office building that housed his firm, having purchased it many years previously for $160,000. He thought it was worth its tax basis of $80,000; but when a real estate broker brought him an offer of $50,000, he sold at that figure even though he felt he might get $80,000 by holding off for a while. He felt that the opportunity to relieve his cash situation and also reduce his income by the tax loss would offset the prospect of getting an additional $30,000 at some future time.

☐ (2) *Lowering Price in Return for Purchase of Stock.* Builder B wanted to sell his apartment house to investor C in order to get the equity money with which to launch a larger project. B thought the property was worth a million dollars, at which price he would have had to pay a capital gains tax of $100,000. C's real estate advisor thought that C should be able to get the property for $800,000. The trade was made at the lower figure after C agreed to put up $150,000 in cash to acquire stock in the corporation in which B intended to undertake his new project. The sale of stock in the new corporation and the $50,000 tax saving resulting from the reduced sale price brought B the capital he needed without capital gains tax. What's more he had just as much cash as he would have had if he had obtained his asking price. In addition, C had an extra kicker by way of a participation in B's big new project.

☐ (3) *Use of Higher Estate Tax Valuation for Higher Depreciation.* A movie actress inherited an apartment building from her grandmother. She thought that the building was worth about $60,000. The inheritance tax appraiser took the position that the building was worth $90,000. The higher figure was accepted after the movie actress was told by her advisors that the depreciation on a $90,000 valuation would be worth more to her in income tax savings than the small estate tax which would be payable on the difference between the $60,000 exemption and the $90,000 valuation. (Tax rules under the *Tax Reform Act of 1976* would now also be a factor, as the basis may not step up.)

☐ (4) *Exchange for Heavily Financed Property.* The party "trading up" to a more heavily financed property is treated, in effect, as if he paid cash for the excess amount of debt, and so his basis is increased by that amount.

Take the case of an individual who owns a building that has a basis of $16,000. There is no mortgage on the property, and it has risen in value to

$150,000. He trades up for an apartment house valued at $450,000 which is subject to a mortgage of $300,000. Now he has a total basis for the new property of $316,000 (his original basis plus the amount of new debt). If 80 percent of the value is allocated to the building, his basis for depreciation is about $250,000, as compared to his original $16,000 basis. Yet he did not have to pay any tax on the exchange.

☐ (5) *Long-Term Lease Better Than Sale.* Jones owned an office building which he had held for some time and which had been substantially depreciated. He was offered $500,000 for the building but rejected the offer when he found how much he would have to pay in tax. The offer was made by a well-rated, listed corporation which wanted the building. Mr. Jones accepted a long-term lease commitment from this corporation instead and on the basis of the lease he was able to get tax-free cash by mortgaging the building with the assurance that the rentals coming in over a period of time would pay back the money.

[¶104] ACCOUNTING METHODS AND TAX SAVINGS

The method of tax accounting which you use can create substantial tax savings and help retain funds for use in the business. The Appendix at the end of the book summarizes the various tax accounting methods and capsulizes their advantages and disadvantages. You can change your overall method of accounting from the cash receipts and disbursements method to an accrual method. To obtain the Commissioner's consent, you file an application within 180 days from the beginning of the taxable year for which you want to make the change [Reg. §1.4446-1(e)(3)(i)]. A request filed within nine months after the beginning of the taxable year for which the change is requested may be considered timely if good cause is shown [*Rev. Proc. 70-27,* CB 1970-2, 509]. However, any change will be reviewed for possible tax avoidance or evasion.

CHAPTER 2

How to Determine Real Estate Costs

PART A: TAX TREATMENT

[¶201]   **ACQUISITION
                       AND OPERATING COSTS**

The costs of acquiring and operating property are subject to differing tax treatment. The buyer-operator will be concerned with whether certain expenses incurred are currently deductible or whether they must be capitalized.

[¶202]   **REAL PROPERTY TAXES**

Taxes levied against real property are a primary source of government revenue in every American community. Once levied against real estate, taxes usually become a lien and may be enforced by the sale of the property or some interest in it. A determination of the tax burden which a piece of real estate will have to carry is a primary element in determining its desirability for acquisition and its value. Since real property tax rates vary from year to year and assessing practices may be changed from time to time, the tax burden which a parcel of real estate will be required to carry in the future can only be an estimate.

To arrive at a tax rate a local government usually takes these steps: (1) It sets a budget (the amount of money it will have to raise), (2) determines the total valuation of taxable property within its confines, and (3) arrives at the tax rate by dividing the amount to be raised by taxation by the total assessed valuation. The tax rate applied to the value of a particular parcel of real estate as determined by assessment gives the amount of taxes which will be charged to it. Thus, we see that the budget or, over the long term, whether local government is economical or extravagant will determine the real estate tax burden. Whether a particular piece of real estate carries a fair share of that burden will depend on how it is valued by the assessing authorities.

[¶203]   DEDUCTIONS: WHEN TO TAKE DEDUCTIONS; ACCRUING REAL PROPERTY TAXES

If you sell or buy property, you will have to know not only what to deduct but when to deduct property taxes. If you are on the accrual basis and you are either buying or selling a parcel of real estate, the following rules apply: (1) If the other party to the transaction (buyer or seller) held the property when the tax became a lien or the other party became personally liable, your share of the deduction accrues on the date of the sale. (2) If not, the general rule applies and the deduction accrues on the lien date [Sec. 164 of the Code].

If you are on the cash basis the following rules apply:

1. If the other party to the transaction (buyer or seller) held the property when the tax became a lien or the other party became personally liable, it is assumed that your share of the tax was paid on the date of sale (regardless of when actually paid).
2. If not, the general rule applies and you deduct your share of the tax when actually paid [Sec. 164 of the Code].

Example: In White County the real property tax year is the calendar year. The real property tax is a personal liability of the property owner on June 30 of the current year but is not payable until February 28 of the following year. Doe, a cash-basis taxpayer who had owned property in White County on January 1, sells to Roe on May 30. Roe retains ownership for the balance of the year. A tax equal to 149/365 or January 1 to May 29 is imposed on Doe and is considered paid on the date of sale. Doe may deduct in the year the sale occurs or the year he actually pays. Roe is charged a tax equal to 216/365 for May 30 to December 31. He may deduct in the tax year when he actually pays the tax.

Example: In Brown County the real property tax year is the calendar year. The real property tax becomes a lien on January 1 and is payable on April 30. It is not treated as a personal liability of the owner. Smith, a cash-basis taxpayer, is the owner of the property on January 1 and pays the tax on April 30. On May 1 Smith sells the property to Jones who retains it until September 1 when he sells to Brown. Smith pays a real property tax equal to 120/365 or January 1 to April 30. He may deduct only in the year the tax was actually paid. Jones pays to the extent of 123/365 or May 1 until August 31 and is considered to have paid on the date of sale. He may deduct in the year of sale or the year when actually paid. Brown pays to the extent of 122/365 or September 1 to December 31. He is also considered to have paid on the date of sale and can deduct in the year of sale or in the taxable year when the tax is actually paid.

Example: In Green County the real property tax year is the calendar year. The tax becomes a lien on June 30 and is payable on September 1. Lake, who is on the cash basis and owned the real property on January 1, sells it to Rivers on July 15. The tax is imposed on Lake to the extent of 195/365 or January 1 to July 14. He may deduct in his taxable year when the sale occurs or when the tax is actually paid. Rivers pays to the extent of 170/365 or July 15 to December 31. He may also deduct in his taxable year when the sale occurs or when he actually pays the tax.

[¶204]   LOCAL BENEFIT TAXES

Special Assessments: No deduction is allowed for taxes specially assessed against local benefits if they tend to increase the value of the property assessed [Sec. 164(c)]. These taxes can be added to the cost of the property. There are two important exceptions to the rule of nondeductibility in this area:

1. You can deduct the part of the tax which goes toward maintenance and interest charges with respect to the benefit. But you, the taxpayer, must show the allocation.
2. Taxes levied by a special taxing district are deductible. However, the special district must generally cover the whole of at least one county and usually at least 1,000 people must be subject to the taxes levied by that district. Also, to get the deduction, the district must normally levy its assessments annually at a uniform rate on the same assessed value of real estate as is used for purposes of the real property tax generally.

Where both nondeductible special assessments and deductible general taxes are levied, you must make an allocation. Otherwise, you will not get any deduction.

[¶205]   FEES AND COMMISSIONS

Attorneys' fees, brokers' commissions, and other expenses incurred by a lessor to procure a lessee may be amortized over the entire lease period, regardless of whether the lessor is an accrual- or cash-basis taxpayer [*IT 3251,* CB 1939-1, 113]. If the lease is cancelled, the unamortized portion is immediately deductible in the year of cancellation. Similar fees and commissions incurred by a lessee to obtain a lease must be capitalized and the deductions amortized over the lease period, regardless of whether the lessee is an accrual- or cash-basis taxpayer [*King Amusement Co.,* 15 BTA 566, 44 F.2d 709, *cert. den.* 282 US 900; *Appeal of Walter & Co.,* 4 BTA 142]. Commissions paid by a lessor for managing his property or collecting rents are deductible business expenses [Sec. 1.162-1]. Where an owner incurs expenses and commissions in obtaining a loan on his property, such expenses are amortized and deducted over the life of the loan. Normally costs to purchase would be capitalized. Costs of sale reduce the sales proceeds (or increase the basis). They are not current deductions, for investment property.

[¶206] TITLE COSTS

Costs and legal fees relating to the perfection, defense, or removal of a cloud on title are nondeductible capital expenditures which increase the basis of the property. Costs relating to the protection of *income or rents* (as differentiated from the protection of mere ownership) are deductible business expenses [*Friend,* 40 BTA 768 aff'd 44 F. 2d 709. (7th Cir., 1941) cert. den. 314 U.S. 673]. The right to the deduction runs only to the owner; a lessee cannot normally deduct the cost of defending a suit involving the lessor's title (a property interest) even though he is thereby protecting his own right to the property's income [*Central Material & Supply Co.,* 44 BTA 282 aff'd 126 F. 2d 542 (10th Cir. 1942)]. In the case of costs which involve both title and income, the litigation is allocated between deductible income protection expense and nondeductible title protection expense [*Murray,* 21 TC 1049 aff'd 232 F. 2d 742 (9th Cir. 1956) *cert. den.* 352 U.S. 872)]. The dividing line between deductibility and nondeductibility is often slight and depends on the facts. Where costs are incurred in defending a suit to recover stock and income-producing real estate as a means to protect income, one court has held that the expenses directly involved perfection of title rather than protection of income [*Shipp,* CA-9, 217 F.2d 401 (9th Cir. 1954)].

[¶207] INTEREST

Current mortgage interest is deductible when paid or accrued regardless of whether business or residential property is involved [Sec. 163(a)]. This applies where the taxpayer has a legal or equitable proprietary interest, even though he is not personally liable on the mortgage [Reg. §1.163-1(b)]. But where a mortgage is assumed as part of the purchase price, any interest accrued prior to purchase is not deductible and must be capitalized.

INTEREST EXPENSE LIMITATIONS

Although the prior rules restricted prepaid interest to situations which did not result in "a material distortion of income," the new *Tax Reform Act of 1976* will simply turn cash basis taxpayers into accrual basis taxpayers. This rule eliminates much of the controversy, but it may result in harsh overall effects [Sec. 461 (g) of the Code]. This new rule would cover points and other types of artifices which attempt to disguise a transaction which actually is prepaid interest.

The Committee Reports indicate that the rules under this new provision, under Sec. 461(g), do not necessarily mean that level payments of interest must be made. Obviously, greater payments of interest would be made initially. Prepaid interest considerations under wraparounds are also covered.

These rules apply to business and non business interest. These rules will apply to individuals, Sub S corporations, estates, trusts, partnerships, and corporations. Variable interest rates may be subject to tight scrutiny, although they are not necessarily prohibited.

Points, as indicated, will also be included in these limits. However, there are exceptions for points paid to purchase a principal residence. Points which are paid by a cash basis taxpayer for his principal residence, and secured by that residence, can be deductible if:

1. The payment is business-like in nature according to normal transactions.
2. The deduction is reasonable for the general geographic area. [Sec. 461(g)(2) of the Code].

The effective date is generally for amounts paid after December 31, 1975. There is, however, an exception with regard to amounts paid before January 1, 1977, where they are paid persuant to a contract which was binding or a written loan commitment which was binding and existed on September 16, 1975.

[¶208]   **CARRYING CHARGES FOR**
UNIMPROVED AND UNPRODUCTIVE REAL ESTATE

An election may be made to capitalize rather than deduct carrying charges (interest, taxes, etc.) [Sec. 266 of the Code] for unimproved or unproductive real estate. Consistency is not required until the property is converted to productive use or improved. Charges may be capitalized in one year and deducted the next. But all charges of the same type must be treated consistently. Once a property is converted to productive use or improved, the charges must be treated as unused expenses.

How to Use the Election. Tailor the election to your tax bracket. If income for the taxable year in which the charges were paid or accrued has been high, elect to deduct so as to offset present high income. But where little income is received, e.g., during construction, you might capitalize to increase depreciation deductions in later years.

See also the discussion at paragraph ¶2008 as to capitalization of interest and taxes during construction (Sec. 189 of the Code).

[¶209]   **LESSEES: ABANDONMENT AND
                       OBSOLESCENCE DEDUCTIONS**

A lessee who abandons his leasehold or discontinues his business may be able to write off the remaining cost of improvements he installed either via an abandonment loss or by a deduction for obsolescence. But he must comply strictly with the statutory rules, as illustrated by the case of *Zwetchenbaum,* 21 TCM 1493, aff'd 326 F.2d 477 (1st. Cir. 1964).

Zwetchenbaum was a lessee who operated a retail store in a downtown area. Over a period of years, he put in about $194,000 worth of improvements which became a permanent part of the property and for which he took an annual depreciation deduction. Then poor business drove him to the suburbs, although 15 years remained on his lease. He actively sought a new tenant and tried to terminate the lease but was unsuccessful on both counts. So he deducted the unrecovered cost of the leasehold improvements in the year he moved.

The court held that he could take only his normal depreciation deduction, even though he was unable to put the assets to their fullest economic use. The lessee must first show that the improvements have been abandoned, retired, or permanently withdrawn; and as long as he continues to search for a new tenant, none of these can be established, since a new tenant might be able to use the premises as remodelled. In any case, a claim for obsolescence must be rejected here because obsolescence never occurs in a single year and hence could not justify a one-time deduction.

What to Do. Under the present provisions of the tax law, there are two ways to take a faster write-off for depreciable property than that permitted by the normal depreciation methods.

☐ (1) *Abandonment Deduction.* The theory here is that the property has lost all its useful value and has been permanently discarded or abandoned. The user must show an irrevocable intent not to use or sell the property. This is difficult to show in the case of permanent improvements. The court in the above case indicated that a sufficient showing would be made if the premises were subleased for the remaining period of the lease to a tenant who could make no use of the improvements (and presumably where the rent paid by the subtenant reflected this fact). Another way to show abandonment would be to tear out the improvements; this might be warranted when the value of the deduction was greater than the cost of removal [Reg. §1.167(a)-8].

☐ (2) *Obsolescence Deduction*. This is permitted in addition to the regular depreciation deduction when the useful life of the improvement has been shortened by economic changes, etc. The term is defined to mean a process that occurs over a period of several years. The taxpayer in the above case could not use this approach since he had taken the whole deduction in one year. He might have argued that the shift of business to suburban areas would make the downtown area unsuitable for business use in a few years and so the useful life of the improvements he had installed had been reduced. If the court agreed, he could have taken an additional deduction for obsolescence while still trying to rent the premises.

[¶210]   PLAN OF DEMOLITION CAN SHORTEN USEFUL LIFE

When an owner abandons his property, he is entitled to a deduction for its entire adjusted basis. But there has to be an actual abandonment, not just an intention to abandon or the completion of some of the steps toward that end. However, as an alternative, since the property's useful life is now known, it can be used in redetermining the depreciation for the current year which could be substantial.

For example, Cosmopolitan Corporation owned several converted brownstones in New York City. It decided to demolish them and build a modern office building. Planning and arranging to get the tenants to move stretched over a two-year period. When Cosmopolitan couldn't get the necessary financing, it leased the land to Tishman Realty which was to put up the office building. It was then that the buildings were abandoned. The Tax Court disallowed an abandonment loss before the buildings were abandoned. But IRS agreed that if the Court was satisfied that the buildings had a remaining useful life of only 18 months on January 1 of a given year, the taxpayer could deduct two-thirds of the remaining basis as depreciation in that year (12 months being two-thirds of the 18-month remaining useful life.) [See *Cosmopolitan Corp.*, 18 TCM 542(1959) 1959-122; *Keller Street Development Co.*, 323 F.2d 166 9th Cir. 1963).]

Buildings Acquired with Intention to Demolish. Where you acquire a building and the land on which it stands with the intention of demolishing the building, you may not get any depreciation deductions since the cost of the building merely increases the cost of the nondepreciable land. But you may be entitled to depreciate buildings even though they were bought with the intention to demolish where you hold the buildings for rental income for the time being

[*Nash,* 60 TC 503 1974]. However, the depreciation was allowed only to the extent of net rental income, 1.165-3(a)(2)(i). Here's how to figure your depreciation deductions under these circumstances: Allocate part of the basis of the property to the buildings and depreciate the buildings over the period during which they are held for rental purposes. The amount allocated must not exceed the present value of the right to receive rentals from the buildings over the period of their intended use for that purpose. You determine the present value of that right at the time the buildings are first used for rental income. Your depreciation deductions cannot be greater than your net rental income.

[¶211]
LESSOR'S COSTS:
IMPROVEMENT TO OBTAIN A TENANT

An improvement made by a lessor to obtain a lessee is generally capitalized and deducted by way of annual depreciation over its useful life. But the deduction may be accelerated over the lease period if the improvement was made especially for a specific lessee and will have no value after the lease ends. Similarly, a loss resulting from the undepreciated cost of a building which is demolished (either by the lessor to procure a lessee or by the lessee) is amortized over the lease period as part of the cost of the lease [*Anahma Realty Corp.,* 42 F.2d 128; *Berger,* 7 TC 1339, *acq.*].

It may be better to have the tenant make the improvements. The landlord amortizes them for tax purposes over the life of the property; the tenant, over the life of the lease, which is usually shorter. And the landlord loses nothing when the tenant makes the improvements. They are not taxable to him at the time, nor do they affect his basis. (This assumes the improvements are not in lieu of rent.) If the value of his property is increased by these improvements, he pays only the gain when he sells the property.

It may be to the landlord's advantage to give a proportionate reduction in rent to have the tenant make the improvements. The tenant benefits because the reduction in rent will pay the cost of the improvements. And he will have the advantage of the depreciation deductions in addition.

From the landlord's standpoint, the rent he gives up—which would be taxed as ordinary income—will be returned to him, subject only to the possible capital gain tax, when he sells the property. But it is important not to require improvements in lieu of additional rent; if they are, the value of the improvements will be taxed immediately as rent income.

[¶212]
REAL ESTATE TAXES — SUMMARY:
CHECKLIST OF DEDUCTIBILITY OF REAL ESTATE TAXES
IN SPECIAL SITUATIONS

☐ (1) *Tenancy in Common.* If you are a tenant in common, you deduct only your proportionate share of the tax even if you pay the entire tax.

☐ (2) *Tenancy by the Entirety*. Either tenant can take the deduction if he pays the tax [*Nicodemus,* 26 BTA 126, *acq.*].

☐ (3) Joint Tenancy. Arguably, the one who pays the tax can take the deduction.

☐ (4) *Mortgagee*. If you are a mortgagee, you cannot deduct taxes you pay on the property for periods prior to your acquiring title to the property. If the taxes are paid before foreclosure, they represent an additional loan on the property. If they are paid after foreclosure, they represent additional cost of the property [*Schieffelin,* 44 BTA 137].

☐ (5) *Back Taxes Paid by Buyer*. The buyer gets no deduction for any back taxes he pays. The sum he pays is added to the purchase price [Reg. §1.164-6].

☐ (6) *Future Taxes Paid by Seller*. The future portion is not deductible by the seller. It reduces his sales proceeds.

PART B: APPRAISAL OF REALTY

[¶213]   **DETERMINING MARKET VALUE**

The purpose of an appraisal is to determine the market value of the real estate being appraised. The handbook of the American Institute of Real Estate Appraisers defines market value as the highest price, estimated in terms of money, which the property will bring if exposed for sale in the open market, allowing a reasonable time to find a purchaser who buys with knowledge of all the uses to which it is adapted and for which it is capable of being used.

Put another way, the value of a particular property basically is made up of the future benefits that the owner of the property can expect to receive in the form of rental or other income. In determining the future benefits from property, an owner will consider the current use of the property and all other uses that it may be capable of in the foreseeable future. Property presently used as farmland may be usable for a residental subdivision in five or ten years and at a later date for commercial or industrial sites.

Market value is not the same thing as *market price*. Market price represents the actual dollar price put on a property at the time of a transaction. This may be higher or lower than the value which an individual appraiser might place on the property. The difference may be due merely to differences of opinion or it may be due to the fact that the property, to the particular buyer or seller, has a greater or lesser value because of some special consideration, such as the financing which a buyer could obtain or the need of the seller to raise cash.

[¶214]   **ASSESSMENT METHODS**

Various methods of appraisal are used to determine assessed valuation. Some communities take assessed property at a fraction of its current market value. Others take the value to be the amount for which the property would sell at a forced sale. Others assess property at its full market value. Full market value assessment is being used by more and more communities.

The assessor usually separates the value of land and buildings. Land values are set on the basis of the value of a typical lot — one of a size which is standard or common in laying out land in the community. Using this standard as a base, the assessor tries to value odd-size and special-location lots in relationship to that standard. Depending on prevailing subdivision practices in the development of the community, the standard lot will usually have a 20- to 50-foot width and a 100- to 125-foot depth. One method of determining variations from a standard 100-foot depth lot is the 4-3-2-1 depth rule, which determines variations for lots having less depth or more depth than 100 feet in this way:

Depth of Lot in Feet	Percent of Standard Lot Value	Depth of Lot in Feet	Percent of Standard Lot Value
25	40	125	109
50	70	150	117
75	90	175	124
100	100	200	130

In valuing buildings the assessor must consider age, depreciation, type, size and character, suitability to the location, and various other factors. Most assessors start out with cost per foot of cubical content or cost per square foot of floor space. This rule of thumb will vary with different types of buildings — loft, factory, fireproof, nonfireproof, elevator and walk-up apartments, office buildings of various heights, etc. The size of the building is determined, and the appropriate square-foot or cubic-foot factor is applied to arrive at an estimate of the replacement cost of the building. Then, based on age, an allowance is made for accrued depreciation. Assessors also consider the rent a building is able to produce. In fact, many assessors treat this as the paramount factor on the basis that an improved piece of real estate is never worth more than its capitalized rental value unless the value of the land alone is greater. In some communities, land increases in value while buildings almost always decline. Thus, sometimes buildings are only valued at the amount they add to the value of the land, and this may decline until it becomes a nominal amount.

An assessment must be equitable. All parcels of real property should be treated in substantially the same way. The assessed value should impose on each parcel of real estate a portion of the community tax burden which is no greater than the ratio which the true value of the particular piece of real estate bears to the total value of all the real estate in the community. This objective is never fully achieved. Reassessment cannot be carried out as rapidly as values change and as new buildings are added to the total real estate in a community. For this reason, there must be procedures by which taxpayers can have their assessments reviewed if they think they are being asked to carry a greater share of the community tax burden than is proper or fair.

[¶215]   **REDUCTION OF ASSESSMENT**

Wherever a taxpayer feels that his real property has been assessed too high, local law affords him an opportunity to petition for a reduction of the assessment. Such a proceeding is usually initiated by making a protest to the taxing authority itself with an application for correction. Only after such an application is denied, either in whole or in part, may a proceeding for judicial review of the assessment be initiated. When tax officials turn down a property owner's protest, this action is usually subject to review by a court in an appeals proceeding. This is a proceeding whereby the tax officials are called on to produce their records and to certify them to the court so that the court may determine whether the officials have proceeded according to the principles of law which they are required to follow in the performance of their assessing duties.

Local tax authorities usually have forms of application to be used in asking for a review of an assessment.

If an application of protest is rejected, the next step is to initiate a proceeding in the appropriate court to review the final assessment. The grounds on which an assessment may be reduced usually are:

1. overvaluation,
2. inequality, or
3. illegality.

Overvaluation can be established by showing that the assessment of real property has been set at a sum which is higher than the full and fair market value of the property.

Inequality, which somewhat overlaps overvaluation, can be established by showing that the assessment was made at a proportionately higher valuation than the assessment of real estate of like character in the same area. To obtain relief it usually is necessary to show that the assessment is out of proportion as compared with valuations in the municipality generally. To prove inequality, it is necesary to examine a considerable number of parcels of real estate for the purpose of comparing the market values of these properties with their assessed valuation and ascertain the ratio of assessed value to market value in each instance. You have a case of inequality if such a study shows that the ratio of assessed values to market values generally is substantially lower than the ratio between the assessed value and the market value of your property.

Illegality exists when the assessment has been levied in an irregular manner or on a basis erroneous in law or in fact other than an error in the evaluation itself. An example of an illegal assessment is the inclusion on the tax roles of an assessment of a parcel of real estate which is legally exempt from taxation.

To seek a reduction of a real estate assessment, you would normally take these steps:

(1) Examine the assessor's report. If this is predicated on some error of fact, such as an incorrect description of the property, an incorrect statement of its actual income or expenses, or any other error concerning the property itself, submit proof of the correct facts.

(2) Find out what the property cost. Compare the actual cost of the property with the assessment. If the purchase price is substantially below the assessed value to be challenged and the date of purchase is not too remote from the tax date, this comparison will be relevant as long as it can be established that the property was purchased in an arm's-length transaction.

(3) Study the records of income received from the property and the expense of operation over several years prior to the tax date. The earning capacity of income property is the most significant single factor in determining its market value for purposes of seeking reduction of a tax assessment.

(4) Make a comparison of sale prices and assessed valuations and of estimates of market value and assessed valuations for other comparable properties in the area. This kind of a comparison will have been made by others, and so a great deal of the necessary information may be obtained in that way rather than through the laborious, costly method of getting appraisals on a large number of properties.

(5) Consult experts. The rules of each locality will vary. The testimony of expert witnesses is usually the most important proof in court proceedings to seek reduction of real estate taxes. You may want to use the testimony of a building expert as well as a real estate expert. The real estate expert will testify as to sales of comparable property and to the value the property would have in the market place. The building expert would testify as to the sound structural value or reproduction cost, less depreciation of the building.

[¶216]   **ADMINISTRATIVE ERRORS**

For you to check for administrative errors, it will be necessary to understand the assessing practices used by your local authorities. This information can be obtained from a responsible official in the local assessing office.

CHAPTER 3

Tax Benefits For Homeowners, Condominium Unit Owners And Cooperative Tenant-Stockholders

[¶301]   **TAX BENEFITS OF HOME OWNERSHIP**

Homeowners, condominium unit owners and cooperative tenant-stockholders all enjoy tax benefits that can make investment in one of these forms of ownership a wise one. Each form has its own distinct advantages depending on the circumstances of the individual investor. This section is devoted to a comparison of the tax benefits available to home, condominium, and cooperative owners. Generally speaking, the tax treatment of single family homeowners and condominium owners is almost identical. Cooperatives vary as to their tax treatment.

It should come as news to no one that our income tax laws strongly favor home ownership. What is more, the tax advantages of home ownership are open to the little man, the man on a salary who has to go out and raise the money to buy his home as well as to the big investor whose financial resources are such that he can choose to finance his purchase either with the proceeds of a mortgage loan or by selling some of his securities.

Here is a rundown summary of some tax benefits of home ownership:

A homeowner can take tax deductions for the *interest* he pays on his mortgage — the limitations on the tax benefits of investment interest don't apply to money borrowed to buy a home. He also is entitled to take tax deductions for the *real estate taxes* he pays. He can make a *tax-free sale* of his home if he buys another home within the required time and meets other requirements. Even if he sells and does not buy another home, he is taxed at favorable *capital gains* rates on his profit rather than at higher ordinary income rates. As extra icing on his cake, his monthly mortgage amortization payments can be considered as *savings* and his home can be considered as a protection against *inflation*.

[¶302] SALE OF OLD RESIDENCE AND PURCHASE OF NEW RESIDENCE

If you sell your principal residence after December 31, 1974 and buy or build a new residence, you can escape tax on the gain by complying with the rules of [Sec. 1034 of the Code].

If you buy a new home, the purchase must be accomplished and use made of the home within 18 months before or after the sale of the old residence. If you build, you must begin construction within 18 months after the sale. However, you have up to 24 months after sale of the old residence to *occupy* the new one.

Gain on sale of the old residence will be recognized unless both homes (old and new) are your principal residences. Summer homes, for example, do not count.

The term "residence" includes a trailer, a co-op or condominium apartment or house, and a houseboat. Gain is not recognized if your spouse owns the old and/or new residence or if you own them jointly. However, in such cases a consent by the appropriate spouse(s) must be signed to get tax-free treatment.

Qualifying for Tax-Free Treatment of Gain on Sale of Old Residence. No tax is due on the transaction unless the "adjusted sales price" of your old home exceeds the "cost" of the new home. The "adjusted sales price" is arrived at by subtracting selling expenses such as commissions and expenses for work performed on the old residence in order to assist in the sale (so-called fix-up expenses) from the selling price of the old residence. Expenses to assist in the sale reduce sale prices for these purposes only if performed within 90 days before the sale and paid within 30 days after the sale. The "cost" of the new residence is what you actually paid for it plus brokers' commissions or other purchasing expenses. Mortgages are included in the sale and purchase prices.

If you *exchange* residences, the result is about the same. For an even exchange (no boot, i.e., only real estate is involved, no cash, loans, or personalty), there is no tax due and the new residence is given the same tax basis as the old. If you receive or give boot, certain adjustments have to be made. For example, if you receive $1,000 cash, the old residence cost $20,000, and value of the new is $25,000, your gain is $6,000 ($26,000 received minus cost of old residence). The transaction is treated as if you had sold the old residence for $26,000 and bought the new residence for $25,000. Therefore, $1,000 of the gain is recognized. If you had given $5,000 boot, there would be no gain and no tax since you would have received $25,000 (value of new home) and paid out $25,000 ($20,000 basis of old house plus $5,000 cash).

Where you have sold your old residence and bought another without the recognition of gain, the same procedure may be repeated, but only if eighteen months has elapsed between the two sets of transactions. Involuntary sales during the period have no effect.

[¶303]   **REAL ESTATE FORMS**

The forms that follow have been reprinted with permission of Publisher—©REALTORS National Marketing Institute® of the National Association of REALTORS 1975.

EXCHANGE RECAPITULATION

Figure 3-1 allows for the summarizing of exchange considerations so far as market value, existing loans, equity, and proceeds received, if any. There is also an adjustment for commissions, closing costs, loans, and so on.

For example, if Owner A trades his Building A-1 for B's Building B-1 and the facts are:

(A)

	A-1	B-1
Fair Market Value	$400,000	$450,000
Loan	− 300,000	300,000
Equity	$100,000	$150,000

(B) Differences in equities ($150,000 − $100,000 = $50,000)

(C)

	A-1	B-1
Equities Less:	$100,000	$150,000
Commission	28,000	31,500
Transfer Costs	1,000	1,000
Net Equity	71,000	117,500

Then the form reflects the equity (Col. 4) and adjusts for transfer costs (Col. 10) and commissions (Col. 9).

CASH FLOW ANALYSIS SHEET

Figure 3-2 (page 25) emphasizes the cash considerations in real property. It allows for adjustments on mortgages and principal and interest payments. It works off net operating income, adjusting for the items noted; it also has an analysis of sales proceeds to determine actual cash flow after a sale.

ANNUAL PROPERTY OPERATING DATA FORM

Figure 3-3 (page 26) provides a worksheet to present gross scheduled rental income, the adjustments for vacancy, and the operating expenses, to therefore reach the net operating income figure. It also allows for debt service computations, and therefore cash flow production.

INTERNAL RATE OF RETURN WORKSHEET

Figure 3-4 (page 27) allows for the computation of the internal rate of return; that is, allowing for discounting factors as a result of the time value of money. Interpolation is also provided for under the form.

INDIVIDUAL TAX ANALYSIS FORM

The form in Figure 3-5 (page 29) to provide for the projected net taxable income and tax due by the taxpayer in question. It allows for an emphasis on real estate transactions, along with other income, when computing taxable income for Federal purposes.

EXCESS DEPRECIATION SHEET

The sheet in Figure 3-6 (page 30) allows for computation of depreciation, and then allows for excess (amount over straight line depreciation). It is useful when computing recapture.

[¶304]   AVOIDING GAIN ON SALE OF RESIDENCE BY REINVESTING IN A CONDOMINIUM OR COOPERATIVE

When an individual sells his principal residence and reinvests the proceeds in a condominium apartment that he uses as his new principal residence, any gain on the sale is tax free if the purchase of the condominium apartment is made within a period beginning 18 months before the date of the sale and ending 18 months after that date. A similar privilege applies to reinvestment in a cooperative apartment [*Rev. Rule. 60-76,* CB 1960-1, 296].

In the case of a cooperative, there is a problem of determining the amount of your investment. Is your investment only what you paid for your co-op stock? If so, chances are you have invested considerably less than the sales price of your old residence, and part or all of the gain on the residence would be taxable. Or does the investment in the co-op also include your share of the mortgage on the co-op property? Then you may very well have invested as much as the sale price of your residence.

Where your share of the mortgage is allocated to you by the co-op, that mortgage share is part of the price you paid for the co-op, says the Treasury [*Rev. Rul. 60-76*]. Here is the arrangement in the case on which the Treasury ruled. The purchase-money mortgage indebtedness of the co-op was allocated among the

FIGURE 3-1. EXCHANGE RECAPITULATION SHEET

Date _____

Property 1	Market Value 2	Existing Loans 3	Equity 4	Cash Gives (In) 5	Cash Gets (Out) 6	Paper Gives 7	Paper Gets 8	Comm. 9	Trans. Costs 10	Net Equity 11	New Loan 12	Old Loan 13	Net Loan Proceeds 14
A-1	$400,000	$ 00,000	$100,000	$50,000	-	-	-	$28,000	$1,000	$ 71,000			
B-1	450,000	300,000	150,000	-	$50,000	-	-	31,500	1,000	117,500			

24

FIGURE 3-2. CASH FLOW ANALYSIS

Date_____

Name_____ Purpose_____

Mortgage Data

	Encumbrances	Amount			Remaining Term	Payment Period	Interest Rate	Payment Period	Remarks
1	1st Mortgage								
2	2nd Mortgage								
3	3rd Mortgage								
		(1)			(2)	(3)	(4)	(5)	(6)

		Year:			Year:	Year:	Year:	Year:	Year:
4	Initial Investment								
5	1st Mortgage								
6	2nd Mortgage								
7	3rd Mortgage								
8	Total Encumbrances								
9	Principal Reduction								

Ownership Analysis of Property Income: Taxable Income

10	Total Gross Income								
11	− Vacancy & Credit Loss								
12	− Operating Expenses								
13	Net Operating Income								
14	− Non-Operating Expense								
15	− Interest								
16	− Depreciation								
17	Taxable Income								

Cash Flows

18	Net Operating Income								
19	− Princp. & Int. Pymts.								
20	− Funded Reserves								
21	− Capital Additions								
22	Cash Flow before Taxes								
23	− Income Tax								
24	Cash Flow after Taxes								

Analysis of Sales Proceeds Year:

	Adjusted Basis			Excess Depreciation		Tax on Gain	%	
25	Original Basis			Total Depr.		Excess		
26	+ Capital Improvements			S/L Depr.		Cap. Gain		
27	+ Costs of Sale			Excess Depr.		Cap. Gain		
28	Sub-Total					Total Tax Liab.		
29	− Depreciation			Gain		Sales Proceeds		
30	− Partial Sales			Sales Price		Sales Price		
31	AB at Sale			− AB		− Sales Costs		
32				Gain		− Mortgage		
33				− Excess		Proceeds before Taxes		
34				Cap. Gain		− Total Tax Liab.		
						Proceeds after Taxes		

FIGURE 3-3. ANNUAL PROPERTY OPERATING DATA

Purpose _____ Date _____

Name _____

Location _____ Price $ _____

Type of Property _____ Loans $ _____

Assessed/Appraised Values Equity $ _____

			FINANCING				
Land	$_____ ____ %						
Improvement	$_____ ____ %		Balance	Payment	Period	Interest	Term
Personal Property	$_____ ____ %	Existing $_____				%	
Total	$_____ 100 %	1st $_____				%	
		2nd $_____				%	
Adjusted Basis as of _____ $_____		3rd $_____				%	
		Potential					
		1st $_____				%	
		2nd $_____				%	

		%	2	3	Comments
1	GROSS SCHEDULED RENTAL INCOME				
2	Plus: Other Income				
3	TOTAL GROSS INCOME				
4	Less: Vacancy and Credit Losses				
5	GROSS OPERATING INCOME				
6	Less: Operating Expenses				
7	Accounting and Legal				
8	Advertising, Licenses and Permits				
9	Property Insurance				
10	Property Management				
11	Payroll - Resident Management				
12	Other				
13	Taxes-Workmen's Compensation				
14	Personal Property Taxes				
15	Real Estate Taxes				
16	Repairs and Maintenance				
17	Services - Elevator				
18	Janitorial				
19	Lawn				
20	Pool				
21	Rubbish				
22	Other				
23	Supplies				
24	Utilities - Electricity				
25	Gas and Oil				
26	Sewer and Water				
27	Telephone				
28	Other				
29	Miscellaneous				
30					
31	TOTAL OPERATING EXPENSES				
32	NET OPERATING INCOME				
33	Less: Total Annual Debt Service				
34	CASH FLOW BEFORE TAXES				

FIGURE 3-4. INTERNAL RATE OF RETURN WORKSHEET

Date _____

Name _____ Property _____

Net Sale Proceeds $_____ Investment Amount $_____

End of Year	Cash Flow	Discount at 5%		Discount at 10%		Discount at 15%		Discount at 20%	
		P.V. of 1	Amount	P.V. of 1	Amount	P.V. of 1	Amount	P.V. of 1	Amount
1		.952381		.909091		.869565		.833333	
2		.907029		.826446		.756144		.694444	
3		.863838		.751315		.657516		.578704	
4		.822702		.683013		.571753		.482253	
5		.783526		.620921		.497177		.401878	
6		.746215		.564474		.432328		.334898	
7		.710681		.513158		.375937		.279082	
8		.676839		.466507		.326902		.232568	
9		.644609		.424098		.284262		.193807	
10		.613913		.385543		.247185		.161506	
11		.584679		.350494		.214943		.134588	
12		.556837		.318631		.186907		.112157	
13		.530321		.289664		.162528		.093464	
14		.505068		.263331		.141329		.077887	
15		.481017		.239392		.122894		.064905	
16		.458112		.217629		.106865		.054088	
17		.436297		.197845		.092926		.045073	
18		.415521		.179859		.080805		.037561	
19		.395734		.163508		.070265		.031301	
20		.376889		.148644		.061100		.026085	
Reversion Year____									
Reversion Year____									
Reversion Year____									
TOTALS									

INTERPOLATION

% Rate	$ Present Value Amount

Smaller _____ $ _____ ──────▶ $ _____

Larger _____ $ _____ Investment Amount $ _____

Absolute Difference _____ − $ _____ x $ _____] + Smaller Rate _____ %

FIGURE 3-4 (CONTINUED)

Date _____

Name _____   Property _____

Net Sale Proceeds $ _____   Investment Amount $ _____

End of Year	Cash Flow	Discount at ___ %		Discount at ___ %		Discount at ___ %		Discount at ___ %	
		P.V. of 1	Amount	P.V. of 1	Amount	P.V. of 1	Amount	P.V. of 1	Amount
1									
2									
3									
4									
5									
6									
7									
8									
9									
10									
11									
12									
13									
14									
15									
16									
17									
18									
19									
20									
Reversion Year ___									
Reversion Year ___									
Reversion Year ___									
TOTALS									

INTERPOLATION

	% Rate		Present Value Amount
Smaller	$		$
Larger	$		Investment Amount $
Absolute Difference	$	x $	÷ Smaller Rate %

FIGURE 3-5. INDIVIDUAL TAX ANALYSIS

Name_____ Date_____

LINE		(1)	(2)	(3)	(4)	(5)	(6)	(7)	(8)	(9)
		PRESENT INCOME POSITION			PROPERTY			PROPERTY		
1	GAINFUL OCCUPATION									
2	Exemptions									
3	Deductions									
4	Total Lines 2 & 3									
5	Taxable Income Gainful Occupation (L1 - L4)									
6	TAX LIABILITY GAINFUL OCCUPATION									
7	Dividends									
8	Interest									
9	Other Income									
10	TOTAL SECURITY INCOME (L7 + L8 + L9)									
11	Total Gainful Occupation & Security Income (L5 + L10)									
12	TAX LIABILITY GAINFUL OCCUPATION & SECURITY									
13	REAL ESTATE TAXABLE									
14	TOTAL ORDINARY INCOME (L11 + L13)									
	TAX LIABILITY ORDINARY INCOME									
16	EXCESS DEPRECIATION RECAPTURE									
17	Other Recapture									
18	TOTAL RECAPTURE INCOME (L16 + L17)									
19	Total Lines 14 & 18									
20	TAX LIABILITY INCLUDING RECAPTURE									
21	CAPITAL GAINS TAXABLE									
22	TOTAL TAXABLE (L21 + (L19 or L14))									
23	TOTAL TAX LIABILITY									
24	Tax on Security Income (L12 - L6)									
25	Tax on Real Estate (L15 - L12)									
26	Tax on Recapture (L20 - L15)									
27	Tax on Capital Gains (L23 - L20)									
28	Income Listed Above (L1 + L10 only)									
29	All Other Income									
30	TOTAL INCOME (L28 + L29)									
	Less Total Tax Liability									
32	Net After Tax									
33	Overall Rate (L31 : L30)									

FIGURE 3-6. EXCESS DEPRECIATION

Date _____

PROPERTY _____

Original Cost $_____	x _____% = Improvements $_____
+ Cap. Impr. _____	x Total Depreciation _____%
TOTAL $_____	= Total Depreciation $_____
– Depreciation _____	Useful Life _____ Years
+ Selling Costs _____	Accelerated Method _____
= Adjusted Basis $_____	Straight Line _____%/Year
Selling Price $_____	Sale Date _____
– Adjusted Basis _____	Purchase Date _____
= Realized Gain $_____	

Enter Time Period From Purchase Date to 1/1/64	Enter Time Period From Purchase Date to 1/1/70	Enter Time Period Property Held From Purchase Date to Sale Date
		Holding Period _____ Months
_____Years + _____Months To 1/1/64	_____Years + _____Months To 1/1/70	_____Years + _____Months
Straight Line / Accelerated	Straight Line / Accelerated	Straight Line / Accelerated
_____% / _____%	_____% Prior to 1/1/64 _____%	_____% Prior to 1/1/70 _____%
	_____% _____%	_____% _____%
	_____% _____%	_____% _____%
	_____% Accelerated Depreciation	_____% Accelerated Depreciation
	_____% Straight Line	_____% Straight Line
	_____% Excess x Improvements =	_____% Excess x Improvements =
	$_____ Excess Depreciation	$_____ Excess Depreciation
NO RECAPTURE PRIOR TO 1/1/64	**120 Months**	**200 Months**
	_____ Holding Period	_____ Holding Period
	_____% To Ord. Income	_____% To Ord. Income*
	x Excess $_____ Ordinary Income	x Excess = $_____ Ordinary Income

Ordinary Income Recaptured Prior to 1/1/70 $_____	Realized Gain $_____
Ordinary Income Recaptured After 1/1/70 $_____	Total Ordinary Income Recaptured $_____
TOTAL $_____	Capital Gain Realized $_____

Note: If improvements have been added, use another form then combine for totals.
*If the property involved is non-residential, ignore holding period and enter 100.

tenant-stockholders in proportion to the fair market value of each apartment. Each tenant-stockholder, under his lease, was obligated to pay his portion of the co-op's mortgage payment (principal and interest). To secure performance of this and other obligations, the tenant-stockholder, had to pledge his stock interest with the co-op. And, in the event of liquidation, each tenant-stockholder's distributive share of the corporate assets would be reduced by the unpaid balance of his proportionate share of the mortgage debt.

[¶305]   SALE BY INDIVIDUALS 65 YEARS OF AGE OR OLDER

Taxpayers 65 or over before the date on which they sell or exchange their residences can elect to exclude from their gross income that portion of their gain that is attributable to the first $35,000 of the *adjusted sales price*. (Prior to 1/1/77, the rule was $20,000.) To be eligible for this treatment, the seller must have owned and used the property involved as his principal residence for five of the last eight years before the sale or exchange.

If the home sells for $35,000 or less, the entire gain is tax free. If the adjusted sale price is more than $35,000, you compare $35,000 to the total adjusted sale price to find what percentage of that adjusted sale price $35,000 is. Then you apply that same percentage to the total gain to find the tax-free portion. [Sec. 121 of the Code].

> *Example:* Say the adjusted sale price is $50,000; $35,000 is 70% of $50,000. If the total gain is $9,000, 70% of that, or $6,300, is a tax-free gain. The remaining $2,700 of gain is taxable.

Special Limitations and Requirements. This tax-free gain is available to a taxpayer and his spouse only once during their lifetimes. This rule applies even if a previous sale or exchange was made by you or your spouse before you were married to each other.

If you and your spouse before your marriage each owned and used a separate residence and if after your marriage both residences are sold, whether or not in a single transaction, an election to exclude the gain may be made as to either residence (but not as to both) if the age, ownership, and use requirements are met.

Here is an example of what happens where there is a divorce and remarriage by one spouse:

> *Example:* Assume that while A and B were married, A sold his separately owned residence and made an election to avoid the tax. Pursuant to the requirement (discussed below), B joined in the election. Subsequently, A and B are divorced and B marries C. While B and C are married, C sells his residence. C *is not entitled to make an election* since an election by B, his spouse, is in effect at the time of such sale.

To qualify for the tax-free exclusion, you must show ownership and use for 60 full months or for 1,825 days (365 x 5). Short, temporary absences for vacation or other seasonal absences (although accompanied with rental of the home) can count as periods of use.

"Adjusted Sales Price" and the Tax-Free Gain. Determining the amount of gain on the sale or exchange of a residence which is excludable depends on the "adjusted sales price." Where the adjusted sales price is $35,000 or less, the entire gain may be excluded. Over that figure, only a portion of the gain may be excluded.

The "adjusted sales price" is arrived at by subtracting selling expenses, such as commissions, and expenses for work performed on the old residence to assist in the sale (so-called fix-up expenses) from the selling price of the old residence. Expenses to assist in the sale reduce the sales price for these purposes only if performed within 90 days before the sale and paid within 30 days after the sale. Mortgages are included in the sales price.

So, for example, if you sell your principal residence for $35,400 and it costs you $400 to fix up the property for sale, the adjusted sales price is $35,000.

Special Situations. Here's how various special situations are handled in connection with the tax-free gain for the 65 or over:

Property Held Jointly by Husband and Wife. If (1) a residence is held by a husband and wife as joint tenants, tenants by the entirety or community property, (2) they file a joint return, and (3) either spouse satisfies all the requirements (i.e., age, ownership, and use of the residence), then both spouses are treated as satisfying all the requirements. Thus, although only one spouse meets the requirements, the tax-free gain will be available on the sale of the jointly owned property.

Property of Deceased Spouse. The holding period and use of a residence of a deceased spouse carries over to the surviving spouse if the deceased spouse met those requirements before death during the eight-year period before the sale by the survivor. These carryover rules do not apply, however, if the surviving spouse is married at the time of the sale or if an election made by the deceased spouse is in effect with respect to any other sale or exchange.

Tenant-Stockholder in a Cooperative. An individual who holds stock as a "tenant-stockholder" in a "cooperative housing corporation" can be eligible to make an election to get tax-free gain on the sale or exchange of his stock. The ownership requirements are applied to the holding of the stock and the use requirements are applied to the house or apartment which the individual was entitled to occupy because of such stock ownership.

So, if he owned the stock and used the apartment or house as his principal residence for at least five of the eight years before the sale (and, of course, if he's

65 or over), he can elect to avoid tax on the gain on the sale of his stock within the $35,000 limitation.

Involuntary Conversions. Destruction, theft, seizure, requisition, or condemnation of property is treated as the sale of property for the purposes of this section. So, tax on the gain resulting from these involuntary conversions can be avoided if the age, use, and holding period requirements are met.

Property Used Only in Part as Principal Residence. Where you can satisfy the ownership and use requirements with respect to a portion of the property sold, then the law applies only to as much of the gain from the sale or exchange of the property as is attributable to that portion. For example, an attorney uses a portion of his principal residence as a law office for a period of more than three of the eight years preceding the sale of that residence. He cannot avoid the tax on as much of the gain as is allocable to the portion of the property used as a law office.

Determination of Marital Status. Marital status is determined on the date of the sale or exchange of the residence. An individual who on the date of the sale or exchange is legally separated from his spouse under a decree of divorce or of separate maintenance is not considered as married on that date.

Combining a Tax-Free Replacement with a Tax-Free Sale. You can reinvest the proceeds from the sale of a residence or the amount realized in an involuntary conversion. If you meet the reinvestment rules (i.e., you reinvest at least the amount you realized), you avoid a tax on the gain.

> *Example:* You are over 65, have owned your present residence for the last 15 years, and have used it as your principal residence during all that time. You sell the residence and the adjusted sales price is $50,000. Your gain is $15,000. Since $35,000 is 70 percent of the $50,000 adjusted sales price, you can elect to avoid tax on 70 percent of your $15,000 gain, or $10,500. The remaining $4,500 gain is taxable.

But you can avoid the tax on the $4,500 gain, too. If you reinvest the full adjusted sales price in a new residence within 18 months, you avoid the tax on the gain. Since, however, you elected to take $10,500 of the gain tax free, you need not reinvest the full adjusted sales price to avoid tax on the $4,500 portion of your gain. You can reinvest only $39,500 (the $50,000 sales price less the $10,500 gain you picked up tax-free) and get the full $4,500 balance as tax-free. If you reinvest less than $39,500, then the difference between the amount you reinvest and $39,500 (but not more than $4,500) will be taxable. If, for example, you reinvest $38,000, you'll have $1,500 of taxable capital gain.

[¶306]   CONDOMINIUM-UNIT OWNERS: TAX BENEFITS

These are the tax benefits for condominium-unit purchasers:

Real Estate Taxes. A condominium-unit owner can take an itemized deduction for the real estate taxes assessed against his unit [Sec. 164 of the Code].

Interest. An itemized deduction can be taken by the unit owner for the interest he pays on the mortgage debt incurred to purchase his unit [Sec. 163 of the Code].

Casualty Loss. A deduction for a casualty loss to his property by reason of fire or storm for the amount of the loss in excess of $100 per casualty will be allowed [Sec. 165(c)(3) of the Code].

Nonrecognition of Gain. If the condominium unit is his principal place of residence and he sells it and purchases another condominium unit, single-family home, or co-op unit which he uses as his principal place of residence, the unit owner pays no tax on his gain provided he pays as much or more for his new principal place of residence than the adjusted sale price of his old unit [Sec. 1034 of the Code]. The new unit must be purchased within 18 months of the date of the sale of the old unit (24 months if the new unit is newly constructed).

Senior Citizens' Exemption. If the condominium unit owner is 65 years or older on the date he sells his old unit and the old unit has been his principal place of residence for at least five of the eight years immediately prior to the sale, he can exclude that portion of the profit that the sum of $35,000 bears to the adjusted sale price of the unit [Sec. 121 of the Code]. So, for example, if the adjusted sale price is $50,000, he can exclude from income 70 percent of his gain. Any portion of the gain attributable to the first $35,000 of the adjusted sale price is tax free.

Involuntary Conversion. If the condominium unit is condemned or sold under threat of condemnation the owner can defer any profit realized by treating the disposition as an involuntary conversion [Sec. 1033 of the Code]. Nonrecognition of gain under these circumstances would apply if the condominium unit owner replaces the converted property with another place of residence within two taxable years following the termination of the tax year in which the conversion occurred. The excess of the condemnation proceeds over the cost of the new residence is currently taxable.

Gift Tax. A condominium unit owner can transfer his unit to himself and spouse as tenants by the entirety without receiving any consideration for the transfer and without having the transfer treated as a taxable gift. Under Sec. 2515(a) of the Code, the creation of a tenancy by the entirety in real estate is not a transfer for gift tax purposes unless the donor elects to have the transfer treated as a taxable gift.

Note: It should be noted here that the same rule would not apply to a similar transfer of an interest in a co-op dwelling unit where, under state law, that type of interest is considered to be personal property and not real estate.

Long-Term Capital Gain. The owner of a condominium unit who sells his unit after he has held it for more than nine months in 1976 (one year after 1977) is taxed on his gain at favorable long-term capital gain rates.

Installment Reporting. If the condominium owner makes an installment sale of his unit he can qualify for installment reporting provided he does not receive more than 30 per cent of the sale price in the year of sale and the sale otherwise qualifies [Sec. 453(b) of the Code].

[¶307]   CONDOMINIUM-UNIT OWNERS
WHO RENT OUT THEIR UNITS PART OF THE YEAR: TAX BENEFITS

If a condominium apartment owner treats his unit as an investment for rental income, he gets the usual benefits of deducting interest and tax payments. If he is in a 50 per cent tax bracket, this means that the government is paying one-half these charges for him. As the first owner in a new development, he also may deduct for depreciation using the fastest methods of accelerated depreciation permitted under the Code (200 per cent declining-balance or sum-of-the-years-digits). (This method assumes the residential, nontransient test of 30 days or more is met.) On top of these deductions, those portions of his monthly charges that go for ordinary operating maintenance and repairs are also deductible.

When you take all these benefits into consideration and then add that you might pick up a condominium apartment — with a cash investment of $5,000 or less, you can understand why many professional men and business executives are saying that if one condominium apartment is good, two — one to live in and one to rent (or both to rent) — are even better.

Benefits of Tax-Sheltered Rental Income Without Management Problems. A condominium apartment unit owner who uses his apartment for rental income gets the benefits of being a landlord with few or none of a landlord's headaches. For one thing, his cash investment is, as we have seen, quite small. Since each apartment unit requires only a small cash outlay, he can spread his money around to pick up different units in different parts of the development or in several developments. This makes his position quite flexible. When he sells, he can space his sales to suit his needs. And his market should be a favorable one — even allowing for temporary setbacks. You might say, for example, that he has a ready-made market in his tenants.

Another great advantage that a condominium-unit owner has is that he doesn't have to participate in any management duties. A professional management company will be running the show for him as well as for his fellow condominium unit owners.

To top things off, his investment enjoys the same favored treatment that other rental real estate gets under the Code, as well as the same type of safety and chances for appreciation in value that other well-chosen multifamily real estate investments show in a booming market.

[¶308]   CO-OPS: TAX ADVANTAGES

The man who owns stock in a cooperative apartment or housing corporation may deduct his proportionate share of the interest and real estate taxes paid by the corporation. This proportionate share is based on the proportion of the total stock he owns; and the interest that is deductible can relate to any debt incurred by the corporation to acquire, construct, alter, rehabilitate, or maintain the building and land.

Qualifying for Tax Deductions. The cooperative must be bona fide; that is, the stockholder's ownership must give him the right to live in an apartment or house on the property owned or leased by the corporation. He need not actually live there, but he must have the right to do so if he wants.

The following requirements must be met:

a. Stockholders are entitled to no distribution other than out of corporate earnings and profits (except on liquidation).
b. Stockholders are the source of 80 percent of the corporation's gross income for the taxable year in which the deduction is taken.
c. Only one class of stock is outstanding: the stock issued to the tenant-stockholders.

As to the last requirement, an exception is made in favor of governmental agencies and entities; and under this exception as liberalized by the 1969 tax law, stock owned and apartments leased by governmental entities and agencies authorized to acquire share of stock in cooperative housing corporations to provide housing facilities are not taken into account. Included within the meaning of the exception are shares of stock owned and apartments leased by the United States or any of its possessions, a state or any political subdivision, or any agency or instrumentality of the foregoing empowered to acquire shares in a cooperative housing corporation for the purpose of providing housing facilities.

As a convenience, a tenant-stockholder may pay the corporation a lump sum periodically to cover interest, taxes, maintenance, overhead, and amortization payments on the mortgage. He is allowed to compute the portion of the payment allocable to interest and taxes and deduct it. This is a helpful exception to the general rule that interest must be segregated in order to be deductible. The basis used for the computation is the corporation's total expenses. From that, the tenant-stockholder computes his own share of the interest and taxes.

The following illustration shows how it is done: Assume the tenant-stockholder owns 10 percent of the stock and is in a 70 percent tax bracket. At the beginning of the year, he pays the corporation $1,600 as his share of the estimated expenses of $16,000 for the year. The actual expenses turn out to be only $15,000. Our tenant-stockholder's share is reduced to $1,500. The extra $100 is either refunded to him or he leaves it with the corporation as an installment on his share of next year's expenses. Here is the way he computes his deduction.

Corporation's Expenses During the Year

Interest	$ 5,500		
Real Estate Taxes	5,000		
Maintenance	3,500		
General Overhead	1,000		
Total	$ 15,000		
Tenant's Share of Total (1/10)			$ 1,500
His Share of Interest (1/10 of $5,500)	$ 550		
His Share of Taxes (1/10 of $5,000)	500		
Total Deduction	$ 1,050		
Tax Savings (70% of $1,050)			735
Tenant's Net Cost for the Year			$ 765

How about housing corporations that change to cooperative ownership during the year? Does the 80 percent requirements apply to the entire year or only to the portion after the change? IRS has ruled that the 80 percent requirement applies to the entire Year [*Rev. Rul.* 55-556, CB 1955-2, 57].

[¶309]   **CONVERSION OF BUILDING TO**
COOPERATIVE FORM OF OWNERSHIP — CAPITAL GAIN

If the owner of an apartment building desires to sell off separate units and thus sells the individual apartments, he risks ordinary income treatment on his gain if he holds them for sale to customers in the ordinary course of business from the time that he adopts the plan to convert to a cooperative. But if he sells to a cooperative corporation composed of the new purchasers of the apartments who are the corporation's stockholders, it would seem that he has held the property for rental purposes up to the time of sale. By dealing with the cooperative corporation from its formation (as the representative of the purchasers), the seller probably preserves the character of his property as rental property to the time of sale, and he should get a capital gain.

However, if he is active in the new corporation, he will have additional problems.*

[¶310]   TAX DEDUCTIONS FOR TENANT-STOCKHOLDERS THROUGH CALENDAR-YEAR REPORTING BY CO-OP CORPORATION

Use of the calendar-year accounting period by a co-op apartment house results in more deductions for tenants, most of whom are also on the calendar-year basis. For tax purposes, a co-op does not qualify as such unless 80 percent or more of its gross income for its taxable year comes from tenant-stockholders. Until the co-op's tax year has ended, we do not know whether it has met that 80 percent requirement. And until it has met that requirement, the tenant-stockholders cannot deduct their proportionate shares of the co-op's interest and taxes.

Take this situation: A co-op had a taxable year ending September 1975. Tenants' taxable years end December 31, 1974. Until September 1975, it was not known whether the co-op met the 80 percent test for its year running from October 1, 1974, through September 30, 1975. So the tenants, on their 1974 tax returns (due April 15, 1975), could not deduct their proportionate shares of the interest and taxes contained in their October, November, and December 1974 maintenance charges paid to the co-op.

The best bet is to have co-op and tenants have the same tax year. In the vast majority of cases that would be the calendar year. If, however, the co-op does have a fiscal year other than a calendar year, be sure to file a refund claim as soon as the co-op's tax year ends and it is clear it has met the 80 percent test. In the example above, as soon as September 30, 1975, rolled around and it was clear that the co-op met the 80 percent test, the tenants could file refund claims or amended return for 1974, claiming as deductions their proportionate shares of the co-op's interest and taxes for October, November, and December 1974 [*Rev. Rul. 59-257,* CB 1959-2, 101].

[¶311]   FIGURING DEPRECIATION FOR A CO-OP APARTMENT

A tenant-stockholder in a cooperative housing corporation can depreciate his stock if he leases his apartment to another or uses it wholly or partly for business purposes [Sec. 216(c) of the Code]. Thus a cooperative owner is placed on the same footing as the owner of a private residence or of a condominium apartment.

*See Mark Lee, Levine, *Real Estate Transactions* (West Publishing Co., St. Paul, Minn., 1976, Supp. 1977), Tax Planning, Chapter 16.

IRS has issued Regulations on the subject of computing the basis for depreciation [Regs. § 1.216-2]. The Regulations cover three different situations:

1. original ownership of stock;
2. subsequent ownership of stock;
3. conversion to business use during ownership.

Original Owner of Stock. If you buy an apartment in a new cooperative or in a building just converted to cooperative use, you have to compute the depreciation to which the cooperative is entitled. Then you compute your pro rata share based on your proportionate ownership of stock. The maximum depreciation deduction is available to you only if you use the entire apartment in a trade or business (for example, a professional suite) or if you hold the entire apartment for the production of income (for example, if you rent it out). If you use the apartment only partly for business, then only a pro rata amount of depreciation may be taken. In such case, the allocation usually can be made on any reasonable basis: for example, by a comparison between the number of square feet devoted to business use and the square footage devoted to personal use or by the number of rooms devoted to each use.

How Depreciation Deduction Works Out for an Original Stockholder. Since, in general, a tenant-stockholder is entitled to take as depreciation his share of the depreciation allowable to the cooperative [Reg. §1.216-2(b)(1)] if you are an original stockholder and have always used your cooperative apartment only for business or for rent, it is easy enough to work out what your share of the depreciation comes to. Here is how it is done:

Let us say we are dealing with a co-op that constructed an apartment building at a cost of $250,000 ($200,000 for building, $50,000 for land). When construction was completed, the building had an estimated 50-year useful life and an estimated $20,000 salvage value. Tenant-Stockholder Smith, an original stockholder, owns 10 percent of the total outstanding stock. Assuming Smith has used his apartment solely for business (or for rent), his depreciation is computed this way [1.216-2(d)(1)]:

Co-op's basis in building	$200,000
Less estimated salvage value	20,000
Co-op's basis for depreciation	$180,000
Annual (straight-line) depreciation on building (1/50 of $180,000).	3,600
Smith's share of depreciation for the year (1/10 of $3,600)........	360

If the co-op is entitled to claim accelerated depreciation, the tenant-stockholder is also entitled to use that type of depreciation; and this is true regardless of the method of depreciation the co-op or the other stockholders actually use.

Subsequent Owner of Stock. If you bought your apartment from a previous tenant, the procedure is the same as above except that you compute the building's basis for depreciation as if it were related to your cost of the stock. The effect of this procedure is to permit increased depreciation deductions to owners who purchase at higher prices than originally established. (If prices decline, it works the other way, too!)

Assume that one year later you buy Smith's stock (his 10 percent interest) at $150 per share. You use the apartment for the entire year for business or rent. Here is how your depreciation would be figured [Sec. 1.216-2(d)(3)]:

Your $150 per share price times total outstanding shares (assumed to be 1,000)	$150,000
Plus co-op's mortgage debt	135,000
	$285,000
Less amount attributable to land (assumed to be 1/5 of $285,000)	.57,000
	$228,000
Less salvage value	$ 20,000
Basis for depreciation	$208,000
Annual (straight-line) depreciation (1/49 of $208,000)	4,245
Your share of depreciation (1/10 of $4,245)	425

Conversion to Business Use. If you start out using the apartment as a residence only and then convert part or all of it to business use, you can begin to take a deduction for depreciation. The general rule is that you depreciate from the lower of (1) adjusted basis or (2) fair market value at the time of the conversion.

Under Reg. §1.216-2(b)(3), to determine the fair market value, you take the cooperative's basis adjusted as if straight-line depreciation had been used. If the resulting figure is lower than the cooperative's actual adjusted basis, you must use that figure unless you can show that attributing such a fair market value is unrealistic as, for example, where there has been substantial appreciation in the value of the building. In that case, as in the case where the cooperative's adjusted basis is actually lower, you would use the cooperative's adjusted basis.

Once having arrived at the proper basis, you follow the appropriate procedure described above to determine the amount of the deduction.

Commercial Space Excluded. Many residential cooperative corporations rent out ground-floor space to retail shops or for other commercial uses. Under Section 1.216-2(d)(2), where this occurs, the depreciation deductions must be reduced proportionately by the amount of space so used. Also, appropriate adjustments must be made in respect to prepayments and delinquencies on account of the cooperative's management obligation [Reg. §1.216-2(b)(1), (2)]. In addition, the total depreciation can not exceed the stockholder's basis for that part of the stock allocable to depreciable real estate.

[¶312]   BASIS OF CO-OP APARTMENT STOCK

Tenant-stockholders may deduct for tax purposes the amount of their monthly carrying charges equal to their porportionate share of the co-op's real estate taxes and mortgage interest. The balance of the monthly charges, in much the same manner as an apartment dweller's rent, is not deductible. But a portion of the balance of that carrying charge could increase the tenant-stockholder's basis for his co-op stock (thus cutting down on any taxable gain when he sells it in the future). To get this step-up in basis, the proprietary lease between the co-op and the tenant-stockholder must provide that the portion of the carrying charge that is to be applied by the co-op to paying off the principal on its mortgage should not be credited to the co-op's income but should be credited to its paid-in surplus. Where this is done, the amount so designated may be considered a contribution by the tenant-stockholder to his corporation's capital, stepping up his basis for his stock. The co-op, too, would benefit from this arrangement. The contribution to capital is eliminated from its income and, after taking into account its operating costs and depreciation, it may very well have no taxable income.

[¶313]   TAX BENEFITS FOR TRANSFERRED EMPLOYEES AND BUSINESSMEN ON THE MOVE

Here is a checklist on the important tax deductions under Sec. 217 of the Code available to transferred employees and self-employed individuals. A $3,000 limit applies to the sum of items (3) to (6), with a $1,500 limit on items (3) and (4).

☐ (1) Travel. The cost of travel, including meals and lodging, from the old to the new residence for the transferee and his family. If traveling by car, the transferee may deduct 7ᶜ per mile.

☐ (2) *Possessions*. The costs of moving all household goods and personal effects. Insurance is also included.

☐ (3) Pre-move House Hunting. The expense of house-hunting trips, including the cost of meals and lodging.

☐ (4) *Temporary Lodging Expenses*. The expense of temporary lodging in the general location of the new job for a period of up to 30 days after obtaining employment.

☐ (5) *Cost of Selling Old Residences*. This includes selling expenses and closing costs, appraisal fees, brokerage commissions, legal fees, title costs, and transfer stamps.

☐ (6) *Buying New Residence*. Loan placement charges other than points that are deductible as interest and legal escrow, recording and appraisal fees.

The above deductions depend on the satisfaction of two conditions: (1) the new place of employment must be 35 or more miles farther from the former residence than was the former principal place of work and (2) the employee must be a full-time employee for 39 or more weeks in the new job location during the 12 months immediately following his arrival there. The 39-week test is not waivable except in the case of death, disability, involuntary separation from service, or transfer for the benefit of the employer after getting full-time employment in which the employee might reasonably have expected to satisfy the requirement. The requirement for self-employed persons is 78 weeks during a 24-month period of which not less than 39 weeks are during the 12-month period described above.

[¶314]　　TAX DEDUCTIONS FOR HOME-OFFICE EXPENSES

Under Sec. 162 of the Code, you can deduct part of the cost of maintaining your home or apartment as a business expense if you use it for conducting your business. (However, new Sec. 280(A) of the Code and existing Sec. 183 of the Code add tough qualifying tests. Generally, the office in home must be for the *convenience* of the employer, *regularly* used for clients or customers, and an *exclusive* room must be for business use.)

This type of deduction is particularly favorable for the professional or other self-employed person who maintains no office outside the home and segregates a specific room as space within the home where he carries out his business activities. However, the availability of the home office deduction is not so clear for a person who has access to an outside office or who is not self-employed. It has been that a home office deduction will be disallowed where a person has an outside office available to him and he conducts the business of his employer only incidentally at home [*Bodzin,* 509 F. 2d 679 (4th Cir. 1975, *cert. den.* 75-1 USTC]. Consequently, where you maintain an outside office, you probably will not be able to deduct the expenses of your home office unless you can meet the tests noted.

For years after 1975, the taxpayer will not be allowed deductions for an office in the home, except to the extent the taxpayer meets specific tests, (Sec. 280(A) of the Code) that is:

a. It is his principal place of business, *or*
b. It is a place of business which the taxpayer uses for his patients, clients, or customers, in meeting or dealing with the taxpayer's normal course of business, *or*,
c. In the case of a separate structure, which is not attached to the dwelling, it is used in connection with the taxpayer's trade or business.

Additionally, in the case of an employee, the above mentioned rules apply only if there is an *exclusive* use of the area in the home, and which is for the convenience of the employer. The *area* must be exclusively used for the taxpayer's trade or business or investment use. It cannot be used in conjunction with normal household use, such as the split use as a den and office.

Under the discussion of Sec. 280(A), infra, relative to vacation homes, the rule on *exclusive* use of the portion of the home will *not* apply to a taxpayer whose trade or business is selling products at retail, where the dwelling unit is the *only* location of that trade or business. However, the ordinary and necessary expense rules (Sec. 162 of the Code) allocable to the space will apply. Further, the space must be used on a *regular* basis; it must also be separate space when used as storage.

In any event, even if the tests are met, the *expenses* must be allocated; the only amounts that can be deducted are those expenses attributable to business or investment use. Further, the allowable expenses attributable to the business use under this section cannot be greater than the income derived from the business [Sec. 280(A) of the code]. This section is effective for years after 1975.

Example: If we assume the taxpayer used one tenth of his home for business, and the expenses for the home were:

A.

*Taxes	$2,000
*Interest	4,800
Repair/Maintenance	500
Insurance	400
Others	200
TOTAL	$7,900

*Deducted anyway, as itemized deduction, if not claimed here.

B. 1/10 × $7,900 = $790 deduction

C. Assumes income is not less than $790.

[¶315]   **RESORT/VACATION HOMES**

☐ The current change in the *Tax Reform Act of 1976* tightens the effect of Sec. 183 of the Code by adding a new Code Section 280(A), captioned "Disallowance of Certain Expenses in Connection With Business Use Of Home, Rental of Vacation Homes, Etc."

☐ Section 280(A) provides under (a) that, except as otherwise provided in the Section, where a taxpayer who is an individual or an electing small business corporation (notice that it excludes a corporation, at least by *direct* language), no deduction otherwise allowable will be allowed to the extent there is a dwelling which is used by the taxpayer as his personal residence in excess of given limits. The Section is designed to make it clear that this Section is an overriding section.

☐ There are exceptions to allow deductions for interest, taxes, and casualty losses. These items would be deductible, if they qualify, whether the home was for rental or for personal use.

☐ The Section further provides for limitations on the maximum amount of deductions, where Section 280(A) is applicable. The deductions are limited to the amount of gross income derived from the property, reduced by the deductions which would otherwise be allowed, such as interest, taxes, and casualty losses.

☐ Section 280(A) can come into play where the residence is used on a *personal* basis. However, since this test has been subject to an interpretation as to how much would eliminate the use for business use as opposed to personal use, Section 280(A)(d) provides that where a taxpayer uses the dwelling unit for his own personal use for the greater of 14 days or 10 percent of the number of days during each year that such property is used for rental, the limitations under 280(A) apply.

☐ Section 280(A) is tied to Sec. 183 of the Code with regard to the 2 out of 5 year rules. (If a property produces profit 2 out of 5 consecutive years, there will be a presumption that it is for profit purposes). [Sec. 280 (A)(f) of the Code].

☐ There is an additional *de minimus* rule relative to a rental that is less than 15 days during the year. In such case, there is no deduction allowed which would otherwise be allowed because of rental property; *and,* the rental gross income is also *not* included in the taxpayer's gross income under Section 61 of the Code. In other words, the expenses and income are considered a wash.

☐ This rule emphasizes the importance of timing of income and deductions. Once again, the personal use of the residence reemphasizes the potential argument that it is not a profit-motive use. This change also indicates the general tightening up on items which are arguably personal deductions, as opposed to investment or business deductions.

☐ The vacation home is also defined under this Section to include, very broadly, a house, apartment house, boat, trailer, condominiums, or any similar properties.

☐ There is also a provision for *allocating expenses* among the rental and personal use time. The personal use, as opposed to the rental use expenses, are allocated based on a ratio of such expenses relative to the number of days the home is actually rented as opposed to the number of days it is actually used (personal and rental). Therefore, if the home is used 30 percent personally, 30 percent of the allocable expenses would be personal and would not be deductible. (Subject to exceptions, i.e., interest, taxes, and casualty losses.)

☐ A rental day would not include a situation where the home is merely *available* for rent, but in fact is not rented.

☐ The Code attempts to define what constitutes personal use; it includes instances where the taxpayer or certain other related parties use the home, any individual who uses the home under a reciprocal arrangement, anyone who uses the home for less than a fair rental charge, and various other circumstances.

(1) *Income from* property $2,900
(2) *Expenses*

A.Interest	$2,400
Taxes	1,200
Repair	400
Insurance	300
Others	100
	$4,400

B.	*Number	Percent
Days Rented	273	75%
Days Personal	92	25%
	365	100%
*Rounded		

The rules are:

C. *Tier One:* Taxpayer may deduct all in this tier.
These are amounts that are deductible, even without business.

1. Interest/Taxes	$3,600

2. These reduce the Income from the other property, after looking to the rental use only:

Personal use (25%)	
25% (x) $3,600	(900)
Business use	$2,700
3. Rental	$2,900
Expenses - Tier one	$2,700
(Business part)	
4. Balance	$ 200

Tier Two:

1. Other expenses, not in Tier One and not affecting basis. (Repair, Insurance, Others) ($800 × 75%)	$ 600
2. Balance of Tier One (#4 above) Non-Deductible ($600 − $200)	$ 400

Tier Three: Expenses that affect basis (i.e., depreciation). — Not allowed: No income left.

RESULT: Expenses are deductible in the order noted, up to a maximum of the gross income, except that tier one is allowed.

A rental day would not include a situation where the home is merely *available* for rent, but in fact is not rented.

The Code attempts to define what constitutes personal use; it includes instances where the taxpayer or certain other related parties use the home, any individual who uses the home under a reciprocal arrangement, anyone who uses the home for less than a fair rental change, and various other circumstances.

[¶316]   HOBBY LOSSES:
NON-BUSINESS AND NON-INVESTMENT ACTIVITIES

The hobby loss rules under Section 183 of the Code provide a presumption in favor or the taxpayer that if the taxpayer had a profit in two out of five consecutive tax years from the activity, it would not be deemed to be a hobby (i.e., non-business). That is, the taxpayer has a presumption in his favor. (See also the example in the prior section).

For the taxpayer to come within the provisions of the Section 183(e) of the Code, the taxpayer was required to elect to postpone his determination as to whether the activity was a hobby, and to thereby extend the Statute of Limitations. That is, to see if he generates income.

One problem with the extension is the extension arguably allowed the Service to come in and review *other areas* beyond the Section 183 issue.

The *Tax Reform Act of 1976* provision, under Section 183(c)(4) of the Code, provides that if the taxpayer makes an election, as mentioned, the Statutory period for the assessment of any deficiency attributable to that activity will not expire before the expiration of two years after the date prescribed by law for filing a tax return. However, the extent of the waiver is only to the hobby loss item, and to items affected by this issue, such as adjusted gross income and the deductions that are affected by adjusted income. The effective date for this section is for taxable years beginning after December 31, 1969, in most circumstances.

[¶317]   TAX-EXEMPT STATUS OF HOMEOWNERS

The problem in this area has been to determine whether home-owners associations would be tax-free. The previous determination by the Government, under its rulings, has been that the homeowners associations would not fit the Section 501(c) category, i.e., these were not exempt. To be exempt, a taxpayer must fit the definition of an exempt organization under the Code. Since a condominium is for private owners, it could not meet the Code definition of an entity. The result: it *was* taxed as a corporation. To avoid these problems, the rules, noted below, were passed:

☐ There have been numerous rulings that have allowed the associations to avoid, under given circumstances, the paying of income tax on contributions to the association. These were under a trust theory, escrowing, contributions to capital, agency, or other theories.

☐ To alleviate the problem in this area, Section 528 of the Code is added. It provides for tax exempt status for condominium management associations and residential real estate management associations.

☐ This rule only protects the association relative to income which is generated with regard to *exempt* function activities, which include dues, fees, and assessments from the member's owners.

☐ To the extent the income is taxable, that is, not exempt income, the entity is taxed as a corporation. (It is not allowed to use the corporate surtax exemption. However, the 30 percent capital gains rule would apply.)

☐ The exempt howeowners association includes:

a. A condominium management association or residential management association, if it meets additional requirements.
b. The organization must be organized and operated for the acquisition, construction, management, maintenance and care of the associations property.
c. 60 percent or more of the gross income of the organization for the tax year must consist solely of amounts received as membership dues, fees, or assessments, generally from the owners.
d. 90 percent or more of the expenditures of the organization must generally be with regard to the property which is the subject of the exemption.
e. No part of the net earnings of the organization can inure to the members of the organization.
f. The organization must elect to have this special section apply [Sec. 528(c)(1) of the Code].

☐ Most of the dwelling units must be used as residences in the case of the condominium management association or substantially all the lots or buidings must be used by the individuals for a residence of exempt status is sought for a residential real estate management association [Sec. 528(c)(3) of the Code].

Effective date: The amendment generally applies to tax years beginning after December 31, 1973.

The above provisions do not apply to a Section 216 — cooperative association. However, Section 216(c) is amended to provide that depreciation is allowed with regard to property in a cooperative association. [This should eliminate the contrary position in *Park Place, Inc.* 57 TC 767 (1972).]

Thus, if a condominium can meet the rules noted, it will not be taxed as a corporation, for its normal activities.

CHAPTER 4

Tax Benefits of Real Estate Depreciation

[¶401]   **DEPRECIATION DEDUCTIONS**

In real estate investments depreciation and amortization play decisive roles. Often, the difference between a profitable and nonprofitable transaction results from the interplay of these two elements.

Depreciation deductions can provide a tax-free return of your investment. To the extent that depreciation exceeds amortization payments, you can have a tax-free cash flow. That is why in appraising a real estate investment, in setting up financing, in building, in leasing, in selecting the depreciation method to be used, it is essential that these elements be carefully scrutinized.

The tax benefits of real estate depreciation are of great importance to real estate investors. In the following material, you will find out just how tax shelter is obtained through depreciation deductions that real estate investments throw off.

[¶402]   **WHO CAN TAKE DEPRECIATION DEDUCTIONS?**

The person who takes the economic loss because of the decrease in value is the one entitled to take the depreciation deduction. Normally, that means the owner of the property. For this there must be an investment. This does not necessarily mean actual out of pocket money. Debt may be part of the basis. [See *Atlantic Coast Line Ry. Co.,* 31 BTA 730 81 F. 2d 309 (4th Cir. 1936). cert. den. 298 U.S. 656]. Legal title alone is not sufficient. [See *Gladding Dry Goods Co.,* 2 BTA 336.].

A lessee would be entitled to the depreciation deduction, as opposed to the lessor, where the rental payments were, in effect, payments of the purchase price [*Rev. Rul. 55-25*, CB 1955-1, 283]. Property that does not cost anything has no basis and therefore does not result in any depreciation deduction [*Detroit Edison Co.* 45 BTA 358, 131 F. 2d 619 (6th Cir. 1942). (aff'd BTA), 319 US 98 (aff'd 6th Cir.)]. This would also apply where the Code provides for a zero basis. For example, property contributed to a corporation by persons who do not make the contribution in the capacity of stockholders is considered to have a zero basis [Sec. 362 (c) of the Code].

The depreciation deduction may be claimed by any person or taxable entity owning a capital interest in the property. These are: individuals, whether citizens or aliens, residents or nonresidents; corporations, whether domestic or foreign; partnerships and joint ventures; fiduciaries and beneficiaries of estates and trusts; heirs, legatees, and devisees; life tenants; and any other entities that are subject to tax [Reg. 1.167]. Depreciation deductions to recover paving costs have been allowed where the paving was needed to make a warehouse accessible [*D. Loveman & Son Export Corp.,* 34 TC 776, aff'd 296 F 2d 732 (6th Cir. 1962) *Cert. den.* 369 U.S. 860].

Where the owner of depreciable property dies, the allocable portion of depreciation for the taxable year, computed on the basis of the number of months to the date of his death, is taken by his executor or administrator on his final return. The deceased's estate computes the depreciation from the date of death and uses a new basis for computation: the value of the property at the date of death or, if elected, the alternate valuation [Sec. 1014 (a) for decedents dying before 1977. (After 1977, see the rules under basis, *infra.*)].

A life tenant is entitled to the deduction as if he were the absolute owner of the property (Reg. § 1.167(h)-1(a)). After the life tenant's death, any remaining deduction is allowed to the remainderman.

Where the owner of a depreciable property dies, the allocable portion of depreciation for the taxable year, computed on the basis of the number of months to the date of his death, is taken by his executor or administrator on his final return. For decedents dying before January 1, 1977, the deceased's estate computes the depreciation from the date of death and uses its own basis for the computation (see ¶ 603 for how estates' basis is determined).

[¶403]   **WHAT PROPERTY IS DEPRECIABLE?**

Generally, depreciable property is property used in trade or business or held for the production of income which is subject to physical decay or obsolescence and has a definite useful life [Sec. 167 of the Code]. The asset need not be earning income nor bringing in money as long as it is used in trade or business or held for the production of income [*Hardwick Realty Co.*, 7 BTA 1108 aff'd 29 F.2d 498 (1929), cert. dismissed 279 U.S. 876]. Holding a single piece of rental property is enough to give you a depreciation deduction.

You cannot take a deduction for personal assets. But a property can be used for a dual purpose. For instance, suppose a building has two apartments. You rent one and occupy the other as your residence. You can take a depreciation deduction for the portion that is used in business (i.e., rented to a tenant) but not for the residential half.

> *Example:* John purchases a house. The house costs $25,000. It has a life of 20 years. Five thousand dollars is allocable to the land and hence is not deductible. Assume no salvage value. That leaves $20,000. Since half of this house is allocated to a business purpose, Johnson can depreciate on one-half of the house, or $10,000, over a period of 20 years.

Land is not depreciable as it has no limited useful life. When you buy improved property, you have to allocate your purchase price among the land and the buildings and other improvements.

Former Residence. What was formerly your personal residence can be converted into income-producing property. In *Smith*, TC Memo 1967-28, the taxpayers permanently abandoned their residence and offered it for sale but made no attempt to rent it. They not only took depreciation deductions, but also deductions for repair and maintenance expenses. The Tax Court okayed the deductions. In an earlier case, *Neave*, 17 TC 1237, the Tax Court ruled that merely offering a former residence for sale was insufficient to convert it from personal use. However, this case also involved a very short temporary rental.

Vacant Building. Under Sec. 167(a)(2) of the Code, the property held for gain from its disposition is depreciable as well as property held for the purpose of producing recurring income [*Mitchell*, 47 TC 120]. A vacant building bought as a rental investment, but never rented, never producing income, and then sold at an attractive price is depreciable during the period you own it.

[¶404]   **ELEMENTS OF DEPRECIATION**

Before you can determine the amount of your depreciation deduction, you must know the following three elements:

1. The method of depreciation that you will use,
2. The amount you can recover (depreciable basis), and
3. The period over which you can take deductions (useful life).

(1) Depreciation Methods. There are several methods by which to calculate the depreciation deduction. Sometimes the rate at which you take depreciation deductions can vary considerably from one method to another. The accelerated depreciation methods, of course, permit the fastest recovery of cost. [Sec. 167(c) of the Code].

(2) How Much You Can Recover. The amount recoverable through depreciation usually is what you pay for the property (cost) reduced by the amount which you estimate you will realize on disposition of the property (salvage). Where the property is tangible personal property which is eligible for the 20% first-year writeoff, this too has to be deducted from the cost to arrive at the amount recoverable. Section 179 of the Code is discussed in ¶ 415.

(3) Useful Life. The last element is useful life, the period over which you can take depreciation deductions. The length of the depreciation period will have the greatest effect on the amount of your annual depreciation deductions. This usually is the area where disputes with IRS arise.

Back in 1942, IRS issued Bulletin F which listed the useful lives of various types of assets. These guidelines were used until 1962 when IRS, in *Rev. Proc. 62-21*, issued depreciation guidelines. *Rev. Proc. 62-21* replaced the item-by-item listing of Bulletin F with broad classes of assets which had shorter lives than those listed in Bulletin F.

IRS used the reserve ratio test to check up on the useful lives claimed by taxpayers. This test was rather complicated and had the effect of discouraging use of the guidelines. As a result of difficulties arising out of using the reserve ratio test and other problems, IRS adopted the Asset Depreciation Range (ADR) system. [See Rev. Proc. 77-10, IRB 1977-12, and the book's Appendix which explains the ADR concepts.] The Revenue Act of 1971 authorized a new class life system which combined the provisions of the ADR system with parts of the guidelines.

For determining an asset's useful life, you can now elect to use the class life system or you can use depreciation rates based on all the facts and circumstances surrounding your situation. Although you may use the old Bulletin F as a guide, it should be noted that IRS has not used it for examining depreciation since 1962. [Reg. § 1.167(a)-11.]

[¶405]   DEPRECIATION METHODS

Straight-Line Depreciation. With this method, the depreciation expense is the same from period to period. The formula followed for this method is:

$$\frac{(\text{Cost} - \text{Salvage Value})}{\text{Estimated Life}} = \text{Depreciation Expense}$$

Example: If the improvement costs $20,000, has a salvage value of $200, and an estimated life of 20 years, the depreciation expense for the year would be computed as follows:

$$\frac{(\$20,000 - 200)}{20} = \$990$$

The straight-line method is essentially an accounting concept which, to a great extent, depends on a hypothesis. It is based on a conjecture that the depreciation will be at a constant rate throughout the estimated life. Despite this unscientific approach in a scientific world, the straight-line method is followed by many taxpayers and is recognized as a method of depreciation by the Internal Revenue Service. [Sec. 167(b)(1) of the Code]. This method of depreciation is available for all new or used property.

Declining-Balance Depreciation. Under this method, the amount of depreciation expense decreases from period to period. It is favored by economists because it takes note of the fact that real depreciation in value is greatest in the first year and becomes progressively less as the asset ages. Therefore, the largest depreciation deduction is taken in the first year. The amount then declines steeply over succeeding years until the final years of estimated useful life when the depreciation charge becomes relatively small. This method of depreciation as to realty can be used only with respect to new residential rental properties (200 percent declining balance), new commercial (150 percent declining balance) and used residential, with 20-year remaining life, or more (125 percent declining-balance).

While the true declining-balance method requires the application of a complex formula if you are going to use the maximum declining-balance depreciation, there are various percentages to use, (i.e, the 200 percent method), you need not go through these mathematical computations. Instead:

1. Determine the straight-line percentage rate;
2. Double it;
3. Apply it to your full basis (undiminished by salvage value) to get your first year's deduction.

In the second year,

1. Reduce your basis by the previous year's depreciation deduction;
2. Apply the same percentage rate to the new basis you arrived at in step (1).

In the third year and later years, repeat the same process.

Example: Taking the earlier facts, 20 years = 5 percent per year. Two times 5 percent = 10 percent. 10 percent × $20,000 = $2,000. In the second year, it is ($20,000 - $2,000 = ($18,000) × 10 percent = $1,800, and so forth.

Sum-of-the-Digits Depreciation. Here, diminishing rates, expressed fractionally, are applied to the total depreciable value. Determination of the fractional rate to be used each year may be made as follows:

1. Obtain the sum of the years' digits. On a ten-year life, add this way: $1 + 2 + 3 + 4 + 5 + 6 + 7 + 8 + 9 + 10 = 55$.
2. The first year's depreciation will be 10/55 x $10,000; the second year's depreciation will be 9/55 x $10,000; the third year's depreciation will be 8/55 x $10,000; and so on.

This method is permited by the Internal Revenue Service only on property acquired and first put into use after 1953. [Sec. 167(b)(3) and (c) of the Code]. Here is how it works:

Assume: Cost, $10,600; salvage value, $600; life, 10 years.

Year	Depreciation
1st	$ 1,818.18
2nd	1,636.36
3rd	1,454.55
4th	1,272.73
5th	1,090.94
6th	909.09
7th	727.27
8th	545.45
9th	363.64
10th	181.82
	$10,000.00

Under this method, the asset is depreciated over the estimated life, and in the first three years more of the cost is recovered than with the 200 percent declining balance method. All of the cost of the asset is recovered over its useful life, but this is not so in the declining-balance method. The sum-of-the-years-digits method will give a more rapid return of capital than the percentage declining-balance method.

[¶406] **DEPRECIATION RATES**

Agreement Covering Depreciation Allowance. Written agreements as to useful life and depreciation rates may be made between the taxpayer and IRS and are binding on both parties unless new facts can be shown justifying a change. Any such change would be prospective only and would not affect previous taxable years [Sec. 167(d) of the Code]. In the absence of an agreement to the contrary, the taxpayer has the privilege, as indicated, of switching at any time from the declining-balance to the straight-line method (Sec. 167(e)). Unless there is ''clear and convincing basis for a change'' from the amount of deduction taken by a taxpayer, the Internal Revenue Service will not question a depreciation allowance [*Rev. Rul. 53-90,* CB 1953-1, 43]. Application for agreement is made to the director for the district in which your return is required to be filed.

[¶407] COMPARISON OF DIFFERENT DEPRECIATION METHODS

Here's how straight-line, declining-balance, sum-of-the-years-digits, and declining-balance with a switch to straight-line depreciation methods work on a piece of property with a ten-year life, assuming a $10,000 cost and no salvage value.

Year	Straight-Line	Declining-Balance	Sum-of-Digits	Declining-Balance Switch to Straight-Line
1st	$ 1,000	$ 2,000	$ 1,818	$ 2,000
2nd	1,000	1,600	1,636	1,600
3rd	1,000	1,280	1,455	1,280
4th	1,000	1,024	1,273	1,024
5th	1,000	819	1,091	819
6th	1,000	655	909	655
7th	1,000	524	727	655
8th	1,000	420	545	655
9th	1,000	336	364	655
10th	1,000	268	182	655
	$10,000	$ 8,926	$10,000	$ 9,998

[¶408] DEPRECIATION AVAILABLE FOR DIFFERENT TYPES OF PROPERTY

Here is a rundown on the different methods of depreciation available with respect to different types of property for realty:

☐ (1) *Straight-Line*. This method of depreciation is available for all types of new and used properties, real or personal.

☐ (2) *125 percent Declining-Balance*. This depreciation method is available for (a) used real property acquired before July 25, 1969; (b) used residential rental property acquired after July 24, 1969, with a useful life of 20 years or more; (c) new or used personalty.

☐ (3) *150 percent Declining-Balance*. This method is the fastest available for (a) used real property acquired before July 25, 1969; (b) new nonresidential rental properties constructed after July 24, 1969; (c) used personalty.

☐ (4) *Sum-of-the-Years-Digits*. This method of depreciation is available only for (a) new real estate constructed before July 25, 1969; (b) new residential rental properties; (c) new personalty.

☐ (5) *200 percent Declining-Balance*. This depreciation method is available only for (a) new real estate constructed before July 25, 1969; (b) new residential rental properties; (c) new personalty

☐ (6) *Straight-Line Using Short Useful Life*. This method of depreciation is available for rehabilitation expenses for low- or moderate-income residential rental properties. Expenditures are depreciated on a straight-line basis using a 60-month useful life. This method may also come into play with historic structures. See ¶ 2109.

What is New Residential Rental Property Within Meaning of Depreciation Rules? New residential rental property is residential rental property with respect to which the taxpayer is the first user. At least 80 percent of the gross rental income from the property in the taxable year must be rental income from dwelling units. While a "dwelling unit" can be a house or apartment used to provide living accommodations in a building or structure, a unit in a hotel, motel, or other establishment, more than one-half the units of which are used on a transient basis, is not a dwelling unit. For purposes of the 80 percent test, if part of the building is occupied by the taxpayer, the gross rental income includes the rental value of that portion of the building, but it does not count as residential use for the 80 percent test. Interest subsidy payments under the FHA Section 221(d)(3) and 236 programs are not included in gross income for this purpose.

The property may be situated within the U.S. or any of its possessions or in a foreign country if that country's laws provide a method of depreciation for the property which is comparable to the 200 percent declining-balance or the sum-of-the-years-digits method. In the event such a method is provided and it results in a depreciation allowance which is greater than that under the 150 percent declining-balance method but less than the fastest method available under Section 167 of the Code, the depreciation deduction is limited to that provided by the foreign country's law.

[¶409] CHOOSING A FORM OF ACCELERATED DEPRECIATION

Assume that, after due consideration, you have definitely decided to adopt one of the accelerated methods of depreciation. Which form of accelerated depreciation should you use?

If you are the first user of new residential rental real property, you are allowed to use either the 200 percent declining-balance or sum-of-the-years-digits method of figuring depreciation. Either method will return your basis much faster than the conventional straight-line method.

Consider these rules when you pick your method. Then pick the method that fits your requirements:

1. Depreciation the first two years will be greater under the 200 percent declining-balance method than under the sum-of-the-

digits method. By the third year, the digits method will catch up. Thereafter, the digits method will pull ahead.
2. At halfway mark in the property's life, you'll have recovered about two-thirds your cost under the 200 percent declining-balance method; about three-quarters, under the digits method.

[¶410]   SWITCHING DEPRECIATION METHODS

You can usually switch from a declining-balance to the straight-line depreciation method and get automatic approval of the switch. (You would usually switch near the halfway mark because then you'd get bigger deductions under straight-line.) To get automatic approval of the switch, you must file Form 3115 within the first 90 days of the taxable year in which you want the change to become effective and, in addition, meet other conditions. You will not be able to switch where you have entered into an agreement with the Commissioner prohibiting such a switch.

How to Figure When Switch Should Be Made. The depreciation rate to be used on the declining-balance method and on the straight-line method should be determined when the asset is first acquired. The time of the switch from the declining-balance method to the straight-line method should be carefully ascertained. Safeguards should be posted so that the change is made during the proper year, otherwise the asset will not be exhausted over its estimated life.

[¶411]   BASIS FOR DEPRECIATION AND SALVAGE VALUE

The basis for depreciation (i.e., the capital amount on which you figure your deductions) is the adjusted basis [under Sec. 1011 *et seq.*] for the purpose of determining the gain or loss on the sale or other disposition of the property [Sec. 167(g)]. Normally, this means your basis is what you paid for the property. But where you have trade exchanges, gifts, and other forms of acquisitions, there are special rules.

To the original basis for the property, from time to time should be added the cost of improvements, additions, and betterments. Any deductible loss or damage from casualty must be subtracted.

Where both depreciable property and nondepreciable property (such as land and buildings) are acquired for a lump sum, the basis for depreciation of the depreciable property is its proportionate part of the total cost, based on the ratio of the total cost to total value at the time of purchase [Reg. §1.167(a)-5].

A mortgage on the property at the time of acquisition does not reduce the basis; it is immaterial whether the property was taken subject to the mortgage or the mortgage was assumed. If property is repossessed because of default by the purchaser, the allowance for depreciation after the repossession should be computed upon cost at time of repossession, not upon original cost (*Crane,* 331 US 1). [Sec. 1038 of the Code].

If property that is used for personal reasons, such as a personal residence, is converted to rental property, the basis for depreciation is its fair market value at the time it was converted or its adjusted basis on that date, whichever is *less* [Reg. §1.167(f)-1]. The same basis would be used for computing any loss on the sale of property that was converted from residential to rental property before its sale [Reg. §1.165-3(b)]. For a discussion of basis of property acquired by inheritance or gift see ¶603.

> *Example:* Johnson purchased a residence in 1965 for $25,000. Of this amount, $15,000 was allocable to the building. The property was used as residence until 1/1/74, at which time it was converted to rental property. Its fair market value on that date was $22,000, of which $12,000 was allocable to the building; and its estimated life was 20 years. The basis for depreciation starting on 1/1/74 is $12,000, the amount then allocable to the building which is less than $15,000, the cost of the building; the annual amount deductible for depreciation on the straight-line basis is $600, one-twentieth of $12,000. The basis to be used for the entire property in computing loss on a subsequent sale would be $22,000, not $25,000.

A careful ledger should be kept of all construction costs, such as direct labor, manufacturing overhead, etc., so that a depreciation basis can be computed. If due to the construction of the asset there are assessments against the company or taxpayer, the amount of the assessment increases the basis.

All charges are to be included in determining basis. Freight charges, cost of installation, and special lines and services all go into determining the cost of the asset. However, on property which was not used in a trade or business but is converted to business use, the basis for depreciation is the fair market value at the time of the conversion or the cost of the property, whichever is lower.

If you act as your own builder or general contractor in putting up your own building or a capital improvement, you do not get a depreciation deduction on your equipment used on the job. [*Comm. v. Idaho Power Co.,* 418 U.S.1 (1974)]. The depreciation allocable to that job is added to the cost of your improvement [*Rev. Rul. 59-380,* CB 1959-2, 87].

Salvage Value. Salvage value must be taken into account in computing the annual allowance under all but the declining-balance method of depreciation. Salvage value is the net amount realizable from the sale of an asset, usefulness of which has been exhausted, over and above the cost of dismantling or removing [Sec. 1.167(a)-1(c)]. Furthermore, in no event can an asset (or account) be depreciated below a reasonable salvage value [Reg. §1.167(b)-2; *Massey,* 364 US 92]. Use a realistic value taking into consideration your use of the property, your retirement and maintenance practice, and the proceeds which experience has indicated you can expect. Junk or scrap value can be used only if your policy is to use depreciable property for its full serviceable life [*Special Ruling,* 5/18/55]. At one time it was thought that the concept of salvage value did not apply to real estate; but in a series of cases, beginning with *Casey,* 38 TC 357, the Tax Court held otherwise.

The reason for not deducting salvage from basis where declining-balance depreciation is used is that this method will leave an undepreciated balance at the end of the estimated useful life. This amount is the salvage value, bearing in mind the requirement that it must be reasonable.

To the extent salvage eventually realized exceeds the estimate which was used in computing the basis for depreciation, the excess is Section 1231 income (assuming no recapture) in the year of realization. If it is less than the estimate or if the declining-balance method was used so there is an unrecovered basis at the end of the useful life, the unrecovered amount is a fully deductible loss when the asset is sold or abandoned. [Sec. 1231 of the Code].

Where you switch from declining-balance to straight-line, estimated salvage must be subtracted from unrecovered basis, to which the straight-line method is thereafter applied [Reg. §1.167(e)-1(b)].

Either salvage or net salvage may be used in determining depreciation allowances, but the practice selected must be consistent, and treatment of costs of removal must be consistent with the practice followed. [See Reg. §1.167(b)-1, 2 and 3.]

When an asset is retired or disposed of, appropriate adjustment must be made in the asset and depreciation reserve accounts.

A special salvage rule, applicable only to depreciable personal property with a useful life of three years or more, permits you to ignore salvage up to 10 percent of the basis of the property [Section 167(f)].

[¶412]   **CLASS LIFE SYSTEM**

The Code has a "Class Life System." It:

1. Authorizes IRS to accept depreciation based on lives for business equipment (tangible personalty) acquired after 1970 that are not more than 20% shorter nor 20% longer than the "guideline lives" fixed by the Treasury in July 1962.
2. Provides for a half-year averaging convention as exemplified by the following alternative methods:
   a. all eligible property obtained during the taxable year is deemed to be acquired at midyear or
   b. each asset placed in service during the first half of the taxable

year is deemed to be acquired on the first day of the same year, while each asset placed in service in the second half of the year is deemed to be acquired on the first day of the next taxable year.

3. Permits a deduction for expenditures for repair and maintenance based on a percentage of the assets in a guideline class on which depreciation under the Class Life System is elected. It will not be necessary to prove that such expenditures do not have to be capitalized.

4. Sets up an Office of Industrial Economics which will analyze the annual information submitted by taxpayers using the Class Life System and constantly revised the guideline classes, guideline lives, and repair allowances and set up new guidelines and allowances where appropriate.

5. Reserve ratio test is no longer used. [See Rev. Proc. 77-10 in the Appendix. This explains the new ADR lines.]

How to Decide Whether to Adopt System. To determine whether it pays to sell or trade in your old equipment and buy new to get the higher depreciation under the Class Life System, take a careful look at the arithmetic. How much depreciation are you getting out of the old? How much will you get with the new? How much is any loss on the sale of the old worth? What are the estimated expenses with the old? With the new? What are the estimated cost savings, if any, through the higher efficiency of the new?

The approach will be different depending on whether or not the tax basis of the old equipment is higher than its present value. If it's not and you trade it in on the new equipment, you avoid the recapture of the gain as ordinary income under Section 1245 of the Code — the gain carries over to the new equipment and is not realized until the new property is sold.

On the other hand, if the basis is higher than the present value and you trade in the old property, you can't claim the loss, so that you would be looking to sell the property to realize the loss (and to avoid having IRS look on it as a trade-in anyhow, the sale should be to a third party).

Gauging the Savings in Purchase of Used Equipment. Under the Class Life System, you have to be extra careful in situations where you buy relatively small quantities of used equipment along with more substantial purchases of new equipment. The danger is that if the System is elected, it will apply to both used and new assets. The result could be that the used equipment would be subject to the same useful life range as the new equipment; whereas, as used equipment it actually has a shorter useful life. However, there is an exception: If the used assets exceed 10 percent of the total basis of all assets placed in service in the year. In such case, lives for used assets may be determined *without* regard to the new asset depreciation ranges.

[¶413]   **FASTER WRITE-OFF DUE TO TECHNOLOGICAL,
ECONOMIC AND POLITICAL CHANGES**

You can get faster depreciation on property whose economic value can be cut off by rapidly changing economic, technological, or political forces. A 50 percent deduction of the cost of a flying field and buildings was upheld for an air-training setup with a useful life of more than two years. Reason: It was built under a short-term government contract for a two-year training program [*Riddle,* 12 TCM 44, 1953].

An investor was allowed to depreciate a building over 20 years, although construction itself was good for 50 years, where a two-story building was erected to carry taxes in anticipation that it would be scrapped and replaced by a larger building as soon as economically feasible. This prospect was good enough to warrant an annual charge-off of 5 percent instead of 2 percent. [*Adda, Inc.* 9 TC 199 aff'd 171 F.2d 367 (2nd Cir. 1948)]. But note that acquisition with intention of demolishing may cost you any depreciation of an existing building; the cost of the building merely increases your cost for the nondepreciable land [*Lynchburg Nat. Bank,* 20 TC 670, *aff'd* 208 F.2d 757 4th Cir. 1970].

Where it appears that the actual useful life of your building will be considerably shorter than your original determination would indicate, you can depreciate the building using the shorter useful life, provided you can show clearly and convincingly obsolescence greater than you originally figured [*Offshore Operations Trust,* 32 TCM 985 (1973)].

Obsolescence can be caused by improvements, inventions, business expansion and contraction, relocation, etc. Obsolescence, unlike depreciation which reflects physical wear and tear, connotes a functional lessening of value resulting from external forces [*Real Est. Land Title Tr. Co.,* 309 US 13]. If it can be predicted (not the usual case), depreciation can be accelerated because obsolescence shortens useful life. Obsolescence is not the same as abandonment; the latter implies an overt act by which the taxpayer permanently discards the property (this doesn't mean mere nonuse). Obsolescence accelerates a loss, which still must be spread; abandonment gives rise to a full loss in the year it takes place [*Anheuser-Busch, Inc.,* 120 F.2d 403 8th Cir., 1941]. To accelerate depreciation, a taxpayer may have to prove the obsolescence was caused by factors over which he had no control; a shutdown of business due to an illegality is insufficient [*Haberle,* 280 US 384].

[¶414] **NONDEPRECIABLE PROPERTY BECOMING DEPRECIABLE;
TRAP IN FIRST-USER RULE**

When property which was not depreciable at the time of original use becomes depreciable property after 7/24/69, it cannot be treated as new property, the original use of which began with the taxpayer. Therefore, the taxpayer cannot use the fastest methods of accelerated depreciation with respect to the property if it is residential rental property or the 150 percent declining-balance method if it is new nonresidential rental property. [Sec. 167(j)(6)(B) of the Code].

Suppose you acquire a brand-new residence for your own use. You cannot claim depreciation deductions since depreciation on a personal residence is not a business (deductible) expense. A few years later, you move and rent the house, either partially or completely. Under the above provision, you won't be able to take accelerated depreciation. Formerly, IRS ruled that you could take accelerated depreciation under these circumstances. Since the property was never used by anyone else, you were the first user. Inasmuch as the property had not previously been eligible for depreciation deductions, you could choose accelerated depreciation [*Rev. Rul. 60-67,* CB 1960-1, 117].

The right to use accelerated depreciation has been limited to property not previously used by someone other than the taxpayer who claimed the deduction [Sec. 167(c) of the Code].

Here is an example of how you can run into this tax trap and how to avoid it:

Assume you have started a new business. Like many others, you use the sole proprietorship form of business so that the expected initial losses can be set off against personal income. When the profits start coming in, you incorporate the business to protect those profits from the individual income tax rates. The incorporation, of course, is tax free [Sec. 351 of the Code].

If you want the corporation to get the benefit of accelerated depreciation, do not acquire depreciable property for the business while you are operating it as a sole proprietorship. A corporation that receives depreciable property in a tax-free exchange is not the "first user" of the property as required by Section 167. Consequently, the corporation will not be entitled to accelerated depreciation [*Rev. Rul. 56-256,* CB 1956-2, 129; Sec. 1.167(c)(6)).

It might be well to protect yourself either by renting instead of buying during the proprietorship period or by forgoing the proprietorship entirely and incorporating immediately. If you are reasonably well satisfied that profits will be coming along fairly early in the operation, immediate incorporation will not hurt; the initial losses can be taken care of through carryovers.

[¶415] SPECIAL FIRST-YEAR DEPRECIATION ALLOWANCE

There is a special 20 percent first-year depreciation allowance which applies only to tangible personal property [Sec. 179 of the Code]. However, it is frequently available to real estate investors, for example, where a real estate operation requires a significant expenditure for personal property items, as in the case of a motel. Also, IRS treats certain items as personal property even though they are deemed fixtures and part of the real estate under local law. Typical examples are refrigerators and individual air conditioners.

The first-year allowance permits you to write off as much as $2,000 ($4,000 on a joint return) in addition to regular depreciation in the year the personal property is acquired [Sec. 179 of the Code]. This is based on a 20 percent deduction on a maximum annual investment of $10,000 ($20,000 on a joint return).

The effect of the 20 percent first-year writeoff when used with 200 percent declining-balance depreciation is to step up the recovery of investment by about 10 percent over the first half of the life of the property. Under the 200 percent declining-balance method, about 65 percent of cost is recovered in the first half of the life of the asset. Adding the 20 percent first-year writeoff, the recovery over the first half of the life of the property is boosted to about 72 percent. With the sum-of-the-digits method, the first half of the useful life recovery is boosted from about 73 percent to about 79 percent.

The immediate 20 percent writeoff is available on the purchase of both new and secondhand property. You still get your ordinary depreciation deduction on the balance of the cost.

The first-year writeoff plus the 150 percent declining-balance method can give better results than the 200 percent declining-balance or the digits methods (without the first-year writeoff) on property with an equal useful life.

Here are some *technical rules* you have to follow to be eligible for the special 20 percent first-year writeoff:

(1) The property you buy has to have a useful life of at least 6 years.

(2) The property has to have been bought after 1957.

(3) You cannot buy property from a related party between whom losses are disallowed, e.g., a corporation in which you own 50 percent or more of the stock; a partnership in which you own a more-than-50 percent interest (nor can the partnership or corporation buy from you); a trust of which you are the grantor or beneficiary; certain relatives. As to relatives, however, the prohibition applies only to transactions between spouses, ancestors, and lineal descendants (e.g., parents, children, and grandchildren). So you can make purchases from a brother or sister and from in-laws. When applying the constructive ownership rules to find if you own 50 percent of the stock of a corporation, for example, holdings of spouse, ancestors, and lineal descendants are the only relatives' holdings that count. [Sec. 179(d)(2) of the Code.]

(4) The property cannot be purchased from a corporation with which the purchaser files a consolidated return. The entire group filing a consolidated return is entitled to only one 20 percent deduction.

(5) The first-year writeoff does not apply to property received by gift or inheritance.

(6) If you trade in property as part of your purchase, that part of the basis of the new property which is a carryover of the basis of the traded-in property does

not count in applying the 20 percent writeoff. For example, assume you buy a new machine for $10,000, paying $7,000 in cash and trading in your old machine. If the old machine had a basis to you of $1,500, your basis for the new machine is $8,500. But your 20 percent writeoff applies only to $7,000, giving a $1,400 first-year writeoff.

(7) Where partnerships are concerned the dollar limitation of $10,000 is applied to the partnership, and the individual partners divide the permitted deduction (portion of the $10,000) [Sec. 179(d)(8) of the Code].

IRS Regulations Clarify First-Year Depreciation in Certain Areas.
IRS shows how to handle certain aspects of Sec. 179 of the Code 179 depreciation.

☐ (1) *When Deduction Is Available.* You can elect the full 20 percent writeoff in only the first year that depreciation deductions are available to you on that property. If you do not use averaging conventions, you can claim depreciation on property from the day you put it into service. If you put it into service on December 27, you could claim five days' ordinary depreciation — and the full 20 percent deduction. For example, you would claim 20 percent of a $10,000 qualified property, even on December 27 (20 percent × $10,000 = $2,000). You would also claim your normal depreciation for 5/365 ths of the year, against the $8,000.

☐ (2) *Tangible Personal Property.* As noted, Sec. 179 applies only to tangible personal property. Assets accessory to operating a business are personalty even though they may be deemed fixtures and so real estate under local law. Examples are machinery, printing presses, transporation or office equipment, refrigerators, individual air conditioning units, and grocery counters. Structural components of buildings are real estate (e.g., wiring, plumbing systems, central heating or central air conditioning machinery, pipes or ducts) and do not qualify.

☐ (3) *Electing Additional First-Year Allowance.* Under Sec. 1.179-4(a), a separate statement need not accompany a return to serve notice that special first-year depreciation is being claimed on the return. Simply compute the amount of first-year "bonus" depreciation as a separate item.

[¶416]   **ACCOUNTING FOR DEPRECIATION**

Depreciation is an annual deduction. You should deduct the proper depreciation allowance each year because you cannot increase your depreciation deduction later by failing to take the deduction in earlier years [Reg. §1.167(a)-10(a); *Young,* TC Memo 16 TCM 1012 (1957) aff'd 268 F. 2d 245 (9th Cir. 1959), Sec. 1016 of the Code]. The fact that you did not depreciate in a prior year will not prevent you from taking the proper current depreciation deduction in a later year.

> *Example:* Gray should depreciate $5,000 on his building in 1974. He fails to do this. In 1975, he can again depreciate $5,000 on the building. This time, he does so. However, he cannot get the deduction in 1975 that he should have taken in 1974.

If you buy or sell a depreciable asset during the taxable year, you can only deduct a *part* of its annual depreciation allowance.

> *Example:* Green buys a depreciable building during the year. He buys it on April 1. Green is a calendar-year taxpayer. He pays $10,000 for the building. It has a useful life of 20 years. Assume no salvage value. The annual depreciation allowance would be $500. However, Green has only held the asset for three-fourths of the year. Therefore, he is only entitled to take $375 depreciation for the year.

[¶417]   SPECIAL FIVE-YEAR DEPRECIATION FOR POLLUTION CONTROL FACILITIES

A taxpayer (including an estate or trust) can elect (under the regulations) to amortize a certified pollution control facility over a period of 60 months [Sec. 169(a) of the Code]. The amortization deduction is limited to pollution control facilities added to plants or other properties which were in operation before January 1, 1976. The amortization deduction is allowable only for the proportion of the cost of the property attributable to the first 15 years of its normal useful life. Where a property has a normal useful life of more than 15 years, you, in effect, treat the facility as if it were two separate facilities. One facility, representing the portion of the total cost attributable to the first 15 years of useful life, is eligible for the 60-month amortization. The other facility, the remaining cost, receives regular depreciation based on the entire normal useful life of the property. If the property has a normal useful life of 15 years or less, the total cost of the property is eligible for the 60-month amortization.

Facilities That Qualify. The amortization deduction is available only with respect to a "certified pollution control facility," generally defined as appropriately certified depreciable property which is a separate identifiable treatment facility used to abate or control water or atmospheric pollution or contamination by removing, altering, disposing, storing, or preventing the creation or emission of pollutants, contaminants, and wastes or heat [Sec. 169(d) of the Code]. A building is not a pollution control facility unless it is exclusively a treatment facility. A pollution control facility does not include any facility which serves any function other than pollution abatement. Facilities which only diffuse pollution, as distinct from abating it, are not pollution control facilities. The *Tax*

Reform Act of 1976, Sec. 169(d)(1)(C) of the Code, provides that the facility can not significantly:

1. Increase the output or capacity, extend the useful life, or reduce the total operating costs of such plant or facility or other property (or any unit thereof) or,
2. Alter the nature of the manufacturing or production process or facility.

Examples: A smokestack on a plant whose height was increased to disperse pollutants over a broader area is not a pollution control facility, while a device which is contained in a smokestack and actually abates the emission of pollutants is a pollution control facility. A facility that removes certain elements from fuel is not a pollution control facility.

Certifications. The amortization deduction is available only with respect to a pollution control facility which is certified by the appropriate state and federal authorities. [Sec. 169(d)(a) of the Code]. In the case of water pollution, the state certifying authority means the state water pollution control agency as defined in the Federal Water Pollution Control Act, and the federal certifying authority is the Secretary of the Interior. In the case of air pollution, the state authority is the air pollution control agency as defined in the Clean Air Act, and the federal authority is the Secretary of Health, Education, and Welfare. An interstate agency authorized to act in place of a state certifying authority is treated as the certifying authority of the state.

It is necessary with respect to any pollution control facility for the state authority to certify to the federal authority that the facility has been constructed, reconstructed, or erected or acquired in conformity with the state program or requirements regarding the abatement or control of water or air pollution or contamination.

Original User. The amortization deduction is available only with respect to a facility whose original use commences with the taxpayer before January 1, 1969. (If the plant was *not* in operation before January 1, 1969, there are special effective date limitations [Sec. 169(d)(4)(B)]. Only that portion of the basis of property constructed, reconstructed, or erected by the taxpayer is taken into account for purposes of the amortization deduction.

How to Make the Election to Amortize Over 60 Months. The election must be made either (1) within the month following the month in which the facility is completed or acquired or (2) within the first month of the tax year following the year in which the facility is completed or acquired.

A statement of election to amortize the pollution control facilities should be attached to the return for the year in which the first month of the 60-month amortization period occurs. It should include the following:

1. A description clearly identifying each separate certified pollution control facility for which the election is being made.
2. The date on which the facility was completed or acquired.
3. The period of useful life of the facility from the date the property was placed in service.
4. The date on which amortization is to begin.
5. The date on which the plant or other property to which the facility is connected began operating.
6. The total cost incurred and expended for the facility.
7. A description of any wastes to be recovered as a result of the operation of the facility; an estimate of the proceeds and profits to be realized from the sale of the wastes; a detailed schedule showing computation of the estimate.
8. A detailed computation of the amortizable basis of the facility as of the first month for which the deduction is taken.
9. A copy of the application for certification of the facilities and a copy of the federal certification. If certification has not yet been received, a statement to that effect should be attached.

The *Tax Reform Act of 1976* has broadened the allowance to cover equipment that prevents the emission or creation of pollutants while the plant is operating. (The *Tax Reform Act of 1976* also allows the investment credit on qualified property, even if Sec. 169 of the Code is *also* used.)

[¶418]   SPECIAL FIVE-YEAR DEPRECIATION FOR REHABILITATION EXPENDITURES

Under Section 167(k) of the Code, capital expenditures made for the rehabilitation of existing buildings used for low- and moderate-income rental housing can be depreciated on a straight-line basis over a 60-month period if the additions or improvements have a useful life of five years or more. This five-year writeoff gives the investor in rehabilitated housing great tax shelter.

As to qualified property for which rehabilitation expenditures are made before January 1, 1978, an election can be made to compute depreciation by using straight-line depreciation, a useful life of 60 months, and no salvage value in lieu of any other method. If an election is properly made and in effect to use this method as to any portion of the basis of property, no deduction for depreciation or amortization will be allowed as to that portion of the basis of the property under any other provision of the IRC. Thus, for example, the additional first-year depreciation allowance for small businesses permitted under Section 179 would not be available as to that portion of the basis of property for which a proper election was in effect.

In addition, if the expenditures are pursuant to a contract entered before January 1, 1978, then such expenditures qualify for Section 167(k) treatment. Once the election is made, you get the full 60 months to depreciate. (It should be noted that this extension reflects congressional concern and further extensions may occur in the future.) To determine whether rehabilitation expenditures are incurred before the deadline, each dwelling unit will be considered separately. Regardless of the method of accounting used by the taxpayer as to other items of income and expense, an expenditure is incurred for the purposes of the election on the date that expenditure would be considered incurred under the accrual method of accounting.

Election by Partnership. An election to use the 60-month depreciation as to property held by a partnership must be made by the partnership (Sec. 703(b)).

Excess Depreciation as Item of Tax Preference. Under Sec. 57 of the Code, the amount by which the depreciation deduction taken for a taxable year using the 60-month useful life exceeds the amount of the depreciation deduction which would have been allowable for the taxable year if the taxpayer had depreciated the property under the straight-line method for each taxable year of its useful life (determined without regard to the 60-month useful life provided for by Sec. 167(k)) for which the taxpayer has held the property constitutes an item of tax preference subject to the minimum tax on tax-preference income (see ¶421).

Recapture of Excess Depreciation. Additional depreciation of rehabilitation expenditures after one year after they were incurred is subject to recapture to the extent that they exceed the amount of depreciation adjustments which would result from straight-line depreciation without regard to the 60-month useful life (Sec. 1245 and 1250).

Expenditures for Which Special Five-Year Tax Writeoff Is Available.
Expenditures for which the special 60-month depreciation is available include amounts chargeable to a capital account for depreciable property with a useful life of five years or more, in connection with the rehabilitation of an existing building for low- and moderate-income rental housing. [Sec. 167(k)(1) of the Code]. Expenditures do not qualify unless, following the completion of rehabilitation, the dwelling unit is held for occupancy on a rental basis by tenants meeting the income requirements set up for this type of housing. Expenditures incurred to purchase land, the existing building, or any interest in the building (e.g., a leasehold interest) do not qualify. Likewise, expenditures attributable to a commercial unit (e.g., a grocery store) do not qualify. But an expenditure need not actually be made on a dwelling unit or a building provided it is incurred in connection with the rehabilitation of an existing building and is not attributable to

a commercial unit. For example, expenditures to pave a parking lot for use by the tenants might qualify. Such expenditures must meet the requirements set up as to minimum and maximum amounts of rehabilitation expenditures that may be taken into account.

New Construction. Expenditures for new construction do not qualify. But expenditures may qualify if the foundation and outer walls of the existing building are retained. Other relevant factors in making the determinatin may include the amount paid to acquire the existing building and the amount of material remaining for the existing building. The question will be determined as one of fact.

Enlargement of Existing Buildings. Expenditures for the enlargement of the total area occupied by the dwelling units in a rehabilitated building do not qualify. But expenditures for the construction of a related facility, such as a garage sidewalk or parking lot, may qualify.

What is Low- and Moderate-Income Rental Housing for Which Rehabilitation Expenditures May Qualify for 60-Month Writeoff?

In this context, "low-income rental housing" refers to any dwelling unit in a building which is held for occupancy by families and individuals of "low or moderate" income. If a dwelling unit fails to qualify as low-income rental housing at any time during the 60-month election period, the election is considered revoked by the taxpayer as to that unit. If a dwelling unit is rented for one or more periods during the taxable year beginning after the date the property attributable to rehabilitation expenditures allocated to such unit is placed in service, the dwelling unit will be considered low-income rental housing only if it is occupied by families and individuals of low or moderate income during each such period. If a dwelling unit is not rented for some period during the taxable year beginning after the date the property attributable to rehabilitation expenditures allocated to such unit is placed in service, the dwelling unit will be considered low-income rental housing only if, at all times during that period, the rental at which the unit is offered indicates that the unit is held for occupancy by families and individuals of low or moderate income. Generally, if the rental at which the unit is offered does not exceed 30 percent of the low- or moderate-income level for the number of persons occupying comparable units, the unit will be considered low-income rental housing.

What Is a Dwelling Unit for Purposes of 60-Month Writeoff?

The term "dwelling unit" means a house or an apartment used to provide living accommodations in a building or structure and containing the usual facilities found in a principal place of residence (e.g., kitchen and sleeping accommodations). A unit in a hotel, motel, inn or other establishment more than half of the dwelling units in which are used on a transient basis does not qualify. Generally, a unit will be considered used on a transient basis if the normal rental term is less than 30 days.

Maximum and Minimum Amounts of Rehabilitation Expenditures That May Qualify. The amount of rehabilitation expenditures that may be taken into account as to any dwelling unit is subject to the following limitations. In the case of a partnership, the limitations apply to the partnership, not to the individual partners. The taxpayer must maintain detailed records which permit specific identification of the rehabilitation expenditures paid or incurred as to each dwelling unit:

Minimum Amount. The taxpayer must pay or incur rehabilitation expenditures of more than $3,000 as to any dwelling unit over a period of two consecutive years in order to qualify.

Maximum Amount. The maximum amount of expenditures as to any dwelling unit which may be taken into account is $20,000. Property attributable to amounts in excess can be depreciated according to the usual methods. All amounts as to which a property election has been filed are taken into account, including expenditures covered by an election which has been revoked.

Allocations Rules. Expenditures attributable to more than one dwelling unit will be allocated among those individual dwelling units in the same ratio as the area of each such dwelling unit bears to the total area of all dwelling units to which the expenditures are attributable. Expenditures for related facilities attributable solely to dwelling units, such as parking facilities for tenant use, are to be allocated among the dwelling units to which they relate in the manner described. Expenditures for commercial units or for related facilities attributable solely to commercial units are not to be allocated to dwelling units. Expenditures for common areas such as stairways, halls, and entranceways are to be allocated among the particular dwelling and nondwelling units to which they relate.

How to Make the Election to Take the 60-Month Writeoff. An election under Section 167(k) to take the special five-year depreciation is made by attaching a statement to the income tax return filed for the first taxable year in which you compute the depreciation deduction using a 60-month useful life.

An information statement should be attached to the income tax return filed for each subsequent taxable year in which you compute depreciation. The 60-month election period begins with the date the property is placed in service, unless you adopt an averaging convention in accordance with Reg. §1.167(a)-10(b), which permits the use of some other date.

Generally, no election may be made until all conditions and limitations have been met. But, if the amount expended does not exceed the minimum amount of $3,000 per unit in the taxable year in which the property is placed in service and in the immediately preceding taxable year, you can make the election for the taxable year in which the property is placed in service by filing the election in the prescribed time and manner by enclosing a separate written statement showing an intent to fulfill the $3,000 minimum the succeeding taxable year. Provision is also made for making the election by filing an amended return.

When Election Must Be Filed. The election must be filed no later than the time prescribed by law (including extensions thereof) for filing the taxpayer's return for the taxable year in which the property is placed in service provided the expenditures meet the statutory requirements in that year, taking into account expenditures of the preceding taxable year for purposes of the $3,000 minimum amount limitation.

The statement required for subsequent years must be filed no later than the time prescribed by law (including extensions thereof) for filing the return for such subsequent years. If the taxpayer does not file a timely return for the year in which the property is placed in service, the election should be filed at the time the taxpayer files his first return for such year.

If the taxpayer fails to make an election within the prescribed time, no election may be made as to such property by filing an amended return or in any other manner.

If an election is filed with an amended return, it must be filed no later than the time prescribed for filing a return for the first taxable year following the year in which the property is placed in service.

The election may be made for any taxable year ending after July 24, 1969, even though the prescribed period for filing an election for such taxable year has expired. The provisions dealing with the time for making an election apply for purposes of determining the beginning of the 60-month election period.

If the taxpayer is permitted to revoke an election as to any property within the 90-day period, the taxpayer may adopt any method of depreciation permitted for such property, beginning with the date the property was placed in service, using the estimated useful life of the property on such date and determined without regard to the provisions permitting the 60-month writeoff.

When Election May Be Revoked. An election may be revoked by the taxpayer at any time prior to the time prescribed by law (including extensions thereof) for filing a tax return for the last taxable year in which any portion of the 60-month election period falls.

The revocation of an election does not affect taxable years for which a tax return was filed computing a depreciation deduction. A revocation is effective on the date specified by the taxpayer. Once an election is revoked, it may not be reinstated.

Failure to Meet Requirements as Revocation of Election; Effect of Revocation. An election is considered revoked if at any time during the taxable year

1. The unit is rented to a person or persons outside the definition of low or moderate income,
2. such unit is not held for occupancy by families and individuals of low or moderate income,

3. more than half the dwelling units in the building are rented on a transient basis, or

4. expenditures which are required in order to meet the $3,000-minimum-amount limitation for the preceding taxable year are insufficient.

The revocation is deemed to occur on the first day during the taxable year that the dwelling unit does not meet the requirements. Revocation of an election does not affect prior taxable years for which a tax return computing a depreciation deduction was filed if all the conditions were met for those years. Once an election is considered revoked, it may not be reinstated.

Effect of the Revocation. The taxpayer may not compute the depreciation deduction using the 60-month useful life for any portion of any taxable year beginning after the date on which a revocation is effective. The depreciation deduction allowed for the taxable year in which a revocation is effective is the amount the deduction would have been for that year if no revocation had occurred, multiplied by a fraction consisting of (1) the number of days in the taxable year prior to the date of the revocation over (2) the number of days of the 60-month period which fall within such year. Taxpayer will continue to use straight-line depreciation using the estimated remaining useful life and salvage value of the property, determined without regard to the provisions of Section 167(k) which permits the 60-month writeoff as of the date the revocation is deemed to occur. If a taxpayer wants to adopt another method of depreciation following a revocation of an election, the new method of depreciation would be a change in the method of accounting requiring consent of IRS [Section 446(e)]. Generally, the straight-line method of depreciation, using the property's remaining useful life determined without regard to the provisions permitting a 60-month writeoff, will be the only method which will be accepted following a revocation.

[¶419]   TWO METHODS OF SAVING TAX DOLLARS BY BOOSTING DEPRECIATION DEDUCTIONS

Here is a rundown on two methods by which you may be able to boost your depreciation deductions:

(1) Converting "Real Estate" Into Personal Property. The tax law bars the use of the 200 percent declining-balance or sum-of-the-years-digits depreciation method on commercial real estate factories, office buildings, stores, and warehouses and other commercial buildings. It limits you to 150 percent declining-balance depreciation on new commercial property and straight-line on used property. However, 200 percent declining-balance depreciation continues to be available for new personal property, and you can still use 150 percent declining-balance depreciation for used personal property if it has a useful life of three or more years.

Obviously, whether you can use the depreciation rules applicable to real estate or those applicable to personal property is going to make a big difference in your tax liability and your cash flow. What is more, items of personal property generally have shorter useful lives than realty. The availability of these shorter useful lives can greatly increase the depreciation available in the early years.

Further, as to personal property (but not for real property), you may get a special 20 percent first-year depreciation allowance. This tax break, of course, is of relatively greater importance to the small business, but in any business, it is a source of dollar savings.

The tax law requires you to pay an additional tax, on so-called tax-preference income, in excess of given amounts:

a. for individuals it is for preference in excess of $10,000 or half of tax paid (the greater of the two);

b. for corporations, it is for preferences in excess of $10,000 or the full tax paid (the greater of the two).

Included in the tax-preference income subject to this tax is accelerated depreciation on real estate; indeed, anything faster than straight-line is subject to this bite. But fast depreciation on personal property is not within reach of the special 15 percent tax with one exception-personal property subject to a lease.

Putting these routes to tax savings together yields significant results.

Example: You put up a new building with wall to wall carpeting. The carpet cost $20,000. If it becomes part of the building, the building has a useful life of 40 years, and you use composite depreciation, this $20,000 item will, in the first year, give you all of $750 in depreciation (using 150 percent declining-balance depreciation). You will save half that amount if you are in the 50 percent tax bracket. That's good money, and you will not want to throw it away. On top of that, you will add $250 to your tax-preference account.

If the carpet retains its character as personal property, you get that special first-year deduction. This reduces your basis to $16,000; but using 200 percent declining-balance and a useful life of 10 years, you come out with $7,200 in first-year depreciation ($4,000 plus $3,200). So you save $3,600 in taxes if you are in that same 50 percent tax bracket.

There are many types of property used in business that are not clearly either real or personal property. It has been important in the past to distinguish between personal and real property because of the shorter useful life of personal property and the special 20 percent first-year depreciation allowance which is available only for tangible personal property. But the fact that the tax law cuts down on the use of accelerated depreciation for real estate and imposes a new minimum tax on tax-preference income in which is included depreciation of real estate taken in excess of straight-line make it more important than formerly that, in planning ahead for new ventures or in reviewing your accounts as they now stand, you make sure that you are not passing up the savings which can result from transmuting items that may now be carried in your real property accounts into the personal property accounts.

Here are examples of situations where property which may be included in your real property accounts may qualify as personalty:

☐ *Air Conditioners.* Although central air conditioning is part of the build-ing, temperature and humidity machines required for the operation of other machines or for the processing of materials and foodstuffs are not considered part of the building. This is so even if the machinery incidentally provides for the comfort of employees or serves to an insubstantial degree areas where the environmental conditions are not essential.

☐ *Fixtures Relating to Business.* Fixtures that become real property under local law when they become fixed to a building may also qualify. Examples of these fixtures are: printing presses, individual air conditioners, refrigerators, shelves, counters, and similar assets accessory to the business.

☐ *Machine Foundations.* Specially designed flooring or slabs that are used for machine foundations are considered part of equipment and not realty. Where a whole floor is specially constructed as a foundation, the excess cost over the standard floor can be listed as equipment.

☐ *Outside Fixtures.* Items such as gasoline pumps and hydraulic lifts will qualify as equipment even though permanently fixed to the land.

☐ *Storage Tanks.* If a water storage tank serves a process requirement exclusively, it is equipment. If a general purpose tank is used also for a proces-sing requirement, the allocated portion can qualify. The same rules would apply to concrete reservoirs.

☐ *Special Structures.* A building is defined as any structure or edifice enclosing a space within its walls. However, certain structures are so closely combined with the machinery or equipment which they support, house, or serve that they must be retired, replaced, or abandoned with the machinery or equip-ment; e.g., special purpose buildings such as oil and gas storage tanks, grain storage bins, silos, fractioning towers, blast furnaces, coke ovens, brick kilns, coal tipples, and chicken coops. These can be excluded and be considered equipment.

☐ *Special Piping Systems.* When used for production purposes, these systems will qualify as equipment; e.g., compressed air, water processing, or special drainage systems. Also included are electric power supply systems that serve processing requirements. But only those systems that serve the building or normal human occupancy requirements are considered part of the building.

(2) Using Component Depreciation. The fastest method of depreciation available for commercial real estate is the 150 percent declining-balance depreciation on new and straight-line on used commercial buildings. This change could spell the difference between a good deal and a not-so-good deal. For example, on a $1 million building with a 40-year life, double-declining-balance would give you $50,000 in depreciation the first year; 150 percent declining-balance would give you 25 percent less or $37,500. The after-tax difference for the individual or corporation in the 50 percent tax bracket would be $6,250. This would represent a substantial part of the "profits" or cash flow of an investor buying the land and building for $1.2 million, putting in $300,000 of his own money, and giving a mortgage for the balance. Percentagewise, the difference would be even greater for the investor in used commercial property.

You can improve the picture considerably if, instead of using composite depreciation, that is, taking the building as a whole and applying a useful life to the whole building in line with IRS guidelines; you set up separate depreciation accounts for the components as follows:

	Useful Life	Cost
Building (shell)	40 years	$120,000
Wiring	12 years	20,000
Plumbing	12 years	12,000
Roof	12 years	8,000
Elevator	12 years	10,000
Paving	8 years	5,000
Air Conditioning	8 years	20,000
Ceilings	8 years	9,000
Floor	8 years	10,000
		$214,000

This would result in first-year depreciation aggregating $19,000 using 150 percent declining-balance.

Instead of using the separate component accounts, you used the composite method to depreciate the building as a whole, you could use a shorter useful life for the building than the 40 years used above for the shell. To figure the composite life of the building, you would take the useful lives of the components, weigh them on the basis of cost, and so arrive at a composite life for the entire building. Using the figures in our example as the average, the life of the composite building would be 26.88 years. Using this and 150 percent declining-balance depreciation would give first-year depreciation of $11,942. Contrast this with the $19,000 depreciation you were able to get with component depreciation.

If you had used the 200 percent declining-balance method of depreciation in the example with the composite method, your first-year depreciation would have been $15,923. In other words, using the component method even though limited to 150 percent declining-balance, you come out 19 percent better in terms of depreciation in the first year than if you had used the 200 percent declining-balance method, as permitted under the previous law, along with the composite method.

The minimum tax on tax preferences imposed by the 1969 tax law hits depreciation on real estate in excess of straight-line. Just as the component method of depreciation increases your depreciation deduction when you use 150 percent declining-balance, it increases your tax-preference income. So you should work out the arithmetic according to your particular tax situation.

It goes without saying that the faster you use your depreciation, the faster you run out of it. But that has always been part of the game. You use your depreciation while it lasts, in theory, get more when you run out of it, and keep the tax collector at bay.

Component Depreciation of Used Buildings. Formerly, IRS would not accept component depreciation for used real estate. Later, IRS ruled that you can depreciate a building by the component method even though it was a used building when you acquired it. However, you must make a proper allocation to each asset, and the ADR class life system must not be used for the building [*Rev. Rul. 73-410,* CB 1973-2, 53].

The facts presented to IRS showed that the taxpayer purchased land and building for a lump sum, that qualified appraisers allocated the costs between the land and the individual components of the building, and that a separate useful life was used for each component. IRS ruled that used real property can't be depreciated in separate component account unless the cost of acquisition is "properly allocated to the various components based on their value and useful lives are assigned to the component accounts based on the condition of the components at the time of acquisition."

To make sure you are on the right track, figure your depreciation deductions by way of the component and the composite methods. If you come out ahead with component depreciation, have the necessary allocation made by an expert appraiser and keep his report on file.

[¶420]   DEPRECIATION OF LAND PREPARATION COSTS

Under a revenue ruling [*Rev. Rul. 74-265* CB - 1974-1,56], you are allowed a depreciation allowance for some of your land preparation costs. Here is how the rule works.

As you know, Section 167 of the Code permits a depreciation allowance for the exhaustion of and wear and tear on property held for the production of income. Usually this does not cover deductions for the land itself but is restricted to improvements to the land, such as buildings [Reg. §1.167(a)-(2).].

IRS has ruled that it can determine that land adjacent to buildings may have a useful life. How is this determined? Well, if the replacement of your buildings will require the physical destruction of your land preparation immediately adjacent to those buildings, you may treat that land preparation, consisting of the shrubbery and ornamental trees, as depreciable property under Section 167 of the

Code. However, the balance of the landscaping — clearing and grading, topsoil, seeding, and planting shrubbery and ornamental trees around the boundaries of your land — will not be affected by replacement of the buildings. The cost of landscaping these areas will not be subject to the depreciation allowance. Instead, the cost of this land preparation is added to your basis.

Land not adjacent to a building is unaffected by the building's life so that it does not have a determinable life. As a result, a depreciation allowance for the preparation of such land is not applicable.

Land adjacent to a building will be destroyed when the building is replaced. The preparation of such adjacent land has a useful life contemporaneous with the building's and may therefore be depreciated for tax purposes.

In *Aurora Village Shopping Center, Inc.* 29 TCM 126 (1970), the Tax Court ruled that some of the grading costs incurred by the taxpayer were depreciable but it disallowed others.

Necessity for Supporting Allocation of Costs Between Land and Buildings. Aurora's architect, in planning a shopping center, recommended that the plateau of the building site be raised to make the shopping center more conspicious to passing traffic. The architect also recommended that the grading of the parking area be no greater than 3 percent to avoid discomfort to female patrons. It cost Aurora about $52,000 to get these jobs done. Aurora allocated $42,000 of this amount to its depreciable basis of the building. IRS allowed only $21,000 of this amount, and the Tax Court agreed with IRS. The Court stated that Aurora had grading costs that were attributable to building costs but that Aurora also had costs attributable to the cost of land. Although Aurora relied on an accountant to make the allocation, the accountant did not testify, and no reason was given for his absence. Neither did anyone else who could shed some light on the allocation testify. The Court had no basis for making an allocation more favorable than that made by IRS.

What to Do. To sustain your allocation of grading costs between land and buildings, you must show that the costs you allocate to the buildings are directly associated with them. While you can prevail where the grading is necessary for the proper setting of the buildings, you must prove your case. The burden will be on you if you're put to the test. You can't leave the court in a position in which it has no basis for making an estimate as to which costs are attributable to buildings and which to the land.

[¶421]   EXCESS DEPRECIATION AS ITEM OF TAX-PREFERENCE INCOME SUBJECT TO MINIMUM TAX

There is an element in the tax structure that real estate men have to take into consideration when figuring what the depreciation deductions that the different methods of depreciation open to them are worth. A 15 percent minimum tax is imposed on specific items of tax-preference income. The minimum tax applies (with individuals) only to the extent that the total tax preferences for the year exceeds $10,000 or one-half your regular tax (as adjusted for certain tax credits). Among the items that consititute tax preferences within the operation of this provision are accelerated depreciation on real estate and accelerated depreciation on personal property subject to a lease.

What Is Tax-Preference Income Subject to the Minimum Tax? Only the items listed in the statute are considered tax-preference income subject to the imposition of the minimum tax. In dealing with your depreciation deductions, you are going to have to consider not only the fact that those deductions may constitute tax-preference income, but you are also going to have to take into consideration your entire picture — all the other items of tax preferences that you have. Here is a rundown on tax-preference items for individuals:

1. accelerated depreciation on real estate;
2. accelerated depreciation on personal property subject to a lease,
3. excess depreciation over straight-line for housing rehabilitation expenditures;
4. amortization over accelerated depreciation on pollution control equipment;
5. amortization over accelerated depreciation on railroad rolling stock;
6. the amount by which the fair market value exceeds the option price on the exercise of a qualified stock option;
7. bad debt deductions of financial institutions;
8. the excess of percentage over cost depletion;
9. one-half of capital gains to the extent they exceed the net short-term capital loss for individuals and the ratio of the difference of corporate regular rate less their special tax rate and the general corporate tax rate for corporations;
10. intangible drilling costs in connection with productive oil and gas wells in excess of the amount that would have been deductible if the cost had been capitalized and amortized over 10 years;
11. excess of itemized deductions over 60 percent of adjusted gross income (excluding casualty and medical items).

Preferences From Foreign Sources. Generally, the 15 percent minimum tax applies only to preferences derived from domestic sources. However, tax benefits of stock options and capital gains derived from sources outside the U.S. are subject to the tax if the foreign country either does not tax these items or taxes them at preferential rates.

[¶422]   MINIMUM TAX AND HOW IT WORKS

Whether you are considering excess depreciation deductions as an item of tax preferences or any other item of tax preference income, keep in mind that you have no problem as long as the total of all your tax preferences does not exceed $10,000. What is more, even if you exceed the $10,000 limit, you can only be hit with a 15 percent tax.

How the Minimum on Tax Preferences Work. You add all your tax-preference income and subtract either the $10,000 exemption or one-half of your regular federal income tax, whichever is greater. (The regular tax must first be reduced by any tax credits for foreign tax, retirement income, investment, work incentive program and political contributions.) The regular tax of a corporation can be used in full; it does not include the penalty tax imposed for unreasonable accumulation of earnings or the personal holding company tax.

> *Example:* Suppose you have $100,000 of excess real estate depreciation from commercial property, $50,000 of excess depreciation for housing rehabilitation expenditures, and $50,000 worth of other items of tax preferences; your regular income tax bill comes to $50,000.
>
> The amount of the tax on your tax-preference income would be figured as follows: you subtract from the total of your tax preferences ($200,000) the exemption ($10,000) or one-half your regular income tax ($25,000). This leaves you a balance of $175,000 and 15 percent of this sum ($26,250) is the tax on your tax-preference income. So your total tax bill would be $50,000 plus $26,500 = $76,250.

No Basis Adjustment. The fact that accelerated depreciation in excess of straight-line depreciation is subject to the minimum tax does not mean that the tax paid on this preference is added to the basis of the property.

Deductions, Carryovers, and Carrybacks. Generally, no deductions are allowed for purposes of the minimum tax because they are allowed with the computation of the regular tax and to allow them again would amount to a double tax allowance.

How It Works: Where there is an operating loss carryover, the 15 percent tax is not due on the lesser of

1. an amount of tax preferences over $10,000 which is equal to the operating loss carryover where the operating loss carryover is less than the total of otherwise taxable preferences or
2. the amount of tax preferences over $10,000 where the operating loss carryover is greater than the totals of otherwise taxable preferences.

The "saved" 15 percent minimum tax will be due in any subsequent year in which the operating loss that was previously used to offset the minimum tax actually applied as a carryover to reduce regular taxable income.

If the operating loss carryover used to reduce taxable income in a subsequent year exceeds the amount of operating loss which offset the minimum tax in the earlier year, the part of the operating loss carryover which exceeded the previous minimum tax is treated as the first part of the carryover to reduce taxable income in the carryover year. Thus, the taxpayer is benefited since there is, to this extent, no need to pay the minimum tax previously saved. [Sec. 56(b) of the Code].

If an operating loss expires after 7 years without having been capable of being used to offset ordinary income, the minimum tax will never be paid.

An operating loss *carryback* cannot serve to reduce a minimum tax on tax preferences for an earlier year.

[¶423] ACCELERATED DEPRECIATION AS ITEM OF TAX PREFERENCE

The amount that accelerated depreciation of real estate contributes to your tax-preference income for each year is the amount of accelerated depreciation taken in that year in excess of the amount that straight-line depreciation would have yielded for each year of the useful life of the property [Sec. 1250 property]. In figuring the useful life of the real estate for this purpose, the special 60-month writeoff period for rehabilitation expenditures for low- and medium-income housing is disregarded and the excess of depreciation taken becomes an item of tax preference. As to certified pollution control facilities, the excess of amortization taken for the year under the 60-month writeoff over the amount that would otherwise be allowable as depreciation under Section 167 is subject to recapture.

Accelerated depreciation taken for personal property subject to a lease is an item of tax preference where the property is depreciable personal property or other nonreal property subject to depreciation recapture under Section 1245. If the property is in the hands of a corporation other than a personal holding company or a Subchapter S corporation, the 15 percent tax for tax preferences does not apply.

[¶424] MINIMUM TAX AND RELATED TAXPAYERS

Here is how the tax on tax-preference income applies to related taxpayers.

Husband and Wife. Where husband and wife file separate returns, each receives a $5,000 exemption.

Controlled Groups. With members of a controlled group of corporations, as defined for the purpose of the corporate income Surtax [Sec. 1563(a)], the

$10,000 exemption is divided equally among the members unless they agree to some other allocation.

Estates and Trusts. Tax preferences are attributed to an estate or trust on the one hand and the beneficiaries on the other hand in the same ratio as the income allocated to each except for depreciation or depletion specifically allocated in the governing instrument, which are attributed as allocated. The $10,000 exemption available to the trust or estate is allocated in the same proportions.

Subchapter S Corporations. Items of tax preference are apportioned among the shareholders as losses are apportioned under Section 1374(c)(1); they are not treated as preferences of the corporation. However, where capital gains are taxed to both the corporation and the shareholder (under Section 1378), the capital gains tax preference is subject to the minimum tax at both the coporate and the individual level. In such case, the amount treated as capital gain by the shareholder is reduced by the tax imposed under Section 1378, and by the 15 percent minimum tax imposed at the corporate level.

Regulated Investment Companies. These companies are not subject to the minimum tax to the extent they pass through to shareholders amounts attributable to tax preferences. However, their shareholders are subject to the minimum tax on preferences passed through to them. In addition, the shareholders are deemed to have received other tax preferences in proportion to the amounts of income of regulated investment company and other distributions made to them.

[¶425] HOW THE MINIMUM TAX ON TAX PREFERENCES FIGURES IN YOUR TOTAL TAX PICTURE

The way the minimum tax on tax preferences is set up, you're able to use a pretty large amount of tax-sheltered deductions (including depreciation deductions) each year and become subject to the 15 percent tax only when your tax-preference items exceed the protected amount, i.e., when the total of your tax preferences exceed either the $10,000 exemption or one half your regular taxes.

The More You Make, the More You Are Protected Against the Minimum Tax. The way the minimum tax works out is that the higher your tax bracket, the higher your regular income tax, the more tax shelter you can get for your depreciation and other tax deductions without paying the minimum tax. For example, if your regular tax comes to $30,000 you can take $15,000 worth of excess real estate depreciation deductions without paying any minimum tax at all. If your regular tax is higher than that, then you can take still more tax-preference income without paying the 15 percent tax. What's more, if you're in the 70 percent tax bracket and the 15 percent tax does apply to some part of your tax-preference income, you're only going to be paying the 15 percent on the unprotected part of your tax-preference income, but you will not be paying the 70 percent tax on one half of that income.

If you are shooting for avoiding the 15 percent tax altogether, your basic strategy will be to see that your tax-preference income is in balance with one half your regular tax liability. Since you have to have $10,000 worth of tax-preference income before the 15 percent tax comes into play, you might distribute property that generates tax preferences to your family in such a way that no member of the family is within its reach. Or you might consider switching from accelerated depreciation to straight line.

Absence of Tax Savings No Bar to Liability for Minimum Tax. You can be stuck with the 15 percent tax on tax-preference income even though your tax preferences did not save you any tax dollars. For example, if you wind up with a net loss by reason of your tax preferences, which cannot be carried backward or forward because it is not an operating loss, you are still liable for the 15 percent tax.

Effect of Depreciation Recapture on Liability for Minimum Tax. The fact that by reason of depreciation recapture some or all of the tax savings realized from this item of tax-preference income will be nullified does not mean that you do not have to pay the 15 percent tax.

Depreciation Recapture. Back in 1964, Congress enacted IRC § 1250, which recaptures depreciation on the sale of depreciable real property at a gain. To the extent the gain reflects previously deducted depreciation, the gain is ordinary income. Any remaining gain is normally capital gain. The Code also provides for depreciation recapture covering depreciable personal property (i.e., nonreal estate property) [Sec. 1245 of the Code].

Before the adoption of the 1969 Tax Reform Act, real estate depreciation recapture applied to all types of real estate in a uniform manner; and, if the real estate was held 21 months or more, the proportion of "additional" depreciation which was recapturable as ordinary income was reduced by 1 percent per month for each full month thereafter the property was held. Thus, real estate depreciation was phased out gradually; and if you held on to the property long enough, you could realize all your gain as capital gain and none of it would be treated as ordinary income.

The *1969 Tax Reform Act* changed this picture. Real estate depreciation recapture no longer applies across the board in a uniform manner to all types of properties. Indeed, with some real estate — all depreciable real estate other than residential rental properties — there's 100 percent recapture no matter how long you hold on to the property.

[¶426]   PRE-1969 DEPRECIATION RECAPTURE PROVISIONS MAY STILL APPLY

The 1969 tax law provides for the application of the earlier and more liberal depreciation recapture provisions to property the sale of which was subject to a building contract in existence before July 26, 1969, even though the actual transfer took place after that date. They also apply to federally assisted projects (e.g., FHA § 221(d)(3) and §236 programs) and to other publicly assisted housing programs under which the investor's return is limited. Also, since the 1969 depreciation recapture rules apply only to depreciation taken after December 31, 1969, depreciation taken before that date is subject to recapture under the earlier rules, discussed below.

How Pre-1969 Real Estate Depreciation Recapture Works. "Additional" depreciation taken after 1963 is subject to recapture as follows:

1. If real estate is sold when it has been held not more than one year, any realized gain is taxable as ordinary income to the extent of all depreciation taken by or allowed to the seller.
2. If sold in the first eight months of the second year — i.e., the 13th through the 20th month of the holding period — gain is taxable as ordinary income to the extent of additional (excess) depreciation. Additional depreciation is the difference between the depreciation actually taken or allowed (e.g., some form of accelerated depreciation) and the straight-line rate of depreciation for that period.
3. If sold at the end of the 21st full month of ownership or thereafter, the proportion of additional depreciation which is to be treated as ordinary income is diminished by 1 percent per full month after excluding the first 20 months. Thus, at the end of ten years of ownership, no ordinary income would result on the sale. This works out because from the 21st month through the 120th (the end of 10 years) is a period of 100 months. Reducing the additional depreciation subject to recapture by 1 percent per month for 100 months brings us to a point, at the end of the 100 months, where no part of the additional depreciation is subject to recapture.

Note: We are dealing with "full" months in applying these rules. If property was sold after being held, say, 20 months and 25 days, the entire additional depreciation could be recovered as ordinary income (i.e., the rules in (2), above, rather than the rule in (3), above). Similarly, if property was sold after being held 30 months and 20 days, 90 percent of the additional depreciation could be taxable as ordinary income. Since 30 months is 10 more months than 20 months, the amount of additional depreciation subject to ordinary income is reduced by 10 percent (1 percent for each full month; the 20 days do not count).

Example: Suppose a low-income apartment was constructed in 1969 for $300,000 and depreciated according to the double-declining-balance method. Assume $50,000 is allocated to land and $250,000 to the building, and a 50-year life is used. At the end of 4 years (48 full months), it is sold for $350,000. The seller's gain would be taxed as follows:

Selling price		$350,000
Original cost	$300,000	
Depreciation taken	37,663	
Basis		262,337
Gain		$ 87,663
Depreciation taken	$ 37,663	
Depreciation on straight-line basis		
(2% a year for 4 years)	20,000	
Additional depreciation		
subject to recapture	$ 17,663	
Percent recaptured (48th full month)	72%	
Amount recaptured (ordinary income)		12,717
Amount taxable as capital gain		$ 74,946

In any case where the total gain is less than the depreciation subject to recapture, the full gain is taxable as ordinary income — but no additional amount is taxable.

[¶427]   DEPRECIATION RECAPTURE RULES

The tax law strongly favors investments in residential rental properties, not only by permitting the fastest methods of accelerated depreciation with respect to such properties while limiting other new properties to the 150 percent declining-balance method, it also favors residential rental properties by applying softer depreciation recapture rules to them.

Under the provisions of Section 1250 as amended in 1969, accelerated depreciation taken in excess of allowable straight-line depreciation with respect to all forms of depreciable real estate except residential rental property is subject to recapture as ordinary income to the extent of gain resulting from the sale. As to residential rental property, a 1 percent per-month reduction in the amount subject to recapture is allowed after the property has been held for *100* full months. As to government-assisted residential rental properties, the more liberal pre-1969 recapture rules apply. As to property, the sale of which was subject to a binding contract in existence before July 26, 1969, the earlier recapture provisions (discussed below) still apply even though the transfer took place after that date.

[¶428]   FIGURING AMOUNT OF
ADDITIONAL DEPRECIATION AFTER 1969 AND BEFORE 1976

If a useful life (or salvage value) was used in determining your depreciation for any taxable year, that life (or value) is used in determining the straight-line depreciation for that period. However, a method of depreciation might have been used as to which a useful life was not taken into account — for example, the units of production method. Or, you may have used a method as to which salvage value was not taken into account — for example, the declining-balance method or the amortization of a leasehold improvement over the term of a lease. In these situations for the purpose of determining the straight-line depreciation for the applicable period, you use the useful life or salvage value which would have been proper if depreciation had actually been determined under the straight-line method. For this purpose, useful life or salvage value is determined by taking into account for each taxable year the same facts and circumstances as would have been taken into account if you had used such method.

Example: On January 1, 1971, a calendar-year taxpayer sells real estate which he purchased for $10,000 on January 1, 1969. Throughout the period he held the property, he computed depreciation under the 200 percent declining-balance method and used a useful life of 30 years. Salvage value was not taken into account. If he had computed depreciation under the straight-line method he would have used a salvage value of $1,000. The depreciation on the property under both methods is as follows:

Year	Declining Balance	Straight Line
1969	$ 667	$ 300
1970	622	300
1971	581	300
Total Depreciation	$1,870	$ 900

The additional depreciation for the property is $970, that is, the depreciation actually deducted minus the depreciation which would have resulted for that period under the straight-line method ($900).

[¶429] **RECAPTURE OF DEPRECIATION —
TAX REFORM ACT OF 1976**

Under Section 1250(a)(1) of the Code), for additional depreciation after December 31, 1975, the Tax Reform Act of 1976 provides that all excess depreciation on residential property is recaptured. Thus, the percentage rules for reduction of recapture of excess depreciation on residential realty are eliminated for depreciation after 1975.

A sketch history of the depreciation recapture rule is:

a. There is a special rule that *all* depreciation, not just excess, will be recaptured if the property is held for 12 months or under.

b. 1964-1969, recapture on all *excess* depreciation, reduced by one percentage point for each full month held over 20 months.

c. The depreciation recapture for *commercial* property is on all excess depreciation for years (generally) 1970 and on.

d. Depreciation recapture on *residential* property, (generally) for years 1970 and on, is full recapture on excess depreciation, reduced by one percentage point for each full month held over 100 months.

e. Commencing after 1975, there is full recapture of excess depreciation on residential property, along with commercial property. (Residential real property was not under this rule, under the 1969 Act.)

The rules noted are modified under Section 1250(a)(1)(B) of the Code for Federally Assisted Housing Projects with respect to which a mortgage is insured under 221(d)(3) or 236 of the *National Housing Act* or housing financed or assisted similarly under state or local laws; it also provides an exception for low income rental housing with respect to which a depreciation deduction for rehabilitation was allowed under Section 167(k) of the Code. There is also an exception with regard to the *Housing Act of 1949* and also with regard to low rental housing for occupancy by families or individuals under Section 8 of the *U.S. Housing Act of 1937* or similar laws under state and local laws.

The holding period does *not* continue, when computing the 1 percent rule for each full month property was held if the property is being foreclosed. The holding period of the property is determined as if the taxpayer ceased to hold the property on the date of the beginning of the proceedings for foreclosure. This rule is applicable to years after December 31, 1975. [Sec. 1250(d) of the code].

[¶430] REDUCING OR POSTPONING DEPRECIATION RECAPTURE

The effect of the stiff recapture provisions can be softened by using various techniques for postponing gain such as, for example, installment sales, tax-free exchanges, and refinancing.

If you hold your real estate long enough before disposing of it, you may be able to come out without any depreciation recapture and still benefit from the tax advantages of accelerated depreciation in the early years of your holding. As to depreciation taken after 1963 and before 1970, after you have held any depreciable property more than 20 months, the amount of excess depreciation subject to recapture is reduced by 1 percent for each full month. So, no pre-1970 depreciation is recaptured if you hold the property for 10 full years.

As to depreciaiton taken after 1969 with respect to government-assisted residential rental property (e.g., FHA §221(d)(3) and 236 programs) acquired before 1976, the amount of excess depreciation subject to recapture is reduced by 1 percent per full month in excess of 20 months. At the end of 10 years, there's no recapture.

As to residential rental housing other than government-assisted housing or for low- or moderate-income rental housing and which qualify for the five-year writeoff, the amount of post-1969, pre-1976 excess depreciation subject to recapture is reduced by 1 percent per month after 100 months. If you hold the property for 16 years and 8 months, there's no recapture.

Here we give you a rundown on some of the important ways open to real estate men to ease the bite of or postpone depreciation recapture.

(1) Tax-Free Exchanges. Tax-free exchanges of like-kind property can be used to unlock your "locked in" position, since you postpone the tax on your gain and, consequently, the effect of the recapture provisions. You may want to trade up your property and finance the difference between your equity in your old property and the value of the new.

(2) Refinancing. Another avenue that you might consider is the advisability of refinancing. Refinancing can help you raise the cash necessary for another investment, get the benefits of interest deductions, and, at the same time, retain the benefits of accelerated depreciation.

(3) Income Averaging. The tax law liberalizes the old income averaging provision in two basic ways that can help real estate investors as well as other investors:

1. It lowers from 33⅓ percent to 20 percent the percentage by which an individual's income must increase over the 4-year base period before the averaging provision becomes available.
2. It extends income averaging to long-term capital gains.

If you elect to use income averaging (1) you cannot use the alternative capital gains rate, nor (2) the 50 percent maximum tax on personal service income. As to the first limitation, it is now 25 percent for the first $50,000 of capital gains and 35 percent for the remainder.

What it all comes down to is that, before you elect to use income averaging, you will have to do some arithmetic to figure out how much you will gain by income averaging and how much you will lose, if anything, by the loss of the alternative capital gains rate and the earned-income ceiling.

(4) Sale After End of Holding Period. If you sell when the holding period is exactly 1 year or less, the entire depreciation (including straight-line) can be recaptured as ordinary income. If the holding period is 1 year and 1 day, only as much of the depreciation as exceeds straight-line is recapturable as ordinary income. As to residential rental property, for depreciation prior to 1976, there is a phase-out of recapture; and for each full month in excess of 100 months, the recapture is reduced by 1 percent. What is required here is a full month; part of a month does not count. Keep in mind that a sale of real estate generally is considered to occur on the day of the closing, i.e., the day when title passes.

Low- and Moderate-Income Rental Housing. When you invest in federally assisted low- and moderate-income rental housing [FHA §221(d)(3) and 236 programs] or in other publicly assisted housing programs, the pre-1969 recapture rules apply (but the sale may be a tax-free sale to tenants or occupants or to a tax-exempt organization). The pre-1969 recapture rules apply provided the property is constructed, reconstructed, or acquired before January 1, 1976. Under these rules, depreciation is recaptured in full if the sale occurs in the first twelve months and there is a phase-out of the recapture of the excess of acceleration over straight-line depreciation after 20 months. The recapture is reduced at the rate of 1 percent per month until 120 months, after which no recapture applies.

Sale During the 20-Month Holding Period. Keep the *full-month* concept in mind for pre-1976 depreciation. For each full month of holding period in excess of 20, you knock off an additional 1 percent from the amount of additional depreciation (i.e., excess of accelerated over straight-line depreciation) that's subject to recapture at ordinary income rates. Here, too, timing becomes important. For example, if you acquire property on the 16th of the month, each full month of ownership will end on the 16th of succeeding months. So, if you are setting a closing date near the middle of the month when you dispose of the property, make sure it is the 16th or later. Otherwise, 1 percent of the additional depreciation that you could otherwise pick up at capital gain rates will become ordinary income.

Where construction is nearing completion and the end of the month is approaching, it may be worthwhile to push hard to put the property into service before the end of the month. If you do, you pick up almost a whole month in holding period because your holding period then starts on the first day of the month. That speeds up the completion of the first year's holding period if there's going to be an early sale; it gets you past the 20-month holding period, after which less than the full additional depreciation is subject to recapture; or it gives you an additional edge of 1 percent reduction in additional depreciation subject to recapture when you dispose of the property sometime after you've held it for a period that exceeds 20 months.

(5) Should you Make a Gift (lifetime transfer) or Let the Property Pass by Inheritance? Here are the factors to consider:

    a. The *pre-1977* gift tax rate is three fourths of the estate tax rate.

    b. Making a lifetime gift prior to 1/1/77 generally got the property and the gift tax paid on it out of the estate (the estate tax paid on property in the estate does not reduce the estate subject to tax).

    c. Making a lifetime gift gets the income from the property into the hands of the donee (whose income tax bracket is presumably lower than the doner's).

    d. A lifetime gift does not result in Section 1250 (depreciation recapture) income. But the donee takes the donor's basis for the property; so, on a subsequent disposition, the donee may realize Section 1250 income. And the donor's holding period is "tacked on" to the donee's holding period.

e. When property passes on death, there is no Section 1250 income realized. Furthermore, the beneficiary who receives the property gets a basis for it that is equal to the market value at the time of death *if death was prior to 1//77*. Thereafter, basis to the beneficiary is generally the decedent's basis. Plus pre-1977 appreciation, plus taxes attributable to post 1976 appreciation. And any potential Section 1250 income that was present when the decedent held the property disappears if death is prior to 1/1/77. A new holding period begins to run for death prior to 1/1/77.

In each case, you'll have to analyze these factors in view of your own situation. But keep this in mind: Where other indications point to a lifetime gift, the potential Section 1250 income to the donee need not always be a deterrent. Remember that your holding period before the gift carries over to him. So, if he holds the property for some time thereafter (especially where you already had a substantial holding period), he will be approaching the 10-year limit. And the potential ordinary income on recapture keeps diminishing.

(6) Purchase of Stock Versus Sale of Assets. There are many considerations that arise in determining whether or not to operate a business in corporate or unincorporated form. If you incorporate and subsequently sell stock rather than assets, you avoid any impact of Section 1250.

Purchase of Assets Rather Than Stock. On the other side of the coin, we have the tax considerations of the purchaser. Before the 1969 tax law, where asset values had appreciated, a corporate purchaser could buy stock rather than assets and within two years liquidate the purchased corporation. Under Section 334(b)(2), the basis of the assets acquired in the liquidation would be stepped up to the price paid for the stock. The purchaser in many cases is willing to buy stock. But under Section 1250, the corporation being liquidated will have to pick up as taxable income as much of the Section 1250 profit as is equal to the difference between its basis and the market value of the assets (as reflected by the purchase price paid for the stock) at the time of liquidation.

If assets rather than stock are sold, the sellers will have to pick up the Section 1250 gain — either in a 12-month liquidation (Section 337) or via an ordinary liquidation followed by a sale of the assets. In either case, the corporation being liquidated will pick up the Section 1250 gain — in a 12-month liquidation, when it sells the assets within the 12-month period; in an ordinary liquidation, when it distributes the assets. In the second situation, we have to worry about *Court Holding Company* [324 US 331, 33 AFTR 593 (1945)]. Under that case, the stockholders of the seller must be able to show that they negotiated on their own behalf (not the corporation's) when they sold the property received in liquidation. Otherwise, the entire gain (not only the recaptured depreciation) can be taxable to the corporation.

(7) Sale of Depreciable Real Estate Used in Business. Since the sale of a Section 1231 asset might very well result in ordinary income under Section 1250, timing a sale in a year to coincide with the availability of an ordinary loss may be desirable, since the loss will offset ordinary income to the extent that Section 1250 applies to the sale of Section 1231 assets.

[¶431]   REAL ESTATE SUBJECT TO DEPRECIATION RECAPTURE

Depreciation recapture applies in the following ways:

Commercial, Industrial and Office Buildings. Under the 1969 Tax Reform Act, 100 percent of the excess of accelerated over straight-line depreciation is subject to recapture with respect to all properties other than residential rental properties, including commercial, industrial, and office buildings. This rule applies to depreciation for periods subsequent to December 31, 1969, with respect to properties acquired before December 31, 1969, as well as to properties acquired after that date, except as noted above.

> *Example:* Your gain on a sale of an office building is $15,000. Additional depreciation after 1969 is $1,500 and for earlier periods additional depreciation was $3,000. Your holding period is 30 months. All the additional post-1969 depreciation ($1,500) is recaptured as ordinary income. As to depreciation taken in the pre-1970 years, 90 percent (120 months - 30 months) of the $3,000 additional depreciation gives you $2,700 recaptures as ordinary income. The way it works out is that $4,200 ($1,500 (+) $2,700) of the $15,000 gain is recaptured as ordinary income; the rest is capital gain.

Residential Rental Properties. The entire excess of accelerated over straight-line as to new residential properties is recaptured as ordinary income if the property is disposed of within 100 months. Thereafter, the amount recaptured as ordinary income is reduced by 1 percent for each month if it is depreciation prior to 1970. (After 1975, the 100 month rule on post 1975 depreciation on residential realty of most types is eliminated. That is, all post 1976 excess depreciation is subject to recapture). If the property is sold after a holding period of 16 years and 8 months, the entire gain on the sale will be long-term capital gain for depreciation post 1969 and pre 1976.

Government-assisted low- and moderate-income rental properties are subject to the recapture rules in effect before the 1969 tax law.

[¶432]   AMOUNT OF RECAPTURE WHERE PROPERTY CONSISTS OF SEVERAL ELEMENTS

Where property is made up of separate elements is sold or disposed of, special rules are provided for figuring the amount of depreciation recapture.

Under these rules, where real estate has been improved or has had different parts of the property added or put into service before the completion of the entire property, the property is divided into separate elements. When the property or any element is sold or disposed of, each separate element is treated as a separate property; the recapture is figured based on the depreciation attributable to that element, using a separate holding period for that element. Under the 1969 law [Sec. 1250(f) of the Code], effective for taxable years ending after July 24, 1969, you figure the amount of recapture attributable to any element as follows:

Aside from the fact that the Tax Reform Act of 1976 changed the recapture rules for residential property, as noted earlier, by deleting rule for each month over 100 months, the amount of depreciation recaptured as ordinary income attributable to any element is the sum of (1) the amount (if any) determined by multiplying (a) the amount which bears the same ratio to the lower of the gain or the additional post-1969 depreciation on the entire property as the additional post-1969 depreciation for that element bears to the additional post-1969 depreciation for all elements by (b) the applicable percentage for such element plus (2) the amount (if any) determined by multiplying (a) the amount which bears the same ratio to the lower of the additional pre-1970 depreciation on the whole property or the excess of the gain over the additional post-1969 depreciation, as the addition pre-1970 depreciation for such element bears to the additional pre-1970 depreciation for all elements, by (b) the applicable percentage for such element [Sec. 1250(f)(3) of the Code]. You make your determinations as to any element if the element was a separate property as follows:

(A)	(B)	(C)	(D)
Additional post-1969 depreciation for the element.	÷ Additional post-1969 depreciation for all elements	× Lower of gain (under post-1969 rules) or additional post-1969 depreciation on whole property	× Applicable percentage for the element (under applicable percentage rules for for post-1969 depreciation)

Plus

(E)	(F)	(G)	(H)
Additional pre-1970 depreciation for the element	÷ Additional pre-1970 depreciation on all elements	× Lower of additional pre-1970 depreciation on whole property or excess of gain over additional post-1969 depreciation on whole property	× Applicable percentage for the element (determined under applicable percentage rules for pre-1970 depreciation)

Example: You sell real estate for $90,000. The adjusted basis is $37,500. Additional post-1969, pre-1976, depreciation comes to

$6,000. Additional pre-1970 depreciation is $24,000. Gain is $52,500. Excess of gain over post-1969, pre-1976 depreciation is $46,500. The property is made up of three elements (I, II, III). The additional post-1969 and pre-1970 depreciation and applicable percentage for each element, determined as if each element was a separate property, are:

Post-1969, Pre-1976 Depreciation

Element	Additional Depreciation	Applicable Percentage
I	$3,000	80
II	1,500	100
III	1,500	100
Total	$6,000	

The amount of gain for each element of property of post-1969 depreciation is figured as follows:

I	$3,000/$6,000	×	$6,000	×	80%	=	$2,400
II	$1,500/$6,000	×	$6,000	×	100%	=	$1,500
III	$1,500/$6,000	×	$6,000	×	100%	=	$11,500
Total Amount Recaptured							$5,400

Pre-1970 Depreciation

Element	Additional Depreciation	Applicable Percentage
I	$15,000	50
II	4,500	80
III	4,500	60
	$25,000	

The amount of gain for each element of property of pre-1970 depreciation is figured as follows:

I	$15,000/$24,000	×	$24,000	×	50%	=	$ 7,500
II	$ 4,500/$24,000	×	$24,000	×	80%	=	$ 3,600
III	$ 4,500/$24,000	×	$24,000	×	60%	=	$ 2,700
Total Amount Recaptured							$13,800

Total amount of post-1969 and pre-1970 depreciation recapture comes to:

Element	Post-1969 Depreciation	Pre-1970 Depreciation	Total
I	$2,400	$ 7,500	$ 9,900
II	1,500	3,600	5,100
III	1,500	2,700	4,200
Total	$5,400	$13,800	$19,200

[¶433]   DEPRECIATION RECAPTURE RULES CAN APPLY IN UNEXPECTED SITUATIONS

Just in the case of Section 1245 (recapture of depreciation of personal property), the section, Section 1250, affecting real estate is broad enough to cover more than sales and exchanges; it can even create taxable situations where otherwise the transaction would be tax free. Generally, Section 1250 applies to sales and exchanges and other dispositions subject to a number of exceptions and modifications, the more important of which are as follows:

Gifts are not taxable events — but the recapture potential in the hands of the donor is transferred to the donee. So, when the donee disposed of the propery, he could have ordinary income based on excess depreciation taken by the donor. But the donor's holding period is tacked on to the donee's period. So, if they had a combined holding period of more than ten years, there'd be no depreciation recapture.

Transfers at death are not taxable events. Under pre-1977 Law, the recipient takes as his basis the fair market value of the property at the time of the decedent's death, there is no transferred basis, and the law forgives the ordinary income potential that arose from depreciation taken by the decedent. The post '76 rules do not provide for this step up of basis.

Charitable contributions of real property have to be reduced by the amount that would have been taxable income under the recapture rules had the property been sold at market value.

Tax-free incorporations, etc. [Sec. 351]; reorganizations [Sec. 361]; and liquidations of subsidiaries [Sec. 332] do not give rise to taxable events except to the extent of "boot."

Distributions to partners by a partnership generally do not create a taxable event for depreciation recapture. But the potential ordinary income in the distribution will carry over to the partner to be applied when he disposes of the property.

Corporate distributions normally not taxable to the corporation can be taxable to it to the extent that the depreciation recapture provisions apply. The situations involved are: (1) distributions of dividends in kind, (2) distributions in partial or complete liquidation, and (3) sales made by corporation during the course of a 12-month [Sec. 337] liquidation.

Disposition of a principal residence does not create any recapture problem, whether or not the residence is sold for cash or exchanged for other property. For purposes of this exception, "principal residence" has two meanings: (1) it may be a principal residence as defined in Section 1034 which permits tax-free exchanges, or (2) it may be a principal residence as defined in Section 121 which refers to a residence of a person attaining the age of 65 before he disposes of a house which he has owned and used as his principal residence for five out of the past eight years.

Like-kind exchanges and involuntary conversions proceeds reinvested under the tax-deferral rules generally do not give rise to taxable events under the recapture section except to the extent that gain would be recognized under the like-kind or involuntary conversion rules. There are two important cases, however, where otherwise unrecognized gain is subject to recapture:

1. Where the owner of converted property uses the money obtained from the conversion to buy stock to acquire control of a corporation owning property similar or related in service or use to the converted property. Although under Section 1033(a)(3)(A) this use of the funds creates no taxable gain, Section 1250 says gain to the extent of the funds so used is subject to recapture.

2. Where the properties received in the tax-free exchange consist partly of Section 1250 property and partly of other property (e.g., vacant land), as much of the gain as exceeds the fair market value or cost of the Section 1250 property received is subject to recapture.

Sales during a 12-month liquidation period are generally tax free. But to the extent of ordinary income potential in the property sold, the corporation will be taxable under the rules of Section 1250. If the company takes back installment notes and thus delays reporting the gain, when the notes are distributed to the stockholders in the liquidation, the corporation will have to pick up the same amount of ordinary income that it would have realized had it sold the notes.

[¶434] **SPECIAL HOLDING PERIOD RULES**

To determine the percentage of additional depreciation that can be taxed as ordinary income, you must use the special holding period rules set forth in Section 1250. In all other respects, as in determining the amount of straight-line depreciation, the usual holding rules set forth in Section 1223 apply. (Keep in mind that, while as to all real estate other than residential rental property, the tax law provides for 100 percent recapture of excess depreciation regardless of how long the property has been held, as to residential rental properties, there is a gradual phaseout of recapture if the property was held for the specified time prior to 1976). These rules are as follows:

1. For property acquired by the taxpayer, the holding period begins on the day after the date of acquisition.

2. For property constructed, reconstructed, or erected by the taxpayer, the holding period begins on the first day of the month in which the property is placed in service (i.e., used in a trade or business, or for the production of income, or for personal use).

3. For property where the basis is transferred from the former owner because it was acquired by gift or in a tax-free transaction, the holding period of the new owner includes that of the former owner.

4. For property acquired in exchange for a principal residence and where recapture did not apply, the holding period of the new property includes the holding period of the former property.

[¶435] **AGREEMENT WITH
IRS COVERING DEPRECIATION ALLOWANCE**

Agreement can be made with IRS respecting estimated useful life, method and rate of depreciation, and salvage.

Application for agreement is made to the Director for the District in which your return is required to be filed [Reg. §1.167(d)-1]. Application must be in quadruplicate and include in practical detail information as to:

a. Character and location of the property;

b. Original cost or other basis and date of acquisition;

c. Proper adjustments to basis, including depreciation accumulated to the first taxable year to be covered by the agreement;

d. Estimated useful life and estimated salvage value;

e. Method and rate of depreciation;

f. Any other facts and circumstances pertinent to making a reasonable estimate of the useful life of the property and its salvage value.

The agreement binds both parties until facts and circumstances not taken into account in making the agreement are shown to exist. The party wishing to modify or change the agreement has the burden of proving the new facts or circumstances.

Because the agreement is binding, it is probably better to rely on following a consistent practice in setting up your depreciation schedules. Consistency is adequate protection against a challenge by the Commissioner. For information about the content and handling of the agreement, see Reg. §1.167(d)-1. When new circumstances arise, you are permitted to modify your agreement if the Treasury agrees that these new depreciation rules are a new factor which justifies modifying the agreement. If the new rules give you a better break, notify the District Director of the Internal Revenue Service that you want to modify your agreement and spell out the changes you want to make in a letter sent by certified mail [Reg. §1.167(d)-1].

CHAPTER **5**

Casualty Loss Tax Deduction

[¶501] **WHAT IS A CASUALTY LOSS?**

Losses on business or nonbusiness property which result from an accident, fire, storm, drought, shipwreck, or other casualty are generally deductible [Sec. 165 (c) (3) of the Code]. Even if you cannot use the full deduction in the current year, there is still the possibility of getting all of the benefit over the years. Since casualty losses are subject to the net operating loss carryover provisions, any part of the loss not used one year may be carried back three years or ahead for seven years. The deduction and the carryover are available to an individual, a married couple, or an estate or trust. Members of a partnership share casualty losses. A corporation does not have to rely on the casualty loss. It is entitled to deduct losses in most events.

In *Matheson* [18 BTA 674 aff'd, 54 F. 2d 537 (2nd Cir. 1931)], a casualty was defined as "an event due to some sudden, unexpected or unusual cause." But in *Heyn* [46 TC 302 acq. 1967-1CB2], the Tax Court ruled that you can get the deduction although the loss may have been foreseeable and even preventable by the exercise of due care.

Casualty losses do not include losses due to progressive deterioration of property through a steadily operating cause *Fay* [42 BTA 206, Aff'd, 120 F. 2d 253 (2nd Cir. 1941)], *Durden* [3 TC].

The deductible loss is limited to property. If you pay damages for personal injuries to others, you cannot take a casualty loss deduction [*Mulholland*, 16 BTA 1331].

If your property loses value because it is in or near a disaster area, (i.e., mud slide area) you cannot take a deduction for that loss. The loss must occur in relation to your property, not someone else's [see *Stoll,* 5 TCM 731 (1959))].

The expenses incident to a casualty, such as the cost of moving or rental of temporary living accommodations, are not allowed as a casualty loss deduction.

Deductible Casualty Losses: Losses due to bomb damage [IT 3519, CB 1941-2, 96; see *Ebner*, TC Memo 1958-108)]. Losses to home caused by a sudden settling of the land due to excessive rainfall (note his is not erosion) [*Hester*, TC Memo 1954-176]. Losses of trees due to drought [*Buttram v. Jones*, 87 F. Supp. 322]. Losses due to an earthquake [A.R.R. 4725, CB 111-1, 143]. Losses due to fire [IRC Sec. 165 (c) (3)]. Losses due to shipwreck [IRC Sec. 165 (c)(3)]. Losses due to storm [IRC Sec. 165(c)(3)]. Damage to a grain mill by unusual river ice formation [*Stewart City Mills*, 44 BTA 173]. Losses due to a mine cave-in [*Rev. Rul.* 55-327, CB 1955-1, 25.]. Losses due to deep sinking of land caused by a subterranean disturbance [*Grant*, 30 BTA 1028]. Losses caused by vandalism [*Banigan*, 10 TCM 561]. Losses due to a quarry blast [*Durden*, 3 TC 1]. Losses due to "sonic boom" when an airplane breaks the sound barrier [*Rev. Rul. 59-344*, CB 1959-2, 74]. Losses due to termite destruction if the attack is sudden. The important concept is suddenness [*Rosenberg*, 198 F.2d 46; *Buist*, 164 F. Supp. 218; compare *Rogers*, 120 F. 2d 244]. Although there was previous termite damage and it was stopped, later termite damage revealed in annual inspection is deductible as being sudden [*Kilroe*, 32 TC 1304]. Losses due to landslide [*Heyn*, 46 TC 302].

Disallowed Casualty Losses: Damage to property of another [*Stoll*, 5 TCM 731. See also *West*, 163 F. Supp. 739]. Cost of defending a damage suit [*Oransky*, 1 BTA 1239]. Erosion loss [*Texas and Pacific Ry. Co.*, TC Memo 1943-507]. Loss caused by moths [Rev. Rul. 55-327, CB 1955-1, 25]. Wrongful seizure of property [*Hughes* 1 BTA 944]. Loss of trees resulting from Dutch elm and other diseases [*IRS Field Release No. 56*, August 5, 1957]. Damage done by rats [*Banigan*, 10 TCM 561].

[¶502]　　　　　　　**ESTABLISHING CASUALTY LOSS**

You must be able to prove your loss to obtain a deduction. You should be prepared to show: (1) the nature of the casualty and when it occurred; (2) that the loss was the direct result of the casualty; (3) that you were the owner of the property; (4) the cost or other adjusted basis of the property, evidenced by a purchase contract or a comparable instrument; note that you must also show improvements; (5) depreciation allowed or allowable; (6) values before and after the casualty; (7) the amount of insurance or other compensation received or recoverable, including the value of repairs, restoration, or cleaning up provided without cost by disaster agencies.

[¶503]　　　　　　　**DECREASE IN VALUE**

The difference between the value of the property immediately before and immediately after the casualty (limited to your basis) is usually the key to how much you can deduct. It becomes a matter of proof. With considerable amounts involved, the best bet is to use competent appraisers [Reg. §1.165-7(a)(2)].

The costs of repairing, replacing, or cleaning will not be a deduction. However, where the repairs do nothing more than restore the property to its pre-casualty condition, the cost of repairs may be accepted instead of an appraisal in the determining of the amount of the loss [Reg. §1.165-7(a)(2)(ii)]. In many cases, this is the practical solution accepted by the courts. See *Harmon*, 13 TC 373; *Jenard*, 20 TCM 346.

[¶504]   **WHEN TO DEDUCT A CASUALTY LOSS**

A casualty loss is deductible in the year it occurs. The deduction should be taken in that year and not in any other year, regardless of whether or not the damages are actually repaired or replaced that year. The loss must be fixed by an identifiable event which occurred in the year the deduction is taken [Reg. §1.165-1(d)(1)].

If in the year in which the casualty occurred, there is a claim for reimbursement (e.g., insurance) and there is a reasonable prospect of recovery, you cannot deduct that portion of the loss for which you may be reimbursed until it becomes reasonably certain that reimbursement will not be received [Reg. §1.165-1(d)(2)(i)]. The loss, then, will only be deductible in the taxable year in which the claim is adjudicated or otherwise settled [Reg. §1.165-1(d)(2)(iii)]. If a loss is deducted in one year and a reimbursement is received in a later year, no recomputation of tax is made for the prior year; the reimbursement is included in the year received and is treated as a recovery of an amount previously deducted [Reg. §1.165-1(d)(2)(iii)].

[¶505]   **DEDUCTIBLE CASUALTY LOSS**
          WITHOUT PHYSICAL DAMAGE TO PROPERTY

The District Court in *Stowers* [169 F. Supp. 246 D.C. Miss., 1959] held that one can get a casualty loss deduction even if his property is not damaged. In that case, there was a sudden cave-in of land near the taxpayer's residence. As a result, the street was closed, and the taxpayer lost access to his own house. That was enough to create a casualty loss, said the Court.

The Treasury admitted that since the property's access (except for a rear entrance served by a small alley) was cut off, its value was reduced by some $7,000. But it had disallowed the deduction because there was no physical damage to the property itself. The court disagreed, and held that loss of use is sufficient to give the deduction.

Not all cases arising from indirect property damage have been resolved as favorably to taxpayers, however. In *Kamanski v Commissioner,* 477 F. 2d 452

(9th Cir, 1973), 73-1 USTC para. 9371 (9th Cir. 1973). a homeowner whose property was not directly injured by a landslide which destroyed the surrounding neighborhood claimed he was entitled to a casualty loss deduction. The Tax Court disallowed the loss, saying it was a personal loss, not a casualty loss. The Ninth Circuit affirmed, stating that the loss claimed was based on market predictions, not on damage actually caused by the casualty and that therefore the loss claim must wait until such time as the loss is actually incurred — not on the present predicted loss.

[¶506]   AMOUNT OF CASUALTY LOSS

The method of computing a casualty loss is the same regardless of whether the loss was incurred in a trade or business or in an transaction entered into for profit (Reg. §1.165-7(a)(1)).

Personal Casualty Loss. The amount of the deduction for each casualty under IRC § 165(c)(3) is the lesser of two figures: (a) the difference between the value of the property before the casualty and after the casualty (including any salvage) or (b) the amount of the adjusted basis of the property. Your adjusted basis for personal property will probably be your cost plus your additions to the property since you are not allowed a depreciation deduction for such property. The lesser of these figures must then be reduced by insurance payments you receive and the $100 floor imposed by the tax law. No matter which figure you use, you must deduct this compensation whether it is insurance, relief from disaster agencies or the Red Cross, or any other compensation. You do not have to reduce for food, medical supplies, or other forms of subsistence which are not replacements of lost property.

> *Example:* Suppose your house which cost $35,000, not including the cost of land, is destroyed by fire. Just before the fire your property (house and land) was worth $60,000 (fair market value). Say you insurance proceeds from the fire total $28,000. Here's how your figure your deductible loss:

Property value prior to casualty	$60,000
Minus: Property value (land) after casualty	20,000
Value or property destroyed	$40,000
Loss (lesser amount of property destroyed ($40,000) or adjusted basis or property [$35,000])	$35,000
Minus: Insurance proceeds and $100 floor	28,100
Allowable casualty loss deduction	$ 6,900

Business Property. IRS' position on the treatment of casualty losses to business property is revealed in its regulations [Reg. §1.165-7(a)].

Under IRS regulations, losses to business property are required to be computed in the same manner as losses for nonbusiness property. The amount of the deduction, therefore, is the lesser of: (a) the difference between the fair market value of the property before and after the casualty or (b) the adjusted basis of the property. This lesser amount is further reduced by any insurance received. But, if the property is fully destroyed and the fair market value is less than basis, you can deduct basis.

Trees and Shrubs. If trees, shrubs, or buildings are integral parts of your property not used in a trade or business, you compute the loss caused by damage by computing what happened to your entire property [Reg. §1.165-7(b)(2)(ii)].

[¶507]   **DISASTER AREA CASUALTY LOSS**

Section 165(h) applies to any loss attributable to disaster which occurs during the period following the close of the taxable year and on or before the time prescribed by law for filing the income tax return for the taxable year and in an area subsequently determined by the President to be a disaster area. Such a loss may be deducted for the taxable year immediately preceding the taxable year in which the disaster occurred.

The way it works out is that if a disaster occurs within 3½ months after the close of a taxable year, you may take your disaster loss deduction either on your tax return for the preceding year or for the current year. If you're on a calendar-year basis, you can make your election at any time within a period of three months after the regular due date for filing your return. The fact that you've filed your return for the year of the loss doesn't prevent you from filing an amended return for that same year to show the losses resulting from the disaster. If the election is properly made, the casualty to which the election relates will be deemed to have occurred in the taxable year immediately preceding the taxable year in which the casualty actually occurred, and the loss to which the election applies will be deemed to have been sustained in such preceding taxable year.

Time and Manner of Making Election: The election must be made by filing a return, an amended return, or a claim for refund clearly showing that the election provided by Section 165(h) has been made. The return or claim should specify the date or dates of the disaster and the city or town, county, and state in which the property which was damaged or destroyed was located at the time of the disaster. As already indicated, the election must be made on or before the later of (1) the fifteenth day of the third month following the month in which the date prescribed for the filing of the income tax return (determined without regard to any extension of time granted for filing such return) for the taxable year immediately preceding the taxable year in which the disaster actually occurred falls or (2) the due date for filing the income tax return (determined with regard to any extension of time granted for filing such return) for the taxable year immediately preceding the taxable year in which the disaster actually occurred. An election is irrevocable after such later date.

6

How Real Estate Sales
Are Taxed

[¶601]   **TAX RULES**

Sales of exchanges of real estate almost always results in a gain or loss [Secs. 1001 and 1002 of the Code]. Whether or not the gain is taxable or the loss is deductible depends on the nature of the transaction-some transactions are tax free. Whether you have a capital gain or loss or ordinary income or an ordinary deduction depends on the nature of the property and your status as investor or dealer [Sec. 1221 of the Code]. Furthermore, you must have held the property more than six months before you can have a long-term capital gain or loss. (In 1977, the holding period must be greater than 9 months; it changes to a greater than 12-month rule for 1978 and thereafter.)

[¶602]   **BASIC TAX PLANNING**

Because real estate values tend to hold up even after the property has been held a number of years, real estate investors have been able to trade off ordinary depreciation deductions (which reduce ordinary income) for more favorable capital gain tax rates. Depreciation deductions taken during the time the property is held reduce the basis of the property to the owners. When they sell (assuming that values have held up), they have a capital gain for the difference between the reduced basis and the selling price. If effect, they are recovering their depreciation deductions via the gain. But this technique is, to some extent, limited by the recapture provisions of the tax law, discussed earlier.

[¶603]   **BASIS**

Basis of property will depend on the manner of its acquisition. The original basis must be adjusted for improvements to and depreciation of the property during the period of ownership.

(1) Property Acquired by Purchase. The cost of a purchase is a capital expenditure [IRC Sec. 263]. For future tax purposes, the unadjusted basis is computed as follows: if acquired on or after March 1, 1913, the basis is cost. If acquired before March 1, 1913:

a. The basis for determining gain is either cost less depreciation to March 1, 1913, or fair market value as of March 1, 1913, whichever is higher, and

b. The basis for determining loss is cost (IRC Secs. 1012 and 1053). The basis at time of sale is adjusted for depreciation, etc.

Example: The basis of property acquired for $20,000 on December 1, 1923 is $20,000 less depreciation. But assume it was acquired on March 1, 1911, and its value on March 1, 1913, was $22,000, while its depreciated cost on that date was $16,000. Its basis for gain is $22,000 while its basis for loss is $16,000.

(2) Property Acquired by Gift. For future tax purposes, the unadjusted basis is computed as follows: If acquired after December 31, 1920:

a. The basis for determining gain is the same as it would be in the hands of the donor or last preceding owner by whom it was not acquired by gift, and

b. The basis for determining loss is the donor's basis or fair market value at date of gift, whichever is lower [IRC Sec. 1015].

For gifts made after September 1, 1958, or gift property held unsold at that time and prior to January 1, 1977, gift tax paid is added to basis so long as the total adjusted basis is not in excess of fair market value. For gifts post December 31, 1976, the gift tax added to the basis is that portion of the gift tax attributable to appreciation [Sec. 1015(d)(6)]. If property was acquired from a decedent before death (death occurring after December 31, 1953) and the property was included in the decedent's gross estate, the recipient's basis is the value at date of death or optional valuation (value six months after death), reduced by amounts allowed him for depreciation [IRC Sec. 1014(b)(9)] if death was prior to 1977. (After December 31, 1976, basis is generally the adjusted basis of the decedent, increased for appreciation prior to 1977, and taxes attributable to post 1976 appreciation.)

Example: The basis of property given on November 10, 1920, when it was worth $5,000 is $5,000. If given on April 3, 1921, and the donor had purchased it for $3,000, the basis for gain or loss is $3,000 (since the fair market value exceeds the donor's cost). If the property was taxed in the donor's estate (because of retained ownership rights or for some other reason) on a valuation of $4,000, the donor having died on May 9, 1954, the donee's basis would be $4,000 less depreciation already claimed by the donee (i.e., prior to the donor's death).

(3) Property Acquired from a Decedent. For future tax purposes, the unadjusted basis is the fair market value at *date of death* or optional valuation date (six months after death) [IRC. Sec. 1014] for death prior to 1977. (For post 1976, see below.)

> *Example:* If inherited property worth $3,000 at date of death in 1975 was valued for estate tax purposes at its value of $2,000 six months after death, its basis on future sale is $2,000.

New Rules on Basis of Property Acquired from a Decedent. Under the Tax Reform Act of 1976, the step-up or increase in basis as a result of inheriting property has been removed. [Secs. 1014, 1023 and 1024 of the Code].

Thus, property that is acquired from a decedent after 12/31/76 will have a basis that is *not* increased for all of the appreciation that occurred since the date that the decedent acquired the property.

The above rule is *modified* to the extent that there are transitional rules to allow for appreciation that occurred prior to the change that took place by the Tax Reform Act of 1976. In summary, the general concept is to allow the appreciation that occurred *before* the 12/31/76 date to be added to the basis of the decedent. However, the question becomes "how does one know how much appreciation took place before the cutoff and how much occurred after that date?" One way to approach the problem would be to have *all* property appraised as of 12/31/76. This solution was not acceptable.

The alternative proposal was to assume that all appreciation occurs pro-rata. Thus, if property appreciated $20,000 from the time of purchase to the date of death, and if the property was held 365 days before 12/31/76 and 365 days after that date (date of death of the decedent in question), it would be presumed that half or $10,000 occurred *prior* to the cutoff (12/31/76) and thus the basis to the beneficiary would be the decedent's adjusted basis, increased for the $10,000 amount (appreciations before the tax law change as of 12/31/76).

There are other adjustments to this concept. In general they are:

a. If the property in question involves stock or other securities that are readily tradeable on an established market, the valuation to use as to the *appreciation* is the value on 12/31/76.

b. This rule assumes the property has increased in value; the rules mentioned cover appreciation.

c. Basis is also increased by death taxes, federal and state, that are payable on the net post 1976 appreciation of the property. (However, the basis cannot in any event be increased in excess of fair market value of the property.)

d. The basis rules will not limit the appreciation on up to $10,000 of household assets. [Sec. 1023(b)(3)].

e. There is also a special rule that allows the full appreciation to be part of the new basis to the beneficiary, up to a maximum of $60,000 amount. Thus, if a party died with $60,000 of assets (fair market value), the new rules limiting the increase in basis to a beneficiary will not apply.

f. There is also special adjustments with regard to depreciation. In essence, depreciation before the 12/31/76 cutoff date will not be subject to the adverse rule of no step up, but depreciation after 12/31/76 will be affected. Thus, the depreciation before the 12/31/76 date will be added to the basis of the property, but the post 12/31/76 depreciation will not be part of the basis.

(4) Property Acquired as Compensation for Services. This results in immediate taxable income to the recipient [IRC Sec. 61(a)(1)]. The measure of this income is the fair market value of the property at the date of acquisition; fair market value may be presumed to be the stipulated price of the services rendered [Reg. §1.61-1]. For future tax purposes, the basis is the fair market value at the date of acquisition, adjusted for depreciation.

Example: A gives B property worth $1,000 in lieu of a cash fee of $1,000 for services rendered. B's basis is $1,000. If the property is depreciable and B deducts a total of $500 for depreciation before selling the property, his basis for gain on the sale is $500.

(5) Property Acquired as a Liquidating Dividend. This results in immediate tax consequences to the extent of capital gain or loss in the amount of the difference between the adjusted basis of the stock and fair market value of the real estate [IRC Sec. 331]. For future tax purposes, the basis is the fair market value at the date of acquisition, adjusted for depreciation.

Example: Suppose real estate valued at $10,000 is distributed to X on liquidation of a corporation. X paid $6,000 for his stock; capital distributions totaling $1,000 have reduced his basis to $5,000. He has a $5,000 gain on liquidation (excess of $10,000 value of real estate over $5,000 adjusted basis of stock). His basis for the real estate is $10,000; if he later sells it for $12,000, he will have a further gain of $2,000 on the sale (assuming no adjustments to his basis).

(6) Property Acquired as Full or Partial Satisfaction for Indebtedness. This may or may not involve immediate tax consequences. If the exchange is equal, there will be no immediate tax consequences. For future tax purposes, the basis is the fair market value at the date of acquisition, adjusted for depreciation.

(7) Acquisition of Mortgaged Realty. These may or may not involve immediate tax consequences. First, at the mortgagee:

    a. If the **mortgagee** (creditor) acquires the property by foreclosure, the Regulations provide that a taxable gain or loss results to the extent of the difference between the amount of the mortgagor's obligation as applied to the bid price and the fair market value of the property which is presumed to be the bid price [Reg. §1.166-6(b)].

    b. If the property is acquired by a voluntary conveyance from the mortgagor to the mortgagee, the receipt of the property by the mortgagee is considered payment of debt and not a sale or exchange. Gain or losss is the difference between the balance due and the fair market value of the property. In a loss transaction, the mortgagee may deduct the unpaid portion as a bad debt [Reg. §1.166-6(a)]. Thus property acquired by a voluntary conveyance can result in either a taxable gain or a bad debt deduction.

The mortgagee's gain, loss, or bad debt deduction is taxable or deductible when realized — usually after the mortgagor's redemption period (which varies in different states) expires. For future tax purposes the unadjusted basis is the same as for a purchase (see above) — usually cost.

The mortgagor can have taxable gain to the extent the discharge from liability (the loan-debt) is greater than the mortgagor's adjusted basis [*Rev. Rul.* 76-111, 1976-1 CB 214].

(8) Acquisitions by Repossession. These involve immediate tax consequences to the mortgagee. Section 1038 of the Code limits the amount of realized gain on repossessions. This limitation applies whether the real property is sold on an installment sale or a deferred-payment sale and regardless of whether or not under local law title had passed to the buyer. Application of Section 1038 is mandatory, not elective.

Under Section 1038, the gain on repossession is to be realized to the extent of collections made on the sale of the real property, less amounts previously picked up as taxable income. However, the amount of income to be realized is not to exceed the total potential profit on the original sale reduced by income previously picked up and payments made by the seller on the repossession.

(9) Acquisition Through Purchase of Tax Lien. Here there is a common transaction involving no immediate tax consequences. A tax lien bought at public auction is a purchase (see above) and the price, which is considered fair market value, is a capital expenditure (Section 263). For future tax purposes, basis is the same as for any purchase — usually cost plus the expenses of acquisition (such as legal and recording fees), adjusted for depreciation.

    Example: A tax lien is purchased for $10,000. This is considered the fair market value of the property. Say the cost of acquisition was

$250, and depreciation totaling $2,000 was deducted before the property was sold. Basis for gain or loss on the sale would be $8,250.

[¶604] **ALLOCATION OF BASIS**

If the holder of a large tract of land sells a single parcel or if he subdivides and sells individual lots, he must allocate a portion of his basis to the property sold for the purpose of ascertaining gain or loss. Such allocation must be made ratably to each portion according to its fair market value at the time of acquisition, on the basis of its highest and best use [*Sevier Terrace Realty Co.*, 21 TCM 1289, *aff'd* 327 F.2d 999 (9th Cir. M64)]. Assessed values, appraisals, and comparable sales are often used as guides for determining value at acquisition. If you make a fair allocation among the different properties you buy, the court will be apt to go along with your figures [*Almac's Inc.*, 20 TCM 56(1961)]. Where, and only where, a fair allocation is impossible, there is no recognizable gain until all payments received on resale or other disposition exceed the total (unallocated) basis. Nor is there any recognizable loss until the entire group is sold [*Orvilletta, Inc.*, 47 BTA 10].

Sometimes an allocation will have to be made because the seller retains some interest in the property sold, through the creation of restrictive covenants or conditions. [See *Black*, 38 TC 673, where restrictions against use for commerical or industrial purposes and against a sale outside the buyer's family without first offering it to the seller resulted in a disallowance of the loss. However, the retention of the covenants and restrictions accounted for the reduction in the sales price].

[¶605] **DETERMINING GAIN OR LOSS**

While the amount of gain or loss seems easy to determine (i.e., sale price less your basis, Secs. 1001 and 1002), there are some rules which are important:

Sale Price. The amount realized on a sale for tax purposes includes the amount of cash received plus the fair market value of any other property you receive [Sec. 1001]. Mortgages on the property which the purchaser either assumes or takes subject to are added to the sale price [*Crane v. Comm.*, 331 U.S. 1(1947)].

Basis. Basis is generally the original cost of the property plus the value of any improvements put on the property by the seller and minus depreciation taken by him. [Secs. 1011 and 1012]. The manner in which the property was acquired will also affect its basis.

Selling Expenses. Expenses, such as recording fees and transfer taxes, commissions and all the other expenses of the sale including legal fees, reduce the sale price. If you realize a capital gain, the selling expenses reduce that gain; they are not deductible against ordinary income. A dealer in real estate, however, does deduct all his selling expenses as ordinary and necessary business expenses. However, having no capital gain, this does not necessarily prove of aid.

[¶606]   **ACQUISITION COSTS**

Acquiring title to realty involves various costs, and a question arises as to their deductibility. Generally, capital expenditures are not deductible [Sec. 263], whereas trade or business expenses are deductible [Sec. 162]. Thus, the cost of the property and the costs involved in acquiring the property or perfecting title are "capital expenditures" and as such are not deductible. They are added to basis. Included in this category are fees paid to surveyors, architects, lawyers, and legal fees involved in perfecting, defending, or removing a cloud on title [III-2 CB 157; *Louisiana Land & Exploration Co.,* 7 TC 507, aff'd 161 F. 2d 842 (5th Cir. 1947) Rev. Rul. 75-151, 1975-7 IRB 12. Regs. §1.263 (a)(2)]. Legal fees to protect income are deductible. Where a suit involves both, prorate between the deductible and the nondeductible.

Improvements made to the property increase basis. They are not deductible. There may be a question when trying to determine when there is an improvement and when there is a repair. Reg. §1.162-4.

[¶607]   **TIMING**

The timing of capital gains realization, the deferral of earned income, the acceleration or deferral of tax-preference income assume tremendous importance in minimizing taxes and legitimate tax avoidance.

[¶608] **DEPRECIATION AND AMORTIZATION: INTERPLAY**

Investors often look at their return from real estate investments this way: How much am I getting on the cash I invested? In arriving at this return, keep these factors in mind:

1. Depreciation is based on the full cost of the property — not only the cash paid — including all mortgages.
2. Depreciation deductions require no cash outlay.
3. Mortgage amortization payments (the amount paid to reduce the mortgage principal) do require cash outlays but are not deductible for tax purposes.

Where the depreciation deductions exceed the amortization payments, the difference is possible cash that comes back to the investor, tax free. But where the amortization payments exceed the depreciation deductions, the taxable income from the property will exceed the cash returned to the investor. (At this point, he may want to sell and get capital gain or he may seek refinancing to reduce the amortization payments.)

Here's a simple example to show how the interplay of depreciation and amortization works. Use some arbitrary figures for the sake of illustration: gross rents, $100,000; operating costs (including mortgage interest) $40,000; depreciation, $10,000; mortgage amortization, $6,000. Taxable income would be $50,000 ($100,000 rents less the $40,000 operating costs and $10,000 depreciation). Cash flow before taxes, however, would be $54,000 ($100,000 rents less the $40,000 operating costs and the $6,000 mortgage amortization). $4,000 of the $54,000 is called tax free. (This $4,000 is the excess of depreciation over amortization.)

[¶609]   **FIGURING THE TAX**

After computing the net gain on a transaction, the next step is to compute your tax. Individuals report long-term capital gains in one of two ways:

1. *Regular Way:* Subtract (deduct) 50 percent of the net long-term capital gains from your regular income; the total is taxed at ordinary income rates [Sec. 1202 of the Code].

2. *Alternative Method:* This method is even better than the first if you are in an over-50 percent tax bracket. This section taxed the first $50,000 of long-term capital gains at 25 percent and the balance is taxed at 35 percent. Obviously, capital gains are normally to be preferred to ordinary income. (We must also consider the effect of the minimum tax on tax-preference income as well, since the untaxed portion of capital gains is counted as an item of tax-preference income subject to the minimum tax. This holds true for both corporations and individuals) [Sec. 1201 of the Code].

Capital Gains Tax for Corporations. The capital gains rate for corporations is 30 percent. If your corporation has an income of less than $50,000, it can still pay the regular tax on the capital gains. Under "temporary" rates, that may become permanent, corporations pay 20 percent on the first $25,000 of taxable ordinary income, 22 percent on the next $25,000 and 48 percent on any ordinary income over the $50,000.

Capital Gains Tax for Individuals. For an individual, the *alternative* tax is a means of cutting his taxes to a 25 percent rate when his regular tax rate is at the over-50 percent level. The maximum alternative tax operates at two levels or rates: first, on gains of $50,000 or less; second, on gains of $50,000 or more. On gains of less than $50,000 the maximum alternative tax rate is 25 percent. Bear in mind that only half of long-term gains are normally taxable. This means that whenever your taxable income puts you above the 50 percent tax bracket, it will pay you to use the alternative method.

When do you reach the over-50 percent tax bracket?

1. If you are married and file a joint return or you are a surviving spouse, your taxable income in excess of $52,000 is taxed at a rate ranging from 53 percent on taxable income of from $52,000 to $64,000 on up to 70 percent on income in excess of $200,000.

2. If you are the head of a household, your taxable income in excess of $38,000 will be taxed at a rate ranging from 51 percent on income up to $40,000 to 70 percent on income in excess of $180,000.

3. If you are unmarried and not a surviving spouse or the head of a household, income in excess of $38,000 is taxed at the rate of 55 percent, and you reach the 70 percent rate at the $100,000 level.

4. For married individuals filing separate returns, amounts in excess of $26,000 are taxed at the rate of 53 percent and 70 percent rate is reached at the $100,000 level. (See Appendix.)

Here is how individuals figure their tax by the 25 percent alternative method: When you use the 25 percent alternative method of computing your tax, that is, on the first $50,000 of gains, you follow these steps:

1. Eliminate your long-term capital gains from your taxable income and figure the tax on what is left.

2. Find 25 percent of the total net long-term gains in excess of net short-term losses.

3. Add the results in (1) and (2). That is your total tax.

Capital Gains in Excess of $50,000. The 2 percent alternative tax rate is of value on the first $50,000 of gains in a given tax. Once you get beyond the $50,000 level, by the alternative method, you take half of the excess and add that to your regular income to be taxed at your regular rate(s), which, as you know, go as *high as* 70 percent. Capital gains in excess of $50,000 have what amounts to a maximum rate of 35 percent on the full amount of the gain, and the alternative capital gains tax at this level is dead for all practical purposes (that is, the alternative tax is 35 percent, the same as taxing 50 percent of gain at a 70 percent rate). The first $50,000 of gain also affects your rate, to push you up to the 70 percent maximum.

[¶610] MINIMUM TAX*

The Tax Law in Internal Revenue Code of 1954 (as amended) [26 USCA, (IRC 1954] provides for a minimum tax on what is referred to as tax preference income [Sec. 56 of the Code].

The essence of the minimum tax, so that one might see the forest as opposed to being lost in the trees, is simply that the tax law has structured a type of tax that is *in addition* to the normal or regular tax that one might pay on "regular income."

The Code provides that certain types of income produce benefits which thereby should generate an additional or minimum tax level. These types of special items of income or deductions are sometimes referred to as tax preference items, sometimes loosely labeled tax preference income.

Under Section 57 of the Code, the types of tax preferences include such things as excess depreciation on real property, excess depreciation on personal property subject to a net lease, certain stock options, capital gains, and a few additional items added by the *Tax Reform Act of 1976.*

In concentrating on the general concept of tax preference, the essence of Section 57 of the Code, and the new tax provision, is an additional or minimum tax on these types of items, which will result in a minimum tax produced by taxing that excess by 15 percent.

That is, there is a 15 percent (up from the prior 10 percent which existed prior to the *Tax Reform Act of 1976*) on the tax preference items that exceed, for an individual, the sum of $10,000 or half the regular tax liability. In other words, the taxpayer, an individual, in addition to his normal taxes, will be required to pay an additional 15 per cent tax on any of the tax preference items that exceed (1) the $10,000 amount, or if greater, (2) half the regular tax liability.

> *Example:* If the tax preference items produced from one or all of the tax preference items exceed $10,000, this amount would be taxed at 15 percent. Thus, if we assume tax preference of $40,000 subtracting from this the $10,000 (assuming that this amount is greater than half of the regular tax liability), the additional tax would be 15 per cent of $30,000 or an additional $4,500.

A further change made by the 1976 law, beyond increasing the tax rate from 10 percent to 15 per cent, is the addition of three more items of tax preference. The new law provides that itemized deductions, that is, those which are below line (from adjusted gross income to reach taxable income), to the extent they exceed 60 percent of the adjusted gross income, excluding certain items such as medical and casualty deductions, are tax preference items.

*Reprinted by permission of the Colorado Lawyer from Volume 6, No. 1, *The Colorado Lawyer,* page 90, 1977. ©The Colorado Bar Association, 1977. All rights reserved.

Example: If adjusted gross income was $10,000, and the tax prefer-
ence itemized deductions constituted $8,000, 60 percent of the
$10,000 would be $6,000. Since the itemized deductions ($8,000)
exceed $6,000 by $2,000, (that is $8,000 of itemized deductions less
than $6,000 or 60 percent of the $10,000 adjusted gross income),
there would be $2,000 of preference.

The new tax law adds intangible drilling and development costs which
exceed the deduction that would be available assuming that one used a capitalized
method in amortizing them on straight line method.

Finally, the new tax law added as a tax preference item excess depreciation
an all personal property which is subject to a lease (not just the personal which is
subject to a *net* lease, which was the prior restriction before the *Tax Reform Act of
1976).*

The effective date for individuals and non-corporations is for years 1976
and thereafter. Taxpayers must face this in the current year!

You should be aware that there are additional preferences. There is a
different treatment for corporations, and there are additional interpretive problems on the tax preference issue.

In summary the minimum tax rules are:

☐ Under Section 56(b) of the Code, the tax rate on tax preference income,
(discussed below) has been changed from 10 percent to 15 percent under §
56(b)(1)(B) of the Code.

☐ The exemption has been changed from $30,000 to $10,000 *or* one-half
of the regular income tax paid by the taxpayer, the greater of the two. (This is for
individuals and noncorporate taxpayers.) [Sec. 56(b)(1)(A) of the Code].

☐ As for corporations, the $30,000 amount is reduced to $10,000 *or* the
total amount of the regular taxes paid by the corporation (as opposed to one-half
for an individual.

☐ Generally speaking, the effective date is for tax years beginning after
December 31, 1975, again with certain exceptions, especially for corporations.

☐ Similar to the previous law, the 1976 act allows the deferral of part of all
of the minimum tax in which the taxpayer also has a net operating loss which can
be utilized for future years. Section 56 states the rules for determining the regular
tax with regard to the amount exempted. In general, this is the tax imposed by the
Code for income taxes, reduced by foreign income tax credit, retirement income,
investment, work incentive program credit, contributions to candidates, credit
for personal exemptions, credit regarding the purchase of a new residence, and
certain other adjustments.

☐ Section 57(a) of the Code, adds addition of items to the list of tax
preference items. It now includes excess itemized deductions. That is, the excess
of the itemized deductions, excluding medical expenses and casualty items, over

60 percent of the adjusted gross income. (With regard to estates and trusts, there are certain additional adjustments.)

In addition to the excess itemized deductions, intangible drilling costs, paid or incurred in connection with productive oil and gas wells, in excess of the amount that would have been deductible if the cost had been capitalized and amortized over ten years or over the life of the wells, is also a tax preference item [Sec. 57(a)(11) of the Code].

The excess of allowable depreciation (excess depreciation over the straight line amount, for all personal property subject to a lease (is a tax preference item).

These new rules apply with regard to individuals and non-corporate taxpayers. They do not include corporations.

Further, the previous rules prior to the 1976 act, tax preference items continue. (The items of tax preference include many others; the capital gain deduction, excess depreciation on real estate, etc.) Again, generally speaking, the effect of these new tax preferences is for years ending after December 31, 1975.

[¶611]   **MAXIMUM TAX (MAXI)**

Under the 1976 act, the maximum tax rules, taxing earned income at a maximum of 50 percent, will continue to apply [Sec. 1343 of the Code]. However, the maximum tax will now also apply to annuities, deferred compensation, and pension. (This excludes lump sum distribution.) These rules are effective for 1977 and future years.

When making the computation for maximum tax, the earned income items are computed and then reduced by:

a. Deductions which are allocable to personal service income, and
b. The full amount of tax preference items (not reduced for a $30,000 amount). [Sec. 1348 (b)(2) of the Code].

In place of looking to "earned income," we look to personal service taxable income as a result of the new definition. (As noted, there is now the inclusion of certain *passive* types of income, such as pensions and annuities.) The effective date for this amendment is for taxable years beginning after December 31, 1976.

CHAPTER 7

Taking Real Estate Profits at Favorable Capital Gains Tax Rates

[¶701]   **CAPITAL GAIN AND LOSS**

When you have a profit on your sale or exchange, you want it to be a long-term capital gain. The obvious reason is that it costs less-normally at least 50 percent less than what you would pay in taxes if the gain was not a long-term capital gain.

A capital gain results if what you sell is a capital asset—or is treated for tax purposes as such. If you have held the property for more than six months (9 months, 1977; 12 months 1978 and after) before the sale, it is long-term.

[¶702]   **CLASSIFICATION OF PROPERTY**

The tax consequences of the disposition of real estate are affected by the *classification* or type of realty involved.

(1) Investment Realty. This is property held primarily for investment, as differentiated from trade or business, residential— personal use, or dealer's realty. Investment property is considered a capital asset (like securities held for investment), and gain or loss realized on disposition gives capital gain or loss [Sec. 1221 of the Code].

(2) Trade or Business Property. This is depreciable property or realty used in a trade or business which has been held for more than six months (see new excess of 9 months, excess of one year rules, *supra*) and is neither property includable in the owner's inventory nor dealer's realty [Secs. 1231 and 1221 (2) of the Code]. Rental property is classified as trade or business realty, as is realty purchased for such purpose but never so used and even idle realty. But if the realty is incapable of being used in business because of zoning restrictions, it is not trade or business realty. A personal residence may become trade or business realty if converted to rental or income-producing use before its disposition. Trade or business realty is not a capital asset, and its sale or exchange produces either a gain taxable at capital gain rates or an ordinary loss which is fully deductible. Gains from the sales of exchanges or such property are offset against losses from similar sales or exchanges. The net gain (that, after adding all gains and losses *together*) is taxed as capital gain, but a net loss (i.e., after adding all gains and losses together) is fully deductible as an ordinary loss [Sec. 1231 of the Code].

(3) Residential Realty. This is property used as a personal residence. The sales, exchange, or other disposition of personal residential relaty results either in taxable capital gain or nondeductible loss [Sec. 1221, 1001, 1002, 165(c) (3) of the Code].

(4) Dealer's Realty. This is realty held primarily for resale and includable in the owner's inventory. The classification of dealer may be pinned to an owner who would not normally consider himself such—whether it will stick depends on the facts in each case, the owner's actions, etc. Dealer's realty is not a capital asset, and gains or losses resulting from sales or exchanges are ordinary gains (fully taxable as ordinary income) or ordinary, fully deductible losses [Sec. 1221(1) of the Code].

[¶703]   TRADE OR BUSINESS PROPERTY

Trade or business property are not capital assets; under Section 1231 of the Code, they are treated as such if held the proper time: excess of (1) 6 months, 1976 and prior; (2) 9 months for 1977 dispositions; (3) 12 months for 1978 and thereafter. If the sales net to a gain, as to this trade or business property [Sec. 1231], the gain is treated as long-term capital gain. If it nets to a loss, you benefit again (taxwise, at any rate); the loss is an ordinary loss that reduces income taxes at the ordinary (rather than the special capital gain) tax rates.

You apply capital gain treatment to the net figure of all gains and losses in this trade or business category; it is better to have all sales at a gain in one year and all sales at a loss in another year. That way, all the gains get the full benefit of the capital gain treatment and all the losses are free to offset ordinary income.

Here is an example showing you how separating the years of gain and loss can work out. Take an owner of two apartment houses. He can sell one at a profit of $100,000 and the other at a loss of $30,000. His other ordinary taxable income is $50,000 a year. If he sells the two houses in different years, he can end up with more money than if he sells both in the same year. Here's how to work out the figures:

Both houses sold in one year:

Ordinary income each year is $50,000. Tax (assuming a joint return)
  each year is $17,060.
  Subtracting two years' taxes ($34,120) from two years' income
  ($100,000) gives a two-year, after-tax ordinary income of .. $ 65,880
Net capital gain of $70,000 is taxable at $___, giving an
  after-tax income of .... ———

Total two-year, after-tax income is .... $_____

One house sold in each year:

In first year, the $50,000 ordinary income is reduced by the
  $30,000 loss on the house sold in first year. Tax on the
  remaining $20,000 is $4,380, giving an after-tax ordinary
  income of 15,620
In second year, the other house is sold at $100,000 gain. Tax is
  $_____* giving after-tax gain of .... ———
Ordinary income in second year is $50,000. Tax is $17,060, giving
  after-tax income of 32,940
Total two-year, after-tax income is $123.560

[¶704]   **HOLDING PERIOD**

Your holding period is extremely important whether you are selling a capital asset or trade or business property Section 1223 of the Code. It is the difference between getting long-term and short-term capital gain. To get long-term gain, you need a holding period of more than six months. (See paragraph 703).

Measuring the Period. Your holding period begins the day after you acquire title to the property; it ends when you pass the title to a purchaser. But if you make an unconditional contract of sale, i.e., the purchaser cannot cancel the deal if title is not clear, and the purchaser takes possession of the property before title closing, then your holding period may end when he moves in. Normally a

*Under the 1969 Tax Reform Act, the 25% alternative tax rate is good only on the first $50,000 of gains in a given year. Once you get beyond the $50,000 level, starting in 1972, you take half of the excess and add that to your regular income to be taxed at your regular rate(s), which, as you know, go as high as 70%.

Capital gains in excess of $50,000 in 1972 and subsequent years will have what amounts to a maximum rate of 35% on the full amount of the gain.

holding period doesn't end until title passes; you could put off the closing date until you are in a long-term holding.)

If you took an option to purchase property and exercised it, you do *not* add the length of time you held the option to the time you owned the property when you determine your holding period. You must hold the property for the long term period *after* you exercised the option and acquired title if you want long-term capital gain. Alternately, you also can get long-term capital gain if you hold the *option* itself for long term and then sell it if the property would have been a capital asset had you owned it instead of the option. But make sure that the option you sell is the same as the option you bought. Do not acquire title to the property and then give a new option. If you do that, you will be treated as acquiring the land and selling it immediately, which would mean that you did not hold the *property* long term [Sec. 1234 of the Code].

[¶705]   CAPITAL GAINS TAX — ALTERNATIVE METHOD

The *alternative* capital gain tax for individuals is continued for the excess of net long-term capital gain over net short-term capital gains up to $50,000 of gains per return ($25,000 for married persons filing separately) without regard to the taxpayer's tax preferences. As to net long-term capital gains above the $50,000 level, one-half is included in ordinary income to affect the progressive income tax rates. (See also paragraph 609.)

Where an individual has capital gains in excess of $50,000, he has three tax computations: First, he determines his tax on ordinary income, then he figures the tax on the first $50,000 of capital gains, and, finally, he figures the tax on the amount in excess of $50,000.

To determine his tax on his capital gains over $50,000, he must, in effect, determine what his tax would be on these gains if one-half of them was added on top of ordinary income. This requires a tentative tax computation first on ordinary income plus one-half of $50,000 of capital gains. Second, a tentative tax would be computed based on total income including one-half of all capital gains. The difference between these two amounts is his tax liability on those capital gains over $50,000.

There has been a gradual phaseout of the alternative tax on net long-term capital gains in excess of $50,000 which provides a gradual upward transition in the maximum effective rate on capital gains not eligible for the 25 percent alternative tax to 29.5 percent in 1970, 32-½ percent in 1971 and, finally, 35 percent in 1972 and thereafter.

[¶706]   STATUS

Dealers are taxable as any other business person. However, dealers may also be investors as to *some* property. Unless they exercise some ingenuity in segregating their assets, they may have ordinary income whenever they sell property.

The Factors. *Each case* depends on its own facts and generally there are no Rulings issued on this, per Rev. Proc. 72-9, 1972-1 CB 721, Rev. Proc. 73-15, 1973-1 CB 141. There are various factors usualiy found by the courts to be significant as to dealer status. Bear in mind that all factors are important, not merely the number of sales made. For cases that have discussed some of the following factors, see *Frank Taylor, Inc.* [32 Tem 362, TC Memo 1973-82]; *Maddux Construction Co.* [54 TC 278 (1970)].

Here are some factors considered:

(1) *Degree of activity.* The size and number of sales involved, the regularity, and past activities are all considered.

(2) *The purpose for which the property was acquired and held.* Even though the taxpayer has purchased property for ultimate resale, this alone will not make him a dealer. In almost every purchase of property, the taxpayer hopes for a rise in its market value and a resale if such a rise does occur. But, if the taxpayer acquired the property involuntarily, say by inheritance or as security for a debt, the argument that his purchase was incidental to a real estate business is not present as a factor.

Under Section 1221(1) of the Code you are entitled to capital gains instead of ordinary income when you sell a piece of property at a profit if the property is a capital asset. In defining "capital asset," Section 1221(1) says that the term does not include property held by a taxpayer primarily for sale to customers in the ordinary course of his trade or business. The United States Supreme Court has ruled that "primarily" as used in Section 1221(1) means "principally" or "of first importance" and not "substantially" [*Malat,* 383 US 569, *vac'g and rem'g* 9th Cir., 347 F.2d 23]. In reaching this determination, the High Court said that the purpose of Section 1221 is to differentiate between the "profits and losses arising from everyday operation of the business" and the "realization of appreciation in value accrued over a substantial period of time." Under this decision, you can get capital gain treatment even though you always intended to sell if the income projections from the property didn't stand up or if someone came along and made an offer for the property that was too attractive to turn down. However, to assure capital gains, your actions in relation to the property during the holding period must be in accordance with an investment purpose or, at least, consistent with that purpose. If you have a loss, you will generally want to argue that it is an ordinary loss, such as being tied to your trade or business. See *Corn Products,* 350 US 46(1955). *W.W. Windle Co.,* 65 TC 694 (1976).

(3) *The existence of other income and full-time businesses.* If this is so, it indicates that the taxpayer is devoting his time and efforts elsewhere, not to real estate—especially where real estate income is low compared with other income.

(4) *The length of time the property is held.* If the taxpayer sells shortly after the six-month holding period (necessary for long-term capital gains), it may indicate he is not investing in real estate on a long-term basis but is more interested in short-term sales to customers.

(5) *The extent of sales activity by the owner.* Hiring an office or a broker, advertising the property for sale, and spending money to achieve sales can indicate the existence of a real estate business. Note that acts done for him by a third party are attributable to the taxpayer.

(6) *The owner's representations.* Any actions on the owner's part connecting him with the real estate business are held against. him. This could include holding himself out as a real estate man (either to the public or on his tax return) or joining a dealers' association.

(7) *Rental property.* If the taxpayer has held the property for years for its rental value, this indicates that although he is in the business of owning and renting property, he is not in the business of selling it. But rental of property is not necessarily inconsistent with holding it for sale if the renting is made to realize income while planning or trying to sell.

(8) *Purchase of other property.* If you purchase other real estate at the same time you sell or soon afterwards, this may indicate that you are continuing a business rather than disposing of an investment.

(9) *Subdividing and developing.* Almost any activity on this score makes you subject to a claim that you are a dealer.

(10) *Liquidation.* If the taxpayer can show that he is merely liquidating an investment, then he may get capital gain treatment. But he will argue that in almost any case; and the analysis of the other factors above will, in reality, concern itself with whether the taxpayer was in the business of selling real estate or merely liquidating an investment in it. Yet, this "liquidation of investment" theory still has vitality and has been reaffirmed. [See *Charles E. Tibbals* 17 TCM 228; *Altizer Coal Land Co.,* 31 TC 70; *Wm. T. Minor, Jr.,* 18 TCM 14 (1959) 1959-4]. Even if the liquidation argument is a valid one, you have to be sure that the taxpayer has by subdividing and improving to increase the profit on his sale not gone beyond the steps necessary. [See *S. G. Achong,* 246 F.2d 445 (9th Cir. 1957).]

What You Should Do. From the time you start your investments in real estate, you must set up your activity so as to minimize any claim against you as a dealer. You should check over the factors outlined above to make sure you do not do anything harmful. Enter into fewer transactions which involve more money rather than many transactions involving less money in each; spread your gains over different years (to avoid too much real estate gain in any one year); hold the property for long-term periods for rental income; refrain from purchases of new property at the same time you sell. Document your position by records, where your intent to invest, not resell, is clear. Be consistent in your treatment: Do not claim depreciation, sell at a loss, and claim the property was for "resale"!

[¶707]   SPECIAL PROBLEMS OF REAL ESTATE PROFESSIONALS

Problems of the Real Estate Man. People connected with real estate in more than an investment capacity face greater problems than investors. To achieve capital gain treatment, they must do more than convince a court that they are not in a separate real estate business. They have to establish that their real estate "investment" activity is separate from their full-time professional activity in real estate.

Attorneys and Brokers. Lawyers, particularly those connected with real estate in the exercise of their profession, and brokers cannot hide behind their professional activities. Actually, you consider their real estate investment activities as you would those of any other businessman to see whether they are in a side business of dealing in real estate [*J. M. Philbin,* 26 TC 1159.] However, the taxpayer in this case involved continuous sales and purchases].

Brokers and Builders. These are people in a full- or part-time business of owning real estate for resale or of building it for purposes of sale. Dealers in real estate, unlike those in securities, are not allowed statutory rules for segregation of investments. But, it is possible for a real estate dealer to get capital gain treatment on his investment real estate. The fact that you are normally a dealer makes it harder; but if you can establish that the property is not the type of land you usually sell, you hold it for a long period, and you do not subdivide, you may then be able to get a capital gain. But the fight will be an uphill one [see *W. Linton Atkinson,* 31 TC 1241 (1959)]. Builders face a slightly different problem. They must establish that the property they build for investment is rental property. Here a long-term holding period is generally essential. But even this may not be enough. If you're in the business of constructing apartment houses for resale, then you may find it easier to establish "investment" status for a shopping center you erect adjacent to your housing project and which you hold [see *Maddux Construction Co.* 54 TC 127B (1970)].

Applying the Dealer Investor Rule. As indicated above, you can be both a dealer and investor. IRS has actually ruled that you can subdivide part of a tract and sell lots (making you a dealer as to those) and still be an investor as to the remaining undivided tract [*Rev. Rul. 57-565,* CB 1957-2, 546].

Tax Alternatives You Might Consider. There are alternatives which you might try if you fear dealer treatment and want more than you could get from sale of the whole property in one transaction.

(1) *Rent.* If you sold a tract outright to another, he might have to obtain mortgage financing in order to purchase, or you might have to take a purchase-money mortgage. But instead, consider renting on a long-term basis, say to a builder who will construct and then himself rent or sell the building. You will have ordinary income on the rental payments, but you've spread these payments over a long-term period and so may have lowered your tax bracket. Since your lessee gets a deduction for his rental payments, his ability to pay you may be better than if he purchased from you. You also have the land and building on expiration of the lease (this will not be income to you); and if you then sell, your long-term holding of the property may negate any argument that you are a dealer.

(2) *Contingent Sale.* You might be able to find a developer willing to gamble on his ability to resell who will purchase for a percentage of his resale price. Since you've sold the entire tract without any subdivision or development activity on your part, you'd think you were entitled to a capital gain. Actually, you may be walking a tightrope. Here it's important to avoid any trace of a joint venture between you and the developer. Since he's a dealer, if you were in a joint venture with him, you may be tainted as a dealer too [see *Bauschard,* 31 TC 910, *aff'd (6th Cir. 1960) 279 F.2d 115*]. Try to find an independent party with whom you've had no prior dealings in order to avoid the inference that you set up a joint venture when you purchased the property.

(3) *Sale to Several Builders.* Instead of subdividing and selling individual lots, with possible dealer treatment resulting from your subdivision activity, you might sell the tract in large parcels to a few builders. This way, you may get more than you could from one sale. Here your position is that you've had no subdivision or development activity. But this might boomerang since the act of dividing among the builders themselves has been considered a subdivision. You may be able to get around this by getting the builders to form a partnership.

(4) *Use of a Corporation.* Here you sell the property to your corporation. Although it will be a dealer, you hope to get a capital gain at the time of transfer and thus to have ordinary income only on the profit added to the property by the corporation's efforts. If you transfer the property to the corporation for its stock, then you want to have a taxable transaction, not a tax free transfer under Section 351 of the Code.

Here there are several risks, if you plan to sell the stock of the corporation, you have a collapsible corporation (see Levine, *Real Estate Transactions, supra*). And if you sell depreciable property, Section 1239 of the Code provides that you will have *ordinary* income on a sale to the corporation if you own 80 percent or more of the corporation, directly or indirectly.

(5) *Devise the Property.* Finally, you would hold on to the property until your death. This means your heir will be liquidating property he involuntarily acquired.

[¶708]   **SUBDIVISION SALES**

In trying to avoid the "dealer" problem, you can consider Section 1237 of the Code which permits capital gains to be realized from subdivided property if three conditions are met: (1) You were not otherwise a dealer during the taxable year of sale, never held the subdivided tract or any part of it primarily for sale to customers, and did not hold any other real property as a dealer in the year of sale. (2) No substantial improvements increasing the value of the property were made by you or related entities. Nor could such improvements be made by a lessee if the improvement constituted income to you or by a governmental body, if the improvement constituted an addition to your basis for the property. (3) You held the subdivided realty for at least five years, unless the property was inherited.

As indicated, you cannot make substantial improvements to the property if you want [Sec. 1237(a) (2) of the Code]. According to the regulations, an improvement which does not increase the value of a lot by more than 10 percent is not substantial. Only those lots in the tract increased by more than 10 percent in value may lose §1237 treatment. Shopping centers, other commercial or residential buildings, hard-surface roads, and utilities such as sewers, water, gas, and electric lines are substantial improvements. But temporary field offices, gravel roads, surveying, draining, levelling, clearing operations and filling are not.

Sale of Fill. However, if you sell fill taken from your land, you can get favorable capital gains treatment for your profit from the deal, that is, assuming you have held the land for the long-term period and you are not in the business of selling fill. Or you may be slapped with ordinary income. It all depends on how the deal is set up.

In two Tax Court cases two farmers were forced to sell portions of their land to the state for use in an interstate highway project. In each case, the farmers entered into written agreements to supply dirt fill from portions of their land for use in the construction of the highway. Both reported the profit as long-term capital gains, treating the sale of the fill as the sale of property held for more than six months. However, one farmer's profit received favorable capital gain treatment [*Collings,* 56 TC 1074, (1971)], while the other farmer was slapped with ordinary income treatment [*Ellis,* 56 TC 1079]. But *Ellis* was reversed by the 7th Cir. in favor of the taxpayer; nevertheless, the uncertainty remains].

To be accorded capital gain treatment (assuming, that you are not in the business of selling fill, and that you have owned the land for long-term holding, there must be a sale "of the soil in place."

The agreement which Farmer Collins entered for the sale of his dirt fill and as a result of which Collins got capital gains treatment provided that the buyer was required to purchase "all earth and granular materials" from certain clearly specified locations. The agreement required Collins to sell all the soil in place on specified areas of his land, and so he was entitled to favorable long-term capital gains treatment of his profits.

Farmer Ellis' agreement provided that the buyer of the fill was to excavate down to an average depth of 12 feet below the existing ground level but did not specify either the length or breadth of the excavation nor the amount of soil to be excavated. Further, the agreement required that the excavated fill material "meet Indiana State Highway specifications and shall be approved by their engineers" for Ellis to be paid. The Tax Court denied Ellis capital gains treatment on the ground that his agreement did not amount to an unconditional sale of all the soil in place. The agreement was conditional in nature in that it required the approval of the fill by the appropriate state engineers. The agreement also failed to specify clearly either the area to be excavated or the amount of fill to be extracted. [See Levine text, cited earlier, Sec. 632 and 137, Note 36. However, again, Ellis was reversed on appeal.]

Necessary Improvements. Even if an improvement would be considered substantial under the above rules, it still does not knock out §1237 treatment if it is necessary. It's necessary if all of the following conditions are met:

1. You held the lot for at least ten years.
2. The improvement is a water, sewer, or drainage facility or a road.
3. You can show that the property would not otherwise have been marketable at the prevailing local price for similar building sites.
4. You elect to neither deduct the expense nor add it to the basis of any lot sold for purposes of determining your gain. This results in the loss of any tax benefit for these expenses. [Regs 1.1237-1(c), Sec. 1237 (a) (2) of the Code].

Here's an example of when a substantial improvement can become a necessary improvement. You donate to your city a strip of land which is part of your undeveloped tract to allow the city to extend a street into your property. This may result in a special assessment for paving expenses. This assessment would be a substantial improvement to the retained land since you would add the assessment to the basis. But you can make it a necessary improvement and still come within the rules of Section 1237 by electing not to add the assessment to your basis [Regs. 1.1237-1].

CHAPTER 8

Tax Credits

[¶801]   **HISTORY OF INVESTMENT TAX CREDIT:
AMOUNT-PERCENTAGE**

The *1971 Revenue Act* restored, with some modifications, a credit against tax. The credit was restored at a 7 percent rate. (It is as of May 1977, 10 percent; there is talk it may go even higher.) It covers an investment in most tangible depreciable personal business property (other than buildings or their structural components.) The credit offsets, dollar for dollar, the buyer's tax without affecting his basis for purposes of depreciation or his right to take accelerated depreciation. It applies to property acquired after 8/15/71, or acquired after 3/31/71 and before 8/16/71 if ordered after 3/31/71. Where property is constructed or erected by the taxpayer, the credit applies to property whose construction was begun after 3/31/71 or was completed after 8/15/71. If construction was begun before 4/1/71. Only the construction costs incurred after 8/15/71 are eligible for the credit. You get the full credit subject to the limitations discussed below in the year in which the property is put into service—even if on the last day.

As noted, the 7 percent amount was increased to 10 percent for most acquisitions in 1975 and 1976. The *Tax Reform Act of 1976* has extended the 10 percent rule.

[¶802]   **PROPERTY QUALIFYING FOR THE CREDIT**

To qualify for the credit the investment must be in property which is:

1. depreciable property,

2. having a useful life of at least three years, and
3. tangible property which is
   a. personal property; or
   b. property used as an integral part of manufacturing, production, or extraction *or* of furnishing transportation, communications, electrical energy, gas, water or sewage disposal services, or which consists of a research or bulk storage facility for fungibles used in connection therewith; or
   c. elevators and escalators if construction, reconstruction, or erection is completed by taxpayer after June 30, 1963 or if acquired after that date and original use commences with taxpayer after that date.

Structural Components of a Building. There is no definition of structural components of a building in the law. However, under the Regulations (Sec. 1.48-1(e)(2), structural components which do not qualify for the credit include, for example, such parts of a building as walls, partitions, floors and ceilings, as well as any permanent coverings therefore such as paneling or tiling, and other components relating to the operation and maintenance of a building. The term "building" does not include such structures as oil and gas storage tanks, grain storage bins, silos, fractionating towers, blast furnaces, coke ovens, brick kilns, and coal tipples (so-called "special purpose" buildings).

Lodging Facilities. Property which is used predominantly to furnish lodging or in connection therewith generally does not qualify for the investment credit. But it can qualify if it is a nonlodging commercial facility which is available to nonlodgers on the same basis as to lodgers or is used by a hotel or motel where the predominant portion of the accommodations is used by transients. "Predominant portion"" and "transients" are the key words. IRS says that "predominant portion" means "more than one-half" and the accommodations will be considered used on a transient basis if the rental period is normally less than 30 days.

[¶803] **QUALIFIED INVESTMENTS**

The credit is 10 percent of the qualified investment-subject to the various limitations discussed below. To have a qualified investment there must be an acquisition of property that qualified for the credit. The amount of the qualified investment also depends on whether the investment is in brand-new or second-hand property.

Used v. New Property. If the accquired property is new, there's no limitation on how much you can invest in one year and still have it eligible for the credit (subject, of course, to the other limitations.)

If the property is used, however, you can include as qualified investment property only purchases up to $100,000 in one year (prior rule was $50,000 of *used* property). If you buy more than $100,000 worth of property in one year, you can select whichever items you wish to designate (within the $100,000 limitation) as qualifying property.

Placed in Service. Property is eligible for the investment credit in the year in which it is placed in service. According to the Regulations [Sec. 1.46-3] property is placed in service when it becomes depreciable or when it is in a condition or state of readiness or availability for a specifically assigned function (whether or not in your business), whichever occurs earlier. Thus, a certain amount of flexibility is possible in the case of used property by controlling these factors in order to stay within the $100,000 annual limitation.

If depreciation is deferred to the following year because of an averaging convention or because of the method of depreciaton used (e.g., completed contract, unit of production, retirement), nevertheless, the credit is available in the earlier year if the property is placed in a condition of readiness for a specific function in that year.

How Much Is Your Investment? With new property, the amount of your investment is basis. If you trade in old property for new, you take the basis for the old plus any additional amount you pay and figure the credit on the total. If you trade in a machine on which you claimed a credit in the past, there may be a recapture of part of the previous credit. With acquisitions of used assets, the basis of your credit is cost, not basis. On a trade-in, the only part that would qualify for the credit is the cash you pay in addition to the trade-in. What is more, if used assets are acquired to replace other property that was disposed of (in a transaction that's not a tax-free trade-in), the cost of the acquired property has to be reduced by the basis of the disposed-of property.

If the recapture rules apply on a disposition of property to make way for replacement used property, the cost of the acquired used property is not reduced by the basis of the disposed-of property.

Included in basis (or cost for used property) are all items properly included in your basis for depreciation (Reg. § 1.46-3(c)(1)).

Useful Life. If you qualify for the credit, the amount of qualified property is:

Useful Life if	Amount Qualified for credit
1. 3 years, but less than 5	1/3
2. 5 years, but less than 7	2/3
3. 7 years, or more	3/3

[¶804]   **RECAPTURE OF INVESTMENT CREDIT**

If you dispose of an asset before the useful life on which the credit was figured has run you have to refigure the credit (sec. 47 of the Code). Any excess credit you took is added to your current *tax*.

Suppose you buy an asset for $6,000. Its useful life is ten years. Your credit is 600 (10% of $6,000). But in the sixth year you sell. That entitles you to a credit of only two-thirds of cost ($4,000.) Your credit is 400 (10% of $4,000) rather than $600. The $200 difference is added to your tax in the year of sale.

The recapture rules apply when you dispose of the asset. A disposition includes a sale, trade-in, exchange, gift distribution, involuntary conversion, casualty, theft, in-kind dividend or contribution to a corporation, contribution to a partnership or a sale by a partner or Subchapter S stockholder of his interest in the firm. (See also the Levine text, noted *supra.*)

Occurences Triggering Recapture of Investment Credit. Here are some prime instances:

(1) *Cessation.* The asset ceases to be Section 38 property. For example, a business asset is switched to personal use or the percentage of use of an asset between personal and business changes after the year the credit was taken.

(2) *Property Destroyed by Casualty.* Recapture applies if Section 38 property is disposed of or otherwise ceases to be qualified due to its destruction or damage by casualty or theft on or after 8/15/71. However, qualified replacement property may get the investment credit.

(3) *Lease of Property.* While mere leasing of an asset escapes recapture, a lease treated as a sale will not. Also, leased property ceases to be Section 38 property to the lessor if, after the credit year, it does not qualify as such in the hands of the lessor, lessee or sublessee (Reg. Sec. 1.47-2(b)(1)). Further, recapture may occur in a sale-leaseback subject to certain exceptions.

(4) *Corporate Liquidations.* Recapture can be triggered by corporate distributions in liquidation, sale by a corporation in a "tax-free" Section 337 liquidation and also in a Section 333 (one-month) liquidation where the sole shareholder continues to use the property in business [Rev. Rul. 73-515, CB 1973-2,7; Regs. S 1.47 (3) (f)(1)(ii)(d)].

(5) *Subchapter S Corporations, Partnerships, Estates.* Recapture applies in cases of contributions of property to Subchapter S corporations or to certain partnerships, sales of stock by a Subchapter S corporation, sale of a partnership interest or sale by a beneficiary of an interest in a trust or estate. A corporation electing under Subchapter S may trigger recapture. But see below.

Exceptions to Recapture. Some principal examples include:

(1) *Death Transfers.* There's no recapture when an asset is transferred because of the death of an individual taxpayer nor in the case of a death transfer of a partner's interest or of the stock of a Subchapter S corporation or even in a joint tenancy to the surviving owner.

(2) *Corporate Transfers in Tax-Free Reorganization.* This takes place in a tax-free reorganization or liquidation [Section 381(a)] if the acquiring corporation succeeds to the tax attributes of the transferor corporation.

(3) *Change in the Form of Conducting Business.* Recapture is avoided where a proprietorship or partnership is changed into a corporation provided the transferor retains a substantial interest in firm. Shareholders retaining substantial interest in a corporation while others sell all their stock are not subjected to recapture.

(4) *Reselection of Used Property.* The $100,000 limit on used Section 38 property can be bypassed on early disposition by reselecting excess used property for the earlier year to take the place of the disposed property.

[¶805]   CARRYOVER OF UNUSED CREDITS

To the extent a credit cannot be used in the current year because of the tax liability limitation, it can be carried back for three years and then carried forward seven years. The unused credit is applied to the earliest year first and then in order to subsequent years until exhausted. There is a specific order of priority as follows: Pre-1971 carryovers are first applied until exhausted (pre-1971 carryovers can be carried over for ten years), then the regular credits for the tax year, and, lastly, post-1970 carryovers, but all only to the extent that the maximum credit amount allowable for the tax year is not exceeded. In addition, the 20 percent limitation on post-1968 carryovers is abolished for years beginning with 1972. A first-in/first-out rule applies on carryovers after 1976 (TRA 1976; Section 46(a) and (b).

[¶806]   INVESTMENT CREDIT ON LEASED PROPERTY

A lessor of *new* property can elect to pass the credit through to the lessee under certain conditions discussed below. This can be a valuable sales tool in the hand of companies which engage in equipment leasing. And the tax advantage can make the difference to a lessee in determining whether to lease or buy. The lessor must make a timely election, however, by filing *with the lessee* a signed statement which contains the consent of the lessee and certain other information. The statement must be filed on or before the due date (including any extensions) for the lessee's return in the year possession of the property is transferred to the lessee. Once the election statement is filed with the lessee, the election is irrevocable.

The property must qualify in the hands of the lessor as new property eligible for the credit. It must also be such that it would have qualified for the credit as new property if it had been acquired by the lessee. Thus, the lessee must have been the original user of the property. A lessee is the original user as long as he is the first person to use the property for its intended function. Thus storage, testing, or previous attempts at leasing by the lessor will not preclude the lessee from being treated as the original user.

Reconditioned property will not qualify for the passthrough of the credit since it is not new property. Property which has been reconstructed by the lessor is new property in his hands and will qualify for the credit without regard to the lease. However, IRS says that *neither reconditioned nor reconstructed property* will qualify for the passthrough of credit to the lessee because the lessee is not the original user of the property.

Most of the other limitations on eligibility apply to both lessor and lessee. The useful life limitation, that is, of course, the life used for depreciation, is applied to the property in the hands of the lessor.

General Election. Lessors who engage in numerous leasing transactions with a single lessee can make a general election covering all their transactions with a particular lessee. The election must be filed on or before the due date (including any extensions) for the lessee's tax return in the year of possession under the lease of the first property which is eligible for the general election. And once filed as to the property, it is irrevocable as to all transfers under lease to that lessee during that entire taxable year of that lessee.

How It Works. As to leased property where the lessor elects to pass the credit through to the lessee the credit is based on the fair market value of the property as of the date when possession of the property is transferred to the lessee. However, in the case of leases between corporations both of which are members of the same affiliated group, the credit is based on the lessor's basis. These rules apply to leases entered into after November 8, 1971.

The full investment credit on *new* qualified property may be passed through to the lessee, subject to the following limitation: the property may not have a class life of more than 14 years and be leased for less than 80% of its class life (except in the case of a "net lease" which would not be subject to the aforementioned limitation). (Sec.48(d) of the code). Where the limitation applies, the lessor can pass through to the first lessee of the property only that portion of the credit which the period of the lease bears to the class life of the property. The portion of the credit which cannot than be passed through to the lessee can be taken by the lessor. Since the entire credit is available in the year the property is placed in service, the result may be a tax saving in the first year which exceeds that year's expenditure. Recapture can apply, however.

[¶807]   TAX LIABILITY LIMITATIONS ON INVESTMENT CREDIT

The credit is applied in full against your tax liability up to $25,000 in any taxable year. The credit can never exceed the tax liability. But if your tax liability exceeds $25,000, any remaining credit can only be applied against one-half of the excess. Any unused credit is available as a carryback for three years and then as a carryforward for seven years.

In the case of married taxpayers, the $25,000 figure is cut to $12,500 on a separate return. There is an exception, however, where your spouse makes no investments which would qualify for the credit and has no credit carryovers to that year. But in making this determination, IRS will consider that your spouse made a qualifying investment even if the spouse is only an indirect beneficiary of the credit.

[¶808]   CASUALTY LOSS LIMITATIONS ON INVESTMENT CREDIT

Another limitation covers reinvestment of casualty insurance proceeds. If property is stolen or destroyed or damaged by fire, storm, shipwreck, or other casualty, the amount spent on replacement property must be reduced by any insurance recovery or the adjusted basis of the destroyed property, whichever is smaller.

[¶809]   INVESTMENT CREDIT— TAX REFORM ACT OF 1976, ESOP, FIFO AND OTHERS

As noted, the rate change for the credit from 7 percent to 10 percent is extended through 1980 by the *Tax Reform Act of 1976* [Sec. 46 (a) of the Code]. The change for used property ($100,000, maximum to qualify) remains and is extended through 1980.

There is an additional possible 1½ percentage points increase in the credit relative to the tie-in of the investment credit and an employee stock ownership plan (ESOP) [Sec. 46 (f) of the Code].

The *Tax Reform Act of 1976* also provides a first-in first-out treatment for the investment credit. It allows the taxpayer to use the oldest investment credit that has accrued, but has not been used. (FIFO — first-in first-out prevents the expiration of the investment credit from lack of use.) This rule applies for 1976 and later years [Sec. 46(a) and (b) of the Code].

There are special rules for investment credit generated from movies, television films, tapes, vessels, and certain other items. The effective date of the investment credit changes by the *Tax Reform Act of 1976* varies somewhat on certain of the special items, but generally applies to years after December 31, 1975.

[¶810]   POLLUTION CONTROL—INVESTMENT CREDIT

The Tax Reform Act of 1976, under Section 169 of the Code, allows the investment credit even for the portion of certified pollution control equipment that is amortizable on a rapid basis under Section 169 of the Code. The above rule is change from the prior law, which would not allow both the Section 169 of the Code rapid amortization and the investment credit.

Under the new provision, the equipment which meets the Section 169 of the Code test, as long as it is placed in service after 1976, will qualify for the investment credit, providing it has a useful life of at least 5 years.

The percentage that qualifies is 50 percent of the amount of the basis which is amortizable under Section 169 of the Code. This rule is generally applicable to property acquired by the taxpayer after December 31, 1976, with some exceptions.

CHAPTER 9

Involuntary Conversions

[¶901]   TAX ASPECTS OF INVOLUNTARY CONVERSIONS

Where property is destroyed, condemned, or threatened with condemnation and you then have a gain or loss because you received insurance or condemnation proceeds, you have the equivalent of an exchange. The nature of the gain or loss will be either ordinary or capital, depending on the nature of the converted property.

Where the property converted was a capital asset held for more than six months (prior to 1977, see *supra*), a capital gain or loss is incurred. If the property was used in your trade or business and held for long-term, the gain or loss is treated as Section 1231 gain or loss (sale or exchange of trade or business property). In that event, the gain or loss is combined with other Section 1231 gains — net gain being long-term capital gain, net loss being ordinary loss [Reg. §1.123-1(e)].

A Tax Court case [*Tri-S Corp.*, 48 TC 316, *aff'd* 400 F.2d 852, (10th Cir. 1968)] shows how property may be changed from property held for development, subdivision, and sale into a capital asset so that gain on conversion may be taxed at a favorable capital gain rate.

Tri-S, a residential land developer, had purchased a tract of raw land for development purposes. Thereafter, it was notified that condemnation proceedings would be instituted to take part of the property. Tri-S thereupon negotiated with the condemning authority for the sale of the parcel with the closing to take place six months after it received the notice of intention to condemn. The Tax Court held that Tri-S was entitled to treat the gain realized on the sale as a capital gain on the theory that once it received notice of the intention to condemn, Tri-S no longer held the parcel for development, subdivision, and sale in the regular course of business. It seems that once the notice of intention to condemn was given, any subsequent improvement of the property could not be recouped in condemnation proceedings. Thus, the property was no longer held for development and sale in the regular course of business and could be treated as a capital asset.

A sale to the condemning authority was treated the same as a sale to a third person. Actually the argument adopted would apply even if the property had been taken by condemnation rather than by sale, assuming a substantial interim period between the notice of intention to condemn and the actual taking of possession or title by the condemning authority. The nature of the gain realized, whether ordinary income or capital, is determined by the nature of the holding of the property at the time possession is taken by the condemning authority, not by the nature of the holding at the time of the notice of intention to condemn.

In most jurisdictions, there is some procedure available whereby the public authorities can protect themselves against the improvement of property they contemplate taking. Once the public authorities avail themselves of this procedure, the developer would not hold the property for development and sale in the regular course of business, and any improvements made could not be recouped if the property actually had been condemned.

[¶902]   **TIME LIMITS FOR REPLACEMENT**
OF CONVERTED PROPERTY

The replacement property must be purchased within a period running from the date of the disposition of the converted property or the earliest date of the threat or imminence of condemnation (whichever is earlier) and ending two years after the close of the taxable year in which any of the gain on conversion is realized [Sec. 1033 (a)(3)(B)(i) of the Code]. Where *real estate* is condemned after 12/31/74, there is a 3-year replacement rule [*Tax Reform Act of 1976*, Sec. 1033 (f) of the Code]. If you cannot find replacement property within the required time, you may apply for extra time. And even if the application for an extension is filed after the expiration of the original period, it will be considered provided you have a good reason for not filing earlier [Reg. §1.033(a)-2]. But if the owner of converted property dies before the proceeds have been invested in other property, his legal representative have no right to the tax-free replacement privilege [*Rev. Rul.* 64-161, CB 1964-1 (Part I), 298, revoking *Rev. Rul. 58-407, CB 1958-2, 404*].

To qualify for tax-free treatment, you have to "purchase" replacement property within the required time. Suppose you contract to buy a qualified parcel, make a down payment, have the deed placed in escrow until closing, but do not actually close title until more than three years after the condemnation. Will the replacement qualify so as to defer the tax on your gain? No, says the Tax Court since there is no purchase. To have a purchase, the burdens and benefits of the property have to pass. Here, although you may have assumed the investment risk, you have assumed nothing else. The seller retains title; he has the burden of paying taxes and insurance and the benefits of possession [*Estate of H.L. Johnston,* 51 TC 290 *aff'd* 430 F.2d 1019 (6th Cir. 1970)].

Date When Condemning Authorities Given Right of Possession and Property Owner Given Right to Proceeds as Controlling. When you are transferring property, whether it be through condemnation or through some other disposition, for purpose of knowing when title actually passes, you should always look to the date that the benefits and burdens of the property are transferred and not rely on the date that the deed is actually delivered. Here's why: Under threat of condemnation, you are offered $50,000 for a parcel of land you own. You refuse the offer and the state authorities get a condemnation judgment in the amount of $50,000 and then deposit the money with the court. You appeal, but in spite of this, under local law, you have the right to the money. About a year later you settle for an additional $10,000 and reinvest all of the proceeds in similar or related property. The tax on your gain will be deferred if title to the property passed as of the settlement date. If it passed as of the date of judgment, the gain is taxable because the replacement of the property was too late. How do you make out? The Tax Court says no deferral.

Even though technically title to the property may not have transferred until the year of settlement when the deed was delivered, for all practical purposes it passed when judgment was entered, because at that time the state authorities were given the right of possession and you were given the right to purchase proceeds ($50,000) without any strings [*Harry D. Aldridge,* 51TC 475].

Tax-Free Replacement by Way of Purchase of New Property, Sale to Public Authorities, and Leaseback from Public Authorities. You may be able to work out a tax-free deal by purchasing land to replace your condemned building and land and immediately selling the new property to the condemning authorities who then build on the land to suit your specifications and lease this land and building back to you. Here's an example:

Suppose a manufacturing company realizes a gain when it sells its manufacturing plant and the land on which it stands to a municipality under threat of condemnation. For the purpose of replacing the property sold, the company then buys a tract of unimproved land and immediately conveys it to the municipality. The municipality builds a manufacturing plant on the land to suit the company's specifications with funds obtained through the issuance of industrial revenue bonds. The building is completed before the end of the period within which the property taken by condemnation must be replaced if the company is to be able to take advantage of Section 1033. The company then leases the land and building for a 20-year period, paying rent equal to the principal and interest on the municipality's bonds. Under the agreement between the company and the municipality, the company is obligated to purchase the land and the building for a nominal price at the end of the lease term. Also, under the provisions of the lease with the municipality, the burdens and benefits of ownership fall on the company.

IRS has ruled that the transaction qualifies for tax-free treatment because the arrangement with the municipality amounts to a purchase of replacement property with financing being provided through the municipality [*Rev. Rul. 68-642*, 1968-2 CB 337].

[¶903]　　　TIME WHEN PERIOD BEGINS TO RUN

Knowing when a condemnation is threatened or imminent is very important for tax purposes. In the first place that starts the period during which you can invest in similar property and avoid a tax on any gain on the condemnation. Thus, you can anticipate the actual condemnation and get your new property before you get the condemnation award. In addition, gain realized on a *sale* made under the "threat of, or imminence of" condemnation may also be reinvested tax free or, if not reinvested, is eligible for capital gain treatment if the sale was of Section 1231 property. At one time, IRS held that no threat occurred until a public body having the authority to condemn land indicated by public resolution or act that specifically designated land would be condemned [*Rev. Rul. 58-557,* CB 1958-3, 402]. Now, however, IRS has changed its tune. It agrees that a threat exists when a property owner learns through a newspaper or other news medium of a decision to acquire his property. However, he must obtain confirmation of this news items from a government representative of the body involved. And he must have reasonable grounds to believe this [*Rev. Rul. 63-221,* CB 1963-2, 332].

IRS' ruling followed a decision by the Tax Court reaffirming its decision in *Maixner,* [33 TC 191], that a liberal interpretation must be given to Section 1033. The reaffirmance was announced in *Carson Estate Co.,* [22 TCM 425 (1963)]. There, the Board of Supervisors of Los Angeles County authorized the instituting of condemnation proceedings to acquire land for a park. Taxpayer's land was included. Taxpayer negotiated with representatives of the Board to sell the land to the County after assurances from the Board that the land would otherwise be condemned. The Treasury refused to consider the sale as an involuntary conversion because there was no public resolution or public act. The Tax Court held in favor of the taxpayer, saying that a threat exists when there is a declaration of intention to condemn private property for public use, and such was clearly the case here.

A sale made under threat of condemnation may be made either to the condemning authority or to a third party. Although Section 1033 doesn't specifically authorize private sales, the Fifth Circuit has approved such a rule [*Creative*

Solutions, 320 F.2d 809 (1963)], and IRS apparently has gone along by failing to raise the issue in a case involving this type of situation [*Kress & Co.,* 40 TC 142 acq. 1965-2 CB 5].

[¶904]   **ACHIEVING TAX-FREE GAIN ON AN INVOLUNTARY CONVERSION**

As noted, Section 1033 of the Code rule permits you to reduce or avoid any tax on an involuntary conversion. To do so, you must replace the converted property with other properties "similar or related in service or use" to the converted property. It is a functional test. But back in 1958, a liberalizing amendment applicable to condemnation of real property (only) held either for productive use in a trade or business or for investment was adopted under which such property may be replaced with property of a "like kind" Section 1033(g)* of the Code. This like-kind test permits a much broader selection of replacement property than the similar-or-related test. For example, under the like-kind test, replacement of unimproved property by improved property, city real estate by a ranch or farm, or a leasehold with at least 30 years remaining for a fee are all permitted [Reg. §1.103(a)-1].

The similar-or-related test, not the like kind test, continues to apply to real estate, and of course, all other property within Section 1033 of the Code, in two situations:

(1) *Purchase of Stock.* Where the proceeds of the converted property are used to purchase stock to acquire control of a corporation which owns the replacement property. In purchasing control, you must obtain stock possessing at least 80 percent of the total combined voting power of all classes of stock entitled to vote and at least 80 percent of the total number of all other classes of stock of the corporation [Sec. 1033(a)(3)(A) of the Code].

There is no limit stated in the regulations as to the value of the replacement property owned by the corporation whose control is being purchased. Nor is there any reference to the effect of other property in the corporation. It may be possible to acquire a going business or a substantial amount of nonqualifying property along with a nominal amount of replacement property. In such case the Treasury will probably attempt to upset the transaction as a sham to avoid recognition of gain.

(2) *"Dealer" Property.* Where the converted property was held by one engaged in the business of buying and selling such property. Section 1033(g)* of the Code only applies to property for investment or trade or business use.

[¶905]   **APPLYING THE SIMILAR-OR-RELATED TESTS**

Knowing what meets the test of similar or related property has been a difficult problem for both the owner-investor and the owner-user of property. A

---

*1976 TRA redesignated this as Section 1033(f).

number of different tests have been used by the Tax Court and the various Federal Circuit Courts, including the: (1) "functional" test and the (2) "same general class" tests.

Under the functional test, the actual end-use of the property is the only consideration in deciding whether or not the owner uses the property or only holds it as an investment.

Under the same general class test, the original and replacement properties are considered in light of the owner's relationship to them.

A related test has been developed by the Second and Sixth Circuits, and IRS has announced that it will follow this in owner-investor (but not owner-user) situations. This test can be called the "owner-comparison" test and is illustrated by the following decisions:

Case #1—Office Building and Apartment Building Held Similar. The first of the two cases, *Liant Record, Inc.,* [22TCM203, TC Memo 1963-53], and deals with property converted prior to 1958. The taxpayer owned an office building which was condemned. With the proceeds, it bought three apartment buildings. Both the office building and the apartment buildings were held for investment, not for taxpayer's own use. Comparison of the original and replacement property showed the following:

(1) *Management.* The office building has been managed by an independent managing firm but under the supervision of one of the taxpayer's officers. The firm collected rent, made minor repairs, and kept a list of prospective tenants. The apartment buildings were being managed by employees of the taxpayer who did similar functions, under the same supervison.

(2) *Tenancies.* The tenancies in both the original and replacement property were on leases running about two years. All space was unfurnished except for three furnished apartments. The taxpayer made alterations in all buildings at the tenants' requests, although more commonly in the office building.

(3) *Services.* Taxpayer cleaned, painted and decorated the public areas of all the properties; it also cleaned the leased property in the office building.

(4) *Investment Risk.* All the properties were in good areas, rent-controlled, with very few vacancies, and with similar insurance coverage.

The first time it heard the case, the Tax Court held the old and new properties were not "similar and related" [36 TC 224]. The Court used the functional test and considered only the actual end-use of the property. Here, the two end-uses were wholly different—one was as an office building, the other, as an apartment building.

But on appeal, the Second Circuit ruled that the proper test was a *comparison of the service and use of the properties to the owner,* whether he used the property for himself or just held it for investment [303 F.2 326]. Service and use to the owner involves comparing: (1) the extent and type of the owner's management activity, (2) the amount and kind of service rendered to tenants, and (3) nature of the business risks involved. The case was sent back to the Tax Court which reversed its original finding and held for the taxpayer, since the office building and the apartment buildings did not substantially differ under the comparison text.

Case #2—Office Building and Hotel Held Not Similar: The second case, which cited the Second Circuit Court's decision in *Liant,* was *Clifton Investment Co.,* [312 F.2d 719 (6th Cir. 1963), *cert. den.* 373 U.S. 921; but see *Rev. Rul.* 71-41, 1971-1 CB 233]. Clifton had sold an office building which it held for rental income to the city under threat of condemnation. It used the proceeds to buy 80 percent of the stock of a corporation which acquired a hotel. The Tax Court, again using the functional test, held that the properties were dissimilar in their end-use and found against Clifton [36 TC 569]. On appeal, the Sixth Circuit followed the Second Circuit in rejecting that test and applying the comparison test. But in this case the comparison test also resulted in a decision against the taxpayer. While both the office building and the hotel were held for rental income, the taxpayer itself managed the former while the hotel required professional management. There were also material differences in the services supplied to the office building tenants and the hotel guests. Thus, Clifton's relationship to the two properties were dissimilar enough to deny the right to a tax-free exchange.

IRS Acquiescence. IRS will follow the owner-comparison test for investment real estate [TIR 612]. The release gives the example of a lessor of property used for light manufacturing who replaces it with property leased out for a wholesale grocery warehouse. The two properties would not be similar or related in use under functional test but they are under the owner-comparison test. (Some commentators describe these tests as: (1) owner-user functional test and (2) investor-lessor functional test.)

[¶906]   DEDUCTING LOSSES

If an involuntary conversion results in a loss, regardless of whether a replacement was purchased, the loss in recognized. There is nothing in Section 1033 of the Code limiting the recognition of a loss sustained in an involuntary conversion.However, the loss must be taken at the time of the involuntary disposition and cannot be deferred by a replacement.

[¶907]   FIGURING TAXABLE GAIN

An election for nonrecognition of gain may be made by not reporting the entire gain in the return for the year in which the gain is realized but including in gross income only that gain which exceeds the cost of the replacement. If the converted property is not replaced within the specified time limit or if the replacement costs less than was anticipated, an amended return must be filed recomputing the tax for the year in which the election was made. (Failure to report the entire gain is an election.) If no election was made in the year of gain, an election may still be made within the replacement time period by filing a refund claim. Where the election has been made, the time for assessing a deficiency attributable to an involuntary conversion gain, or to deficiencies respecting basis of acquired property in anticipation of a conversion, is three years from the date the Secretary or his delegate is notified of the replacement or of an intention not to replace [Sec. 1033(a)(3)(C),(D)].

If a proper election to avoid the recognition of gain is made, two possibilities governing the extent of the nonrecognition of gain exist:

1. All the money received from the involuntary conversion may be used to purchase the replacement. No gain is recognized.
2. Only some of the money received may be used to purchase the replacement. Gain is recognized but only to the extent of any excess.

Here are illustration of the rules governing whole and partial nonrecognition of gain:

Example: Assume that White received a $100,000 condemnation award for his warehouse, which had an adjusted basis of $60,000. Within the specified time limit he purchased or built another warehouse at a cost of $100,000 (or more). Although his gain on the condemnation award was $40,000, he wholly avoids the recognition of any taxable gain.

Example: Now consider Black: He also received $100,000 for his condemned property having an adusted basis of $60,000. But he only partially replaced the involuntarily converted property with a building costing $75,000. Although his gain on the converted property was $40,000, he realized taxable gain only to the extent that the $100,000 received exceeded the cost of the $75,000 replacement, or $25,000.

Example: Gray also received $100,000 for involuntarily converted property having a $60,000 adjusted basis. But his partial replacement cost him only $50,000. His actual gain ($40,000) was less than the excess of money received over replacement cost ($50,000). His taxable gain is therefore $40,000, the lesser amount. In other words, taxable gain is the lesser of (a) actual gain or (b) the excess of money received over replacement cost.

A conflict has arisen in this situation: Suppose the state condemns your property, giving you an award of $200,000. At that time your basis is $80,000, but there's a $50,000 mortgage on the property. Instead of paying you the $200,000, the state pays you $150,000 and pays the mortgagee $50,000 to wipe out the mortgage debt. How much do you have to reinvest in similar property to avoid tax on the gain: $150,000 or $200,000? The Ninth Circuit says $150,000 if you are not personally liable on the mortgage [*Babcock,* 259 F.2d 689 (1958)]. This disagrees with the IRS, which would require the $200,000 to be reinvested [Reg. §1.1033(a)-2(c)(11)]. In this author's opinion, the Government's position is the stronger.

If you are personally liable on the mortgage, you will have to reinvest the $200,000 because it will be considered that you had received the $200,000 and used $50,000 to pay off your liability.

[¶908]   **TRANSFER OF EASEMENT UNDER THREAT
OF CONDEMNATION**

As discussed, you may realize either a gain or loss in consequence of a condemnation or involuntary conversion of your property. Your gain or loss is capital or ordinary depending on the nature of your property [*Casalina Corp.,* 60 TC 694 (1973)].

Under Section 1033 you can reduce or avoid any tax on an involuntary conversion by replacing the converted property with property of like kind. Where proceeds are received as a result of granting an easement under threat of condemnation and the granting of the easement deprives the owner of all or practically all the beneficial interest in the property or a specific part of the property, any gain realized from the involuntary conversion is recognized for tax purposes only to the extent that the amount realized exceeds the cost of the replacement property [*Rev. Rul.* 54-575, CB 1954-2, 145].

[¶909]   **TAX TREATMENT OF FEES INCURRED IN
OBTAINING AN AWARD**

Suppose that to get the best possible award for the property, you incur expenses for legal, engineering and appraisal fee. You replace the property and make the appropriate election to have any gain recognized only to the extent that the award exceeds the cost of the replacement property [Sec. 1033(a)(3)(A)]. IRS has ruled that you may offset the amount of the condemnation award by the legal, engineering and appraisal fees incurred by you, thereby reducing your taxable gain on replacement by the amount of the offset [*Rev. Rul.* 71-476, CB 1971-2, 308].

The legal bill should be itemized. The part of the fees that was incurred for the money dispute is a capital expenditure. The amount spent for contesting the extent or legality of the taking is currently deductible.

Suppose you incur legal fees in fighting the condemnation of your property. If the legal fees are incurred in getting more money for your property than the authorities offer, you cannot take a current deduction for those fees; you must capitalize them [*Madden,* 57 TC 513; rev'd 514 F.2d 1149 (9th Cir. 1975); *Cert. den.* 424 U.S. 912 (1976)]; the 9th Cir. applied the nature and origin test and held the legal fees to resist condemnation were inherently related to the sale; they were required to be capitalized. But if you incur legal fees in contesting not only the amount of the award but also the actual legality of the taking or the extent of the taking, you might be able to support a current deduction.

[¶910]   SEVERANCE DAMAGES

Where the condemnation award is made for the estimated loss of the land actually taken, the portion of the cost allocable to the land taken is the basis for determining whether or not a taxable gain or loss has been sustained. Where the amount awarded is divided into two parts, one for the value of the property taken and the other as a "severance" damage to the property retained, the part awarded for severance damages does not enter into the computation of any gain on the condemnation unless the award is higher than the cost or other basis of the retained property. If the severance damages do not exceed such costs (or other basis), the only effect is to reduce the basis of the retained property. But if this type of damage is greater than the basis of the retained property, then, to the extent of the excess, it is taxable gain.

A condemnation award was divided between compensation for land taken and for damages due to loss of high rental income in a preferential area. It was held that the severance damages awarded were paid in recognition of the injury sustained by taxpayer's remaining properties and taxpayer could apply them against the basis of these properties [*Pioneer Real Estate Co.,* 47 BTA 886].

The entire award is considered as payment for the land condemned unless the taxpayer shows that part represents severance damages to his remaining land [*Seaside Improvement Co.,* 105 F. 2d 990 (2nd Cir. (1939), *cert. den* 308 U.S. 618; however, the condemnation award referred only to term "land"; also BTA found that condemnation did not decrease the value of the remaining land. *Rev. Rul.* 59-173, CB 1959-1, 201]. But see *Johnston* [42 TC 880 (1965)], holding that the fact that the award was made in a lump sum because of state law was a mere formality that did not change the substance of what occurred, which was that part of the award represented the value of the land and part was for severance damages. The facts demonstrated that during the negotiations the severance damages were a major issue.

Since the splitting of a condemnation award between payment for the property taken and severance damages may result in a postponement of any taxable gain on the transaction, it is advisable to set up the contract with the condemning authority in such a way that it will result in the most favorable tax situation to the owner [see *Greene,* 173 F. Supp. 868]. If the contract is silent as to the amount of the damages, the court may allow reasonable damages [*Beeghly,* 36 TC 154; but see *Rev. Rul.* 59-173, CB 1959-1, 201]. Taxable gain, at the taxpayer's election, is not recognized if the proceeds of the award are used to purchase property similar to that condemned within the proper time [Sec. 1033(a)(3)(b)]. If you reinvest the severance money in similar property, no gain will be recognized [*Rev. Rul.* 69-240, CB 1969-1, 199; *Rev. Rul.* 73-35, 1973-1 CB 367].

[¶911]　　TAX-FREE REINVESTMENT OF SEVERANCE MONEY

Where you obtain an award of severance damages because you can no longer use your remaining property in the same manner as before, you might invest the proceeds in other property that will permit you to continue using the property in the same manner [*Rev. Rul.* 69-240, CB 1969-1, 199]. The rule has been applied where severance damages obtained for the condemnation of part of a farm were used to purchase adjacent land to replace the land taken.

[¶912] INVOLUNTARY CONVERSION OF CORPORATE PROPERTY

If property held by a corporation is condemned, the corporation may reinvest the proceeds and postpone tax on any realized gain. Sometimes, however, the shareholders may want the proceeds distributed to them so they can reinvest on their own. This might also occur when the corporation owns only one parcel of property and its condemnation just about puts the corporation out of business. If the corporation picks up the gain on the condemnation, it will have a tax to pay. Then, if it liquidates, the stockholders have a second tax to pay (presumably, the basis for their stock is less than what they'll receive in the liquidation). The rule is the replacement must be by the one who suffers the loss. If a partnership suffers the condemnation, it, and not the partners, must make the replacement [*Rev. Rule* 66-191, 1966-2 CB 300; Regs. §1.1033(a)-2(c); see also *Varner,* 32 TCM 97, TC Memo. 1973-27]. Since a condemnation is a sale or exchange, at first blush there seems to be an easy way out: use a 12-month liquidation (Sec. 337). Where sales of the corporation's property take place during the 12-month period after adopting the liquidation resolution and everything is distributed to the stockholders during that 12-month period, the corporation is not taxed on the gain. *Net result:* one tax payment (by the stockholders on liquidation).

Proper timing in this transaction is vital. The sale or exchange takes place when title vests in the governmental authority and the right to compensation is established [*Rev. Rul.* 59-108, CB 1959-1, 72]. It makes no difference that the actual amount of compensation has not yet been established. So you must look to the law under which the condemnation takes place to find when the title passes and the right to compensation is established. You should time the adoption of your plan of liquidation so that the act that transfers title and gives you the right to compensation takes place within 12 months after your adoption of the liquidation plan. You have to have your complete liquidation take place within that 12-month period, too. Since you probably will not have yet received the actual condemnation proceeds, you can transfer the claim for those proceeds to your stockholders in the liquidation.

A difficult problem arises in jurisdictions where it is sometimes impossible to know exactly when title passes to the condemning authority. For example, under some New York statutes, title passes on the filing of a map in the county clerk's office. Even though the property owner has no way of knowing beforehand when this will occur, he is barred from using a Section 337 liquidation as a result (*Driscoll Bros*. [221 F. Supp. 603 (D.C. N.Y. 1963)] *Dwight* [328 F.2 973, (2d Cir. 1964]. One taxpayer faced with this result tried to argue that a single tax was nevertheless payable because (1) the corporation distributed its claim to compensation prior to payment by the city and (2) the corporation was out of existence when final payment was made. It lost on both counts [*Wood Harmon Corp.*, 311 F. 2d 918 (2d Cir. 1963)].

What to Do. Here are three alternatives which might be helpful in cases where exact knowledge of the condemnation may not be available until it is too late to qualify for a Section 337 liquidation:

(1) Proceed with a normal plan of liquidation as soon as you get wind of the condemnation. Only a single capital gain tax (on the stockholders) would then be payable. The problem here is that the shareholders may have to pay the tax before they receive the award.

(2) Adopt a plan of liquidation. When sufficient time goes by to make it unlikely that title and possession of the property will be taken by the condemning authorities to meet the 12-month requirement for a completed liquidation, abandon the plan and continue operations until such time as you're reasonably sure when title and possession of the property will be acquired by the condemning authorities. Then adopt a new plan of liquidation and carry it out within the 12-month period.

(3) Adopt monthly resolutions to liquidate and then cancel them if the order of condemnation (or other act which passes title) does not occur during the month. This eliminates the possibility that the passage of title will not take place until more than 12 months have passed, making the liquidation ineligible under §337. The validity of this method is uncertain but it may be effective.

(4) Once you suspect a condemnation may occur, adopt a plan of liquidation but provide in the resolution that the plan is not to become effective unless

the property is condemned and then it is to become effective automatically on the same day. This sequence was found to create a Sec. 337 liquidation in a case where the corporation wanted to avoid that result because a loss was involved [*Adams,* 38 TC 549]. But the same reasoning should apply if you seek the advantages of Section 337.

[¶913]   **PARTIAL CONDEMNATION**

It is not unusual to have only part of your property condemended. That may leave you with remaining property that you can no longer use for your present business or investment purposes. Here's what you can do.

Sell the balance of your property and reinvest the combined condemnation and sales proceeds in a new property of like kind. You avoid being taxed on any gain on the condemnation and sale that way. IRS has changed its previous position on this point and has agreed to follow a Tax Court decision which allowed the avoidance of tax on gain on the sale of the remaining property [*Rev. Rul.* 59-361, CB 1959-2, 183].

The property condemned need not be physically attached to the remaining property provided you used the two properties as one economic unit and can't use the remaining property without the condemned part. For example, in a Tax Court case [*Masser,* 30, TC 741, acq. 1959-2 CB 5], the owner of a freight terminal used the lots he owned across the street to store his semitrailers when not in use. Because they were nearby, he could move the semitrailers into the terminal in order to unload freight from them into delivery trucks. When the lots were taken by condemnation, the lack of the nearby parking area made it impossible to continue operating the freight terminal. So the taxpayer sold the freight terminal and used the proceeds from that sale and those from the condemnation to buy a new terminal with adjacent parking facilities. The Tax Court treated both condemnation and sale together as an involuntary conversion and allowed the avoidance of tax by reinvestment.

IRS has indicated that the same principle would apply where part of a golf course is condemned and the remaining part is sold because it can no longer be used as a golf course. This reverses its earlier position on this matter [*Rev. Rul.* 57-117, revoked by *Rev. Rul.* 59-361, Supra].

[¶914]   **REFUND OF TAXES PAID**

Say your property was condemned in 1973 and you received the full award of $100,000. Your gain was $60,000. In 1973 you reinvested in the proper type of property to the extent of $70,000. At this point, you did not expect to reinvest the remaining $30,000. On your 1973 tax return, you elected to avoid your gain on the involuntary conversion to the extent of your reinvestment by $30,000 and that $30,000 was less than your total gain, that $30,000 was taxable. So, you paid a tax on that $30,000.

The tax law lets you avoid tax on the gain or involuntary conversions if you made the proper reinvestment by the close of the second year following the first year in which any part of the gain on the involuntary conversion was realized [Sec. 1033(a)(3)(B)]. (Now 3 years, not 2, if within Section 1033(f), involuntary conversion of realty by condemnation; see *Supra*). So in your case, since the entire gain was realized in 1973, you had until the end of 1975 to make a proper reinvestment. Suppose in 1974 you decided to reinvest that remaining $30,000. Could you get your tax back? Yes, says IRS, if you spelled out the details on your 1974 tax return and filed a claim for refund for overpayment of 1973 tax [*Rev. Rul.* 63-127, CB 1963-2,333].

[¶915]   **AVOIDING SECTION 1033 OF THE CODE:
SWAPPING CAPITAL GAINS FOR ORDINARY DEDUCTIONS**

Whenever you can trade capital gains for ordinary deductions, you have a good deal. Ordinary deductions offset income which is taxed at much higher rates. When you elect to avoid the tax on an involuntary conversion, your basis for your new property is the basis you had for your old property. Your depreciation deductions on your new property (the ordinary deductions) are very small. But if you paid the capital gains tax and reinvested the proceeds, the basis for your new property would be what you paid for it. So, you'd be getting large depreciation deductions. And with new property, you'd also be allowed to use accelerated depreciation— stepping up your deductions in the early years still more.

The Arithmetic. Say you had an apartment building with a basis of $100,000 that was condemned to make way for a new highway. You received an award of $300,000. Your gain was $200,000 and the capital gains tax on that was $50,000.* If you reinvested the $300,000 in a new building and elected to avoid the tax, your basis for the new property is $100,000. Assuming (for the sake of illustration) that there would be no salvage value, you would deduct that portion of the $100,000 which was allocable to the building over its remaining useful life. If 80 percent was allocable to the building and you were a tax payer in a 70 percent bracket, that would give you a total deduction of $56,000 (70 percent of $80,000).

But if you elected to pay the capital gains tax, you would have a $300,000 basis for the new property and $240,000 of that would be allocated to the building (again, assuming no salvage value and an 80 percent allocation to the building). In a 70 percent tax bracket this would mean a recovery via depreciation deductions of $168,000. But that cost you a $50,000 capital gains tax. So your net

*Spreading gain.

deduction was $118,000. And that was more than double the $56,000 deduction you would get by avoiding the capital gains tax. Accelerated depreciation would allow you to recover about two-thirds of the cost allocable to the building in about half its useful life. (But, also consider the time value of the earliest taxes paid.)

The Other Side of the Coin. The economics of the situation will not always allow you to pay current taxes in exchange for future tax savings. You may need the full $300,000 to reinvest in the new building and may not afford to shell out $50,000 in capital gains taxes, to boot. There may, however, be room to borrow the tax via a mortgage on the building. This could still be worthwhile since the interest is tax deductible. But, your tax bracket may not be so high that the savings would warrant a current big payout of capital gains tax.

[¶916]   "TACKING" OF HOLDING PERIOD

The holding period of the converted property is tacked to the holding period of the replacement purchased with the conversion proceeds. Section 1223(1)(A) of the Code provides that "an involuntary conversion described in Section 1033 shall be considered an exchange."

[¶917]   FIGURING BASIS

In computing gain or loss from an involuntary conversion, it is necessary to start with the basis of the converted property. If the converted property is replaced, the basis of the replacement is related to that of the converted property. Here are the rules:

(1) Basis of Involuntarily Converted Property Where There Is No Replacement. The usual rules in determining the basis for purposes of computing gain or loss apply to Section 1231 assets, that is, cost of the property adjusted for depreciation and other items [Sec. 1012 and 1016]. Generally, the method by which the property was acquired (purchase, exchange, gift, inheritance, etc.) determines the method for computing the property's basis. Gain or loss from the involuntary conversion of a Section 1231 asset is the difference between the property's basis (adjusted for depreciation, depletion, etc.) and the proceeds received.

> *Example:* Able's condemned factory had an adjusted basis of $80,000. He received a $100,000 award. Gain is the difference between the adjusted basis of the property ($80,000) and the proceeds ($100,000)—or a $20,000 capital gain. (If a replacement is purchased, see below.)

Basis of Property Involuntarily Converted Directly Into Other Property. The basis of the new property is the same as that of the involuntarily converted property, adjusted at the time of the conversion, because no gain is recognized. In other words, there is a direct exchange, and the new property takes the basis of the old, adjusted at the time of the conversion.

> *Example:* Baker's condemned warehouse had an adjusted basis of $80,000. He received new property having a fair market value of $100,000. The new property takes the same basis as the old—$80,000. No gain is recognized unless and until the new property is sold.

(3) Basis of Replacement Property Purchased With Proceeds of Involuntary Conversion (a) If there is a gain—i.e., the money received exceeds both the basis of the involuntarily converted property and the cost of the replacement—the basis of the replacement is its cost less the unrecognized gain on the conversion. If the money received equals or is less than the cost of the replacement, no gain is realized if a proper election is made, and the basis of the replacement is its cost less the unrecognized gain. If several replacement properties are purchased, the aggregate basis as determined above must be allocated among the replacement properties in proportion to their respective costs.

> *Example:* Champ's apartment house had an adjusted basis of $80,000 when it was destroyed by fire. He received $100,000 insurance proceeds and purchased another building for $90,000. He elected that gain be recognized only to the extent of the excess. The basis of the new building is its cost ($90,000) less the unrecognized gain on the conversion ($10,000, which is the difference between the $20,000 realized gain and the $10,000 recognized gain), or a basis for the replacement property of $80,000.

(b) If there is a loss—that is, if the amount received is less than the adjusted basis of the involuntarily converted property—the loss is fully recognized at the time of the conversion. If he purchases a replacement costing more than he received on the conversion, the basis of the replacement is its cost or other basis, depending on the manner of acquisition.

> *Example:* Everett's factory was totally destroyed by fire. It had an adjusted basis of $100,000, but he received only $80,000 insurance proceeds. He takes his loss in the year of the involuntary conversion. He then buys another building for $100,000. The basis of the replacement building has nothing to do with the loss suffered on the involuntary conversion—the basis is merely its $100,000 cost.

(c) If there is a mortgage, either on the involuntarily converted property or on the replacement property, the mortgage is included in the proceeds received or in the cost of the replacement for purposes of computing both gain or loss and the basis of the property. However, items such as collection fees and mortgage interests are deductible, and capital items such as legal fees increase basis.

> *Example:* Franklin received a $100,000 condemnation award for property having an adjusted basis of $80,000. He used $50,000 to satisfy a mortgage on his property and then purchased a replacement costing $90,000, on which there was a $40,000 mortgage. The mortgages do not affect his gain ($10,000 capital gain if he made an election to have gain recognized *only to the extent of the excess not invested).*

[¶918]   CONDEMNATION—OUTDOOR ADVERTISING DISPLAYS

Outdoor advertising displays have been an issue as to whether they constitute real property. Under the *Tax Reform Act of 1976,* beginning after 1970, the taxpayer can make an irrevocable election to treat this as real property; *it will* therefore qualify under Section 1033(f) of the Code. (This rule will not apply to the extent investment credit or additional first year depreciation was claimed on the property.) The election is irrevocable.

10

Tax-Free Real Estate Exchanges of Business or Investment Real Estate

ADVANTAGE OF THE TAX-FREE REAL ESTATE EXCHANGE

More and more brokers and real estate men are becoming aware of the money-making advantages in exchanges of real estate properties, especially in view of the increased impact of capital gains under the present tax law.

An exchange provides the real estate owner with a method of achieving some favorable tax results he might not otherwise get by selling his property outright. It also allows the owner to trade his property and receive a new one immediately. An owner who is interested in continuity can exchange for a new property throwing off an income instead of selling outright and then having to wait, perhaps for months, until a suitable replacement property can be found.

Finally, tax-free exchanges are an excellent way of solving the problems created by a tight-money market. If you want to sell your property, take out most of the value, and reinvest in a new property, it will be hard to find a buyer who is able to put up just cash for the value of the property. And if your prospective buyer cannot get a loan in order to pay you the full cash value of the property, you'd have to take back a purchase-money mortgage. Thus, while eventually (as the mortgage is paid off) you'd pull out your full equity from the old property, you might find yourself with insufficient immediate funds to reinvest in new property. But on a tax-free exchange, two potential sellers who are both locked in by a tight-money situation can pull out the full equity they have in a property by trading with each other because after the trade each has fully reinvested his previous equity.

[¶1002]   **HOW TAX-FREE EXCHANGES WORK**

Section 1031 of the Internal Revenue Code provides that no gain or loss on an exchange is recognized if property held for productive use in a trade or business or for investment is exchanged solely for property of a like kind, which also is going to be held for productive use in a trade or business or for investment. If real estate is exchanged, then the property received is considered of like kind as long as it is real estate (improved, unimproved, farmlands, etc.) and both the property given up and the property received are trade or business or investment properties and not held for resale or as a residence.

This test is applied separately to each of the parties to the exchange. Thus A may give B a hotel he held for rental purposes and receive investment farmland; A does not have any taxable gain. But if B's intention is to resell the farmland (dealer concept), then the land may be held for resale to customers by B, and so B can have a taxable exchange even though A does not have a taxable gain.

If you have a tax-free exchange, then the basis of the property you receive is the same as that of the property you transferred. You add the time you held the old property to the new one for purposes of your holding period for the new property. [Sec. 1223 of the Code].

Boot. If in addition to real estate you receive boot (nonqualified property such as stocks, cash, a residence), gain is recognized to the extent of the boot. So, if you transfer investment real estate with a basis of $20,000 and worth $100,000 for investment real estate worth $80,000 and $20,000 cash, you have $80,000 gain, but only $20,000 of it, the boot, is taxable. Your basis for the new property is still $20,000 (the basis of the old property, decreased by the amount of the boot received and increased by the gain recognized on the exchange). If you transfer property subject to a mortgage, the amount of the mortgage debt is treated as cash received. But if you *transfer* cash in the exchange or take the new property subject to a mortgage, that increases your basis for the new property.

Mortgages on Both Sides. Suppose both parties exchange properties subject to mortgages. Then each receives boot in the amount of the mortgage on the property he trades away, but he is entitled to deduct from this boot the amount of the mortgage on the new property he gets for purposes of determining his gain presently recognized. So, assume D transfers an apartment house worth $200,000 but subject to a mortgage of $100,000 (his equity is $100,000) and with an adjusted basis of $50,000 for E's tract worth $250,000, which is subject to a mortgage of $175,000 (E's equity is $75,000) and $25,000 cash. E's basis in the tract is $25,000.

D has a gain of $150,000. He has received a tract of land worth $250,000, cash of $25,000, and has been relieved of a $100,000 mortgage. From this total of $375,000, he deducts his basis of $50,000 and the $175,000 mortgage to which he takes subject on the property he receives. This gives him a gain of $150,000. But this $150,000 gain is recognized only to the extent of the $25,000 cash since this is the only boot D has received. (The mortgage liability on the old property, $100,000, is offset by the mortgage of $175,000 on the tract.) D's basis for the new property is $125,000: his old basis of $50,000, plus $175,000 (the mortgage he takes subject to the new propery), minus $100,000 (the mortgage on the property he transfers).

E has a $225,000 gain, computed as follows: He receives an apartment house worth $200,000 and is relieved of a $175,000 mortgage on his old property. From this $375,000 total is subtracted his basis of $25,000 for his old property, the $100,000 mortgage to which he is subject on the apartment, and the $25,000 cash he is paying. His gain is $225,000.

But this gain is recognized only to the extent of $50,000. The boot he receives is $175,000, which is the mortgage on his old property. But he subtracts from this amount the mortgage on his new property ($100,000) and the cash he gives to D ($25,000). E's basis for the apartment house is $25,000: $25,000 (his old basis), plus $25,000 (cash he transferred) plus $100,000 (mortgage on his new property), plus the gain recognized to him ($50,000), minus $175,000 (mortgage on tract he transferred to D). [Reg. §1.1031(d)-2].

Formula for Finding Basis of New Property. To find your basis of the new property after you have traded your old property for it:

Start with:	Adjusted basis of your old property
Add:	Cash paid; Any other "boot" paid; Mortgage or trust deed assumed or taken subject to; Recognized gain
	Total
Subtract:	Mortgage or trust deed on old property assumed or taken subject to by the other party; Cash received; Any other "boot" received
Result is:	Basis for new property

[¶1003]   WHEN AND HOW TO AVOID A TAX-FREE EXCHANGE

If you do not take over property which has a higher mortgage or you cannot get a more favorable land-building ratio, you will not be able to raise your basis. Here, it may be worthwhile to pay the capital gain tax to raise your basis and then take higher depreciation deductions against ordinary income. This is something you must calculate in advance. Determine how much the money you use to pay the tax would be worth to you in after-tax yield if invested (after a tax-free exchange) and compare this with the tax savings you'd get from the higher depreciation deduction resulting from a taxable exchange. You will also want to have a taxable transaction if you want to realize a *loss*. To make the transaction taxable, sell to one party and buy from another in separate transactions.

[¶1004]　　TAX REASONS FOR EXCHANGE OF PROPERTIES

The most realistic reason why you may try to go into a tax-free exchange, particularly in view of the tax law, is the postponement of capital gain taxes on the appreciation in value of the property. If the property has risen in value or if property values have stayed constant and your basis has been reduced by depreciation deductions, you would have a capital gain on sale of the property. For example, say the property cost you $20,000 and you took $5,000 of depreciation. If you now sell for $25,000, you will have a $10,000 gain. (Your basis is now $15,000, and you have received $25,000.) This gain will be taxed at capital gain rates unless you are a dealer in the property or the property is subject to Section 1250 of the Code which recaptures depreciation on the disposition of depreciable real property at a gain.

Thus, the owner of the property has a great incentive to find some method by which he can dispose of the property and yet not pay a tax on his capital gain. He would like to be able to reinvest the full value of the old property in the new property that he eventually will get. And he would like to raise his basis for the new property in order to take large depreciation deductions on that property, particularly when he has used up his depreciation on the old property. A good solution to many of these problems is the tax-free exchange.

[¶1005]　　MEETING THE PARTIES' REQUIREMENTS

If an exchange of real estate is to serve the parties' needs, they should not only be aware of the methods by which the value of the properties can be measured, but also of how to evaluate the properties in terms of the reasons for which the exchange is being made. One way of looking at the exchange technique is that it is a method of exchange between persons rather than the exchanging of properties. Many exchanges make sense only when the particular needs of the individuals involved are understood. The true value of the property, for the purpose of the exchange, often depends on the position of the individual who is going to receive it.

How will the spendable income of the recipient, both present and future, be affected by this exchange? An investor who will be able to double his depreciation deduction without increasing his equity will often be willing to take a property at a somewhat overvalued price. Another person, paying taxes in the highest bracket, will turn down high-income, low-depreciation property even at a bargain price.

What are some of the factors and ingredients which make up the total so-called "exchange value" picture of a typical income property? These generally fall into three groups as follows: (1) those making up the cash income and cash expense picture of the property. (2) Those making up the property's capital position — i.e., amortization of debt, extent of actual depreciation, "hidden" values such as a leasehold interest held at declining rentals. (3) Those giving the property its "relational values" — i.e., factors which make it of interest to a particular investor because of high current income, high depreciation, etc.

Here's a rundown on the important factors that a party entering into an exchange of real estate should give careful consideration to in order to arrive at a true evaluation of the transaction in terms of his particular situation and requirements:

Cash Income and Expense. This data is the basic "bread and butter" picture of the property. The investor to whom the property is offered will want to know both the audit income and the scheduled income from the property.

Audit Income. This is derived from an actual accounting of the income of the property for prior years. Information of this type is derived from the individual's income tax returns and/or from his records of the property. In some cases his warranted statement of income is accepted.

Scheduled Income. This is an intangible-type projection of income which the property owner hopes he will receive for the coming year. When this method is used, the sophisticated property owner who is contemplating an exchange would, in his final analysis, estimate true income by allowing a percentage vacancy factor. In establishing the expenses of the property, the sources of information are the same as those used to establish the income. We are safe in assuming that any property owner is prudent enough to report maximum expenses on his property as an income tax deduction. What better source of information could we find than an income tax report?

Capital Structure. The extent to which property is mortgaged has important tax consequences in the exchange. To the party "trading up," highly leveraged property is his opportunity to increase the fair market value of his holdings. The party "trading down" sees his obligations lessened but also may have a tax problem since he is obliged to recognize gain on the exchange to the extent of his reduction in debt. But even apart from these considerations, the capital structure of the property may add or detract from its value for exchange purposes. For example, a property with a standing mortgage will be attractive to an investor who requires a large cash flow in the immediate future. Or an owner of property subject to several small mortgages may be anxious to acquire property with only one lien, which would make refinancing or additional financing much easier.

Similarly, sophisticated investors frequently seek out properties with "hidden" values which will not appear on a balance sheet or profit and loss statement. An investor may own a leasehold interest in an office building for which he pays a rental which declines over the years. Other things remaining equal, income will increase proportionately. Yet this will not be reflected in the current income of the property.

Finally, the prospective recipient of the property will want to know the extent of actual depreciation or obsolescence of the property. He must make some estimate of the property's remaining life in order to know how soon he must recoup his investment.

Relational Values. These are values which can be said to be created by the exchange itself — the value is created by the right person holding the right property at the right time. The most obvious are those arising out of the individual's tax structure. But there are other relational values, too. Some are connected with the time factor — an investor may want to exchange immediate income for long-term appreciation in order to build an estate, or he may want just the opposite. Values may be connected with the management factor — an investor who wants to remain completely passive with respect to the property will frequently be prepared to pay slightly above the theoretical market price. Finally, value may arise from transferring the risk factor from one who seeks security in his investments to one who is anxious to assume risks because of the prospect of very substantial gain.

Valuation for Financing. While it is true that two overvalued properties can sometimes be exchanged because the mutual inflation of values cancels out, if an exchange is contemplated on the basis of inflated prices, there may be difficulty in obtaining loans to generate the cash required to balance equities, and the exchange cannot be accomplished.

[¶1006]   **FINANCING THE EXCHANGE**

By exchanging real estate instead of selling it in the usual way and financing the deal with a mortgage loan, it is possible to make deals in a tight-money market and with cash-poor buyers that might not otherwise be possible. The tax-free exchange technique makes it possible for a property owner to switch investments and increase financing without the loss of capital resulting from the capital gain tax he would have to pay on his profit if he sold the property. When money is tight, a property owner who wants to sell his property, take out most of its value, and reinvest in a new property might find it difficult to obtain a buyer who can put up the necessary cash. By making a tax-free exchange, he and his opposite party can pull out the full equity they have in their respective properties.

While a real estate exchange can substantially reduce financing requirements, it frequently doesn't eliminate the need for financing. The equities of the parties usually don't exactly offset each other, and the resulting imbalance may be settled by a cash payment or by financing. Here are three ways of overcoming this imbalance:

(1) Loan Commitment. One approach to easing the path to getting the necessary financing is to contact your loan sources as soon as an exchange is contemplated in order to obtain tentative loan commitments. In this way, the parties are made aware of the terms and conditions of the proposed loan and exactly what their monthly payments and interest rates will come to.

(2) Financing by Real Estate Broker. The real estate broker who represents the parties can sometimes furnish the financing required to make an exchange possible. Frequently, the commissions are sufficient to meet the financing requirements.

The procedure is this: The broker lends the amount of his commission to one of the principals. The principal receiving the funds gives the broker a note for value received. The note may be secured by property involved in the exchange or any other property owned by the principal. Sometimes the broker may invest money over and above the amount of his commissions, either as a lender or as a principal having an interest in one of the properties.

(3) Carryback Financing. In any exchange of properties of unequal value, the owner of the higher-priced property realizes taxable gain to the extent of his boot. If the difference is great enough, the boot is likely to equal the entire realized gain, so that the tax-free nature of the exchange does him no good. In such event, the investor can reduce or delay his tax by installment reporting provided he receives less than 30 percent of the price at the time of the exchange. The answer is carryback financing — a purchase-money mortgage large enough to prevent the 30 percent limit from being reached. At the same time, this financing is what makes it possible for the other party to trade up to a more valuable property, using only the equity in his present holding.

[¶1007]   BROKER'S ROLE IN PROPERTY EXCHANGES

In order to create "exchange situations," the real estate broker will have to use some time-tested rules. Essentially, what is necessary is an alertness to the methods of finding participants in an exchange transaction, getting them interested in an exchange, developing an exchange even when one of the parties wants cash, and taking advantage of the opportunities offered by cooperating with other brokers.

Setting Up the Deal. First, the broker should go over his own listings to see if two prospective sellers would be interested in an exchange. Often, the customers for a trade are parties who at first wanted to sell their properties. As an initial step, you should ask prospective clients listing property with you exactly what they plan to do with the proceeds of the sale. If they plan to reinvest in new property, you may be able to work out an exchange.

If you have reached the point where you think you have a deal, it's important to set all the terms so that both parties can understand exactly what will happen. This means that you will have to be able to explain financing, cash requirements, etc. In this connection, make sure that the exchange is not based on cash values. Usually you should not put a value on each property in the exchange contract. Instead, just mention the terms of the exchange; for example, one party is exchanging a building subject to a $50,000 mortgage for a building subject to a $30,000 mortgage and $5,000 cash. In this way, you will protect the parties from having the inflated valuation figures considered as actual value for estate and property taxes.

Three-Way Exchanges. Suppose an exchange would be accepted by one of the parties but the other party is interested only in cash on the sale. In such case, the broker will try to work out an exchange and get cash to the party who wants it by setting up a three-way exchange. For example, Green has a property that White is willing to trade for, but Green does not want White's property. Here the broker gets Black, who is interested in buying White's property, into the deal. Green and White exchange properties, and then Green sells Black the property he got from White. Green has a taxable gain on the sale to Black.

In arranging three-way exchanges, the broker has to be careful to distinguish a nontaxable exchange from a taxable purchase and sale. Take the case where A wants to buy B's property for cash; B wants to exchange it for C's property; and C wants to sell for cash. There are three possible ways to effect the three-party transaction:

1. B can sell to A for cash and then buy C's property.
2. A can buy C's property and then exchange it for B's property.
3. B can exchange properties with C, who then sells to A for cash.

Situation (1) is clearly a sale and purchase, and B (the only party who both starts and ends with a property) must pay tax on any gain realized on the sale to A.

Situations (2) and (3) both can qualify as tax-free exchanges provided the various steps are carried out in the right order. Situation (2) is illustrated by the *Alderson* case [317 F.2d 790 (1963)]; situation (3) is illustrated by the *Baird Publishing* case [39 TC 608 (1962), *acq,* 1963-2 CB 4].

The Alderson Exchange. This began as a straight cash sale from Alderson to Alloy. After the contract was made, Alderson found land (the Salinas property) which he wanted in exchange for his. So, the contract with Alloy was amended to provide that (1) Alloy would acquire the Salinas property and exchange it for Alderson's property and (2), if the exchange didn't take place before a given date, the original cash sale would be made.

Alderson's daughter, acting in his behalf, made the arrangements for transfer of the Salinas property to Alloy and deposited $19,000 as a down payment. This amount represented the difference between the price of the Salinas property and the price which Alloy had contracted to pay for the Alderson property. At simultaneous closings, Alloy took title to the Salinas property, paying the rest of the purchase price, and then exchanged it for Alderson's land.

The Tax Court held that this was really (1) a sale by Alderson to Alloy for cash and (2) a purchase by Alderson of the Salinas property for cash. The Ninth Circuit held just the opposite, that this was (1) a purchase by Alloy of the Salinas property for cash and (2) an exchange between Alloy and Alderson. The Tax Court based its decision primarily on the *method* used — namely, the negotiation for the salinas property by Alderson (through his daughter) rather than by Alloy. The Ninth Circuit rejected this as being too narrow. It relied on *intention* and *legal obligation*. It found that Alderson's intent from the beginning was to transfer his property in a tax-free exchange if at all possible, and it gave this finding great weight. In addition, there never was a fixed obligation on the part of Alloy (once the original contract was amended) to pay cash; it merely had to exchange the Salinas property or pay cash. Since it did the former, it didn't have to do the latter. The Court also made clear that it is perfectly all right for one party to acquire property solely for purposes of an exchange. [See also *Leslie Coupe,* 52 TC 394 (1969).]

The Baird Exchange. Baird was a publisher occupying its own building. The Baptist School Board was anxious to buy the property to round out its holdings on the block. Baird refused to sell despite attractive offers on the specific ground that it did not want to incur the capital gain tax on the substantial profit it would realize. An enterprising real estate broker then proposed that he (the broker) construct a building and trade it for Baird's building, which would constitute a tax-free exchange. The broker could then sell to the School Board.

Baird agreed, and a contract was drawn giving the broker the right to sell the property subject to Baird's occupancy of it rent free until the broker provided a substitute building, which was to be constructed subject to Baird's approval and within a reasonable time. A price of $50,000 was put on Baird's property; the difference between the cost of the building and the purchase price would be paid to Baird in cash.

Subsequently, the broker sold the property to the School Board for $60,000. The $50,000 price it owed to Baird was deposited in an escrow account. Of this amount, $33,000 was used to put up the new building and the remaining $17,000 was paid to Baird in cash. Baird's basis for the property exchanged was $2,000, so that the total gain was $48,000. Since boot is taxable up to the amount of gain realized, Baird reported as capital gain only the $17,000 received in cash.

Baird took the position that it had entered into an agreement with the broker to exchange properties and that it had no interest in what the broker would do with the property he received. The Treasury argued that the deal was really a cash sale between Baird (by the broker acting as its agent) and the School Board and that the broker then constructed a building for Baird. Therefore, argued the Treasury, the entire profit of $48,000 was taxable gain. The test applied by the Treasury in determining if a transaction is a cash sale or an exchange of property is as follows: In an exchange, no fixed money price or value is placed on either property. In a sale, there is either a money consideration or the equivalent in property. Since Baird had placed a fixed price on its property, this was a sale.

The Court, however, went along with Baird and found a true exchange for two reasons: First, Baird had consistently said the only acceptable deal would be one involving an exchange. Second, the relationship between Baird and the broker was not an agency one — that is, Baird did not in fact authorize the broker to sell the property on Baird's behalf. The agreement really was that Baird would sell its building to the broker in exchange for another building to be built by the broker. The broker was under no duty to account to Baird for the price it received for selling Baird's property to another.

The court did not agree with the Treasury's test to distinguish a sale from an exchange. Giving dollar values to the respective properties does not always make the deal a cash sale. Dollar values are involved whenever "boot" is exchanged, and the statute permits this in a tax-free exchange.

Still another example of a three-way tax-free exchange occurred in *Mays, 246 F. Supp. 375 [D.C. Tex, 1966]*. In that case, W.A. Mays, a Texas cattle rancher, signed an agreement to transfer a ranch he owned in Texas and other real estate plus about $213,000 in cash to a charitable foundation in exchange for a New Mexico ranch owned by the foundation. The foundation wanted cash. Any profit it made on this deal was tax exempt, anyway. The exchange was conditioned on the foundation's finding a buyer for the property. So, the very same day, the foundation entered into an agreement with Agridustrial, a financing company 100 percent owned by Mays and his family, to sell it the exchanged property for $500,000. IRS held that this was a taxable sale by taxpayer to his controlled corporation. IRS put a sale price of $500,000 on the New Mexico ranch. This was the amount realized by the foundation for the Texas ranch, according to IRS. But the District Court sided with taxpayer. In holding the exchange tax free under §1031(a), the Court reasoned as follows:

1. Mays held the New Mexico ranch for use in his business of cattle raising, as he had done with his Texas ranch;
2. the corporate entity of Agridustrial Financing (the family corporation) should not be disregarded as it had been active for ten years and had substantial assets. Further, it could not be considered as a conduit for the exchange of the properties involved;
3. the facts indicated an exchange between taxpayer and foundation — not a sale to Agridustrial for cash.

The Court concluded that since the transactions had been executed in a legal manner and were not simulated, they should be given their normal effect. Therefore, this was a nontaxable exchange under §1031 and Mays realized no taxable gain.

Working Relationship Between Broker and Speculators or Syndicates. To make these three-way exchanges, brokers have found that it is a good thing to keep a working relationship with one or more speculators in the real estate community. For instance, one investor might own small houses and raw land which he wants to trade for an apartment house. The apartment house owner wants the small house but isn't interested in the land. Here, you can get the speculator to agree to take the land for a specified price, which will go to the apartment house owner. Some brokers, instead of just using a speculator, will have a working relationship with a syndicate, which will make cash offers for properties offered in a trade which the other party to the trade does not want.

Splitting Commissions. Many brokers who handle exchanges do so because of the cash benefits to them in getting two commissions, one for each property. Sometimes, brokers can increase their volume by being alert and willing to split fees with other brokers. One broker was told of a three-story brick building by another broker who had a listing to sell it for $60,000. At a meeting, another broker told him about a client who had three small houses and wanted to trade for a bigger one. Our broker worked out an exchange between the two owners, and the three brokers involved split the commissions three ways. So, our broker, by ingenuity, had created his commission without having a listing on either of the properties.

Interbroker Deals. Just how do brokers get together to talk about exchanges? Many communities have developed periodic meetings between exchange-oriented brokers. They have luncheons at which they discuss properties they want to exchange. And they will have an exchange bulletin for the listing of properties. Swapping clubs are particularly numerous in southern California, where property turnover is considerable. These clubs are also helpful in giving brokers opportunities to study trading techniques and methods.

CHAPTER 11

Deferring Tax on Sales

[¶1101]   **FOUR KEY ADVANTAGES**

Deferring a taxable gain frequently works out to your advantage. For example, you may incur serious tax penalities if you allow the profits on a sale to bunch up in one year. Other reasons for deferring a taxable gain include:

1. Taking payments over a period of time may facilitate the sale and improve the price. If the tax can't be similarly deferred, you have created a cash liability against a paper profit.
2. Deferment of a long-term capital gain may provide the opportunity to offset it with a loss realized in the future.
3. If a profitable sale takes place in the year of an operating loss, you may want to push the gain ahead because you would rather have it taxed at the favorable capital gains rate than used to reduce the amount of loss which can be carried back against a previous year's ordinary income.
4. An individual will save tax by deferring gain to years when his tax bracket will be low.

[¶1102] **NINE WAYS OF DEFERRING TAX ON PROFITS FROM A SALE**

Here are nine ways of deferring tax or eliminating it all together on profit resulting from a sale:

1. Elect the installment method under [Sec. 453 of the Code.]

2. Use a deferred payment sale not on the installment basis (any sale in which part or all of the purchase price is payable in a year subsequent to the year of sale).

3. Make a contingent sale in which payment is made dependent on future profits or production.

4. Borrow money on your property.

5. Place a mortgage on your property and then give the property to charity or to other donees.

6. Place property under an option, which defers realization of gain.

7. Use an escrow arrangement.

8. Lease property instead of selling it.

9. Work out a tax-free exchange.

[¶1103] **INSTALLMENT SALES**

This is the most commonly used method of deferring sales income. It is the easiest to use because the law sets out definite rules that you have to follow. But it is very important to make sure you do follow the technical rules.

This method allows you to spread your profit over the installment payments made by the purchaser by treating a fixed percentage of each installment as profit on the sale. If the sale resulted in a capital gain, each installment is reported as a capital gain.

[¶1104] **ELECTING INSTALLMENT REPORTING**

While the rule requiring that the election to use the installment method be made on the tax return for the year of sale seems simple enough, IRS and the courts have had differences of opinion as to which returns fall under this description. Here's a rundown of how the courts now stand on the various types of returns:

(1) Amended Return. Installment sales can sometimes be reported on an amended return even though omitted from the original return [*Reaver*, 42 TC 72, *Rev. Rul.* 65-297, 1965-2 CB152, acq. 1965-2 CB 6].

(2) Amended Return After Election of Deferred Sale. However, even if the taxpayer elected to report a deferred sale on his original return, he can change his election on an amended return [*Mamula,* 41 TC 572, rev'd 346 F. 2d 1016 (9th Cir. 1965); it is not an election; Ivan Pomeroy, 54 TC 1716 (1970)].

(3) Return for Year in Which First Payment Made. If the sale takes place in one year but no payments are made until the following year, the sale must be reported on the return for the year of sale [*Ackerman*, 318 F.2d 402 (10th Cir. 1963)].

(4) Late Return Due to Negligence. If the return is filed late due to the taxpayer's negligence, he can still elect the installment method [*C' de Bacca*, 326 F.2d 189 (5th Cir. 1964)].

(5) Late Return Due to Mistake. The Tax Court has held that if a late return is filed because the taxpayer erroneously believed it need not file a return, the taxpayer can still use the installment method of reporting [*McGillick Co.*, 42 TC 1059 acq. 1965-2 CB 6].

To determine the year of sale, look to execution of the deed; mere completion of the contract of sale doesn't complete the sale. Passing of the title to the real property is usually the important thing, and that doesn't occur until the closing or a few days thereafter. Normally, the initial payments for computing the 30 percent limitation are the payments in the year of closing.

The 30 percent test is to be met in the year of "sale or other disposition." In *Stuart*, TC Memo 1960-234, the Tax Court ruled that the signing of a binding executory contract was a "sale or other disposition" of property. However, the Third Circuit reversed on the ground that a contract is an option rather than a sale where the buyer can terminate the agreement by forfeiting the payments previously made [*Stuart*, 300 F.2d 872 (1962)].

For a contract for the sale of real estate to be held a disposition of the property, it would have to require the buyer to accept title in any event and pay the purchase price. The seller would have to retain the right to enforce specific performance. Otherwise, you must consider the year of title passing as the year of the sale for installment reporting purposes.

[¶1105]   QUALIFYING FOR INSTALLMENT REPORTING

To qualify, the payments in the year of sale (including installments) must not exceed 30 percent of the total selling price of the property. (Sales price includes mortgages which the purchaser assumes or takes subject to and without deducting the selling expenses in determining whether the 30 percent test has been met).

Under the tax law, certain types of indebtedness are treated as payments received in the year of sale and taken into account in determining whether the 30 percent rule has been exceeded. Included are bonds or debentures with interest coupons attached, in registered form, payable on demand or in any other form designed to make it possible to trade them readily in an established securities market. Ordinary promissory notes are not treated as payments received in the year of sale, even though they may be assigned by one party to another [Sec. 453(6) of the Code].

Installment Computation for Sale of Realty. The contract price is divided by the total profit; the resulting percentage is the percent of each payment received that must be reported by the seller as income. Contract price is in essence the entire amount the seller will receive (excluding payments on existing mortgages, except to the extent they exceed the seller's basis). That is, it is sales price less mortgages assumed or taken subject to, and the excess of seller's mortgage over his adjusted basis.

We assume a selling price of $25,000 and a cost basis of $15,000. The buyer assumes an existing $5,000 mortgage and gives his own mortgage for the balance due, payable over a 20-year period. The down payment is $5,000, and payments in the first year total $1,000, of which $600 represents interest. Thirty percent of the selling price of $25,000 would be $7,500; and since a total of only $6,000 was received in the year of sale (less then 30 percent), the sale qualifies for installment reporting.

Here is the computation for the first year.

Selling price	$25,000	
Cost basis	15,000	
Gain	$10,000	
Payments received		$6,000
Less interest (reported as ordinary income)		600
Principal amount received		$5,400
Selling price	$25,000	
Less mortgage assumed	5,000	
Contract price	$20,000	
Profit percentage ($10,000 profit ÷ $20,000 contract price)	50%	
Reportable gain (50% × $5,400)		2,700

In subsequent years, 50 payments of each payment on the remaining $4,600 due would be reported as capital gain.

If the taxpayer was on the accrual basis and did not use the installment sales method of reporting the gain, the reportable gain would be $10,000 instead of only $2,700. And if he was a cash-basis taxpayer and didn't use installment method reporting, his reportable gain could also be $10,000 or somewhat less if the buyer's mortgage was worth less than face value.

Election to use the installment method must be made on the tax return for the year of sale. You can't start with another method and later switch to the installment method. However, this doesn't affect your right of choice as to **other** transactions. You have a separate election for each transaction.

[¶1106]   IMPUTED INTEREST ON INSTALLMENT SALES

Formerly, it was possible when making an installment sale of real estate to omit interest from the contract altogether. Instead of getting a specific amount of interest on the unpaid balance, the interest element in the deal was reflected in the purchase price. In that way, instead of getting fully taxed interest, you got additional, favorably taxed capital gains.

Back in 1964 the law put a damper on this technique in certain cases where the sale price exceeds $3,000 by imputing an interest character to a portion of each installment. The law calls it "unstated interest." The unstated interest is then taxable as ordinary income to the seller and is deductible by the buyer as an interest expense.

What Sales Are Covered. For a sale or exchange to be covered by the imputed interest rules, there must be a contract for the sale or exchange of property under which some or all of the payments are due more than one year after the date of the sale or exchange. Once this requirement is met, the rules can apply to all payments which are due more than six months after the date of sale or exchange.

The imputed interest rules apply to the seller only if some part of the gain from the sale or exchange of the property would be considered as gain from a capital asset or as gain from depreciable property. If the property is sold at a loss or if no gain is recognized, the rules will nevertheless apply if, had there been a gain, some part of it would have been considered as gain from a capital asset or from depreciable property. And the fact that gain is ordinary income because of the application of the depreciation recapture provisions [Secs. 1245 and 1250] makes no difference.

The rules do not apply in the case of payments with respect to patents, which are treated as capital gain under present law, nor in the case of property which is exchanged for annuity payments which depend in whole or in part on the life expectancy of one or more individuals, nor in the case of certain payments which are not treated as installments, such as those for timber, coal, and iron ore where the property is treated as sold as the timber is cut or as the coal or iron ore is withdrawn.

How to Determine Unstated Interest. Basically, the law provides that IRS is to set a proper rate at which interest is to be imputed. IRS must also prescribe a second rate of interest which must be at least 1 percent below the rate at which interest is imputed. (IRS has designated a rate of 6 percent simple interest.) If the rate of interest specified in the contract is below this second rate or, of course, if no interest is specified, there is a "total unstated interest" and the rules apply. Thus, if a contract provides interest at 3½ percent and since the IRS "higher" rate seems to be at least 6 percent, the 3½ percent would be disregarded. So, you might pick up an additional amount as capital gain instead of ordinary income by setting an interest rate in the contract that equals IRS' second-or lower-interest rate. (Presumably, the contract price will be adjusted accordingly.) On the other hand, of course, the buyer will be getting a smaller interest deduction. But that can also enter into the negotiations for the purchase price.

Amount of Unstated Interest. Once we determine that there is a total unstated interest, we have to determine its amount. This will then be apportioned equally to the installments under the contract. Here is how to determine the proportion of each payment considered interest:

(1) Determine the present value of each installment payment using the specified interest rate. This is done by discounting each payment from its due date back to the date of the sale or exchange. Thus, the present value of a payment is the amount which, if left at interest at the prescribed rate from the date of the sale to the due date of payment, would have increased to an amount equal to the amount of the payment [Sec. 1.483-1 (g)].

Payments are to be discounted on the basis of six-month brackets from the nearest date which marks a six-month interval. Payments due not more than six months from sale are excluded; thus, their present value is 100 percent.

(2) Deduct the sum of all the present values from the sum of all the payments under the contract. The resulting figure is the total unstated interest under the contract.

(3) This amount is then spread pro rata over the total payments involved so that the same percentage of each payment is deemed to be imputed interest. Technically, this is done by applying a fraction to each payment, the numerator of which is total unstated interest under the contract as arrived at in Step (2) above and the denominator is the sum of all the payments to which the rules apply.

You can't avoid the application of these rules by paying with a note. The note will not be considered to be payment, and the rules will be applied to payments under the note.

Indefinite Amounts Due. Where some or all of the payments are indefinite in amount as of the time of sale, the unstated interest for each indefinite payment will be determined separately as received based on elasped time between sale and receipt. This might be the case where payments are dependent in whole or part on future income derived from the property. A similar rule holds true where there is a change in the amount due under the contract. The unstated interest is recomputed at the time of the change.

[¶1107]   REPORTING IMPUTED INTEREST

Imputed or unstated interest is treated as interest for all purposes of the tax law — and not as part of the selling price of property (unless charged to a capital account under Section 266 — carrying charges). A seller on the cash basis reports unstated interest when received; a seller on the accrual basis reports it when due. A cash-basis purchaser deducts it when paid; an accrual-basis purchaser accrues it when due [Reg. §1.483-2(a)].

Imputed Interest Rules Can Endanger Installment Sale Reporting. In adition to its stated effect, the imputed interest rules can also have far-reaching side effects. *Reason:* any amount treated as interest under this provision is treated as interest for *all* purposes. For example, in a typical installment sale, there's a 30 percent down payment in the year of sale. This is the maximum amount you can receive and still have the sale qualify for installment reporting. But if any part of the installments due in future years is held to be interest payments because this new provision applies, this could reduce the selling price to a point where the down payment exceeds 30 percent. Then the sale will not qualify as an installment sale, and the entire gain could be taxable in the year of sale. [Regs. 1.483-2(a)(2); *Robinson, Raymond U. Comm.*, 54 TC 772 (1971), 439 F.2d 767 (8th Cir. 1971)].

[¶1108]   **DISPOSITION OF INSTALLMENT OBLIGATIONS**

If an installment obligation is sold or otherwise disposed of, there is gain or loss in the amount of the difference between the basis of the obligation and the proceeds in the case of a sale or the fair market value of the obligation in the case of any other disposition. For example, if unrecovered cost is $75 and unrealized profit $50, and the dealer sells for $100, he has a $25 gain. If he gives the obligation away, and it is worth $90, he has a $15 gain. In either case, the gain is capital gain if the original transaction gave rise to capital gain, and ordinary income if the original transaction gave rise to ordinary income. However, modification of the selling price doesn't constitute a disposition [*Rev. Rul. 55-429*, CB 1955-2, 252, *Rev. Rul.* 72-570, 1972-2 CB 241.]

If the holder of the obligation dies, those who receive the installments uncollected at the time of his death (his executor or his heirs) report the gain in the year received, the same way he would have reported it if he had lived [Secs. 691(a)(4)(c); 453(d)(3) of the Code].

Gain or loss on the disposition of an installment obligation will not be recognized if the disposition is part of a nontaxable transaction, such as a tax-free incorporation under [Sec. 351 of the Code]. Nor will gain be recognized to the distributing corporation in the tax-free liquidation of a subsidiary, or if the obligation is distributed in a special 12-month [Sec. 337] liquidation and gain or loss would not have been recognized in a sale or disposition of the obligation on the day of such distribution [Sec. 453(d)(4) of the Code].

[¶1109]   **INSTALLMENT SALE CHECKLIST**

If you want to take advantage of installment reporting, you have to avoid those pitfalls that may result in your losing the right to use that method of reporting. In this checklist, we assume that the property now has an adjusted basis of $10,000 and that you can sell it for $80,000. We further assume that you are a taxpayer in the 32 percent bracket (married, joint return).

If you sell for cash, your profit is $70,000, on which you must pay a capital gains tax of $15,270, leaving you with $54,730. If, instead, you take $8,000 in cash now and take back a purchase-money mortgage for the remaining $72,000 at 6 percent interest, payable over a nine-year period, this is how it would work out:

You now qualify for the installment method of reporting. Each year, the interest you get is ordinary income. The balance (amortization) is divided as follows: one-eighth of each annual payment is a tax-free return of capital, the other seven-eighths is capital gain. In the year of sale, you have $7,000 capital gain, which in your bracket is subject to a tax of $1,120. And in each of the next nine years, assuming your other income remains steady, you will report the same figures. Now, your total tax is $11,200, a net saving to you of $4,070 over what you would have had to pay on a cash sale.

Here are the common pitfalls that can kill the deal for you and how you can avoid them:

☐ **Buyer Gets Bank Mortgage for Balance.** Where the buyer gets a bank mortgage for the $72,000 balance, paying the same, the transaction will be treated as a cash sale taxable in full in the year of the sale.

What to Do: Seller can take back the mortgage himself, payable over more than one tax year.

☐ **Buyer Takes Over Existing Mortgage and Gives Seller Second Mortgage.** Let's say there's an existing mortgage of $30,000 which the buyer takes over. He pays $5,000 cash and gives the seller a second mortgage for $45,000.

Here, the excess of the old mortgage over a basis ($20,000) will be treated the same as cash. So, the seller is treated as having received more then 30 percent of the selling price in the year of sale and he cannot report on the installment basis.

What to Do. Make sure that the excess of the existing mortgage over basis plus cash received will not total more than 30 percent of the selling price. On our facts, any cash paid in the year of sale should be limited to $4,000 or less.

☐ **Buyer Pays Part of Purchase Price in Cash and the Rest in Securities and a Promissory Note.** There's no mortgage on the property. The buyer pays $15,000 at closing, gives the seller securities worth $10,000, and a note for $55,000.

Under these circumstances, the seller is treated as having received an initial payment of $25,000. This is more than 30 percent of the selling price, and he's not entitled to use the installment method of reporting.

What to Do. The seller should take the buyer's note for $65,000 secured in part by the pledge of securities. This reduces the initial payment to $15,000.

☐ **Buyer Makes More Than One Cash Payment.** A contract of sale is signed in 19X1 at which time the buyer pays $10,000. The title is closed in 19X2, at which time the buyer pays another $15,000. The seller takes back a mortgage for $55,000

Under these circumstances, the 19X1 payment is treated as part of the payment in the year of sale 19X2 and brings the initial payment to more than 30 percent. No installment reporting.

What to Do. Make sure that all payments prior to, and during, the year of sale don't exceed 30 percent. The payment at closing should not exceed $14,000.

☐ **Buyer Makes Cash Payment and Gives Purchase-Money Mortgage Calling for Payments Beginning in Year of Sale.** Title closes on January 2, 19X1. They buyer pays $15,000 down and gives a purchase-money mortgage for $65,000, payable in five annual installments beginning on November 1, 19X1. On November 1, the buyer pays the first installment of $13,000.

Here, the seller got $28,000 in the year of sale. This is more than 30 percent of the selling price. No installment reporting.

What to Do. Watch out for Payments in the year of sale. Remember, *all* payments of principal prior to and during that year must not exceed 30 percent of the selling price.

☐ **Buyer Makes Prepayment in Year of Sale.** The sale is in 19X1, and buyer pays $24,000 at the closing. The seller takes back a mortgage for the balance, with the first payment due on January 1, 19X2. In December, 19X1, the buyer prepays an installment, which includes $1,000 amortization.

Since payments in the year of sale exceed 30 percent of the selling price, seller is not entitled to installment reporting.

What to Do. Make sure that the contract of sale and mortgage bond or note have a provision barring prepayment of installments in the year of sale. If the buyer tries to prepay, do not accept the money.

[¶1110]   OPTIONS

An option payment is another method of postponing tax. The option usually provides for forfeiture of the option price if the option is not exercised. If exercised, the option price is credited to the purchase price. Options are practically down payments. But there is no income when they are received. Until the option period expires, you do not know how it will finally be applied. If it is forfeited, you then have ordinary income. If it is exercised, it is added to the sales price. But a word of caution. You want to be sure the option contract states what will happen if it is forfeited and if it is exercised. Otherwise, you will be taxed as soon as you receive the option payment [Reg. § 1.1234-1].

Or, you can lease properties with an option to buy. Here there is the option plus possession by the buyer during the option period. This method must be used with great caution. The courts will strike down disguised sales in the forms of leases with options to buy; e.g., where the option price is only nominal or the rental price is larger than normal rentals for the type and value of the property involved.

If called a sale, the "purchaser-lessee" will have his "rental" payments treated as part payment of the purchase price. The purchaser will not be allowed a deduction for rent, but will be allowed a deduction for depreciation [*Chicago-Stoker Corp.*, 14 TC 441; *Rev. Rul. 55-540,* CB 1955-2, 39].

[¶1111]   CONDITIONAL OR CONTINGENT SALES PRICE— OPEN SALE TRANSACTIONS

This is a sale where the consideration recieved by the seller is incapable of valuation with the result that the transaction is not considered closed and no income is realized until the seller recovers his basis for the property. Any excess over basis is capital gain if the property qualifies as a capital asset. The classic case involved a consideration of 60ᶜ a ton on all iron ore mined by a corporation. The Court held that no valuation could be attached to this agreement since there were no maximum and minimum requirements as to the amount of ore to be mined [*Burnett v. Logan*, 283 US 404 (1931)].

Similarly, the promise of a corporation to pay a percentage of its profits for a number of years was held to be indeterminate, with the result that the transaction was not considered closed (*Yerger*, 55 F. Supp. 521). The same result should follow where the consideration is contingent on net profits to be received from real property which is the subject of the sale. No gain will be realized until the seller's basis is recovered.

You will get an argument from the Treasury on this, though. It insists there rarely is a situation where value is indeterminable [*Rev. Rul. 58-402*, 1958-2, CB 1958, 15, Regs. 1.453-6 (a)(2)].

[¶1112]   DEFERRED SALES

This method may be used where the seller receives only part of the sale price in the year of sale. If the purchaser's debt for the balance is not evidenced by any note but is merely in the contract of sale, then the courts may say it has no fair market value. The seller is taxable on the sale only when the cash amounts he receives cumulatively exceed his basis in the property [*Ennis*, 17 TC 465].

But an arrangement such as this may be unsatisfactory; the seller ordinarily wants some sort of bond or note for protection. So, we usually use installment sale reporting. However, if the seller wants more than 30 percent of the sales price in the year of sale, you can't have an installment sale. Then the deferred sale method may still be available.

If the seller can show that the notes he receives are not worth their face value, he only picks up the cash received plus the fair market value of the notes as the amount received on the sale. However, the Service may oppose this. [*Warren Jones Co.*, 1975-2 USTC para. 9732 (9th Cir. 1975).] Assume his basis is $10,000 and the sale price is $40,000 ($15,000 cash, a $15,000 mortgage, and $10,000 notes secured by a second mortgage). The seller may claim that he has a gain in the year of sale of only $25,000 by valuing the notes at only $5,000 or half of their face amounts.

You can use the deferred sales method whether you report for tax purposes on the cash or the accrual basis because the Regulations give you permission to do so. But if you sold a hotel and its furniture and equipment, you couldn't use the deferred sales method of reporting gain on the furniture and equipment if your regular accounting method is the accrual method. *Reason:* There's no provision for such treatment in the Regulations [*Castner*, 30 TC 1061 (1958)].

If you use the deferred sale method of reporting, you will not have capital gain on the *deferred part* even if you have a capital gain on the original sale! Treasury and the Tax Court say that if the notes are worth less than face, you pick up the notes at their value and compute your capital gain or loss at that time. In later years when you realize more than the value you assigned to the notes, that realization does not come from a *sale or exchange*, hence it must be reported as ordinary income [*Culbertson*, 14 TC 1421, See Levine, cite *supra*, Section 533].

[¶1113]   **ESCROW ARRANGEMENTS**

You can intentionally postpone delivery of title. In case of real property, the sale usually occurs on the closing or settlement date. Receiving a down payment or earnest money does not of itself fix the date of sale. You will generally not be taxed at that time if title *or* possession does not pass. A true escrow arrangement, with some of the purchase price set aside to be paid over to the seller together with the balance of consideration at the closing date provided seller furnishes a marketable title and otherwise complies with the contract, will defer the tax on the entire transaction until the closing or settlement date [*Waggoner,* 9 BTA 629 non acq; VII-1 CB 41; *Holden,* 6 BTA 605]. This case (Holden) held the other way, although it supports the general proposition. Here, there was no contract requiring payment to be withheld; it was only a request by the seller that proceeds not be paid until later. The taxpayer was clearly in constructive receipt of the funds. But if you give possession to the buyer before title passage, chances are the sale for tax purposes took place when you gave possession [*Scruggs*, 281 F. 2d 900, (10th Cir. 1960)].

[¶1114]   **TAX-FREE SALE OF LOW- AND
                       MODERATE-INCOME HOUSING**

Under [Sec. 1039 of the Code], no gain will be recognized to the initial investor in these housing projects (e.g., FHA Sec. 221(d)(3) and Sec. 236 programs) where the properties are sold to the tenants or occupants or to a tax-exempt organization managing the property to the extent that the investor reinvests the proceeds from the sale in other similar government-assisted housing [Sec. 1039(a) of the Code]. The sale or disposition must be approved by HUD and be made within the required reinvestment period. The reinvestment period is the period beginning one year before the date of the approved disposition and ending either one year after the close of the first taxable year in which any part of the gain from the approved disposal is realized or at the close of a later date designated on application of the taxpayer and subject to the terms and conditions specified by the Secretary.

To take advantage of these provisions of the tax law, you will have to make your election to do so in accordance with IRS regulations [Sec. 1039(a)(2) of the Code]. You will be taxed only to the extent that the net amount you realize on the disposition is greater than the cost of the other qualified housing project. In figuring the net amount you realize, you're entitled to subtract the expenses paid or incurred which are directly connected with the disposition and the amount of taxes (other than income taxes) paid or incurred which are directly attributable to the disposition.

Your basis for the project is carried over and becomes part of your basis for the new project in which the funds are invested (depending on whether or not you also invest additional funds in the second project) [Sec. 1039(d) of the Code]. The holding period for the first property is taken into account in determining how long the second property is held in this case, but only to the extent the proceeds from the sale of the old project are reinvested in the new project.

CHAPTER 12

Tax Consequences of Individual, Joint and Partnership Ownership of Real Estate

[¶1201]   **CHOICE OF OWNERSHIP FORMAT**

In almost any new real estate venture, one of the first questions you will be faced with is the form of ownership you should use. Should the property be held by you individually, in common or joint tenancy or by the entirety with others, or in partnership form? In determining which is the best form of ownership, you will want to carefully study the tax consequences of each form and on this basis decide which best suits your situation.

[¶1202]   **TAX SHELTER FOR INVESTORS IN**
                  REAL ESTATE SYNDICATES

Syndicating (combining investors) ranges from simple joint-ownerships to large, sprawling limited partnerships and corporations. There are many ways to set up a real estate syndicate, to split the profits, to provide for the interest earned by the promotors, syndicators, and managers, and to fulfill the many different purposes served by syndicates, ranging from ownership to financing, leasing, and management. Syndicates, especially those on a partnership basis, are operated in a manner calculated to make them free of federal corporation taxes. This permits distribution of most of a venture's earnings to the participants. Even more important, partnership tax rules allow each syndicate participant to share in the tax shelter generated by the project.

Real estate syndicates are frequently organized in the form of limited partnerships because this type of organization combines the benefits of the passthrough of profits and losses to the individual investors for income tax purposes and limited liability on the part of the passive investors (the limited partners) and retains the management of the enterprise in the hands of the syndicator(s) (the general partner(s)).

The general partner(s) manages the partnership affairs. The limited partners who invest their funds as silent partners do not take an active part in management and have no personal liability beyond their investment or other commitment made. In this way, a limited partnership offers the advantages of centralized management and limited liability for the investors. Transferability of limited partnership interests, subject to consent of the general partners, and the continuance of the partnership can be provided [*see Philip Larson,* 66 TC 159 (1976)].

[¶1203]   **SEVERALTY AND CO-OWNERSHIP OF PROPERTY**

Special problems arise when realty is acquired in the individual form, or jointly by a group of investors, or by married persons. An understanding of the forms of co-ownership is important from a tax planning standpoint. The different forms give rise to income, gift, and estate tax problems. (Corporate acquisitions often do not involve these problems, provided the corporate entity is bona fide for tax purposes.) There are methods of acquiring real property in non-corporate/partnership form:

1. Individual
2. Joint tenancy
3. Tenancy in common
4. Tenancy by the entirety

These are forms of common ownership ordinarily confined to small-scale real estate businesses. They avoid double taxation, but they can create considerable management and control problems where there are a number of people involved. The forms of joint ownership normally are not considered partnerships; they cannot elect to be taxed as corporations. Here are the tax problems involved.

Individual Ownership. This type of ownership exists where a lone investor acquires the property solely in his or her own name. He is taxed on the income just once. His net income from real estate is added to his other income and he pays a tax on the total. If he has losses, they reduce his other income. Broadly speaking, the individual may acquire:

a. Complete ownership, called the fee simple.
b. Ownership subject to a spouse's dower, curtesy, community, or statutory rights.
c. Ownership subject to a future reversionary interest.

There are no special problems if the investor acquired complete ownership or is unmarried, or if the realty is located in a state which does not recognize dower, curtesy, or community rights. (Dower is a wife's right to a life estate in the husband's property after his death; curtesy is a husband's right to a life estate in the wife's property after her death; community rights are the rights each spouse has in the other's property; statutory rights are the rights of a spouse to a share in the other's estate.) Tax problems arise if the realty is located in a state which recognizes dower, curtesy, or community rights. From an income tax standpoint, payments for the release of such rights are neither deductible expenses nor additional property costs. Property passing to a spouse under dower, curtesy, community, or statutory right has a basis under the death tax rules. See paragraph 603. From a gift tax standpoint, payments for the release of such rights under either an antenuptial (agreement before marriage) or separation agreement may be subject to gift tax (less the martial deduction; there is no gift tax if the settlement payment was an arm's-length business bargain without donative interest, or in release of the wife's right to support, or pursuant to a decree of a divorce court. From an estate tax standpoint, property rights of the surviving spouse are includable in the decendent's estate (subject to the marital deduction); but there is no gift tax on community property severed in contemplation of death or on payments for release of a wife's right to support during her lifetime (as distinguished from amounts payable at a husband's death). Estate tax problems also arise if ownership of the realty is subject to a future reversionary interest. [Secs. 2036 and 6203]

Joint Tenancy. Where two or more individuals have the same ownership interest in a single parcel of realty (each owns undivided interests) with the right of survivorship (the survivor gets all), we have a joint tenancy. In some states there is a presumption that a joint tenancy is created when realty is acquired by two or more persons. This presumption may be rebutted by stating in the deed that the acquisition is as tenants in common. From an income tax standpoint, each joint tenant reports his own share of income and gain or loss; but if one pays more than his share of costs, he may take the full deduction. From a gift tax standpoint, if one joint tenant pays the entire cost, one-half of the cost is a taxable gift. However, the creation of a joint tenacy in realty between husband and wife postpones the gift tax (unless an election is made immediately to tax it as a gift) until the joint tenancy is ended other than by death. (There is no gift tax if the joint tenants divide the proceeds in proportion to their contributions.)

From an estate tax standpoint, the gross estate of a deceased joint tenant dying before 1/1/77 includes the value (at the date of death or optional valuation date) of the entire realty less the portion paid by the survivor (Sec. 2040 of the Code) for deaths prior to 1/1/77. For deaths after 12/31/76, between husband and wife, one half of a prior gift after 1976, that *was* taxed, is in the estate of the decedent-joint tenant/spouse; the surviving spouse gets the deceased's interest in the realty on the death of the other joint/spouse.

Tenancy in Common. There is a tenancy in common where two or more persons each have the same right to possession (but there may be unequal shares of ownership) with no rights of survivorship (the interest of a deceased tenant in common passes as an asset of his estate). Both joint tenants and tenants in common may transfer normally their interests, but they cannot transfer a specific portion of the realty. Where a joint tenant transfers his interest, the transferee becomes a tenant in common with the remaining joint tenants; when a tenant in common transfers his interest, the transferee becomes a tenant in common with the other tenants in common. In most states the presumption today is that a tenancy in common is created when realty is acquired by two or more persons. From an income tax standpoint, each tenant in common reports income and gain or loss according to his own share of ownership. From a gift tax standpoint, liability arises from the gift of an interest in a tenancy in common or if one tenant in common pays more than his share of costs. From an estate tax standpoint, the interest of a deceased tenant in common is taxed as part of his estate at its value at the date of death or optional valuation date [Sec. 2040 of the Code]; and the heirs get the interest in the realty at an income tax basis equal to the value used for estate tax purposes if death is prior to 1/1/77 [Sec. 1014(b) of the Code]. Death after 12/31/76 results in the new basis rules applying, as mentioned earlier.

If any tenant in common purchases not only his share but also a share for another and then the tenant dies, only his interest in the property is included in his gross estate since he is deemed to have made a gift, for gift tax purposes, of the share bought for the other tenant. The advantage in the use of this form is that, like a partnership, provision can be made for continuance on the death of a participant and transferability of shares. The tenancy must avoid any centralized control to keep single tax treatment. (Where there's centralized control, the Treasury may argue the tenancy is really an association to be taxed as a corporation—see the discussion under Partnership, below).

An exclusive management contract, even for a term of years, would not be considered centralized control so long as the agent's duties involve ministerial functions such as collecting rents, making periodic accountings, seeing to minor repairs, and making and enforcing short-term leases. [*See Burton S. Ostrow,* 15 TCM 957 (1956); this case involved a trust that was *not* taxed as an association— corporation as centralized management was missing; the duties were only ministerial and this was not centralized management.]

Tenancy by the Entirety. This form of ownership exits where realty is owned by a husband and wife provided they were married at the time of the acquisition and carries the right of survivorship. In some states there is a presumption that a conveyance to a husband and wife creates a tenancy by the entirety, but there may be nonrecognition for tax purposes if this type of tenancy was created for "income juggling" after negotiations were completed for sale of the realty at a gain. *Both* tenants together *can* end a tenancy by the entirety, but *one cannot.*

From an income tax standpoint, married persons will normally file joint returns; if separate returns are filed, each tenant reports his own share of the income and gain or loss, but if one paid more than his share of the costs, he may take the full deduction. State laws control in determining the method of reporting income and gain or loss. So local law governs if a state follows the common law rule that a husband is entitled to all income from realty, or if a state's law provides that income is to be divided between husband and wife. (Again, this is not important if the tenants file a joint return.)

From a gift tax standpoint potential liability can arise if one spouse furnishes all or most of the cost. However, the gift tax on realty is postponed (unless an election is made to tax it immediately as a gift) until the tenancy by the entirety is terminated other than by death. The gift is taxed to the extent that the proportion of the total consideration furnished by one spouse, multiplied by the total proceeds at termination, exceeds the amount received by such spouse [Sec. 2515 of the Code].

From an estate tax standpoint, the gross estate of a deceased tenant by the entirety includes the value (at date of death or optional valuation date) of the entire realty less the portion paid by the survivor [Sec. 2040 of the Code] if death is prior to 1/1/77. If death is after 12/31/76, see the rules noted earlier for joint interests.

[¶1204]　　　　　　　　　　　　**PARTNERSHIPS**

This is the most common form of unincorporated business involving more than one individual. The most usual form is the general partnership which involves the combining of several individuals into one business. Each normally has a voice in management and each can bind the business by his acts.

For tax purposes, the partnership is a conduit. This means that in itself it is not a taxpayer. It merely computes its profit or loss and then each partner reports on his own tax return his share of the partnership's profits or losses.

Each partner picks up his share in the tax year with or in which the partnership year ends [Secs. 702, 704, 706, and 708 of the Code]. If both partnership and partners have the same tax years (e.g., the calendar year), the partners pick up their share of the partnership's 1975 profits (for example) on their personal 1975 returns. Keep in mind that usually—in new partnerships, at any rate—partners and the partnership will have the same tax year. To have different tax years, you need a good business purpose and you must get permission from the Treasury.

Partnership profits or losses retain their same nature when picked up by the partners. So, if the partnership should have some long-term capital gains, for example, each partner would pick up his share as a long-term capital gain.

A big advantage of the partnership—especially in real estate operations—is the fact that it is a single non-tax entity. Only one tax is paid—by the partners. The advantages of high depreciation, for example, are passed directly to the partners. Thus where the cash profit is greater than the tax profit, the excess cash can be paid out to each partner tax free. For example, gross rents might be $100,000. All cash expenses might be $50,000. Amortization payments might come to $10,000. And depreciation might be $20,000. The cash left is $40,000 ($100,000 gross rents less $50,000 expenses and $10,000 amortization). But the taxable profit is $30,000 ($100,000 less the $50,000 expenses and the $20,000 depreciation). So, while $40,000 may be distributed to the partners, they pay tax on only $30,000. On the other hand, if the property was held by a corporation, the corporation would have to pay a tax on $30,000. And if it distributed any profits, they'd be taxed again in the individuals' hands.

Because of this advantage in partnerships, the Treasury looks at them very carefully to see if they are not so set up as to resemble corporations. This may arise in some syndications. If it is set up so as to resemble a corporation, the partnership may be taxed as an association (i.e., as a corporation) [*See Zuckman,* 75-2 USTC ¶ 9778 (1975)].

[¶1205] LIMITED LIABILITY FOR GENERAL PARTNER AND RETAINING TAX ADVANTAGES

If instead of having the sponsor serve as the general partner in his individual capacity, the general partner is a corporation, the sponsor-builder also enjoys limited liability. But where this is done, the setup must meet requirements in addition to the usual requirements for conduit tax treatment. *Rev. Proc.* 72-13, IRB 1972-2 tells us what must be present before IRS will consider issuing an advance ruling:

(1) Limited Partner's Ownership of Stock in Corporate General Partner. The limited partners will not own, directly or indirectly, individually or in the aggregate more than 20 percent of the stock of the corporate general partner nor any affiliates as defined in [Sec. 1504 of the Code] dealing with affiliated groups. The attribution rules set forth in [Sec. 318 of the Code] apply in determining stock ownership.

(2) Net Worth of Corporate General Partner. The Revenue Procedure spells out the capital requirements of the corporate general partner as follows:

    a. If the corporate general partner has an interest in only one limited partnership and the total contributions to that partnership are less than $2,500,000, the net worth of the corporate general partner at all times will be at least 15 percent of such total contributions or $250,000, whichever is less.

    b. If the total contribution to the partnership is $2,500,000 or more, the net worth of the corporate general partner at all times will be at least 10 percent of such total contributions. In computing the net worth of the corporate general partner, for this purpose, its interest in the limited partnership and accounts and notes receivable from and payable to it will be excluded.

c. If the corporate general partner has interests in more than one limited partnership, the net worth requirements set forth in (a) and (b) will be applied separately for each limited partnership and the corporate general partner will have at all times a net worth at least as great as the sum of the amounts required under (a) and (b) for each separate limited partnership exclusive of any interest in any limited partnership and notes and accounts receivable from and payable to any limited partnership in which the corporate general partner has any interest.

d. In computing the net worth of the corporate general partner in (a), (b), and (c), the current fair market value of the corporate assets must be used. See also Rev. Proc. 74-17, IRB 1974-22, for more on this same problem of advance rulings. (No ruling issued unless additional tests are met. *Levine, Sec.* 779.)

(3) Investors Not Required to Purchase Security of Corporate General Partner. The purchase of a limited partnership interest does not entail either a mandatory or discretionary purchase or option to purchase any type of security of the general partner or its affiliates.

(4) Compliance With State Statute. The organization and operation of the limited partnership must comply with state statutes.

[¶1206]   DEALINGS BETWEEN PARTNER AND PARTNERSHIP

Transactions with individual partners are treated the same way as transactions with any other individual [Sec. 707(a)]. However, no deduction is permitted with respect to losses from sales or exchanges between the partnership and a partner owning more than a 50 percent interest in the firm or its profits [Sec. 707(b)(1)]. And losses from sales or exchanges between two partnerships are disallowed if they have common partners owning more than 50 percent interest in the capital or profits. A gain on a subsequent sale or exchange by the transferee will be a non-recognized gain up to the amount of the disallowed loss [Sec. 267(d)].

There is a special rule for treatment of gain on a sale or exchange of property between a partnership and a partner owning more than 80 percent of capital or profits, or between partnerships which have common partners owning more than 80 percent of the capital or profits of both firms. In these transactions, the gain is ordinary income if the property is other than a capital asset in the hands of the transferee [Sec. 707(b)(2)].

[¶1207]   PARTNERSHIP BASIS

If contributions are in cash, there is no problem. The basis of the partners' interests are the amounts they paid in. If contributions are in property, each partner's interest takes the basis of the property contributed by him. The partnership takes the partner's basis.

Where the tax basis of contributed property differs from the value at which it is contributed, the deductible depreciation allowed for tax purposes will not accurately reflect the economic depreciation sustained by the firm. For example, if depreciable property with a tax basis of $27,000 and a ten-year estimated life is contributed at its current value of $42,000, the yearly tax deduction will be only $2,700. But the annual "economic loss" will be $4,200.

If the value was less than cost at the time of contribution, the partnership's depreciation deduction would exceed its economic loss. If, in the above example, the basis was $50,000 instead of $27,000, the annual deduction would be $5,000 as against an economic loss of only $4,200.

To carry this one step further, suppose the partnership sold the property after one year for $30,000. Reverting to our original basis of $27,000, there would have been a taxable gain of $5,700 ($30,000 less $27,000 basis reduced by one year's depreciation of $2,700). Yet, this tax would be paid on what was actually an economic loss of $7,800 (only $30,000 received for $37,800 economic value remaining after reducing $42,000 value at time of contribution by $4,200 economic depreciation for one year).

[¶1208]   PARTNER'S CAPITAL CONTRIBUTIONS

No gain or loss is recognized to either a partnership or the partners on the partners' contributions of capital to the partnership in exchange for their partnership interests [Sec. 721 of the Code]. This applies to contributions of property as well as cash. It applies whether the contribution is made by an incoming partner for a new interest or by an existing partner to increase his interest [Sec. 721 of the Code; Reg. §1.721-1].

Recognition for tax purposes is postponed until the contributed property is disposed. This may occur by the partner selling his interest, by the partnership selling the property, or by a partner selling property after it has been distributed to him.

An increase in a partner's share of partnership liabilities or his assumption of partnership liabilities is treated as a contribution of money [Sec. 752 of the Code]. For example, suppose a building subject to a $5,000 mortgage is distributed to one partner; the other partners receive assets equal in value to the value of the building but without any offsetting liability. Let's assume there are four partners in all. This would be treated as a contribution of $3,750 by the partner who received the building. Before the distribution, his share of the $5,000 liability was one-fourth, or $1,250. Assumption of the entire $5,000 adds $3,750 to his liability. The mechanics of the transaction would be a reduction of the basis of all partnership interests to the extent of the distributions and then an increase in the basis of the assuming partner's interest by the portion of the liability for which the other partners are no longer liable.

[¶1209]   **SALE OF PARTNERSHIP INTEREST**

The sale or exchange of a partnership interest results in capital gain or loss to the transferor partner except to the extent the proceeds are attributable to the selling partner's pro rata share of unrealized receivables [Sec. 751] and substantially appreciated inventory [Sec. 751] items [Sec. 741].

[¶1210]   **BASIS OF SUCCESSOR PARTNER'S INTEREST**

A deceased partner's interest is taxed in his estate. His successor's tax basis for the interest is the estate tax value. However, any part of this value attributable to a right to receive income with respect to the decedent [Sec. 691] must be subtracted from the successor's basis [Secs. 742 and 1011 of the Code].

Thus the successor's basis cannot include value attributable to income items as defined in Sec. 736(a). (See the discussion below entitled "Payments to Retiring or Deceased Partner.") But value attributable to the decedent's interest aside from income items is not subject to this limitation and is therefore part of the successor's tax basis.

[¶1211]   **FIGURING TAX BASIS ON TRANSFER OF SHARE**

The purchaser's basis for an interest in a partnership generally is his cost [Sec. 742 of the Code]. If the partnership assets have appreciated in value and the partnership subsequently sells some of its assets at their appreciated value, the buyer will be taxed for a gain that he never actually realized. Similarly, even though the appreciated assets remain unsold, the buyer will be unable to take the benefit of depreciation of these assets to the full extent of the consideration which he paid.

If a purchaser pays par for a partnership interest, he may be paying considerably more than the undepreciated portion of the syndicate property allocable to his share in the syndicate. This is so because the syndicate has been taking depreciation deductions in prior years when he was not a syndicate member.

The Code does provide some relief for the buyer by permitting a writeup of the basis of the appreciated property by the partnership at the time the buyer purchases his interest but only in respect of the buyer. Section 743 of the Code provides for such an adjustment but only if the partnership has filed an election under Section 754.

A syndicate in trust form presents a different basis problem. Assume the syndicate has new property which qualifies for accelerated depreciation. Later, a syndicate member sells part or all of his interest to a new buyer. It is likely that the new buyer will take as his basis, for his share of the trust property, the price he paid for the interest. This may step up his basis for depreciation but at the same time it may prevent him from using the accelerated depreciation method available to the original syndicate members. This may be true because, as the new syndicate share buyer, he arguably does not own new property of which he is the "first user" [Regs. 1.167(c); *Levine, Mark, "Shoptalk" J. Tax* 256 (Ap. 1975)].

[¶1212] TAX TREATMENT OF GAIN ON SALE OF PARTNERSHIP INTEREST

Section 741 of the Code makes the sale or exchange of a partnership interest a sale or exchange of a capital asset except as otherwise provided in Section 751 of the Code requiring a selling partner to reflect that part of his gain which is represented by his share of depreciation recapture under Sections 1245 and 1250 as an "unrealized receivable" to be "considered realized from the sale or exchange of property other than a capital asset." The result is that part of the gain realized on the sale or exchange of a partnership interest may have to be reported as ordinary income. Any balance of the gain would qualify for long-term capital gain treatment if the partnership interest was held more than six months. (The holding period is "greater than 9 months" for 1977 dispositions and greater than 1 year for sales or exchanges in 1978 and thereafter.) [Sec. 1223 of the Code].

[¶1213] PAYMENTS TO RETIRING OR DECEASED PARTNER

Payments to either a retiring or a deceased partner are allocated first to payment for his interest in the firm, including goodwill if the partnership agreement so provides, and inventory [Sec. 736].

Payments for the partner's interest in the inventory and capital assets are distributions by the partnership and therefore capital in nature. The firm is not allowed to deduct the payments in computing income; and except to the extent they are allocable to substantially appreciated inventory, they are capital gain to the retiring partner (or whoever is the recipient if we are dealing with a deceased partner).

Payments in excess of those allocated to inventory and capital are allocated to the interest in income items. These payments are ordinary income to the recipient and deductions to the firm, either as a guaranteed payment if not based on firm income, or as a distributive share of income if based on income [Secs. 702, 704 of the Code].

[¶1214]　　　　　　**PARTNERSHIP DISTRIBUTIONS**

Generally, no gain or loss is recognized to the partnership when it distributes cash or property to the partners [Sec. 731; Reg. §1.731-1]. The partner is not taxed on a distribution of cash except to the extent the amount exceeds the adjusted basis of his partnership interest. To that extent, the gain will be recognized, whether or not his interest is liquidated. Loss is not recognized to the partner unless his interest is completely liquidated and the distributed items consist entirely of cash, unrealized receivables, and inventory. Gain or loss, where recognized, is treated as gain or loss from the sale of a capital asset, except where special rules for payments in liquidation of the interest of a retiring or deceased partner come into play [Sec. 736 of the Code].

[¶1215]　　**REALLOCATING DEDUCTIONS AMONG PARTNERS**

Where property is contributed by a partner to a partnership at a value different from its tax basis to the contributor, it may be advisable to include in the partnership agreement a provision to utilize the elections on contributed property offered by Section 704(c)(2) of the 1954 Code. Under this section, a partnership agreement may provide that depreciation, depletion, or gain or loss be shared by the partners so as to reflect the difference between the basis of the property to the partnership and its fair market value at the time of the contribution. The reason for including such a provision in the partnership agreement is illustrated by the following example:

> *Example:* B and D form a partnership on an equal basis. D contributes $50,000 in cash. B contributes machinery that cost him $5,000 but is currently valued at $50,000. The estimated life of the machinery is ten years. The partnership will be allowed an annual tax deduction for depreciation of the machinery of only $500 (10 percent of $5,000), although the actual economic depreciation to the partnership is $5,000 (10 percent of $50,000). If the partnership agreement fails to include a provision for allocation, the depreciation is treated as if the partnership had purchased the contributed property; the tax deduction of $500 (and the economic loss) is divided equally between B and D [Sec. 704(b) of the Code]. The partnership agreement may, however, provide for a more equitable method of allocation of the depreciation between the partners [Sec. 704(c) of the Code].

[¶1216] MAKING SPECIAL ALLOCATIONS AMONG PARTNERS

Partners can share partnership profits and losses in any way they see fit as long as the principal purpose of the allocation is not the avoidance of income tax. Thus, a special allocation in a real estate limited partnership agreement of an item of income, gain, loss, deduction, or credit should stand up under IRS scrutiny provided the principal purpose of the allocation is not tax avoidance [Sec. 704 of the Code; Reg. §1.704-1(a)]. A principal test for determining whether an allocation amounts to improper avoidance is whether the allocation has substantial economic effect, that is, whether the allocation may actually affect the dollar amount of the partners' shares of the total partnership income or loss independent of the tax consequences [Sec. 1.704-1(b)(2)]. The substantial-economic-effect test should be the dominant criterion for recognition of a special allocation [*Orrisch* 55, TC 395 (1970)]. There has been some uncertainty in this area. Therefore, the Tax Reform Act of 1976 added to Section 704 of the Code. It provides that for *special* allocations, that is an adjustment of the partnership income and loss among partners *different* from a *pro rata* ownership of the partnership percentages, special allocations have been and are permitted, subject to the rules noted below.

Section 704(b) of the Code provides that if partners distribute a share of income, gain, loss, deduction, or credit (or item thereof), it shall be determined in accord with the partner's interest in the partnership, taking into account all facts and circumstances, if the partnership agreement does not provide as to the partner's distributive share of these items or the allocation under the agreement does not have ''substantial economic effect.'' In other words, a special allocation is allowable providing it has substantial economic effect and the partnership agreement provides for the same.

Effective date for this new *statement* on special allocations is for tax years ending after December 31, 1975.

[¶1217] ALLOCATION OF ALL DEPRECIATION TO LIMITED PARTNERS

Here are two examples of allocations of all depreciation to the limited partner and how they work out in terms of whether they will stand up under IRS scrutiny.

(1) Example of Allocation That Should Stand Up. Take the case of a limited partnership owning a $1-million apartment building subject to a no-recourse mortgage of $800,000. The limited partner puts in $200,000. The general partner does not put in any money. The profits are split 50-50. All depreciation deductions go to the limited partner. At a sale, the *gain is to be charged back first to the limited*

partner, who took the losses in that amount, and the remainder is to be split 50-50. The proceeds of the sale are to be allocated according to the final capital account.

This allocation may stand IRS attack. The general partner has nothing to lose. Although the limited partner can only lose $200,000, he can take depreciation deductions in excess of that sum. Any loss in excess of the $200,000 would be borne by the no-recourse lender and not by the partnership. In the event of a sale or foreclosure, depreciation deductions in excess of contributions would be taxed as a so-called "phantom gain," since the gain would be less than the face amount of the mortgage and the mortgage would be considered proceeeds [*Rev. Rul.* 76-111, 1976-13]. Inasmuch as neither the general partner nor the limited partner could bear this loss, they should be entitled to decide between themselves who will get the tax benefits.

(2) Example of Allocation That May Not Stand Up. Suppose the general partner contributes land worth $100,000 with a basis of $100,000. The limited partner contributes $100,000 to put up a building worth that amount. The limited partner gets all the depreciation allocated to him since it is his money that will be used to put up the building. As to everything else, the general and limited partner share equally.

During a two-year period, $30,000 in depreciation is claimed and there is $70,000 of net rental income.

PARTNERSHIP BALANCE SHEET AFTER TWO YEARS

Cash		$ 70,000
Building	$100,000	
Accumulated Depreciation	−30,000	
		70,000
Land		100,000
		$240,000

If the land and building are sold for $240,000 and distributions are made according to the partnership agreement on a 50-50 basis, this is how the partners would come out. The general partner receives $120,000 in cash. His basis for his partnership interest is $135,000 (100 (+) 35 gain). He comes out with a capital loss of $15,000. The limited partner receives $120,000 in cash. His basis for his partnership interest is $105,000. (100,000 − 30,000 Deprec., + 35,000 gain). So he has a capital gain of $15,000.

Actually, the general partner has a cash gain of $20,000 ($120,000 − $100,000). He has also paid tax on $20,000 worth of income ($35,000 [his share of rental income] − $15,000 [capital loss] = $20,000 [net taxable income]—not adjusted for character of gain or loss).

The limited partner also had a $20,000 cash gain. But his total taxable income was $20,000 ($35,000 [share of net rental income] − $30,000 [depreciation deduction + $15,000 [capital gain from the dissolution of the partnership]).

So it appears that although all the depreciation was allocated to the limited partner, the dollar amounts of actual partnership income were not affected by the allocation.

Thus under these circumstances, IRS probably would not recognize the allocation on the ground that it is without substantial economic effect, other than the tax consequences.

How to Turn Results Around. IRS would probably recognize the allocation of depreciation if, in addition to the allocation of all depreciation to the limited partner, the partnership agreement provided that the partners on liquidation would share in the partnership assets *according to their capital account balances.*

Under our figures, the general partner would receive $135,000 and the limited partner would receive $105,000. Thus the limited partner would actually suffer the economic loss attributable to the decline in value of the building. The limited partner's share of net rents would come to $35,000. This sum, less the $30,000 of depreciation allocated to him, would give him a taxable and actual gain of $5,000. The allocation of depreciation thus would have substantial economic effect and would actually affect the dollar amount of the partner's ultimate share of partnership income.

Remember, it is important that risk of economic loss be with the partner to whom depreciation was allocated. If this is true, IRS should recognize the disproportionate allocation.

What to Do. The point is that the partnership agreement should provide that items are to be shared by the partners in different proportions so that the allocation reflects economic realities and is not merely a device to escape taxes.

[¶1218] PASSING THE SUBSTANTIAL-ECONOMIC-EFFECT TEST

Suppose we look at some figures to see how the substantial-economic-effect test works out under different circumstances.

Assume a real estate partnership between A and B. The land is worth $100,000; the building is worth $400,000; straight-line depreciation is taken on the building using a 40-year life. During the first three years, income equals expenses except for depreciation and the partners share profits and losses equally.

BALANCE SHEET AFTER THREE YEARS

Land		$100,000
Building	$400,000	
Depreciation	−30,000	370,000
Total		$470,000
Capital: A ($250,000 − $15,000)		$235,000
B ($250,000 − $15,000)		235,000

Special Allocation of Total Depreciation Deduction. After year three, the partnership agreement is amended; and in the fourth, fifth, and sixth years, the total depreciation deduction is specially allocated to partner B.

Can this special allocation stand up? To sustain it, we have to find a substantial economic effect of the special allocation agreement aside from its tax consequences. Look at who bears the economic burden of the depreciation if the building is sold for an amount less than its original cost.

Sale Price Equal to Adjusted Basis. Suppose the property is sold for its adjusted basis at the end of the sixth year and the property had a fair market value that equaled its adjusted basis at the time the special allocation agreement was made. Here is how the partnership balance sheet would look at the end of year six and before the distribution:

BALANCE SHEET AFTER SIX YEARS AND BEFORE
Distribution

Assets (land and building net of 6 years' depreciation)	$440,000
Capital: A	235,000
B ($235,000 − $30,000)	205,000
	$440,000

As you can see from these figures, if the partnership distributes its cash according to the capital balances, the special allocation has substantial economic effect in that Partner B bears the full reduction in value of the property since the special allocation agreement was made. But, if the proceeds are equally divided, Partner A bears one-half of the decline and the special allocation to Partner B does not affect the dollar amount of the partners' shares of total partnership income or loss independently of tax consequences.

Sale Price Greater Than Adjusted Basis. Now, suppose the fair market value of the property is not the same as the adjusted basis at the time of the special allocation agreement. Suppose that the fair market value of the property in the above example was equal to its original cost of $500,000 at the time of the special allocation agreement and that it later declines some $30,000 in value. Let's also assume that under the special allocation agreement taxable gain is to be first reported by Partner B to the extent of his special allocation.

TAXABLE GAIN ON SALE

Sale price	$470,000
Basis (end of year 6)	440,000
Taxable gain	$ 30,000

BALANCE SHEET BEFORE DISTRIBUTION

Cash	$470,000
Capital: A	$235,000
B ($235,000 − $30,000 + $30,000)	235,000
	$470,000

Here you see that Partner B does not bear the burden of the diminution in value of the property equal to the special allocation made to him where the basis for distribution is either capital account balances or percentage ownership. If the special allocation agreement called for a distribution based on capital account balances, the property would have to decrease in value by $60,000 before Partner B would have to bear the $30,000 economic burden of his special allocation.

Sale price ($500,000 − $60,000)	$440,000
Basis	440,000
Taxable gain	None

BALANCE SHEET

Cash	$440,000
Capital: A	235,000
B ($235,000 − $30,000)	205,000
	$440,000

Suppose the amended partnership agreement provided that any decline in value of the property from the date of the special allocation agreement was to be borne by Partner B to the extent of his special allocation. The allocation could result in Partner B's ultimate participation in partnership assets being reduced accordingly as follows:

Sale price ($500,000 − $30,000)	$470,000
Basis	440,000
Taxable gain	$ 30,000

Assuming the $30,000 taxable gain was allocated equally to Partners A and B on the theory that it resulted from the first three years of depreciation and that there actually was no decline in value during that period, the balance sheet would look like this:

BALANCE SHEET BEFORE LIQUIDATION

Cash	$470,000
Capital: A ($235,000 + $15,000)	250,000
B ($235,000 − $30,000 + $15,000)	220,000
	$470,000

Here, a distribution based on capital account balances results in B's share of the proceeds being reduced by his special allocation if a decline in value to that extent is actually sustained.

Assume the property is sold for $490,000 (a $10,000 decline from the time of the special allocation agreement):

Sale price	$490,000
Basis	440,000
Taxable gain	$ 50,000

Allocated to partners in the order in which depreciation was claimed:

A	$ 15,000
B ($15,000 + $20,000)	35,000
	$ 50,000

BALANCE SHEET BEFORE DISTRIBUTIONS

Cash	$490,000
Capital accounts: A ($235,000 + $15,000)	250,000
B ($235,000 − $30,000 + $35,000)	240,000
	$490,000

If the distributions are made on the basis of capital account balances, Partner B suffers the burden of the actual decline in value since the making of the special allocation agreement.

B's overall taxable income since the special allocation is composed of:

Depreciation claimed	$30,000
Gain reported	20,000
Actual depreciation and B's economic loss	$10,000

Any loss *in excess* of the special allocation would be borne by Partners A and B in their regular profit-and-loss ratios:

Sale price		$450,000
Basis		440,000
Taxable gain		$ 10,000
Allocated: A	$	5,000
B		5,000
	$	10,000

BALANCE SHEET BEFORE DISTRIBUTIONS

Cash	$450,000
Capital accounts: A ($235,000 + $5,000)	$240,000
B ($235,000 − $25,000)	210,000
	$450,000

The economic loss since the making of the special allocation agreement is ($500,000 − $450,000) $50,000. This loss should be borne as follows:

PARTNER B

Decline in value to extent of his special allocation ($500,000 − $470,000)	$30,000
One-half of·balance ($470,000 − $450,000)	10,000
	$40,000

PARTNER A

One-half of decline in excess of B's special allocation: one-half
of $470,000 − $450,000 .... $10,000

A distribution based on capital account balances results in losses being borne by the partners as follows:

SPECIAL ALLOCATION OF LOSSES

	A	B	Total
Value of equity at time of special allocation agreements	$250,000	$250,000	$500,000
Distribution	240,000	210,000	450,000
Economic loss	$ 10,000	$ 40,000	$ 50,000

Bearing the Economic Burden of Depreciation. It appears that the special allocation of depreciation to Partner B results in economic consequences to B only where an economic loss is sustained by the partnership. If the property appreciates in value, the special allocation does not affect the dollar amount of the partners' share of the total partnership income. But, you can see from the above, Partner B has borne the risk of loss, a risk that is commensurate to the special allocation made to him. Thus, he has borne the economic burden of the depreciation.

[¶1219]   **SPECIAL ALLOCATIONS AND
ADMISSION OF NEW PARTNERS**

A and B form a partnership for the construction of a building. A and B both contribute $50,000, of which sum $20,000 is deductible by the partnership at the end of year one.

BALANCE SHEET AT END OF FIRST YEAR

Land and building ($100,000 − $20,000)	$80,000	$100,000
A Capital ($50,000 − $10,000)	$40,000	$ 50,000
B Capital ($50,000 − $10,000)	40,000	50,000
	$80,000	$100,000

Assume that C will invest $50,000 for a one-third interest in the partnership. C wants the tax deductions attributable to his contribution to be allocated to him. A and B agree. C contributes $50,000, of which $40,000 is added to the cost of the building and $10,000 is currently deducted. The $10,000 deducted is allocated to C.

BALANCE SHEET AFTER C'S ADMISSION TO PARTNERSHIP

	Basis	Fair Market Value
Land and building ($150,000 − $30,000)	$120,000	$150,000
A Capital ($50,000 − $10,000)	$ 40,000	$ 50,000
B Capital ($50,000 − $10,000)	40,000	50,000
C Capital ($50,000 − $10,000)	40,000	50,000
	$120,000	$150,000

If, after C's admission to the partnership, the property is sold for $140,000 and there is an economic loss of $10,000 and a tax gain of $20,000, the capital accounts of the partners would shape up as follows in the absence of provisions in the partnership agreement to the contrary:

CAPITAL ACCOUNTS AFTER SALE OF PARTNERSHIP PROPERTY

	A	B	C	Total
Balance before sale	$40,000	$40,000	$40,000	$120,000
Taxable gain	6,667	6,667	6,666	20,000
Balance (and amount distributed) ..	$46,667	$46,667	$46,666	$140,000
Original contribution	50,000	50,000	50,000	150,000
Economic loss	$ 3,333	$ 3,333	$ 3,334	$ 10,000

As you can see, although Partner C was allocated $10,000 of tax loss on being admitted to the partnership; he did not bear the risk of that loss. When the loss was actually sustained, it was borne equally by Partners A, B, and C. Hence, the allocation of the $10,000 tax deduction to C did not have a substantial economic effect. To give substantial economic significance to the special allocation of the $10,000 to C, it appears that C must bear the risk of the first $10,000 of economic loss sustained by the partnership. The effect of a provision in the partnership that Partner C bear the risk of the first $10,000 of economic loss sustained by the partnership would be as follows:

EFFECT OF ALLOCATION OF RISK OF FIRST ECONOMIC LOSS TO C

	A	B	C	Total
Balances before sale	$40,000	$40,000	$40,000	$120,000
Taxable gain	10,000	10,000	-0-	20,000
Balance (and amount distributed)	$50,000	$50,000	$40,000	$140,000
Original contribution	50,000	50,000	50,000	150,000
Economic loss	$ -0-	$ -0-	$10,000	$ 10,000

As you can see, C bears the risk of the $10,000 special allocation and has in fact, suffered the $10,000 loss sustained by the partnership. Thus, the allocation appears to have substantial economic effect.

[¶1220]   RETROACTIVE ALLOCATIONS-PARTNERSHIPS

As to retroactive allocations, the law has not been clear. There has been confusion as to whether these were allowable because of the case of *Norman Rodman,* 32 TCM 1507, 1973-227. This case arguably allowed retroactive allocations because the taxpayer had claimed a share of losses, based on a retroactive allocation. However, it was later discovered that the "loss" by the partnership was in error; there was a gain! Nevertheless, the government attempted to force retroactive allocation. The government was successful in this position, at tax court level. (However, on appeal the government backed off this position as too many other taxpayers could assert this concept as to losses.)

There appears to be some statutory authority under Sections 704, 706, 708 and 761(c) of the Code for retroactive allocations. Section 761(c) of the Code allows the partnership to amend its partnership agreement to effect an allocation.

The *retroactive* allocation rules have now been clearly modified by the Tax Reform Act of 1976 to provide that retroactive allocations will *not* be allowed.

The effective date for the statutory change as to retroactive allocation rules is for tax years beginning after December 31, 1975. However, the Committee Reports specifically state that no inference should be drawn as to the propriety or impropriety of a *previous* retroactive allocation. [Secs. 704, 706(c) and 761 of the Code].

[¶1221]   PARTNERSHIP LOSSES

The Code limits a partner's deduction of his distributive share of the partnership's losses. He can deduct only to the extent of his adjusted basis for his partnership interest at the end of the partnership year in which the loss occurred. Any excess over his basis becomes deductible at the end of the partnership year or years in which repayment to the partnership is made [Sec. 704(d) of the Code; Regs. 1.752-1(a)(1) as to limited partners].

Here is an example: A partner's basis is $2,500; his distributive share of the firm's 1974 loss is $3,500. In 1975, he contributes $1,500. The deductible loss in 1974 is $2,500; the basis becomes zero. The remaining $1,000 of loss is allowed in 1975 against his $1,500 contribution, and the $500 excess of contributions becomes the new basis for his partnership interest.

If the partner wanted to deduct his full share of the loss in the year sustained, he would have to contribute $1,000 before the close of that year. This would raise his basis to $3,500, enough to cover his share of the loss. Or he could make the contribution in a later year, if he wished, and take the deduction in that year.

[¶1222]   **OPTIONAL ADJUSTMENT TO BASIS**

Because of the possible difference between the partnership's basis for its property and the fair market value when a partnership interest is sold or is redeemed, the tax law permits the partnership to elect to adjust the basis of its assets. The election can be made by the partnership only — even though only certain partners may benefit. Once the election is made, it must be applied to later similar transactions, even if the adjustment of basis is unfavorable (downward).

Transfer of a Partnership Interest. If a partnership interest is sold or exchanged or there is a payout as the result of the death of a partner and the partnership has made the election to adjust the basis of its assets, [Sec. 754 of the Code] the basis of the partnership's property must be increased or decreased, as the case may be, by the difference between the transferee partner's basis for his interest and his proportionate share of the partnership's basis for its property. Even if the partnership has not made the election, a partner who recieves a distribution of assets (other than cash) within two years after the transfer of the partnership interest to him may have an adjustment to the basis of the distributed property similar to that required if the election had been made [Sec. 732(d) of the Code].

The adjustment may be required at any time if at the time of the transfer the fair market value of partnership property exceeds 110 percent of its basis to the partnership. Here is an example:

	Assets			Capital Accounts	
	Adjusted Basis	Market Value		Adjusted Basis	Market Value
Securities	$12,000	$15,000	Smith	$12,000	$18,000
Land and Buildings	18,000	33,000	Jones	12,000	18,000
Cash	6,000	6,000	Brown	12,000	18,000
Totals	$36,000	$54,000		$36,000	$54,000

Smith sells his partnership interest to Robinson for $18,000. With the election in effect, Robinson gets a $6,000 adjustment upward in the basis of property held by the partnership. This figure is the difference between his basis for his partnership interest, $18,000 (the amount he paid), and one-third of the total basis of partnership property, which is $12,000. Section 743 provides the adjustment.

Here is the allocation of the adjustment to partnership property:

	Basis	Market Value	Difference	Percent	Increase in Basis
Securities	$12,000	$15,000	$ 3,000	16-2/3	$1,000
Land & Buildings	18,000	33,000	15,000	83-1/3	5,000
Totals			$18,000	100%	$6,000

The increase in basis is available only to Robinson. If the securities (a capital asset) were sold for their market value, $15,000, Jones and Brown would each have a capital gain of $1,000. But Robinson, because of the increase of his securities basis by $1,000, would have no gain.

In the case of depreciable property retained by the firm, the effect of the adjustment would be to increase the depreciation of Robinson's interest in the property.

The adjustment with respect to Robinson's interest would be downward if he paid less than his proportionate share of the partnership's basis for its property. The computation would be made along the lines set forth above.

[¶1223] ADJUSTMENTS ON A DISTRIBUTION OF PROPERTY

With the Section 754 of the Codes election in effect, a distribution of property will necessitate an adjustment to the partnership's basis for its remaining assets [Sec. 734 of the Code]. Since the adjustments are partnership adjustments, they will affect all of the continuing partners. A partner whose interest is liquidated won't be affected.

Gain by a partner on a cash distribution, whether or not in liquidation of his interest, increases the basis of partnership assets. The amount of increase is the amount of the partner's gain on the distribution [Sec. 734(b)(1)(A)].

The basis of partnership assets increases also on a distribution of property to a partner, whether or not in liquidation of his interest, if the partnership's basis for the property exceeds his basis for his partnership interest. The amount of the adjustment is the difference between these two bases [Sec. 734(b)(1)(B)]. Here is an example:

	Assets			Capital Accounts	
	Adjusted Basis	Market Value		Adjusted Basis	Market Value
Securities	$12,000	$15,000	Smith	$13,000	$17,000
Land and Buildings	21,000	30,000	Jones	13,000	17,000
Cash	6,000	6,000	Brown	13,000	17,000
Totals	$39,000	$51,000		$39,000	$51,000

Assume Smith's interest, valued at $17,000, is liquidated by distribution of the securities, worth $15,000, plus $2,000 cash. The securities are capital assets.

Smith's basis for the securities will be $11,000 (basis of his partnership interest, $13,000, less the $2,000 cash). The partnership's basis for the land and building will increase by $1,000 (excess of its basis for the securities, $12,000, over Smith's basis for the securities after the distribution, $11,000). This increase will be available to Jones and Brown.

The example assumes all capital assets are of like character. If the partnership did not have property "like" the distributed property after the distribution, the adjustment would be postponed until it acquired such property. To illustrate, if the distributed property were inventories instead of securities, the $1,000 adjustment could not be made until the partnership acquired new inventories.

[¶1224]   **TERMINATION OF PARTNERSHIP**

Termination of a partnership closes its taxable year. The death of a partner with a resulting bequest of his interest, entry or withdrawal of a partner, and sale of a partnership interest do not of themselves close the taxable year [Sec. 708 of the Code].

A provision in the partnership agreement closing the firm's accounting year upon death of a partner will not be effective for tax purposes with respect to the remaining partners if any of them continues the business in partnership form. Nor can a provision in state law for termination upon death of a partner close the partnership year for tax purposes if the business is continued in partnership form.

Termination for tax purposes is governed by the provisions of the Code, which apply automatically. Neither the partners' preferences and intentions nor state law has any effect.

If the agreement in a two-man partnership provides for winding-up and liquidation upon the death of one partner, the partner's death will close the year. You can avoid this, if you want, by a provision in the agreement for continuation of the deceased partner's interest in the firm until the normal closing of the partnership year or until a suitable date beyond his death.

What Constitutes Termination? The partnership is considered terminated only if: (1) none of the partners continues the business in partnership form or (2) within a 12-month period, 50 percent or more of the total interest in the firm's capital and profits is sold or exchanged [Sec. 708 of the Code].

The second of these two tests will be easier to apply. With respect to the first test, there might be some difficulty about deciding whether some of the partners had continued the business in partnership form. The difficulty would come in determining how broadly you are going to interpret the term "business." If some of the partners carry on some of the specific business transactions of the old partnership in a new partnership, this would almost surely be deemed a continuation of the old partnership. The answer is not so easy where the new partnership, while not completing any of the old firm's business, engages in a type of business that is similar to the business of the old firm.

In the computation to determine whether the required 50 percent of a partnership interest has been sold within 12 months, you probably could not count duplicating sales. Say there was a sale of a partner's 25 percent interest, followed by another sale of the same interest during the year. The statute says 50 percent of the "total" interest; thus this double sale would still be a sale of only 25 percent of the "total" interest.

New capital contributions and withdrawals of partners can complicate values of the different interests in the underlying assets to determine whether the 50 required percent has been sold.

Effects of Closing by Termination. Closing can affect the year in which the partners should report their distributive shares of the firm's income or loss. Also affected is the determination whether an election to adjust the basis of partnership assets in the case of distributions and transfers of interests. Code sections 734, 743, and 754 provide for the election.

Automatic termination may bring problems with respect to basis, recognition of gain or loss, "bunching" of two years of partnership income into one individual year, and other matters that are likely to arise when an old firm is dissolved and a new one created. However, for new partnerships, the "bunching" problem may not be too important under the new law, since the partnership and partners will be on the same taxable year.

The partnership's taxable year closes with **respect to a partner** who sells or exchanges his entire interest and to a partner whose interest is liquidated. The taxable year of a deceased partner's interest will not close merely as a result of his death. When the partnership year closes **with respect to a partner**, his distributive share of income or loss is determined as of the date *he* ceased to be a partner. The partnership year with respect to the *other partners* and the determination of their distributive shares is *not* affected [Sec. 706(c) of the Code; Regs. 1.706-1(c)(21)].

If only a portion of a partner's interest is liquidated or sold, the partnership year with respect to his interest is not closed. But the partner must take into account his varying interest in computing his distributive share of income or loss for the full year [Sec. 706(c)(2)(B) of the Code].

Planning: If a retiring partner wishes to defer reporting his distributive share until a subsequent tax year, he may be able to do so by retaining a small part of his interest beyond the end of the current year. If he disposes of his entire interest during the partnership's taxable year, he will have to report his distributive share for that year in his personal return for the year. On the other hand, if he disposes of less than his entire interest, his distributive share is not determined until the close of the partnership's taxable year. If that carries beyond the end of his own tax year, the effect will be to postpone part of his tax.

Example: A partner reporting on a calendar-year basis sells his entire interest in a partnership reporting on the basis of a fiscal year ending June 30. The sale is made on November 30, 1975. The partner must report for 1975 not only his distributive share for the partnership fiscal year ending June 30, 1975, but also his distributive share for the short period ending November 30, 1975. If instead the partner sold **Less** than his entire interest, although he would still report his distributive share for the partnership fiscal year ending June 30, 1975, in his personal return for 1975, he would report nothing more in that year. His distributive share for the full partnership fiscal year ending June 30, 1975, would not be taxable until 1976.

[¶1225]   **COLLAPSIBLE PARTNERSHIP**

The "collapsible partnership" rules provide that if, in connection with the transfer of a partnership interest or the distribution of partnership property, a partner received any money or other property in exchange for his share of (1) the unrealized receivables of the partnership or (2) substantially appreciated inventory items, such amounts are to be treated as ordinary gain or loss to the transferor or distributee. Where, in a distribution, a partner receives more than his share of unrealized receivables or substantially appreciated inventory items, the partnership is treated as having sold such items, with the result that the ordinary gain or loss in this case is considered as being realized by the partnership as constituted after the distribution. An exception to these rules is provided where a distributee receives property he contributed to the partnership. With respect to the distribution of such property, neither he nor the partnership is considered as having ordinary gain or loss [Sec. 751(b)(2)(A) of the Code].

"Unrealized receivables" are defined as: (1) any rights to payment for goods to the extent amounts received would not be treated as payment for a capital asset or (2) any right to receive payment for services rendered or to be rendered [Sec. 751(c)]. In other words, if the payment would be ordinary income to the partnership, the right is an "unrealized receivable." But if the payments have already been taxed to the partnership, the rule doesn't apply [Regs 1.751-1(c)].

"Substantially appreciated inventories" covers more than is usually embraced in the term "inventory." For this purpose, "inventory" includes in addition to stock-in-trade and other property held primarily for sale to customers in the ordinary course of trade or business, any other property belonging to the partnership which would not be considered a capital asset, real property, or depreciable property used in trade or business. Thus, where a real estate partnership is a "dealer" in real estate, the properties it holds for sale would constitute inventory for this purpose. A partnership asset will be considered "inventory" if its use by either the partnership or a selling or distributee partner conforms to this definition.

Take an example. Assume we have a partner who is a real estate dealer and a partnership which is not. The partnership owns a parcel of unimproved real property. In the hands of the partnership, it is a capital asset; in the partner's hands, it is not. Distribution of the real estate to the partner or sale of his partnership interest makes the real estate inventory item in the partnership's hands.

If the real estate has substantially appreciated in value, the best hope for avoiding the ordinary income rate is for the partnership to sell the real estate before the partner sells his partnership interest. Or, if it is a question of a distribution, the thing to do would be to sell the real estate before the distribution and distribute the proceeds. If the item in question has not substantially appreciated in value, then the parties can do as they like without fear of the ordinary income rate being applied on grounds of this special rule.

Substantial appreciation means market value in excess of (1) 120 percent of the adjusted basis to the partnership and (2) value in excess of 10 percent of the fair market value of *all* partnership property other than money [Sec. 751(d) of the Code; Regs. 1.751-1(d)].

[¶1226] MAKING SURE THAT LIMITED PARTNERSHIP INTERESTS PAY OFF IN TAX SHELTER

Depreciation deductions, interest deductions, etc., especially in the early years of a project, usually generate paper losses. The partnership form permits the pass through of these paper losses to the individual partners, who thereby acquire substantial tax shelter. This explains the great attraction that limited partnership interests in real estate have for investors looking for tax shelter. There is no tax at the partnership level; both income and losses are passed through to the individual partners.

The flow-through to the individual partners of their distributive shares of the taxable income and loss is provided for under Section 702 of the Code. Section 704(a) of the Code permits the partners to determine by the partnership agreement their distributive shares of income, gain, loss, deductions, or credit of the partnership, provided the principal purpose is not to avoid or evade the federal income tax.

The tax shelter that a limited partner gets from the paper losses that a real estate project generates can be severely cut down by the erosion of the basis of his partnership interest. A partner (whether general or limited) cannot deduct his share of the partnership losses if it exceeds his basis in the partnership interest [Sec. 704(d) of the Code]. A general partner's basis includes his share of the partnership debts as well as the amount of his investment in the partnership. So he can include the amount of his share of the mortgage obligation. But a limited partner is not liable for partnership obligations, and his basis in his partnership interest is limited to the amount of his investment. If the project produces tax losses, he soon cannot benefit from them since his basis is quickly reduced to zero. In most projects, most of the funds are furnished by the lender, and the relatively modest size of the limited partner's investment is quickly chipped away by the tax losses generated. Were this the whole story, the limited partnership syndicate would not be the great tax shelter and fund raiser for real estate enterprises that it is. In fact, however, it is possible to pass on to the partners large chunks and even all the paper losses that the enterprise generates.

How to Lift the Lid on the Tax Shelter the Enterprise Generates.

Where none of the partners has any personal liability as to a partnership liability, all the partners, including the limited partners, are considered as sharing such liability under Section 752(c), in the same proportion as they share profits [Reg. §1.752-1(e)]. For example, where the partnership acquires real estate subject to a mortgage and neither the partnership nor any of the partners (general or limited) has any liability on the mortgage obligation, all the partners are considered as sharing proportionately in the losses generated by the enterprise, and each can take tax deductions accordingly. Under the *Tax Reform Act of 1976,* this rule will not be applicable when dealing with certain farming groups, equipment leasing, movies and oil and gas ventures; however, real estate is specifically *not* subject to these limitations. See ¶1227 dealing with the "at risk" rules.

Here are two methods of precluding personal liability.

(1) *No-Recourse Note and Mortgage.* Include in the mortgage note a provision that the liability of the maker and of the partners is limited as set forth in the mortgage of even date therewith and include a no-recourse provision in the mortgage. Thus, the mortgage should contain a provision that neither the grantor nor any general or limited partner will be personally liable for the note secured by the mortgage nor for the violation of any covenant, condition, or warranty set forth in the note or mortgage and that any such liability will be collectible only out of the security described in the mortgage.

Keep in mind that loans for low- and moderate-income rental housing [FHA §221(d)(3) and 236] projects are obtainable without personal liability. Among the great advantages these projects offer is the tax shelter they generate.

(2) *Use of Nominee.* You could use a corporation as the debtor on the mortgage, for the partnership, but argue that it is merely acting for the partnership, as its agent or nominee. Another method is of great danger due to case decisions [*William Strong* 66 TC 3(1976); *Moline Properties, Inc. v. Comm., 319 U.S. 436 (1943); Harrison Property v.* U.S., 73-1 USTC Para. 9292 (1973)]. The courts are tending not to treat the corporation as a mere nominee. The result: the corporation will be subject to all of the normal corporate rules, such as taxation of gains and a non-pass through of losses.

[¶1227]   **AT RISK LIMITATIONS**

The use of non-recourse, non-risk type loans, for increasing basis, has been greatly restricted by the *Tax Reform Act of 1976.*

New Section 465 of the Code has been added to the law. Generally speaking, this limits deductions for investors to the amount the investor has "at risk" in the venture. The "at risk" limitations under Section 465 of the Code affect numerous areas, including:

a. motion picture films or video tapes
b. farming as defined under [Sec. 464(e) of the Code]
c. leasing of any property [Sec. 1245 of the Code]
d. exploring for or exploiting, oil and gas resources, as a trade or business or for the production of income. [Sec. 465(c) of the Code].

This rule applies in the case of a taxpayer, excluding a normal corporation, but not excluding a subchapter S corporation. It also does not exclude a personal holding company as defined under [Sec. 542 of the Code].

Any loss from such activity which is limited by this Code Section will be treated as a deduction allowable to such activity in the first succeeding taxable year where basis is sufficient to support the loss.

Amounts which are considered "at risk", as defined under Section 465 (b) of the Code, include the amount of money and the adjusted basis of other property contributed by the tax payer to the activity and amounts borrowed with respect to such activity. The borrowed amounts include these transactions where the taxpayer is personally liable for the repayment of the amount or has pledged property, *other than* property used in the activity, as security for the borrowing to the extent of the fair market value of the taxpayer's interest in such property.

The property classified as "borrowed" will not include any property where the security for such property is, directly or indirectly, financed by the indebtedness which is secured by the property which is the property subject to the transaction question — the "at risk" issue.

Borrowed amounts will not include the amounts borrowed from any person who has an interest, other than an interest as a creditor in that particular activity or one who has a relationship to the taxpayer specified within Section 267(b) of the Code (related).

The taxpayer is not considered "at risk" with respect to amounts protected from loss through non-recourse financing, guarantees, stop-loss agreements, or similar Section 465 (b)(4) of the Code.

The effective date for this rule is generally for tax years beginning after December 31, 1975.

[¶1228]   PARTNERSHIP AT RISK LIMITATIONS

Section 704(d) of the Code was amended to provide that a partner may deduct losses, under the general rule, up to the amount of his adjusted basis and to the extent of any items for which he has liability. However, the amendment indicates that a partner's adjusted basis will *not* include that *portion* of the partnership liability where the partner has no personal liability.

However, there is a specific provision under Section 704(d) of the Code which states that the limitation mentioned, on loss limitations, will not apply ''to any partnership, the principal activity of which is investing in real property (other than mineral property).'' The effective date is generally for years beginning after December 31, 1975. Thus, partnerships in real estate and real estate ventures, in general, do not suffer from these new rules requiring ''At Risk'' capital. This means that real estate is one of the few viable tax shelters that remains, at this juncture.

[¶1229]   USING LIMITED PARTNERSHIP AS CONDUIT FOR TAX PURPOSES

In setting up a real estate syndicate, you want to preserve for the investors the tax advantages that lie in the property — the right to make the best use of depreciation charges by offsetting depreciation against income from the property and the benefit of only a single tax on the income from the property.

The partnership form is used in real estate syndicates because, when properly set up, it avoids double taxation and passes the high depreciation deductions directly through to the individual investors. In order to facilitate the operation of the partnership, the syndicator will try to give it some of the powers and characteristics of a corporation. But too many corporate characteristics in the partnership can result in taxation as a corporation. The general rule has always been that the Treasury will treat an organization as an association and tax it as a corporation if it more nearly resembles a corporation than a partnership.

What is desired is a syndicate with some of the characteristics of a corporation which is still not taxable as an association. Treasury Regulations spell out when an unincorporated group is a partnership and when it is a corporation for tax purposes.

When is there a partnership? The Regulations have made it possible to set up an unincorporated real estate syndicate with reasonable certainty that it will be treated as a partnership and not as a corporation for tax purposes. The following list of corporate characteristics enables you to tell, from the number present in your organization, whether it is taxable as a partnership or an association, if a numbers test is employed:

1. Associates.
2. An objective to carry on a business and divide the profits from it.
3. Continuity of the life of the entity on the death, insanity, bankruptcy, retirement, resignation, or expulsion of any member.

4. Centralization of management.
5. Limited liability.
6. Transferability of interests.

As a practical matter, the first two characteristics are present in both corporations and partnerships, so the Treasury is concerned with only the last four characteristics. The Regulations, [Sec. 301.7701-2(a)(3)] say that an organization will not be taxable as an association unless it has more corporate than noncorporate characteristics. If there are no other significant factors aside from the four corporate characteristics (continuity, centralized managment, limited liability, and transferability of interest) and no more than two of these characteristics are present, your partnership is taxable as a partnership and not as a corporation. (However, this area may be changing: see Levine article, *infra,* this section of the text).

[¶1230]   **AVOIDING TAXATION OF LIMITED PARTNERSHIP AS CORPORATION**

Before we weigh the various characteristics, first examine each and see when the Regs say a corporate characteristic is present.

(1) Continuity of Life. To avoid continuity of life, the withdrawal of a member (by death, insanity, bankruptcy, retirement, resignation, or expulsion) should cause a dissolution.

If the organization is to continue for a stated time (or until the end of a particular project) and there is no provision for prior termination — either at death, insanity, etc., or at will of any partner—there is continuity. But if, despite the agreement, state law allows any partner to dissolve the partnership at will, there is no continuity.

Limited partnership law or the agreement often provides that the retirement, death, or insanity of a general partner of a limited partnership causes a dissolution of the partnership unless the remaining partners agree to continue the partnership. In these circumstances, there is no continuity of life [Reg. §301.7701-2(b)]. The Regulations go even further and say that a limited partnership subject to a law corresponding to the Uniform Limited Partnership Act lacks continuity of life. This means that in some cases a limited partnership can provide for continuation on the death of a general partner by agreement of the remaining general partners and still avoid continuity of life for tax purposes.

(2) Centralized Management. This corporate characteristic exists if any person or group of less than all the members has continuing and exclusive authority to make independent business decisions for the organization. In order

for there to be centralization, these decisions must be necessary for the conduct of the business and not subject to ratification by the other memberrs. But the Regulations say that a general partnership cannot have centralized management, since the act of any partner within the scope of business binds all the partners. Even if the partners in a general partnership agree that their managment powers will be centralized in a few of them, this agreement would not be binding on outsiders who have no notice of it.

A large-scale limited partnership will still have centralized management. The Regulations [Sec. 301.7701-2(c)] say that limited partnerships subject to a statute corresponding to the Uniform Limited Partnership Act generally do not have centralized management but that centralized management does exist in such a limited partnership if substantially all the interests in the partnership are owned by the limited partners. This means that a small-scale limited partnership might not have centralized management but a large-scale partnership will.

(3) *Limited Liability.* For the corporate characteristic of limited liability to be absent, one of the members has to have personal liability. In a limited partnership, with only the general partners having liability to outsiders, the limited partnership has personal liability even if only general partners have personal liability. The Regulations [Sec. 301.7701-2(d)] say that the general partner in a limited partnership does not have personal liability, *only*, when he has no substantial assets *and* is also merely a dummy acting as agent for the limited partners. Even if he has no substantial assets (other than his interest in the partnership), he still has personal liability if he is not a dummy. It makes no difference whether the personally liable partners contributed services or capital to the partnership for their interests in it.

(4) *Transferability of Interest.* Transferability exists if all those members owning substantially all the interests in the organization have the power to substitute an outsider for themselves. For there to be transferability, they must possess this power without the consent of the other members. Also they have to be able to give their transferee all the attributes of their position in the organiza- tion. Transferability does not normally exist if a member·can assign only his right to share in the profits and not his right to participate in the management of the organization. And transferability does not usually exist if under state law a transfer of a member's interest results in dissolution of the old organization and formation of a new one.

The Main Impact of the Regulations on Associations. A limited part- nership formed under the Uniform Limited Partnership Act will normally not have continuity; and, unless the general partners have no substantial assets and are dummies, it also will not have limited liability. Right there two corporate characteristics are absent; and, ordinarily, at most only centralized management and free transferability would be present. In that case, under the rule in the regulations, your organization would be taxable as a partnership. And, if there is any fear that the general partners might be considered dummies, you could tie up transferability to ensure that two corporate characteristics (namely, continuity and transferability) would be absent. In any event, if a real estate limited partnership is set up under the Uniform Limited Partnership Law, you are fairly sure of getting partnership treatment for tax purposes.

Remember that under the Regulations an overall approach will be taken and other factors besides the usual corporate characteristics may also be considered. In addition, the Regulations give some examples of what kind of partnership setup will be taxable as an association and what kind will be taxable as a partnership.

Assume that 3 individuals form an organization which is a limited partnership under state law to acquire and operate real estate. Each invests $100,000 in the organization, and together they solicit $5,000,000 in investment capital from 30 limited partner, so there is no continuity present. The organization is a limited partnership. The organization dissolves on the death, insanity, or retirement of a general partner, so there is no continuity present. Assume the organization is a limited partnership and substantially all the interests in the organization are owned by the limited partners; management is centralized in the general partners. The liability of the general partners is unlimited, and they are personally capable of assuming a substantial part of the obligations of the organization. So the characteristic of limited liability is not present. A limited partner can assign only his right to receive profits and cannot assign his interest without consent of the general partners, so transferability is not present. Here, only the characteristic of centralized management is present. Thus, the organization is taxed as a partnership.

Now, assume that these individuals form an organization which is a limited partnership under state law. The purpose is to acquire and operate real estate. Each of the 3 individuals is a general partner, each invests $50,000 in the organization, and, $5,000,000 of investment capital is then raised through the sale of 900 limited partnership interests. Assume that the limited partnership interests are freely transferable. There is centralized management since substantially all the partnership interests are owned by limited partners. Assume that the general partners have substantial assets — so limited liability is not present. Finally, the organization will continue for 40 years, unless a general partner dies, becomes insane, or retires during such period. If that happens, the remaining general partners can continue the business of the partnership for the balance of the 40-year period under a right stated in the certificates. This does not constitute continuity, so the only corporate characteristics present are centralized management and transferability. Thus, the organization is taxable as a partnership.

[¶1231]   "CORPNERSHIP"—A LIMITED PARTNERSHIP WITH CORPORATE ATTRIBUTES

A vast $80,000,000-plus real estate investment was lauched in the form of a limited partnership giving investors reasonable assurance of continuity of life, limited liability, and free transferability of interests. The setup is backed by a private IRS ruling that the enterprise will be taxed as a partnership, not as a corporation.

This enterprise offers investors substantially all the advantages of investment in a corporate enterprise without the disadvantage of double taxation. What's more, it offers participation to tens of thousands of investors in a giant real estate enterprise, rivaling in size some of our corporate giants. An examination of the prospectus shows a very carefully thought-out plan for dealing with those troublesome areas that might make the partnership taxable as a corporation:

Continuity of Life. On the death of a general partner or the sale of his interest, the partnership is terminated; but the remaining general partners will form a new partnership to continue the business. Two of the four general partners are corporations; presumably perpetual in existence. A further provision in the partnership agreement provides for termination on December 31, 2069, unless the general partners by *unanimous* vote decide to terminate earlier.

Centralization of Management. Reg §301.7771-2(c)(4) says that centralized management does not generally exist in a limited partnership subject to the Uniform Limited Partnership Act or a similar law but that centralized management can exist if substantially all the interests in the partnership are owned by the limited partner. The latter is not the case with this limited partnership, and so it appears that this element is missing.

Limited Liability. The individual general partners or associates are personally liable and have substantial assets. The corporations which are general partners also appear to have substantial assets. Hence, the limited liability characteristic of a corporation is missing.

Transferability of Interests: The offering consists of 81,700 units of $1,000 9 percent junior mortgage bonds and 10 participation interests representing undivided economic interests in the limited partnership interest held by the one initial limited partner. Holders of participation interests are not limited partners nor otherwise members of the partnership.

It is contemplated that there will be a public market for the participation interests and that they will be freely transferable. This, however, would not be true of the limited partnership interest as such. The corporate characteristic of free transferability of interests is also apparently lacking.

[¶1232]   **WEIGHT OF CHARACTERISTICS TEST**

The prior discussion reviews the Regulation's position [and the Morrisey case, 36-1 USTC ¶9020, 296 US 344 (1935)] as to whether a partnership will be recognized as such.

However, the following article by this author reviews the most important recent case on this subject (Larson), and the possible "Writing on The Wall" to evidence a shift to a new test of *weighing* the characteristics:

THE TAX DEFINITION OF AN ASSOCIATION OR A PARTNERSHIP: THE LARSON "ANSWER"*

Most practioners are familiar with the basic concept of determining whether an entity is a corporation-"association" or a partnership, for tax purposes. Notwithstanding the local-state law definition of whether an entity constitutes a corporation or partnership, the federal tax law provides its own definition and determination on this issue.

A corporation has been referred to "as an artifical being, intangible, invisible, and existing only in contemplation of law." *Dartmouth College v. Woodward* 17 U.S.518, 4 Wheat. 518, 4 L. Ed. 629 (1819). This definition, for state law purposes, implies the concept of creation. The corporation comes into being because of state allowing the entity. Nevertheless, even though state law allows for the creation of this entity, federal tax law determines the status of the entity for federal tax purposes.

Under the now famous *Morrissey Case,* 296 U.S. 344, 56 S.Ct. 289, 80 L.Ed. 263, 36-1 USTC Para. 9020 (1935), the Supreme Court listed corporate characteristics which should be considered when making a determination as to whether an entity will be treated as a corporation for tax purposes. These items have been ingrafted in the Internal Revenue Code of 1954, as amended, under Section 7701 and the regulations under 301.7701, *et seq.*

The essence of the Morrissey decision and the regulations is that there are six characteristics which are used to test whether an entity will be an association-corporation or a partnership. These characteristics are:

1. Associates — two or more parties.
2. The entity must have an objective to carry on business and to divide the gains derived from that business.
3. There must be a continuity of life — that is, e.g., a perpetual existence or a given continuation of existence.
4. There must be centralization of management. See for example *Glensder Textile Company v. Comm.,* 46 BTA 176 (1942).
5. Limited liability must be present. That is, the exposure to the shareholders is limited in most circumstances to their investment.
6. Free transferability of the shares of the corporation generally exists.

*Reprinted with permission of the Publisher, *Real Estate Securities and Syndication Institue® Review,* article by Mark Lee Levine. See also the follow-up on this article in *Real Estate Securities and Syndications Institute Review,* p. 1 (May, 1977) by Levine.

Once again, the six characteristics noted above are characteristics which are prevalent in an association. The test under the *Morrissey* position is whether *more* corporate characteristics than non-corporate characteristics exist. If the latter point is true, the entity will be classified, for tax purposes, as an association, notwithstanding that state law might treat it as a partnership for the purposes of its statutes.

Because the two characteristics first mentioned, that is, (1) associates and (2) having an objective to carry on a business for profit and to divide the same are common to partnerships and corporations, these two characteristics are omitted in the examination as to the association-partnership status determination.

The latter four characteristics are reviewed to make the determination. If three of the four or four of the four characteristics exist, the entity, according to the Regulations, will be classified, for federal tax purposes, as an association and will be taxed accordingly.

This brief background exemplifies those principles familiar to most practitioners.

Most tax practitioners are also familiar with the deluge of rulings and procedures issued by the Service with regard to the interpretation under the Morrissey Case and the regulations noted. For example, there is the basic Service position illustrated in Revenue Procedure 72-13, IRB 1972-2. This procedure emphasizes the Service's position that it will not issue a favorable ruling to recognize a limited partnership as such if there is a corporation as the sole general partner in a limited partnership, unless certain basic tests are met. These tests are sometimes referred to as the shareholder test and the equity test. Under the shareholder provision, the investing limited partners cannot own more than 20 percent of the stock in the sole corporate general partner including any of its affiliates. As to the equity test, the Service has taken the position that if a corporation is a general partner in a partnership, the net worth of the corporation at all times must be maintained to at least 15 percent of the investment in the partnership, of two-hundred and fifty thousand dollars ($250,000), whichever is less, and subject to certain other limitations and exceptions.

The above information has been provided for basic background. The Service has issued other rulings with regard to restrictions on advance rulings on limited partnership status. Under Rev. Proc. 74-17, IRB 1974-22, the Service has held that advance rulings for limited partnership status will not be made unless the general partners have at least 1 percent interest in each material item of partnership income, gain, loss, deduction, or credit; the aggregate deductions to be claimed by the partners for the first two years of operation cannot exceed the amount of equity capital invested in the limited partnership; and, the creditor who makes a non-recourse loan to the limited partnership cannot have or acquire, as a result of making the loan, a direct or indirect interest in the limited partnership.

To avoid going further into the rudimentary concepts of this area, suffice to say that the Service has been very active in developing rules in this area as to whether a given entity constitutes a partnership for tax purposes.

The problem. Larson and Other muddy waters. The problem in this area generally arises with regard to limited partnerships which invest in properties that provide a high level of tax shelter for the limited pratners. In the real estate area, with various real estate ventures throwing off tax deductions in the form of operating losses, often due to accelerated depreciation and interest deductions the Service has watched many operations with a jaundice eye. Most *apropos* in this area is the recent case of *Phillip G. Larson, et al. v.* Comm. 65 TC-, No. 10, CCH Dec. 33, 471, issued Oct. 21, 1975.

In that decision, the issue was whether the entity in question constituted a partnership for tax purposes.

The taxpayers owned limited partnership interests in real estate syndications created under the California Uniform Limited Partnership provisions of their state.

There was a sole corporate general partner in each of the partnerships. This sole general partner was an unrelated independent corporation. This entity was organized to underwrite these partnerships and other partnerships, and to manage properties owned by the partnership.

Factually, the corporation which was acting as the general partner did not have an equity investment in the partnership in question. Both of the partnerships provided that the corporate general partner's interests were in a subordinate position to the investors (limited partners). The general partner would participate after the limited partners received a return of their after-tax investment. In fact, at the time of the trial, the general partner's interest in one partnership was completely unsubordinated.

As anticipated at the formation of the partnerships, the limited partnerships sustained losses and the taxpayers deducted those losses in accord with the partnership rules. However, the Service supported the position that the losses were not deductible because the entities should be taxed as associations and not as partnerships.

Factually, it is important to note that the interest held by the limited partners, as to their income rights, was transferable, subject to the consent of the general partner. However, the consent could "not be unreasonably withheld." (This is traditional language in many partnership agreements).

There are certain other provisions with regard to transferability of the interest.

The Tax Court, in a shocking decision, as far as many practitioners were concerned, in its decision issued October 21, 1975, held the two limited partnerships in question were to be treated as associations, not as partnerships! In a very unusual move the Tax Court withdrew the opinion on November 7, 1976, in accord with the motion for reconsideration which was filed by the petitioner-taxpayer and I.R.S. (Both the petitioner-taxpayer, the I.R.S. and the Court had stipulated at the start of the trial that the case was to be tried on the I.R.S. regulations. The first opinion was based on the "law," rather than the regulations.)

On reconsideration, a new decision was issued on April 27, 1976, 66 TC-21 (1976), CCH Dec. 33, 793.

The opinion on reissue, announced by Judge Tannenwald, stated the ground rules for the new decision *as to the Larson Case*. It was to be based on the Kintner Regulations. These regulations under Treas. Reg. Sec. 301.7701-2, *et seq.*, repeat the six characteristics mentioned earlier.

The Court stated that its decision was based upon these characteristics, not upon any other test.

The Court, when reviewing these characteristics, held that the partnerships would be taxed as partnerships because they did not contain sufficient corporate characteristics. The partnerships had two of the four corporate characteristics. They therefore would not be treated as associations.

When reviewing the continuity of life test, the Court held there was no continuity of life. Under California law, the bankruptcy of the general partner would cause the dissolution of the partnership, notwithstanding that the partnership might be reconstituted by vote of the partners. (The partnership agreement contained a provision to reconstitute the partnership.)

The Court held that there was no limited liability. The general partner had personal liability for the debts of the partnership. Therefore, the limited liability characteristic, a characteristic of corporations, was not present in the partnerships. Treas. Reg. 301.7701-2(d)(2). Under this Regulation there is a *conjunctive* test. A general partner is considered not to have personal liability only when (1) he has no substantial assets, except those in the partnership, which could be reached by creditors. However, as an *additional part* of this test, (2) there must be a showing that the corporation is merely a dummy, acting as agent for the limited partners. This additional requirement was stressed by the Court. Even though the limited partners had the power to remove the general partner, the general partner was not a dummy or nominee. The general partner had the power to direct the activity of the partnership. Therefore, the conjunctive test of *both* a lack of substantial assets *and* acting as merely a dummy was not met. Limited liability was not present! (Incidentally, the I.R.S. included *non-recourse* loans in all computations of the corporation's liabilities.)

The Court held that centralization of management existed. The general partner had the power to administer the partnership affairs under California law and under general partnership law. Treas. Reg. Sec. 301.7701-2(c)(4).

The characteristic of transferability of interests was met. Even though formal consent was necessary from the general partner, that consent could not be "unreasonably withheld" (whatever that means). This was merely a "procedural" rather than a substantive limitation. The transferability of interest characteristic was present.

Once again, with only two of the four characteristics present, the entities, in the reissued opinion, were held to be partnerships for tax purposes. (In golf and here, low scores win!)

Had nothing further been said in the Larson Case, aside from the history of the issuing of the opinion and the withdrawing of the same, possibly the merit of reviewing the Larson Case might have been somewhat limited. However, of what importance is it that:

1. There were a number of concurring opinions. Dawson, Featherston, Irwin, Goffee, and Willis concurred.

2. There were dissenting opinions issued by Raum, Drennen, and Simpson. Their dissent was based on the overall "resemblance" test of corporate characteristics. They argued that the regulations do not impose a rigid numerical test. The dissenting opinions emphasized the importance of the *weight* of the characteristics not the numerical test.

3. There was further dissent by Simpson, Drennen, and Sterrett on the issue that the even-split rule of the regulations, in this case, the majority held two corporate characteristics existed and two did not. The dissent sponsored the position that this numeritive test would apply only in the instance where there were not other significant characteristics that might tip the scale in favor of determining that corporation-association existed. (During the course of the trial, the I.R.S. had argued that in addition to looking at the four corporate characteristics, the Court should also consider other items that were common to corporations. The I.R.S. pointed out that the interests, in one case, were registered with the California Department of Corporations, as are corporate stocks, the interests in both ventures were sold by NASD members who also sell corporate stocks. The interests were referred to as "units," which compares to corporate shares.)

4. There was dissent as to whether limited liability did or did not exist.

5. Quealy dissented by arguing that the regulations were invalid. The Court was not bound by the position under Treas. Reg. Sec. 301.7701.

6. As if this was not enough, there were other opinions on the same issue.

7. Insomnia, exposure, and trepidation were further spawned in this author not simply as the offspring of the number of dissents and concuring opinions, not that they are not of crucial importance, but the problem or irritation lies in the words of the majority. The

majority of the Court, through the opinion by Judge Tannenwald, held that it would have been inclined to find that the two entities in question were corporations if the overall corporate resemblance test had been applied. This text examines the weight of each characteristic as opposed to a mere numbers test. The Court made it clear: It would have been inclined to find that the entities were associations!

Although there are other more comforting decisions which exist, such as Zuckman, 75-2 USTC Para. 9778 (1975), wherein the partnership was treated as a partnership for tax purposes, the decision in Larson should not allow any practitioner to rest easy.

Conclusion. Although Larson created great turmoil at the time of its first issuance, some relief was engendered when that decision was withdrawn, in a very unusual act by the Tax Court. The reissuance of the opinion in favor of partnership status does not eliminate the perplexing problems in this area. The river of problems stirred by Larson makes one point obvious: the waters are not clear. If opinions are meant,among other purposes, to provide order from chaos, Larson fails this function. Larson produced further apprehension and uncertainty. It has been engendered by the Court's language as to the "corporate resemblance test." Fuel of apprehension and uncertainty has been added to the fire of confusion by the great number of dissenting and concurring opinions.

Possibly the muddy waters will clear after the appeal of this case. In either event, clarification is needed. Practitioners, investors, and related parties must have some basis to act.

Chaos that has been illuminated and/or produced by the Larson Case will result in greater uncertainty in the real estate and other tax shelter areas. If direct participation programs are to be discouraged, production of this type of uncertainty is the wrong way!

Legislation may be forthcoming. [RESSI has proposed a new form of entity, a Real Estate Venture, which may eliminate some of the problems.]

[¶1233]   SAVING TAX DOLLARS FOR SYNDICATORS

The syndicator should plan his share of the deal from the very beginning. If he takes a percentage of the partnership as compensation for his services, he has ordinary income at that point unless he can convince IRS that he has received his partnership share in exchange for his contribution of a contract right to buy the property. A partnership interest is ordinary income when it is received in exchange for services. But it is a capital asset when received in exchange for property, and the partnership interest is not taxable on receipt in such a case. So by acquiring a contract right to buy the property and transferring it to the partnership in exchange for his partnership interest, the syndicator will attempt to show that the partnership interest has been recieved in exchange for a transfer of property (i.e., the contract right) to the partnership. If the partnership interest is a capital asset in the hands of the syndicator, he can hold it for the necessary long term period and then sell it at a long-term capital gain.

So suppose the syndicator takes a percentage of the profits in exchange for his services. Formerly, it was thought that he avoided an immediate tax provided he received an interest in *future* profits only and no interest in capital [*Herman M. Hale, 24 TCM 1497 (1965)*] it was ruled that where a mortgage broker received an interest in the profits of a joint venture for his services in securing financing for the venture, the fair market value of the interest was taxable to him as ordinary income in the year he received it. Since he sold his interest some three weeks after he received it, the price he realized was taken to be its fair market value. The Seventh Circuit agreed with the Tax Court that the interest in profits was a valuable property interest and that, since it was received in return for services, it was compensation and taxable as ordinary income. The Seventh Circuit made it clear that for an interest in profits to be taxable as ordinary income when received in return for services it must have a determinable market value.

Even with *Diamond,* a syndicator should still be able to receive as compensation for his services an interest in the profits of the properties tax free. As pointed out by the Seventh Circuit, in many situations the interest in profits will have only a speculative value. *Diamond* established the value of his interest when he sold it.

Here are some ideas for avoiding ordinary income where a syndicator receives a right to share in profits in return for his services, in view of *Diamond.* The syndicator should (1) refrain from selling his interest in the year he receives it or in immediately succeeding years, (2) set up his deal so that his right to share in the profits is conditioned on his performing future services, (3) make his right to share in profits contingent on the occurrence of an uncertain future event, (4) place absolute or conditional restraints on his right to transfer his interest, (5) use a minimum amount of equity in capitalizing the partnership, and (6) complicate the deal so as to make value not readily ascertainable.

The Diamond result can now arise from Section 83 of the Code, would tax this type of interest if it is freely transferable or not subject to a substantial risk if forfeiture, assuming it could be valued.

[¶1234]   JOINT VENTURES

The joint venture is a business form that is particularly adaptable for special-purpose investments and projects that require large sums of capital and specialized experience. An experienced operator who is short of captial or doesn't want to risk all of his capital in one venture may use a joint venture arrangement to team up with one or more investors who have the necessary capital. The joint venture form is used most often in the building field. A particular project may be too big and the risks too great for a single general contractor or builder, or the combination of equipment and supervisory personnel may produce important savings in the costs of contruction. Syndicates, for example, are a form of joint venture; and they, are widely used for investment purposes. (Although outside of the tax area, syndicators must be leary of the potential of violating the federal and State Securities laws.)

Joint ventures are in many ways like partnerships, and they are *treated as such for tax purposes.* The main distinction between a joint venture and a partnership is that the joint venture is a special assocation for a specific enterprise or project — such as constructing or designing a building or large-scale land development — with *no intention* on the part of the associates to enter into a *continuing* partnership relationship or to assume partnership obligations and liabilities. Joint venturers cannot represent their associates and incur liabilities on their part as freely and broadly as can partners.

A joint venture agreement should make it clear that there is an intent to associate as co-adventurers for a defined purpose, and it should spell out a joint interest in the subject matter of the venture, a sharing of profits and losses, and a right to an accounting. The mere ownership of property as joint tenants or tenants in common will not result in a joint venture.

As already noted, a joint venture is ordinarily treated as a partnership for tax purposes [Sec. 761 of the Code; Regs. 301.7701]. As with other entities taxed as partnerships, if there are too many corporate characteristics, the entity will be considered as association taxable as a corporation. Partnership treatment combines the advantage of an immediate write-off of losses with the elimination of the second tax at the corporate level. However, a corporation may offer other tax advantages which may in a particular situation outweigh the tax advantages of a partnership-joint venture arrangement. Before deciding on either form, both forms should be considered.

A joint venture may be in the form of an association of individuals, partnerships, or corporations, or some combination of these. Some joint ventures actually incorporate, sometimes for tax reasons and sometimes to avoid unlimited liability exposure.

[¶1235] USING A SUBCHAPTER S CORPORATION AS A PARTNER TO INCREASE TAX AND BUSINESS FLEXIBILITY

If your real estate corporation qualifies and elects to be treated as a Subchapter S corporation, instead of being taxed as a separate entity, its taxable income is picked up by its stockholders, and each pays his individual tax on the portion of the corporations's income allocable to him. (Corporations, not electing Sub S are discussed subsequently.) The same is true for losses whether or not the profits are actually distributed to the stockholders. Each picks up his pro rata share (just as partners do). Profits you pick up without getting actual distribution increase the basis for your stock, and losses passed on to you decrease your basis [Sec. 1376(a) and (b) of the Code].

To get the benefits of Subchapter S treatment, the election must be properly made, and the corporation must meet all the statutory requirements. Here, a real estate corporation with substantial rental income—so-called "passive investment income" — can run into trouble, since a corporation which derives more than 20 percent of its gross receipts from passive investment income is not qualified to receive Subchapter S treatment [Sec. 1372(e)(5) of the Code]. Another limitation is the requirement that the corporation must have no more than ten shareholders (15 limit after 5 years of existence).

The formation of a partnership using a Subchapter S corporation as a partner (general or limited) is one method of coping with these limitations. This type of setup offers sound tax-planning opportunities, since it can be used to overcome the serious limitations in using a Subchapter S corporation as the basic form of doing business and affords the operator increased all-around flexibility.

Flexibility in Capital Structure and Financing. The capital structure of a Subchapter S corporation limits financing possibilities. As we have seen, you can have only ten shareholders (except as noted where the number of shareholders can go to 15 after 5 years of existence). (Also, if a shareholder dies, new shareholders-beneficiaries can generally come in up to a maximum shareholder rule for the company of 15 [Sec. 1371(c) of the Code].) Using a partnership as the basic form of doing business and Subchapter S corporations as some of the partners overcomes these limitations while retaining the tax benefits of the Subchapter S election. *The Tax Reform Act of 1976,* adds a few exceptions for special trusts, such as a revocable trust made during life, temporary use (60 days) if a testamentary (death) trust and a voting trust. For details see Section 1371(f) of the Code.

The partnership is not strapped with limitations on the number or type of participants. There usually is no statutory limit on the number of partners, with many jurisdictions allowing corporations to be partners (this is the approach taken by the Uniform Partnership Act). Thus, by using the partnership, participation by trusts, regular corporations, and other Subchapter S corporations is possible. Also, a greater number of participants can invest in the enterprise. Under this setup, each corporation would proportionately pick up as its income or loss the net profits or losses of the partnership. This income or loss would, in turn, pass through to the individual stockholders.

Opportunities for Sheltering Passive Income. If your corporation has sufficient passive investment income to put in jeopardy its right to Subchapter S treatment, the active income from a partnership of which it is a member can be sufficient to prevent the corporation's disqualification. As a partner, the corporation's distributive share of the partnership income is not deemed to be passive income unless the underlying income of the partnership falls into the passive category [Reg. §1.61-13(a)]. By the same token, if the partnership produces passive income, the corporation's active income from other sources may be sufficient to prevent its disqualification.

Flexibility in Management, Transferability, and Taxes. In addition to the advantages already mentioned, you also have the basic advantages of using Subchapter S corporations. These include limited personal liability, continuity of entity, transferability of interests, centralization of management, choice of fiscal year, passthrough of start-up losses, single tax (including capital gains), and avoidance of personal holding company and accumulated earnings penalties.

Subchapter S Shareholder's Basis. The shareholders' basis is limited to what they invest. If, for example, a Subchapter S corporation applies for a mortgage, a share of the mortgage is *not* picked up as part of the shareholder's basis. The shareholder's basis is not increased by the mortgage debt, and the amount that may be passed through as a loss is limited even though a shareholder endorses the Subchapter S corporation's mortgage notes. (Compare this to a partnership!)

As to a partner, when a loss cannot be taken because of a zero basis in the partnership interest, the loss may be taken at some later date if the basis is increased. As to a stockholder in a Subchapter S corporation, the results are different. If, because of low basis, the loss is not taken in the year it is incurred, it is lost forever and cannot be used at some future date. This is one of the disadvantages of using a Subchapter S corporation where the investors have a small investment and, consequently, a small basis [Sec. 1374 (c)(2) of the Code].

Avoiding Pitfalls. Where the Subchapter S corporation is used to shift income to lower-bracket members of a family, IRS may attempt to reallocate income where the allocation is unreasonable or unrealistic [Sec. 482 of the Code].

[¶1236] TAX-SHELTERED PROFITS IN APARTMENT BUILDINGS

The *1969 Tax Reform Act* favors apartment buildings and makes this type of investment a good tax shelter. Investments in apartment buildings are set up in the form of limited partnerships for two good reasons: (1) During the period of construction and in the early years of operation when there are "losses"; the partnership form permits the passthrough of the losses to the investors. They can be used to offset the investors' other income and so save taxes. (2) When the loss period is over, the partnership form avoids the double taxation inherent in the corporate form. There is no tax at the partnership level as in the corporate set up — only a single tax at the investor level.

We put the term "losses" in quotes because as in any real estate deal where depreciation is an element of the "loss," it's only a paper or tax loss. In fact, all the time the property is being depreciated for tax purposes, it may in actuality be increasing in value. And, the tax "loss" will actually keep money in the investor's pocket which he would otherwise have to pay to IRS. The higher the investor's tax bracket, the more tax money he saves.

A private offering may be made of limited partnership interests specifying the total dollar amount of the partnership interests, the number of units offered, and the dollar amount of each unit. The project will be described; a summary rundown will be given on the project, financing, building, manager, architect, general partners and their contributions, limited partners and their contributions, and allocation of benefits and liabilities. A description of the proposed offering will be given; projections of tax benefits and a schedule of income and expense items and other pertinent date will be given.

Accelerated Depreciation. The availability of accelerated depreciation is the big thing in these deals. On new residential projects, 200 percent declining-balance is still available. Thus, if you use a 33-1/3-year life and 200 percent-declining-balance depreciation, the partnership gets and passes through to the investors, as a depreciation deduction in the very first year 6 percent of the entire cost of the building. This is so even though the building is 90 percent or more financed with borrowed money so that the 6 percent may actually represent 50 percent or more of the equity investment.

Special Benefits in Low- and Moderate-Income Housing. The tax shelter in real estate deals may be offset by the recapture (by methods faster than straight-line) of depreciation as ordinary income when you sell or dispose of the property in certain ways. Tax Reform Acts removed the limitation on recapture as to all real estate, except federally or municipally assisted low- and moderate-income rental housing. This, offers additional incentive for investing in low- and moderate-income housing.

Equity Buildup. The investor not only gets the tax shelter, but he is building equity, too. The mortgage is being amortized, the land value figures to increase, and, as we have suggested, the building itself despite depreciation for tax purposes, may indeed be expected actually to appreciate in value.

High Leverage Made Higher. Apartment houses have high loan value, and federally and municipally assisted low- and moderate-income deals have the highest loan values and so the highest leverage. The loan may, in some cases, be as high as 95 percent of the recognized cost of the project.

[¶1237]   TAX AND OTHER BENEFITS FOR INVESTORS FROM NET-LEASE DEALS

High-tax-bracket investors are often offered net lease investments that give them the chance to cash in on a highly leveraged setup, great tax shelter, and secure real estate backed by a high-credit-rated tenant.

How Investors Reap Great Tax and Other Benefits. The lease is set up so that the rental payments over the lease term are sufficient to amortize from 90 to

100 percent of the debt and, in addition, to provide a cash flow on the equity investment. The investors share in the cash flow that the project produces and also reap a harvest of tax benefits that are especially advantageous to high-tax-bracket investors.

The large tax deductions against ordinary income generated by depreciation and interest deductions create paper losses which, especially in the early years of the project, are sufficient to shelter the investors' income, not only from the project but also from other sources.

Where the deal involves net-leased residential rental real estate, the investors benefit from the especially high tax deductions against ordinary income generated by the project. In effect, what occurs is that ordinary income is converted into capital gains. The 200 percent-declining-balance and the sum-of-the-years-digits depreciation methods are open.

If the property that is net leased is new commercial property, the fastest method of depreciation open is the 150 percent-declining-balance method, and all excess depreciation is recaptured on the sale of the property.

Beware of Investment Interest Limitations. Under Section 163(d) of the Code, investment interest under the *Tax Reform Act of 1976* is limited even further.

[¶1238] LIMITATIONS ON INTEREST DEDUCTIONS: TAX REFORM ACT OF 1976

The limitation under Section 163(d)(1) of the Code provides that investment interest shall be limited to $10,000 (as opposed to the old $25,000 rule of investment interest) in excess of net investment income and certain other items.

Net investment income is defined in Section 163(d)(3)A. (It is, generally defined as investment income, excluding the interest deduction factor.) [*See also* Sec. 163(d)(1)(B) of the Code.]

If the taxpayer is a trust, the $10,000 amount does not apply and the limitation is net investment income.

Under Section 163(d)(2), the amount of disallowed investment interest for any taxable year is treated as investment interest paid or accrued in succeeding years.

In addition to the amounts noted, the taxpayer is allowed an additional $15,000 worth of investment interest deduction where interest is incurred by the taxpayer to acquire stock in a corporation or a partnership interest, where the taxpayer, his spouse, and his children own or acquire fifty percent or more of all capital interests in the partnership. (Actually, the $15,000 is the highest amount, because the addition is $15,000 *or* the amount of interest paid or accrued on the indebtedness to acquire the interest.) [Sec. 163(d)(7) of the Code.] Generally speaking, the effective date is for tax years beginning after December 31, 1975.

The rules, prior to the *Tax Reform Act of 1976,* will continue as to the definition of investment interest [Sec. 163(d) of the Code]. This includes interest paid or accrued on debt to carry property held for investment (passive), as opposed to an active business.

Investment interest limitations apply to investment items, not active businesses. (It may be an interpretive problem to determine whether the business is *active.*)

Investment interest *also* includes transactions subject to a *net* lease, as defined under 163(d)(4)! (A net lease is defined as a lease where the ordinary and necessary business expenses [Sec. 162 of the Code] are less than 15 percent of the rental income *or* the lessor is guaranteed in whole or in part against loss of income)! It should be apparent that this will have an adverse effect on net leases.

How Lessee Also Benefits. A quick listing of some of the important reasons why a high-credit corporate-lessee would go for a net-lease deal would include the following:

1. Leasing rather than owning can result in favorable government contract cost allocations and profit computations.
2. Assuming that the leased property is not shown on the corporation's balance sheet, improved asset-to-liability financial ratios result.
3. Leasing rather than owning can avoid debt indenture restrictions and limitations.
4. In effect, 100 percent financing can be obtained through a leasing arrangement.
5. The lease effectively converts the cost of nonamortizable elements (intangibles, land, etc.) into tax-deductible charges.

How to Handle Renewal and Purchase Options. Since the lease arrangement does not permit the lessee to benefit from the residual value of the property, the parties can include in their agreement an option to purchase the property or an option to extend or renew the lease. It is important to avoid fixing unrealistically low figures here. Otherwise, the transaction may be treated as a financing deal rather than as a true lease, in which event the investors would be held to be lenders rather than owners and therefore not entitled to depreciation deductions.

[¶1239] PARTNERSHIP ORGANIZATION AND SYNDICATION FEES

There was no prior statutory law, per se, in this area. The issue was whether the partnership syndication fees and organization fees would be currently deductible or whether they must be capitalized and amortized over some period of time. There have been numerous cases in this area which have affected the deductibility of these items. The deductibility was limited in *Jackson E. Cagle, Jr.*, 63 T.C. 86 (1974).

Under the Tax Reform Act of 1976 provisions, the deductibility of syndication and organization fees is limited. Section 709(a) of the Code provides that no deduction is allowed with regard to the cost to *promote* the sale of an interest in the partnership.

Organization expenses are also limited under Section 709(b) of the Code. However, organization expenses may, at the election of the partnership, be written off over a sixty-month period.

Organization expenses are defined under Section 709(b)(2) of the Code to include expenditures which are incident to the creation of the partnership, chargeable to a capital account, and of a character which, if expended incident to the creation of the partnership, having an ascertainable life, would be amortized over such life.

These rules are generally effective for tax years beginning after December 31, 1975. However, there is authority for the position that syndication expenses were not deductible previously. In other words, this may have been just a clarifying amendment.

CHAPTER 13

Tax Treatment of
Real Estate Investment Trusts

ORGANIZING A REIT

To avoid being taxable as an association, a trust must show that either there are no associates or the trust was not formed to carry on a business and divide its profit [Reg. §301.7701-2(a)(2)]. (A real estate investment trust must also pass the income tests as set forth in Section 856(c) of the Code). (See below).

In the ordinary syndicate situation where promoters solicit investment in an enterprise, it is pretty clear that there are associates. And you are going to have a tough time showing there is no conduct of a business. So, it will be very hard to operate a syndicate as a trust, unless the trust can qualify for treatment as a real estate investment trust. The corporate characteristics are normally present.

To be entitled to obtain the special "conduit" tax treatment afforded to REIT's, a REIT must comply with all the statutory requirements. These requirements are somewhat modified by the *Tax Reform Act of 1976*. They are as follows:

1. *Unincorporated Trust or Association.* It must be a common-law business trust, having all the attributes of a corporation. It cannot be either a corporation or a limited partnership. [Except see #5, *infra.*]

2. *At least 100 Beneficial Owners.* It must have at least 100 beneficial owners. (This, alone, may kill the use of a REIT for most investors.) Owners can include individuals, trusts, estate, partnerships, and corporations.

3. *Transferable Shares.* Ownership of a REIT must be evidenced by transferable shares or by transferable certificates of beneficial ownership. (Again, many small groups will not choose a REIT due to this requirement.)

4. *Management by Trustees.* The trustees may be individuals or corporations and may hold property in their own name or in the name of a nominee. The trustees must hold legal title to the trust property and have continuing and exclusive authority over management of the trust's properties and affairs.

5. *Association Taxable as a Corporation Except for REIT Provisions.* A corporation, prior to the *Tax Reform Act of 1976,* could qualify as a REIT. On the other hand, a REIT could not qualify either unless it would (apart from the REIT provisions) be considered as if it was a corporation for tax purposes under Reg. §301.7701-2. The *Tax Reform Act of 1976* now allows corporations to qualify, excluding banks and insurance compaies.

6. *No Active Business Enterprise.* A REIT is a public investment vehicle and is not intended to participate actively in business. Again, this may destroy the effective use of a REIT for many practitioners. Consequently, it must limit itself to a passive position. A REIT previously could not hold property primarily for sale to customers in the ordinary course of trade or business. The *Tax Reform Act of 1976* will not disqualify such REIT, but it will tax, at 100 percent the income from such property [Section 857(b)(6) of the Code]. In addition, less than 30 percent of the annual gross income of a REIT can be derived from sales of securities held for less than long-term and sales of real estate held for less than four years (except for involuntary conversions).

7. *Personal Holding Company Limitation.* A REIT cannot be more than 50 percent owned by five or fewer individuals. A trust cannot qualify as a REIT if it is a personal holding company. (With this restriction, many investors will choose another entity.)

8. *Election.* A trust must elect to be treated as a REIT on its tax return for the first taxable year in which it wants the treatment, even though it may have otherwise qualified for a prior year. An election once made is irrevocable for all succeeding taxable years. If an electing REIT does not distribute 90 percent of its ordinary income or does not comply with the other requirements, it will be taxed in that year as a corporation, except as modified by the Tax Reform Act of 1976. (See paragraph 1302). The Act allows a deficiency dividend procedure, which if applicable, avoids disqualification. [Sec. 859 and 6697 of the Code.]

9. *Distribution of Income.* A REIT must distribute annually to its shareholders at least 90 percent of its ordinary taxable income. (This will go up to 95 percent after 1979. *Tax Reform Act of 1976* [Sec. 856(c)(2) and 857(a)(1) of the Code; *see* infra ¶1304]. The trust then pays a tax only on the income that it retains. If it distributes all its income, it pays no tax. To the extent that it distributes capital gains to its shareholders, no tax is payable by

the trust. On retained long-term capital gains, it pays the capital gains tax.

[¶1302] TAX ADVANTAGES OFFERED BY REIT TO ITS INVESTORS

REITs enable small investors to get the tax and economic advantages of real estate investments which might otherwise be available only to large investors. REITs spread the risk among many investors and provide diversification (as to type and location) of investments and professional management. By pooling the resources of many individuals, they enable investors to finance projects they could not undertake singly. They also provide liquidity by establishing a market for their shares.

Proper use of a REIT means that you can set up an organization with the attributes of a corporation (centralized management, limited liability, continuity of interest, and transferability of shares) and, at the same time, you can get single-tax treatment for the beneficiaries of the trust, similar to the tax treatment given to partners in a large-scale partnership (except that losses cannot be passed through to the beneficiaries).

The market value of the properties that a REIT carries in its portfolio usually will not reflect the accelerated depreciation that the REIT takes for these properties. So, the REIT can make substantial distributions to its shareholders out of its net cash flow. Given professional and skilled management, the investments made by a REIT should perform on a relatively high level. Since REITs have a good deal of flexibility in timing their sales, they're in a position to select the most favorable time to sell. (A REIT must hold a real estate asset for four years before selling to get capital gain treatment.)

Since, as stated above, a qualified REIT gets ''conduit'' tax treatment only if it annually distributes at least 90 percent (except as noted) of its ordinary taxable income to its shareholders, an investment in a REIT is most attractive to one looking for current income. In effect, REIT shareholders benefit from all the tax shelter that real estate offers, including deductions for interest payments, depreciation, and operating expenses; and when they get their annual cash distribution, only a small part of it might be taxable as ordinary income. The rest may come to them tax free as a return of capital or part tax free and part taxable at capital gain rates.

A REIT may designate as ''capital gains distribution'' only the excess of its net long-term capital gains over its net short-term capital losses, so that every distribution of this kind is long term. The shareholder may report it as a long-term gain without regard to his individual holding period. Shareholders are not allowed any deductions, credits, or exclusions for these distributions.

Shareholders are treated almost the same as real estate partners, with one important difference: Partners can pick up their shares of a partnership tax loss to the extent of their respective basis. But losses of a REIT are not distributed to its shareholders, and it can have no operating loss carryover.

Late Dividends. A REIT may meet the 90 percent rule by distributing some of the dividends to the shareholders in its next taxable year. [*See* Secs. 859 and 6697 of the Code, added by the *Tax Reform Act of 1976,* which liberalized this rule; see also *Supra.*] Thus, under Section 859 of the Code, a dividend deficiency rule allows qualifying distributions to issue by the corporation in subsequent years, if an adjustment results (i.e., determination by Court) which causes an increase in the dollars that the REIT was required to pay out to comply with the 90 percent rule, noted above, or causes a decrease in the amount of dividends that were already distributed for that particular year. (This rule applies if no fraud existed.) If the correct adjustment for distributions is made, the REIT is not disqualified [Sec. 859(g)].

[¶1303]   **HOW REIT INCOME IS TAXED**

As already pointed out, a REIT can be treated as a corporation and be subject to the corporate income tax rates, unless it annually distributes 90 percent (except as noted) or more of its ordinary income or otherwise meets the tests noted earlier. As a qualified REIT, it only pays a tax on the income that it retains and does not distribute as dividends. If it distributes all of its income, it pays no tax. While the trust pays tax at the favorable capital gains rate on long-term capital gains, a qualified REIT avoids tax to the extent it distributes the capital gains to the beneficiaries.

Beneficiaries: The ordinary income of the trust that is distributed to beneficiaries is taxable to them as ordinary income. Beneficiaries are not allowed any deductions, credits, or exclusions for these dividends received. Long-term capital gain distributions received by beneficiaries are taxed to them as capital gains.

[¶1304]   **REAL ESTATE INVESTMENT TRUSTS —**
        SUMMARY OF THE TAX REFORM ACT OF 1976 CHANGES

The earlier mentioned rules have been somewhat modified by the Tax Reform Act of 1976. Although noted earlier, they can be summarized:

☐ The prior rules, under Sections. 856(c) and 857(b) of the Code provide that a REIT will lose its tax favored status if the source of its income does not consist of at least 90 percent gross receipts from passive income. Seventy-five percent of the gross income must also come from real estate.

— Under the *Tax Reform Act of 1976* new provisions, even though the REIT could not meet the 90 percent and 75 percent tests, this will not disqualify the REIT if it discloses this in the return, no fraud or evasion is involved, and the amount of failure to meet the test is small and is due to reasonable cause [Sec. 857(b)(5) of the Code]. The effective date is for tax years after the date of enactment (10/4/76). However, there are exceptions which the reader is advised to investigate.

— To the extent there is income different than as required, there is a 100 percent tax on the net income of the amount (difference) by which the REIT fails to meet the 90 percent and 75 percent tests.

☐ Under Section 856(g) of the Code, a new addition, the REIT can revoke its election for any tax year after the first tax year for which the election is made. However, if the election is revoked, there is a five-year waiting period for a new election. (This is similar to the five-year rule with Subchapter S Corporations.)

☐ New Sections 857(a) and (b)(6) of the Code provide that even if a REIT holds property for sale to customers in the ordinary course of business, (which it previously could not do), it will not lose its election. However, the REIT is subject to a 100 percent tax on the income from such property. This rule is effective for tax rules beginning after 10/4/76.

☐ Under Section 856(c)(2) of the Code, the current 90 percent gross income test for a REIT (a REIT must drive *90 percent of its income* from *passive* sources), will remain through 1979. After this date, the new percentage test for passive income is 95 percent.

☐ Also, after 1979, the REIT will be required to distribute 95 percent of its taxable income, as opposed to the current 90 percent rule; the latter rule will remain effective until the end of 1979 [Sec. 857(a)(1) of the Code].

☐ The definition of *rents* from real property has been changed under the *Tax Reform Act of 1976,* Section 856(d) of the Code. It now includes:

a. rents from interest in real property.

b. charges for services customarily furnished or rendered in connection with the rental of real property, whether separately stated or otherwise, and

c. rent attributable to personal property which is leased under, or in connection with the lease of real property, but only if the rent attributable to such property for the taxable year does not exceed 15 percent of the total rent for the taxable year attributable to both real and personal property under such lease. [Sec. 856(d)(1) of the Code].

☐ Sections 859 and 6697 are added to the Code to allow a deficiency dividend procedure. The prior law, before this amendment, provided for a requirement that 90 percent of the REIT taxable income be distributed in the REIT's year. The Act allows a procedure to correct a previous failure to make that distribution. This rule would apply assuming there is no fraud or evasion.

☐ Generally speaking, a REIT cannot use a net operating loss. However, if the REIT eliminates the election, it can utilize a carry forward of a net operating loss, for a loss which arises in the year in which it was a REIT. This rule allows for an 8 year carryforward, with some modifications [See Secs. 172(b)(1), (d)(7), and 857(b)(2) of the Code].

There is a new provision under Section 857(b)(3)(A) of the Code which allows the REIT, for years after 10/4/76, to offset its ordinary losses against undistributed net long term capital gain.

CHAPTER 14

Corporations

[¶1401]   TAX ASPECTS OF REAL ESTATE CORPORATIONS

The tax law offers the owners of closely held or family real estate corporations many new opportunities for using their corporations as wealthbuilding machines. There are many provisions to be watched and taken into account. Many affect the corporation directly; many, the individual owners; and many, both.

The following material focuses on the items the owners will need to be familiar with in order to extract maximum benefits and hold possible adverse effects to a minimum.

[¶1402] TAX FACTORS TO CONSIDER BEFORE INCORPORATING

In addition to these general economic and legal advantages, use of the corporate form involves a number of important tax considerations that must be taken into account in deciding what form of operations is best suited to your needs. For example:

(1) Corporations take their own deduction for charitable contributions, but the rate is only 5 percent.

(2) The corporation takes a deduction for funds it expends for its stockholder-employees, which it can accumulate in pension or profit-sharing trusts or use to pay for medical expenses, group term insurance, wage continuation plans, and health and accident insurance. These benefits are not taxable to the stockholder-employees, within specified limits.

(3) Compensation to officers and employee stockholders is subject to Social Security tax.

(4) Stockholders usually have freedom to assign their stock without consulting anyone, but earnings can't be assigned separately from the stock.

(5) Income is taxed to the corporation; stockholders are taxed only on dividends distributed to them, reduced by the dividend exclusion [Sec. 116 of the Code] and credit.

(6) Stockholders are not taxed on accumulations. However, a penalty tax (§531) may apply if the purpose is to avoid taxation and the accumulation is beyond $150,000.

(7) A corporation uses the alternative computation for capital gains [Sec. 1201 of the Code]; but, unlike for individuals, there's no deduction of 50 percent of the excess of long-term gain over short-term loss [Sec. 1202 of the Code].

(8) Exempt interest distributed by a corporation would be fully taxable income to the stockholders.

(9) Death benefits up to $5,000 can be received tax free by stockholder-employees' beneficiaries [Sec. 101 of the Code].

(10) Corporations are subject to various state taxes, although deductibility of these on the federal return lessens cost.

(11) After the 20 percent, 22 percent and 48 percent corporate rates in the individual rate brackets are reached, the corporation can be a temporary tax shelter.

(12) In the corporate form, a latent capital gains tax is paid when accumulated earnings are cashed in by liquidation or sale of stock. If stock is held until death and then sold by the family, capital gains tax on the accumulation of earnings is avoided, except as modified by the *Tax Reform Act of 1976.*

(13) The division of income among more than one corporation can bring substantial tax benefits.

You also may be able, beyond accumulations, to get some money to the shareholders without a dividend tax. This is done by setting up part of your capitalization as debts to the stockholders. Interest to the stockholders would be taxable to them but deductible to the corporation. Return of principal would not be income to the stockholder-creditors. But you have to be very careful here. Besides making sure that your securities (debts) have a fixed maturity date and all the other attributes of securities, you have to pass the thin-corporation hurdle. If the capitalization of the corporation is inadequate, the securities will be treated as stock. You may have to show that the "debt" was to be repaid in any case and not, as stock is, put at the risk of the venture.

[¶1403] INCORPORATING REAL ESTATE; TAX-FREE TRANSFER OF PROPERTY TO NEWLY ORGANIZED CORPORATION

Section 351 of the Code permits a tax-free transfer of real estate to a newly organized corporation if, immediately after the transfer, the individuals making the transfer have control, i.e., they own 80 percent or more of the value of all issued and outstanding stock.

Where, in addition to receiving stock on the transfer, the individuals also receive money, gain would be recognized but only to the extent of the money received.

The assumption of any mortgage debt by the corporation or the mere acquisition of property subject to a mortgage is *not* treated as money received from the individuals unless it can be shown that the principal purpose of the assumption or acquisition was tax avoidance or that it had no bona fide business purpose [Sec. 357(b) of the Code].

However, even absent these purposes, where the mortgage debt exceeds the transferor's basis for the property, the transferors are subject to tax on the transfer to the extent of such excess. If the property was a capital asset, the gain would be capital gain [Sec. 357(c) of the Code].

The basis of the stock received is the same as that of the property transferred decreased by any money received (assumption of liabilities or acquisition of property subject to the same — [Sec. 358(d) of the Code] and increased by the amount of any gain recognized [Sec. 358(a) of the Code].

There may, however, be some situations in which you would want to have a taxable transaction. This would occur if you owned the property individually and it appreciated substantially in value before you transferred it to the corporation, and the corporation contemplates a resale which would be taxed at ordinary income rates. With a taxable transaction, you could raise the basis of the property in the hands of the corporation at the cost of a capital gains tax to you, assuming you can show that you are not a dealer in the property. You might also want a taxable transaction where the corporation will have enough income to be taxed at the 48 percent bracket. Here you pay a capital gains tax, but the corporation then gets higher depreciation deductions to offset against its ordinary income.

You can set up a taxable transaction by giving more than 20 percent of the stock of the corporation to an outsider in exchange for services.

You also have to watch out for Section 1239 of the Code, which converts any gain on the sale of depreciable real estate by an individual to his controlled corporation (or between two controlled corporations) from capital gain into ordinary income. Control is effected through "related parties." Related parties include (1) a husband and wife, (2) an individual and a corporation, 80 percent or more in value of the outstanding stock of which is owned, directly or indirectly, (i.e., by a corporation, Sections 318 and 1239(b)(2)) by or for such individual, *or* (3) two or more corporations that meet the 80 percent test, noted.

In general, stock owned by a member of the family, as defined in Section 318, is deemed to be owned by the taxpayer, when testing for the 80 percent or more test as to corporation control.

Transfer of Mortgaged Property to Corporation. As indicated above, if you have a mortgage on property that exceeds your basis and transfer the property to your corporation in a tax-free exchange, the corporation assuming the mortgage or taking subject to it, you will have a tax on the transaction. The excess of the mortgage over your basis gives you a gain [Sec. 357(c) of the Code]. But you can have a tax even if the mortgage does not exceed your basis. That happens if the transfer was made to avoid tax or there was no bona fide business reason for the transfer. Then the amount of the mortgage is treated as boot and taxable to the extent it does not exceed gain [Sec. 357(b) of the Code].

[¶1404]   CAPITAL STRUCTURE OF CORPORATION

The major goal here is to keep the capital at a minimum. One popular method is to have the stockholders supply most of the capital by loans. The danger is that IRS will refuse to recognize the heavy debt capitalization as genuine [Sec. 385 of the Code]. In that case, it will declare the debt (or a substantial part of it) to be equity capital. Result? Payments made as interest will not be deductible and repayments of "debt" may be dividend income to the recipients. Likewise, the risk element will become perhaps greater than it should be in a new business.

Although IRS has recognized the validity of debt-equity ratios as high as 3 or 4 to 1, the "thin" capitalization problem remains a big tax worry.

One suggestion that may help calls for the stockholders to buy property and lease it to the corporation rather than lend the corporation the money to buy the property. The stockholders would put up some cash in exchange for stock in order to provide working capital. The rent charged for the property would have to be fair in amount, based on current market rates.

Since the corporation's financing would not be entirely equity, the "thin" capitalization danger might be eliminated. The stockholders get the same tax benefits they would have had with debt financing. They have the corporate protection they sought, without having to pay the corporate tax to get it.

The only difference is that corporate profits paid to them, instead of being deductible by the corporation as interest, would be deductible as rent. It is possible that, having put up whatever cash was necessary to acquire the property, the stockholders might not have enough funds left to furnish the working capital needed to properly launch the enterprise.

The obvious solution would be to borrow the money from a bank. The corporation might borrow this money with the stockholders as guarantors and the property as collateral. The guarantor feature is necessary because it is the stockholders who own the collateral.

[¶1405] TAX AND OTHER ADVANTAGES OF USING A CORPORATION

Acquiring property as an individual means only one tax on the profits. Property acquired in corporate form will eventually mean two taxes: one against the corporation, the other against the individual. However, there may be a saving in corporate owning for a high-bracket taxpayer.

1. If the profits can be held in the corporation without incurring either the personal holding company or accumulated earnings penalty surtax and the corporation remains in operation for the three-year period required to avoid the "collapsible" rules of [Sec. 341 of the Code], the individual tax will be only the 25 percent - 35 percent rules discussed earlier as to the capital gains rate payable on either sale or liquidation.

2. A great advantage in corporate ownership of real estate lies in the paying off of the mortgage principal. More of the earnings will be left after tax at the 48 percent corporate rate than after tax at a higher individual rate. More earnings left means more earnings to apply to amortization. This means a faster amortization and a smaller total interest bill, all without extra expense to the investor.

3. The timing of the incorporation of the real estate may be important where you are using accelerated depreciation and are in a high tax bracket. Depreciation deductions will be high in the early years and amortization low. If, as will likely be the case, this leaves you with a loss, it will be better to hold the property individually so that the loss can be used against heavily taxed individual income. As the depreciation deductions go down, amortization will be increasing. Eventually, closing of the gap will eliminate the annual loss. That is the point at which you should incorporate.

It frequently is advisable from an income-tax-savings point of view, depending on the tax brackets of the individuals involved and on the anticipated income to be derived from the property, to incorporate real estate. In this connection, consider, too, that the tax law (Subchapter S) allows incorporation while still retaining many of the tax benefits of an unincorporated business.

From an economic standpoint, the great appeal of the corporate form lies in the fact that the law treats a corporation as an entity in itself, apart from the identity of its stockholders. The general advantages (sometimes disadvantages) of the separate entity of the corporation can be summarized as follows:

1. It continues until dissolved by law (unless statute limits the time).

2. As a separate entity, it can sue and be sued, hold and deal in property.

3. A stockholder has no individual liability; only his capital contribution is involved (exception: some state laws subject bank stockholders to double liability).

4. Stock can ordinarily be sold or otherwise transferred at will.

5. Capital can be raised by the sale of new stock or bonds or other securities.

6. Authority is centered in a board of directors, acting by majority agreement.

7. As a separate entity, a corporation has credit possibility apart from stockholders; in a close corporation, stock is available as collateral.

8. The stockholders are not responsible; managers are employed.

9. A corporation is limited to the powers (express and implied) in its charter from the state.

[¶1406]   WHEN A DUMMY CORPORATION IS NOT TAXABLE AS A SEPARATE ENTITY

Property may be acquired in the name of a dummy for various reasons. For example, this may be done for the purpose of concealing ownership or to avoid liability. Sometimes, a dummy corporation is formed for the purpose of raising money on the property where the rate of interest charged would be usurious if the loan had been made to an individual.

If the corporation is disregarded for tax purposes, the actual parties in interest are taxed. Thus, the owners of the beneficial interest (usually the stockholders), rather than the corporation, report the income and deduct the losses on the realty investment. Where a dummy corporation actually does nothing but hold legal title and does not engage in any business activity, it probably will be disregarded. Whether a corporation will be treated as a viable entity for tax purposes is primarily a question of fact rather than of law. The question is determined according to such matters as the extent of corporate activity, the reasons for forming the corporation, evidence of the parties' intention that the corporation hold the property for the benefit of the stockholders, etc. Another consideration is whether IRS or the taxpayer is contending that the corporation is a viable one. It seems that IRS is given greater latitude in arguing that the corporate form should prevail.

While each case must stand or fall on its own particular facts and circumstances, the following rundown on leading cases dealing with the subject should give you guideposts as to what factors the courts consider to be important in deciding the issues. The rundown is partially based on a talk given at the

Practising Law Institute by Mr. Leonard Blank, a New York tax attorney associated with the firm of David Berdon & Company, certified public accountants.

In the following case, the corporation was treated as a viable entity:

Moline Properties, Inc. [319 US 436, 1943]: In this case the taxpayer tried to bypass the corporation and have gains on sale of real estate taxed on an individual basis. The corporation was formed as a security device, and stock was transferred to a voting trust to secure a loan. While corporate stock was issued, no corporate books were maintained. But the corporation mortgaged property, entered into a lease, and rent checks were made payable to the corporation. In determining that the corporation was a viable entity for tax purposes, the Court pointed out that, at the time of its creation, exercise of control by the stockholder was realizable, since stock was held by a voting trustee appointed by the creditor. What's more, the corporation refinanced the mortgage and entered into a lease.

In the following cases, the corporate entity was disregarded:

(a) *Stewart Forshay* [20 BTA 537, 1930]: The Commissioner sought to tax income to the corporation. Here, stock was issued, but there was no corporate bank account. The Court laid emphasis on an agreement that the corporation could act only on the written authorization of stockholders, on a beneficial ownership resolution, and that leases and contracts were in individual names. Under New York law, the property transferred to the corporation was a mere trust.

(b) *Moro Realty Holding Corp.*, [25 BTA 1135, aff'd 65 F.2d 1013 (2d Cir. 1947)]: In this case, the Commissioner sought to tax income from sales to the corporation. The corporation was formed as an agency for carrying out a syndicate agreement. No stock was issued; no corporate books or bank account was maintained. There was no resolution as to beneficial ownership, but the syndicate agreement stated that the beneficial interest was in the syndicate. The Court stressed this last point, along with the absence of corporate activity.

(c) *John A. Mulligan* [16 TC 1489, (1951)]: IRS sought to tax the income from sales to the corporation. While the corporation originally was a functioning corporation, at the death of the sole slockholder, it was kept at surrogate's direction. Stock was issued, and mortgages were held. The corporation entered into leases, and rent checks were made payable to it. The Court emphasized the surrogate's supervision and that the estate insulated beneficiaries from liability.

(d) *Seattle Hardware Co. v. Squire*, [83 F. Supp. 106, (D.C. Wash., aff'd 181 F.2d 188 9th Cir. 1950)]: The taxpayer sought to establish a valid sale to it by the corporation so as to establish a higher basis. The corporation was organized to avoid shareholder liability during construction. Neither corporate books nor a corporate bank account was maintained. While the corporation mortgaged property, proceeds were paid to a related corporation. The Court pointed out that when the property was "sold" to a related corporation, the proceeds were never paid to the "dummy" corporation. The corporation was a nominal holder; the facts did not support a separate entity.

(e) *National Investors Corp. v. Hoey,* [144 F.2d 466, (2 Cir. 1944)]: Here, the Court held that the corporate entity, although valid when formed, in effect ceased when the reason for its existence terminated. The stockholder sought to deduct the loss on liquidation of the corporation. The loss was due to a decrease in value of securities held by the shell corporation. The corporation was organized for the purpose of consolidating with three subsidiaries and to hold subsidiary shares pending approval of the plan. Stock was issued. The corporation received income in the form of dividends from securities. The Court remanded the case to allow for a determination as to whether a loss occurred when the corporation was viable.

Recently the courts have illustrated to taxpayers that nominee status will be difficult to obtain. Nominee status was denied in *Collins* [514 F2d 1282 (5th Cir. 1975)] and *Wm. Strong* [66 TC 3 (1976)]. *See also* TMM, 76-21, "Straw Corporations, Recent Developments," BNA, par & 1 (1976), Levine, *Supra,* Sec. 798 of the Code.

[¶1407]   CORPORATE TAX RATES

The normal temporary income tax rates for a corporation range from 20 percent on taxable income of $25,000 or less, to 22 percent on the next $25,000, to 48 percent on any excess over $50,000. The alternative capital gains rate for corporations is 30 percent. However, those corporations with taxable incomes of less than or equal to $50,000 (including capital gains) still pay a tax at the rate of 20 percent (on first $25,000) or 22 percent (on next $25,000) on such income.

For individuals, the **alternative** capital gains rate is 25 percent on the first $50,000 and 35 percent on the excess.

These differences in the individual and corporate rate, along with the minimum tax on excess tax preferences (which include the untaxed portion of capital gains), the possibility of increasing exemptions from this tax by dividing tax preferences between shareholders and the corporation, and the 50 percent ceiling on earned and other types of income create possible opportunities for tax savings which you will need to explore.

[¶1408]   OWNERSHIP OF UNIMPROVED PROPERTY

Real estate is often acquired for purposes of development. Real estate held in corporate form lends itself more readily than that held in individual ownership to qualification as "property used in the trade or business" for purposes of nonrecognition of gain resulting from an involuntary conversion [Sec. 1231 of the Code]. The special rules for determining capital gains and losses for business property may make it advisable to keep ownership of business property out of an individual taxpayer's hands. But Section 337 (nonrecognition of gain in connection with corporate liquidation) does not apply to the liquidation of a "collapsible" corporation [Sec. 337(C)(1)(A) of the Code].

[¶1409] DEALERS

The profits of a dealer who holds real estate primarily for sale to customers is taxed at ordinary income rates, rather than at capital gain rates. When a dealer buys realty for investment purposes, he must separate his investment property from his other holdings in order to receive capital gain treatment on a subsequent resale of his investment property. If the dealer is a corporation, investment property might be acquired in the individual form; if the dealer is an individual, investment property might be acquired in the corporate form.

[¶1410] TAXABLE GAIN ON SALE OF CORPORATE PROPERTY

It is quite common for investment real estate to be held by a corporation rather than in the name of an individual. When the time comes to sell the property, however, corporate ownership can create problems. This is so because the corporation is a separate taxable entity. If it sells the property at a gain, it will have to pay a tax, and any subsequent distribution to the stockholder will normally be treated as a dividend, taxable a second time to the stockholder individually. Of course, the distribution problem is avoided if the corporation reinvests the proceeds itself, but this is often not feasible or desirable.

There are a number of ways of avoiding the double tax where (as is frequently the case) the property to be sold constitutes the sole or principal asset of the corporation. The chief alternatives are:

1. Sale of the corporate stock, which can result in a single long-term capital gain if the stock has been held long-term;
2. Complete liquidation of the corporation followed by a sale of the property by the stockholders so that no corporate tax is payable;
3. A 12-month liquidation which permits the corporation to sell the property and make distributions in liquidation after the sale without paying any corporate tax [Sec. 337 of the Code].
4. A one-month liquidation which permits the stockholders to avoid a tax on the unrealized appreciation of corporate property at the price of paying ordinary income tax on accumulated earnings received in liquidation [Sec. 333 of the Code].

Each of these alternatives has pitfalls which must be avoided. In addition, the special rule dealing with collapsible corporations must be considered whenever a sale of corporate property is planned. In brief, this rule provides that if the corporation held the property less than three years, capital gain *may* be converted into ordinary income [Sec. 341 of the Code].

[¶1411]   **MANAGEMENT COMPENSATION**

One way to cut corporate income taxes is to siphon off the corporate "profits" by paying yourself and your co-owners nice salaries. The rub is that if IRS rules that you have paid yourself unreasonable sums and can make its ruling stick, you subject yourself to a form of double taxation. The corporation loses its right to deduct the excessive compensation or payments made to you; but you, as officer-owner, still have to pay a tax on them on the theory that they amount to constructive dividends.

How Reasonableness of Compensation Is Determined: IRS, as already noted, requires that the compensation be reasonable. Reasonable compensation is "only such amount as would ordinarily be paid for like services by like enterprises under like circumstances." Circumstances to be considered are those existing on the date when the services are contracted rather than when the contract is questioned [Reg. §1.162-7(b)(3)]. No single factor is decisive. Circumstances considered important by the courts in determining reasonableness of compensation are: the employee's special qualifications and availability of others to fill the job; the nature, extent, and scope of his work; the size and complexities of the business; a comparison of salaries paid with gross and net income; prevailing rates of compensation for comparable positions, comparably performed in comparable concerns; the salary policy of the taxpayer as to other similarly situated employee; the arm's length element in the compensation deal; consideration for past services and compensation in prior years; and comparison of salaries paid with employee's stock ownership.

Advantages of Corporate Formation Where Low-Bracket Taxpayer Draws Salary: The corporate form may be justified if a low-bracket taxpayer manages the realty and draws a salary for his services. However, the compensation must be reasonable or it will be disallowed, as was true in part in *Langley Park Apts* [44 TC 474 aff'g 359 F 2d 427 (4th Cir. 1966)], *Perlmutter* [373 F.2d 45, (10th Cir. 1967) aff's 44 RC 38].

How Agreement to Reimburse Corporation for Excess Compensation Avoids Risk of Double Taxation: The officer receiving the compensation from the real estate corporation can enter into a reimbursement agreement with the corporation under which he is bound to reimburse the corporation for salary or payments made to him that are disallowed as a deductible expense for federal income tax purposes. If he gets a deduction for his repayment to the corporation, he is in virtually the same position he was in before the payment was made to him, since the deduction will offset a like amount of inclusion of the original payment in his taxable income. Also, since the amount of the excess is returned to the corporation, it, too, comes out even [Rev. Rul. 69-115, CB 1969-1,50]. However, recent cases and the IRS position seem to support this reimbursement agreement if it is made before the refund payments are made and if the refund is binding on the employee. The agreement should also reflect in board resolutions.

Deductibility of Bonuses Paid in Excess of Authority Granted in Minutes: When a closely held corporation pays a bonus to working stockholders which is more than that authorized by its minutes, the Tax Court says that only the amount authorized can be considered a bonus, but the Tenth Circuit says that the amount actually paid is deductible where the sole stockholder approved the payment [*L.R. Schmaus Co.,* 406 F 2d. 1044 (7th Cir. 1969), rev'g TC Memo 1967-197].

[¶1412]   MAXIMUM TAX ON EARNED INCOME

Under the provisions of Section 1348 of the Code, the maximum tax rate applicable to Personal Service income is 50 percent instead of the 70 percent maximum rate applicable to other types of income. Under the *Tax Reform Act of 1976,* for years after 1976, the maximum tax applies to annuities, deferred compensation arrangements of some types and pensions, *non-lump sum.*

For purposes of Section 1348 of the Code, earned income includes not only compensation for personal services but reasonable remuneration for someone engaged in a trade or business in which both capital and personal services are material income-producing factors. In this context, reasonable remuneration cannot exceed 30 percent of the taxpayer's share of the net profits of the business. The maximum tax rate is not available if the taxpayer uses income averaging or if the taxpayer is married and files a separate return.

The maximum rate previously applied to earned income was reduced by tax preferences *in excess of $30,000* in the current year or the average tax preferences in excess of $30,000 in the current and the previous four years, whichever was greater. Thus, tax-preference income over $30,000 reduced earned income on a dollar-for-dollar basis. However, under the *Tax Reform Act of 1976,* personal service income is reduced for deductions allocable to the earned income and *all* tax preference items, *not* just those above $30,000 [Sec. 1348(b)(2) of the Code; *see also* ¶601, *supra*].

Some Choices Where Earned Income and Tax-Preference Income Are High. Suppose you have high earned income from a real estate development company and also have high tax-preference income from investment properties in the form of fast amortization, capital gains, and accelerated depreciation. Do you go for income averaging? Or do you take the maximum ceiling on earned income? As we've already pointed out, you can't have both. If your tax-preference income is sufficiently high to offset your earned income, the maximum tax rate for earned income will be of no use to you, so that you might do better to use income averaging.

Again, suppose your earned income from your development company is offset by your excess tax-preference income from your investment properties (including the untaxed half of capital gains). You might find that although you won't be subject to the minimum tax on tax-preference income, you will be subjecting a large part of your earned income to tax at regular rates, thus substantially boosting your effective tax rate. Here, the various methods for deferring gain may be pursued.

Salaries, Dividends, and Loans From Your Real Estate Corporation; Accumulated Earnings.

The provisions of Section 1348 of the Code bring to light two elements for consideration: the maximum tax rate for personal service income and the requirement, where capital is a material factor, that the compensation paid not only be reasonable but also not come to more than 30 percent of the taxpayer's share of the net profits of the business. In making the determination whether to pay out earnings in the form of salaries or dividends or keep them in the corporation with the idea of building up capital values, the figures will have to be kicked around; and the individual tax rate, maximum tax rate, corporate tax rate, and tax on dividends on the corporate and individual level will all have to be considered along with the penalty tax for unreasonable accumulations [Sec. 531 et. seq. of the Code].

If income is paid out in the form of a *dividend,* tax is imposed not only at the corporate level but also at the individual level. If paid out in the form of *salary* and the amount paid out does not exceed the statutory maximum and is not unreasonable, tax is payable only at the individual level, and the amount of this salary is deductible as an ordinary expense of the corporation.

You may be able to withdraw funds from your closely held real estate corporation in the form of loans from the corporation rather than in the form of compensation or dividends. But you have to make sure that the loans won't be treated by IRS as taxable dividend distributions. Accordingly, withdrawals should be properly and timely recorded as loans. The obligation to repay should be evidenced by promissory notes with fixed maturities and reasonable interest rates. The interest should actually be paid. Deductions for interest paid should be taken on your individual return. (If you use the funds for business purposes, you won't be confronted with the excess investment interest problem.) Interest payments should be shown as an income item in the corporation's return. There should be regular payments on account of the sums withdrawn. The financial statements of the corporation, particularly those furnished banks and creditors, should reflect the loans.

[¶1413]   "TAX-FREE" DISTRIBUTION
                         IN TODAY'S TAX SET UP

Years ago it was the accepted practice that many real estate corporations regularly made distributions that were tax free because of the use of accelerated depreciation. The depreciation deductions kept the earnings and profits at a level where they would not be exceeded by the distributions. The distributions were considered tax free because they were not deemed to be out of "earnings and profits." The result was the avoidance of tax at ordinary income rates (tax-free "dividends") in exchange for a possible postponed tax at capital gains rates (proceeds on the sale of the stock).

The 1969 tax law changed the picture. (The *Tax Reform Act of 1976*, although sweeping, did not change this picture further.) For the purpose of computing its earnings and profits, a corporation must deduct depreciation using the straight-line method or a similar method providing for ratable reductions of depreciation over the useful life of the asset. Such similar ratable methods would include units of production and machine hours but (except in unusual personal property cases) would not include the so-called "forecast of income" method.

In effect, this conforms the law regarding depreciation to present practice regarding depletion. Regulation §1.312-6(c)(1) provides that cost depletion must be used in determining earnings and profits of a corporation that uses percentage depletion in computing its taxable income.

The provision introduced by the 1969 law also applies to corporations which use the rapid methods of amortization under Sec. 168, 169 or 184 of the Code; but it is not intended to affect the amount of depreciation that may be deducted by a corporation under Section 167 or 179 of the Code or the amortization deduction allowable under Section 168, 169, or 184 of the Code in determining taxable income.

Similarly, the provision does not affect the computation of real estate investment trust taxable income in determining whether the trust paid dividends equal to or in excess of 90 percent of its taxable income; but the provision will apply to a real estate investment trust for the purpose of computing its earnings and profits and, therefore, the taxability of distribution to shareholders or holders of beneficial interests in such a trust.

When property depreciated under this rule is sold, the amount of gain or loss taken into earnings and profits is to be adjusted to compensate for any difference between the tax return depreciation deductions and the earnings and profits depreciation deductions up to the time of sale.

[¶1414]   **LOSS OFFSET AND CAPITAL LOSS CARRYBACK**

Sometimes a real estate investment is expected to show a loss, especially in the first years of operation. If the property is acquired by a corporation owning other properties, the corporation can use the loss to offset other income. Unless such a situation exists, however, losses won't pay off in a corporation except as carryovers to offset future income. If the property is acquired in the individual form, the loss can be used to offset the individual's other income. Thus an individual might be able to lower his tax bracket by acquiring the property in his own name. The corporate loss may, however, be available to the individual stockholders if the corporation is eligible to and does elect Subchapter S.

Capital Loss Carryback Corporations. Formerly, no carryback of capital losses was available either for individuals or for corporations. A three-year capital loss carryback for a net capital loss is provided for a corporation for any taxable year in addition to the five-year capital loss carryforward allowed corporations.

The carryback, however, is not available for a capital loss arising in a year for which a corporation is treated as a Subchapter S corporation. Also, the carryback is reduced by the number of years a corporation elected Subchapter S treatment in the years preceding the taxable year.

> *Example:* If a real estate coporation was treated as a Subchapter S corporation in 1973 but not in 1972 or 1974, and if it sustained a capital loss in 1974, it could carry the loss back to 1972 but not to 1973.
>
> The rule in [Section 381(b)(3) of the Code] which applies to the carryback of a net operating loss generally in the case of tax-free corporate acquisitions is applied to the carryback of a net capital loss. Under this rule, a corporation acquiring property in a distribution or transfer of the type specified is not allowed to carryback a net capital loss for a year ending after the date of distribution or transfer to a taxable year of the distributor or transferor corporation. Such a post-acquisition net capital loss, however, could be carried back by the acquiring corporation to its own preacquisition taxable years.

Individuals and non-corporations. Capital loss carrybacks are not available for individuals; they can only be carried *forward,* until used.

[¶1415] USING APPRECIATED PROPERTY TO REDEEM STOCK OR PAY DIVIDENDS

Under provisions of Section 311 of the Code, corporations face a tax on appreciated property used to redeem stock. This rule adds another exception to the general rule that a corporation does not realize gain when it distributes appreciated property. There have been three exceptions to this general rule:

1. LIFO inventory [Sec. 311(b) of the Code].
2. property subject to debt in excess of basis [Sec. 311(c) of the Code], and

3. recapture income.

Some Routes Still Open: If a corporation has appreciated property which it would like to distribute when it is no longer needed in the business without having to pay a capital gains tax on the appreciation, it can still distribute it:

1. as a dividend,
2. in complete or partial liquidation,
3. in complete termination of the interest of a stockholder holding a 10 percent or more interest,
4. in redemptions to pay death taxes [Sec. 303 of the Code], and
5. in certain redemptions from private foundations [Sec. 311(d) of the Code].

There are two other situations which are apt to be of more limited application in a closely held corporation: distribution of the appreciated stock of a 50 percent-or-more subsidiary and distributions under antitrust decrees [Sec. 311(d)(2)(D) of the Code]. Management that has appreciated property which it no longer needs must keep its eye open to dispose of it in one of the tax-free ways.

Under the provisions of Section 311 of the Code, your corporation will realize a gain when it distributes appreciated property in redemption of its stock, but it will not realize a gain where it distributes appreciated property as a dividend without surrender of stock or where the distribution is made in partial or complete liquidation of the corporation [Sec. 311(d) of the Code]. Likewise, the rule does not apply to a distribution in complete termination of the interest of a stockholder holding at least 10 percent of the stock of the corporation, the distribution of the stock of a 50 percent-or-more-owned subsidiary, and under various other circumstances. Also, the rule does not apply to an REIT where a stockholder demands the redemption [Sec. 311(d) of the Code].

[¶1416] AVOIDING DOUBLE TAX BY SALE OF CORPORATE STOCK

The simplest way of avoiding the double tax is by a sale of stock. The present stockholders merely sell their holdings to the new group of owners. From the sellers' point of view, this is also the most advantageous method since it gives them a clean capital gain (provided the long-term holding period is met and there are no collapsible corporation problems) and also an easy way to report on the installment basis. But prospective buyers in the real estate field usually shy away from stock purchases. They prefer to buy assets — the property itself. They do not wish to buy a corporation which may have unknown liabilities nor do they wish to be burdened with the job of liquidating the corporation — a necessary step when they want the purchase price of the stock to be the basis for depreciation. (If such liquidation were not pursued, the old basis, which is usually lower than the cost of the stock, would have to be used as the basis for depreciation.)

A sale of stock therefore is frequently not possible. So we must turn to one of the methods involving liquidation of the corporation by the sellers.

[¶1417]   **TAX-FREE ONE-MONTH LIQUIDATION**

If you meet the requirements of [Sec. 333 of the Code], you can avoid any tax on the liquidation of a corporation. What happens is that the basis of the stockholders' stock becomes the basis of the property received in the liquidation. So, where the property is appreciated property — i.e., worth more than the basis of the stock — the tax on the gain is postponed until the stockholder disposes of the property.

One big advantage of a Sec. 333 liquidation is that the stockholders can turn around and make an installment sale and use the installment method of reporting the gain. This approach is not available in situations where the corporation has to be liquidated to avoid a double tax on the transaction (i.e., either the 12-month [Sec. 337] liquidation or liquidation followed by resale under Section 331).

The problem with Section 333 generally is that it is only useful where the corporation does not have any accumulated earnings and profits to speak of and little or no cash or stock and securities acquired after 1953. Where earnings and profits are present, there will be ordinary income to the distributees in the liquidation. And where the cash and post-1953 stock and securities are distributed, there can be capital gain. So, the advantage of Section 333 is really restricted to those cases where the corporation has highly appreciated property other than stocks and securities acquired after 1953 but has had little or no income — which is frequently the case with real estate corporations.

How the One-Month Liquidation Rules Work. To have the provisions of Section 333 apply, you need the adoption of a plan of liquidation. Written consent of the stockholders within 30 days of the adoption of the plan, and a distribution in complete redemption of all the stock interests that takes place within one calendar month.

Section 333 applies only to those stockholders who file consents. But, in the case of noncorporate stockholders, 80 percent of the voting power (other than stock held by corporations) have to consent. In the case of corporate stockholders, 80 percent of the corporate stockholders have to consent (stock held by a corporation owning 50 percent or more of the combined voting power at any time after 1953 is not counted in this calculation).

The election to come within Section 333 is made on Form 964, which must be filed in duplicate with the District Director. A copy of the form must be attached to the shareholder's return for the year of liquidation.

Failure to file the election turns the liquidation into a standard Section 331 liquidation. Neither the Treasury nor the courts can waive the election requirement. Adoption of the plan of liquidation can be a date other than that of the formal plan of liquidation [*Shull*, 291 F.2d 680, (4th Cir. 1961), *rev'g* 34 TC 533].

Also, keep in mind that you usually cannot change your mind once you choose the one-month liquidation route, though you subsequently discover you made a mistake and, as a result, wind up with a higher tax. The Fifth Circuit, reversing the Tax Court, has held that you can revoke your election where there is a mistake of fact as to the amount of retained earnings [*Meyer Estate*, 200 F.2d 592, (5th Cir. 1953)]. However, the Sixth Circuit held that where there is a mistake of law, not of fact, the taxpayers are stuck with their election [*Raymond*, 269 F.2d 181, (6th Cir. 1959)].

In the first case, the stockholders were unaware that the books erroneously understated earned surplus and did not account for a large dividend received by the corporation 15 years earlier. This was a mistake of fact. In the latter case, the taxpayers thought they could reduce profits by writing off good will. This was a mistake of law.

How Stockholders Are Taxed in One-Month Liquidations. First, of course, each stockholder has to determine the amount of the gain (i.e., the difference between his basis for the stock in the liquidated corporation and the total fair market value of everything received in the liquidation distribution). Then he determines the portion of the gain that is taxable. That amount is the larger of the following two amounts:

1. His ratable share of the corporation's accumulated earnings and profits through the end of the month of the distribution;
2. The total of cash and the value of stock and securities acquired after 1953 distributed to him.

If the stockholder is a corporation, the larger of (1) or (2) is taxable to it as a capital gain (long- or short-term depending on the holding period). The remainder of the gain is not taxed.

If the stockholder is not a corporation and the larger amount is (1), then the entire amount is treated as a dividend. Where, however, the amount in (2) is larger than (1), then to the extent of the total arrived at in (1), the gain is taxable as a dividend. The excess of the amount in (2) over the amount in (1) is treated as capital gain (long- or short-term depending on the holding period). Any gain in excess of the larger of (1) or (2) is not taxable.

How to Boost Bias — and Depreciation — via a One-Month Liquidation. The one-month [Sec. 333] liquidation can do more than merely avoid a tax on liquidation of a corporation. It can boost your basis for depreciation on property distributed from the corporation.

Assume, for example, that you formed a corporation several years ago to build and own an office building. You weren't concerned about the corporate tax then because depreciation charges (using the 150 percent declining-balance method) almost always exceed the operating income of the building for the first several years at least. Your corporation showed an annual tax loss. The corporation has not accumulated any cash but has sustained itself. However, due to depreciation, taxes, and interest deductions, there is a deficit.

Now, several years later, two things have changed: Depreciation charges are dipping below operating income so there's a tax at the corporate level and the property has substantially appreciated in value. You'd like to eliminate the first and take advantage of the second.

A liquidation under Section 333 avoids any capital gains tax on the distribution because the corporation (1) has neither cash or securities which were purchased after 1953 nor (2) earnings or profits.

While appreciated property often gives rise to collapsible corporation problems, assume your corporation owns a single piece of rental property and none of its shareholders are real estate dealers. Then you escape collapsible treatment under the relief provisions of Section 341(e)(3). So you are ready to use the one-month liquidation provided you can find a way to maintain or increase the depreciation charges.

After the liquidation, the 150 percent declining-balance method will no longer be available to the shareholders because the original use of the property does not begin with them. But the straight-line method may be used. And although you may initially think that depreciation deductions on the straight-line method are only two-thirds of those with the declining-balance method, you may even find that your depreciation deductions increase. *Reason:* You will probably be able to increase the depreciable basis of the property (perhaps you can change the allocation between land and building) or shorten the useful life of your property.

Regulation §1.334-2 says that the basis of assets received in a Section 333 liquidation is (a) the basis of the stock surrendered plus (b) liabilities assumed by the shareholders. Normally, the only liability assumed will be the unamortized portion of the mortgage. However, the shareholders' basis for the property will be increased (over the corporation's adjusted basis) by the amount of deficit incurred by the corporation during its life. This deficit often arises as a result of

1. deducting (instead of capitalizing) interest and taxes during construction of the building,
2. taking depreciation deductions in excess of the mortgage amortization, and
3. incurring actual losses in operations financed by loans or additional capital.

Furthermore, Reg. §1.334-2 provides that the basis is to be allocated between land and building in proportion to their relative market values. So if the circumstances justify an increase in the building-to-land ratio, the basis for depreciation will be stepped up even further.

[¶1418]
AVOIDING DOUBLE TAX BY WAY
OF A 12-MONTH LIQUIDATION

To avoid the problems created by a simple liquidation, Congress put a relief provision [Sec. 337] in the 1954 Code. Under Section 337, if a corporation in complete liquidation distributes all its property (except assets retained to meet creditors' claims) *within 12 months* after adoption of a plan of liquidation, gain or loss on sales or exchanges of property by the corporation during that period will not be recognized or taxed to the corporation. By eliminating the tax at the corporate level, the double tax is avoided.

This permits a liquidating corporation to sell — without taxable gain or loss — its noninventory assets. The tax-free treatment is limited to sales of *property* (which is carefully defined), so as to eliminate double taxation of corporate earnings **only where sales are incident to liquidation.**

Section 337 is not an elective section. If you liquidate under its rules, it applies. So, if assets have appreciated, the corporation (in order to avoid tax on gain) should adopt a plan of liquidation before making any sales and then liquidate within a 12-month period. If assets have depreciated, the corporation (in order to obtain deductible loss) should sell the property before adopting a plan or delay completion of the liquidation for more than 12 months from the date of adoption of the plan.

Section 337 requires that there be a plan of complete liquidation and that the tax-free corporate sales take place within the 12-month period beginning on the date of adoption of the plan. (Of course, there has to be a complete liquidation within that 12-month period, too.) While the usual procedure is first to adopt the plan of liquidation and then go through with the sale, the Regulations concede that if both the sale and the adoption of the plan of liquidation occur on the same day, Section 337 applies even if the sale occurs earlier in the day than the adoption of the plan [Reg. §1.337-1]. Sometimes, the time of the formal adoption of the plan will be ignored and a practical approach used. That occurred in one case where the company's only asset was condemned and the corporation decided to accept the award without contesting it. The check was received the same day. Two months later, the formal liquidation resolution was adopted. But the court said that the practical adoption of the plan occurred when it was decided to accept the award. *Reason:* With its only asset gone, the company couldn't do anything but liquidate [*Mountain Water Co.*, 35 TC 418 (1961)]. (But do not chance this route!)

Limitations on the Use of Section 337. You cannot use the 12-month liquidation route where you have a collapsible corporation, a one-month [Section 333] liquidation, or a tax-free liquidation under Section 332. Nor does it apply where all the assets are distributed to creditors [*Rev. Rul. 56-387,* CB 1956-2, 189]. Furthermore, where the property disposed of by the corporation during the

12-month period is depreciable, part or all of the benefits of Section 337 can be lost.

Sale of Depreciable Property. A sale that would otherwise produce capital gain (in situations outside Section 337) can now produce all or part ordinary income. Under Section 1245, post-1961 depreciation on personal property reflected in the gain is taxable as ordinary income to the extent the depreciation does not exceed the gain. Similarly, all or part of post-1963 excess depreciation on real property may be taxed as ordinary income under Section 1250. Where a corporation during the 12-month period of the Section 337 liquidation sells depreciable property, it may realize ordinary taxable income despite the rules of Section 337. To the extent that the sale would have produced either Section 1245 or 1250 income had the sale not taken place during a Section 337 liquidation period, the gain is taxable as ordinary income to the corporation during the Section 337 period. (In other words, where Sections 1245 or 1250 applies, it supersedes Section 337.) What's more, if the company takes back installment notes and thus delays the reporting of the taxable gain, when the notes are distributed to the stockholders in liquidation, the corporation will have to pick up the same amount of ordinary income that it would have realized had it sold the notes.

Collapsible Corporations. If you meet the Section 341(b) definition of a collapsible corporation, you can't use a 12-month liquidation as the corporation pays tax on the gain. But in that case, you still get a capital gain on liquidation after the corporation pays a capital gains tax on the sale of its assets. In other words, you pay a double capital gains tax — a tax on the gain on the corporate level plus a tax on the remaining gain that is distributed in liquidation. [See *Rev. Rul. 58-241*, CB 1958-1, 179].

Installment Obligations. Using a Section 337 liquidation does not solve the installment sale problem. If the corporation receives installment notes on the sale of its property and then distributes them in complete liquidation, the stockholders have to pick up the value of the notes when they receive them in liquidation even though they won't realize the proceeds of those notes for a number of years.

Timing Distributions. Just because Section 337 requires that all assets (other than those held back to pay corporate debts) must be distributed within 12 months of the adoption of your liquidation plan, that doesn't mean you have to rush into making the distributions as soon as the assets are available for distribution. As long as you get the assets out of the corporation to the stockholders within 12 months, you avoid double taxation on the sale of the corporation's property. So, the next step is to look over the stockholders' tax picture.

Where the 12-month period after adoption of the plan of liquidation cuts across two taxable years of the stockholders, you can have the corporation split its distribution over the two taxable years. In the first year, an amount equal to the stockholders' basis for their stock can be distributed to them without tax. After that, any additional distribution will result in capital gain.

Losses: Sales by a corporation during a 12-month liquidation period are not taxable. But not only gains are affected; losses are, too. You can't deduct losses. So, what you try to do is sell the loss property before adopting the plan of liquidation. That gives the corporation a deduction [*Virginia Ice, 30 TC 1251*]. Where you've already adopted the plan of liquidation and then discover you have some depreciated property, consider abandoning the property. Section 337 applies only to sales and exchanges, not abandonment. So, an abandonment loss would seem to be available.

Not only do you have to watch out for losses that can arise on the current sale of corporate property, but you must be sure not to overlook the carryback loss you may have from operations. That may give rise to a claim for refund. Since all assets other than those needed to meet claims have to be distributed, failure to distribute the refund claim to the stockholders within the 12-month period (to the extent that the refund exceeds the reasonable needs of the corporation to meet claims against it) can upset the Section 337 qualifications of the entire liquidation. Fortunately, however, although a federal statute [31 U.S.C. Section 203] prohibits the assignment of claims against the United States, the courts have held that this prohibition does not apply where a corporation assigns its claims to its shareholders in the process of the complete liquidation of the corporation [*Kinney-Lindstrom Foundation, Inc., 186 F. Supp. 133, D.C. Iowa, 1960*].

Complete Distributions. Because Section 337 requires a complete distribution in liquidation during a 12-month period, problems sometimes arise when all the stockholders cannot be located. It is a common solution to this problem to distribute the property to trustees for all the stockholders. In this connection, it is important to make sure that the trustees are acting as trustees for the stockholders and not as trustees for the corporation. An unpublished letter ruling said that a distribution to the trustees in the following circumstances would meet the requirements of Section 337:

1. The trustees are approved by all the stockholders who can be located.
2. The trustees are selected by the corporation and approved unanimously at a stockholders' meeting by the stockholders.
3. The trustees are appointed by a court of competent jurisdiction.

[¶1419] CONVERTING ORDINARY INCOME TO CAPITAL GAIN ON 12-MONTH LIQUIDATION

Suppose that during the 12-month period after the adoption of a plan of liquidation, the corporation comes into a lot of cash. This could easily come about after it sold most of its property. At that point, assume it still has time within the 12-month period to liquidate. So it invests this cash in securities whose value increases during the next two or three months. At that point, the corporation sells its securities and realizes a substantial gain. But this sale took place within the 12-month period and therefore should be tax free to the corporation under Section 337. The gain on the securities sale will be reflected in the gain the stockholders realize on the liquidation. But that gain will be long term. So, the net effect is to convert a short-term gain to a long-term gain.

A variation of this technique is one where the corporation would distribute the securities to the stockholders in the liquidation. Here, the value of the securities received would be included in the amount received in liquidation, and the appreciation would be taxable as a long-term gain. The basis of the securities would be stepped up to market value; so a sale by the stockholders of the securities immediately after the liquidation would result in no gain or loss. The net effect again would be one long-term capital gain on the securities' appreciation.

[¶1420]   **MORTGAGES**

Under the tax law, loans repaid by a corporation can sometimes be considered a distribution of dividends, and taxed to the recipient as dividend income. If it is expected that the property will be mortgaged for the individual's benefit, ownership in the individual form might be preferable. However, state laws often permit a higher rate of interest to be charged to corporations than to individuals. If mortgage money is tight, it may be easier to borrow as a corporation than as an individual.

Handling Limitation on Deductibility of Interest on Loans to Carry Investments. Under the *Tax Reform Act of 1969,* modified by the *Tax Reform Act of 1976,* as noted earlier, excess investment (not business) interest is limited as to its deductibility. This rule applies to individuals; it also applies to stockholders of Subchapter S corporations but only at the stockholders level; it does not apply to corporations. These distinctions in its application open up various possibilities for avoidance or reduction of the impact: Investment property kept within a regular corporation may be carried without regard to excess investment interest (see ¶1238).

[¶1421]   **JOINT VENTURE CORPORATIONS**

An individual, partnership, or corporation engaged in the real estate business may want to take on a real estate venture (a large-scale building project, land development, or other venture) but may find it lacks the necessary skill, technology, facilities or equipment, supervisory personnel, financial resources, or other essential ingredient to go it alone. To accomplish its objectives, it may seek to work out arrangements with other compatible individuals, a partnership, or corporation. These arrangements might, of course, take the form of some sort of contractual relationship, but contractual arrangements might not always be satisfactory. Those in a position to make an important contribution to the enterprise may insist on a management and ownership interest as the price of their participation.

If the interested parties on both sides are corporations, a permanent union via an acquisition or merger may be the indicated solution where the new activity is likely to become dominant in either or both corporations. But if the new activity merely operates to create a narrow community of interest, the corporations may not be ripe for a permanent union. They might under these circumstances try for a partnership or joint venture agreement. As far as corporations are concerned, a few jurisdictions still take the position that a corporation lacks the power to be a partner. In those jurisdictions, a joint venture can be used because there's no question of the power of corporations to enter joint venture agreements. However, the nature of a joint venture is limited in duration and if the participants are individuals or partnerships it will leave them exposed to unlimited liability.

Hence, if the venture promises to be a long-range, large-scale operation with considerable risks, rather than a one-shot proposition of marginal importance and risk, the participants may want the advantages of incorporation. To meet this need the joint venture corporation has evolved. The corporate form, besides offering limited liability and perpetual existence, also, of course, offers a familiar framework for financing and controlling the enterprise.

A joint venture corporation is essentially a special type of close corporation. In it the participants seek the safety of the corporate form with the flexibility and other benefits of the partnership or joint venture — personal voice in management policy, assurance of the maintenance of a pro rata share in the enterprise, a choice of participants, and the exclusion of unwanted outsiders.

Joint venture corporations have been used to a large extent in operations of a highly speculative or risky nature where the limitation of liability and stability of the corporate form make them particularly attractive.

Cumulative voting provisions, separate classes of stock with separate directorial representation, and provisions requiring greater than a majority vote for action by the board of directors or stockholders have been used to give each participant power in determining policy. Stock transfer restrictions have been used to keep out unwanted participants, and agreements among the corporate stockholders have been used to cover appointment and removal of officers and dividend and other corporate policies. These provisions have been used in the articles of incorporation, the bylaws, and in stockholder agreements.

[¶1422]   **PERSONAL HOLDING COMPANY**

If there is a danger that a corporation might be classified as a "personal holding company," it might be better to avoid the corporate form. Undistributed personal holding company income is subject to a 70 percent tax, in addition to other taxes [Code Sec. 541]. A personal holding company in essence involves a corporation that generally produces passive type income (i.e., interest from notes generally).

To be a personal holding company (PHC), at least 60 percent of the adjusted ordinary gross income [Sec. 543(b)(2)] to the company must be PHC income. Generally, as noted, this means passive type income [Sec. 542(a)(1)].

Also, the PHC test requires that at any time during the last half of the year, more than 50 percent in value of the outstanding stock must be owned by five or fewer individuals. [Sec. 542(a)(2)].

Again, if Sections 541 *et. seq.* are applicable, there is a 70 percent tax on the indistributed PHC income. (For more details on this area, which is outside the intended scope of this text, see Levine, §680 and Bitter and Eustice, Chapter 17.)

[¶1423]
ACCUMULATED EARNINGS TAX

You can accumulate $150,000 of the earnings of a corporation without distributing them as dividends. You must be able to show that any accumulation beyond that is for the reasonable needs of the business. If you can't, then you have to distribute dividends or pay an accumulated earnings tax. In the case of holding or investment companies, you can't show reasonable need and are limited to only $150,000 before being subject to the accumulated earnings tax. These include corporations whose principal activity is owning real estate for income or for sale. But even when you get past the $150,000 accumulation mark, there still may be situations where accumulation in the corporation saves money — i.e., where the corporate tax plus the accumulated earnings and liquidation taxes may still cumulatively be less than the shareholder's bracket.

If accumulations of corporate earnings in excess of the $150,000 exemption of Section 535 of the Code can be justified, it may be possible to: (a) avoid or postpone a secondary income tax at the stockholder level and (b) use the growth corporation's stock for more favorable capital gain tax treatment in the future.

Under these circumstances, earnings may be reinvested in other realty rather than distributed through dividends. Stockholders avoid the secondary tax at high income rates and may later sell their appreciated stock at more favorable capital gain rates. However, if retention of earnings cannot be justified, the accumulated earnings will be taxed; even if you cannot avoid the tax, it may be better to pay it than to distribute the money to a high tax bracket taxpayer-shareholder.

If the tax applies, the rates are, per Section 531: (a) 27½ percent of the accumulated *taxable* income not in excess of $100,000 and (b) 38½ percent over said $100,000.

How to Avoid Penalty Taxes by Reason of Unreasonable Accumulation of Earnings.

Where the decision is made to have real property placed in the hands of a corporation, care should be taken to avoid the tax on unreasonable accumulation of earnings resulting in penalty taxes. Monies accumulated to provide for mortgage payments are deductible in determining the applicability and the basis of this penalty tax. It would thus be prudent, if and when unencumbered real estate is transferred to a corporation, to have the corporation transfer, in addition to stock, stock securities that will be secured by a mortgage to the individual transferors. This may also result in greater after-tax dollars from the income of the property. But if the corporation is merely holding title to property subject to a net lease, it may well be classified as a "holding or investment company," in which event the sum retained for the reasonable needs of the business would not qualify as a deduction in computing the accumulated earnings tax [Sec. 535(C) of the Code] and it will be difficult to avoid the penalty tax. The ownership, management, and maintenance of an office building leased to several tenants would seem to qualify as a business that would not be subject to the taint of a mere holding or investment company [Reg. §1.355-1(d)].

Accumulated Earnings Escape Hatch Under 1969 Tax Reform Act.

The *1969 Tax Reform Act* offers a tool to help with the accumulations problem. Earnings can be retained to redeem the stock of a deceased stockholder but only to the extent of Section 303 of the Code redemption needs of the business; that is, the amount needed or reasonably anticipated to be needed to make a redemption of stock included in the estate of a deceased stockholder up to the maximum amount permitted in a so-called Section 303 redemption (one to pay death taxes and administrative costs).

Here is a new way to finance buy-outs. To the extent that the corporate tax rate is lower than that of the shareholders, the added permissible accumulation enjoys tax shelter. Instead of being paid out in the form of dividends at ordinary income rates, it is ultimately paid out to the estate of the deceased stockholder at capital gains rates computed on the basis of the stock in the estate's hands and not what it was in the hands of the deceased stockholder. In other words, the estate has a stepped-up basis.

The corporation should decide whether it wishes to take advantage of this accumulations escape hatch. If it does, the policy should be reflected in the corporate minutes and records.

15

Subchapter S Corporations

**TAX ASPECTS OF
SUBCHAPTER S CORPORATIONS**

The Internal Revenue Code, Subchapter S [Sec. 1371 to 1379 of the Code] provides for an election by which certain small business corporations can avoid corporate taxation. Under these rules, the corporation is not taxed at all. Its taxable income is picked up by its stockholders and each pays his individual tax on the portion of the corporation's income allocable to him. The provision is similar in its treatment of losses. It makes no difference whether the profits are actually distributed to the stockholders. Each picks up his pro rata share (just as partners pick up their distributive shares regardless of distribution) [Sec. 1373(a) of the Code]. Profits you pick up without getting actual distribution increase the basis for your stock; losses passed on to you decrease your basis [Sec. 1376 of the Code].

Benefit from these provisions can be realized in several situations:

1. The stockholders want to keep earnings in the business and their tax brackets are lower than the effective corporate rate. [Where the individual's rates are higher, it might still be cheaper to pay a salary (assuming it was reasonable) up to the point where the individual's rates reach the corporate rate level and leave the rest in the business.]

2. The corporation has losses and the individual has profits. By electing to have the individual taxed directly, he can offset the losses of the corporation against his personal profits.

3. Another advantage is the availability of pension or profit-sharing plans and other fringe benefits which, even under the 1974 pen-

sion reform law, can be more beneficial for an over-5 per cent stockholder-employee than a Keogh plan is for partners or sole proprietors.

Some important tax advantages you may be able to achieve by electing to have your corporation qualify under Subchapter S are:

1. retention by earnings in the business by paying lower individual than corporate rates;
2. offsetting individual profits with business losses;
3. pension and profit-sharing plans and other fringe benefits for corporate shareholders;
4. deferring tax on corporate profits by postponing final payment on corporate income through adoption of different tax years;
5. passing the entire year's income tax liability to lower-bracket family members by transferring stock any time before the end of your tax year;
6. choosing year of corporate taxable income despite different tax years by cash distributions made within two and one-half months after the end of the corporate tax year;
7. distributing long-term capital gain and ordinary losses of Subchapter S corporation in different tax years by election of Section 337 liquidation and allocating gain to tax year following loss;
8. avoiding the collapsible corporation rule by letting the corporation sell assets, yet turning ordinary income into capital gain and passing it through to the shareholders;
9. combining 12-month liquidation and installment sale, yet eliminating double tax and resulting in capital gain.

State Tax Problems Created for Subchapter S Corporations.

Although the election available to corporations to be taxed as partnerships can give great tax advantages, don't overlook possible increased state taxes that may arise as a result of the election. The rules vary from state to state.

[¶1502] ELECTING SUBCHAPTER S TREATMENT

Special rules have been issued by IRS outlining how to make the election to be a Sub S Corporation [Reg. §1.1372-2]:

(1) Form. The election is to be made on Form 2553.

(2) Signature. The election is to be signed by the person or persons authorized to sign tax returns and filed with the District Director with whom the tax return would be filed.

(3) Consents. Attached to the election should be the consents of all the stockholders. This should be in the form of a statement signed by all the shareholders consenting to the election and giving the following information: names and addresses of the corporation and all the shareholders, number of shares owned by each shareholder, and dates on which the stock was acquired. All the necessary consents are not signed if a beneficial owner of stock in the corporation has not signed. Thus, the election has been knocked out where one of the record shareholders was also engaged with his brother in another business, and the two brothers often invested jointly on an informal basis without any written agreement. The shares of the corporation in question that were issued to the shareholders of record were paid for with a check issued by the real estate company carried on by the record shareholder with his brother and charged to the drawing account of each brother, and each brother reported income from the sale of the stock. The Tax Court ruled that the brother who was not owner of record was a beneficial owner and that his failure to file a consent to the Subchapter S election invalidated the election [*Harold Kean,* 51 TC 337 aff'd in part 469 F.2d 1183 (9th Cir. 1972)]. However, the 9th Cir. held the court abused its discretion in refusing to allow taxpayer an extension to file a consent after the decision under Regs. §1.1372-3(c).

Where a new stockholder comes into the corporation, under the *Tax Reform Act of 1976,* for years after 1976, he must elect, within 60 days, to *terminate* the election or it will *continue* [Sec. 1372(e)(1)]. There is usually some time lapse between the death of a stockholder and the appointment of an executor or administrator; therefore, an estate which becomes a stockholder in a Subchapter S Corporation has 60 days after the earlier of:

1. the day on which the executor qualifies; or
2. the last day of the taxable year of the corporation in which the decedent died, to affirmatively refuse to consent to the election.

(4) Time of Election. The election must be made in the first month of the taxable year in which it is made or during the month before that month.

A new corporation has one month from the time it begins to elect Subchapter S for its first year. The Regulations interpret this to mean the corporation has until the close of the day preceding the same numerical date of the month following the date it begins to make the election. For instance, if the business starts in the middle of the month, say January 14, it has to make its election by the day before the corresponding date in the following month — February 13. If there is no such corresponding date in the following month, then the election must be made by the end of the following month. For example, if the corporation begins business on January 30, it must make its election by February 28 (or 29). This requirement of timeliness is strictly construed [*Pestcoe,* 40 TC 195].

The first month of its taxable year does not begin until the corporation has shareholders, acquires assets, *or* begins doing business [Reg. §1.1372-2(b)].

[¶1503]   QUALIFYING FOR SUBCHAPTER S TREATMENT

For a corporation to be eligible for treatment as a Subchapter S corporation it must meet all the following requirements:

1. be a domestic corporation;
2. not be a member of a parent-subsidiary affiliated group;
3. have no more than ten stockholders (up to 15 shareholders, after it has been in existence for 5 years or if needed due to new beneficiaries—stockholders due to death of a shareholder);
4. have only individuals or estates as stockholders; however, the *Tax Reform Act of 1976* allows, as shareholders:
   a. a trust which is owned by the grantor of the trust;
   b. a voting trust; and
   c. a trust with respect to stock transferred to it pursuant to the terms of a will, but only for 60 days from the date the stock is transferred to said trust. (In (b) each beneficiary is treated as one shareholder) [Sec. 1371(f)];
5. have no nonresident alien stockholders;
6. have only one class of stock;
7. derive no more than 80 percent of its gross receipts from sources outside the United States;
8. derive no more than 20 percent of its gross receipts from "passive investment income" (personal holding company-type income, i.e., rents, royalties, etc.).

For Subchapter S purposes, the shareholders of the corporation are the beneficial owners of the corporate stock and not merely the owners of record [*Harold Kean,* 51 TC 337; *Kates,* 27 TCM 1423 (1968)]. The election was held invalid in the case, since the partnership owned part of the stock. The question of "beneficial ownership" may be raised to make the Subchapter S election void. For this reason, it might be a good idea to enter into a shareholders' agreement providing:

1. that the record owner is the real owner of the stock and that no other person owns any interest whatsoever in the shares purchased by the shareholder; however, it would appear that a holder of record might often act for a beneficial owner. (But, avoid being a disqualified type of trust!);
2. that the shareholder will not pledge the securities as a loan without first informing the other shareholders (lenders can be "beneficial owners");
3. that in the event the election is lost because of the failure of any one stockholder to reveal beneficial interests in his stock, he will

reimburse the other stockholders to the extent of the loss of the tax benefits they would have received had the election been valid.

Some Important Situations in Which the Personal Holding Company Rule is Not a Bar. A corporation does not qualify for Subchapter S treatment where more than 20 percent of its gross receipts is from rents, royalties, interest, dividends, annuities, or capital gains from stocks or securities. But there are important cases where the personal holding company rule will not be a bar:

(1) *Builders, Real Estate Brokers, and Mortgage Brokers.* In these real estate operations, the primary source of income is not from rentals and therefore Subchapter S can be used.

(2) *One-Shot Capital Gains.* Formerly, it was possible to make a Subchapter S election just for the purpose of getting the corporation's net long-term capital gains (i.e., the excess of long-term capital gains over short-term capital losses) into the hands of shareholders at the cost of only one capital gains tax. The following year the election was revoked (by doing some disqualifying act) to return to regular corporate tax treatment and get the benefit of the corporate tax shelter (where the corporate rates are lower than the individual stockholder's rates). This maneuver was aptly termed a "one-shot" election. So, if a corporation owning several properties expected to realize an unusually large capital gain from the sale of some of them, the gross sale price increasing its gross income to a point where rental income was 20 percent or less, it could elect Subchapter S treatment. This would permit the gain to be passed through to the stockholders. They could end up with the proceeds at the cost of one capital gains tax. The following year, assuming the arithmetic ordinarily did not make Subchapter S status advantageous, the election could be given up and the corporation could revert to a regular corporation which would pay regular corporate taxes.

However, Section 1378 takes the shine out of a "one-shot" election by imposing a tax on a Subchapter S corporation where:

1. the net long-term capital gains exceed $25,000 and 50 percent of the corporation's taxable income for the year and
2. the taxable income for the year is more than $25,000. (*Note:* A Subchapter S corporation's "taxable income" combines ordinary income—or loss—and capital gains.)

Example: Suppose you have a corporation that has a taxable income of $40,000, including net long-term capital gains of $30,000. Since net long-term capital gains exceed $25,000 and 50 percent of taxable income (which is over $25,000), Section 1378 applies.

(3) Installment Sale of the Real Estate. Suppose you expect to liquidate all the corporation's real estate next year. The corporation can use a 12-month [Sec. 337] liquidation. But suppose the sale is an installment sale. If the installment paper is distributed in the liquidation, the stockholders have to pick up *the* value

of these installment obligations right away and pay a tax on them. They are taxed before they actually receive the proceeds from the purchaser.

If you elect Subchapter S, you can have the corporation make the sale and realize the gain, report via the installment method as the payments are received, and the gain each year is passed through to the stockholders. Net result: one capital gains tax (as under Sec. 337) but payable as the installments are received. *Note:* The Subchapter S corporation has to be kept in existence while the installment payments are received. If there is imputed interest, the interest after a few years may exceed 20 percent of gross receipts. Then the corporation would automatically lose its Subchapter S status. One solution might be to spell out the interest payment schedule in the sales agreement so that the 20 percent rule is not violated until perhaps the last year of payment. You'd have to work out the arithmetic in each case to see whether it pays to use this approach. Also, be leary of Section 1378 of the Code problem, noted earlier (large capital gain by Sub S).

[¶1504]   **NUMBER OF SHAREHOLDERS —
SUBCHAPTER S CORPORATIONS**

For purpose of determining the *number* of shareholders, the *Tax Reform Act of 1976* provides the following shall be treated as *one* shareholder [Sec. 1371(c)]:

1. Community property of a husband and wife, under applicable community property laws of the state;
2. The stock is held by a husband and wife as joint tenants, tenants by the entirety, or tenants in common.
3. On the date of death of a spouse, stock described above, by reason of such death, is held by the estate of the deceased spouse and the surviving spouse, or by the estates of both spouses by reason of both of their deaths in the same proportions as held by the spouse before such deaths, or,
4. On the date of death of the surviving spouse, stock described above, by reason of such death, is held by the estates of both spouses in the same proportions as it was held by the spouses before their deaths.
5. These rules apply for tax years ending after 1976.

[¶1505]   **USING A SUBCHAPTER S CORPORATION TO SPLIT INCOME**

A Subchapter S corporation can act as an income-splitting device because it permits a division of ownership between a father and his minor children. This reduces taxable income because of additional standard deductions and personal exemptions. In addition, a taxable income is split among several taxpayers.

How a Builder Can Use Subchapter S. Suppose Bob Builder anticipated income of $25,000 from his real estate operations. He has never incorporated because the standard corporation might create a double tax liability. He could avoid the double tax problem by using a Subchapter S corporation which would be treated similar to a partnership for tax purposes, but he has never seen any advantage to this.

Key to Tax Savings. Now assume he organized a Subchapter S corporation with himself and his three minor children as stockholders, the children's stock to be held under a custodial arrangement. The primary tax saving arises because Builder is entitled to claim his unmarried children as dependents as long as they are under 19 or are full-time students, even though they have income in excess of their personal exemption. The children in turn are entitled to claim their own personal exemptions in their own return.

Be Sure to Achieve Economic Reality. The Tax Court has held that the use of a Subchapter S corporation to split income would be recognized only where the deal had economic reality [*Duarte,* 44 TC 193].

What to Do. If you make stock transfers in Subchapter S situations, make sure you cross all the t's and dot all the i's. If there are distributions to stockholders, make sure all the transferees get their shares. Where minors are involved and custodianships are set up, make sure the custodian sets up bank accounts for the minors and the distributions are deposited in those accounts. Pay taxes due for the minors from these accounts. Have the custodian exercise his right to vote in the corporation by appearing in person at the corporation's annual meeting or exercising a proxy. In short, do all that any stockholder can do in any corporation.

[¶1506]   **TAX TREATMENT OF SUBCHAPTER S's**
TAX-PREFERENCE INCOME

A Subchapter S corporation's tax-preference income is generally treated as the tax-preference income of the stockholders rather than of the corporation. Items of tax preference are apportioned among the stockholders in a manner consistent with the manner in which operating losses are apportioned. If, for example, a Subchapter S corporation had tax preferences of $90,000 and there were three equal stockholders, the $90,000 would be passed through, $30,000 to each.

Since under Section 1378 of the Code a Subchapter S corporation often can only pass through tax free to its stockholders $25,000 of long-term capital gains, any excess of capital gains over and above $25,000 (less the corporation's capital gains tax) is taxable both to the Subchapter S corporation and to the stockholders. Where the Subchapter S corporation is taxable on its long-term capital gains, it is also subject to the minimum tax on the capital gains as tax preference, it is entitled to the exemption, too. [Secs. 57(a)(9)(b) and 58(d)(2) of the Code; see ¶422].

As for the stockholders, they're taxed on the capital gains passed through the Subchapter S corporation to them less the amount of the tax paid by the corporation on the amount of capital gains over $25,000. If the corporation has to pay a minimum tax, the amount of this tax also reduces the amount of capital gains passed through the corporation to the stockholders. The amount of capital gains passed through to the stockholders is considered tax-preference income to them even though part of it has already been taxed as tax-preference income to the corporation.

CHAPTER 16

Collapsible Corporations

[¶1601]   TAX ASPECTS OF COLLAPSIBLE CORPORATIONS

The attempt to convert ordinary income into capital gain via a corporate structure is thwarted to a great extent by the "collapsible" corporation rules [Sec. 341 of the Code]. Under these rules, the capital gain that would otherwise result from the sale of corporate stock, the liquidation of a corporation, or the distribution from a corporation in excess of its earnings and profits becomes ordinary income.

Keep in mind that if you fall within the "collapsible corporation" rules of Section 341, you have ordinary income even if you can show that you could have had capital gains had you never incorporated. That's what the Supreme Court determined in response to that contention [*Braunstein*, 374 US 65, 1963]. So you have to watch the technical rules of Section 341 carefully and then plan accordingly to avoid getting caught in the snare they create for the unwary.

How the Collapsible Rules Work. Section 341 defines a "collapsible" corporation as a corporation that is formed or availed of principally to:

1. Manufacture, construct, or produce property; or
2. Purchase property that (in the corporation's hands) is inventory, stock in trade, property held primarily for sale to customers, unrealized receivables or fees, or Section 1231(b) assets (trade or business property) and hold this purchased property for less than three years; or
3. Hold stock in a corporation so formed or availed of with a view to
   (a) having the shareholders sell or exchange the stock (in liquida-

tion or otherwise) or having a distribution made to the shareholders before the corporation realizes a substantial part of the taxable income to be derived from the property and (b) having the shareholders realize gain attributable to the property.

For real estate purposes, the term ''collapsible corporation'' generally means a corporation formed or availed of principally for the purchase or construction of real estate with a view to selling the property *or* the stock of the corporation before the corporation realizes any substantial income from the property.

There is a presumption that a corporation is collapsible if at the time of the sale, exchange, or distribution of the fair market value of its ''Section 341 assets'' is

1. 50 percent or more of the fair market value of its total assets, excluding cash, obligations which are capital assets (includes government obligations described in Section 1221(5)), and stock in another corporation; and
2. 120 percent or more of the adjusted basis of its ''Section 341 assets.'' However, absence of these conditions will not give rise to a presumption that the corporation was not ''collapsible.''

Gain realized by a shareholder with respect to his stock in a collapsible corporation, won't be subjected to the ordinary income rates by reason of Section 341 unless:

1. The shareholder owned (directly or indirectly) more than 5 percent in value of the oustanding stock of the corporation at any time after the commencement of the manufacture, construction, or production of the property or at any time after the purchase of the property. For this purpose, the constructive ownership rules apply; i.e. the taxpayer is treated as owning the stock owned by his or her family, including his or her spouse, lineal descendants and their spouses, ancestors, and brothers and sisters of whole or half blood and their spouses [Sec. 341(e)(8) of the Code].
2. More than 70 percent of the gain is attributable to the property so manufactured, constructed, produced, or purchased; and
3. The gain is realized within three years following the completion of such manufacture, construction, production, or purchase.

[¶1602] COLLAPSIBLE CORPORATIONS TAX TRAP

The collapsible corporation rules [Sec. 341 of the Code] may convert what would normally be long-term capital gain on the sale of stock of a corporation or on a distribution in complete liquidation of a corporation into gain from the sale of a noncapital asset. Because of the provisions of Section 341, real estate investors as well as builders and developers of property must be careful to avoid having the owning corporation tainted as a "collapsible corporation."

The statute provides that you have a collapsible corporation if a corporation is availed of principally for the construction or *purchase* of a building or stock in a corporation which builds or buys real estate with a view to the sale by the stockholders of their stock or the liquidation of the corporation prior to the realization by the corporation of a substantial portion of the income to be derived from the property.

Section 341 assets include real property used in a trade or business that is held for a period of less than three years. Thus, where receiving rental income is classified as a "trade or business," you may be in trouble — especially where the real property is the only asset of the corporation and it has appreciated in value to an amount in excess of its basis. [See Sec. 341(c) of the Code as to presumption of a collapsible corporation where fair market value of Section 341 assets is 50 percent or more of the fair market value of total assets and 120 percent or more of the adjusted basis of such assets].

Of course, where the particular stockholder owns 5 percent or less of the oustanding stock of the corporation or the property is held for a period of three years or more, the statute may be avoided. It may also be avoided where it can be established that 70 percent or less of the gain realized on the sale of the stock is attributable to the purchased or constructed property. However, this may be difficult where practically the only asset of the corporation is income-producing real estate.

As a planning technique, therefore, it may well be advisable to have the property purchased in the name of individuals. However, some degree of relief from the collapsible corporation problem is provided in the Code. Under Section 341(a), the taxpayer is given a capital gain on the sale and certain liquidations of what would otherwise have been a collapsible corporation. Section 341(a) concerns itself with a comparison of the increase in net worth of the corporation with the unrealized appreciation of ordinary income assets. The dealer status of certain stockholders also figures in the calculation.

If the unrealized appreciation of "ordinary income" assets of the corporation is not more than 15 percent of the corporation's net worth (on a market value basis), you can collapse the corporation and get capital gain. You can either

1. sell your stock,
2. have a complete liquidation,
3. have the corporation sell assets followed by a liquidation and avoid double taxation under Section 337, or
4. have a one-month liquidation under Section 333 (avoiding recognition of gain except as to earnings and profits and cash and securities).

"Ordinary income" assets are those assets which, if sold at a gain by the corporation, would result in ordinary income to the corporation. If a shareholder owns more than 20 percent of the corporation's stock, ordinary income assets of the corporation also include those corporate assets which, if held by that shareholder and sold by him, would result in ordinary income to him. That provision is aimed at dealers who use separate corporations.

But as to securities held by a corporation, they do not become ordinary income assets merely because a securities dealer is a more-than-20 percent-stockholder. If the dealer holds his stock in the corporation in his investment acount as provided in Section 1236(a) (which lets dealers in securities segregate securities held for investment and treat those segregated securities as investments), then the securities held by the corporation do not become ordinary income assets.

In some cases, the corporation will not qualify for the special rule if transactions in similar corporations are carried out by stockholders owning more than 5 percent of the corporation's stock.

How the Collapsible Rules Can Work to Allow or Disallow Capital Gain Treatment. The following example shows how these rules will be applied either to allow or disallow capital gain on the sale of stock in what would otherwise be a collapsible corporation.

> *Example:* Assume the sole asset of a corporation is appreciated land and the corporation is not a dealer in land. Since there are no ordinary income assets here, gain on the sale of the corporation's stock will result in capital gain if (1) a no-more-than-20 percent stockholder is a dealer in land and (2) a no-more-than-20 percent stockholder owns or has owned within the preceding three years more than 20 percent of the stock of a corporation, more than 70 percent in value of whose assets are property similar or related in service to the land of this corporation.
>
> If a more-than-20 percent stockholder is a dealer in land, then none of the stockholders can get capital gain (the corporation's appreciated ordinary income assets will not pass the 15 percent test).
>
> If a more-than-20 percent stockholder is not a dealer now but has sold within the past three years similar stock interests in corporations having similar property, then, as to him, his activities will be taken into account to determine if he is a dealer and he cannot get capital gain.
>
> If a more-than-5 percent but not-more-than-20 percent stockholder is a dealer, then he has ordinary income even though the other stockholders get capital gain.
>
> Sales of stock cannot be made back to the corporation, so this provision does not apply to redemptions. Also, a more-than-20 percent stockholder cannot make a sale to a related person (that is,

spouse, ancestor, lineal descendant, or corporation in which he has 50 percent control).

Three-Year Waiting Period. Where you have a real estate development corporation that has built a number of units on a specific parcel of land and, before selling a substantial number of these units, the corporation is liquidated or its stock is sold, the collapsible corporation rules prevent this from resulting in a conversion of what normally would be ordinary income (sale of the units) to capital gain. One way to avoid collapsible corporation tax treatment in this type of situation is to hold onto the property for three years after completion of construction. The obvious drawback to this approach is that you may pass up some very lucrative offers. In some cases, of course, you have to weigh the size of the offer against the loss of capital gains treatment and then decide whether the deal is for you. But what do you do if, say, six months before the completion of the three-year holding period you get an attractive offer for the property?

What to Do. IRS has ruled that you can get capital gain treatment if you enter into a contract of sale before the completion of the three-year waiting period provided title to the property does not pass until after the end of the three-year period and you retain all the risks and benefits of ownership until you actually convey title [*Rev. Rul. 67-100*, CB 1967-1, 76]. What this means in simpler language is that you don't have to wait until the three-year period is completed to accept the offer. You only have to postpone the transfer of legal title until then.

CHAPTER 17

Tax Angles in Leasing

[¶1701]   **LEASING**

A lease is a contract between the landlord (lessor) and the tenant (lessee). The effect of the lease upon the parties is twofold:

1. it determines the legal rights and duties of one to the other, and
2. it serves as a basis for the tax treatment of both parties under the Internal Revenue Code.

Therefore, it is only logical that both parties will try to shape the various provisions in the lease so that each will get the maximum advantage — legally, as well as taxwise. The importance of the wording of the lease cannot be overemphasized since it may determine upon whom the tax burden will fall, when the tax will be imposed, which party will be entitled to tax deductions for certain items, whether or not such deductions will be allowed at all, when the deductions may be claimed, and many other subsidiary questions. In the balance of this chapter, you will find a detailed discussion of the problems of both parties — landlord and tenant.

[¶1702]   **TAX CONSEQUENCES OF PAYMENTS**
                     BETWEEN LESSOR AND LESSEE

In negotiating for a lease, the parties must keep in mind the various types of payments that are or may be payable under it. These include not only rent, but also bonuses or additional rental payments, security deposits, cancellation payments, etc. The *landlord* wants to know which of these payments will be taxable income to him and if they can be spread over the lease term to prevent "bunching" of income in a single year. The *tenant* wants to be sure he can deduct all the payments he makes under the lease. If the property is leased at a bargain rental, there may be unexpected tax consequences for both parties. And if there is an option to purchase, there may be a risk that the Treasury will call the transaction a sale rather than a lease, with the result that the payments from the tenant to the landlord will become transfers of capital rather than deductible expenses.

[¶1703]   TAX TREATMENT OF IMPROVEMENTS BY LESSEE

Improvements made by the lessee are not deductible since they are considered capital expenditures. The lessee recovers his improvement expenses by amortizing them over their useful lives or over the lease period, whichever is shorter [Reg. §1.167(a)-4]. In some cases, however, improvements made by a tenant instead of paying rent may be deducted by the tenant. It depends on the intent of the parties.

If the improvements were begun after July 28, 1958, *renewal periods are to be taken into account* in determining the period over which amortization is to take place if the initial term of the lease remaining upon the completion of the improvements is less than 60 percent of the useful life of the improvements. Even if you do not meet the 60 percent rule, you can still amortize over the initial term if you can establish that, as of the taxable year of the improvements, it is more probable that the lease will not be renewed than that it will [Sec. 178(a) of the Code].

> *Example:* You put up a building on property you lease. The building has a 35-year life. The lease has 21 years to run, with a renewal option of 10 years. Since the 21-year original term is 60 percent of the 35-year life of the building, you can write off your building cost over 21 years, unless there is reasonable certainty you'll renew the lease.

> *Example:* You put up an improvement with a 30-year life on the leasehold having a remaining term of 15 years with a 20-year renewal period. The 15-year remaining term is only 50 percent of the life of the improvement. So, you have to use the combined terms of the lease (35 years) in your computation. Since the building's life of 30 years is less than the combined term, you depreciate over the 30-year period. However, you can still use the 15-year period if you can prove it is more probably that you will not renew the lease than that you will.

[¶1704]   TAX TREATMENT OF IMPROVEMENTS BY LESSOR

Another phase of the lessor's tax problems deals with improvements. Improvements made by the lessor are generally capital expenditures and not deductible [(Sec. 263(a) of the Code)]. It may be advisable to have the lessee make the improvement in return for a smaller rent. Improvements by the lessee are not included in the lessor's taxable income if they are not rent [Sec. 109], nor is the lessor's basis affected thereby [Sec. 1019]. In this way, the lessor realizes no income when the improvement is made, nor does he realize income at the termination of the lease [Sec. 109]. At the same time, the rental value may subsequently increase as a result of the improvement. On subsequent sale, any gain resulting directly from the lessee's improvement will be taxable at more favorable capital gain rates. The rental should be reasonable rather than no rent or radically reduced rent, and there should be no intimation in the lease that the lessee's improvement will be considered rent — otherwise the lessee's improvement may be construed as immediately taxable income to the lessor as rent paid in kind [*IT 4009,* CB 1950-1, 13].

Whether improvements are deemed rent is up to the *intent* of the parties. If they intended that the lessee's improvements shall be in lieu of rent or as a substitute for rent, it will be rental income to the lessor. Their intent will be seen from the terms of the lease and the surrounding circumstances.

[¶1705]   PAYMENTS MADE BY LESSEE FOR CANCELLATION OF LEASE

If the tenant pays a lump sum to the landlord in order to cancel the lease, the payment is a deductible expense in the year paid. The landlord must report the payment as ordinary income in the year received, since it is regarded as rent [Reg. §1.61-8(b); *Hort*, 313 US 28 (1941)].

Where there is a security deposit and the landlord receives that in payment for cancelling the lease, the security deposit may be deducted by tenant for tax purposes [*Bradford Hotel Operating Co.,* 244 F. 2d 876 (1st Cir. 1957)].

[¶1706] PAYMENT OF BONUS OR WAIVER OF RENT BY LESSOR FOR CANCELLATION OF LEASE

If the landlord makes a cash payment to the tenant to cancel the lease and obtain immediate possession of the property, the payment is not immediately deductible but must be amortized. If the landlord (on accrual basis) waives rent that is past due and unpaid, this may be treated the same as if the rent had been collected and then a cash payment had been made to the tenant [*Cosmopolitan Corp.,* 18 TCM 542 (1959)]. The tenant is entitled to treat payments for cancellation of a lease as a sale or exchange taxable in the year of receipt [Sec. 1241 of the Code]. The period over which the landlord must amortize the cancellation payments will depend on his intention when he makes the payment and on what he actually ends up doing with the property.

Landlord's Own Use. If the landlord cancels the lease so he can use the property himself, than he amortizes the cancellation payment over the unexpired term of the lease.

New Building. If the landlord demolishes the old building and puts up a new one that he rents to a new tenant, the courts disagree over the period during which the cancellation payments must be deducted. Ordinarily, taxpayers have been required to amortize the cancellation payment over the life of the new building (since the old lease is cancelled with a view to its construction) rather than over the remaining years of the cancelled lease. But the *Cosmopolitan* case, supra, said that the cancellation payment should be deducted over the life of the 50-year lease given on the new building. The old lease was cancelled and the land was leased to a new tenant who then put up a new building. But in a case where the owner maintains control of the new building and makes leases with different tenants, it is hard to see this case applying. He'd probably have to amortize over the life of the new building.

New Lease. If instead of constructing a new building the owner makes a new long-term lease, his cancellation payments are probably deductible over the term of the new lease, rather than the shorter unexpired term of the old lease.

[¶1707] TAX TREATMENT OF PAYMENTS BY TENANT IN ADDITION TO RENT (NET LEASES)

Generally if the lessee pays the expenses of his landlord, such payments are considered rent to the lessee and income to the landlord [Reg. §1.162-1].

Real Estate Taxes. If these are paid by the tenant, they are deductible as rent (Reg. §1.162.11). Taxes are deductible in the year paid, but payments for local improvements must be amortized over the term of the lease [*IT 2164*, CB IV-1, 34].

Mortgage Payments. If these are paid by the lessee on behalf of the lessor, the lessee must capitalize and amortize them over the lease term. [Reg. §1.162-11].

Income Taxes. If both the lessee and the lessor are corporations, federal income taxes paid by the lessee for the lessor come under a special rule if the lease (1) was entered into before January 1, 1954, or (2) is a renewal or continuation pursuant to an option contained in such a lease on December 31, 1953. In such case, the taxes paid by the lessee for the lessor are not deductible by the lessee and are not taxable to the lessor [Sec. 110 of the Code].

[¶1708] TAX TREATMENT OF PAYMENTS MADE BY LESSEE TO OBTAIN LEASE (BONUS PAYMENTS)

If the landlord receives a bonus for entering into the lease, the payment is taxable income to him when received, whether he is on the cash or accrual basis. Thus it is considered the same as advance or additional rental. On the other hand, the lessee must capitalize bonus payments (as well as commissions and other expenses incurred in acquiring the lease) and amortize them over the term of the lease.

The lessor can avoid having the bonus taxed in one lump sum by spreading it over all or part of the lease and designating it additional rent. Of course, this means he receives the payment in installments. The lessee will normally not object to this since he must amortize in any event.

[¶1709] ADVANCE RENTALS, BONUS PAYMENTS, AND SECURITY DEPOSITS

The difference between an advance rental and a security deposit is essentially this: An advance rental is money which belongs to the landlord. It's his to do with as he wishes. A security deposit, on the other hand, is not the landlord's property. It is like money in trust to be paid to the landlord only on certain conditions such as a default in rent. That is why escrow arrangements are often used in this area. If the security money is given to the landlord, he acts as a fiduciary and must account to the tenant. He (the landlord) does not own these funds and he generally must keep the funds in an interest-bearing account.

A landlord, whether on the cash or accural basis, reports advance rentals as income in the year of receipt [Reg. §1.61-8(b)]. The tenant, however, must take the deduction in the year to which the rent applies.

Example: Mallin entered into a lease with Jones, the lessee. The lease is to run for ten years. On the signing of the lease, Jones pays Mallin $4,000 — two years' rent (the yearly rental is $2,000). The $4,000 is income to Mallin in the year received (when the lease was signed). Jones, however, must deduct $2,000 in each of the first two years.

A contingency providing for the refund of the advance rental on certain conditions will not mean any different treatment to an accrual basis landlord. He still must include the advance rental when received [*New Capital Hotel, Inc.*, 28 TC 706, *aff'd* 261 F.2d 437 (6th Cir. 1958)].

A security deposit, unlike an advance rental, is not taxable on receipt. This is so even though the money is deposited with the lessor and the lessor has temporary use of the money [*Mantell*, 17 TC 1143 acq. 1952-ICB 3]. A security deposit becomes income if and when appropriated by the lessor because of rent default or some other reason.

[¶1710]   BARGAIN RENTALS AND RENT-FREE APARTMENTS

Giving an apartment rent free or at a bargain rent can create tax problems for both landlord and tenant. So you have to plan carefully to get the tax results you want. Here are some common situations to look out for.

When There's a Gift. When an apartment is given rent free (especially when the building is owned by an individual and the apartment is given to a relative), the landlord can lose a portion of his deduction for maintenance and operating costs of his building. *Reason:* Treasury says he's no longer in business of renting as to the apartment occupied rent free. A proportionate part of his expenses are disallowed [*see Walet, Jr.*, 31 TC 461, *aff'd* 272 F.2d 694, (6th Cir. 1960)]. [*See also Tax Reform Act of 1976*, adding Sec. 280 (A) of the Code; *see also* Sec. 183 of the Code].

Apartment as Compensation. If you show that the use of the apartment is given as compensation for services rendered, the landlord does not lose any part of his maintenance and operating expenses. The landlord probably has rental income equal to the rental value of the apartment and an offsetting deduction for compensation paid; so there's a washout. The tenant, has compensation income. But within a family, if the tenant's tax bracket is lower than the landlord's, this could be a method to shift income.

What to Do. Make sure you can show that the use of the apartment is being given in exchange for services. In one case a deal where the landlord's sister was given an apartment in exchange for services in directing the remodeling of the apartment house and acting as rental agent was approved [*Rolland*, 18 TCM 702, *aff'd* 285 F.2d 760, (6th Cir. 1961)].

Stockholder-Tenants. Where a corporation owns the building and a stockholder lives in one of the apartments at a bargain rental, the courts have looked to see if the stockholder performs services and if he does, the difference between the going rental for a similar apartment and the lesser rental paid by the stockholder is taxed as compensation. [*Peacock*, 256 F.2d 160, (5th Cir. 1958); *Dean*, 187 F.2d, (5th Cir. 1940.)].

Look Out for Possible Dividend. The Treasury has taken the position that the bargain portion of the rent is a dividend where the corporate apartment is occupied by a stockholder [*Rev. Rul. 58-1*, CB 1958-1, 173].

[¶1711]   **LEASES BETWEEN RELATED PARTIES
AND CONTROLLED CORPORATIONS**

If the lessor and lessee are related persons, the remaining useful lives of the improvements must be amortized over the life of the property and without regard to the terms of the lease [Sec. 178(b) of the Code].

Related persons include:

1. an individual and his (or her) spouse, ancestors, and lineal descendants;
2. an individual and a corporation 80 percent or more of the stock of which is owned by the individual;
3. two corporations if 80 percent or more of the stock of each is owned by the same individual and one of the corporations is a personal holding company or a foreign personal holding company;
4. a grantor and a fiduciary of any trust;
5. a fiduciary of a trust and fiduciary of another trust if the same person is a grantor of both trusts;
6. a fiduciary and beneficiary of the same trust;
7. a fiduciary of a trust and a beneficiary of another trust if the same person is a grantor of both trusts;
8. a fiduciary of a trust and a corporation if 80 percent or more of the stock of the corporation is owned by the trust or by the grantor of the trust;
9. a person and a tax-emempt organization (one qualifying under Section 501 of the Code) if the person controls the organization or members of his family do;
10. corporations of an affiliated group that are eligible to file a consolidated return [Sec. 178(b)(2) of the Code].

[¶1712]   **AMORTIZATION OF LEASEHOLD COSTS**

Lease acquisition costs include bonus payments to the landlord or payments to the tenant in possession. These must be capitalized by the tenant and amortized over the life of the lease [Reg. §1.162-11]. It makes no difference if the tenant is on the cash or accrual basis.

If the lease contains an option to renew and was obtained after July 28, 1958, or is between related parties, the special rules of [Sec. 178(a) of the Code] are applicable. Two separate tests are applied:

The 75 Percent Test. If the lease contains renewal options, and if less than 75 percent of the cost of acquisition is attributable to the initial term remaining on the date of acquisition, then the tenant must spread the amortization over the remaining initial term plus the renewal term. This rule, however, will not apply if the tenant can show that it is more probable than not that the lease will not be renewed. For purposes of allocating the cost between the initial and renewal term, a provision in the contract probably isn't sufficient. The allocation should be based on the opinion of a qualified appraiser. [Sec. 178(a)(2) of the Code.]

The "Reasonable Certainty" Test. Even where 75 percent or more of the cost of acquisition is attributable to the remaining initial term, the tenant will still have to include the renewal terms in the amortization period if there is a "reasonable certainty" that the lease will be renewed.

> *Example:* You pay $10,000 to acquire a lease for 20 years with two options to renew for 5 years each. $8,000 of the cost is allocable to acquiring the originial 20-year term. You can write the $10,000 off over the 20-year period, unless there is a reasonable certainty that you will renew.

> *Example:* Same as above, but only $7,000 is paid for the original 20-year term. You have to write the $10,000 off over the full possible 30-year term, unless you can show that it is more probably that you will not renew than that you will.

[¶1713]   LESSEE'S RIGHT TO DEDUCT REPLACEMENT COST

Occasionally, a lease will require you to replace, repair, or otherwise maintain leased furnishings and equipment. This kind of clause is most prevelant with hotels. You may be able to deduct the cost of replacements as a current expense if the replaced items have relatively short lives and similar expenditures can be expected in subsequent years as were made in the years of the lease [*Illinois Central Ry.*, 90 F.2d 458. (7th Cir. 1937); *Manger Hotel Corp.*, 9 TCM 873].

[¶1714]   RETAINING DEDUCTIBILITY OF RENT PAYMENTS UNDER LEASE WITH OPTION TO PURCHASE

At the very outset, a lease containing an option to purchase must be scrutinized with great care. While the lease may describe the tenant's payments as rent, the details of the transaction may indicate they are really installments paid on a deferred purchase of the property. The law permits rentals to be deducted only if they are paid for property to which the taxpayer has not taken or is not taking title, or in which he has no equity [Sec. 162 of the Code; *Berry*, 52 TCM 271]. If it is a purchase, the tenant must capitalize the payments and take deductions in the form of depreciation.

Similarly, under a deferred purchase, the "lessor" doesn't get rent income but a return of capital and capital gain or less (unless he is a dealer in which event he has ordinary income or loss).

> *Example:* Evans, who is not a dealer, enters into a ten-year lease with an option to purchase agreement with Black, the lessee. The rent is $10,000 a year. At the end of the tenth year, Black has the option of buying the property for $5,000. Evans' adjusted basis for the property is $60,000. A court may find that this is not a lease with an option but an installment sale. The $105,000 is not rental income to Evans. $60,000 is a return of capital. $45,000 is capital gain (excluding interest).

There is no statutory provision to tell you when a lease with an option to purchase becomes an installment sale. However, the cases in the field give you some rules of thumb. The important considerations are the amount of rent called for in relation to the fair rental value of the property and a comparison of the "rent" with the option purchase price. [*See Haggard*, 241 F.2d 288 (9th Cir. 1957)].

Some examples of lease-option arrangements that were deemed sales include: a rental of $680,000 payable over a 68-year period with an option to buy for $10 at the end of the lease term [*Oesterreich*, 226 F.2d 798, (9th Cir. 1955); *Wilshire Holding*, 288 F 2d 799]; a ten-year lease calling for annual rent of $19,000 with an option to purchase at the end of the lease at $75,000 — the annual "rent" being more than 25 percent of the "purchase" price, the Court concluded a sale was intended [*Elliot*, 262 F. 2d 383 (9th Cir. 1959)].

But the Ninth Circuit now agrees that in such a lease-option agreement not all the "rent" is necessarily payment of principal. Part may be interest on the unpaid balance of principal. In the *Wilshire* case, the Ninth Circuit determined that the maximum interest rate allowed by the state — 12 percent — should be used to find what part of the rental paid was really interest.

[¶1715]   **DEPRECIATION OF LEASEHOLDS**

If instead of purchasing a fee interest in a parcel of real estate, the buyer were to purchase a leasehold interest — that is, purchase for a stated sum of money a lease on the particular piece of property that permits subleasing to other tenants — a reasonable allowance for exhaustion is permitted. This simply consists of an aliquot part of the cost of the lease based on the term of the lease [*See Minneapolis Security Bldg. Corp.*, 38 BTA 1220]. (The allowance was based on the term of the lease, not the *shorter* life of the building.)

Where an owner of improved property leases it to another person, he is nevertheless entitled to take a deduction for depreciation of the property. However, where by the lease terms, the lessee is required to return the property at the end of the term in as good a condition as it was at the beginning of the term (*not* excluding ordinary wear and tear), it is doubtful that the lessor-owner can take any deductions for depreciation as he will not have suffered any economic loss [*G.C.M. 11933*, CB XII-2, 52]. Of course, neither can the lessee take any deduction for depreciation, although he can deduct the cost of restoring the property to its original state in the year of restoration (*O.D. 516*, CB 2, 112]. [On a related point, forcing the lessor to treat a payment by the lessee to lessor, in lieu of a duty to restore, as ordinary income [*see Sirbo Holdings, Inc.* 509 F.2d 1220 (2nd Cir. 1975)].

[¶1716]   DEPRECIATION DEDUCTIONS BY PURCHASER OF FEE SUBJECT TO LEASE

Another special situation arises when the lessor sells his fee interest subject to an existing leasehold. The question is whether the purchaser can depreciate any improvements on the property. This will depend on whether the lessor or the lessee constructed them.

Improvements Constructed by Lessor. If the lessor put up the improvements prior to making the lease (and has been depreciating them), the purchaser of the fee steps into his shoes and continues to take the depreciation deductions.

Improvements Constructed by Lessee and Having Useful Lives Exceeding the Term of the Lease. In this type of situation, the Treasury has allowed a *purchaser of the fee*, subject to a lease, to allocate a part of the cost to the purchase-date value of the revisionary interest in the lessee's improvements [*Rev. Rul. 60-180*, CB 1960-1, 114]. However, the Treasury does not allow a depreciation deduction during any part of the term of the lease. It is presumed, therefore, that depreciation may be taken by the new lessor when he gets the improvements when the lease ends. (The Service's position on this point appears very weak).

Improvements Constructed by Lessee and Having Useful Lives Less Than the Term of the Lease. In this situation, the Treasury has consistently said that the purchaser has no depreciable interest in the improvement if the term of the lease extends beyond the remaining useful life of the improvement [*Rev. Rul. 55-89*, CB 1955-1, 284]. The reasoning used is that an allowance for depreciation is available only to persons who would suffer an economic loss resulting from the deterioration and physical exhaustion of the improvement.

However, in *World Publishing Company* [299 F.2d 614 (8th Cir. 1962)]; the company paid $700,000 for a piece of property subject to a lease that had about 28 years to go. The lessee, under the original lease, had constructed a building on this property that at the time of the sale to World Publishing had a remaining useful life of less than the 28-year remaining term of the lease. World argued that $300,000 of the purchase price represented the fair market value of the building constructed by the lessee and it should be entitled to depreciate this amount. The Tax Court held that depreciation was only available where the building was erected by the landowner and not by the lessee. The Eighth Circuit disagreed and found that World had made an investment in the property. The Court reasoned that to allow a deduction in a case where the building was erected by the vendor-lessor and deny it where the tenant was the builder would be to exalt form over substance.

[¶1717]   DEPRECIATION DEDUCTIONS BY LESSEE

Where the lessee improves the property during the term of his lease, he is permitted either to (1) amortize the cost of the improvements over the term of the lease or (2) if the useful life of the improvements is less than the remaining term of the lease, depreciate the improvements over such useful life.

The accelerated methods of depreciating property cannot be used if the cost of the improvements is amortized over the term of the lease, since the accelerated methods are only available when the deduction is for depreciation, not amortization in lieu of depreciation [Reg. § 1.167(a)-4]. The deduction for amortization of the leasehold improvement is similar to a deduction for depreciation on the straight-line method, using the term of the lease as the life of the property.

[¶1718]   DEPRECIATION DEDUCTIONS BY LESSEE WHO PURCHASES FEE INTEREST

Very often, a lessee who makes improvements may decide to buy the fee from the owner of the land. When he does so, he has to make an allocation of his purchase price if the remaining life of the improvement is longer than the remaining term of the lease. One part of the purchase price reflects the market value of the land at the time of the purchase. The other part equals the value at the time of the lessee's purchase of the lessor's right to acquire the improvements at the end of the lease term. The amount allocated to this value of the lessor's right to get the improvements is added to the lessee-purchaser's remaining cost basis of his lease. This total amount then becomes the basis for his improvement and is recovered via depreciation over the remaining estimated life of the improvement.

If the lessee-purchaser had been recovering the cost of his improvements through amortization deductions, he can still do so until the date of the purchase. But thereafter, he can only use depreciation [*Rev. Rul. 60-180*, CB 1960-1, 114; *Millinery Center Building Corp.*, 350 US 456, 1956].

This problem arises when the improvements have useful lives greater than the term of the lease. Where the improvements are shorter, the lessee would have been using depreciation. So this would not change. Nor would it affect the basis for depreciation, since the lessor never had any right to the improvements (they'd have been used up before the lease ended) and the purchase price should be equal to the fair market value of the land.

Example, you hold a lease for 40 years and erect a building on the property at a cost of $100,000. The building has an estimated useful life of 50 years and you are taking deductions of $2,500 a year. At the end of 10 years, you purchase the fee for $25,000. The land has a fair market value of $20,000 at that time and the balance of $5,000 may be considered the value of the lessor's right to acquire the improvements at the end of the lease term. This $5,000 which you paid for the right of the leassor to acquire the improvement at the end of the lease is added to your unamortized cost of the improvement ($75,000), giving you a new basis for depreciation ($80,000).

[¶1719]   GROUND LEASES

Where the seller does not wish to keep the land as an investment, use of a ground lease with a fixed redemption date (not granted by statute) may be better than a purchase-money mortgage for tax purposes. With a mortgage, the seller would have to receive 30 percent or less of the sales price in the year of sale in order to be able to spread out his income via an installment sale. And if he wanted more than 30 percent, he'd have to pay a tax on his entire gain immediately.

Furthermore, since the title to the land is then in the purchaser, the seller's remedies for nonpayment of the mortgage involve expensive and time-consuming procedures.

However, use of a ground lease enables the seller to receive the entire sales price of the house at once (even if it's more than 30 percent of the total value of the property) and still pay only the tax on the gain attributable to the building. What's more, since the house purchaser is a tenant and not a mortgagor of the land, he can be evicted for nonpayment, which is a much simpler procedure than mortgage foreclosure (varies in some jurisdictions).

Be careful in fixing the redemption price of the land to make it reasonable in terms of the actual value of the land. Otherwise, IRS may say that you have a sale of the land at the time the redemption price is fixed because the low price will lead the buyer to choose to redeem.

From a tax point of view, the tenant may also come out ahead. Payments of mortgage principal (if the tenant purchased instead of leased) would not be a deduction to the purchaser — only interest would be deductible. But the full yearly rental payments would be a deduction to the tenant, and actually, part of these payments would represent the amortization that the tenant would have had to pay had he bought the land outright instead of entering into a rental arrangement.

[¶1720]   **ABANDONMENT OR OBSOLESCENCE**
              DEDUCTIONS BY LESSEE

A lessee who abandons his leasehold or discontinues his business may be able to write off the remaining cost of improvements he installed either via an abandonment loss or by a deduction for obsolescence. But he must comply strictly with the statutory rules, as illustrated by the case of *Zwetchenbaum* [21 TCM 1493, *aff'd* 326 F.2d 477 (1st. Cir. 1964)].

Zwetchenbaum was a lessee who operated a retail store in a downtown area. Over a period of years, he put in about $194,000 worth of improvements which became a permanent part of the property and for which he took an annual depreciation deduction. Then poor business drove him to the suburbs although 15 years remained on his lease. He actively sought a new tenant and also tried to terminate the lease but was unsuccessful on both counts. So he deducted the unrecovered cost of the leasehold improvements in the year he moved.

However, the court held that he could take only his normal depreciation deduction, even though he was unable to put the assets to their fullest economic use. The lessee must first show that the improvements have been abandoned, retired, or permanently withdrawn. As long as the lessee continues to search for a new tenant, none of these can be established, since a new tenant might be able to use the premises as remodelled. The obsolescence did not occur suddenly.

Under the present provisions of the tax law, there are two ways to take a faster write-off for depreciable property than that permitted under the normal depreciation methods. They are as follows:

(1) Abandonment Deduction. Here, the theory is that the property has lost all its useful value and has been permanently discarded or abandoned. The user must show an irrevocable intent not to use or sell the property. This is difficult to show in the case of permanent improvements. The court in the above case indicated that a sufficient showing would be made if the premises were subleased for the remaining period of the lease to a tenant who could make no use of the improvements (and presumably where the rent paid by the subtenant reflected this fact). Another way to show abandonment would be to tear out the improvements; this might be warranted when the value of the deduction was greater than the cost of removal [Reg. §1.167(a)-8].

(2) Obsolescence Deduction. This is permitted in addition to the regular depreciation deduction when the useful life of the improvement has been shortened by economic changes, etc. The term is normally defined to mean a process that occurs over a period of several years.

[¶1721] CAPITAL GAIN ON ASSIGNMENT OF LEASE BY LESSEE

Selling a profitable lease may enable you to get some of your future income from the property as capital gain. But to achieve this result, you have to assign the lease and step out of the picture entirely. If you merely sublet, even for the balance of the term of the lease, what you receive is rent and fully taxable as ordinary income.

Example: A lessee agreed to sublet the premises for the balance of the lease term. A new agreement between all three parties — landlord, lessee, and sublessee — was drawn, requiring the sublessee to make monthly payments to landlord (equivalent approximately to the rent originally called for) and additional payments to the lessee. The Tax Court said that the monthly payments alone distinguish this case from cases where lump-sum payments were held capital gain. In addition, there was no indication that the landlord released the lessee from any liability as tenant under the original lease. Also, the lessee retained the right of re-entry should the sublessee break any conditions of the new agreement. All these circumstances point to a sublease, not a sale of the lease. Hence, payments received are taxable as rent [*Voloudakis*, 29 TC 1101, *aff'd* 274 F.2d 209, (9th Cir. 1960)].

Example: A lessee, the M corporation, held a 99-year lease for certain property. The lease agreeement contained an option to purchase the fee at any time during the first ten years. After five years of the lease had run, M corporation sold the leasehold to N corporation for cash in an amount sufficient to purchase the property under the option, and M corporation intended to exercise the option before the end of the ten-year period. The agreement with N corporation provided that M corporation was to retain the option to purchase under the lease and that if the original lessor refused to sell to M, N would exercise the option on behalf of M. IRS held that the agreement between M and N created a lessor-lessee agreement and so the payment to M was an advance rental, taxable as ordinary income in the year received [*Rev. Rul. 57-537*, CB 1957-2, 52].

[¶1722] DEPRECIATION RECAPTURE ON SALE OF LEASEHOLD AND LEASEHOLD IMPROVEMENTS

Since a leasehold interest is ordinarily a capital asset, sale of the entire interest results in capital gain. Moreover, payments by a lessor to a lessee for cancellation of the lease results in a sale or exchange [Sec. 1241 of the Code]. However, if the disposition or cancellation is made after December 31, 1963, part of the gain may be treated as ordinary income because of recaptured depreciation [Sec. 1250]. Here's how Section 1250 works.

Suppose you buy a leasehold, or you erect a building or other improvement on leased property. In either case, you'll amortize your costs over the period of the lease or, in the case of improvements, over the shorter of the lease period or the useful life. Suppose, however, the leases have renewal periods. The Code today has rules for including or excluding the renewal periods in figuring your amortization or depreciation. You can generally ignore the renewal periods where (a) in the case of an improvement you erect, the remaining initial term of the lease is at least 60 percent of the useful life of the improvement, and (b) in the case of a lease you acquire, at least 75 percent of the cost of the lease is attributable to the initial term.

But if you dispose of the lease, under Section 1250 of the Code, the recapture provisions can apply. To figure what your excess depreciation is, you apply a straight-line method that takes into account the renewal periods — even though, under the rules above you did not have to take the renewal periods into account in figuring amortization or depreciation. But the renewal periods you take into account do not have to exceed two-thirds the original period on which your depreciation was based.

> *Example:* A leasehold improvement was amortized on the basis of a ten-year initial lease term. The lease was renewable for an additional nine years. But the period taken into account for figuring the straight-line depreciation for depreciation recapture purposes would be 16 and two-thirds years — i.e., ten years plus two-thirds of ten years. But if the useful life of the improvement were only fifteen years, then the period taken into account would be fifteen years.

As this example indicates, Section 1250 was drafted in such a way that for purposes of applying the recapture rule, a lessee must use the useful life of the improvement. *Here's why:* Under Section 178, you can use the remaining original term of the lease, instead of useful life, to amortize the cost of an improvement, if that original term is at least 60 percent of the useful life of the improvement. But for Section 1250(b)(2)(B), you have to add renewal terms up to two-thirds of the period used for figuring your depreciation. Since two-thirds of 60 percent is 40 percent, you end up using the useful life of the improvement.

When you're amortizing the cost of a leasehold, the effect is the same — you must end up using the entire lease period including renewals in applying Section 1250.

It may be possible to use a shorter period than useful life in computing recapture depreciation. That would be where the lease was for a short term and provided for no renewals (since the statute provides for extending the initial term only by adding renewal terms). This may be impractical, however, since a lessee would normally not want to put up an improvement that would last a long time unless he were assured of the right to renew the lease. And when we come to related parties, Section 178 of the Code requires the lessee in that case to use the useful life of the improvement for depreciation purposes regardless of the length of the lease or renewal periods. So in figuring the depreciation taken or available on disposition, the related-party lessee would be using the useful life of the improvement in any case.

[¶1723] OWNING AND LEASING: COMPARING AFTER-TAX BENEFITS

It's all a matter of arithmetic. On one hand, a corporation will be saving the net after-tax rent cost. On the other hand, it will have after-tax operating expenses and loss of income on the money invested in the plant. However, it will have an additional release of cash equal to the tax saving resulting from the depreciation deduction. If the net costs of owning the building are less than the after-tax rent costs, the corporation will be ahead by switching to ownership. If the residual value of the property is added to the total of the cash saved during the life of the building, you have the total value of the plant as an investment.

> *Example:* Assume a simplified example where a corporation pays rent of $100,000 per year. It can buy a plant with a 25-year life for $600,000. Land is worth $100,000; the building, $500,000. Realty taxes and other expenses would come to $30,000. If the corporation invested the $600,000 cash at 6 percent, it would make $36,000 a year — $17,280 after taxes, assuming a 48 percent corporate tax rate.

As a lessee, the corporation's after-tax cost of its rent was		$52,000
As owner, its after-tax expenses are	$15,600	
Its after-tax loss on investment of the cost of the plant is	17,280	32,800
So, its after-tax cash outlay as an owner is reduced by		$19,120
But, in addition, the depreciation deduction of $20,000 (1/25 of $500,000) reduces the income tax and releases additional cash of		10,000
That makes the total cash benefit per year to the corporation as a result of owning instead of leasing a total of		$29,120

On a 25-year basis, the savings will total $728,000. At the end of 25 years, however, the building (theoretically) is worthless — it has been completely depreciated. But it should be possible to determine what the building will be worth in 25 years — whether it will have some resale value or whether land values will hold up enough to make demolition and reconstruction feasible.

In our example, we've used straight-line depreciation. Declining balance is more favorable in the early years. New commercial real estate can be depreciated under the 150 percent declining-balance method; for used commercial real estate, only straight-line depreciation is available. Using the declining-balance method, depreciation is reduced yearly and so is the cash benefit. (In the event of an early sale, the recapture provisions of the tax law would apply.)

The corporation might consider paying only partly in cash and giving a mortgage for the rest. Whether this is advisable depends on whether the company can earn more with the money it doesn't put into the building than it will pay for mortgage money. (Internal rate of return considerations were ignored along with other variables, for simplification.)

CHAPTER 18

Tax and Economic Benefits of Sale-Leasebacks

[¶1801]   **AN OVERVIEW**

Sale-leaseback deals have become an established method of putting real estate on a tax-deductible basis, releasing cash for other business purposes, and supplying good investment opportunities in real estate for institutional and other investors.

What's involved in a sale-leaseback is the sale of property by the owner to an investor with an agreement to lease back the property to the seller.

Often, the sale-leaseback accomplishes the equivalent of mortgage financing, but the seller of the property, since he is in the position of a lessee, is entitled to tax deductions for the rental payments that he makes to his purchaser. As in the case of a mortgage, the seller-lessee keeps the use of the property (although he will lose it when his lease expires) and pays a constant net rental which can be conceived of as representing both interest and mortgage amortization. But in the case of a mortgage, the owner only gets a tax deduction for the interest that he pays, not for mortgage amortization.

In a sale-leaseback, since the rentals paid to the purchaser are, in effect, equivalent to interest and amortization on a mortgage, mortgage payments are now put on a tax-deductible basis. This may more than compensate for the loss of the depreciation deduction by the seller.

The investor-purchaser owns the building and is entitled to depreciate it. He is fully taxable on the rent he receives, and part of this rent represents amortization of his investment. But his depreciation of the property may provide enough of a tax deduction to make up for this.

Nowadays, sale-leasebacks are often entered into with institutional, tax-exempt investors. But deals are still worked out even where the investor is not tax exempt, particularly where short-term leases and high building-to-land valuation ratios exist. In this way, the investor shelters from taxation, by way of the depreciation deduction, most of the portion of the rent which represents amortization and recovers this "amortization" in a short period of time.

[¶1802] SALE-LEASEBACK: BUILDING WITH TAX-DEDUCTIBLE MONEY BY USING A SALE-LEASEBACK

The University of Washington leased a large tract of property it owned in the center of Seattle to Roger Stevens and Al Glancy, who set up a company, University Properties, Inc. They leased the property from Washington University for 35 years. For the first 4 years, they committed themselves to a total rental of $6.8 million. Thereafter, they paid percentage rentals with a guaranteed minimum of $1 million a year. The percentage payments were:

— Seventy-four percent of the first $400,000 of gross rental income from commercial space and 80 percent of all additional gross rental income from such space;

— Thirty-five percent of the first $800,000 of gross rental income from office space and 38 percent of all additional gross rental income from such space.

At the current rental rates and occupancy of the tract, these percentages produced annual income to the University of approximately $1.2 million. As the property was improved, the rental income was to go up for both parties.

University Properties agreed to spend at least $2 million to modernize the tract during the first 4 years of the lease. Washington University was obligated, as rentals were received, to put into a new building fund 35 percent of the gross rents received during the first 4 years and 15 percent of the gross rents received thereafter. As University Properties modernized and improved the leased properties, it became entitled to be reimbursed from the new building fund. Thus, in the first 4 years, the lessee obligated itself to pay the lessor $2 million more than the scale of percentage rates presumably required, and the lessor committed itself to put $2,380,000 into the new building fund.

This, in effect, puts the modernization on a tax-deductible basis. The lessee can suggest new buildings and improvements, which can be undertaken only with the lessor's consent. *All costs of such new buildings or improvements are to be paid out of the new building fund.*

The tax consequences of these lease provisions should be as follows:

— The lessee can deduct in full all rentals paid. The obligation to pay $6.8 million of rent during the first 4 years is definite. It is not subject to any reduction or rebate. None of these rentals constitute loans to the lessor. The lessee must spend $2 million on modernization. This $2 million is to be reimbursed from the new building fund. No part of the rental payment is to be repaid.

— The lessee's modernization expenditures initially constitute a leasehold improvement, subject to amortization in equal annual amounts over the term. As the lessee receives reimbursements from the new building fund, its leasehold investment is reduced and finally extinguished. When reimbursement exceeds the amortized cost, the lessee will have taxable income: the lessee's prior amortization deductions have reduced its remaining cost below the amount of the final reimbursements.

[¶1803]   ADVANTAGES AND DISADVANTAGES TO BUYER-LESSOR

Advantages:

(1) The buyer-lessor gets a rental return from the property which is evenly spread over the term of the lease. (Interest on a mortgage is greater in the earlier years and so creates an unequal tax burden.) What's more, the rental return will be partially tax free because of the depreciation deductions available to the buyer. So the net rental may be greater than the net interest plus amortization of principal which would be received under a mortgage. The annual net yield may range from 5 percent to 10 percent or more before income taxes assuming there are no outstanding loans. Furthermore, the return is based on a relatively long and definite period of time and it enjoys a relatively high degree of safety.

(2) In the case of an institutional lender, the usual loan-to-value ratios don't apply; and, in effect, a 100 percent loan can be made. This widens the market for the institution's funds.

(3) When the lease is over, the buyer-lessor has full ownership and possession of the land and improvements remaining on it. If the value of the property has gone up, the buyer-lessor can take advantage of the increase in value at the end of the lease by re-renting the property at an increased rental or by selling the property at a price which reflects its increased value.

(4) If the buyer-lessor wants to dispose of his investment, it may be easier for him to sell the fee interest subject to the lease than to sell a mortgage. In addition, sale of Section 1231 property would create an ordinary loss while sale of a mortgage at a loss normally would create a capital loss.

(5) The buyer-lessor may have a relatively carefree investment. Indeed, all management problems can be left to the lessee by a net lease. (But, if the lessee is a poor manager, this may reduce the lessor's security or the value of the property.)

(6) The buyer-lessor is provided with an offsetting tax benefit against all his earned income (including rent from the property) for the current year, since he is entitled to apply one of the available depreciation schedules to the real estate — except, of course, the land.

(7) If there is a loan against the property, the interest paid on this loan provides the buyer-lessor with an additional deduction against current income.

Disadvantages:

(1) The buyer-lessor takes the risk that the seller-lessee may go broke and, as a result, he may lose rental income and may have to find a new tenant.

(2) The ownership of the property requires a certain amount of management from the buyer-lessor. How much, depends on the terms of the lease. Even though the lease requires a minimum of management duties, the buyer-lessor still must cope with some of the problems of ownership. For example, someone has to take care of possible condemnation, destruction of the premises, or formation of a new assessment district.

(3) The buyer-lessor takes the risk that the property will be less valuable when the lease is over than it was when the deal was made.

(4) The buyer-lessor takes the risk that his tax position may change.

[¶1804] ADVANTAGES AND DISADVANTAGES TO SELLER-LESSEE

Advantages:

(1) The capital which would otherwise be tied up in the ownership of property is freed for use for other purposes. The seller-lessee can use the capital in his business for further operating capital, debt retirement, or investment purposes.

(2) Credit is less directly tied up than in borrowing, and the balance sheet looks more favorable. Since the property is no longer owned by the seller-lessee, its financial statement will contain no reference to a fixed asset; and, since the fixed asset has been converted to cash, the seller-lessee's liquid position greatly enhances its borrowing capacity.

(3) Restrictive covenants of the loan type are seldom required in a sale-leaseback transaction.

(4) The seller-lessee occupies facilities that are tailored to its needs under the protection of a long-term lease at a fixed rental. A fixed rent, in the event of an inflationary period, means that the seller-lessee discharges his lease obligations with "cheap dollars." In addition, capital improvements built by the sell-lessee may be amortized over the period of the lease. Frequently, this results in an amortization in excess of depreciation because the lease term is so much less than the expected useful life of the improvement.

(5) The seller-lesee has the tax advantage of being able to deduct the amount of his rent payments from income. (The total amount of rent paid by the seller-lessee is a deductible item for income tax purposes.) This places the seller-lessee in the position of, in effect, being able to take depreciation deductions for the land without running the risk that the depreciation deductions will be questioned. The seller-lessee can be sure of his rent deductions provided the sale-leaseback was at arm's length.

(6) The annual return from the cash realized on the sale may more than compensate for the interest figured into the rent.

(7) The seller-lessee does not have to get the approval of its funding sources to make the deal as it would if it were borrowing money.

(8) If the seller-lessee reserves the right to sublet the premises, the seller-lessee may be in an extremely flexible position, since it may be able to secure other desirable quarters and still offset its financial obligations under the terms of the lease.

(9) All these advantages can add up to peace of mind to the seller-lessee, especially where the transaction solves a sticky financial problem for the company.

Disadvantages:

(1) The seller undertakes the obligation of the lease. The lease usually is a long-term lease, for a fixed period of time, and at a specified amount of rent. The obligation to pay rent may become tough under adverse business conditions. Usually the aggregate rental payments made over the primary lease term amount to at least the total value of the property.

(2) The seller-lessee usually gives up all right to the property when the term of the lease is over. This means that it has to relocate or renegotiate for continued occupancy of the premises at that time. It also means that, if the value of the property increases, the seller-lessee does not get any benefit from that increase at the end of the lease. But a recapture or renewal provision giving the seller-lessee the right to reacquire the property either at the end or during the lease term may be included in a sale-leaseback agreement.

(3) If there is an unexpected need for major additions or improvements, the seller-lessee must either finance the cost or amortize it over the remaining period of the lease or negotiate with the buyer-lessor to have him finance it. If the latter path is followed, an increase in the rent can be expected.

(4) If the price paid by the buyer-lessor for the property is in excess of the adjusted cost basis of the property, the seller-lessee incurs an income tax liability which may not be offset by other aspects of his tax structure applicable to the year of sale.

(5) Tax laws may change and adversely affect the seller-lessee.

[¶1805]   **SETTING UP A SALE-LEASEBACK TO AVOID
HAVING IT TREATED AS A LOAN**

In setting up a sale-leaseback transaction it is important to structure the deal in such a way that it won't be deemed by IRS to be in fact a secured loan. If the transaction is considered a disguised loan, the tax consequences to the parties can be quite severe.

IRS isn't bound to consider a transaction a sale-leaseback simply because it is formally characterized as such by the parties. The economic reality of the deal must have the substance of a sale-leaseback. Where there is a substantial disparity between the fair market value of the property and the sale price, this tends to show that title was conveyed as security for a loan and that the deed should be regarded as a mortgage. However, the value of an attractive rental under a sale-leaseback and the repurchase option can mitigate against a finding that the parties really intended a loan and not a sale.

A repurchase option made part of a sale-leaseback deal can put the seller-lessee in the same position he would have occupied had he obtained ordinary mortgage financing. Thus, for example, the seller-lessee may be deemed not to have parted with the beneficial ownership of the property where he can, under the repurchase option, reacquire the property at a price that is nominal in relation to the value of the property at the time the option may be exercised or which is a relatively small amount when compared with the total payments required to be made. If the seller-lessee must exercise the option or, because of the economic realities of the circumstances, an economic compulsion to exercise the option is present, IRS will probably take the position that a mortgage loan was in fact made. But the Fifth Circuit has taken the view that the economic relation between the value of the property and the option price is only one factor in determining the intention of the parties to create a loan or a sale-leaseback situation [*Benton,* 197 F.2d 745].

Whether the seller-lessee is under an economic compulsion to repurchase at the time designated for exercise of the option depends in part on the relation between (1) the anticipated value of the property as of the end of the lease term, including wear and tear and absolescence, and (2) the amount the seller-lessee must pay at that time in order to exercise the option. The time when the option may be exercised is also an important factor in making the determination.

An arrangement that permits the buyer-lessor to reap a specified percentage of the anticipated appreciation in the property is a strong indication of ownership by the buyer-lessor.

Where the rental payments are applied against the seller-lessee's repurchase option price, the transaction may be considered a loan since the seller-lessee is acquiring a substantial equity through the payments designated as rent. Rental payments should be realistic and approximate the rentals being paid on similar properties so that the payments don't appear to be a disguise for a loan arrangement.

The value of the option in a leaseback deal depends on the consideration received in exchange for the option. In the absence of any agreement specifically delineating the consideration given for the option, part of the variance between the fair rental value and the actual rents collected can be attributed to the value of the repurchase option.

To avoid a sale-leaseback being considered a loan, the rental payments over the lease term plus the repurchase price should not closely approximate the fair market value of the property.

[¶1806]   SALE-LEASEBACK — OTHER FACTORS

A sale-leaseback usually involves a valuable property with a substantial amount of cash changing hands. No two are exactly alike; all involve a number of factors that require intensive study and evaluation. A mistake cannot be easily remedied. Here are some of the factors that pose problems:

— At what amount should the selling price be fixed? This means more than evaluating at current value. Both parties generally are tied to the property for a long period.

— For economic and tax reasons, the seller may be reluctant to take a loss on sale, but a loss sale may be called for when the value of the property is taken into consideration.

— Amount of rental and length of the lease require evaluation of intangibles. Change in economic circumstances, the neighborhood, or property values could hurt either party.

— Comparison with other methods of financing is required by the seller. Even if a sale-leaseback as agreed on by the parties seems advantageous, it may not be advisable for a particular seller-lessee. Other methods of financing may offer greater benefits.

State law has to be considered. There may be:

1. Restrictions on institutional purchases.
2. Mortgage restrictions in such deals or the transaction may be considered a mortgage and a recording tax sought.
3. Question of legal title if the seller has an option to repurchase.

— The lease, aside from rental amount, length of time, and options, must include provisions covering:

1. Effect of condemnation of property.
2. Subleasing and lessee's primary obligation for rent.
3. Building alterations and security to the lessor against loss.
4. Repair covenants.
5. Insurance coverage.
6. Destruction of the property regardless of insurance coverage.
7. Restoration of the property in case of casualty and use of insurance recovery.

— Default and escape clauses for both parties if one or the other fails to live up to the agreement.

These lease provisions are intimately tied to the original sale-leaseback factors. For instance, a purchaser buying at a high price but protected by a high rental might suffer serious loss if complete destruction of the property allowed the lessee to escape from the lease.

[¶1807]   FORMS OF SALE-LEASEBACK TO INCREASE LEVERAGE AND TAX BENEFITS

New Construction. Here, a builder may arrange financing for a new plant which he is constructing for a business corporation by getting that corporation to agree to lease the property and by interesting an investor in the purchase of the property on completion. In the meantime, the builder will obtain construction financing unless the investor is an insurance company or pension trust which can handle the financing from commencement of construction.

Split Financing. One way for a real estate developer to achieve high-ratio financing for his project is to use "split" financing. The developer sells the land to an institutional investor and the institutional investor leases the land back to the developer. Simultaneously, a leasehold mortgage loan is executed. The developer comes out with 100 percent financing on the value of the land and approximately 75 percent financing on the value of the buildings and improvements. Frequently, financing may aproach 100 percent of the actual cost of the project. The institutional investor will want a kicker to increase its yield above the straight mortgage rate and to provide an inflation hedge. The kicker may be in the form of a participation (say, 2 percent or 3 percent) in the annual effective gross income from the project. Or it might take the form of a participation (say, somewhere from 10 percent to 20 percent) in the increases in gross income over a specified base figure. The base figure will usually be the projected gross income figure with an offset against the income increase by an amount equal to any tax increases. Another type of kicker might be a percentage of the net income from the project after debt service but before depreciation.

The ground lease may be written for a period of anywhere from 30 to 50 years. Renewal options may extend the period up to, say, 99 years. The developer should give particular attention to the provisions of the ground lease as to repurchase and renewal options, rent increases, and reappraisals.

Options to repurchase may be set up with a formula for fixing the price or may call for an appraisal at the time of repurchase by recognized appraisers.

Pension Trusts. These organizations enjoy tax-exempt status. Many pension trusts have used sale-leasebacks, not only where the pension trust is an outsider but also where a corporation sells its property to its own pension trust and takes back a lease. However, this arrangement is now subject to restrictions in the Employee Retirement Income Security Act and should generally be avoided.

Use of the Family. You may want to set up a sale-leaseback with a relative or perhaps with a trust that you create for, say, your children. In this way, by means of the rent deduction, you can shift the income from the property to lower tax brackets. Also, the trust gets a stepped-up basis for the property. Here, too, you must be prepared to show that the property has been sold at a fair and reasonable price and that a reasonable rental is being charged. Otherwise, the sale-leaseback will either be voided for tax purposes or you will only be able to deduct the amount of rentals which is reasonable. If you sell to related parties — a corporation of which you own more than 50 percent, a trust you set up, an exempt organization controlled by you, or your spouse, brothers, sisters, ancestors, or lineal descendants — any loss on the sale is disallowed [Sec. 267 of the Code]. And where you sell depreciable property to a corporation of which you (and certain related parties) own 80 percent or more of the stock or to your spouse, you will have ordinary income on the sale [Sec. 1239 of the Code].

[¶1808] SALE-LEASEBACKS AND BUILD-LEASEBACKS: COMBINING

Just as an operator of improved real estate can sell and leaseback to reduce his investment, so a builder can build and leaseback. By combining this with a sale-leaseback of the land, he can further improve his position. Under this type of arrangement, an institutional investor, like an insurance company, will buy the land and lease it to a builder for a return of, say, 9 percent (depending on the current market) of the cost of the land. It will then lend the builder an additional amount on a mortgage for the construction of an apartment house or office building. Since the lender owns the land, it will usually give a larger mortgage than it would on any other leasehold. The net result to the builder is a smaller investment than would be required otherwise and a higher return.

This is only done in prime locations or for rated tenants. But prime locations are where this type of financing is most needed, since land costs have been boosted to almost astronomical figures. The high cost of land and construction, plus the need to keep rents at a point that will assure initial occupancy of substantially all of the premises, has put a squeeze on profit margins.

[¶1809] GETTING A DEDUCTIBLE LOSS ON A SALE-LEASEBACK

Suppose you sell your property at a loss and lease it back. You might go through the leaseback deal primarily to get the loss to offset other income. But if your leaseback is for more than 30 years, there's a good chance the Treasury will say your loss is not deductible. *Reason:* A 30-year lease, according to IRS, is equal to ownership of the real estate [Reg. §1.1031(a)-1(c)]. So, says the Treasury; you have exchanged one property for property of a like kind — a tax-free exchange under which a loss is not recognized even if you receive cash, too. The Tax Court and the Eighth Circuit have gone along with this argument [*Century Electric Co.,* 192 F.2d 155 (8th dir. 1951) *cert.* den. 342 U.S. 954]. But the Second Circuit has put a twist on this interpretation that can open the way to deductible losses.

First, says the Second Circuit, you look to the cash received on the sale portion of the sale-leaseback deal. Was the cash received equal to the value of the property sold? If it was and if the rent under the leaseback was equal to the fair rental value of the property, then there was a sale, not an exchange. In other words, insofar as parting with the property was concerned, the seller received full value when he received the cash. The lease portion of the deal was not in exchange for the property. The sale is treated separately and the loss is deductible. Since there is no exchange, says the court, there is no need to determine whether the Regulations that say a 30-year lease is equal to ownership of the property are valid [*Jordan Marsh Co.,* 269 F.2d 453 (2d Cir. 1959)].

Caution: This is an important decision and can be very helpful where you can use a tax loss and still want to use the property. Keep in mind, however, the need for firmly establishing values. If it can be shown that the cash received was less than the value of the property or that the rentals were particularly favorable, it may still be established that there was an exchange for the lease plus cash. In that case, you can end up with a nondeductible loss. Note, too, that IRS announced it will not follow the *Jordan Marsh* decision [*Rev. Rul.* 60-43, 1960-1 CB 687]. Thus, IRS sticks to its position that where there is a sale-leaseback and the lease runs 30 years or more,. there is a tax-free exchange of like-kind property.

Even in the case of a lease of less than 30 years, it is possible that a loss may be attacked by the Treasury as being a sham — i.e., the loss is artificial, being created by a low purchase price in order to obtain a favorable lease. To help to avoid attack, it is important to gear both sale price and rentals to fair market value.

[¶1810]   SALE-LEASEBACK WITH STOCKHOLDERS

Take a company that needs working capital. It has a plant that has considerably appreciated in value. One of its stockholders — rather than advance money as a loan — would be willing to buy the plant and lease it back to the company. That gives him a steady income via rent, enables the company to get its working capital, and puts the entire plant and land on a tax-deductible basis. Assuming reasonable rentals, the rent deal should stand up.

While such a deal has many attractions, you have to approach it carefully to avoid several hidden pitfalls.

Look Out for Unexpected Dividends. If the stockholder does not pay full value for the property, he may very well end up with a taxable dividend equal to the difference between his purchase price and the full value of the land and buildings [see Reg. §1.301-1(j)].

Don't Deal with 80 Percent or more Stockholders.

If the corporation is going to sell at a gain, it should avoid a sale to a stockholder who, together with his wife, minor children, and minor grandchildren, (and as enlarged by the *Tax Reform Act of 1976*, taxpayer's parents, adult children and trusts, estates or partnerships where the taxpayer is a beneficiary or partner) owns 80 percent or more of the corporations stock.

Reason: Gain on the sale of the buildings or other depreciable property will be ordinary income; gain on sale of land will still be capital gain (Sec. 1239).

Look Out for More Than 50 Percent Stockholders If You Have a Loss.

Sometimes a sale-leaseback will be worthwhile to establish a loss on the sale that can be used to offset other corporate income. But look out on a sale to a more-than-50 percent stockholder. Losses on such sales are disallowed [Sec. 267].

Note, too, that constructive ownership of stock in this case is much broader than under the 80 percent-or-more-rule, above. Brothers', sisters', parents', trusts', partnerships', and other holdings of the selling corporation's stock can be attributed to the purchasing stockholder.

[¶1811]   **RECAPTURE PROVISION**

To overcome the drawback in a sale-leaseback arrangement that the seller will lose its property at the end of the lease term, either a recapture or a renewal provision may be included. A recapture provision gives the seller-lessee the right to reacquire the property, either at the end of or during the lease term. If the recapture price is nominal, the courts don't consider the original transaction a sale. The courts reason that since the seller will always be ready to take back its property for nothing, it's the same as if there had never been a sale. But where the recapture price is substantial, the courts don't find it so easy to decide whether there has been a genuine sale. They compare the option (recapture) price with the value of the property at the time for exercising the option. The more nearly the option price approaches the fair market value of the property at the time the option is to be exercised, the more likely the courts are to consider the leaseback to be a genuine rental arrangement.

Usually the lease either fixes the option price or the value of the property at the beginning of the lease term and provides that this figure less the rentals paid is to be the option price. Where the option price is stated in the lease, the court may look at the remaining useful life to determine value on the option date. For instance, the Tax Court has disallowed deduction of the rental payments on a 5-year lease of property with a useful life ranging from 12 to 16 years. To the

Court, a low option price for the property useful for 7 to 11 more years meant that the lessee had retained a substantial equity on the original sale.

More frequently, the option price is determined by subtracting the rentals from the value of the property stated in the lease. A provision that the option can be exercised at any point over the life of the lease may bring a variable option price into the picture. Where the option price isn't stated in the lease, the total number of interim rental payments before the option is exercised becomes important. Generally speaking, the deduction for rent can be supported if the rental payments are not materially larger than the depreciation charges. As the spread between the two becomes larger, it will be increasingly harder to sustain the rental deduction. When the rental payments substantially exceed depreciation, the inference is that the excess is being paid to acquire an equity, which will be formally claimed on exercising the option. If the option price is fixed in the lease agreement, that's about all that can be done to protect the rental deduction provided the price is a reasonable estimate of what the value will be on the option date, based on the known facts at the time. And if merely the present value of the property is fixed, the best protection is to tie the rental figure to the depreciation as nearly as can be done.

[¶1812] FARMERS CAN BENEFIT BY USING SALE-LEASEBACKS

A sale-leaseback of farm property may be peculiarly adapted to fill the needs of a farmer whose property can no longer be economically operated as a farm and is not yet ripe for other uses. Suppose, for example, that rising taxes gobble up a farmer's profits. The widening urban fringe has reached his area, and higher tax tags based on potentially higher and better uses have been placed on properties in the area. The farmer wants out. Someone willing and able to carry the land until such time (a period of, say, five to seven years) as it is ready to be put to other uses (subdivisions, shopping centers, etc.) is needed to take it over.

If a developer buys the farm before it is ready for other uses, he faces the prospect of carrying the land for a considerable period of time and getting little or no income from it. Thus, he'll be paying taxes on the basis of its potential use and have high interest payments and other outflow with little or no offsetting income from the property.

How Sale-Leaseback Solves Both Farmer's and Developer's Problems. A sale-leaseback arrangement can go a long way toward solving the problems of both parties. The following example shows you the general features of the arrangement:

Let's say our farmer has a 40-acre tract with some farm buildings. Assume it's worth $4,000 per acre as farm land and about twice that as future subdivision land. The farmer finds a developer who's ready to buy the farm for $320,000 with

10 percent down and 6 percent interest on the unpaid balance. He has another offer of $300,000 with 25 percent down and the unpaid balance at 6 percent, but he chooses the first deal. Under either deal he would get installment reporting and so could postpone full payment of his taxable gain.

The buyer allocates part of the purchase price to the improvements and can depreciate them over their remaining life. The buyer also gets an interest deduction. On our facts, this would amount to $432 per acre or $17,300 per year for the whole package.

The farmer agrees to a leaseback for five years with options to renew for another two years. The rental is fixed at a level which makes it economic to continue farming. We'll say he gets it at 6 percent of its value as a farm. This works out to $240 per acre or a total of $9,600 per year.

The farmer is out of the red. He has $32,000 or so to invest and a return from interest on the land sale which is $7,700 per year more than he's paying in the way of rent. The buyer has $9,600 per year in rental income. He has an experienced tenant in possession and is assured of continuance of the relationship until about the time he's ready to use the land or sell it to a builder. In the meantime he has a degree of tax shelter which may provide enough tax savings to pay carrying costs during the investment period.

CHAPTER 19

Tax Considerations in Foreclosing Mortgages

[¶1901]   **FORECLOSING MORTGAGES**

Mortgage foreclosure situations can have a variety of tax impacts on both parties involved — the mortgagor and the mortgagee. The typical problem concerns the realization of gain or loss to the parties and the nature of that gain or loss. Even before we can consider this problem, we must determine our point of reference; that is, the adjusted basis of the mortgage debt.

[¶1902]   **PROTECTING THE MORTGAGEE'S TAX POSITION**

The mortgagee should protect himself from unfavorable tax results by taking the following steps in the following designated situations:

Mortgagee bids in property at fore-closure	Mortgagee should try to acquire the property for the lowest possible bid. This will result in the largest possible bad debt deduction which may be deductible in full. The low bid will increase the amount of the mortgagee's capital gain on the foreclosure. Paying capital gains tax at a maximum 25 percent rate and charging the resulting bad debt off in full will improve the mortgagee's tax position. (But, beware of redemptions, by state law ignoring for the moment the tax considerations).
Mortgage debt is in excess of amount bid at foreclosure	Gather and preserve evidence that this amount is uncollectible. This will help you sustain a bad debt deduction.

Mortgagee bids in property at foreclosure sale	Fair market value may be shown by selling the property within a short time after foreclosure or by the asking price in a bona fide attempt to sell the property shortly after acquiring it. Another way of establishing market value is to have the mortgaged property appraised. This protects mortgagee from being charged with gain for having obtained property worth more than the amount of the mortgage. Also, if the appraisal shows the property to be worth less than the price at which the property was bid in, the presumption that the property is worth the bid price may be overcome so as to give the mortgagee a deductible loss.
Mortgagee acquires mortgaged property	Avoid getting in mortgaged property for an amount in excess of the principal amount of the mortgage wherever the fair market value of the mortgaged property doesn't exceed that amount. A higher bid may result in being charged with taxable interest. You may be better off getting a deficiency decree against the owner for the interest. In this way, you won't be taxed on interest until received.
Mortgagor surrenders property to mortgagee in cancelation or reduction of debt	Evidence of the fair market value of the property and the owner's inability to pay the excess of that amount over the amount of the debt cancelled will help sustain a bad debt deduction in that amount. It will also prevent being charged with a gain on the theory that the property is worth more than the debt cancelled.

[¶1903]   **MORTGAGEE TAX RESULTS**

Property Bought (Bid In) By Third Party at Foreclosure Sale	Tax Result	Authority
Amount realized less selling costs is higher than adjusted basis.	Ordinary income. (This can occur where mortgage was originally acquired at discount.)	Ogilvie, 216 F. 2d 748.
	If debtor is a corporation, may be capital gain.	Section 165(g).
	If gain is due to partial writeoff in prior year, excess is treated as	See also Toby, 26 TC 610; where interest accrues after the

ordinary income to extent of past tax benefits.

bonds (corporate) are acquired, the interest is or ordinary income; *Shattuck,* 25 TC 416, which makes excess over adjusted basis ordinary income to extent of previously paid delinquent interest.

Where no tax benefit from prior writeoff, equivalent amount may be excluded from income.

Merchants National Bank of Mobile, 199 F. 2d 657.

Amount realized less selling costs is lower than adjusted basis.

Treated like bad debt.

Reg. §1.166-6(a).

Property Bought (Bid In) by Third Party at Foreclosure Sale	*Tax Result*	*Authority*
Fair market value (bid price) of property received is higher than adjusted basis.	Ordinary income to extent of delinquent interest, recovery of prior writeoff, or collections over basis of note.	*Manufacturer's Life Ins. Co.,* 43 BTA 867; *Missouri State Life,* 78 F.2d 778.
	Possible Capital gain where excess not due to any of above factors.	General capital gain/ordinary income rules of Sec. 1221 apply; there must be a sale or exchange; *Elversen Corp.,* 122 F.2d 296; as to the amount of gain (not character) see *West Production Co.,* 121 F.2d 9.
Fair market value of property received is lower than adjusted basis.	Loss treated like bad debt. Also gain or loss may be recognized for the difference between fair market value and amount of debt applied on bid.	Reg. §1.166-6(a) *Nichols,* 141 F.2d 870; *Larson v. Cuesta,* held to be a capital loss 120 F.2d 482.

If property bought for amount that equals adjusted basis of debt, loss may be treated as capital loss.	Same as above.	

Mortgagee Acquires Property by Voluntary Conveyance Without Foreclosure Sale	Tax Result	Authority
Fair market value (bid price) of property received is higher than adjusted basis.	Ordinary income to extent of delinquent interest, recovery of prior write-off, or collections over basis of note.	*Manufacturer's Life Ins. Co.,* 43 BTA 867; *Missouri State Life,* 78 F.2d 778.
Fair market value of property received is lower than adjusted basis.	Loss treated like bad debt.	Reg. §1.166-6(a); *Spreckles,* 120 F.2d 517.

Mortgagee Acquired Property by Voluntary Conveyance Without Foreclosure Sale	Tax Result	Authority
	Where debtor is a corporation and mortgage was bought as an investment, a capital loss may result.	Section 165(g).
Payment is less than adjusted basis of debt.	Treated like a bad debt.	Reg. §1.166-6(a).

[¶1904]   **MORTGAGOR: TAX CONSIDERATIONS**

We've already looked at the various tax consequences and planning techniques of the mortgagee. Now let's consider the borrower's point of view. Here there are three occurrences that can create a different tax impact to the mortgagor. They are:

1. foreclosure,
2. mortgage reduction or cancellation, and
3. abandonment.

[¶1905]   MORTGAGOR ABANDONMENT OF PROPERTY

A mortgagor may abandon mortgaged property to the mortgagee without discharge of the debt. There is no sale or exchange here [see *Crane*, 153 F.2d 504 (2d Cir. 1946)]. However, if there is some type of consideration received at the same time, an abandonment may be a sale or exchange [*Aberle,* 121 F.2d 726 (3rd Cir. 1941); *Blum,* 133 F. 2d 447 (2d Cir. 1943)].

A mortgagor may abandon property worth less than the mortgage rather than surrender it to the mortgagee. But it is very difficult to establish an abandonment loss. The courts may hold, particularly where there is personal liability, no loss was recognized until the foreclosure sale.

Other important factors having an effect on whether or not an abandonment will be recognized are:

1. Extinction of a personal liability may make the transaction a sale [*Rogers,* 103 F.2d 790 (9th Cir. 1939) *Cert. den.* 308 U.S. 580]. Rogers involved (a) voluntary conveyance. [*Rev. Rul.* 73-36, 1973-3IRB 11].

2. A discharge of personal liability implied from recitals of the deed may be treated similarly [*Stamler,* 145 F. 2d 37 (3rd Cir. 1944)].

3. The mortgagee's assumption of liability for taxes and his payment of the mortgagor's attorney fee for obtaining the deed from the mortgagor resulted in having the transaction treated as a sale rather than an abandonment [*Phillips,* 112 F.2d 721; *Blum,* 133 F.2d 447].

To get an ordinary loss, the property owner's best bet is to abandon title by a voluntary conveyance without consideration to the mortgagee. This has been held to have resulted in an ordinary loss [*Commonwealth, Inc.,* 36 BTA 850; *Polin,* 114 F.2d 174; (3rd Cir. 1940); *Jamison,* 8 TC 173 acq. 1947-1CB2)]. If there is no personal liability by the mortgagor, the Service also concedes this point [Levine, *Supra,* Sec. 457 of the Code].

All of these cases involve a potential loss. The issue has been one of the character of the loss: ordinary or capital. If, on the other hand, the mortgage is in excess of the mortgagor's adjusted basis, gain may result from the foreclosure or abandonment [*Rev. Rul.* 76-111, IRB 1976-13].

[¶1906]   MORTGAGOR: FORECLOSURE LOSSES

Sometimes, the tax year in which a loss on property which is foreclosed may be taken presents a problem. Generally, the time of deductibility depends on whether the mortgagor has a right to redeem the property after a foreclosure under local law. However, the precise date of deductibility depends upon the last event that fixes the loss. This requires a factual determination. Here is a table which can help to tell you when to take the loss.

Under These Facts	Your Loss Is Generally Deductible When
If under local law, the property may not be redeemed,	The sale of foreclosure takes place, not the date of the final decree [*Hammel*, 311 US 504].
Where abandonment occurs but mortgagor retains title until foreclosure sale,	The sale of foreclosure takes place [*Green*, 126 F.2d 70 (3rd Cir. 1942)].
If under local law the property may be redeemed,	The right of redemption expires [*Hawkins*, 91 F.2d 354 (5th Cir. 1937)].
But if it can be shown that mortgagor decided to abandon the property (as, for example, where the cost of redemption is more than the property's worth),	The sale of foreclosure takes place [*Realty Operators, Inc.*, 40 BTA 1051, *nonacq* 1940-1 CB8)].
Where there is no personal liability and mortgagor deeds property to mortgagee in year prior to foreclosure sale.	The sale of foreclosure takes place unless it can be shown that the property was worthless at the time conveyed [*Abramson*, 124 F.2d 416 (2d Cir. 1942)] or at some other time before mortgagor relinquished title (*Hoffman*, 117 F.2d 987 (2d Cir. 1941)].

[¶1907]
MORTGAGOR: REDUCTION OR CANCELLATION OF MORTGAGE

Generally, discharge or reduction of the mortgagor's indebtedness may result in the realization of income (Reg. §1.61-12). However, the mortgagor may avoid realizing taxable income on the reduction of the debt if he can qualify the transaction under one of the following exceptions to the general rule:

a. The debt reduction on cancellation constitutes a *gift* by the mortgagee to the mortgagor [*American Dental Company*, 318 US 322; *Liberty Mirror Works*, 3 TC 1018, *acq.* 1944 CB 17].

b. The mortgagor is insolvent both before and after the mortgage debt is cancelled [*Dallas Transfer*, 70 F. 2d 95 (5th Cir. 1934)]. (Also, an insolvent mortgagor who voluntarily conveys property to the mortgagee and realizes a gain isn't taxed on it unless he is solvent after the debt is discharged [*Est. of Turney*, 126 F.2d 712 (5th Cir. 1942)].

c. The reduced mortgage is a purchase-money mortgage which is treated as a voluntary reduction in the cost of the property [*Hirsch*, 115 F.2d 356 (7th Cir. 1940); *see also IT 4018*, CB 1950-2, 20; *Killian Company*, 128 F.2d 433 (8th Cir. 1942)]. Or where a purchase-money mortgagor makes a voluntary reconveyance of the property to the mortgagee [*Nutter*, 7 TC 480, *acq.;* but *see Rev. Rul.* 76-111, 1976-13 and Sec. 443 of the Code].

d. The mortgagor is a corporation or an individual who mortgaged business property and an election was made to have the amount of the debt cancellation excluded from its income and applied to reduce the basis of its property [Reg. §1.108(a)-1;1.1017-1(a); *see also Hotel Astoria*, 42 BTA 759, *acq.* 1946-2CB4].

e. The mortgage adjustment has been made under a bankruptcy or reorganization proceeding.

A voluntary conveyance of the property to the mortgagee in discharge of the mortgage debt may constitute a sale or exchange of the property by the mortgagor [*Kaufman*, 119 F.2d 901 (2d cir. 1941); *Est. of Day*, 117 F.2d 208 (1941)]. But if the mortgagor doesn't have personal liability, there may not be a sale or exchange [*Crane*, 331 US 1].

Loss in such a case is normally measured by the amount that the adjusted basis of the property exceeds the amount of the mortgaged debt. Depending on the nature of the property in the mortgagor's hands, the mortgagor gets either a fully deductible ordinary loss (for property held for investment or used in trade or business) or a capital loss (for property which is a capital asset, e.g., unimproved land held for investment). This brings up an important point regarding the surrender of such property. The **form of surrender** is highly important because if it constitutes a sale, the loss will be a capital loss with restricted deductibility. However, if the surrender of the property can take the form of an abandonment, the loss can be made fully deductible. Any consideration received here by the mortgagor, no matter how slight, is likely to make the transaction a sale which will subject the loss to capital loss limitations.

Under These Facts	Mortgagor's Gain Amounting to	Is Taxable When
Mortgagor delivers mortgaged property worth less than mortgage in full satisfaction of the debt.	The excess of the mortgage debt over the value of the property. [*Rev. Rul.* 76-111, *Supra.*]	The debt is cancelled if you come under the rule of *Kirby Lumber Co.*, 248 US 1 (1931). But many cases have deviated from this rule.

Mortgagor compromises debt with mortgagee by payment of a smaller amount than the mortgage debt, but without conveyance of the property.	The excess of the mortgage debt over the amount of the payment.	The debt is cancelled.
Mortgagor loses property worth less than the mortgage debt in foreclosure. Mortgagor has borrowed money on his property giving a mortgage and has used the proceeds for his own benefit.	The excess of the debt received from the mortgage over the adjusted basis (usually, cost less depreciation) [*Rev. Rul. 76-111, Supra;* Levine, Sec. 443 of the Code].	The sale of foreclosure takes place and the mortgage debt is cancelled [*O'Dell & Sons Co., Inc.,* 169 F.2d 247). (3rd Cir. 1948)]; under New Jersey law, the mortgagee had three months after confirmation of the sale to obtain a deficiency Judgment; some jurisdictions wait until the expiration of a redemption period.
Same as above except that the mortgagor wasn't personally liable on the mortgage.	As above.	*Woodsam Associates, Inc.,* 198 F.2d 357 (2d Cir. 1952).

[¶1908]   ADJUSTED BASIS OF MORTGAGE

Original basis plus or minus adjustments equals adjusted basis.

Original Basis. If you are the original lender or the seller and gave a purchase-money mortgage, your basis is the face amount of the debt. If you bought the mortgage, the basis is your cost.

Adjustments to Basis:

Add	Deduct
Amounts paid by the mortgagee before foreclosure (e.g., interest, taxes, insurance, repairs, attorney's fees, court costs, auctioneer's fees, etc.).	Payments received on principal prior to foreclosure or deductions taken for write-off of partially worthless business bad debts.
Interest accrued and reported (but not collected).	

[¶1909]   GAIN OR LOSS TO MORTGAGEE:
FROM REACQUISITION OF MORTGAGED PROPERTY

If a third party at the foreclosure sale does not make a reasonable bid, the mortgagee may buy the property. For tax purposes the mortgagee's gain or loss is subject to special treatment because the mortgagee's relation to the transaction is dual in that the IRS views him as being both a creditor and a buyer.

As a creditor, the mortgagee is entitled to a bad debt deduction if his bid price is less than the amount of the debt and the portion of the debt remaining unsatisfied after the sale is wholly or partially uncollectible [Reg. §1.166-6(a)(1)].

Figuring Gain on Reacquisition. The fair market value of the property is deemed to be the bid price, unless there is clear and convincing proof to the contrary [Reg. §1.166-6(b)(2); see below]. This means that if the bid price equals the property's fair market value, the mortgagee is allowed a bad debt deduction for his actual economic injury, but there will be no gain or loss. See the following example:

Amount of debt	$200,000
Bid price	100,000
Bad debt deduction	$100,000
Amount of debtor's obligation applied to bid price	$100,000
Fair market value	100,000
Capital loss or gain	0

Obviously the mortgagee's best tax-sheltered position is to be able to have a capital gain and at the same time get a bad debt deduction when he buys the foreclosed property. Assuming that there is clear and convincing proof that the fair market value is not the same as the bid price, the mortgagee would figure as follows:

Amount of debt	$200,000
Bid price	100,000
Bad debt deduction (allowed only when unsatisfied portion of debt is uncollectible)	$100,000
Fair market value	$150,000
Amount of debtor's obligations applied to bid price	100,000
Capital gain	$ 50,000

[¶1910]   **BID PRICE AND MARKET VALUE**

Ordinarily, the amount for which property is bid in by the mortgagee is considered the fair market value [Reg. §1.166-6(b)(2); *Nichols,* 141 F.2d 870 (6th Cir. 1944); *Hadley Falls Trust Co.,* 110 F. 2d 887 (1st Cir. 1940)].

However, in foreclosures by insurance companies, the harsh rule of *Midland Life Insurance Co.,* 300 US 216, may still be applied. This rule held that even though the fair market value of the property bid in by the mortgagee was less than the basis of the debt, the mortgagee realized the full amount of the obligation since that was the amount bid. However, in the *Hadley Falls* case, the First Circuit allowed the mortgagee a capital loss of $5,800 where he bid in the mortgaged property on foreclosure of $56,000 and it was established that the fair market value of the property was $49,200.

Another time when the *Midland* rule may be applied is when there is insufficient evidence of value. So, for example, a mortgagee may be taxed on the excess between the bid (including interest, if any) and the adjusted basis of the debt [*Clarkson Coal Co.,* 46 BTA 688].

CHAPTER **20**

Tax, Financing, and Leverage in Real Estate

[¶2001]   **FINANCING AND LEVERAGE**

Since the basis of real estate includes not only the cash paid but any purchase-money mortgages and any mortgages assumed or taken subject to [*Crane,* 331 US 1], depreciation is figured on the full total. The interplay of this high depreciation deduction, deductible mortgage interest (which goes down each year with constant payment mortgages), and nondeductible mortgage amortization (which increases each year) determines to a great extent the desirability of a real estate investment. Thus, the consideration of these factors can enter into the calculations of both the prospective investor (looking to buy a property) and the present owner (deciding whether the time to sell has arrived or, perhaps, the time to refinance — or maybe both). For example, the present owner may deem it necessary to sell because his depreciation deductions are dropping and his nondeductible amortization is on the increase. Yet, a new buyer may be willing to take over the property because he will be paying a higher price than the seller's basis (since, we assume, values have increased). Although perhaps two-thirds of his purchase price is in the form of mortgages, he'll still get depreciation based on the higher value, and that may make the purchase a worthwhile investment for him.

Leverage is another factor influencing a buyer. If he can buy with very little cash and get most of the purchase price financed, he's in a position to cash in on any rise in value. The entire appreciation belongs to him even though his equity is relatively small. Of course, any decline in value is also borne only by him.

Placing mortgages on property before selling may facilitate sales in several ways: It may enable avoidance of tax in the year of sale and spread the income over a period of years where the installment sale rules might otherwise not apply. Likewise, refinancing of an existing mortgage prior to sale may make the arithmetic attractive to the buyer without penalizing the seller and swing a deal that might otherwise have died.

[¶2002]   TAX CONSEQUENCES OF MORTGAGING OUT

"Mortgaging out" is the term applied to a situation where a builder or investor constructs or purchases property and later is able to mortgage it for a sum equal to or greater than its entire initial cost and so get back his entire investment. This results in a 100 percent leverage situation since the owner continues to receive any profits although he no longer has any cash investment. Mortgaging out is possible because the lender fixes his loan as a percentage of the fair market value of the property at the time of the loan; if that value has risen substantially since the original investment was made, a 100 percent loan-to-cost ratio is possible. Here's a rundown of the tax consequences of mortgaging out:

(1) Keeping the Property. As long as the owner keeps the property, he need pay no tax on any mortgage proceeds, even though in excess of his cost. No taxable transaction has occurred since the owner has merely borrowed money using the property as security. It makes no difference whether or not the owner is personally liable [*Woodsam,* 198 F. 2d 357 (ad. Cir. 1952)].

(2) Selling the Property. When the property is sold, the owner's gain is computed in the usual way, i.e., difference between initial cost and sale price. [Secs. 1001 and 1002 of the Code].

(3) Transferring the Property to a Corporation. When mortgaged-out property is transferred to a corporation by a high-bracket taxpayer, the funds needed to write off the mortgage come from a corporation which may be taxed at lower rate (i.e., 20, 22, or 48 per cent rate). In such a situation, the corporation assumes the mortgage. Section 357(b) of the code takes such a transaction out of the tax-free exchange rule of Section 351 and treats the debt assumed as "boot" where the assumption of the debt is not for a bona fide business purpose or is for tax avoidance.

The Ninth Circuit has permitted a taxpayer to transfer mortgaged-out property to a corporation without being taxable under Section 357(b) on the ground that there was a good business purpose (taxpayer claimed he wanted to be liquid for other real estate ventures) for the transfer [*Easson,* 294 F. 2d 653 (9th Cir. 1961)]. The Fifth Circuit, however, did not permit a taxpayer to transfer encumbered property interests to a new corporation where the purpose behind the transfer was to create funds to pay his own personal income tax liability [*Wheeler,* 342 F.2d 837 (5th Cir. 1965)].

(4) Foreclosing on the Property; Owner Personally Liable. A mortgage foreclosure is often treated as a sale or exchange. If the owner is personally liable on the debt, he will realize gain to the extent that the face amount of the debt plus any other consideration he gets exceeds his basis. (*Rev. Rule.* 76-111, *Supra.*) (It should be noted that in determining the basis, the amount of depreciation allowed or allowable must be taken into consideration.) For example, if his basis is $900,000, mortgage is $950,000, and the property is bid in at the foreclosure sale at $1,000,000 the owner's gain is $100,000. This represents the $50,000 he received when mortgaging out plus the $50,000 surplus he received at the sale. If the property was a capital asset in his hands, his gain is capital gain [*Hammel,* 311 US 504, 1940].

Note what happens if the bid price is less than the face amount of the mortgage. Suppose in the above example the bid price is $925,000. The owner's gain is $50,000 even though he loses the property and receives no cash at that time (because he received a $50,000 gain when mortgaging out). Fair market value in this instance is irrelevant. The mortgagee, of course, suffers a $25,000 loss [Reg. §1.166-3(a)].

(5) Foreclosing on the Property; Owner Not Personally Liable. Suppose in the above situation, the owner is *not* personally liable, the mortgagee having agreed to look solely to the property as security. The argument can be made that on a foreclosure, the owner realizes only the amount of the bid, not the face amount of the debt. That would mean that if the bid price was *less* than the debt, as in the preceding example, the owner would be taxable only on $25,000 (the difference between $900,000 basis and $925,000 bid price). So he would end up with $25,000 tax-free gain (since he actually has a $50,000 gain from mortgaging out). However, the rule apparently is otherwise and the gain to the owner is measured the same as when he is personally liable [*Mendham,* 9 TC 320. *Rev. Rul.* 76-111, *Supra.*].

(6) Voluntary Conveyance by the Owner to the Mortgagee. Now assume that a voluntary conveyance takes the place of the foreclosure. Here again the owner is deemed to have realized an amount equal to the face amount of the debt, and so the entire gain he obtained when mortgaging out is taxable. However, the nature of the gain depends on whether or not he is personally liable on the debt. If he is liable, the transaction is a sale or exchange and capital gain is realized, assuming the property was a capital asset. If he isn't personally liable but receives some consideration in addition to the discharge of the debt, there is also a sale or exchange and capital gain treatment [*Blum,* 133 F.2d 447 (2d. Cir. 1943)]. But if he isn't personally liable and receives nothing, the courts generally hold he is merely relieving himself of a burden and no sale or exchange occurs, so ordinary income is realized.

Suppose mortgaged property is appraised at a value less than the debt at the time it is conveyed to the mortgagee. Apparently the rule is the same as in the case of a foreclosure, viz., fair market value is irrelevant. But see the Supreme Court's note 37 in *Crane* (331 US 1), which states that where the value of the property is less than the debt, an owner not personally liable cannot realize a benefit equal to the amount of the debt. However, that case did not deal with a ''mortgaging out'' situation, where the owner had previously received an actual economic benefit.

[¶2003]   **LEVERAGE AFFECTS THE INVESTOR**

We get leverage when we are able to buy property — for income or to speculate on an increase in value — by paying only a portion of the price in our own cash. The balance is paid either by a purchase-money mortgage from the seller, by an obligation to make further payments pursuant to an installment contract, by borrowing on the security of the property, or by assuming or taking subject to a mortgage debt already existing against the property.

Here's what leverage can do *for* the investor:

(1) When the underlying property increases in value, the owner gets the full benefit even though he has put up only part of the price in cash. Thus, if he buys property for 25 percent in cash and 75 percent in a purchase-money mortgage and the property doubles in value, he quintuples his money, thus:

	Before	After
Value	$10,000	$20,000
Debt	7,500	7,500
Equity	2,500	12,500

(2) If income property yielding 11 percent is purchased for 25 percent cash and 75 percent by a purchase-money mortgage carrying 7 percent interest, we kick up the yield on equity from 11 percent to 23 percent. Here's how:

Cost $100,000
Net income .... $11,000 (11% on full value)
Interest .... $5,250 (7% on $75,000 mortgage)
Net income .... $5,750 (23% on cash investment of $25,000)
                    (Ignoring present value considerations)

But here's what leverage can do *to* the investor:

(1) If the property loses in value, the debt remains fixed and the loss of value is taken in full out of the cash investment. Thus:

	Before	After
Value	$10,000	$8,000
Debt	7,500	7,500
Equity	2,500	500

(2) If the income falls off, the interest burden remains fixed and the loss is taken in full out of the net to the owner. Thus:

	Before	After
Income	$11,000	$7,770
Interest	5,250	5,250
Net	5,750	2,450

The heavier the mortgage, the greater the percentage gain to the owner when the property rises in value or income-producing power; also, the greater the loss when value or rent turns the other way.

[¶2004] **TAX FACTORS DURING LIFE OF MORTGAGE**

Special problems can arise where the debtor and creditor are related, especially if they are a corporate mortgagor and a stockholder-mortgagee. A number of problems can present themselves: accrued interest not paid within 2½ months after the end of the mortgagor's tax year will not be deductible [Sec. 267(a)(2) of the Code]; interest may be deemed too high and unreasonable, hence a dividend distribution; the corporation may be considered "thinly" capitalized and debt (including mortgage debt) treated as stock [Sec. 385 of the Code]; or there may even be a question of the validity of the debt to begin with. Good records and evidence should be maintained.

Where an interest deduction has been disallowed under 2½-month rule, any subsequent payments of interest should be specifically identified as payments of current interest, otherwise the payment may be applied, under the first-in-first-out theory, as a payment of the prior unpaid interest, so that more than one interest deduction may be disallowed [*Lincoln Storage Warehouses,* 189 F. 2d 337 (1950)].

Personal Holding Company Danger. Where the mortgagee is a corporation more than 50 percent owned by 5 or fewer individuals, check to see that its income other than mortgage interest does not come within the sphere of personal holding company income [Sec. 543] so that when added to the mortgage interest the total will not equal more than 60 percent of ordinary gross income [Sec. 542(a)]. If the 60 percent limitation is exceeded, the corporation may be subject to the 70 percent personal holding company tax [Sec. 541].

Contribution of Mortgage Property to a Partnership. This may result in a taxable gain to the contributing partner as a portion of the mortgage debt is shifted to the other partner or partners. Under the Code any decrease in a partner's individual liabilities by reason of their assumption by the partnership is considered a cash distribution [Sec. 752(b)].

Mortgage Money in Excess of Basis of Property. If you get a mortgage on your property that exceeds your basis for the property, there is no taxable gain at that point [*Woodsam Associates, Inc.,* 198 F. 2d 357 (2d Cir. 1952)]. But if you should transfer the mortgaged property to a corporation tax free for stock [Sec. 351] or where the mortgagor is a corporation and the property is transferred in a tax-free separation [Sec. 368(a)(1)(D)], the excess of the mortgage over the basis of the property is taxable to the transferor as capital gain or ordinary income depending on the nature of the asset [Sec. 375(c)].

If a corporation distributes excess mortgage money to its stockholders and the mortgage is insured by FHA or other US governmental agency, distribution is ordinary income to the stockholders regardless of whether or not the corporation has any other earnings and profits [Sec. 312(i)].

Gifts of Mortgage Property: Where there is a gift of mortgaged property, a gift tax may be imposed on the donor to the extent of the value of the equity transferred. Such value is the fair market of the property less any mortgage indebtedness attached to the property. The donee's basis for purposes of gain is the same as the donor's, increased by any gift tax paid, but not in excess of fair market value, for gifts prior to 1/1/77. For gifts after 12/31/76, the basis is increased for gift taxes paid *which are attributable* to the net appreciation (fair market value over the basis). [Sec. 1015(d)(6)]; for loss it is the donor's basis or fair market value at the time of the gift, whichever is lower [Sec. 1015(a)]. Any subsequent payments made on the mortgage by the donee will not affect basis.

Cost of Obtaining a Mortgage. Expenses such as appraisal and legal fees, title costs, loan commissions to brokers, and surveys are costs of obtaining a loan and are not added to the basis of the property involved. These costs are only deductible where business property is involved. They must be prorated over the life of the mortgage. Where the property is sold prior to the full satisfaction of the liability with the mortgage remaining on the property after its transfer to the purchase the unamortized portion of the mortgage expense may be deducted in the year of sale. This issue is raised in [*Anover Realty Corp.,* 33 TC 671].

Points Paid for Mortgage. IRS has ruled that points paid by a mortgage borrower as a ''loan processing fee'' solely for the use of money and not for any specific services rendered by the lender are deductible by the borrowers as interest under Sec. 163 of the Code regardless of the language used [*Rev. Rul. 69-188,* CB 1969-1, 54]. In *Rev. Rul. 69-582,* CB 1969-2, 29, IRS ruled that a cash-basis taxpayer can deduct the amount he pays for points in the year in which he makes the payment, since this would not amount to a material distortion of his income in violation of *Rev. Rul. 68-643,* CB 1968-2, 76. However, points are generally not deductible currently as a result of the *Tax Reform Act of 1976,* for years after 1975, except on a personal residence.

Mortgages Acquired at a Discount. Three separate situations are involved here:

a. Where the original mortgage is taken at a discount (i.e., where the mortgagor pays a premium) and the mortgagor is not a corporation, the gain to the mortgagee is ordinary income. The mortgagee reports this discount income as follows: If he is on the cash basis, he reports the income as received, either all at once or as part of each installment received. If he is on the accrual basis, the discount is spread over the life of the loan.

b. Where the mortgage was issued at par, the mortgagor is not a corporation, and the mortgagee purchases it at a discount in the secondary market, the gain to the mortgagee is ordinary income. The mortgagee will report his gain as a proportionate part of each installment received. However, if the amount of discount income is uncertain or unascertainable, or where it is doubtful that the entire debt will be repaid, the mortgagee may postpone reporting any gain until his total cost has been recovered.

c. A special section of the tax law [Sec. 1232] deals with mortgages issued by a corporation. If the mortgage was originally issued at par and subsequently purchased at a discount, the gain is capital gain provided the mortgagee is not a dealer. If there was an original issue discount, the mortgagee has ordinary income on each collection to the extent the gain is attributable to the period during which he held the mortgage (the gain over the original issue price is spread ratably over the life of the mortgage). The gain attributable to the period preceding his ownership of the mortgage would be capital gain [Sec. 1232(a)(2)].

Where a mortgage is redeemed, sold, or exchanged, the entire original issue discount would be taxed at ordinary rates, unless at the time of original issue of the mortgage no intention to redeem, sell, or exchange before maturity existed.

Property Taxes Deductible by Mortgagor. The mortgagor holds the beneficial interest in the property and can deduct property taxes. Where business or investment property is involved, a business deduction is allowed; otherwise, with reference to a personal residence, only an itemized deduction can be taken. Where a reserve is built up by monthly deposits to cover property taxes, a cash-basis mortgagor will deduct for payment of the taxes when due and paid by mortgagee. An accrual-basis mortgagor may accrue the tax ratably over the period to which the tax relates [Sec. 461(c)].

Deduction of Insurance Expense. Insurance premiums paid by a mortgagor in advance for more than one year on business property are only deductible on a pro rata basis over the period covered by the payment and are not entirely deductible in the year of payment.

Penalty for Prepayment Privilege. This penalty is deductible as interest whether the property is business or investment property or a personal residence [*Rev. Rul. 57-198*, CB 1957-1, 94]. The rule applies when the mortgagor prepays the mortgage in order to refinance it; the penalty need not be amortized over the life of the new loan [(*1201 Shaker Blvd. Co.*, CA-6, 1963)].

The penalty payment is deductible as interest where the mortgagor agreed to sell the mortgaged premises free and clear and paid the mortgage in anticipation of sale.

Depreciation of Mortgages. There must be a capital investment in depreciable property to get a depreciation deduction, since a mortgage is a security interest in property rather than an investment. So a mortgage is not depreciable even where it is a junior lien and the owners have refinanced the first mortgage on such terms as to make a default and the wiping out of the junior mortgage likely [*Tolins*, 22 TCM 137 (1964)].

Assignment of Rents. The mortgagor is still taxable on any income from the property which he may assign to meet payments of interest and principal due. He as the owner must account for all income from which the property during the period of his ownership [*Horst*, 311 US 112], which ends on subsequent sale or expiration of a redemption period of a foreclosure.

[¶2005]   **INTEREST PAYMENTS**

Tax treatment of mortgage interest paid is governed by the use made of the mortgage proceeds, not the nature of the pledged assets. The mere pledge of business assets for a loan does not make interest paid thereon a business expense (deductible by an individual in addition to the standard deduction). The pivotal factor is whether the proceeds of the loan are used to earn business income. Where the interest is considered a personal expense, it is still deductible as an itemized deduction.

You're entitled to deduct for interest payable under a mortgage obligation regardless of whether the property subject to the mortgage is business, or income-producing, or residential property [Sec. 163(a) of the Code]. You may deduct for interest even though you're not the owner of the property provided you're liable for the mortgage obligation, as where you're liable under your personal guarantee of the mortgage obligation of another who has failed to pay the interest due [*K.B. Sherman*, 18 TC 746, 1952]. If the property is owned jointly, the one who pays the interest may deduct it even though he pays more than his share [*IT 3785*, CB 1946-1, 98; *F.C. Nicodemus, Inc.*, 26 BTA 125, 1932]. You may deduct for mortgage interest even though you're not directly liable on the mortgage debt if you have a legal or an equitable proprietary interest in the property that's subject to the mortgage [Reg. §1.163-1(b)]. But where you assume a mortgage as part of the purchase price of the property, you can't deduct for any interest that accrued before you made the purchase — the amount of such interest must be capitalized as an additional cost [*Haden Co.,* 165 F.2d 588 (5th Cir. 1948)].

Interest that accrues after the property has been acquired is deductible in the year paid or accrued [Sec. 163 of the Code; Reg. §1.163-1]. If you're an accrual-basis taxpayer, you get your deduction when the obligation to pay interest accrues, regardless of when you actually pay the interest. A cash-basis taxpayer may deduct for interest payments when he makes them, except that prepayment of interest is generally eliminated, for tax years after 1975, by the *Tax Reform Act of 1976* [Sec. 461(g)].

[¶2006]   PREPAID INTEREST (SOFT-MONEY) DEALS

In 1945, IRS okayed a deduction by a cash-basis taxpayer for interest paid in advance for a period up to five years [IT 3740, CB 1945, 109]. In a ruling published December 16, 1968, IRS revoked IT 3740 in *Rev. Rul.* 68-643 modified by *Rev. Rul.* 69-582, 1969-2 CB 29; there, the loan processing fee (points) paid by a borrower, solely for the use of forebearance of money, was deductible in full in the year of payment. It was allowed as a current deduction without need for proration as required by *Rev. Rul.* 68-643. These facts only involved a prepayment of $1,200; therefore, there was no distortion. Deductions for prepaid interest will be denied cash-basis taxpayers under the *Tax Reform Act of 1976*. If interst is prepaid it cannot be currently deducted. It is as though the taxpayer is on the acccual method.

[¶2007]   TERMINATION OF MORTGAGE
BY PAYMENT OR SETTLEMENT

When property is condemned or destroyed by fire or other casualty, condemnation or insurance proceeds received by the owner in excess of his basis are not taxable to him if, within one year of the close of the year in which the conversion took place, he reinvests the proceeds in property of a similar or related service or use [Sec. 1033(a) of the Code]. Where there is a mortgage, the mortgagee's interest may be paid to him directly and the mortgage thus paid off. How much must the mortgagor reinvest? The Tax Court says only the net proceeds need be reinvested (*Fortee Properties, Inc.,* 19 TC 99; However, the second Circuit reversed the Tax Court on this issue [211 F. 2d 915 (1954)]. It held the word "property" does not only mean the taxpayer's equitable interest, but it also includes a non-assumable mortgage of the owner. The condemnation award to the mortgagee satisfied a non-assumable mortgage, but was taxable gain [*cert. den.* 348 U.S. 826]. *Babcock,* (28 TC 781). This agrees with the Treasury's regulations which would require the entire proceeds to be reinvested [Reg. §1.1033(a)-2(c)(11)]. The Second and the Ninth Circuits split on this issue, the Second reversing the *Fortee* case (211 F.2d 915), and the Ninth affirming the *Babcock* decision (259 F.2d 689). If you are personally liable on the mortgage, you would have to reinvest the entire proceeds. It would be considered that you had received the entire amount and used the amount covering the mortgage to pay off your personal liability.

When an FHA mortgage is taken over by a successor mortgagor, he will have ordinary income if the mortgage is paid off and the FHA makes a distribution to him of part or all of the insurance premiums paid to it on that mortgage. Since the mortgage existed before he took it over and the prior mortgagor paid premiums, the amount he receives from the FHA may be˙more than the total premiums he actually paid. The excess is taxable to him [*Rev. Rul. 58-380,* CB 1958-2, 14]. But a mortgagor during the entire life of the mortgage would not have any income from the premium repayment by the FHA since he cannot get back more than he paid although if the premiums paid were deducted as a business expense the entire amount received back from the FHA is taxable [*see Rev. Rul. 56-302,* CB 1956-2, 19].

Where a mortgagee settles a mortgage debt for less than par, income may be realized by an individual mortgagor (to the extent of the forgiveness) whose mortgaged property was not business property. Where business property is involved or the mortgagor is a corporation, no income is recognized [Sec. 108 of the Code] if an election is made to reduce the basis of certain property held by the taxpayer [Sec. 1017].

If the mortgagee receives less than the par value of the mortgage, the difference between basis and amount realized is treated as a bad debt deduction, business or nonbusiness.

[¶2008]　CONSTRUCTION: INTEREST AND TAXES—LIMITATIONS

☐ Under Section 189 of the Code, added by the *Tax Reform Act of 1976,* Sub-Section (a) provides that, except as otherwise provided in Section 266 of the Code (relative to carrying charges), whether as an individual, electing small business corporation (Subchapter S) or personal holding company, no deduction is allowed for real property construction period interest and taxes. This means this payment is capitalized, to be spread (deducted) over many years.

☐ If any amount is paid or accrued, which otherwise *would* have been allowable, except for the rules noted, the amount is allowable for such taxable year and subsequent years in accordance with the table prescribed in Section 189(b) of the Code. The table lists the portion that can be currently deductible as to construction interest and taxes. The amount currently deductible depends on whether the property is: (1) residential, (2) nonresidential, or (3) low income housing, and the year in question. For example, with residential property, not of a low income type, the amount is 25 percent in 1978.

☐ Section 189 of the Code specifically states that the Section shall *not* apply to any real property acquired, constructed, or carried if such property is not and cannot reasonably be expected to be *held* in a "trade or business" or in an "activity conducted for profit", i.e., your residence. Thus, if you incur $10,000 worth of interest in 1976 to build your residence, you can deduct it. The same $10,000 paid to construct your office building could not be fully deducted in 1976!

The construction period interest and taxes, defined by the Code, includes interest paid or accrued on indebtedness to acquire or construct or carry real property and real property taxes to the extent that they are attributable on the construction period for the property [Sec. 189(e) of the Code].

Residential property is defined under Section 189(e)(4) of the Code to include property in which 80 percent or more of the gross rent is from dwelling units. This definition is important to see when the above categories of interest limitations come into play.

If the property in question has had construction interest and taxes limited, and the property is sold, Section 189(c)(2) of the Code provides that, for the amortization year in which the property is sold or exchanged, a proportionate part of the percentage is allowable for depreciation; the proportion is determined in accord with the convention used for depreciation purposes with respect to such property. In the case of a sale or exchange of the property, the portion of the amount not allowable as a current deduction is treated as an adjustment to basis under Section 1016 of the Code. (It is added to the basis of the property when you sell; it will thus increase the loss or reduce the gain.) This rule is important with regard to gains or losses on the sale. There is a different rule on tax-free exchanges. [Sec. 189(c)(2)(C) of the Code]. This allows the holder to take the future deductions of interest/taxes, overtime, as if no exchange took place.

In the case of nonresidential real property, the rule is effective for construction periods beginning after December 31, 1975. In the case of residential real property, other than low income housing, the rule is effective for years beginning after December 31, 1977. In the case of low income housing, the rule is effective for taxable years beginning after December 31, 1981.

[¶2009]　　　　TAX-EXEMPT STATUS OF
INDUSTRIAL DEVELOPMENT BONDS

Under Section 103(b) of the Code the income from industrial development bonds issued by state and local governments is no longer exempt from federal income tax. But the statute contains several important exceptions to this rule.

Industrial development bonds, within the meaning of the statute, include issues which (1) are to be used in a trade or business by a taxable person (i.e., a person or entity other than a governmental unit or a tax-exempt charitable, religious, or educational organization), and (2) are secured by an interest in property used in a trade or business. The statute applies both to general obligation bonds guaranteed by the state or local government and to revenue bonds.

Tax-Exempt Status Retained for Many Important Purposes. To begin with, income from bonds which are part of an issue of $1 million or less is still exempt from the federal income tax. In addition, the federal income tax exemption still applies to income from a bond which is part of an issue, substantially all the proceeds of which are to be used to provide: (a) residential real property for family units; (b) sports facilities; (c) convention or trade show facilities; (d) airports, docks, wharves, mass commuting facilities, parking facilities, or storage or training facilities directly related to any of the foregoing; (e) sewage or solid waste disposal facilites or facilities for the local furnishing of election energy, gas, or water; or (f) air or water pollution control facilities; or (g) for the acquisition or development of land for an industrial park.

Residential Real Property Exemption. This exemption refers to buildings containing one or more complete living facilities not intended to be used on a transient basis. The facilities must contain complete facilities for living, sleeping, eating, cooking, and sanitation. But facilities which are functionally related and subordinate to the space used for family units are included. Also, a minor portion of a facility may be used for nonfamily purposes.

Sports Facilities Exemption. This exemption applies to bonds issued by a governmental unit to provide such facilities as baseball stadiums, football stadiums, indoor sports arenas, ski slopes, golf courses, tennis courts, swimming pools, and gymnasiums. Facilities directly related to exempt sports facilities are also exempt. However, facilities constructed in connection with, but not directly related to, a sports facility, such as, for example, a ski lodge to be built in connection with the development of a ski slope are not exempt.

Convention or Trade Show Facilities Exemption. This exemption applies only with respect to special-purpose buildings and structures constructed for conventions or trade shows.

Storage or Training Facilities Exemption. Included in this exemption are facilities for flight training. Facilities for storage include conveyors to move products from a ship to a silo or other storage facility on a wharf.

Industrial Park Exemption. In this context an industrial park means a series of sites for industrial (including wholesaling and distribution) plants for which a plan has been developed. Development of land in this context includes providing water and sewage facilities as well as road, railroad, docking, or similar transportation facilities and also power or communication facilities. But, except for the facilities referred to above, it does not include the provision of any buildings or structures.

When Exemptions Do Not Apply. The above exemptions do not apply to industrial development bonds during any period in which they are held by a person who is a substantial user of the facilites constructed with the proceeds.

[¶2010]
REAL ESTATE PAPER
PURCHASED AT A DISCOUNT

If an investor buys a mortgage note or other land obligation at face value, his only profit will come from the interest payments, and these will be reported as ordinary income. Normally, however, real estate paper is bought at a discount from face value and the investor's profit is made up of both interest and discount income. Discount income is ordinary income whether or not the holder is a dealer or investor in such paper [*Phillips*, 295 F.2d 629 (9th Cir. 1961)]. The main question is the method of reporting the discount income; the alternatives are the allocation method and the recovery-of-cost method.

Allocation Method. Each installment payment received by the holder of the obligation is considered to consist partly of return of cost and partly of gain. The proportion is determined by the ratio of discount to face value. Thus if a $1,000 note was purchased for $800 (20 percent discount), each payment would be 80 percent return of cost and 20 percent gain. This method is followed when the amount of the obligation is fixed and there is no reason to doubt that the obligation ultimately will be paid in full. Apparently, even when the obligation is to be discharged by a single payment at maturity, an accrual-basis taxpayer must periodically accrue the discount income for tax purposes [*Vancoh*, 33 BTA 918].

Recovery of Cost Method. Here, payments are considered to be entirely a return of capital until the full cost is recovered. Thereafter, they are wholly gain. This method is permitted if the amount of discount income is uncertain or unascertainable or it is doubtful if the obligation will be paid in full because the maker is a poor credit risk or the underlying security is inadequate [*Willhoit*, CA-9, 308 F.2d 259 (9th Cir. 1962)]. In that case, the investor purchased land contracts which were highly speculative. In Michigan, however, where land contracts are frequently used, an investor who bought them at a discount was required to use the allocation method because the court found he was reasonably certain of recovering his cost. The contracts were secured by shell houses, the value of which had been increased by "sweat equity" to the point where they represented good security for the unpaid installments [*Darby*, 37 TC 839, *aff'd* 315 F.2d 551 (6th Cir. 1963)]. The recovery-of-cost method can also be used with some second deed of trust notes [*Liftin*, 36 TC 909, *aff'd* 317 F.2d 234 (4th Cir. 1963)]. In all cases, holders of the obligations were on the cash basis.

CHAPTER 21

Tax Techniques for Owners of Undeveloped Land and Land Developers

[¶2101]   **TAX POSITION OF OWNERS**
                         OF UNDEVELOPED LAND

Both the owner of undeveloped land and the developer of land must be aware of the tax consequences of ownership (sale, exchange, leasing, etc.) or development of their land. Because each phase of real estate ownership and development carries with it such tremendous tax implications, you should know the various alternatives available so that you can analyze them from a tax point of view. Naturally, properly handling the situation, using the best tax techniques, can result in generating tax shelter.

The owner of undeveloped property is given a special election to capitalize or deduct the carrying charges of his property [Sec. 266 of the Code]. Knowing the proper way to use this election will maximize his eventual gain. For more information about this election and when to make it, see "Electing to Capitalize or Deduct Carrying Charges of Undeveloped Land," ¶2114.

(1) Taxes, Mortgage Interest, and Other True Charges for Carrying the Property. These may be capitalized only as long as the land is unimproved and unproductive. The election to capitalize may apply only to certain types of charges, while the rest may be deducted from ordinary income. The election may be changed each year. Thus the owner can tailor his deductions to the amount of his taxable income. Any excess is capitalized and reduces his eventual taxable gain when he sells. A current deduction will offset ordinary income, while a reduction in eventual gain may be a reduction of capital gain.

(2) Expenses in Development or Construction of Improvements or Additions Up to Time Development or Construction Is Completed.

An example is interest on construction loans. It makes no difference whether the construction or improvement will make the property productive of income subject to tax. These expenses may be capitalized even though the property was originally improved or productive. The election may apply only to certain types of expenses. But, once the election to capitalize is made, it cannot be changed in later years. Investors who have a large personal income can benefit substantially from this election. (Under the *Tax Reform Act of 1976* as discussed earlier, construction interest and taxes may not be deductible, currently, see ¶2008, *supra*).

[¶2102]   LAND AND LAND DEVELOPMENT

People make money in real estate in one of two primary ways. On the one hand, they may buy existing improved properties for income or with the idea of rehabilitating or otherwise modifying the improvements for additional profit. On the other hand, people make money in real estate by speculating in land and by developing it for specific purposes.

There is no doubt that the greatest profit potentials lie in the area of buying undeveloped land and developing it, rather than buying already existing properties where much of the initial profit has already been taken out by the original owner. Of course, the risks are equally great since the speculator and developer are anticipating a future market rather than investing in an already existing one.

On the whole, land generally seems certain to become more valuable as a rapidly increasing population, with rising income, fully motorized, and ranging over large areas to satisfy its living, working, and playing requirements, steadily presses against a fixed supply of land. But in terms of specifics, a lot of land will never really feel the press of a growing population in our lifetime. First of all, fully 80 percent of the land in the United States is outside a 30-mile radius of all existing urban centers of 50,000 or more. Second, a lot of land within that radius will undoubtedly be passed by. Most important of all, a lot of land is overpriced today. This means that one cannot speculate intelligently by merely buying land. It is necessary to measure the price that has to be paid against foreseeable future needs and demands and to judge the effects of the economics of future development and the legal requirements of community control and development.

[¶2103]   FACTORS TO CONSIDER TO ACHIEVE
                 MOST FAVORABLE TAX RESULTS

When buying land, you can increase your leverage and tax benefits by setting up the deal so that you crowd as much in the way of interest payments in the early years as you can. This can work out to your advantage provided you're a high-bracket taxpayer and don't trip over the tax reform provisions limiting the deductibility of investment interest. As you know, interest payments are tax deductible so that if, for example, you're a 50 percent tax-bracket man, every dollar of interest you pay costs you only 50¢.

Mortgage Deal Calling for Interest-Only Payments During Early Years. You might enter into a deal with your seller under which you pay nothing in the way of principal for the early period of the deal. The only payment other than interest is your down payment. Suppose, for example, you pick up a parcel of land at $100,000. You make a down payment of $10,000 and give your seller a mortgage for $90,000 for the balance. The mortgage is to run for 15 years, depending on the market, at 8 percent interest per year. The arrangement calls for you to pay interest only during the first 5 years. In each of the following ten years, you're to pay one-tenth of the principal plus a decreasing amount of yearly interest on the balance.

When you buy the land, you expect to turn it over within 5 years. So, you expect to be out of the deal before you're required to make any amortization payments.

If your expectations are realized and the property triples in value within the first 5 years, you'll sell at $300,000 with a total equity investment of only $46,000 [$10,000 (down payment) and $36,000 (interest payments)]. The tax deductions you'll get for your interest payments will, of course, reduce after-tax cost of your investment still further.

Will the seller go for this type of deal? By making the deal an attractive one to the investor, he should be able to get a good price for the land and a steady and reliable income from the deal. What's more, he doesn't want too much cash in the way of a down payment since he'll probably want to report the deal as an installment sale for tax purposes.

You adjust the purchase price, the interest rate, and the payment schedule to suit both his and your requirements. You might come out with a deal that gives the seller a somewhat higher purchase price than he might otherwise get. The interest rate can be set at market level or somewhat lower, since the seller will be paying taxes on the interest income at ordinary income rates. (You and the seller can adjust the rate and the price by swapping a somewhat lower rate for a somewhat higher price.)

Balloon-Mortgage Loan. Another way to kick up your leverage is to use a "balloon-type" arrangement. You might arrange to pay your seller interest plus very little amortization during the loan term. At the end of the term, the entire principal becomes due. Since you expect to sell before the end of the term, you don't expect the lump-sum payment to cause you any trouble.

Prepaid-Interest Deal. You might be able to work out a deal under which you substitute prepaid interest for a portion of the down payment. You can take a tax deduction for prepaid interest during the remaining months of the taxable year of settlement plus the following 12 months. So, the earlier in the tax year you settle, the more prepaid interest you can deduct. However, you should be careful not to materially distort your income by using this deduction, as the Internal Revenue Service, pursuant to *Rev. Rul. 68-643,* CB 1968-2, 76, modified by 69-582, *Supra,* may disallow the deduction. [See *Sandor,* 62 TC 469 (1974) aff'd 536 F. 2d 874 (9th Cir. 1976)].

Also, for at least years 1976 and after, prepayment of most interest is disallowed [Secs. 163 and 461(g) of the Code; *see* ¶2006, *Supra*].

"Reverse-Interest" Deal. The landowner might go for a so-called "reverse-interest" land deal. Under this type of deal, you would pay a small part of the principal plus interest figured only on the amount of the payment rather than on the prepaid balance of the principal. Regular payments of interest and principal might start in the sixth year. The loan term might run to 25 years. You would expect to sell the property by the end of the fifth year. The rate of interest you'd pay would depend on the money market. The following schedule is for a $100,000 loan at 8 percent interest.

Year	Principal	Interest	Total Payment	Unpaid Balance
1	$1,000	$ 80	$1,080	$99,000
2	2,000	320	2,320	97,000
3	3,000	720	3,720	94,000
4	4,000	1,280	5,280	90,000
5	5,000	2,000	7,000	85,000

Checking Out the Deal. No question about it, when you increase your leverage, you also increase your after-tax profit potential. You can achieve very great leverage by making a small down payment, pushing your interest payments into the early years, and putting off payments of principal as long as possible.

You must be careful not to get in over your head. Make sure you can meet the debt service requirements and the other carrying charges. Check out the liquidity of your position. You might want to put your investment dollars into more than one property and thereby spread the risk.

[¶2104] **REDUCING CAPITAL GAIN ON PIECEMEAL SALE OF LAND**

Suppose you buy a tract that you're going to sell on a piecemeal basis. You want to realize as small a taxable gain as possible when you start selling off the property.

What to Do. You can allocate the purchase price at a higher basis to the frontage than to the rest of the tract since the value of the frontage should be greater than the land in the rear of the tract. In this way, you come out with a smaller taxable gain when you sell off the frontage. Later on, of course, since your basis for the remaining property will be lower, your taxable gain, depending on the sale price, will be commensurately greater [*Clayton,* 15 TCM 105, aff'd. 245 F.2d 238 (6th Cir. 1957)].

If the purchase price is allocated in the original purchase-and-sale agreement by which you acquire the property, IRS will usually go along with the allocation.

[¶2105] DEVELOPER'S INCOME AND BEST TAX RESULTS

The manner in which a developer computes his income is of great consequence to him. He has, at least to some extent, the election to capitalize or to deduct taxes and carrying charges. Before he makes his election, he should know which method of computation will be more beneficial to him. The problem is complicated by the fact that it is frequently difficult to determine which expenses must be capitalized and how much can be deducted annually against income.

[¶2106] LAND COSTS

Where building lots contained in a given tract of land are sold before the contemplated development work is fully completed, the gain should be determined on the basis of the cost of the land plus actual estimated future expenditures for the development of the property in accordance with the terms of the contract of sale [*Mackay,* 11 BTA 569, *acq* VII-2 CB25]. However, any unexpended estimated cost at the end of the project will naturally reduce the cost of sales.

A sample of the items included in the cost of land are:

1. The original acquisition costs; e.g., purchase price, closing cost, attorney fees.
2. Improvements; e.g., construction of roads, streets, sewers, water, and electric lines.

Furthermore, IRS has approved boosting land costs by a developer where he bears the cost of installing water lines in order to induce prospective purchasers to buy his lots. An arrangement was made with the water company which called for the developer to pay the water company a fixed sum. The water company agreed to pay the installation cost to the developer based on 6 per cent of the gross annual receipts from the sale of the water to residents of a sub-division.

Although there may be a repayment of the installation costs to the developer, IRS agrees that the developer can add a pro rata share of the cost of installing the water line as part of the cost of the lots he sells. He can also include the cost of the water meter. This is so, says IRS, because payment to the water company is unconditional and the developer may never get back some of his installation costs — for example, if all the lots are not sold or if houses are not constructed on the lots and so water is not purchased [*Rev. Rul.* 60-3, CB 1960-1, 284].

Sometimes builders or subdividers find it necessary to lay down sewage disposal systems, e.g., where septic tanks cannot be used. They treat the costs involved as an increase in the basis of the land sold and in this way try to deduct their costs. IRS, however, has met this treatment with resistance and has usually maintained that the builder or his controlled corporation has retained rights of ownership in the sewage system and is therefore not entitled to any deduction. The Tax Court allowed the deduction where a builder formed a corporation to run the sewage disposal plant. He then constructed a plant and collecting lines for the corporation. The corporation then transferred it back to him as trustee for the benefit of the various lot owners who would be serviced by the sewage collection system. In these circumstances, the Tax Court is convinced the sewage system was constructed to induce and make possible the sale of the lots and that under the arrangement used the subdividers did not retain full ownership in the sewage system. Since extensive beneficial rights were transferred to the lot owners, the subdivider was permitted to add the sewage system's cost to his basis for the lots sold [*Estate of Collins,* 31 TC 238, acq. 1959-2CB4].

[¶2107]   CAPITAL GAIN ON SUBDIVISION SALES

If you own a large tract of land and subdivide it, chances are you are going to run into a Treasury claim that you are holding the property for sale in the ordinary course of business. So the gain on the sale of lots, as the Treasury sees it, would be ordinary income.

If you åre a dealer in these lots, there is no question: You have ordinary income.

Where you bought the land as an investment and find that the only way you can liquidate your investment is by subdividing, you may convince a court you are not holding the property for sale to customers in the ordinary course of your business. [*Edwards Industries,* 33 TCM 569 (1974)]. But even if you cannot establish that you are merely liquidating an investment, you can still get almost all of your gain as capital gain (if you're not incorporated) if you can come within the rules of Section 1237.

What You Should Know About Section 1237. This section lays down specific rules for keeping your sales out of the dealer category and achieving the capital gain rate. It does not apply to losses. The capital gain rate is available if certain conditions are met:

1. You were not otherwise a dealer during the taxable year of sale and never held the subdivided tract or any part thereof as a dealer primarily for sale to customers. Also, you cannot have held any other real property as a dealer in the year of sale.
2. No substantial improvements increasing the value of the property were made by you or related entities. Nor could such improvements be made by a lessee if the improvement constituted income to you, or by a governmental body if the improvement constituted an addition to your basis for the property.
3. You held the subdivided realty for at least five years, unless the property was inherited.

What Is a Substantial Improvement? As indicated, you cannot make substantial improvements to the property if you want Section 1237 to apply. According to the regulations, an improvement which does not increase the value of a lot by more than 10 per cent is generally not substantial. Only those lots in the tract increased by more than 10 percent in value may lose Section 1237 treatment. Shopping centers, other commercial or residential buildings, hard surface roads, or utilities such as sewers, water, gas, or electric lines are substantial improvements. But temporary field offices, gravel roads, and surveying, filling, draining, leveling, and clearing operations are not substantial.

Necessary Improvements: Even if an improvement would be considered substantial under the above rules, it still does not knock out Section 1237 treatment if it is necessary. It's necessary if all of the following conditions are met:

1. You held the lot for at least ten years.
2. The improvements is a water, sewer, or drainage facility or a road.
3. You can show that the property would not have otherwise been marketable at the prevailing local price for similar building sites.
4. You elect to neither deduct the expense nor add it to the basis of any lot sold for purposes of determining how much your gain is. This results in the loss of any tax benefit for these expenses.

[¶2108]   **COSTS RELATIVE TO BARRIERS**
AND REMOVAL OF SAME FOR
HANDICAPPED OR ELDERLY

New Section 190 of the Code, was added by the *Tax Reform Act of 1976* for individuals and corporations. Under Section 190(a)(1) of the Code, the taxpayer can elect to treat qualified architectural and transportation barrier removal expenses, which are paid or incurred by the taxpayer, during the taxable year, as expenses which are *not* to be capitalized, i.e., they can be written off. This is an elective section. (There are procedures to make the election.)

There is a maximum deduction under this rule of up to $25,000. The effective date is for tax years ending after December 31, 1976 and before 1980.

[¶2109] **HISTORIC STRUCTURES**

The *Tax Reform Act of 1976* provides new Section 191(a) of the Code to allow a five year *write-off* of rehabilitation expenditures incurred with respect to depreciable historic structures, which are used in the trade or business or held for production of income by the taxpayer. This rule is for additions to the capital account after June 14, 1976, and before June 15, 1981. (The rules for recapture of depreciation under Sections 1245 and 1250 of the Code apply.)

Section 280B of the Code was also added by the *Tax Reform Act of 1976* to provide for rules for *demolition* of historic structures.

a. The general rule in the case of a demolition of a certified historic structure provides that *no deduction* otherwise allowable will be allowed to the owner-lessee of the structure for any amount expended for the demolition or any loss sustained on account of the demolition. These amounts are chargeable to the capital account of the taxpayer. They are added to the *land* on which the demolished structure was located.

b. The buildings covered include those structures which are in a registered historic district, unless the Secretary of the Interior has certified, before the demolition, that the structure did not have "historic significance."

c. The effective date is for demolitions commencing after June 30, 1976 and before January 1, 1981.

With regard to *depreciating property after a demolition,* in the case of real property which was partially or wholly constructed, erected, or used on a site which was, after the earlier mentioned June 30, 1976 date, occupied as a certified historic structure, on or after said date, and where that structure was demolished or substantially altered after that date, depreciation is limited to straight line. (Penalty!) This applies to the *portion* of the basis attributable to construction, reconstruction, or erection after 1975 and before 1981.

Depreciation on substantially rehabilitated historic property has been changed to allow the taxpayer to treat the property as though he was the "original user." This means that an accelerated rate of depreciation can be used; the rate depends on whether the property was commercial or residential property. (Prize!)

a. To qualify, the taxpayer must show (1) that the amounts added to the capital account during a 24-month period ending on the last day of the taxable year must be the greater of $5,000 or (2) the adjusted basis of the property (with some adjustments).

b. These provisions apply to additions to the capital accounts after June 30, 1976 and before July 1, 1981 [Sec. 167(o) of the Code].

[¶2110]   **LAND CONTRIBUTION BY DEVELOPER**

If a developer donates land to form a country club adjacent to his subdivision and such land donation enhances the value of the subdivision, he generally cannot claim a charitable deduction for the value of the donated property. The cost of the donated property is treated as part of the cost of the lots sold by him [*Country Club Estates*, 22 TC 1283, *acq.* CB 1955-1, 4]. Similar treatment is given to land turned over to water, sewer, or electric companies for rights-of-way and to land and streets deeded to the locality to obtain government maintenance.

If the subdivision is to be developed by sections rather than all at about the same time, an apportionment should be made on a ratio of the sale price of the various lots or divided equally over the number of lots to be sold if the cost is to be apportioned ratably.

[¶2111]   **CHARITABLE CONTRIBUTIONS OF SCENIC EASEMENT**

Under IRS ruling [*Rev. Rul. 73-339*, CB 1973-2, 68] you can get an income and gift tax deduction where you make a charitable contribution of an open space or scenic easement in perpetuity. To qualify as a charitable contribution, the transfer must not be made with the reasonable expectation of an economic benefit in your trade or business [*Duberstein, Mose*, 363 US 278 (1960)].

Figuring Value of Contribution. The value of the contribution is computed by using the "before and after" approach. Thus the difference between the fair market value of the underlying property before the easement was granted and the fair market value of the property after the grant equals the value of the easement.

[¶2112]   **CONTRIBUTIONS—CONSERVATION**

Under the *Tax Reform Act of 1976*, Section 170 (f) (3) of the Code has been amended, along with Sections 2055(e)(2) and 2522 (c)(2) of the Code.

Under the new provision under Section 170(f)(3)(B) of the Code, a lease, option to purchase, or easement with respect to real property of not less than thirty years duration granted to an organization which is charitable in nature (with certain restrictions), exclusively for conservation purposes, or a remainder interest in real property which is granted to an organization which is charitable in nature (with certain exceptions as to the type), exclusively for conservation purposes, will be allowed a charitable contribution.

Section 170(f) (3) (C) of the Code provides that "conservation purposes" means that preservation of land areas for public outdoor recreation or education, scenic enjoyment, preservation of historical important land areas or structures, or the protection of natural environmental systems.

The effective date for this Act is for transfers or contributions after June 13, 1976 and before June 14, 1977*. These rules also apply with regard to the same type of contributions for estates and gifts.

[¶2113]   CAPITAL GAIN ON TRANSFER OF WATER RIGHTS

Under Section 1231 of the Code, gains or losses from sales or exchanges of real estate used in a trade or business, other than inventory or property held primarily for sale in the ordinary course of business, are treated as gains or losses from the sale or exchange of capital assets if the aggregate of the gains exceeds the aggregate of the losses.

Sale of Water Rights as Sale of Property Used in Trade or Business. Let's say you've owned the land you use for your farming business for over six months. You sell perpetual rights to the water under some of your land. Immediately prior to the sale, you used the water for irrigation purposes in connection with your farming business. In transferring the water rights, you reserve the right to use as much water as necessary to drill for and produce oil, gas, and other minerals as well as the right to use water for normal farming and ranching operations and for domestic use but not for irrigation purposes.

IRS has ruled that the water rights you sold are an interest in real property and qualify as profits which you used in your trade or business and which you held long term. Therefore, said IRS, any gain or loss resulting from this sale is subject to the treatment provided for in [Sec. 1231 of the Code; (*Rev. Rul.* 73-341, CB 1973-2, 306 superseding Rev. Rul. 55-295].

[¶2114]   ELECTING TO CAPITALIZE OR DEDUCT CARRYING CHARGES OF UNDEVELOPED LAND

Usually it is preferable to deduct rather than capitalize your expenses. Deducting gives you an immediate writeoff against your income. When you capitalize, however, you add your expenses to the cost basis of your building, plant, or whatever and only very gradually recover them, via depreciation, over the property's useful life [Sec. 266 of the Code]. This gives you very little immediate benefit.

Frequently, an investor or developer whose land is standing idle or being improved has little or no income to absorb the deductions, so he will find it

*Recently extended.

helpful to capitalize his expenses. Therefore, let's examine the treatment of carrying charges under the election rules as set forth in Reg. § 1.226-1.

Which Expenses Can be Capitalized? Under the Regs, the right to capitalize certain expenses depends on the type of property that you own.

1. If you own *unimproved* or *unproductive property,* you may capitalize annual taxes, interest on your mortgage, and other true carrying charges.

2. Whether or not the property is improved, productive or unproductive, you may capitalize any normally deductible development expenses which you might pay or incur for making additions or improvements to the property up to the time such work is completed. Included within this class of development expenses that may be capitalized are interest on loans, unemployment and Social Security taxes paid on employees' wages, and sales taxes on materials used in the course of construction.

How to Make the Election. The election to capitalize is made annually when preparing your tax return. To make the election all you do is attach to your return a statement listing the charges to be capitalized. Be sure to indicate on this statement which property or project is involved.

Once you make your election to deduct for a particular year, you cannot later file an amended return for that year with a capitalization election statement. The statement must be attached to your original return.

Suppose you elected to capitalize your carrying charges this year. May you change your mind and deduct your expenses next year? Once again, the type of property you own is important.

1. If the land is unimproved or unproductive, you may elect to capitalize the appropriate expenses this year and still deduct them next year. If you want to capitalize the expenses in the following year, you must then make a new election, as outlined above.

2. If the land is developed or improved and you've elected to capitalize, you must continue to capitalize your expenses until work on the project is completed. Once the project is completed, you *must* then deduct your expenses.

There is nothing which says that you must treat equally all expenses qualifying for the election. You can capitalize some expenses and deduct other. The only restriction is that you may not ''split'' a single expense. That is, you may not deduct some of the interest paid on a loan and capitalize the rest. In keeping with this rule, you may not split similar expenses. For example, you cannot capitalize unemployment taxes and deduct Social Security taxes.

If you own more than one parcel, you do not have to show consistency from parcel to parcel. By making the election with regard to one lot, you do not bind yourself to treat the next lot in the same manner.

[¶2115] CARRYING CHARGE TAX DEDUCTIONS FOR BUILDERS AND DEVELOPERS

If you form a corporation to build with the idea of renting or operating the property on completion, the corporation will have taxes and carrying charges to pay while the building is being put up. Thus, in its first year it will have deductible expenses with no income to offset them. The tax loss thus created can, of course, be carried forward for five years to offset income arising in those years. But the corporation's earnings during those five years may be too small to recover the full loss. This may be especially true of a shopping center whose development to full earning capacity may take more than the five-year carryover period.

The corporation could elect to capitalize these costs—i.e., add them to the cost of the building or development. This is permitted by the tax law [Sec. 266 of the Code]. However, if the election to capitalize is made, the costs will be recovered via depreciation—over the entire life of the property—giving the owners very little immediate benefit.

One way the owners can get immediate benefit from these carrying charges is to have the corporation elect under Subchapter S. Under this provision of the law, a corporation with fewer than eleven stockholders can, in effect, be treated as a partnership. When a corporation elects under Subchapter S, its loss is picked up by the stockholders in proportion to their stockholdings in much the same way as partners pick up their proportionate shares of a partnership's losses. Each stockholder then reports his share of the loss on his own tax return. Since the corporation during the building period will have only expenses and no income, it is bound to have a loss which the stockholders can then pick up.

Note: Under Subchapter S, when a corporation gets more than 20 percent of its gross receipts from passive rent, the election to be taxed as a Subchapter S corporation automatically ends [Sec. 1372 (e)(5) of the Code].

Once the building is completed and the rents start coming in, the election will end. But for the period of construction, the stockholders can enjoy the benefits of corporate losses under Subchapter S. Note too that since any rent receipts may be the total receipts of the corporation, it is important that no rent is received in a tax year in which the loss is to pass through to the stockholders under Subchapter S. If necessary, the corporation should end its tax year immediately before it begins to collect rent. A corporation can usually change its tax year once without getting Treasury permission.

If for some reason, you cannot use a corporation qualifying to elect under Subchapter S, you can still have the carrying charges be deductible by the individuals by first forming a partnership to build or develop the property. Later, when the operation becomes profitable, you can then transfer the property to the corporation in a tax-free transaction. (But, watch for other adverse results, such as loss of first user depreciation benefits.)

[¶2116]　TAX ELECTIONS AVAILABLE TO SUBDIVIDER

The subdivider may elect to include taxes and carrying charges in his land costs if they otherwise would be deductible. Some of the items which may be capitalized as noted, are:

1. In the case of unimproved and unproductive real property, annual taxes, interest on a mortgage, and other carrying charges;
2. In the case of real property whether improved or unimproved and whether productive or unproductive, all necessary expenditures of the development of the real property or for the construction of improvements buy only up to the time the development or construction work has been completed. This includes interest on a loan to provide funds for the venture and all payroll and state use or sales taxes (or other similar taxes) paid on materials used in such development or construction work [Reg. Sec. 1.266-1b].

Where a portion of a development has been completed, it is necessary to allocate the above charges between the developed section, which must be expensed, and the undeveloped section, which still may be capitalized.

The election to capitalize is exercised by attaching a statement to the income tax return listing those charges to be included in the land costs.

Keep in mind the new limitations, discussed in 2008 per the *Tax Reform Act of 1976,* which restricts the writeoff of construction interest and taxes.

[¶2117] TAX AND OTHER BENEFITS FROM ACQUISITION OF LAND THROUGH LEASE-PURCHASE CONTRACT

A lease containing an option to purchase must be scrutinized with great care. While the lease may describe the tenant's payments as rent, the details of the transaction may indicate they are really installments paid on a deferred purchase of the property. The law permits rentals to be deducted only if they are paid for property to which the taxpayer has not taken or is not taking title, or in which he has no equity [Code Sec. 162]. If it is a purchase, the tenant must capitalize the payments and take deductions in the form of depreciation.

Example: Edgar has a lease with an option-to-purchase agreement which the Treasury considers a sale. The terms are that he will pay rent of $20,000 per year for the first four years. The fifth year he can pay an additional $20,000 thus purchasing the property in five years. Hence, IRS will only allow an annual depreciation deduction which, assuming a 20-year life, will be $5,000 rather then the $20,000 "rent."

Similary, under a deferred purchase the "lessor" does not get rent income but rather a return of capital and capital gain or loss (unless he is a dealer, in which event he has ordinary income or loss).

Example: Evans, who is not a dealer, enters into a lease with an option-to-purchase agreement with Black, the lessee. It is a ten-year lease, with rent of $10,000 a year. At the end of the tenth year, Black has the option of buying the property for $5,000. Evans' adjusted basis for the property is $60,000. A court may find that this is not a lease with an option but an installment sale, in which case $105,000 is not rental income to Evans. Sixty thousand dollars is a return of capital, and $45,000 is capital gain.

There is no statutory provision to tell you when a lease with an option to purchase becomes an installment sale. However, the cases in the field give you some rules of thumb. The important considerations are the amount of rent called for in relation to the fair rental value of the property and a comparison of the "rent" with the option purchase price. [*See Berry, supra; Haggard,* 241 F.3d 288 (9th Cir. 1957)].

Example: Jones owns property worth $100,000. He leases this property to Brown for five years. The "rent" is $20,000 a year. At the end of four years, Brown is given the option to purchase the property for $20,000. This deal would be very suspect. The Treasury would likely call the transaction an installment sale and disallow an attempted rent deduction by Brown.

Note the indicia of an installment sale here rather than a lease.

1. The rent is high—20 percent.
2. The purchase price is low—20 percent of the property's valuation.
3. Total rent plus purchase price equals the value of the property at the time the "lease" was entered into.

The courts will not be bound by the name put on the agreement; rather, they will look to the reality of the situation. Some examples of lease-option arrangements that were deemed sales include: a rental of $680,000 payable over a 68-year period with an option to buy for $10 at the end of the lease term [*Oesterreich,* 226 F.2d 798 (9th Cir. 1955)]; a 10-year lease calling for annual rent of $19,000 with an option to purchase at the end of the lease at $75,000—the annual "rent" being more than 25 percent of the "purchase" price, the court concluded a sale was intended [*Elliot,* 262 F.2d 383 (9th Cir. 1959)].

There has been some liberalizing in allowing rental deductions by some of the circuit and district courts. Note *Benton,* [197 F.2d 745 (1952)], where the Fifth Circuit in allowing the rent deduction de-emphasized the economic realities in favor of the intent of the parties. Also see the very liberal attitude of the Seventh Circuit in *Breece Veneer and Panel Co.* [232 F.2d 319 (7th Cir. 1956)].

In *Arkansas Bank and Trust Co.* [224 F.Supp. 171 (D.C. Ark. 1964)] the taxpayer was successful in obtaining a rental deduction despite the fact that the option price was much lower than the market value of the property after it was improved by the lessee as required by the lease. The Court there refused to look behind the manifested intention of the parties to create a lease and nothing more. However, in spite of these more liberal attitudes, to be on the safe side it is best to watch the ratio of rent to purchase-option price, the excessiveness of rent, and an unreasonably low purchase price. By handling these factors with care, you may avoid having your rent deduction disallowed.

If Lease Is Called a Sale, Tenant Can Obtain an Interest Deduction:. Where a lease with a purchase option is treated as a sale, the tenant can probably deduct part of his payments as interest expense (in lieu of capitalizing them and taking depreciation). The 1964 tax law added a provision (Sec. 483) which requires that a portion of the purchase price in an installment or deferred sale be treated as unstated interest. This rule applies when (1) the sale is of a capital asset or depreciable property; (2) the sale price exceeds $3,000; (3) and the contract doesn't specify at least the minimum interest rate (now 6 percent) set by IRS. Presumably, this provision will apply to a lease agreement which IRS or a court calls a sale.

The landlord in this case would report a similar amount as interest income (and reduce the amount treated as the sale price). The rule applies whether the landlord realizes gain or loss as a result of a sale.

[¶2118]   **TAX ASPECTS OF OPTIONING LAND**

There are several ways in which you can acquire undeveloped land and walk away from the deal with a minimum loss if it turns sour. You can, for example, try for a purchase-money mortgage for as much of the purchase price as possible and have the mortgage provide for no personal liability on your part. (By statute in some states, you can't be held liable for a deficiency when a purchase-money trust deed or mortgage is foreclosed, but elsewhere this is not true.) Another way to limit your liability is to handle the transaction through a corporate entity.

A third way is to use an option to purchase under which the amount you pay for the option is all that you can lose. If you exercise the option, its cost is added to your tax basis of the property. If you don't exercise the option within the specified time, the cost of the option becomes a deductible loss. It is a capital loss if the property would have been a capital asset in your hands; otherwise it is an ordinary loss. The distinction is important. A capital loss has to be used to offset favorably taxed capital gain. An ordinary loss gives you greater tax benefits since it can be used to offset ordinary income.

An option arrangement can be used to control the realization of gain on the sale of land. Proper timing can turn a potential short-term gain into a long-term gain. Also by separating the years of realization of gains and losses, you can prevent the offset of favorably taxed capital gains by losses otherwise available to offset ordinary income.

Here we give you a rundown on how options to purchase are used to nail down land and enable the investor to walk away from the deal if it turns sour. We discuss some important types of option arrangements and show you how they can be used to advantage.

Options to Purchase and How They Work. When you acquire an option to purchase land, you acquire the right to buy the land at any time within a specified period at the price specified in the option. What you pay for the option depends on the circumstances, but it will always be small compared with the price of the land. If you fail to exercise the option, you lose the amount you paid for it.

What it comes down to is that, with an option, you can tie down a piece of land for a period of time at a small fraction of the cost of the land. If the land appreciates in value—as you expect—you benefit from the appreciated value but still pay only the price specified in the option. You get this benefit without tying up large sums of money and without running the risk of loss-except to the extend of the sum you pay for the option—if your expectations are not fulfilled.

Types of Options and What You Pay for Them. With a straight option, you tie down a piece of land for a specified period of time and have the right to purchase the land during that period at a specified price. In a rising market, you'll probably have to agree to a price that is somewhat higher than the price similar properties in the area are selling for. But you're betting on an increase in value, and you're not paying taxes and other carrying charges on the land. If you do buy, the cost of the option will be applied against the price of the land.

There are variations on the straight option that can be used. For example, you may get an option under which the price at which you can buy the property goes up by a specified amount each year that you hold on to the option without exercising it. Or you may get a declining-credit option or a rolling option.

☐ *Declining-credit Option.* Let's say you get a declining-credit option on a piece of property whose price is $100,000. You acquire the declining-credit option at a cost of 10 percent of the price of the land. So, you pay $10,000 for a five-year option. If you exercise your option to purchase within the first year, you get a full credit of $10,000. If you exercise the option during the second year your credit is reduced to $8,000, and so forth until the fifth year, during which only $2,000 would be applied to the purchase price.

☐ *Rolling Option.* This type of option is frequently used where you're picking up a large tract of land that will be subdivided into building lots. Suppose, for example, the tract is priced at $200,000 and is divided into 10 parcels, each parcel being sold at $20,000. You take an option on the entire tract at $10,000. Under the terms of the option, you can purchase any one of the parcels at $20,000 and apply the entire $10,000 that you paid for the option against the purchase price of the parcel and give up your option to purchase any of the other parcels. Or you can pay the full purchase price of the parcel and retain your option by letting it "roll over" to the next parcel. In this way, you retain your hold on the entire tract for the period of the option, without being committed to purchase the entire tract. You can buy only the parcels you want and let the rest go.

Variations on the rolling option might set up the particular order in which you can purchase the parcels or fix different prices for different parcels.

☐ *Option to Purchase in Stages.* One of the techniques used by developers to assure themselves of an adequate supply of land is the continuous option agreement. This provides for purchase of a tract of land in stages and so enables the developer to avoid tying up most of his capital in land for which he has no immediate need. He can build a small group of homes on the first portion and, when and if they are sold, proceed to the next parcel.

As for the landowner, the benefit of this procedure is twofold: He usually can get a higher price than if he insisted on selling the entire tract outright and, in addition, he received payment over a period of years and thus avoids having to report his entire gain at once. This basically is the same as an installment sale except for the manner of apportioning the gain. In an installment sale, a fixed percentage of each payment is gain. Under the option plan, the seller's basis for the entire tract must be allocated among the various portions sold, and the gain attributable to each portion will be the difference between its basis and its selling price. The allocation of basis cannot be made on a straight-square-foot or acreage formula if, in fact, the various portions of the tract have different fair market values.

☐ *Combination of Installment Sale and Option.* An installment sale contract can be combined with an option agreement for the sale of undeveloped acreage. This is a compromise approach to the problem of selling large tracts to developers who plan to improve the land in stages. The price may be stated per acre, with the exact quantity of land to be determined by survey. The land can be conveyed in stages, with the buyer obligated to purchase a minimum percentage of the total acreage. As to the remaining acreage, he has, in effect, an option which must be exercised in accordance with a fixed schedule of dates. The seller can be assured of a sum which probably represents his entire investment plus a small return. If the developer finds his plan is successful and buys the remaining land, the seller will realize the remainder of his profit. If not, the seller will keep the undeveloped portion of the land. The developer may be given some freedom in choosing lots which will be the most salable; the seller may be protected by a provision which prevents a hodgepodge pattern which would severly limit the market for any land which remained unused.

The tax treatment of the seller's gain would vary depending on whether the tax authorities regard this as a sale of the entire tract or as a partial sale and a partial option. In the case of an installment sale, a fixed percentage of each payment would be gain. In the case of an option, the seller's basis for the entire tract would be allocated among the various portions sold; the gain attributed to each portion is the difference between its basis and its selling price.

□ *Option to Purchase Calling for Escalation of Price.* When the parties enter into an agreement granting an option to purchase under which it is contemplated that the option period may continue for a relatively long period of time, the optionor will want to benefit from any anticipated increase in the value of the property. Thus in an option granted for a period of years, the optionee may be required to pay additional amounts to keep the option open. The option price may escalate at periodic intervals during the option period. The optionee may also benefit under this arrangement if there is an unusual increase in value during the option period.

How to Make the Most Out of Your Deal. Suppose you picked up an option with the idea of speculating on the appreciation in value of the land, with the least amount of cash outlay and greatest amount of profit.

You might decide to sell the land on which you hold the option. If you do so, don't tell the prospective buyer that you have only an option on the land until after the contract is signed, since he may decide to wait till your option expires and then buy from the owner. In this type of deal, you can come out with the difference between the option price of the land and the appreciated value of the land as reflected in its purchase price where your option is a straight option.

Sell the Option, Not the Land. There may be a better way available to you to cash in. If the land goes up in value and you've held the option longterm before you sell, your gain comes to you as a long-term captial gain. Make sure that you sell the option, not the land. Otherwise your gain will be fully taxable as a short-term gain. Since your holding period starts after the date when you exercise the option and buy the property, not from the date when you acquired the option, if IRS successfully contends that, in reality, you've sold the land rather than the option, it will be held that you've exercised the option, bought the land, and almost immediately sold it. Thus, you have realized a short-term gain or ordinary income.

To make sure that you get favorable capital gain tax treatment, be sure to hold on to the option for the required time an sell it without any strings. Don't guarantee title or anything else. If you do, you run the risk of IRS contending that, in reality, you've sold the land rather than the option.

[¶2119] TAX DEDUCTIBLE DEMOLITION LOSSES

Generally speaking, a loss due to the voluntary demolition or removal of a building or machinery is deductible as an ordinary loss [Reg. §1.165-1]. There are certain wrinkles to this rule with respect to the demolition of old buildings. Where the demolition occurs as a result of a plan or intention formed subsequent to the acquisition of the buildings demolished, the loss is normally fully deductible as long as it was incurred in a trade or in a transaction entered into for profit [Reg. §1.165-3(b)]. But where the intent to demolish was formed at the time of purchase, the "loss" on the old building (its undepreciated basis) plus the cost of demolition may not be deducted it must be allocated to the *land* or building as part of its cost basis. This is true even though the intention is not to demolish immediately and any demolition orginally planned is subsequently deferred or abandoned.

[¶2120]   INTENTION OF DEMOLISH

An intention to demolish is evidenced by all the surrounding facts and circumstances; it may be suggested by any of the following:

1. Only a short interval between purchase and demolition.
2. Prohibitive remodeling costs.
3. Zoning or other regulations which prohibit the economic use to which the building would have to be put.
4. General unsuitability for taxpayer's business.
5. Inability at time of acquisition to realize a reasonable profit from buildings.

Countering factors include:
1. Substantial improvements after acquisition.
2. Prolonged use after acquisition.
3. Suitability of building as investment asset.
4. A substantial change in the building or the taxpayer's business after acquisition which then makes demolition desirable [Reg. §1.165-3(c)].

If the building is removed to place the land in a condition desired by a prospective or present lessee, the capitalized costs are treated as part of the cost of obtaining the lease, amortizable over the lease term [*Wm. Ward,* 7 BTA 1107, *acq.* VII-1 CB33; Reg. §1.165-3(b)(2)].

[¶2121]   AMOUNT OF DEDUCTION

Where a demolition loss is allowed, it includes the cost to demolish. [Reg. §1.165-3(a)].

See the earlier discussion for special rules on demolition of historic structures. [*See* ¶2109].

CHAPTER **22**

Tax-Shelter
in Farms and Farmland

[¶2201]　TAX-WISE WAYS TO PROFIT FROM FARMLAND

You may be able to sow the seeds of success to reap a rich harvest in farmland profit in three basic speculative ways:

1. Buy an existing and operating farm.
2. Buy land which is ready for farming and start a farming operation to support the land until it attains a value greater than farm value.
3. Buy run-down land or land which in its natural state is not suitable for farming, spend money to improve it so that it will support profitable crops, and farm it until it ripens into more valuable uses.

Here, we take a look at some of the major considerations which are involved in investing in farm property and the benefits to be derived from special tax treatment accorded farmers.

[¶2202]　TAX BENEFITS AVAILABLE TO FARMERS

One of the best summary statements of the tax advantages to be reaped by gentlemen farmers is found in the original Treasury Tax Reform Proposals in 1969. The Treasury said:

"Over the years more and more and more high bracket taxpayers, whose primary economic activity is other than farming, have exploited ... [special farm tax rules] for the purpose of gaining tax advantages. By electing the special farm accounting rules which follow premature deductions, many of these high bracket taxpayers show "farm losses' which are not true economic losses. These 'tax losses' are then deducted from their high bracket nonfarm income resulting in large tax savings. Moreover, these 'tax losses' which arise from deductions taken because of capital costs or inventory costs usually thus represent an investment in farm assets rather than funds actually lost. This investment quite often will ultimately be sold and taxed only at low capital gains rates. Thus, deductions are set off against ordinary income, while the sale price of the resulting assets represents capital gain.''

While most farm expenses are governed by the general rules that apply to all business expenses, special treatment is provided in certain areas. To be treated as a farmer for tax purposes, you must be a person (an individual, corporation, or partnership) engaged in the operation or management of a farm for gain or profit, either as owner or tenant. "Farming" includes the cultivation, raising, and harvesting of any agricultural or horticultural commodity and the raising, shearing, feeding, caring for, training, and management of livestock, bees, poultry, and fur-bearing animals and wildlife. A "farm" as used in its ordinary, accepted sense includes stock, dairy, poultry, fruit, fur-bearing animals and truck farms, plantations, ranches, nurseries, ranges, greenhouses, or other similar structures used primarily for the raising of agricultural or horticultural commodities and orchards.

Soil and Water Conservation Expenditures.

A taxpayer engaged in the business of farming enjoys a special election to expense (rather than capitalize) money spent on land for soil and water conservation and the prevention of land erosion. The deductible amount in any year may not exceed 25 percent of gross income from farming for that year. However, any excess can be carried over, but only to the extent of the 25 percent limit per year. The option applies to expenses for the treatment of moving of earth on land actually used in farming, either before or during the time the expenditures are made. The land must be used for the production of crops, fruits, or other agricultural products or for the sustenance of livestock. It does not apply to money spent on depreciable facilities or structures. Such items must be capitalized.

This deduction can be added to an operating loss and carried over as a part of that operating loss. Where the expenditures exceed 25 percent of gross income, the excess can be carried over until it has all been deducted, but only against income from farming. However, with the election in operation, this excess can't be added to the basis of the improved land. Thus, when the land is sold, the capital gain is not reduced by the portion of the expenses not deducted because they were in excess of the 25 percent limit. But, even though the land has been sold, these expenses can be deducted against subsequently realized farm income.

This special deduction affords an opportunity to convert ordinary income into capital gain. A person buying a piece of farmland can deduct 25 per cent of his expenses for leveling, grading, clearing brush, building drainage ditches, etc., against ordinary (farm) income. When the property is sold, it will bring a higher price because of the work. But the gain will be taxed at more favorable capital gain rates, subject to potential recapture [Sec. 1252].

Development Expenses. The farmer also has an election, except as noted below, for the *Tax Reform Act of 1976* changes, to capitalize or deduct expenses such as taxes, labor, seed, fertilizer, insurance, interest, etc., during the period of development. Once the productive state is reached, however, he must deduct these expenses currently. There is no option to deduct currently capital expenditures, such as wells, irrigation pipes, drain tile, masonry or concrete tanks, reservoirs or dams, and roads. Capital expenditures in connection with soil and water conservation are an exception.

Fertilizer Costs. The cost of fertilizer and lime was deductible; the amount expended in restoration of soil fertility preparatory to planting should be spread over the years of productivity. Where the land is undergoing a period of declining productivity, fertilizer and lime cost over that period can be amortized. Under Section 180 of the Code, fertilizer costs are deductible in the year they are consumed.

Casualty Losses. Farmers (like other taxpayers) can deduct casualty losses resulting from, for example, hurricanes, tornados, heavy rains, freezing, lightning, floods, storms, droughts, cyclones, landslides, avalanches, dust storms, sinking of land, ice pressure, cave-ins, thaws, severe blizzard and cold, and other such natural causes.

Loss of topsoil from the slow, continuous process of erosion and wasting away of land due to natural causes steadily and progressively working on the soil may lack the elements of "suddenness" and "unexpectedness" necessary to qualify as a casualty [Sec. 165(c) of the Code]. Consequently, it isn't a deductible loss even though it may reduce earning power. But a loss of topsoil due to windstorm, destruction of grazing grasses by drought, or impairment of soil by silt would be good grounds for claiming a deduction. Since the claim must be supported by proof of amount of damage, it would be wise to have a reliable soil conservation expert prepare an analysis and estimate of the damage.

Expenses of Clearing Land. Farmers can elect to deduct currently the expense of clearing land if the purpose is to make the land suitable for farming. [Sec. 182 of the Code]. Clearing land includes such things as eradication of trees, stumps, and brush; the treatment or movement of earth; and the diversion of streams and watercourses.

Expenditures for the purchase, construction, installation, or improvement of structures or facilities subject to depreciation are excluded. So are expenses which are deductible under any other section of the tax law. However, depreciation of property, such as tractors, which will be used in farming as well as in the actual clearing of land is allowed.

The deduction is limited to the lesser of $5,000 or 25 percent of taxable income from a farming business. Usually, there won't be any taxable income from farming during the preparatory period; but if the taxpayer has income from farming operations other than the operation in the preparatory period of development, he can apparently use the deduction to offset income from the other farming operation [Sec. 182(b) of the Code].

[¶2203] HOW TO AVOID LOSS OF TAX SHELTER

To get tax shelter for nonfarming income from the development of farm property, the farming operation must be a business and not a hobby [Sec. 183 of the Code]. Loss deductions for farming undertaken primarily for recreation are not allowed. If it is a hobby, deductions are limited to the gross income from the farming operation exclusive of interest and property taxes. What is more, the deductions which are taken first to reach the gross income limitations are those which are deductible in any event — taxes, interest and casualty losses. To be classified as a business, the profit motive must be the dominant factor.

A Presumption Helps. A presumption of profit seeking arises if for any two of five consecutive taxable years (seven years in the case of horse-breeding activities) the gross income derived from the activity exceeds all the expenses attributable to it. This represents good news for the taxpayer who wants to launch a farm which he fears IRS might attack as not profit motivated. But suppose the farm's first year (or even first few years) ends up in red ink? Few businesses are profitable from their very beginning, after all.

A taxpayer may elect to postpone the presumption of profit-seeking activity, putting off until the close of the fourth taxable year (sixth taxable year for horse-breeding activities) following the tax year in which he first engages in the activity the determination of whether the activity was engaged in for profit and its losses are deductible. In the meanwhile IRS will wait out the extension period without upsetting the taxpayer's claimed deductions or the intervening years [Sec. 183(e) of the Code].

Sustained Losses Will Hurt. Continuous losses over a period of years are unfavorable to a taxpayer's chances of getting his loss deduction, but there are some factors indicating a profit motive. Among these factors are operating on an efficient, economical, and sound scientific basis; marketing large quantities of produce at prevailing prices; following sound business principles and practices; changing from unprofitable crops to those with better prospects; profit sharing with a full-time manager; absence of recreational facilities; and absence of buildings other than ordinary farm buildings (not a country residence).

Another factor that is given great weight is whether the taxpayer has sought professional assistance in his farming operation in an attempt to improve the quality of the operation, reduce costs, and work actively in a businesslike manner toward reducing losses. The investment of additional capital, for instance, to improve existing facilities, is often regarded as a factor which demonstrates an overall profit-seeking intent. So, too, is a taxpayer's withdrawal from a farm which constantly loses money. On the other hand, a taxpayer who passively accepts losses that continue for a long period of time without making an attempt to do something about them will generally be treated as a hobbyist.

Examples of How Taxpayers Saved Their Tax Shelter by Proving Their Farms Were Not Hobbies. Although his farm showed consistent net losses each year, W. Clark Wise was able to convince the Tax Court that he was carrying on his farm operations for a profit. By showing that he spent a regular portion of his time actually laboring and physically supervising the operation, keeping accurate records of his income and expenses, and providing machinery for the operation of the farm, he convinced the Court that he conduced his operation with the objective of rehabilitating his farm to bring it to the point where income would exceed the expenses. The fact that the taxpayer and his family did not use the farm for recreation carried additional weight. The Commissioner's contention that because of its small size (40 acres) the farm could not have been operated profitably under any circumstances was rejected [*Wise,* 16 TCM 361 (1957), aff'd 260 F.2d 354 (6th Cir. 1958)].

Rowe B. Metcalf also convinced the Tax Court that his cattle farm was operated for profit, even though he had continuous losses for 24 years. In addition to other factors (accurate records, a full-time manager, etc.), there was testimony from taxpayer's manager, his herdsman, and various farm experts with whom the taxpayer dealt to the effect that the taxpayer was concerned with making a profit. The Court noted that a long series of losses does not of itself make a hobby out of a business [*Metcalf,* 22 TCM 1402 (1963)].

**[¶2204]   FARMERS' EXCESS DEPRECIATION ACCOUNT
AND RECAPTURE RULES**

For the reasons outlined above, farm operations have been a popular form of tax shelter for the wealthy individual. By currently deducting the types of expenditures outlined, he was able to offset substantial sums against his nonfarm income. In addition, these expenditures enhanced the individual's investment and, on the sale of the farm assets, he usually received capital gain treatment.

Beginning in 1970, all taxpayers (individuals and corporations) have been required to maintain an "excess deduction account" (EDA). The account is increased annually by the amount of farm losses in excess of $25,000 claimed by the taxpayer. (Except as provided by the *Tax Reform Act of 1976,* noted below). The rule applies to individuals only in a year in which they have nonfarm income in excess of $50,000 [Sec. 1251 of the Code].

EDA is reduced in years when there is farm income. The purpose of the EDA is to convert capital gain into ordinary income to the extent that farm losses above the limitations are used to offset nonfarm income.

Recapture Rules. The types of farm property which are subject to recapture to the extent of the EDA include depreciable business property, unharvested crops, and livestock. There is also a recapture of losses on the sale of land to the extent of allowable soil and water conservation expenditures and land clearing expenditures incurred in the current year and the prior four years [Sec. 1245(a) of the Code]. If the sale occurs from six to ten years after the expenditure occurs, the amount recaptured is reduced by 20 percent a year with no recapture after ten years. Gain on sale of depreciable real property, such as building, barns, etc., is subject to the regular recapture rules applicable to depreciable real property [Sec. 1250 of the Code].

How Excess Deduction Account Applies to Partnerships and Subchapter S Corporations.

An EDA incurred by a partnership flows through to the partners. The dollar limitations are applicable to Subchapter S corporations in cases where none of the shareholders who are individuals have farm losses.

How Excess Deduction Account Is Affected by Gift, etc.

Generally, the EDA is eliminated at death and by gift (unless the potential gain on donated farm property is more than 80 percent of the unrealized gain on all farm property held by the donor at the beginning of the year).

Electing Accounting Rules. The recapture rules, like the current deduction limitation rules, do not apply if the taxpayer elects to follow generally applicable business accounting rules (i.e., he uses inventories and capitalizes capital expenses).

[¶2205]   TAX TREATMENT OF SALES AND PURCHASES

The main tax objective in buying a farm is to allocate as much of the purchase price as you reasonably can to depreciable assets to secure maximum future depreciation deductions. If there are unharvested crops, another objective is to allocate a substantial part of the purchase price to them to reduce the amount on which you will have to pay tax when they are sold.

In allocating the basis of farm property, the fundamental rule is that the buyer must allocate the composite purchase price among the assets according to the relative fair market value of all of them at the date of purchase. If the total fair market value of all the assets is greater than the composite purchase price, each asset's basis must be reduced proportionately. But the purchase price is first allocated, dollar for dollar, to cash and cash equivalents before any pro rata reduction is made below fair market value as to the remaining assets.

The cost of land preparation incurred by the seller can be allocated by the buyer to the amounts eventually received from the sale of the crop. The amount of the purchase price allocated to semipermanent crops that come back each year for a period of years without requiring additional planting can be depreciated over their remaining useful life.

A careful appraisal should be made of the value of an unharvested crop at the time of purchase. If possible, such valuation should be incorporated in the purchase contract. A fair allocation might be one based on an expert estimate of the size of the crop, multiplied by the known market price for the crop, minus the costs of maintaining the crop and the costs of harvest—provided the purchase is made after the period during which there are problems of freezing, etc., there is no history of diseases, and there is an ascertainable market for the crop. The best procedure is to have the allocation made by an expert, perhaps a banker or a broker, rather than to make it yourself. Tell the expert what the purchase price agreed on by the parties is and give him a schedule of the property. The expert will than make a report, showing the allocation and the remaining useful life for the depreciation items.

From a selling viewpoint, it is better to sell before harvesting than after, assuming the buyer will pay a fair price that reflects the value of unharvested crops. The profit received for harvested crops is ordinary income; this may turn into capital gain if the farm (held for long-term) and crops are sold to the buyer as a package. Expenses, depreciation, etc., incurred in producing the crop are not deductible; the items must be capitalized. Account must be taken of the investment credit and of depreciation recapture.

A farmer who reinvests the proceeds from the sale of his farm in another farm won't have to pay tax on the portion of the gain allocable to his residence provided the reinvestment is made within 18 months of the sale and includes the entire portion of the sale proceeds attributable to the residence. (Sec. 1034 of the Code). This rule applies also if farm **residence** proceeds were reinvested in a nonfarm residence; it will not apply to the proceeds attributable to the rest of the farm.

How the Taxpayer Benefits From Additonal First-Year Depreciation.

When you purchase a farming operation, you are entitled to use the first-year depreciation rules of Section 179. You can take an immediate deduction of 20 percent of the fair market value allocable to farming machinery and equipment, even though the purchase occurs toward the end of the taxable year, if the farming operation includes such farming machinery and equipment. This additional 20 percent depreciation allowance is limited to qualified property with an aggregate cost of $10,000 ($20,000 for a husband and wife filing a joint return).

These rules apply to tangible personal property with a useful life of six years or more which was acquired by purchase after December 31, 1957, for use in a trade or business or for holding for production of income.

[¶2206]   **TAX DEDUCTIONS FOR GENTLEMEN FARMERS;
FARMING AS A SECONDARY OCCUPATION**

Tax reform has treated gentlemen farmers with gentleness. It says to them, in effect, don't overdo a good thing.

As long as the gentleman farmer has no more than $50,000 in nonfarm income for the year, he generally has absolutely nothing to worry about. Even if he's over the particular level of nonfarm income, he still has absolutely nothing to worry about as long as his farm loss for the year doesn't exceed $25,000. Even if he's over both the $50,000 and $25,000 levels we've mentioned, still the only thing he then actually has to worry about is keeping an EDA to record his farm losses in excess of the $25,000 limit. (Prior to 1976). He keeps this EDA for the day, if that day even comes, when he sells the farm. In the meantime, if, contrary to expectations, the farm should ever turn a profit, the profit goes into the EDA to reduce the amount of accumulated losses.

The minimum tax on so-called tax-preference income, including the previously untaxed portion of capital gains, plus the higher tax rates for capital gains over the $50,000 level in one year serves to narrow the gap between ordinary income rates and capital gains rates for some individuals so that even the potential of having farm losses recaptured isn't so bad, relatively speaking. Also, don't forget that the limitations provided are high enough so that they will have little if any effect or application in the case of many individuals using the farm loss provisions as tax shelters. (See the elimination of this problem, discussed in §2209, under the *Tax Reform Act of 1976*).

[¶2207]   **TAX PROTECTED RETURNS FROM CITRUS GROVES**

Citrus growers have six elements of tax protection going for them, subject to the changes by the *Tax Reform Act of 1976,* noted below:

1. In starting a new grove or in buying in a young one, time and nature add value which cannot be taxed until the grove is sold, at which time the profit on the sale is capital gain.
2. Expenditures incurred for cultivating or maintaining a grove which was planted prior to December 30, 1969, are currently deductible. Such expenses include fertilizer, management and water charges, and spraying and cultivation of the trees.

Under a provision added by the 1969 tax law, as to groves planted on or after December 30, 1969, such expenses if incurred before the end of the fourth year after the planting of the grove must be capitalized. (There's an exception in favor of groves replanted after a freeze, disease, drought, pests, or casualty, planted or replanted before the enactment of the law.) Even before the adoption of the 1969 tax law, the cost of developing and planting a citrus grove had to be capitalized. But there were many current maintenance and cultivating costs, such as the cost of fertilizers and labor for cultivation and management, which were currently deductible but which must now be capitalized if incurred "before the close of the fourth taxable year after planting."

3. Taxes and interest paid are generally deductible.

4. The cost of plantings and trees must be capitalized but may be depreciated over a life expectancy of from 35 to 50 years. As the depreciation guidelines note, due consideration must be given to the geographic, climatic, genetic and other factors which determine depreciable life of trees and vines. Some groves may in fact produce for longer periods than their depreciable lives. Thus, a grove being depreciated on the assumption of a 50-year life expectancy may in fact produce for 75 years.

5. By election, soil and water conservation expenses can be deducted to the extent of 25 percent of farm income as well as leveling, terracing, grading, building drainage ditches, and eradication of brush. But such expenses are "recaptured" as ordinary income on sale of the grove within five years of acquisition and slide off in 20 percent increments for each year longer the grove is held until the tenth year when there is no more recapture.

6. When a grove is sold, the owner realizes his profit as capital gain, except as noted. Any loss on sale is fully deductible.

[¶2208]   ALMOND GROVES

Over the years, well-managed and well-operated almond groves have usually proven to be reliable investments. One reason for this is that the product already has a widespread market acceptance and, unlike new and exotic fruits and nuts, the buying public does not have to be educated. There is always a steady market for almonds, either as whole edible nuts or in various processed forms for home and industrial baking use. While almond groves seldom yield spectacular profits, they do provide a comfortable return on a steady year-by-year basis.

Most experts agree that an investment in this field should begin with all or part of an established grove rather than all new plantings. In short, the keynote should be development of an existing grove rather than the creation of a new one.

There are two advantages here: First, the existing grove will produce income to finance at least part of the expansion. Second, trade contacts are easier to come by when you are operating from an established base.

Almond Groves and Development Expenses. Money spent on planting or developing almond groves within four years after these trees are planted cannot be deducted currently but has to be capitalized. If you plant your whole grove in one year, the costs you must capitalize include those in the year of planting plus all the next three years, rather than being currently deductible during those three years in which you planted no almond trees. If you begin planting in late 1974 but finish in 1975, the expenses you must capitalize include expenditures in 1974, for the next three years, and the portion of the costs incurred in 1978, or the fourth year, that applies to the trees planted in the year the planting was finished.

Unlike the rules applying to citrus trees, these rules apply to almond groves planted on or after December 1970.

Exception for Destruction. If the planting or developing costs were incurred to replant a grove which was damaged or destroyed during your ownership by casualty, freeze, drought, pests, or disease, you don't have to capitalize them. (Sec. 278 of the Code).

Other Deductions Preserved. Despite this provision of (Sec. 278 of the Code), you can still take current deductions for soil and water conservation, land clearing, real estate taxes, and interest.

Other Costs Which Must Be Capitalized. You must capitalize fertilizing, frost protection, spraying, pruning and management costs.

[¶2209]   TIMBERLAND

If timber is held as an investment, profits made from sales on the stump or of standing timber in terms of board feet are taxed as capital gain.

If the owner cuts the timber himself and sells it in the form of logs, pulpwood, or poles, his profits will generally be fully taxable as ordinary income. However, he can still get the benefit of capital gain treatment on his profits from the cutting of the standing timber by electing to be taxed under (Sec. 631 of the Code). This permits him to establish as capital gain on the cutting of the timber the amount of the difference between the cost of the timber to him and the fair market value of the timber at the beginning of the year in which it was cut.

The depletion allowance in Sec. 631 permits tax-free recovery of the investment or capitalized expenditure allocable to trees, as the trees are cut.

There are a number of ways timber may be handled. As the owner of timberland, you may do any of these:

1. Cut the timber yourself for sale or for use in your own or someone else's pulp or sawmill.
2. Sell the timberland outright for a fixed sum.
3. Grant a timber operator for the right to cut all or part of the timber presently on the land for a fixed sum.

4. Grant a timber operator the right to cut timber presently on the land for an agreed-on royalty per 1,000 board feet of timber cut or for a percentage of the proceeds from the timber cut.

Although timber has some of the characteristics of both annual crops, such as vegetables and fruits, and minerals extracted from the ground, such as gas and oil, it is not exactly like either.

Depletion. Because it takes so long to replace itself, timber is treated as a wasting asset entitled to capitalization. Hence, depletion is permitted. Only one method is authorized — depletion based on cost.

Gain from Sale. If the timber is held as an investment, sales are taxed at the capital gain rate, whether made on the stump or in terms of board feet. A gain from the sale of timber held as business property is also taxed as capital gain. But if the timber is sold to customers as logs, pulpwood, or poles in the ordinary course of a trade or business, the gain is ordinary income.

Tax Interplay. Do not forget that the untaxed half of long-term capital gains constitutes a tax preference which reduces earned income eligible for the 50 per cent maximum tax. This may influence your decision to sell in the form of standing timber or logs, depending on relative tax savings. If you elect to use income averaging, however, you cannot use the maximum tax.

Section 631 Election. The special tax treatment of timber income is provided by the [Sec. 631 of the Code] election given to a timber dealer to treat the portion of the profits allocable to appreciation by growth as capital gain while reporting the remaining profits allocable to the sale as ordinary income. The income is divided into two parts: (1) the gain up to the time of cutting and (2) the additional gain on the sale. The excess of the fair market value on the first day of the taxable year in which the timber is cut over the adjusted basis of the timber for depletion is taxed as capital gain in the year of cutting. Then when the lumber is sold, the amount by which the proceeds of sale exceed the fair market value on the first day of the taxable year of cutting is taxed as ordinary income.

Both cutting of timber and the transfer of timber rights with royalty interest retained are eligible for capital gain treatment under [Sec. 1231 of the Code]. The election is made on the return for the taxable year. If made, the cutting timber for sale or for use in a trade or business is then treated as a "sale or exchange" of the timber cut. The election is available to both an owner of timber and the holder of a contract right to cut timber, but the timber must have been owned or the contract right held long term before the beginning of the year. The holder of a contract right can sublease or subcontract and still take advantage of the election. But the election won't apply to a contract to cut timber for hire in return for payment per foot of timber cut. The theory is that if you own no proprietary interest in the logs, you are merely performing a service for compensation. Once made, the election will apply to all timber you own or which you have a contractual right to cut and is binding for all subsequent years. You need the Commissioner's consent to revoke an election or to renew a prior revoked election [Sec. 631(a) of the Code].

Christmas Trees. The Section 631 election extends to "evergreen trees which are more than six years old at the time severed from the roots and are sold for ornamental purposes." This includes Christmas trees. But since sellers of balled nursery stock don't sever the tree from the roots, such stock may not qualify.

When Section 631 Election Doesn't Apply. When a timberland owner enters into a long-term agreement with a paper company in return for annual payments, the Section 631(b) election can't be taken by the owner. It can, however, get regular capital gain treatment of sale of timber in existence at the time of contract under [Secs. 1221 and 1231 of the Code].

In a case in which the election was denied, the taxpayer owned a forested tract. It made a 60-year agreement with a paper company under which the company acquired the rights to timber "growing or to be grown" and took possession and management of the forest. The company made annual payments to the timber owner, based on a specified unit price and a specified volume. These payments were due in advance without regard to either the amount of timber actually cut or available to be cut. For a "disposal of timber" to qualify for Section 631(b) treatment, it must be made under a contract pursuant to which (1) the owner retains an economic interest in the timber and (2) the recovery of his capital investment in the timber is conditioned on severance of the timber.

Capital Gains. The sale of timber already in existence when the agreement was executed gave rise to capital gains. Any payments exceeding the fair market value of that existing timber would not be eligible for favorable capital gains. In addition, any payments under the long-term contract not attributable to the existing timber would be deemed consideration for the use of the land and taxable as ordinary income [*Superior Pine Products,* Ct. Cl. 73-1 USTC 9348 Cert. ten. 414 U.S. 857)]. The report in this case was subject to review by the full court.

To avoid losing out on the benefits of the annual election in such a case, you should peg your contract price to the actual board feet cut, for example. The contract price should depend on the actual amount sold and not be arbitrarily fixed.

Tax Breaks for Christmas Tree Growers. IRS has given a tax break to taxpayers engaged in the business of planting and cultivating Christmas trees for sale when the trees are six years old or more. For tax years ending after May 24, 1971, you can deduct as ordinary and necessary business expenses the costs incurred for shearing and pruning these trees. Formerly, these were treated as capital expenditures and added to the basis of the trees and were recovered via depletion allowances as the trees were cut [see *Rev. Rul.* 71-228, CB 1971-1, 53].

Shearing trees is a maintenance expense which regulates growth. It is begun in the third growth year of Scotch pines, for example. The shearing is then continued annually until the trees are cut and sent to market. If you do not shear every year after the third year, the advantage of prior shearings will be wasted and the trees will be unmarketable. Shearing is thus a necessary expense to avoid loss.

Partnership Election. If you are a member of a partnership which contemplates a Section 631 election, be sure that the firm makes the election, not you or one of the other partners. If the partnership fails to make the election, you will not be entitled to capital gain treatment.

[¶2210] FARMING: CHANGES AS A RESULT OF THE TAX REFORM ACT OF 1976

With farming syndicates, capitalization is required for seed, feed, fertilizer, and other farming supplies. They are deductible only in the year in which they are consumed.

a. There are special exceptions with regard to items which could not be consumed because of fires, drought and other casualties.
b. This rule will not apply to Section 278 of the Code (capital expenditures on citrus and almond groves).

Farm poultry syndicates, in a trade or business, are also limited. Costs for poultry are capitalized and deducted over the useful life, or 12 months, the lessor of the two.

Farming syndicates involved in developing groves, orchards, or vineyards in which nuts or fruit are grown must also capitalize the cost of the planting, cultivating, and maintaining or developing these items.

There are special definitions of "farming syndicates" [See Sec. 464 of the Code]. (Generally, partnerships and corporations). There are further limitations relative to farming tax shelters. The deduction of the feed and related items along with the cost of poultry has an effective date of tax years generally beginning after December 31, 1975. The effective date for the rule on the orchards and similar items applies to those which are planted after 1975.

Corporations involved in the farming business are limited by the new law noted; this is for tax years after 1976, except for Subchapter S corporations and for family corporations [Sec. 477(f) and (g) of the Code].

The existing *excess deductions* account for farm losses is amended under the new law. Because of the complexity in applying the excess deductions account rules, losses which are incurred for taxable years after 1975 do not have to be added to this account [See Secs. 1251(b)(3), 1252, 175 and 1882 of the Code].

Appendix

COMPARATIVE DEPRECIATION TABLES

Comparative Depreciation Tables

The following tables show the annual and cumulative depreciation for various useful lives under the straight-line, 200%-declining-balance, 150%-declining-balance, 125%-declining-balance,* and sum-of-the-years-digits methods. All amounts are expressed as percentages of the basis of the property at the time the useful life begins.

Year	Straight-Line		200%-Declining-Balance		150%-Declining-Balance		Sum-of-Digits	
	Annual %	Cum. %	Annual %	Cum. %	Annual %	Cum. %	Annual %	Cum. %
				3-YEAR LIFE				
1	33.33	33.33	66.66	66.66	50.00	50.00	50.00	50.00
2	33.33	66.66	22.22	88.88	25.00	75.00	33.33	83.33
3	33.34	100.00	7.41	96.29	12.50	87.50	16.67	100.00
				4-YEAR LIFE				
1	25.00	25.00	50.00	50.00	37.50	37.50	40.00	40.00
2	25.00	50.00	25.00	75.00	23.44	60.94	30.00	70.00
3	25.00	75.00	12.50	87.50	14.65	75.59	20.00	90.00
4	25.00	100.00	6.25	93.75	9.15	84.74	10.00	100.00
				5-YEAR LIFE				
1	20.00	20.00	40.00	40.00	30.00	30.00	33.33	33.33
2	20.00	40.00	24.00	64.00	21.00	51.00	26.67	60.00
3	20.00	60.00	14.40	78.40	14.70	65.70	20.00	80.00
4	20.00	80.00	8.64	87.04	10.29	75.99	13.33	93.33
5	20.00	100.00	5.18	92.22	7.20	83.19	6.67	100.00
				6-YEAR LIFE				
1	16.67	16.67	33.34	33.34	25.00	25.00	28.57	28.57
2	16.67	33.34	22.22	55.56	18.75	43.75	23.81	52.38
3	16.66	50.00	14.81	70.37	14.06	57.81	19.05	71.43
4	16.67	66.67	9.87	80.24	10.55	68.36	14.29	85.72
5	16.67	83.34	6.58	86.82	7.91	76.27	9.52	95.24
6	16.66	100.00	4.39	91.21	5.93	82.20	4.76	100.00
				7-YEAR LIFE				
1	14.28	14.28	28.57	28.57	21.43	21.43	25.00	25.00
2	14.28	28.56	20.41	48.98	16.83	38.26	21.43	46.43
3	14.29	42.85	14.58	63.56	13.23	51.49	17.86	64.29
4	14.29	57.14	10.41	73.97	10.40	61.89	14.29	78.58
5	14.29	71.43	7.44	81.41	8.17	70.06	10.71	89.29
6	14.29	85.72	5.31	86.72	6.42	76.48	7.14	96.43
7	14.28	100.00	3.79	90.51	5.04	81.52	3.57	100.00
				8-YEAR LIFE				
1	12.50	12.50	25.00	25.00	18.75	18.75	22.22	22.22
2	12.50	25.00	18.75	43.75	15.23	33.98	19.44	41.66
3	12.50	37.50	14.06	57.81	12.38	46.36	16.67	58.33
4	12.50	50.00	10.55	68.36	10.06	56.42	13.89	72.22
5	12.50	62.50	7.91	76.27	8.17	64.59	11.11	83.33
6	12.50	75.00	5.93	82.20	6.64	71.23	8.33	91.66
7	12.50	87.50	4.45	86.65	5.39	76.62	5.56	97.22
8	12.50	100.00	3.34	89.99	4.38	81.00	2.78	100.00
				9-YEAR LIFE				
1	11.11	11.11	22.22	22.22	16.67	16.67	20.00	20.00
2	11.11	22.22	17.28	39.50	13.89	30.56	17.78	37.78
3	11.11	33.33	13.44	52.94	11.57	42.13	15.56	53.34
4	11.11	44.44	10.45	63.39	9.65	51.78	13.33	66.67

*Available for used residential real estate acquired after 7/24/69 and having useful life of 20 years or more when acquired. (See following page.)

Comparative Depreciation Tables   (continued)

Year	Straight-Line		200%-Declining-Balance		150%-Declining-Balance		125%-Declining-Balance *		Sum-of-Digits	
	Annual %	Cum. %	Annual %	Cum. %	Annual %	Cum. %	Annual %	Cum. %	Annual %	Cum. %
				9-YEAR LIFE (continued)						
5	11.11	55.55	8.13	71.52	8.04	59.82			11.11	77.78
6	11.11	66.66	6.32	77.84	6.70	66.52			8.89	86.67
7	11.11	77.77	4.92	82.76	5.58	72.10	—		6.67	93.34
8	11.11	88.88	3.83	86.59	4.65	76.75			4.44	97.78
9	11.12	100.00	2.98	89.57	3.88	80.63			2.22	100.00
				10-YEAR LIFE						
1	10.00	10.00	20.00	20.00	15.00	15.00			18.18	18.18
2	10.00	20.00	16.00	36.00	12.75	27.75			16.37	34.55
3	10.00	30.00	12.80	48.80	10.84	38.59	—		14.56	49.09
4	10.00	40.00	10.24	59.04	9.21	47.80			12.73	61.82
5	10.00	50.00	8.19	67.23	7.83	55.63			10.91	72.73
6	10.00	60.00	6.56	73.79	6.66	62.29			9.09	81.82
7	10.00	70.00	5.24	79.03	5.66	67.95			7.27	89.09
8	10.00	80.00	4.19	83.22	4.81	72.76	—		5.46	94.55
9	10.00	90.00	3.36	86.58	4.09	76.85			3.63	98.18
10	10.00	100.00	2.68	89.26	3.47	80.32			1.82	100.00
				15-YEAR LIFE						
1	6.67	6.67	13.33	13.33	10.00	10.00			12.50	12.50
2	6.66	13.33	11.56	24.89	9.00	19.00			11.67	24.17
3	6.67	20.00	10.01	34.90	8.10	27.10	—		10.83	35.00
4	6.67	26.67	8.68	43.58	7.29	34.39			10.00	45.00
5	6.66	33.33	7.53	51.11	6.56	40.95			9.17	54.17
6	6.67	40.00	6.51	57.62	5.90	46.85			8.33	62.50
7	6.67	46.67	5.65	63.27	5.32	52.17			7.50	70.00
8	6.66	53.33	4.90	68.17	4.78	56.95	—		6.67	76.67
9	6.67	60.00	4.25	72.42	4.30	61.25			5.83	82.50
10	6.67	66.67	3.67	76.09	3.88	65.13			5.00	87.50
11	6.66	73.33	3.19	79.28	3.49	68.62			4.17	91.67
12	6.67	80.00	2.76	82.04	3.14	71.76			3.33	95.00
13	6.67	86.67	2.40	84.44	2.82	74.58	—		2.50	97.50
14	6.66	93.33	2.07	86.51	2.54	77.12			1.67	99.17
15	6.67	100.00	1.80	88.31	2.29	79.41			.83	100.00
				20-YEAR LIFE						
1	5.00	5.00	10.00	10.00	7.50	7.50	6.25	6.25	9.52	9.52
2	5.00	10.00	9.00	19.00	6.94	14.44	5.86	12.11	9.05	18.57
3	5.00	15.00	8.10	27.10	6.42	20.86	5.49	17.60	8.57	27.14
4	5.00	20.00	7.29	34.39	5.94	26.80	5.15	22.75	8.10	35.24
5	5.00	25.00	6.56	40.95	5.49	32.29	4.83	27.58	7.62	42.86
6	5.00	30.00	5.91	46.86	5.08	37.37	4.53	32.11	7.14	50.00
7	5.00	35.00	5.31	52.17	4.70	42.07	4.24	36.35	6.67	56.67
8	5.00	40.00	4.78	56.95	4.35	46.42	3.98	40.33	6.19	62.86
9	5.00	45.00	4.31	61.26	4.02	50.44	3.73	44.06	5.71	68.57
10	5.00	50.00	3.87	65.13	3.71	54.15	3.50	47.55	5.24	73.81

* Available for used residential real estate acquired after 7/24/69 and having useful life of
20 years or more when acquired.

Comparative Depreciation Tables (continued)

Year	Straight-Line Annual %	Cum. %	200%-Declining-Balance Annual %	Cum. %	150%-Declining-Balance Annual %	Cum. %	125%-Declining-Balance Annual %	Cum. %	Sum-of-Digits Annual %	Cum. %
				20-YEAR LIFE (continued)						
11	5.00	55.00	3.49	68.62	3.44	57.59	3.28	50.83	4.76	78.57
12	5.00	60.00	3.14	71.76	3.18	60.77	3.07	53.90	4.29	82.86
13	5.00	65.00	2.82	74.58	2.94	63.71	2.88	56.79	3.81	86.67
14	5.00	70.00	2.54	77.12	2.72	66.43	2.70	59.49	3.33	90.00
15	5.00	75.00	2.29	79.41	2.52	68.95	2.53	62.02	2.86	92.86
16	5.00	80.00	2.06	81.47	2.33	71.28	2.37	64.39	2.38	95.24
17	5.00	85.00	1.85	83.32	2.15	73.43	2.23	66.62	1.90	97.14
18	5.00	90.00	1.67	84.99	1.99	75.42	2.09	68.70	1.43	98.57
19	5.00	95.00	1.50	86.49	1.84	77.26	1.96	70.66	.95	99.52
20	5.00	100.00	1.35	87.84	1.70	78.96	1.83	72.49	.48	100.00
				25-YEAR LIFE						
1	4.00	4.00	8.00	8.00	6.00	6.00	5.00	5.00	7.69	7.69
2	4.00	8.00	7.36	15.36	5.64	11.64	4.75	9.75	7.39	15.08
3	4.00	12.00	6.77	22.13	5.30	16.94	4.51	14.26	7.07	22.15
4	4.00	16.00	6.23	28.36	4.98	21.92	4.29	18.55	6.77	28.92
5	4.00	20.00	5.73	34.09	4.68	26.60	4.07	22.62	6.47	35.39
6	4.00	24.00	5.27	39.36	4.40	31.00	3.87	26.49	6.15	41.54
7	4.00	28.00	4.86	44.22	4.14	35.14	3.68	30.17	5.85	47.39
8	4.00	32.00	4.46	48.68	3.89	39.03	3.49	33.66	5.53	52.92
9	4.00	36.00	4.10	52.78	3.66	42.69	3.32	36.98	5.23	58.15
10	4.00	40.00	3.78	56.56	3.43	46.12	3.15	40.13	4.93	63.08
11	4.00	44.00	3.48	60.04	3.23	49.35	2.99	43.12	4.61	67.69
12	4.00	48.00	3.19	63.23	3.03	52.38	2.84	45.96	4.31	72.00
13	4.00	52.00	2.94	66.17	2.86	55.24	2.70	48.67	4.00	76.00
14	4.00	56.00	2.71	68.88	2.68	57.92	2.57	51.23	3.69	79.69
15	4.00	60.00	2.49	71.37	2.52	60.44	2.44	53.67	3.39	83.08
16	4.00	64.00	2.29	73.66	2.37	62.81	2.32	55.99	3.07	86.15
17	4.00	68.00	2.11	75.77	2.23	65.04	2.20	58.19	2.77	88.92
18	4.00	72.00	1.94	77.71	2.10	67.14	2.09	60.28	2.47	91.39
19	4.00	76.00	1.78	79.49	1.97	69.11	1.99	62.26	2.15	93.54
20	4.00	80.00	1.64	81.13	1.85	70.96	1.89	64.15	1.85	95.39
21	4.00	84.00	1.51	82.64	1.74	72.70	1.79	65.94	1.53	96.92
22	4.00	88.00	1.39	84.03	1.64	74.34	1.70	67.65	1.23	98.15
23	4.00	92.00	1.28	85.31	1.54	75.88	1.62	69.26	.93	99.08
24	4.00	96.00	1.17	86.48	1.45	77.33	1.54	70.80	.61	99.69
25	4.00	100.00	1.08	87.56	1.36	78.69	1.46	72.26	.31	100.00
				30-YEAR LIFE						
1	3.33	3.33	6.67	6.67	5.00	5.00	4.16	4.16	6.45	6.45
2	3.34	6.67	6.22	12.89	4.75	9.75	3.99	8.16	6.24	12.69
3	3.33	10.00	5.81	18.70	4.51	14.26	3.83	11.99	6.02	18.71
4	3.33	13.33	5.42	24.12	4.29	18.55	3.67	15.65	5.81	24.52
5	3.34	16.67	5.06	29.18	4.07	22.62	3.51	19.17	5.59	30.11
6	3.33	20.00	4.72	33.90	3.87	26.49	3.37	22.54	5.37	35.48
7	3.33	23.33	4.40	38.30	3.68	30.17	3.23	25.76	5.17	40.65
8	3.34	26.67	4.12	42.42	3.49	33.66	3.09	28.86	4.94	45.59
9	3.33	30.00	3.84	46.26	3.32	36.98	2.96	31.82	4.73	50.32
10	3.33	33.33	3.58	49.84	3.15	40.13	2.84	34.66	4.52	54.84

Year	Straight-Line		200%-Declining-Balance		150%-Declining-Balance		125%-Declining-Balance		Sum-of-Digits	
	Annual %	Cum. %	Annual %	Cum. %	Annual %	Cum. %	Annual %	Cum. %	Annual %	Cum. %

30-YEAR LIFE (continued)

Year	Annual %	Cum. %	Annual %	Cum. %	Annual %	Cum. %	Annual %	Cum. %	Annual %	Cum. %
11	3.34	36.67	3.34	53.18	2.99	43.12	2.72	37.38	4.30	59.14
12	3.33	40.00	3.12	56.30	2.84	45.96	2.61	39.99	4.09	63.23
13	3.33	43.33	2.92	59.22	2.70	48.66	2.50	42.49	3.87	67.10
14	3.34	46.67	2.72	61.94	2.57	51.23	2.40	44.89	3.65	70.75
15	3.33	50.00	2.53	64.47	2.44	53.67	2.30	47.19	3.44	74.19
16	3.33	53.33	2.37	66.84	2.32	55.99	2.20	49.39	3.23	77.42
17	3.34	56.67	2.21	69.05	2.20	58.19	2.11	51.50	3.01	80.43
18	3.33	60.00	2.07	71.12	2.09	60.28	2.02	53.52	2.80	83.23
19	3.33	63.33	1.92	73.04	1.99	62.27	1.94	55.45	2.58	85.81
20	3.34	66.67	1.80	74.84	1.89	64.16	1.86	57.31	2.36	88.17
21	3.33	70.00	1.68	76.52	1.80	65.96	1.78	59.09	2.15	90.32
22	3.33	73.33	1.56	78.08	1.70	67.66	1.70	60.79	1.94	92.26
23	3.34	76.67	1.46	79.54	1.62	69.28	1.63	62.43	1.72	93.98
24	3.33	80.00	1.37	80.91	1.54	70.82	1.57	63.99	1.61	95.49
25	3.33	83.33	1.27	82.18	1.46	72.28	1.50	65.49	1.29	96.78
26	3.34	86.67	1.19	83.37	1.39	73.67	1.44	66.93	1.07	97.85
27	3.33	90.00	1.11	84.48	1.32	74.99	1.38	68.31	.86	98.71
28	3.33	93.33	1.03	85.51	1.25	76.24	1.32	69.63	.65	99.36
29	3.34	96.67	.97	86.48	1.19	77.43	1.27	70.89	.43	99.79
30	3.33	100.00	.90	87.38	1.13	78.56	1.21	72.11	.21	100.00

33-1/3-YEAR LIFE

Year	Annual %	Cum. %	Annual %	Cum. %	Annual %	Cum. %	Annual %	Cum. %	Annual %	Cum. %
1	3.00	3.00	6.00	6.00	4.50	4.50	3.75	3.75	5.82	5.82
2	3.00	6.00	5.64	11.64	4.30	8.80	3.61	7.36	5.65	11.47
3	3.00	9.00	5.30	16.94	4.10	12.90	3.47	10.83	5.47	16.95
4	3.00	12.00	4.98	21.93	3.92	16.82	3.34	14.18	5.30	22.25
5	3.00	15.00	4.68	26.61	3.74	20.56	3.22	17.40	5.17	27.37
6	3.00	18.00	4.40	31.00	3.57	24.14	3.10	20.49	4.95	32.32
7	3.00	21.00	4.14	35.15	3.41	27.55	2.98	23.47	4.76	37.10
8	3.00	24.00	3.89	39.03	3.16	30.81	2.87	26.34	4.60	41.70
9	3.00	27.00	3.66	42.70	3.11	33.93	2.76	29.11	4.43	46.13
10	3.00	30.00	3.44	46.14	2.97	36.90	2.66	31.77	4.25	50.38
11	3.00	33.00	3.23	49.37	2.84	39.74	2.56	34.32	4.08	54.46
12	3.00	36.00	3.04	52.41	2.71	42.45	2.46	36.79	3.90	58.36
13	3.00	39.00	2.86	55.26	2.59	45.04	2.37	39.16	3.73	62.10
14	3.00	42.00	2.68	57.95	2.47	47.51	2.28	41.44	3.55	65.64
15	3.00	45.00	2.52	60.47	2.36	49.88	2.20	43.63	3.38	69.02
16	3.00	48.00	2.37	62.84	2.26	52.13	2.11	45.75	3.20	72.22
17	3.00	51.00	2.23	65.07	2.15	54.29	2.03	47.78	3.03	75.25
18	3.00	54.00	2.10	67.17	2.06	56.34	1.95	49.74	2.85	78.10
19	3.00	57.00	1.97	69.14	1.96	58.31	1.88	51.63	2.68	80.78
20	3.00	60.00	1.85	71.00	1.88	60.18	1.81	53.44	2.50	83.28
21	3.00	63.00	1.74	72.73	1.79	61.97	1.75	55.19	2.33	85.61
22	3.00	66.00	1.64	74.37	1.71	63.69	1.68	56.87	2.15	87.77
23	3.00	69.00	1.54	75.90	1.63	65.32	1.62	58.48	1.98	89.75
24	3.00	72.00	1.45	77.35	1.56	66.88	1.56	60.04	1.81	91.56
25	3.00	75.00	1.36	78.71	1.49	68.37	1.50	61.54	1.63	93.19

Year	Straight-Line		200%-Declining-Balance		150%-Declining-Balance		125%-Declining-Balance		Sum-of-Digits	
	Annual %	Cum. %	Annual %	Cum. %	Annual %	Cum. %	Annual %	Cum. %	Annual %	Cum. %

33-1/3-YEAR LIFE (continued)

Year	Annual %	Cum. %	Annual %	Cum. %	Annual %	Cum. %	Annual %	Cum. %	Annual %	Cum. %
26	3.00	78.00	1.28	79.99	1.42	69.79	1.44	62.98	1.46	94.64
27	3.00	81.00	1.20	81.19	1.36	71.15	1.39	64.37	1.28	95.92
28	3.00	84.00	1.13	82.32	1.30	72.45	1.34	65.71	1.11	97.03
29	3.00	87.00	1.06	83.38	1.24	73.69	1.29	66.99	.93	97.96
30	3.00	90.00	1.00	84.37	1.18	74.88	1.24	68.23	.76	98.72
31	3.00	93.00	.94	85.31	1.13	76.01	1.19	69.42	.58	99.30
32	3.00	96.00	.88	86.19	1.08	77.09	1.15	70.57	.41	99.71
33	3.00	99.00	.93	87.02	1.03	78.12	1.10	71.67	.23	99.94
33-1/3	1.00	100.00	.26	87.28	.33	78.45	.35	71.95	.06	100.00

35-YEAR LIFE

Year	Annual %	Cum. %	Annual %	Cum. %	Annual %	Cum. %	Annual %	Cum. %	Annual %	Cum. %
1	2.86	2.86	5.71	5.71	4.29	4.29	3.57	3.57	5.56	5.56
2	2.86	5.72	5.38	11.09	4.10	8.39	3.44	7.02	5.40	10.96
3	2.85	8.57	5.07	16.16	3.93	12.32	3.32	10.34	5.24	16.20
4	2.86	11.43	4.78	20.94	3.76	16.08	3.20	13.54	5.08	21.28
5	2.86	14.29	4.51	25.45	3.60	19.68	3.09	16.63	4.92	26.20
6	2.85	17.14	4.25	29.70	3.44	23.12	2.98	19.60	4.76	30.96
7	2.86	20.00	4.01	33.71	3.29	26.41	2.87	22.48	4.60	35.56
8	2.86	22.86	3.78	37.49	3.15	29.56	2.77	25.24	4.44	40.00
9	2.85	25.71	3.56	41.05	3.02	32.58	2.67	27.91	4.29	44.29
10	2.86	28.57	3.36	44.41	2.89	35.47	2.57	30.49	4.13	48.42
11	2.86	31.43	3.17	47.58	2.77	38.24	2.48	32.97	3.97	52.39
12	2.85	34.28	2.99	50.57	2.65	40.89	2.39	35.36	3.81	56.20
13	2.86	37.14	2.82	53.39	2.53	43.42	2.31	37.67	3.65	59.85
14	2.86	40.00	2.66	56.05	2.42	45.84	2.23	39.90	3.49	63.34
15	2.85	42.85	2.51	58.56	2.32	48.16	2.15	42.05	3.33	66.67
16	2.86	45.71	2.37	60.93	2.22	50.38	2.07	44.12	3.18	69.85
17	2.86	48.57	2.23	63.16	2.13	52.51	2.00	46.11	3.02	72.87
18	2.85	51.42	2.10	65.26	2.03	54.54	1.92	48.04	2.86	75.73
19	2.86	54.28	1.98	67.24	1.95	56.49	1.86	49.89	2.70	78.43
20	2.86	57.14	1.87	69.11	1.86	58.35	1.79	51.68	2.54	80.97
21	2.86	60.00	1.76	70.87	1.79	60.14	1.73	53.41	2.38	83.35
22	2.86	62.86	1.66	72.53	1.71	61.85	1.66	55.07	2.22	85.57
23	2.86	65.72	1.57	74.10	1.64	63.49	1.60	56.68	2.06	87.63
24	2.85	68.57	1.48	75.58	1.56	65.05	1.55	58.22	1.90	89.53
25	2.86	71.43	1.40	76.98	1.50	66.55	1.49	59.72	1.75	91.28
26	2.86	74.29	1.32	78.30	1.43	67.98	1.44	61.15	1.59	92.87
27	2.85	77.14	1.24	79.54	1.37	69.35	1.39	62.54	1.43	94.30
28	2.86	80.00	1.17	80.71	1.31	70.66	1.34	63.88	1.27	95.57
29	2.86	82.86	1.10	81.81	1.26	71.92	1.29	65.17	1.11	96.68
30	2.85	85.71	1.04	82.85	1.20	73.12	1.24	66.41	.95	97.63
31	2.86	88.57	.98	83.83	1.15	74.27	1.20	67.61	.79	98.42
32	2.86	91.43	.92	84.75	1.10	75.37	1.16	68.77	.63	99.05
33	2.85	94.28	.87	85.62	1.06	76.43	1.12	69.88	.47	99.52
34	2.86	97.14	.82	86.44	1.01	77.44	1.08	70.96	.32	99.84
35	2.86	100.00	.77	87.21	.97	78.41	1.04	72.00	.16	100.00

Comparative Depreciation Tables (continued)

Year	Straight-Line		200%-Declining-Balance		150%-Declining-Balance		125%-Declining-Balance		Sum-of-Digits	
	Annual %	Cum. %	Annual %	Cum. %	Annual %	Cum. %	Annual %	Cum. %	Annual %	Cum. %

40-YEAR LIFE

Year	Annual %	Cum. %	Annual %	Cum. %	Annual %	Cum. %	Annual %	Cum. %	Annual %	Cum. %
1	2.50	2.50	5.00	5.00	3.75	3.75	3.13	3.13	4.88	4.88
2	2.50	5.00	4.75	9.75	3.61	7.36	3.03	6.15	4.75	9.63
3	2.50	7.50	4.51	14.26	3.47	10.83	2.93	9.09	4.64	14.27
4	2.50	10.00	4.29	18.55	3.34	14.17	2.84	11.93	4.51	18.78
5	2.50	12.50	4.07	22.62	3.22	17.39	2.75	14.68	4.39	23.17
6	2.50	15.00	3.87	26.49	3.10	20.49	2.67	17.34	4.27	27.44
7	2.50	17.50	3.68	30.17	2.98	23.47	2.58	19.93	4.14	31.58
8	2.50	20.00	3.49	33.66	2.87	26.34	2.50	22.43	4.03	35.61
9	2.50	22.50	3.32	36.98	2.76	29.10	2.42	24.85	3.90	39.51
10	2.50	25.00	3.15	40.13	2.66	31.76	2.35	27.20	3.78	43.29
11	2.50	27.50	2.99	43.12	2.56	34.32	2.27	29.48	3.66	46.95
12	2.50	30.00	2.84	45.96	2.46	36.78	2.20	31.68	3.54	50.49
13	2.50	32.50	2.71	48.67	2.37	39.15	2.13	33.82	3.41	53.90
14	2.50	35.00	2.56	51.23	2.28	41.43	2.07	35.88	3.29	57.19
15	2.50	37.50	2.44	53.67	2.20	43.63	2.00	37.89	3.18	60.37
16	2.50	40.00	2.32	55.99	2.11	45.74	1.94	39.83	3.04	63.41
17	2.50	42.50	2.20	58.19	2.03	47.77	1.88	41.71	2.93	66.34
18	2.50	45.00	2.09	60.28	1.96	49.73	1.82	43.53	2.81	69.15
19	2.50	47.50	1.99	62.27	1.88	51.61	1.76	45.30	2.68	71.83
20	2.50	50.00	1.88	64.15	1.81	53.42	1.71	47.01	2.56	74.39
21	2.50	52.50	1.79	65.94	1.75	55.17	1.66	48.66	2.44	76.83
22	2.50	55.00	1.71	67.65	1.68	56.85	1.60	50.27	2.32	79.15
23	2.50	57.50	1.62	69.27	1.62	58.47	1.55	51.82	2.19	81.34
24	2.50	60.00	1.53	70.80	1.56	60.03	1.51	53.33	2.07	83.41
25	2.50	62.50	1.46	72.26	1.50	61.53	1.46	54.78	1.94	85.37
26	2.50	65.00	1.39	73.65	1.44	62.97	1.41	56.20	1.82	87.19
27	2.50	67.50	1.32	74.97	1.39	64.36	1.37	57.57	1.71	88.90
28	2.50	70.00	1.25	76.22	1.34	65.70	1.33	58.89	1.59	90.49
29	2.50	72.50	1.19	77.41	1.29	66.99	1.28	60.18	1.46	91.95
30	2.50	75.00	1.13	78.54	1.24	68.23	1.24	61.42	1.34	93.29
31	2.50	77.50	1.07	79.61	1.19	69.42	1.21	62.63	1.22	94.51
32	2.50	80.00	1.02	80.63	1.15	70.57	1.17	63.79	1.10	95.61
33	2.50	82.50	.97	81.60	1.10	71.67	1.13	64.93	.98	96.58
34	2.50	85.00	.92	85.52	1.06	72.73	1.10	66.02	.86	97.44
35	2.50	87.50	.87	83.39	1.02	73.75	1.06	67.08	.73	98.17
36	2.50	90.00	.83	84.22	.98	74.73	1.03	68.11	.61	98.78
37	2.50	92.50	.79	85.01	.95	75.68	1.00	69.11	.49	99.27
38	2.50	95.00	.75	85.76	.91	76.59	.97	70.07	.36	99.63
39	2.50	97.50	.71	86.47	.88	77.47	.94	71.01	.25	99.88
40	2.50	100.00	.68	87.15	.85	78.32	.91	71.92	.12	100.00

Comparative Depreciation Tables (continued)

Year	Straight-Line		200%-Declining-Balance		150%-Declining-Balance		125%-Declining-Balance		Sum-of-Digits	
	Annual %	Cum. %	Annual %	Cum. %	Annual %	Cum. %	Annual %	Cum. %	Annual %	Cum. %

45-YEAR LIFE

Year	Annual %	Cum. %	Annual %	Cum. %	Annual %	Cum. %	Annual %	Cum. %	Annual %	Cum. %
1	2.22	2.22	4.44	4.44	3.33	3.33	2.78	2.78	4.35	4.35
2	2.22	4.44	4.24	8.68	3.22	6.55	2.70	5.48	4.25	8.60
3	2.22	6.66	4.05	12.73	3.12	9.67	2.63	8.10	4.15	12.75
4	2.23	8.89	3.87	16.60	3.01	12.68	2.55	10.66	4.06	16.81
5	2.22	11.11	3.70	20.30	2.91	15.59	2.48	13.14	3.96	20.77
6	2.22	13.33	3.54	23.84	2.81	18.40	2.41	15.55	3.86	24.63
7	2.22	15.55	3.38	27.22	2.72	21.12	2.35	17.90	3.77	28.40
8	2.23	17.78	3.23	30.45	2.63	23.75	2.28	20.18	3.67	32.07
9	2.22	20.00	3.09	33.54	2.54	26.29	2.22	22.40	3.57	35.64
10	2.22	22.22	2.95	36.49	2.46	28.75	2.16	24.55	3.48	39.12
11	2.22	24.44	2.82	39.31	2.38	31.13	2.10	26.65	3.38	42.50
12	2.23	26.67	2.69	42.00	2.30	33.43	2.04	28.68	3.28	45.78
13	2.22	28.89	2.57	44.57	2.22	35.65	1.98	30.67	3.19	48.97
14	2.22	31.11	2.46	47.03	2.15	37.80	1.93	32.59	3.09	52.06
15	2.22	33.33	2.35	49.38	2.07	39.87	1.87	34.46	3.00	55.06
16	2.23	35.56	2.25	51.63	2.00	41.87	1.82	36.28	2.90	57.96
17	2.22	37.78	2.15	53.78	1.94	43.81	1.77	38.05	2.80	60.76
18	2.22	40.00	2.05	55.83	1.87	45.68	1.72	39.77	2.70	63.46
19	2.22	42.22	1.96	57.79	1.81	47.49	1.67	41.45	2.61	66.07
20	2.23	44.45	1.87	59.66	1.75	49.24	1.63	43.07	2.51	68.58
21	2.22	46.67	1.79	61.45	1.69	50.93	1.58	44.66	2.42	71.00
22	2.22	48.89	1.71	63.16	1.64	52.57	1.54	46.19	2.32	73.32
23	2.22	51.11	1.63	64.79	1.58	54.15	1.49	47.69	2.22	75.54
24	2.23	53.34	1.56	66.35	1.53	55.68	1.45	49.14	2.13	77.67
25	2.22	55.56	1.49	67.84	1.48	57.16	1.41	50.55	2.03	79.70
26	2.22	57.78	1.42	69.26	1.43	58.59	1.37	51.93	1.93	81.63
27	2.22	60.00	1.36	70.62	1.38	59.97	1.34	53.26	1.84	83.47
28	2.23	62.23	1.30	71.92	1.33	61.30	1.30	54.56	1.74	85.21
29	2.22	64.45	1.24	73.16	1.29	62.59	1.26	55.82	1.64	86.85
30	2.22	66.67	1.18	74.34	1.25	63.84	1.23	57.05	1.55	88.40
31	2.22	68.89	1.13	75.47	1.21	65.05	1.19	58.24	1.45	89.85
32	2.23	71.12	1.08	76.55	1.17	66.22	1.16	59.40	1.35	91.20
33	2.22	73.34	1.03	77.58	1.13	67.35	1.13	60.53	1.26	92.46
34	2.22	75.56	.98	78.56	1.09	68.44	1.10	61.63	1.16	93.62
35	2.22	77.78	.94	79.50	1.05	69.49	1.07	62.69	1.06	94.68
36	2.22	80.00	.90	80.40	1.02	70.51	1.04	63.73	.97	95.65
37	2.23	82.23	.86	81.26	.98	71.49	1.01	64.74	.87	96.52
38	2.22	84.45	.82	82.08	.95	72.44	.98	65.72	.77	97.29
39	2.22	86.67	.78	82.86	.92	73.36	.95	66.67	.68	97.97
40	2.22	88.89	.75	83.61	.89	74.25	.93	67.59	.58	98.55
41	2.23	91.12	.72	84.33	.86	75.11	.90	68.49	.48	99.03
42	2.22	93.34	.69	85.02	.83	75.94	.88	69.37	.39	99.42
43	2.22	95.56	.66	85.68	.80	76.74	.85	70.22	.29	99.71
44	2.22	97.78	.63	86.31	.78	77.52	.83	71.05	.19	99.90
45	2.22	100.00	.60	86.91	.75	78.27	.80	71.85	.10	100.00

Comparative Depreciation Tables (continued)

Year	Straight-Line Annual %	Straight-Line Cum. %	200%-Declining-Balance Annual %	200%-Declining-Balance Cum. %	150%-Declining-Balance Annual %	150%-Declining-Balance Cum. %	125%-Declining-Balance Annual %	125%-Declining-Balance Cum. %	Sum-of-Digits Annual %	Sum-of-Digits Cum. %
					50-YEAR LIFE					
1	2.00	2.00	4.00	4.00	3.00	3.00	2.50	2.50	3.92	3.92
2	2.00	4.00	3.84	7.84	2.91	5.91	2.44	4.94	3.85	7.77
3	2.00	6.00	3.69	11.53	2.82	8.73	2.38	7.31	3.76	11.53
4	2.00	8.00	3.54	15.07	2.74	11.47	2.32	9.63	3.69	15.22
5	2.00	10.00	3.39	18.46	2.66	14.13	2.26	11.89	3.60	18.82
6	2.00	12.00	3.26	21.72	2.58	16.71	2.20	14.09	3.53	22.35
7	2.00	14.00	3.14	24.86	2.50	19.21	2.15	16.24	3.45	25.80
8	2.00	16.00	3.00	27.86	2.42	21.63	2.09	18.33	3.38	29.18
9	2.00	18.00	2.89	30.75	2.35	23.98	2.04	20.38	3.29	32.47
10	2.00	20.00	2.77	33.52	2.28	26.26	1.99	22.37	3.22	35.69
11	2.00	22.00	2.66	36.18	2.21	28.47	1.94	24.31	3.15	38.82
12	2.00	24.00	2.55	38.73	2.15	30.62	1.89	26.20	3.06	41.88
13	2.00	26.00	2.45	41.18	2.08	32.70	1.84	28.05	2.98	44.86
14	2.00	28.00	2.35	43.53	2.02	34.72	1.80	29.84	2.91	47.77
15	2.00	30.00	2.26	45.79	1.96	36.68	1.75	31.60	2.82	50.59
16	2.00	32.00	2.17	47.96	1.90	38.58	1.71	33.31	2.74	53.33
17	2.00	34.00	2.08	50.04	1.84	40.42	1.67	34.98	2.67	56.00
18	2.00	36.00	2.00	52.04	1.79	42.21	1.63	36.60	2.59	58.59
19	2.00	38.00	1.92	53.96	1.73	43.94	1.58	38.19	2.51	61.10
20	2.00	40.00	1.84	55.80	1.68	45.62	1.55	39.73	2.43	63.53
21	2.00	42.00	1.77	57.57	1.63	47.25	1.51	41.24	2.35	65.88
22	2.00	44.00	1.70	59.27	1.58	48.83	1.47	42.71	2.28	68.16
23	2.00	46.00	1.62	60.89	1.53	50.36	1.43	44.14	2.19	70.35
24	2.00	48.00	1.57	62.46	1.49	51.85	1.40	45.54	2.12	72.47
25	2.00	50.00	1.50	63.96	1.44	53.29	1.36	46.90	2.04	74.51
26	2.00	52.00	1.44	65.40	1.40	54.69	1.33	48.23	1.96	76.47
27	2.00	54.00	1.39	66.79	1.36	56.05	1.29	49.52	1.87	78.35
28	2.00	56.00	1.33	68.12	1.32	57.37	1.26	50.78	1.81	80.16
29	2.00	58.00	1.27	69.39	1.28	58.64	1.23	52.01	1.72	81.88
30	2.00	60.00	1.22	70.61	1.24	59.89	1.20	53.21	1.65	83.53
31	2.00	62.00	1.18	71.79	1.20	61.09	1.17	54.38	1.57	85.10
32	2.00	64.00	1.13	72.92	1.17	62.26	1.14	55.52	1.49	86.59
33	2.00	66.00	1.08	74.00	1.13	63.39	1.11	56.63	1.41	88.00
34	2.00	68.00	1.04	75.04	1.10	64.49	1.08	57.72	1.33	89.33
35	2.00	70.00	1.00	76.04	1.07	65.56	1.06	58.78	1.26	90.59
36	2.00	72.00	.96	77.00	1.03	66.59	1.03	59.81	1.18	91.77
37	2.00	74.00	.92	77.92	1.00	67.59	1.00	60.81	1.09	92.86
38	2.00	76.00	.88	78.80	.97	68.56	.98	61.79	1.02	93.88
39	2.00	78.00	.85	79.65	.94	69.50	.96	62.75	.94	94.82
40	2.00	80.00	.81	80.46	.92	70.42	.93	63.68	.87	95.69
41	2.00	82.00	.78	81.24	.89	71.31	.91	64.58	.78	96.47
42	2.00	84.00	.75	81.99	.86	72.17	.89	65.47	.71	97.18
43	2.00	86.00	.72	82.71	.84	73.01	.86	66.33	.62	97.80
44	2.00	88.00	.69	83.40	.81	73.82	.84	67.18	.55	98.35
45	2.00	90.00	.67	84.07	.79	74.61	.82	68.00	.47	98.82
46	2.00	92.00	.64	84.71	.76	75.37	.80	68.80	.40	99.22
47	2.00	94.00	.61	85.32	.74	76.11	.78	69.58	.31	99.53
48	2.00	96.00	.59	85.90	.72	76.83	.76	70.34	.24	99.77
49	2.00	98.00	.57	86.47	.70	77.53	.74	71.08	.15	99.92
50	2.00	100.00	.54	87.01	.67	78.20	.72	71.80	.08	100.00

DEPRECIATION TABLES

Depreciation Tables

Here is a rundown on the different methods of depreciation available with respect to different types of real estate

(1) Straight-Line: This method of depreciation is available for all types of new and used properties.

(2) 125%-Declining-Balance: This depreciation method is available for (a) used real property acquired before July 25, 1969, and (b) used residential rental property acquired after July 24, 1969, with a useful life of 20 years or more.

(3) 150%-Declining-Balance: This method is the fastest available for (a) used real property acquired before July 25, 1969, and (b) new nonresidential rental properties constructed after July 24, 1969.

(4) Sum-of-the-Years-Digits: This method of depreciation is available only for (a) new real estate constructed before July 25, 1969, and (b) new residential rental properties.

(5) 200%-Declining-Balance: This depreciation method is available only for (a) new real estate constructed before July 25, 1969, and (b) new residential rental properties.

(6) Straight-Line Using Short Useful Life: This method of depreciation is available only for rehabilitation expenses for low- or moderate-income residential rental properties. Expenditures are depreciated on a straight-line basis using a 60-month useful life.

The following tables give the straight-line; the 200%-, 150% and 125%-declining-balance; and sum-of-the-years-digits annual depreciation amounts and cumulative totals for assets having useful lives of from 3 to 50 years.

Computing Depreciation

Straight-Line: The cost or other basis of the asset is reduced by the anticipated salvage value. The remainder is then divided by the remaining useful life to find the annual straight-line deduction.

200%-Declining-Balance: The straight-line rate is first determined by dividing the useful life into 100. For example, if the useful life is 10 years, the straight-line rate is 10% (100 divided by 10). This rate is then doubled. The doubled rate is applied to the cost for the first year. The second year, the doubled rate is applied to the remaining (or declining) cost. This process is repeated each year.

At any time when the remaining balance divided by the remaining useful life (straight-line) gives a larger deduction than would result from continuing to apply the 200%-declining-balance rate against the declining balance, you can shift to straight-line. For example, with an asset having a useful life of 20 years, the 200%-declining-balance rate is 10%. If the asset cost $100, $68.62 will have been recovered via depreciation after 11 years, leaving a balance of $31.38. If we continue to apply the 10% rate, the 12th year's depreciation will be $3.14 (10% of $31.38). But if we used straight-line, dividing the remaining balance of $31.38 by the remaining useful life of 9 years, the result would be an annual depreciation for the last 9 years of $3.49.

In computing 200%-declining-balance, you need not consider salvage in determining the annual deductions. But you cannot depreciate below the salvage value. When you switch to straight-line, you must take salvage into account in computing the straight-line deductions.

150%-Declining-Balance: You determine the straight-line rate as above. Then, multiply it by 1.5.

125%-Declining-Balance: First, determine the straight-line rate. Then multiply it by 1.25.

Sum-of-the-Years-Digits: Total the years that make up the useful life. For example, if the useful life is 5 years, add together 1, 2, 3, 4 and 5, for a total of 15. Then, the first year's depreciation is 5/15 of your cost, say, $1,500, or $500. The second year, deduct 4/15 of $1,500, then 3/15 of $1,500, etc. Alternatively, starting with the second year, you can reduce the denominator by the previous year's numerator and apply the fraction to the reduced balance. Thus, in the second year, you'd take 4/10 of $1,000 and in the third year, 3/6 of $600. You cannot switch to straight-line without permission.

First-Year Depreciation

Personal tangible property (i.e., non-real-estate items) get a special first-year writeoff under the tax law. Twenty percent of the cost up to $10,000 ($20,000 on a joint return) can be written off immediately. Then, the balance of the cost is subject to depreciation under the usual rules. Thus, if an asset costs $10,000, $2,000 is written off in the year of acquisition. The cost then becomes $8,000, and that is subject to depreciation under any approved method from the time of acquisition as if the original cost were $8,000.

USEFUL LIVES—CLASS LIFE SYSTEM

The ADR Class Life system allows you to take as a reasonable allowance for depreciation an amount that's based on any period of years you select within a range specified by IRS for designated classes of assets (Sec. 167 (m)(1)). That is, the Class Life ADR table gives you a range of useful lives for various classes of assets from which you can determine your asset's useful life.

This system accomplishes the following: (1) Authorizes IRS to accept depreciation based on lives for business equipment acquired after 1970 that are not more than 20% shorter nor 20% longer than the "guideline lives" fixed by the Treasury in July 1962. (2) Provides for a half-year averaging convention as exemplified by the following alternative methods: (a) the eligible property obtained during the taxable year is deemed to be acquired at midyear or (b) each asset placed in service during the first half of the taxable year is deemed to be acquired on the first day of the same year, while each asset placed in service in the second half of the year is deemed to be acquired on the first day of the next taxable year. (3) Permits a deduction for expenditures for repair and maintenance based on a percentage of the assets in a guideline class on which depreciation under the Class Life System is elected. It will not be necessary to prove that such expenditures do not have to be capitalized. (4) Sets up an Office of Industrial Economics that analyzes the annual information submitted by taxpayers using the Class Life System and constantly revises the guideline classes, guideline lives, and repair allowances and sets up new guidelines and allowances where appropriate. (5) Reserve ratio test is no longer used.

Electing to Use the Class Life ADR System. If you want to use the ADR system, you must elect to do so on Form 4832, which is to be filed with your tax return for the year the assets are placed in service. You may make your election on an amended return, so long as it's not filed later than the due date of the return.

Once you make the election for a year, you must restrict your depreciation on all assets that fall within a guideline class, and are placed in service during the year, to the ADR system.

How to Decide Whether to Adopt System. To determine whether it pays to sell or trade in your old equipment and buy new in order to get the higher depreciation under the ADR Class Life system, take a careful look at the arithmetic. How much depreciation are you getting out of the old? How much will you get with the new? How much is any loss on the sale of the old worth? What are the estimated expenses with the old? With the new? What are the estimated cost savings, if any, through the higher efficiency of the new, etc.?

The approach will be different depending on whether or not the tax basis of the old equipment is higher than its present value. If it's not and you trade it in on the new equipment, you avoid the recapture of the gain as ordinary income under Section 1245 — the gain carries over to the new equipment and is not realized until the new property is sold.

On the other hand, if the basis is higher than the present value and you trade in the old property, you can't claim the loss, so that you'd be looking to sell the property in order to realize the loss (and to avoid having IRS look on it as a trade-in anyhow, the sale should be to a third party).

Gauging the Savings in Purchase of Used Equipment. Under the Class Life system, you have to be extra careful in situations where you buy relatively small quantities of used equipment along with more substantial purchases of new equipment. The danger is that if the system is elected, it will apply to both used and new assets. The result could be that the used equipment would be subject to the same useful life range as the new equipment; whereas as used equipment it actually has a shorter useful life. However, there's an exception if the used assets exceed 10% of the total basis of all assets placed in service in the year. In such case, lives for used assets may be determined without regard to the new asset depreciation ranges.

For your convenience, we include here the following table, which sets forth the asset guideline classes, asset guideline periods, asset depreciation ranges, and asset guideline repair allowance percentages.

Asset guide-line class	Description of assets included	Asset depreciation range (in years)			Annu asset guidel repai allowa percent
		Lower limit	Asset guideline period	Upper limit	

SPECIFIC DEPRECIABLE ASSETS USED IN ALL BUSINESS ACTIVITIES, EXCEPT AS NOTED:

Asset class	Description	Lower	Guideline	Upper	Percent
00.11	**Office Furniture, Fixtures, and Equipment:** Includes furniture and fixtures which are not a structural component of a building. Includes such assets as desks, files, safes, and communications equipment. Does not include communications equipment that is included in other CLADR classes _____	8	10	12	2
00.12	**Information Systems:** Includes computers and their peripheral equipment used in administering normal business transactions and the maintenance of business records, their retrieval and analysis. Information systems are defined as: 1) Computers: A computer is an electronically activated device capable of accepting information, applying prescribed processes to the information, and supplying the results of these processes with or without human intervention. It usually consists of a central processing unit containing extensive storage, logic, arithmetic, and control capabilities. Excluded from this category are adding machines, electronic desk calculators, etc. 2) Peripheral equipment consists of the auxiliary machines which may be placed under control of the central processing unit. Non limiting examples are: Card readers, card punches, magnetic tape feeds, high speed printers, optical character readers, tape cassettes, mass storage units, paper tape equipment, keypunches, data entry devices, teleprinters, terminals, tape drives, disc drives, disc files, disc packs, visual image projector tubes, card sorters, plotters, and collators. Peripheral equipment may be used on-line or off-line. Does not include equipment that is an integral part of other capital equipment and which is included in other CLADR classes of economic activity, i.e., computers used primarily for process or production control, switching and channeling _____	5	6	7	7.
00.13	**Data Handling Equipment, except Computers:** Includes only typewriters, calculators, adding and accounting machines, copiers, and duplicating equipment _____	5	6	7	15
00.21	**Airplanes (airframes and engines),** except those used in commercial or contract carrying of passengers or freight, and all helicopters (airframes and engines) _____	5	6	7	14
00.22	**Automobiles, Taxis** _____	2.5	3	3.5	16.
00.23	**Buses** _____	7	9	11	11.

358

Asset depreciation class	Description of assets included	Asset depreciation range (in years)			Annual asset guideline repair allowance percentage
		Lower limit	Asset guideline period	Upper limit	
0.241	**Light General Purpose Trucks:** Includes trucks for use over the road (actual unloaded weight less than 13,000 pounds) _____	3	4	5	16.5
0.242	**Heavy General Purpose Trucks:** Includes heavy general purpose trucks, concrete ready-mix truckers, and ore trucks, for use over the road (actual unloaded weight 13,000 pounds or more) _____	5	6	7	10
0.25	**Railroad Cars and Locomotives,** except those owned by railroad transportation companies _____	12	15	18	8
0.26	**Tractor Units For Use Over-The-Road** _____	3	4	5	16.5
0.27	**Trailers and Trailer-Mounted Containers** _____	5	6	7	10
0.28	**Vessels, Barges, Tugs, and Similar Water Transportation Equipment,** except those used in marine contract construction _____	14.5	18	21.5	6
1.3	**Land Improvements:** Includes improvements directly to or added to land, whether such improvements are section 1245 property or section 1250 property, provided such improvements are depreciable. Examples of such assets might include sidewalks, roads, canals, waterways, drainage facilities, sewers, wharves and docks, bridges, fences, landscaping, shrubbery, or radio and television transmitting towers. Does not include land improvements that are explicitly included in any other class, and buildings and structural components as defined in section 1.48-1(e) of the regulations. Excludes public utility initial clearing and grading land improvements as specified in Rev. Rul. 72-403, 1972-C.B. 102.		20		
1.4	**Industrial Steam and Electric Generation and/or Distribution Systems:** Includes assets, whether such assets are section 1245 property or 1250 property, providing such assets are depreciable, used in the production and/or distribution of electricity with rated total capacity in excess of 500 Kilowatts and/or assets used in the production and/or distribution of steam with rated total capacity in excess of 12,500 pounds per hour, for use by the taxpayer in his industrial manufacturing process or plant activity and not ordinarily available for sale to others. Does not include buildings and structural components as defined in section 1.48-1(e) of the regulations. Assets used to generate and/or distribute electricity or steam of the type described above of lesser rated capacity are not included, but are included in the appropriate manufacturing equipment classes elsewhere specified. Steam and chemical recovery boiler systems used for the recovery and regeneration of chemicals used in manufacturing, with rated capacity in excess of that described above, with specifically related distribution and return systems are not included but are included in appropriate manufacturing equipment classes elsewhere specified. An example of an excluded steam and recovery boiler system is that used in the pulp and paper manufacturing industry _____	22.5	28	33.5	2.5

DEPRECIABLE ASSETS USED IN THE FOLLOWING ACTIVITIES:

1.1	**Agriculture:** Includes machinery and equipment, grain bins, and fences but no other land improvements, that are used in the production of crops or plants, vines, and trees; livestock; the operation of farm dairies, nurseries, greenhouses, sod farms, mushroom cellars, cranberry bogs, apiaries, and fur farms; the performance of agricultural, animal husbandry, and horticultural services _____	8	10	12	11
.11	**Cotton Ginning Assets** _____	9.5	12	14.5	5.5
.21	**Cattle, Breeding or Dairy** _____	5.5	7	8.5	

Asset guide-line class	Description of assets included	Asset depreciation range (in years)			Annual asset guideline repair allowance percent
		Lower limit	Asset guideline period	Upper limit	
01.22	**Horses, Breeding or Work** _____	8	10	12	
01.23	**Hogs, Breeding** _____	2.5	3	3.5	
01.24	**Sheep and Goats, Breeding** _____	4	5	6	
01.3	**Farm Buildings** _____	20	25	30	5
10.0	**Mining:** Includes assets used in the mining and quarrying of metallic and non-metallic minerals (including sand, gravel, stone, and clay) and the milling, beneficiation and other primary preparation of such materials __	8	10	12	6.
13.1	**Drilling of Oil and Gas Wells:** Includes assets used in the drilling of onshore oil and gas wells and the provisions of geophysical and other exploration services; and the provision of such oil and gas field services as chemical treatment, plugging and abandoning of wells and cementing or perforating well casings. Does not include assets used in the performance of any of these activities and services by integrated petroleum and natural gas producers for their own account _____	5	6	7	1C
13.2	**Exploration for and Production of Petroleum and Natural Gas Deposits:** Includes assets used by petroleum and natural gas producers for drilling of wells and production of petroleum and natural gas, including gathering pipelines and related storage facilities _____	11	14	17	4
13.3	**Petroleum Refining:** Includes assets used for the distillation, fractionation, and catalytic cracking of crude petroleum into gasoline and its other components ____	13	16	19	7
13.4	**Marketing of Petroleum and Petroleum Products:** Includes assets used in marketing petroleum and petroleum products, such as related storage facilities and complete service stations, but not including any of these facilities related to petroleum and natural gas trunk pipelines _____	13	16	19	4
15.1	**Contract Construction Other than Marine:** Includes assets used by general building, special trade, and heavy construction contractors. Does not include assets used by companies in performing construction services for their own account _____	4	5	6	12
15.2	**Marine Contract Construction:** Includes assets used by general building, special trade, and heavy construction contractors predominantly in marine construction work. Does not include assets used by companies in performing marine construction services for their own account except for floating, self-propelled, and other drilling platforms and support vessels used in offshore drilling for oil and gas which are included whether used for their own account or others _____	9.5	12	14.5	
20.1	**Manufacture of Grain and Grain Mill Products:** Includes assets used in the production of flours, cereals, livestock feeds, and other grain and grain mill products _____	13.5	17	20.5	
20.2	**Manufacture of Sugar and Sugar Products:** Includes assets used in the production of raw sugar, syrup, or finished sugar from sugar cane or sugar beets _____	14.5	18	21.5	
20.3	**Manufacture of Vegetable Oils and Vegetable Oil Products:** Includes assets used in the production of oil from vegetable materials and the manufacture of related vegetable oil products _____	14.5	18	21.5	

Asset guide-line class	Description of assets included	Asset depreciation range (in years)			Annual asset guideline repair allowance percentage
		Lower limit	Asset guideline period	Upper limit	
20.4	**Manufacture of Other Food and Kindred Products:** Includes assets used in the production of foods and beverages not included in classes 20.1, 20.2 and 20.3 _____	9.5	12	14.5	5.5
20.5	**Manufacture of Food and Beverages-Special Handling Devices:** Includes assets defined as specialized materials handling devices such as returnable pallets, palletized containers, and fish processing equipment including boxes, baskets, carts, and flaking trays used in activities as defined in classes 20.1. 20.2, 20.3, 20.4. Does not include general purpose small tools such as wrenches and drills, both hand and power-driven, and other general purpose equipment such as conveyors, transfer equipment, and materials handling devices _____	.3	4	5	20
21.0	**Manufacture of Tobacco and Tobacco Products:** Includes assets used in the production of cigarettes, cigars, smoking and chewing tobacco, snuff, and other tobacco products _____	12	15	18	5
22.1	**Manufacture of Knitted Goods:** Includes assets used in the production of knitted and netted fabrics and lace. Assets used in yarn preparation, bleaching, dyeing, printing, and other similar finishing processes, texturing, and packaging, are elsewhere classified _____	6	7.5	9	7
22.2	**Manufacture of Yarn, Thread, and Woven Fabric:** Includes assets used in the production of spun yarns including the preparing, blending, spinning, and twisting of fibers into yarns and threads, the preparation of yarns such as twisting, warping, and winding, the production of covered elastic yarn and thread, cordage, woven fabric, tire fabric, braided fabric, twisted jute for packing, mattresses, pads, sheets, and industrial belts, and the processing of textile mill waste to recover fibers, flocks, and shoddies. Assets used to manufacture carpets, man-made fibers, and nonwovens, and assets used in texturing, bleaching, dyeing, printing, and other similar finishing processes, are elsewhere classified _____	9	11	13	16
22.3	**Manufacture of Carpets, and Dyeing, Finishing, and Packaging of Textile Products:** Includes assets used in the production of carpets, rugs, mats, woven carpet backing, chenille, and other tufted products, and assets used in the joining together of backing with carpet yarn or fabric. Includes assets used in washing, scouring, bleaching, dyeing, printing, drying, and similar finishing processes applied to textile fabrics, yarns, threads, and other textile goods. Includes assets used in the production and packaging of textile products, other than apparel, by creasing, forming, trimming, cutting, and sewing, such as the preparation of carpet and fabric samples, or similar joining together processes (other than the production of scrim reinforced paper products and laminated paper products) such as the sewing and folding of hosiery and panty hose, the creasing, folding, trimming, and cutting of fabrics to produce non-woven products, such as disposable diapers and sanitary products. Assets used in the manufacture of nonwoven carpet backing, and hard surface floor covering such as tile, rubber, and cork, are elsewhere classified _____	7	9	11	15
22.4	**Manufacture of Textured Yarns:** Includes assets used in the processing of yarns to impart bulk and/or stretch properties to the yarn. The principal machines involved are falsetwist, draw, beam-to-beam. and stuffer box texturing equipment and related high-speed twisters and winders. Assets, as described above, which are used to further process man-made fibers are elsewhere				

Asset guide-line class	Description of assets included	Asset depreciation range (in years)			Annual asset guideline repair allowance percentage
		Lower limit	Asset guideline period	Upper limit	
	classified when located in the same plant in an integrated operation with man-made fiber producing assets. Assets used to manufacture man-made fibers and assets used in bleaching, dyeing, printing, and other similar finishing processes, are elsewhere classified _____	6.5	8	9.5	7
22.5	**Manufacture of Nonwoven Fabrics:** Includes assets used in the production of nonwoven fabrics, felt goods including felt hats, padding, batting, wadding, oakum, and fillings, from new materials and from textile mill waste. Nonwoven fabrics are defined as fabrics (other than reinforced and laminated composites consisting of nonwovens and other products) manufactured by bonding natural and/or synthetic fibers and/or filaments by means of induced mechanical interlocking, fluid entanglement, chemical adhesion, thermal or solvent reaction, or by combination thereof other than natural hydration bonding as occurs with natural cellulose fibers. Such means include resin bonding, web bonding, and melt bonding. Specifically include assets used to make flocked and needle punched products other than carpets and rugs. Assets, as described above, which are used to manufacture nonwovens are elsewhere classified when located in the same plant in an integrated operation with man-made fiber producing assets. Assets used to manufacture man-made fibers and assets used in bleaching, dyeing, printing, and other similar finishing processes, are elsewhere classified ---	8	10	12	15
23.0	**Manufacture of Apparel and Other Finished Products:** Includes assets used in the production of clothing and fabricated textile products by the cutting and sewing of woven fabrics, other textile products, and furs: but does not include assets used in the manufacture of apparel from rubber and leather ------------------------	7	9	11	7
24.1	**Cutting of Timber:** Includes logging machinery and equipment and roadbuilding equipment used by logging and sawmill operators and pulp manufacturers for their own account --	5	6	7	10
24.2	**Sawing of Dimensional Stock from Logs:** Includes machinery and equipment installed in permanent or well-established sawmills ----------------------------------	8	10	12	6.5
24.3	**Sawing of Dimensional Stock from Logs:** Includes machinery and equipment installed in sawmills characterized by temporary foundations and a lack, or minimum amount, of lumber-handling, drying, and residue disposal equipment and facilities _____	5	6	7	10
24.4	**Manufacture of Wood Products, and Furniture:** Includes assets used in the production of plywood, hardboard, flooring, veneers, furniture, and other wood products, including the treatment of poles and timber ----------------------------------	8	10	12	6.5
26.1	**Manufacture of Pulp and Paper:** Includes assets for pulp materials handling and storage, pulp mill processing, bleach processing, paper and paperboard manufacturing, and on-line finishing. Includes pollution control assets and all land improvements associated with the factory site or production process such as effluent ponds and canals, provided such improvements are depreciable but does not include buildings and structural components as defined in section 1 48-1(e)(1) of the regulations. Includes steam and chemical recovery boiler systems, with any rated capacity, used for the recovery and regeneration of chemicals used in manufacturing. Does not include assets used either in pulpwood logging, or in the manufacture of hardboard ---	10.5	13	15.5	10

Asset guide-line class	Description of assets included	Asset depreciation range (in years)			Annual asset guideline repair allowance percentage
		Lower limit	Asset guideline period	Upper limit	
26.2	**Manufacture of Converted Paper, Paperboard, and Pulp Products:** Includes assets used for modification, or remanufacture of paper and pulp into converted products, such as paper coated off the paper machine, paper bags, paper boxes, cartons and envelopes. Does not include assets used for manufacture of non-wovens that are elsewhere classified _____	8	10	12	15
27.0	**Printing, Publishing, and Allied Industries:** Includes assets used in printing by one or more processes, such as letter-press, lithography, gravure, or screen; the performance of services for the printing trade, such as book-binding, typesetting, engraving, photo-engraving, and electrotyping; and the publication of newspapers, books, and periodicals _____	9	11	13	5.5
28.0	**Manufacture of Chemicals and Allied Products:** Includes assets used in the manufacture of basic chemicals such as acids, alkalies, salts, and organic and inorganic chemicals; chemical products to be used in further manufacture, such as synthetic fibers and plastics materials, including petrochemical processing beyond that which is ordinarily a part of petroleum refining; and finished chemical products, such as pharmaceuticals, cosmetics, soaps, fertilizers, paints and varnishes, explosives, and compressed and liquified gases. Does not include assets used in the manufacture of finished rubber and plastic products or in the production of natural gas products, butane, propane, and byproducts of natural gas production plants _____	9	11	13	5.5
30.1	**Manufacture of Rubber Products:** Includes assets used for the production of products from natural, syn-thetic, or reclaimed rubber, gutta percha, balata, or gutta siak, such as tires, tubes, rubber footwear, mechanical rubber goods, heels and soles, flooring, and rubber sundries; and in the recapping, retreading, and rebuilding of tires _____	11	14	17	5
30.11	**Manufacture of Rubber Products—Special Tools and Devices:** Includes assets defined as special tools, such as jigs, dies, mandrels, molds, lasts, patterns, specialty containers, pallets, shells, and tire molds, and accessory parts such as rings and insert plates used in activities as defined in class 30.1. Does not include tire building drums and accessory parts and general purpose small tools such as wrenches and drills, both power and hand-driven, and other general purpose equip-ment such as conveyors and transfer equipment _____	3	4	5	
30.2	**Manufacture of Finished Plastic Products:** Includes assets used in the manufacture of plastics products and the molding of primary plastics for the trade. Does not include assets used in the manufacture of basic plastics materials nor the manufacture of phonograph records _____	9	11	13	5.5
30.21	**Manufacture of Finished Plastic Products—Special Tools:** Includes assets defined as special tools, such as jigs, dies, fixtures, molds, patterns, gauges, and specialty transfer and shipping devices, used in activities as defined in class 30.2. Special tools are specifically designed for the production or processing of particular parts and have no sig-nificant utilitarian value and cannot be adapted to further or different use after changes or improvements are made in the model design of the particular part produced by the special tools. Does not include general purpose small tools, such as wrenches and drills, both hand and power-driven, and other general purpose equipment such as conveyors, transfer equipment, and materials handling devices _____	3	3.5	4	5.5

Asset guide-line class	Description of assets included	Asset depreciation range (in years)			Annual asset guideline repair allowance percentage
		Lower limit	Asset guideline period	Upper limit	
31.0	**Manufacture of Leather and Leather Products:** Includes assets used in the tanning, currying, and finishing of hides and skins; the processing of fur pelts; and the manufacture of finished leather products, such as footwear, belting, apparel, and luggage _____	9	11	13	5.5
32.1	**Manufacture of Glass Products:** Includes assets used in the production of flat, blown, or pressed products of glass, such as float and window glass, glass containers, glassware and fiberglass. Does not include assets used in the manufacture of lenses _____	11	14	17	12
32.11	**Manufacture of Glass Products—Special Tools:** Includes assets defined as special tools such as molds, patterns, pallets, and specialty transfer and shipping devices such as steel racks to transport automotive glass, used in activities as defined in class 32.1. Special tools are specifically designed for the production or processing of particular parts and have no significant utilitarian value and cannot be adapted to further or different use after changes or improvements are made in the model design of the particular part produced by the special tools. Does not include general purpose small tools such as wrenches and drills, both hand and power-driven, and other general purpose equipment such as conveyors, transfer equipment, and materials handling devices _____	2	2.5	3	10
32.2	**Manufacture of Cement:** Includes assets used in the production of cement, but does not include any assets used in the manufacture of concrete and concrete products nor in any mining or extraction process _____	16	20	24	3
32.3	**Manufacture of Other Stone and Clay Products:** Includes assets used in the manufacture of products from materials in the form of clay and stone, such as brick, tile, and pipe; pottery and related products, such as vitreous-china, plumbing fixtures, earthenware and ceramic insulating materials; and also includes assets used in manufacture of concrete and concrete products. Does not include assets used in any mining or extraction processes _____	12	15	18	4.5
33.1	**Manufacture of Primary Ferrous Metals:** Includes assets used in the smelting and refining of ferrous metals from ore, pig, or scrap, the rolling, drawing, and alloying of ferrous metals; the manufacture of castings, forgings, and other basic products of ferrous metals; and the manufacture of nails, spikes, structural shapes, tubing, wire, and cable _____	14.5	18	21.5	8
33.11	**Manufacture of Primary Ferrous Metals—Special Tools:** Includes assets defined as special tools such as dies, jigs, molds, patterns, fixtures, gauges, and drawings concerning such special tools used in the activities as defined in class 33.1, manufacture of Primary Ferrous Metals. Special tools are specifically designed for the production or processing of particular products or parts and have no significant utilitarian value and cannot be adapted to further or different use after changes or improvements are made in the model design of the particular part produced by the special tools. Does not include general purpose small tools such as wrenches and drills, both hand and power-driven, and other general purpose equipment such as conveyors, transfer equipment, and materials handling devices. Rolls, mandrels, and refractories are not included in class 33.11 but are included in class 33.1 _____	5	6.5	8	4

364

Asset guideline class	Description of assets included	Asset depreciation range (in years)			Annual asset guideline repair allowance percentage
		Lower limit	Asset guideline period	Upper limit	
33.2	**Manufacture of Primary Nonferrous Metals:** Includes assets used in the smelting, refining, and electrolysis of non-ferrous metals from ore, pig, or scrap, the rolling, drawing, and alloying of nonferrous metals; the manufacture of castings, forgings, and other basic products of nonferrous metals; and the manufacture of nails, spikes, structural shapes, tubing, wire, and cable _____	11	14	17	4.5
33.21	**Manufacture of Primary Nonferrous Metals—Special Tools:** Includes assets defined as special tools such as dies, jigs, molds, patterns, fixtures, gauges, and drawings concerning such special tools used in the activities as defined in class 33.2, Manufacture of Primary Nonferrous Metals. Special tools are specifically designed for the production or processing of particular products or parts and have no significant utilitarian value and cannot be adapted to further or different use after changes or improvements are made in the model design of the particular part produced by the special tools. Does not include general purpose small tools such as wrenches and drills, both hand and power-driven, and other general purpose equipment such as conveyors, transfer equipment, and materials handling devices. Rolls, mandrels, and refractories are not included in class 33.21 but are included in class 33.2 _____	5	6.5	8	4
34.0	**Manufacture of Fabricated Metal Products:** Includes assets used in the production of metal cans, tinware, non-electric heating apparatus, fabricated structural metal products, metal stampings, and other ferrous and nonferrous metal and wire products not elsewhere classified _____	9.5	12	14.5	6
34.01	**Manufacture of Fabricated Metal Products—Special Tools:** Includes assets defined as special tools such as dies, jigs, molds, patterns, fixtures, gauges, and returnable containers and drawings concerning such special tools used in the activities as defined in class 34.0. Special tools are specifically designed for the production or processing of particular machine components, products, or parts, and have no significant utilitarian value and cannot be adapted to further or different use after changes or improvements are made in the model design of the particular part produced by the special tools. Does not include general purpose small tools such as wrenches and drills, both hand and power-driven, and other general purpose equipment such as conveyors, transfer equipment, and materials handling devices _____	2.5	3	3.5	3.5
35.1	**Manufacture of Metalworking Machinery:** Includes assets used in the production of metal cutting and forming machines, special dies, tools, jigs, and fixtures, and machine tool accessories _____	9.5	12	14.5	5.5
35.11	**Manufacture of Metalworking Machinery—Special Tools:** Includes assets defined as special tools, such as jigs, dies, fixtures, molds, patterns, gauges, and specialty transfer and shipping devices, used in activities as defined in class 35.1. Special tools are specifically designed for the production or processing of particular machine components and have no significant utilitarian value and cannot be adapted to further or different use after changes or improvements are made in the model design of the particular part produced by the special tools. Does not include general purpose small tools such as wrenches and drills, both hand and power-driven, and other general purpose equipment such as conveyors, transfer equipment, and materials handling devices _____	5	6	7	12.5
35.2	**Manufacture of Other Machines:** Includes assets used in the production of such machinery as engines and turbines; farm machinery, construction, and mining machinery;				

Asset guide-line class	Description of assets included	Asset depreciation range (in years)			Annual asset guideline repair allowance percentage
		Lower limit	Asset guideline period	Upper limit	
	general and special industrial machines including office machines and nonelectronic computing equipment; miscellaneous machines except electrical equipment and transportation equipment ------------------	9.5	12	14.5	5.5
35.21	**Manufacture of Other Machines—Special Tools:** Includes assets defined as special tools, such as jigs, dies, fixtures, molds, patterns, gauges, and specialty transfer and shipping devices, used in activities as defined in class 35.2. Special tools are specifically designed for the production or processing of particular machine components and have no significant utilitarian value and cannot be adapted to further or different use after changes or improvements are made in the model design of the particular part produced by the special tools. Does not include general purpose small tools such as wrenches and drills, both hand and power-driven, and other general purpose equipment such as conveyors, transfer equipment, and materials handling devices _____	5	6.5	8	12.5
32.1	**Manufacture of Electrical Equipment:** Includes assets used in the production of machinery, apparatus, and supplies for the generation, storage, transmission, transformation, and utilization of electrical energy such as; electric test and distributing equipment, electrical industrial apparatus, household appliances, electric lighting and wiring equipment; electronic components and accessories, phonograph records, storage batteries and ignition systems _____	9.5	12	14.5	5.5
36.11	**Manufacture of Electrical Equipment Special Tools:** Includes assets defined as special tools such as jigs, dies, molds, patterns, fixtures, gauges, returnable containers, and specialty transfer devices used in activities as defined in class 36.1. Special tools are specifically designed for the production or processing of particular machine components, products or parts, and have no significant utilitarian value and cannot be adapted to further or different use after changes or improvements are made in the model design of the particular part produced by the special tools. Does not include general purpose small tools such as wrenches and drills, both hand and power-driven, and other general purpose equipment such as conveyors, transfer equipment, and materials handling devices ----------------------------------	4	5	6	—
36.2	**Manufacture of Electronic Products:** Includes assets used in the production of electronic detection, guidance, control, radiation, computation, test, and navigation equipment or the components thereof including airborne application. Also includes assets used in the manufacture of electronic airborne communication equipment or the components thereof. Does not include the assets of manufacturers engaged only in the purchase and assembly of components --	6.5	8.0	9.5	7.5
37.11	**Manufacture of Motor Vehicles:** Includes assets used in the manufacture and assembly of finished automobiles, trucks, trailers, motor homes, and buses. Does not include assets used in mining, printing and publishing, production of primary metals, electricity, or steam, or the manufacture of glass, industrial chemicals, batteries, or rubber products, which are classified elsewhere. Includes assets used in manufacturing activities elsewhere classified other than those excluded above, where such activities are incidental to and an integral part of the manufacture and assembly of finished motor vehicles such as the manufacture of parts and subassemblies of fabricated metal products, electrical equipment, textiles, plastics, leather, and foundry and forging operations. Does not include any assets not classified in manufacturing activity classes, e.g., does not include assets classified in asset guideline classes 00.11 through 00.4. Activities will be considered incidental to the manufacture and assembly of finished motor vehicles only if 75 percent or more of the value of the products				

Asset guide-line class	Description of assets included	Asset depreciation range (in years)			Annual asset guideline repair allowance percentage
		Lower limit	Asset guideline period	Upper limit	
	produced under one roof are used for the manufacture and assembly of finished motor vehicles. Parts that are produced as a normal replacement stock complement in connection with the manufacture and assembly of finished motor vehicles are considered used for the manufacture and assembly of finished motor vehicles. Does not include assets used in the manufacture of component parts if these assets are used by taxpayer not engaged in the assembly of finished motor vehicles ____	9.5	12	14.5	9.5
37.12	**Manufacture of Motor Vehicles—Special Tools:** Includes assets defined as special tools, such as jigs, dies, fixtures, molds, patterns, gauges, and specialty transfer and shipping devices, owned by manufacturers of finished motor vehicles and used in qualified activities as defined in class 37.11. Special tools are specifically designed for the production or processing of particular motor vehicle components and have no significant utilitarian value, and cannot be adapted to further or different use, after changes or improvements are made in the model design of the particular part produced by the special tools. Does not include general purpose small tools such as wrenches and drills, both hand and power-driven, and other general purpose equipment such as conveyors, transfer equipment, and materials handling devices _____	2.5	3	3.5	12.5
37.2	**Manufacture of Aerospace Products:** Includes assets used in the manufacture and assembly of airborne vehicles and their component parts including hydraulic, pneumatic, electrical, and mechanical systems. Does not include assets used in the production of electronic airborne detection, guidance, control, radiation, computation, test, navigation, and communication equipment or the components thereof _____	8	10	12	7.5
37.31	**Ship and Boat Building Machinery and Equipment:** Includes assets used in the manufacture and repair of ships, boats, caissons, marine drilling rigs, and special fabrications not included in asset guideline classes 37.32 and 37.33. Specifically includes all manufacturing and repairing machinery and equipment, including machinery and equipment used in the operation of assets included in asset guideline class 37.32. Excludes buildings and their structural components _____	9.5	12	14.5	8.5
37.32	**Ship and Boat Building Dry Docks and Land Improvements:** Includes assets used in the manufacture and repair of ships, boats, caissons, marine drilling rigs, and special fabrications not included in asset guideline classes 37.31 and 37.33. Specifically includes floating and fixed dry docks, ship basins, graving docks, shipways, piers, and all other land improvements such as water, sewer, and electric systems. Excludes buildings and their structural components _____	13	16	19	2.5
37.33	**Ship and Boat Building—Special Tools:** Includes assets defined as special tools such as dies, jigs, molds, patterns, fixtures, gauges, and drawings concerning such special tools used in the activities defined in classes 37.31 and 37.32. Special tools are specifically designed for the production or processing of particular machine components, products, or parts, and have no significant utilitarian value and cannot be adapted to further or different use after changes or improvements are made in the model design of the particular part produced by the special tools. Does not include general purpose small tools such as wrenches and drills, both hand and power-driven, and other general purpose equipment such as conveyors, transfer equipment, and materials handling devices _____	5	6.5	8	0.5

Asset guide-line class	Description of assets included	Asset depreciation range (in years)			Annual asset guideline repair allowance percentage
		Lower limit	Asset guideline period	Upper limit	

Asset guide-line class	Description of assets included	Lower limit	Asset guideline period	Upper limit	Annual asset guideline repair allowance percentage
37.41	**Manufacture of Locomotives:** Includes assets used in building or rebuilding railroad locomotives (including mining and industrial locomotives). Does not include assets of railroad transportation companies or assets of companies which manufacture components of locomotives but do not manufacture finished locomotives _____	9	11.5	14	7.5
37.42	**Manufacture of Railroad Cars:** Includes assets used in building or rebuilding railroad freight or passenger cars (including rail transit cars). Does not include assets of railroad transportation companies or assets of companies which manufacture components of railroad cars but do not manufacture finished railroad cars _____	9.5	12	14.5	5.5
38.0	**Manufacture of Professional, Scientific, and Controlling Instruments:** Includes assets used in the manufacture of mechanical measuring, engineering, laboratory and scientific research instruments, optical instruments and lenses; surgical, medical, and dental instruments, equipment and supplies; ophthalmic goods, photographic equipment and supplies; and watches and clocks _____	9.5	12	14.5	5.5
39.0	**Manufacture of Athletic, Jewelry and Other Goods:** Includes assets used in the production of jewelry; musical instruments; toys and sporting goods; motion picture and television films and tapes; and pens, pencils, office and art supplies, brooms, brushes, caskets, etc. __	9.5	12	14.5	5.5

Railroad Transportation:
Classes with the prefix 40 include the assets identified below that are used in the commercial and contract carrying of passengers and freight by rail. Assets of electrified railroads will be classified in a manner corresponding to that set forth below for railroads not independently operated as electric lines. Excludes the assets included in classes with the prefix beginning 00.1 and 00.2 above, and also excludes any nondepreciable assets included in Interstate Commerce Commission accounts enumerated for this class.

40.1	**Railroad Machinery and Equipment:** Includes assets classified in the following Interstate Commerce Commission accounts: Roadway Accounts: (16) Station and office buildings (freight handling machinery and equipment only) (25) TOFC/COFC terminals (freight handling machinery and equipment only) (26) Communication systems (27) Signals and interlockers (37) Roadway machines (44) Shop machinery Equipment Accounts: (52) Locomotives (53) Freight train cars (54) Passenger train cars (57) Work equipment _____	11	14	17	10.5
40.2	**Railroad Structures and Similar Improvements:** Includes assets classified in the following Interstate Commerce Commission road accounts: (6) Bridges, trestles, and culverts (7) Elevated structures (13) Fences, snowsheds, and signs				

Asset guide-line class	Description of assets included	Asset depreciation range (in years)			Annual asset guideline repair allowance percentage
		Lower limit	Asset guideline period	Upper limit	
	(16) Station and office buildings (stations and other operating structures only)				
	(17) Roadway buildings				
	(18) Water stations				
	(19) Fuel stations				
	(20) Shops and enginehouses				
	(25) TOFC/COFC terminals (operating structures only)				
	(31) Power transmission systems				
	(35) Miscellaneous structures				
	(39) Public improvements construction _____	24	30	36	5
40.3	**Railroad Wharves and Docks** _____	16	20	24	5.5
	Includes assets classified in the following Interstate Commerce accounts:				
	(23) Wharves and docks				
	(24) Coal and ore wharves _____	16	20	24	5.5
40.51	**Railroad Hydraulic Electric Generating Equipment** _____	40	50	60	1.5
40.52	**Railroad Nuclear Electric Generating Equipment** _____	16	20	24	3
40.53	**Railroad Steam Electric Generating Equipment** _____	22.5	28	33.5	2.5
40.54	**Railroad Steam, Compressed Air, and Other Power Plant Equipment** __	22.5	28	33.5	7.5
41.0	**Motor Transport-Passengers:**				
	Includes assets used in the urban and interurban commercial and contract carrying of passengers by road, except the transportation assets included in classes with the prefix 00.2 _____	6.5	8	9.5	11.5
42.0	**Motor Transport-Freight:**				
	Includes assets used in the commercial and contract carrying of freight by road, except the transportation assets included in classes with the prefix 00.2 _____	6.5	8	9.5	11
44.0	**Water Transportation:**				
	Includes assets used in the commercial and contract carrying of freight and passengers by water except the transportation assets included in classes with the prefix 00.2. Includes all related land improvements ____	16	20	24	8
45.0	**Air Transport:**				
	Includes assets (except helicopters) used in commercial and contract carrying of passengers and freight by air. For purposes of section 1.167 (a)-11(d)(2)(iv)(a) of the regulations, expenditures for "repair, maintenance, rehabilitation, or improvement" shall consist of direct maintenance expenses (irrespective of airworthiness provisions or charges) as defined by Civil Aeronautics Board uniform accounts 5200, maintenance burden (exclusive of expenses pertaining to maintenance buildings and improvements) as defined by Civil Aeronautics Board uniform accounts 5300, and expenditures which are not "excluded additions" as defined by section 1.167(a)-11(d)(2)(vi) of the regulations and which would be charged to property and equipment accounts in the Civil Aeronautics Board uniform system of accounts _____	9.5	12	14.5	15
45.1	**Air Transport (restricted)**				
	Includes each asset described in the description of class 45.0 which was held by the taxpayer on April 15, 1976, or is acquired by the taxpayer pursuant to a contract which was, on April 15, 1976, and at all times thereafter, binding on the taxpayer. This criterion of classification based on binding contract concept is to be applied in the same manner as under the general rules expressed in section 49(b)(1), (4), (5), and (8) of the Code _____	5	6	7	15
46.0	**Pipeline Transportation:**				
	Includes assets used in the private, commercial, and contract carrying of petroleum, gas, and other products by means of pipes and con-				

Asset guide-line class	Description of assets included	Asset depreciation range (in years)			Annual asset guideline repair allowance percentage
		Lower limit	Asset guideline period	Upper limit	
	veyors. The trunk lines and related storage facilities of integrated petroleum and natural gas producers are included in this class. Excludes initial clearing and grading land improvements as specified in Rev. Rul. 72-403, 1972-2 C.B. 102, but includes all other related land improvements _____	17.5	22	26.5	3
	Telephone Communications: Includes the assets identified below and that are used in the provision of commercial and contract telephonic services such as:				
48.11	**Telephone Central Office Buildings:** Includes assets intended to house central office equipment, as defined in Federal Communications Commission Part 31 Account No. 212 whether section 1245 or section 1250 property _____	36	45	54	1.5
48.12	**Telephone Central Office Equipment:** Includes central office switching and related equipment as defined in Federal Communications Commission Part 31 Account No. 221 _____	16	20	24	6
48.13	**Telephone Station Equipment:** Includes such station apparatus and connections as teletypewriters, telephones, booths, private exchanges, and comparable equipment as defined in Federal Communications Commission Part 31 Account Nos. 231, 232, and 234 _____	8	10	12	10
48.14	**Telephone Distribution Plant:** Includes such assets as pole lines, cable, aerial wire, underground conduits, and comparable equipment, and related land improvements as defined in Federal Communications Commission Part 31 Account Nos. 241, 242.1, 242.2, 242.3, 242.4, 243, and 244 _____	28	35	42	2
48.2	**Radio and Television Broadcastings:** Includes assets used in radio and television broadcasting, except transmitting towers _____	5	6	7	10
	Telegraph, Ocean Cable, and Satellite Communications (TOCSC) Includes communications-related assets used to provide domestic and international radio-telegraph, wire-telegraph, ocean-cable, and satellite communications services; also includes related land improvements.				
48.31	**TOCSC-Electric Power Generating and Distribution Systems:** Includes assets used in the provision of electric power by generation, modulation, rectification, channelization, control, and distribution. Does not include these assets when they are installed on customer's premises _____	15	19	23	
48.32	**TOCSC-High Frequency Radio and Microwave Systems:** Includes assets such as transmitters and receivers, antenna supporting structures, antennas, transmission lines from equipment to antenna, transmitter cooling systems, and control and amplification equipment. Does not include cable and long-line systems _____	10.5	13	15.5	
48.33	**TOCSC-Cable and Long-line Systems:** Includes assets such as transmission lines, pole lines, ocean cables, buried cable and conduit, repeaters, repeater stations, and other related assets. Does not include high frequency radio or microwave systems _____	21	26.5	32	
48.34	**TOCSC-Central Office Control Equipment:** Includes assets for general control, switching, and monitoring of communications signals including electromechanical switching and channeling apparatus, multiplexing equipment, patching and monitoring facilities, in-house cabling, teleprinter equipment, and associated site improvements _____	13	16.5	20	

Asset guide-line class	Description of assets included	Asset depreciation range (in years)			Annual asset guideline repair allowance percentage
		Lower limit	Asset guideline period	Upper limit	
48.35	**TOCSC-Computerized Switching, Channeling, and Associated Control Equipment:** Includes central office switching computers, interfacing computers, other associated specialized control equipment, and site improvements __	8.5	10.5	12.5	
48.36	**TOCSC-Satellite Ground Segment Property:** Includes assets such as fixed earth station equipment, antennas, satellite communications equipment, and interface equipment used in satellite communications. Does not include general purpose equipment or equipment used in satellite space segment property _____	8	10	12	
48.37	**TOCSC-Satellite Space Segment Property:** Includes satellites and equipment used for telemetry, tracking, control, and monitoring when used in satellite communications _____	6.5	8	9.5	
48.38	**TOCSC-Equipment Installed on Customer's Premises:** Includes assets installed on customer's premises, such as computers, terminal equipment, power generation and distribution systems, private switching center, teleprinters, facsimile equipment, and other associated and related equipment _____	8	10	12	
48.39	**TOCSC-Support and Service Equipment:** Includes assets used to support but not engage in communications. Includes store, warehouse, and shop tools, and test and laboratory assets __	11	13.5	16	
	Cable Television (CATV): Includes communications-related assets used to provide cable television (community antenna television services). Does not include assets used to provide subscribers with two-way communications services.				
48.41	**CATV-Headend:** Includes assets such as towers, antennas, preamplifiers, converters, modulation equipment, and program non-duplication systems. Does not include headend buildings and program origination assets _____	9	11	13	5
48.42	**CATV-Subscriber Connection and Distribution Systems:** Includes assets such as trunk and feeder cable, connecting hardware, amplifiers, power equipment, passive devices, directional taps, pedestals, pressure taps, drop cables, matching transformers, multiple set connector equipment, and converters _____	8	10	12	5
48.43	**CATV-Program Origination:** Includes assets such as cameras, film chains, video tape recorders, lighting, and remote location equipment excluding vehicles. Does not include buildings and their structural components _____	7	9	11	9
48.44	**CATV-Service and Test:** Includes assets such as oscilloscopes, field strength meters, spectrum analyzers, and cable testing equipment, but does not include vehicles ___	7	8.5	10	2.5
48.45	**CATV-Microwave Systems:** Includes assets such as towers, antennas, transmitting and receiving equipment, and broad band microwave assets if used in the provision of cable television services. Does not include assets used in the provision of common carrier services _____	7.5	9.5	11.5	2
	Electric, Gas, Water and Steam, Utility Services: Includes assets used in the production, transmission and distribution of electricity, gas, steam, or water for sale, including related land improvements.				
49.11	**Electric Utility Hydraulic Production Plant:** Includes assets used in the hydraulic power production of electricity for				

Asset guideline class	Description of assets included	Asset depreciation range (in years)			Annual asset guideline repair allowance percentage
		Lower limit	Asset guideline period	Upper limit	
	sale, including related land improvements, such as dams, flumes, canals, and waterways _____	40	50	60	1.5
49.12	**Electric Utility Nuclear Production Plant:** Includes assets used in the nuclear power production of electricity for sale and related land improvements. Does not include nuclear fuel assemblies _____	16	20	24	3
49.121	**Electric Utility Nuclear Fuel Assemblies:** Includes initial core and replacement core nuclear fuel assemblies (i.e. the composite of fabricated nuclear fuel and container) when used in a boiling water, pressurized water, or high temperature gas reactor used in the production of electricity. Does not include nuclear fuel assemblies used in breeder reactors _____	4	5	6	
49.13	**Electric Utility Steam Production Plant:** Includes assets used in the steam power production of electricity for sale, combustion turbines operated in a combined cycle with a conventional steam unit and related land improvements _____	22.5	28	33.5	5
49.14	**Electric Utility Transmission and Distribution Plant:** Includes assets used in the transmission and distribution of electricity for sale and related land improvements. Excludes initial clearing and grading land improvements as specified in Rev. Rul. 72-403, 1972-2 C.B. 102 _____	24	30	36	4.5
49.15	**Electric Utility Combustion Turbine Production Plant:** Includes assets used in the production of electricity for sale by the use of such prime movers as jet engines, combustion turbines, diesel engines, gasoline engines, and other internal combustion engines, their associated power turbines and/or generators, and related land improvements. Does not include combustion turbines operated in a combined cycle with a conventional steam unit _____	16	20	24	4
49.21	**Gas Utility Distribution Facilities:** Including gas water heaters and gas conversion equipment installed by utility on customers' premises on a rental basis _____	28	35	42	2
49.221	**Gas Utility Manufactured Gas Production Plants:** Includes assets used in the manufacture of gas having chemical and/or physical properties which do not permit complete interchangeability with domestic natural gas _____	24	30	36	2
49.222	**Gas Utility Substitute Natural Gas (SNG) Production Plant (naptha or lighter hydrocarbon feedstocks):** Includes assets used in the catalytic conversion of feedstocks of naphtha or lighter hydrocarbons to a gaseous fuel which is completely interchangeable with domestic natural gas _____	11	14	17	4.5
*49.223	Substitute natural gas-coal gasification: Includes assets used in the manufacture and production of pipeline quality gas from coal using the basic Lurgi process with advanced methanation. Includes all process plant equipment and structures used in this coal gasification process and all utility assets such as cooling systems, water supply and treatment facilities, and assets used in the production and distribution of electricity and steam for use by the taxpayer in a gasification plant and attendant coal mining site processes but not for assets used in the production and distribution of electricity and steam for sale to				

(*) Asset guideline class 49.223 was added by *RevProc 77-14*, IRB 1977-21, effective for property placed in service in tax years beginning after 12-31-76.

Asset ide-ne ass	Description of assets included	Asset depreciation range (in years)			Annual asset guideline repair allowance percentage
		Lower limit	Asset guideline period	Upper limit	
	others. Also includes all other related land improvements. Does not include assets used in the direct mining and treatment of coal prior to the gasification process itself _____	14.5	18	21.5	15.0
49.23	**Natural Gas Production Plant** _____	11	14	17	4.5
49.24	**Gas Utility Trunk Pipelines and Related Storage Facilities:** Excludes initial clearing and grading land improvements as specified in Rev. Rul. 72-403 _____	17.5	22	26.5	3
49.25	**Liquefied Natural Gas Plant:** Includes assets used in the liquefaction, storage, and regasification of natural gas including loading and unloading connections, instrumentation equipment and controls, pumps, vaporizers and odorizers, tanks, and related land improvements. Also includes pipeline interconnections with gas transmission lines and distribution systems and marine terminal facilities _____	17.5	22	26.5	4.5
49.3	**Water Utilities:** Includes assets used in the gathering, treatment, and commercial distribution of water _____	40	50	60	1.5
49.4	**Central Steam Utility Production and Distribution:** Includes assets used in the production and distribution of steam for sale __	22.5	28	33.5	2.5
50.0	**Wholesale and Retail Trade:** Includes assets used in carrying out the activities of purchasing, assembling, storing, sorting, grading, and selling of goods at both the wholesale and retail level. Also includes assets used in such activities as the operation of restaurants, cafes, coin-operated dispensing machines, and in brokerage of scrap metal _____	8	10	12	6.5
50.1	**Wholesale and Retail Trade Service Assets:** Includes assets such as glassware, silverware (including kitchen utensils), crockery (usually china) and linens (generally napkins, tablecloths and towels) used in qualified activities as defined in class 50.0 ____	2	2.5	3	
70.2	**Personal and Professional Services:** Includes assets used in the provision of personal services such as those offered by hotels and motels, laundry and dry cleaning establishments, beauty and barber shops, photographic studios and mortuaries. Includes assets used in the provision of professional services such as those offered by doctors, dentists, lawyers, accountants, architects, engineers, and veterinarians. Includes assets used in the provision of repair and maintenance services and those assets used in providing fire and burglary protection services. Includes equipment or facilities used by cemetery organizations, news agencies, teletype wire services, frozen food lockers, and research laboratories _____	8	10	12	6.5
.21	**Personal and Professional Services Service Assets:** Includes assets such as glassware, silverware, crockery, and linens (generally sheets, pilowcases and bath towels) used in qualified activities as defined in class 70.2 _____	2	2.5	3	
0	**Recreation:** Includes assets used in the provision of entertainment services on payment of a fee or admission charge, as in the operation of bowling alleys, billiard and pool establishments, theaters, concert halls, and miniature golf courses. Does not include amusement and theme parks and assets which consist primarily of specialized land improvements or structures, such as golf courses, sports stadia, race tracks, ski slopes, and buildings which house the assets used in entertainment services _____	8	10	12	6.5
.0	**Theme and Amusement Parks:** Includes assets used in the provision of rides, attractions, and amuse-				

ments in activities defined as theme and amusement parks, and includes appurtenances associated with a ride, attraction, amusement or theme setting within the park such as ticket booths, facades, shop interiors, and props, special purpose structures, and buildings other than warehouses, administration buildings, hotels, and motels. Includes all land improvements for or in support of park activities, (e.g. parking lots, sidewalks, waterways, bridges, fences, landscaping, etc.) and support functions (e.g. food and beverage retailing, souvenir vending and other nonlodging accommodations) if owned by the park and provided exclusively for the benefit of park patrons. Theme and amusement parks are defined as combinations of amusements, rides, and attractions which are permanently situated on park land and open to the public for the price of admission. This guideline class is a composite of all assets used in this industry except transportation equipment (general purpose trucks, cars, airplanes, etc., which are included in asset guideline classes with the prefix 00.2), assets used in the provision of administrative services (asset guideline classes with the prefix 00.1), and warehouses, administration buildings, hotels and motels _____ 10   12.5   15   12.5

COMPONENT DEPRECIATION

Component Depreciation

The tax law limits you to 150%-declining-balance depreciation on new and straight-line on used commercial properties. You may be able to save tax dollars by figuring depreciation on a component basis rather than by using a composite rate. You might, for example, have separate accounts as follows:

	Useful Life	Cost
Building	40 years	$120,000
Wiring	12 years	20,000
Plumbing	12 years	12,000
Roof	12 years	8,000
Elevator	12 years	10,000
Paving	8 years	5,000
Air conditioning	8 years	20,000
Ceilings	8 years	9,000
Floor	8 years	10,000
		$214,000

This would result in first-year depreciation aggregating $19,000 using 150%-declining-balance.

If you were to use composite depreciation, the life of the composite building would be 26.88 years. Using this and 150%-declining-balance depreciation would give first-year depreciation of only $11,941.

If you had used the 200%-declining-balance method with the composite method, your first-year depreciation would still have been only $15,923.

FIRST YEAR'S DEPRECIATION ON INDIVIDUAL-ITEM BASIS

First Year's Depreciation on Individual-Item Basis

Assume that you build a hotel and incur the costs given for each item. Based on the ADR useful lives and disregarding salvage value, below is a table indicating the first year's depreciation for each item under straight-line and 150%-declining-balance depreciation methods.

Item	Cost	Useful Life	First Year Depreciation	
			S/L	150% D/B
Building & Improvements				
Building only	$500,000	40	$12,500	$18,750
Air Conditioning.	45,000	8	5,625	8,433
Elevators:				
Freight (2)	25,000	12	2,083	3,125
Passenger (4)	40,000	12	3,333	5,000
Boiler & Oil Burner	30,000	8	3,750	5,625
Lighting System:				
Fixtures.	15,000	8	1,875	2,813
Wiring	20,000	12	1,666	2,500
Plumbing:				
Bathtubs, etc.	12,500	12	1,042	1,563
Faucets, valves, etc. . . .	7,500	12	625	938
Pipes:				
Cold water	12,500	12	1,042	1,563
Hot water.	15,000	12	1,250	1,875
Roof—copper	25,000	12	2,083	3,125
Switchboards	5,000	8	625	938
Water tank—metal	10,000	8	1,250	1,875
Fire Alarm &				
Prevention Equipment . .	15,000	8	1,875	2,813
Total Building & Improvements . . .	$777,500			
Furniture, Fixtures & Equipment				
Refrigeration System	11,000	8	1,375	2,063
Kitchen Equipment	20,000	8	2,500	3,750
Laundry Equipment	15,000	8	1,875	2,813
House Cleaning Equipment. .	10,000	8	1,250	1,875
Shades & Screens	10,000	8	1,250	1,875
Blankets & Spreads	6,000	8	750	1,125
Carpets & Rugs	12,000	8	1,500	2,250
Curtains, Draperies & Scarfs .	6,000	8	750	1,125
Spring, Mattresses & Pillows .	6,000	8	750	1,125
Furniture:				
Dining & Guest Rooms . .	24,000	8	3,000	4,500
Lobby.	4,000	8	500	750
Total Furniture, Fixtures & Equipment	$124,000			
TOTAL	$901,500		$56,124	$84,187

DEPRECIATION RECAPTURE

When you own property, you can take large writeoffs via accelerated depreciation that can be used to offset ordinary income and possibly provide you with some degree of tax shelter. These depreciation deductions also reduce your basis in the property. As a result, when the property is sold, any gain (i.e., the difference between the selling price and the adjusted basis) is normally taxed at the more favorable capital gain rate. Thus, depreciation allows the investor to possibly shelter his ordinary income and then convert it to capital gain.

In 1963 Congress put some limitations on this practice (effective in 1964) when it passed Section 1250 of the Code, which provided that excess depreciation (depreciation taken which is beyond what the deduction would be under the straight-line method) was to be recaptured (i.e., treated) as ordinary income if the property was sold within 10 years. However, if the property was held for more than 20 months, the owner could get a break: The recapture potential was phased out at the rate of 1% for each full month the property was held, over 20 months.

In 1969, the Tax Reform Act of that year tightened the recapture rules even further by requiring a longer holding period for residential property (16⅔ years) and providing for the complete recapture of excess depreciation on all other non-residential property, no matter how long they were held.

Then came the Tax Reform Act of 1976, which removed some of the benefits of accelerated depreciation by providing for 100% recapture of excess depreciation on all types (residential, too) of property except low-income rental housing.

In the table that follows you will find the rules as they apply for the years 1963-69, 1970-75 and post-1975. Prior to 1964, depreciation, on real estate, was not subject to recapture.

PRE-1970 (1963-69)

Property	Holding Period	Percentage of Excess Depreciation to Be Recaptured
All types of real property	Less than 12 months	All depreciation (not just excess over straight line) is recaptured
	12 to 20 months	100%
	20 months to 120 months	100% reduced by 1% per month for each full month over 20 months
	Over 10 years	None

POST-1969 (1970-75)

Property	Holding Period	Percentage of Excess Depreciation to Be Recaptured
Sold under binding contract in existence be- for 7/24/69,	12 to 20 months	100%
	20 to 120 months	100% reduced by 1% per month for each full month over 20 months
and government sponsored projects	Over 10 years	None

Property	Holding Period	Percentage of Excess Depreciation to Be Recaptured
Residential rental property (other than the above). including §167(k) expenses	12 to 100 months	100%
	100 to 200 months	100% reduced by 1% per month for each full month over 100 months
	Over 200 months (16⅔ years)	None
Nonresidential, commercial, industrial	Any length of time	100%

POST 1975

Property	Holding Period	Percentage of Excess Depreciation to Be Recaptured
Residential and nonresidential	Less than 12 months	All depreciation (not just excess over straight line) is recaptured
	Any length of time over 12 months	100%
Low-income rental* housing	Less than 12 months	All depreciation (not just excess over straight line) is recaptured
	12 to 100 months	100%
	100 to 200 months	100% reduced by 1% per month for each full month over 100 months
	Over 200 months (16⅔ years)	None

*Included within this category are the following: property on which a mortgage is insured under Section 221(d)(3) or 236 of the National Housing Act; low-income rental housing that qualifies for rehabilitation writeoffs under Section 167(k); property covered by Section 8 of the United States Housing Act of 1937; and property insured under Title V or the Housing Act of 1949.

AFTER-TAX COST OF INTEREST PAYMENTS

The actual cost of interest payments to a real estate investor may be a lot less than he may think because: (1) When you finance a real estate deal by way of a long-term loan, you come in for a tax deduction for your interest payments on the loan. (2) You benefit from repaying the loan in relatively cheap inflation-devalued dollars—thus cutting the cost to you of the borrowed funds. (3) You have the prospect of substantial net after-tax returns from income-producing real estate. (4) With both income-producing property and residential property, you have the prospect of appreciation in value, an appreciation, by the way, which should cover both actual economic appreciation and dollar-value appreciation and for which you get long-term capital gain treatment when you cash in. (5) Income-producing property will give you depreciation deductions based on the total cost of the property—including borrowed funds.

The interest you pay is, as we've already pointed out, tax deductible. The higher the tax rate, the higher your tax bracket, the more valuable your interest deductions become.

The table on page 382 shows you how interest deductions shape up for taxpayers in different tax brackets. In reading this table, keep in mind that the tax law provisions as to investment interest are not taken into account in the table because the particulars of each taxpayer's position would affect the result.

Effect of 1976 Tax Law Interest Provisions: The deduction of excess investment interest by individuals, partners, and members of Subchapter S corporations, but not regular corporations, is limited.

Under Sec. 163(d)(3)(D) of the Code, "investment interest means interest paid or accrued on indebtedness incurred or continued to purchase or carry property held for investment." Therefore since the definition is confined to investment property, interest on a home mortgage is not within the limitation's purview, nor is interest paid on financing for trade or business property.

The Limitations: Prior to the Tax Reform Act of 1976, the deduction for investment interest was limited to $25,000 a year, plus the investor's net investment income, the amount of his capital gains, plus 50% of any interest in excess of these amounts.

The Tax Reform Act of 1976 has tightened this rule. For 1976 and subsequent years, the deductible interest on investment indebtedness is limited to $10,000 a year, plus the investor's net investment income. Eliminated is the offset for long-term capital gain. However, an additional deduction of up to $15,000 per year is allowed if the interest is paid in connection with a qualified acquisition of stock in a corporation, or a partnership interest. (Sec. 163(d)(7)).

Transitional Rule: A transitional rule applies where interest on indebtedness attributable to a specified item of property is for a specified term and was incurred before September 11, 1975 ("or is incurred after September 10, 1975 pursuant to a written contract or commitment that on September 11, 1975, and at all times thereafter, before the incurring of such indebtedness, is binding on the taxpayer.") If applicable, the new limitations will not apply, and the old limitations will continue.

Where an investor has investment interest that is subject to both the new limitation and the transitional or pre-1976 rule, he must distinguish between pre-1976 and post-1975 figures. That is, for all indebtedness incurred pre-1976 and for all pre-1976 carryovers, the old limitation will apply. The new limitation rules apply only for indebtedness incurred post-1975.

Special Rules for Net Lease Properties Continue: Ordinarily, rental income will be considered trade or business income, unless it is derived from property rented under a net lease arrangement, in which case it will be considered investment property and the rent will be included as investment income. For this purpose, a lease will not be considered a net lease if trade and business (Sec. 162 of the Code) deductions account for 15% or more of the rental income.

Investors may elect to exclude from the application of the 15% test all leases of properties that have been in use for more than five years. This election is made on a year-by-year basis. After the election is made, all property that has been in use more than five years may be exempted from the 15% test. As a result, any interest paid in connection with this leased property is not considered investment interest and income from the property is not considered investment income.

Joint Return Taxable Income — After-Tax Cost of Interest Paid

Over	Not Over	7	7½	8	8½	9	9½	10	10½	11	11½	12	12½	13	13½	14	14½	15
$ 4,000—	8,000	5.67	6.08	6.48	6.89	7.29	7.70	8.10	8.51	8.91	9.32	9.72	10.13	10.53	10.94	11.34	11.75	12.15
8,000—	12,000	5.46	5.85	6.24	6.63	7.02	7.41	7.80	8.19	8.58	8.97	9.36	9.75	10.14	10.53	10.92	11.31	11.70
12,000—	16,000	5.25	5.63	6.00	6.38	6.75	7.13	7.50	7.89	8.25	8.63	9.00	9.38	9.75	10.13	10.50	10.88	11.25
16,000—	20,000	5.04	5.40	5.76	6.12	6.48	6.84	7.20	7.56	7.92	8.28	8.64	9.00	9.36	9.72	10.08	10.44	10.80
20,000—	24,000	4.76	5.10	5.44	5.78	6.12	6.46	6.80	7.14	7.48	7.82	8.16	8.50	8.84	9.18	9.52	9.86	10.20
24,000—	28,000	4.48	4.80	5.12	5.44	5.76	6.08	6.40	6.72	7.04	7.36	7.68	8.00	8.32	8.64	8.96	9.28	9.60
28,000—	32,000	4.27	4.58	4.88	5.19	5.49	5.80	6.10	6.41	6.71	7.02	7.32	7.63	7.93	8.24	8.54	8.85	9.15
32,000—	36,000	4.06	4.35	4.64	4.93	5.22	5.51	5.80	6.09	6.38	6.67	6.96	7.25	7.54	7.83	8.12	8.41	8.70
36,000—	40,000	3.85	4.13	4.40	4.68	4.95	5.23	5.50	5.78	6.05	6.33	6.60	6.88	7.15	7.43	7.70	7.98	8.25
40,000—	44,000	3.64	3.90	4.16	4.42	4.68	4.94	5.20	5.46	5.72	5.98	6.24	6.50	6.76	7.02	7.28	7.54	7.80
44,000—	52,000	3.50	3.75	4.00	4.25	4.50	4.75	5.00	5.25	5.50	5.75	6.00	6.25	6.50	6.75	7.00	7.25	7.50
52,000—	64,000	3.29	3.53	3.76	4.00	4.23	4.47	4.70	4.94	5.17	5.41	5.64	5.88	6.11	6.35	6.58	6.82	7.05
64,000—	76,000	3.15	3.38	3.60	3.83	4.06	4.28	4.50	4.73	4.95	5.18	5.40	5.63	5.85	6.08	6.30	6.53	6.75
76,000—	88,000	2.94	3.15	3.36	3.57	3.78	3.99	4.20	4.41	4.62	4.83	5.04	5.25	5.46	5.67	5.88	6.09	6.30
88,000—100,000		2.80	3.00	3.20	3.40	3.60	3.80	4.00	4.20	4.40	4.60	4.80	5.00	5.20	5.54	5.60	5.80	6.00
100,000—120,000		2.66	2.85	3.04	3.23	3.42	3.61	3.80	3.99	4.18	4.37	4.56	4.75	4.94	5.13	5.32	5.51	5.70
120,000—140,000		2.52	2.70	2.88	3.06	3.24	3.42	3.60	3.78	3.96	4.14	4.32	4.50	4.68	4.86	5.14	5.22	5.40
140,000—160,000		2.38	2.55	2.72	2.89	3.06	3.23	3.40	3.57	3.74	3.91	4.08	4.25	4.42	4.59	4.76	4.93	5.10
160,000—180,000		2.24	2.40	2.56	2.72	2.88	3.04	3.20	3.36	3.52	3.68	3.84	4.00	4.16	4.32	4.48	4.64	4.80
180,000—200,000		2.17	2.33	2.48	2.64	2.79	2.95	3.10	3.26	3.41	3.57	3.72	3.88	4.03	4.19	4.34	4.50	4.65
200,000—and over		2.10	2.25	2.40	2.55	2.70	2.85	3.00	3.15	3.33	3.45	3.60	3.75	3.90	4.05	4.20	4.35	4.50

TAX RATES, EARNED INCOME, AND
TAX-PREFERENCE INCOME

In working out the arithmetic of real estate deals, taxes play a vital role. And you need tax figures quickly to check out the deal. The tables in this section are designed to give you that information.

Income Tax Rates: Corporate rates are simple: 20% on the first $25,000 22% on the next $25,000 and 48% on everything over that.* For individuals, the tax brackets stretch over a larger area. One table gives you the individual tax rates and also how much income is left after taxes. Another table shows you the relative values of capital gains, ordinary income, dividends, and tax-free income. With these three tables you can compare the various income tax situations for individuals.

Tax-Free Income: Because part or all of the return from a real estate investment can be tax free, it is important to compare the relative values of tax-free and taxable income. That is shown in a table in this section.

Maximum Tax on Personal Service Income: The maximum tax rate applicable to earned income is 50%, instead of the 70% maximum tax rate applicable to other types of income. Earned income generally includes wages, salaries, professional fees or compensation for personal services and, in the case of a taxpayer engaged in a trade or business where both personal services and capital are a material income-producing factor, a reasonable amount but not more than 30% of his share of the net profits of the business. Earned income does not include lump-sum distributions from employees' trusts or employee annuity plans.

Earned taxable income is defined as that proportion of total taxable income which is in the same ratio (but not in excess of 100%) as the ratio of earned income to adjusted gross income. Thus, if 40% of an individual's adjusted gross income is earned income, 40% of this taxable income is earned taxable income. The 50% limit is not available to taxpayers who use income averaging or to married taxpayers who file separately. The 50% limit is applicable to earned income reduced by tax preferences in excess of $10,000 in the current year. Tax preferences for this purpose are the same as those applicable to individuals under the minimum tax.

If during a taxable year a taxpayer has earned taxable income which exceeds the 50% tax bracket, he figures his tax as follows: (1) Takes the lowest amount of taxable income that is taxed over 50%. Computes the tax on this amount. (2) Takes 50% of the amount by which earned taxable income (as defined above) exceeds the taxable income used in step (1). (3) Computes the regular tax on the entire taxable income and deducts the tax computed on only the earned taxable income. (4) Adds the amounts under steps (1), (2), and (3).

Minimum Tax on Tax-Preference Income: The tax law imposes a minimum tax in addition to the regular tax on individuals and corporations on their tax-preference income. The minimum tax provision doesn't apply unless the tax-preference income exceeds $10,000.

The way the minimum tax works is that a corporation or individual adds all his tax-preference income. From this, the $10,000 exemption or one half the amount of regular federal income taxes, whichever is greater, is subtracted. The remained is then taxed at the rate of 15%.

*Code §11.

Tax-Preference Income: For individuals and corporations, tax-preference income includes the following: (1) Accelerated depreciation on real property in excess of straight line; (2) Depreciation on personal property subject to a lease in excess of straight line; (3) Amortization of pollution control equipment in excess of accelerated depreciation; (4) Amortization of railroad rolling stock; (5) Tax benefits from qualified stock options; (6) Excess bad debt reserves of financial institutions; (7) Depletion costs to the extent they exceed the cost or other basis of the property involved; (8) Capital gains (one-half for individuals and 18/48 for corporations); (9) Amortization of on-the-job training and child care facilities; (10) Itemized deductions (not including medical expenses and casualty losses) in excess of 60% of adjusted gross income; (11) Intangible oil and gas drilling costs in excess of what would be deductible if such costs were capitalized and amortized over 10 years.

How Minimum Tax Provision Works: Suppose a real estate man has tax-preference income, including the untaxed half of his capital gain, amounting to $100,000. His regular federal income tax comes to $80,000. The amount of tax on his preferential income would be worked out as follows:

Tax-preference income	$100,000
Regular taxes ($80,000) × ½ = $40,000, or $10,000, whichever is greater	40,000
Subject to minimum tax	60,000
Minimum tax rate	× 15%
To be added to regular taxes	$ 9,000

ADVANTAGES AND DISADVANTAGES OF VARIOUS ACCOUNTING METHODS

	Advantages and Disadvantages of Various Accounting Methods			
Who May Use	When Income Is Taxed	When Expenses Are Deductible	Advantages	Disadvantages

Cash Method

Who May Use	When Income Is Taxed	When Expenses Are Deductible	Advantages	Disadvantages
Any taxpayer unless inventories necessary to reflect income. Must be used if you have no records or incomplete ones. Can be used in one business although another method is used in other business.	In year cash or property is received. For property, use fair market value. Taxed in year of constructive receipt even if there's no actual receipt (i.e., year income was available to you although you didn't take it).	Year in which payment is made in cash or property. Giving note is not payment; payment can be made with borrowed funds. Certain prepaid expenses must be spread over periods to which they apply even though full amount has been paid, e.g., insurance premiums, rent, fees to negotiate long-term lease. But payment for supplies bought in advance is currently deductible.	You don't pay taxes until you get the income. You can control each year's receipts and payouts and even out income over the years. You can keep simple records.	You don't always match related income and expenses in one year, thus creating distortions. You may not have full control over receipts, and income may pile up in one year. Liquidation or sale of business may create income bunching— all accounts receivable may have to be picked up at one time.

Accrual Method

Who May Use	When Income Is Taxed	When Expenses Are Deductible	Advantages	Disadvantages
Anyone except those with no or incomplete books or records. You must use if inventories are necessary clearly to reflect income unless you can use one of methods discussed below.	In year income is earned—i.e., year in which right to income becomes fixed, regardless of year of receipt. You do not accrue contingent, contested or uncollectible items. Prepaid amounts are income when received even if not yet earned.	In the year all events have occurred which fix the fact and the amount of your liability, regardless of the year of payment. You do not accrue contingent or contested liabilities. But if you pay a liability and still contest it, you deduct it when you pay it. If you get a recovery later, it's income when received.	It matches income and related expenses and tends to even out your income over the years.	Have less leeway than cash-basis taxpayer to defer or accelerate income or deductions. Can still accelerate deductions, however, by advancing repairs and advertising expenditures within desired period, purchasing supplies, getting bills for professional services before year end.

	Advantages and Disadvantages of Various Accounting Methods (continued)			
Who May Use	When Income Is Taxed	When Expenses Are Deductible	Advantages	Disadvantages
		Accrual Method (continued)		
	Special Rule: Accruals to certain related taxpayers must be paid within 2-1/2 months of close of taxable year or accrual or deduction is lost.			
		"Hybrid" Method (see Reg. § 1.446-1(c)(1)(iv))		
Any taxpayer if method clearly reflects income and is consistently used.	Accrual method is used in respect of purchases and sales; while cash methods is used for all other items of income and expenses.	Method is simple; it's not necessary to accrue income items such as interest, dividends. The bother of accruing small expenses is removed. Chief benefit is to small business, such as retail store.	Method is not entirely accurate. Since it is a "hybrid," it does not reflect true income. However, if consistently used and absent any unusual nonrecurring income or expense items, it gives a fairly good comparison of how business is doing from year to year.
		Installment Method		
Installment dealers who elect this method. Seller in casual sale of personal property of more than $1,000 or of real property provided, in either case, no more than 30% of selling price is received in year of sale.	Each year that collections are made, a proportionate amount of each collection (equal to percentage of gross profits on entire sale) is picked up as gross income in the year of collection.	Dealer deducts expenses when paid (if he's on cash basis) or incurred (on accrual basis). On casual sales, expense of sale reduces sale price, thereby having effect of spreading deduction over period of reporting income.	Income is spread over period of collection—so you do not pay taxes on amounts not yet received. If tax rates decline in future, part of profits will bear a lower tax.	Dealers who switch from accrual to installment basis may have to pay a double tax on some receivables —unless they sell all receivables before the switch. Tax rate may go up; in which case, some profits will bear a higher tax.

384

Advantages and Disadvantages of Various Accounting Methods (continued)

Who May Use	When Income Is Taxed	When Expenses Are Deductible	Advantages	Disadvantages
Deferred Payment Sales Method				
Any cash-basis tax-payer on sale of personal property. Any cash- or accrual-basis taxpayer on sale of real estate.	At time of sale, seller picks up cash and <u>fair market value</u> of buyer's obligations. If total exceeds basis of sold property, difference is taxable. In later years as obligations are collected, difference between amount received and value at which obligations were originally picked up is taxable at time of collection.	Used generally with casual sales, so expense of sale reduces sale price and is thus spread over period of collection.	Can use where installment sale reporting is not possible —i.e., where more than 30% of sale price is received in year of sale. Useful in somewhat speculative deals where value of buyer's obligations is contingent on future operations and they have little or no ascertainable present value.	You may be in for a long and costly argument with IRS as to value of obligations. Even though original sale gave capital gain, gain on collection of the obligations in future years will be taxable as an ordinary income.
Long-Term Contract Methods				
Percentage of Completion Method				
Taxpayers who have contracts which take more than a year to complete, usually construction contracts. There are two long-term contract methods: (1) percentage of completion and (2) completed contract, and IRS permission is needs to switch to or from either.	A portion of the total contract price is taken into account each year according to the percentage of the contract completed that year. Architects' or engineers' certificates are required.	All expenses made during the year allocable to that contract are deducted, with adjustments made for inventories and supplies on hand at the beginning and end of the year.	Income from long-term contract is reflected as earned. Income bunching in one year is avoided.	Accurate estimates of completion are difficult to make in some cases. If expenses are irregular as compared with income, there may be distortion of income in the interim years, although the final total will work out accurately.

Who May Use	When Income Is Taxed	When Expenses Are Deductible	Advantages	Disadvantages
		Long-Term Contract Methods (continued)		
Completed Contract Method				
	The entire contract price is picked up as income in the year the contract is completed and accepted.	Expenses allocable to specific contracts (that would exclude general administrative costs) are not deductible until year of completion when income is picked up.	Income can be reflected more accurately—all the figures are in when the computation is made. Avoids estimates in interim years which may turn out to be wrong.	Bunching of income or losses in one year is possible if a number of profitable or unprofitable contracts are all finished in one year. A steady flow of completed contracts from year to year overcomes this problem. (There may be some argument with IRS as to proper year of completion in some cases.)

REAL ESTATE INVESTOR'S TAX EVALUATOR

Real Estate Investor's Tax Evaluator

	Deal #1	Deal #2
Rental Income	$ _____	$ _____
Expenses:		
Interest	$ _____	$ _____
Amortization	_____	_____
Real estate taxes	_____	_____
Other taxes (including income taxes)	_____	_____
Insurance	_____	_____
Payroll costs	_____	_____
Repairs	_____	_____
Other expenses	_____	_____
Total Expenses	$ _____	$ _____
Depreciation:	_____	_____
Present basis for depreciation	$ _____	$ _____
Method of depreciation		
(a) 200%-declining-balance	_____	_____
(b) 150%-declining-balance	_____	_____
(c) Sum-of-the-digits	_____	_____
(d) Straight-line	_____	_____
Investment Credit:	$ _____	$ _____

Taxable Income: Income less expenses (not
   including amortization) and depreciation
   using alternate methods

	Deal #1	Deal #2
(a) _____	$ _____	$ _____
(b) _____	_____	_____
(c) _____	_____	_____
(d) _____	_____	_____
Income Taxes:		
Sole proprietorship	$ _____	$ _____
Partnership	_____	_____
Corporation	_____	_____

HOW TO FIGURE THE YIELD ON INVESTMENTS PROPERTIES

Prime property should sell to yield about 2 points higher than the prime mortgage interest rate. The prime mortgage interest rate is the lowest rate of interest available on mortgage loans secured by prime properties with triple-A national tenants under long-term leases. Properties with strong tenants under leases running to 10- to 15-year terms should yield 3 points higher than the prime interest rate. Secondary properties having reasonably sound tenants under short-term leases should yield 4 points more than the prime interest rate. Marginal properties should give you a yield of 5 points over the prime interest rate.

Of course, these are only rules of thumb and should only be used as such.

REAL ESTATE INVESTOR INFORMATION

Here are rules of thumb as to what real estate may be worth in relation to the net income and gross rents it throws off. These rules of thumb should be used only as rough indicators. They should be modified and refined in light of the specific circumstances involved in each piece of property, each negotiation, and each deal.

How Many Times Annual Rent

Residences	9 to 10
Apartment Houses	7 to 9
Stores (Services)	7 to 9
Stores (Self-Operating)	8 to 10
Net Leases	9 to 15 (depending chiefly on credit rating)
Warehouses	10 to 12
Loft Buildings	10 to 12
Office Buildings	8 to 12

HOW MUCH RETURN ON EQUITY IN REAL ESTATE

Here are the components in determining how much yield you should get on cash put in real estate. The percentage rates assigned vary with money conditions, quality of real estate, and individual judgment. Thus, they are merely illustrative.

1. Safe rate (that is, current rate of return on investments having the greatest liquidity and safety, such as long-term United States Government bonds) . 8.0%
2. Risk rate (reasonable allowance for continued ability of property to earn current income) . 3.0%
3. Penalty for nonliquidity (relative salability, rentability, and collateral value of the property) . 2.5%
4. Burden of management of funds rate (cost involved in managing the investment) . 2.5%
   Total rate of capitalization . 16.0%

These factors might be offset (to make a lower yield acceptable) by the following additional considerations:

5. Tax protection — depreciation making a large portion of the income tax free for a period of years . 1%
6. Amortization return — the scaling down of mortgage debt, which though taxable is offset by depreciation and promises an early refinancing to produce tax-free cash or an increased yield through lower financing charge 1%

What the Professionals Have Been Paying

Syndicators are hunting for bargains throughout the country. Here's an analysis of what a group that caters to small investors and buys the kind of property which medium-sized investors might swing on their own or with a partner or two has been paying and the kind of yield and financing it has been getting.

Type of Property	Cash Distribution	Mortgage Reduction	Total Dist. & Mortgage Reduction	Tax-Free Cash per $1,000
4-sty apt house — 16 apts.	$118.12	$54.64	$172.76	$36.00
3-sty brick apt house — 6 apts	100.00	29.70	129.70	53.76
6-sty apt house	99.80	35.58	135.38	29.24
1-sty taxpayer consisting of 7 stores	101.01	26.59	127.60	29.57
2-sty bldg — 9 stores & 15 offices	65.56	30.00	95.56	48.96
4-sty brick walk-up apt & store bldg — 26 apts & 4 stores	97.58	61.64	159.22	26.62
6-sty converted apt house — 38 apts	99.14	30.27	129.41	49.71
2-sty taxpayer — 10 stores & 3 offices	78.04	Free & Clear	78.04	45.00
5-sty brick apt house & garage — 54 apts	89.29	50.57	139.86	56.98
5-sty apt house	91.64	29.94	121.58	34.72
6-sty apt bldg	96.14	31.82	127.96	47.79
11-sty apt house — 123 apts	77.43	77.93	155.36	64.12
5-sty apt house — 30 apts plus 1 sty commercial bldg — 6 stores	82.26	38.60	120.86	59.48
Regional shopping center — 3 stores plus restaurant	64.04	24.00	88.04	73.18

* Ignoring Internal Rate of Return Concepts

HOW MUCH IS LEFT AFTER TAXES

How Much Is Left After Taxes

Example of use of this table: Find how much an unmarried individual who is not head of a household has left from a taxable income of $35,000.

Amount from line $32,000−$38,000 under column for single persons	$21,710
Percentage from that line (50%) times excess of $35,000 over $32,000 ($3,000)	1,500
After-tax income	23,210

Single Person			Head of Household		
Taxable Income	After-Tax Income*	Plus This % of Excess	Taxable Income	After-Tax Income*	Plus This % of Excess
$ - $ 500	--	86	$ - $ 1,000	--	86
500 - 1,000	430	85	1,000 - 2,000	860	84
1,000 - 1,500	855	84	2,000 - 4,000	1,700	82
1,500 - 2,000	1,275	83	4,000 - 6,000	3,340	81
2,000 - 4,000	1,690	81	6,000 - 8,000	4,960	78
4,000 - 6,000	3,310	79	8,000 - 10,000	6,520	77
6,000 - 8,000	4,900	76	10,000 - 12,000	8,060	75
8,000 - 10,000	6,410	75	12,000 - 14,000	9,560	73
10,000 - 12,000	7,910	73	14,000 - 16,000	11,020	72
12,000 - 14,000	9,370	71	16,000 - 18,000	12,460	69
14,000 - 16,000	10,790	69	18,000 - 20,000	13,840	68
16,000 - 18,000	12,170	66	20,000 - 22,000	15,200	65
18,000 - 20,000	13,490	64	22,000 - 24,000	16,500	64
20,000 - 22,000	14,770	62	24,000 - 26,000	17,880	63
22,000 - 26,000	16,010	60	26,000 - 28,000	19,020	59
26,000 - 32,000	18,410	55	28,000 - 32,000	20,200	58
32,000 - 38,000	21,710	50	32,000 - 36,000	22,520	55
38,000 - 44,000	24,710	45	36,000 - 38,000	25,720	52
44,000 - 50,000	27,410	40	38,000 - 40,000	25,760	49
50,000 - 60,000	29,810	38	40,000 - 44,000	26,740	48
60,000 - 70,000	33,610	36	44,000 - 50,000	28,660	45
70,000 - 80,000	37,210	34	50,000 - 52,000	31,360	44
80,000 - 90,000	40,610	32	52,000 - 64,000	32,240	42
90,000 - 100,000	43,810	31	64,000 - 70,000	37,280	41
Over $100,000	46,910	30	70,000 - 76,000	39,740	39
			76,000 - 80,000	42,080	38
			80,000 - 88,000	43,600	37
			88,000 - 100,000	46,560	36
			100,000 - 120,000	50,880	34
			120,000 - 140,000	57,680	33
			140,000 - 160,000	64,280	32
			160,000 - 180,000	70,680	31
			Over $180,000	76,880	30

* Lower Amount in First Column

How Much Is Left After Taxes (continued)

Married Filing Joint Return; Surviving Spouse			Married Individuals Filing Separately and Estates and Trusts		
Taxable Income	After-Tax Income *	Plus This % of Excess	Taxable Income	After-Tax Income *	Plus This % of Excess
$ - $ 1,000	--	86	Not over - $ 500	--	--
1,000 - 2,000	860	85	$ 500 - 1,000	430	85
2,000 - 3,000	1,710	84	1,000 - 1,500	855	84
3,000 - 4,000	2,550	83	1,500 - 2,000	1,275	83
4,000 - 8,000	3,380	81	2,000 - 4,000	1,690	81
8,000 - 12,000	6,620	78	4,000 - 6,000	3,310	78
12,000 - 16,000	9,740	75	6,000 - 8,000	4,870	75
16,000 - 20,000	12,740	72	8,000 - 10,000	6,370	72
20,000 - 24,000	15,620	68	10,000 - 12,000	7,810	68
24,000 - 28,000	18,340	64	12,000 - 14,000	9,170	64
28,000 - 32,000	20,900	61	14,000 - 16,000	10,450	61
32,000 - 36,000	23,340	58	16,000 - 18,000	11,670	58
36,000 - 40,000	25,660	55	18,000 - 20,000	12,830	55
40,000 - 44,000	27,860	52	20,000 - 22,000	13,930	52
44,000 - 52,000	29,940	50	22,000 - 26,000	14,970	50
52,000 - 64,000	33,940	47	26,000 - 32,000	16,970	47
64,000 - 76,000	39,580	45	32,000 - 38,000	19,790	45
76,000 - 88,000	44,980	42	38,000 - 44,000	22,490	42
88,000 - 100,000	50,020	40	44,000 - 50,000	25,010	40
100,000 - 120,000	54,820	38	50,000 - 60,000	27,410	38
120,000 - 140,000	62,420	36	60,000 - 70,000	31,210	36
140,000 - 160,000	69,620	34	70,000 - 80,000	34,810	34
160,000 - 180,000	76,420	32	80,000 - 90,000	38,210	32
180,000 - 200,000	82,820	31	90,000 - 100,000	41,410	31
Over $200,000	89,020	30	Over $100,000	44,510	30

* Lower Amount in First Column.

How Much $1 of Additional After-Tax Income Is Worth

Tax-free income includes municipal bonds, life insurance return. special income earned abroad, etc.

Ordinary income includes interest on taxable bonds, dividends (not considering the $100 exclusion), compensation, net rental income, etc.

Capital Gains: The returns indicated in this table are applicable only with respect to the first $50,000 of capital gains. The maximum tax on these gains is 25%. (The maximum tax on the amount in excess of $50,000 is 35%.) The return also does not take into account any tax on capital gains as tax-preference income.

Income on Joint Return	Tax-Free Income	Ordinary Income	Capital Gains	Net of Capital Gains over Ordinary Income
$ 4 - 8,000	$1.00	$ .81	$ .905	12%
8 - 12,000	1.00	.78	.89	14
12 - 16,000	1.00	.75	.875	17
16 - 20,000	1.00	.72	.86	19
20 - 24,000	1.00	.68	.84	24
24 - 28,000	1.00	.64	.82	28
28 - 32,000	1.00	.61	.805	32
32 - 36,000	1.00	.58	.79	36
36 - 40,000	1.00	.55	.775	41
40 - 44,000	1.00	.52	.76	46
44 - 52,000	1.00	.50	.75	50
52 - 64,000	1.00	.47	.75	60
64 - 76,000	1.00	.45	.75	67
76 - 88,000	1.00	.42	.75	79
88 - 100,000	1.00	.40	.75	88
100 - 120,000	1.00	.38	.75	97
120 - 140,000	1.00	.36	.75	108
140 - 160,000	1.00	.34	.75	121
160 - 180,000	1.00	.32	.75	134
180 - 200,000	1.00	.31	.75	142
200 - 400,000 400 and over	1.00	.30	.75	150

Tax Consequences of Payments, Deposits, Improvements, and Alterations*

Here we give you a handy table from which you can tell at a glance what the tax consequences of payments, deposits, improvement, and alterations by landlord and tenant are to both the landlord and tenant.

	Effect on Landlord	Effect on Tenant
Deposit of security by tenant	No immediate tax effect on landlord or tenant if deposit is properly restricted. If forfeited, it is treated for tax purposes the same as a payment of the obligation for which it is forfeited would have been treated.	
Payment by tenant to renew	Rental income to landlord.	Cost of renewed lease amortizable by tenant over life of lease.
Payment by tenant to modify	Rental income to landlord.	Cost of modified lease amortizable by tenant over life of lease.
Payment of broker's commission by tenant	None.	Amount amortizable by tenant over life of lease. In case of premature cancellation of lease, amount not recovered deductible in year of cancellation.
Payment of broker's commission by landlord	Amount amortizable by landlord over life of lease. If lease prematurely cancelled, amount not recovered deductible in year of cancellation.	None.
Payment of bonus by tenant to landlord for lease	Taxable when received by landlord as additional rental income.	Amortizable by tenant over life of lease.
Advanced payment of rent by tenant	Additional rental income to landlord.	Amortizable by tenant over life of lease.
Payment by landlord to cancel	Amortizable over life of lease. If made for purpose of selling premises, amount of payment is added to basis of property for purpose of figuring gain on sale.	Amount is received by tenant as realized on sale or exchange of lease and reportable as capital gain.
Payment by tenant to cancel	Additional rental income to landlord.	Deductible by tenant as rent.
Payment of taxes, interest, insurance and operating costs by tenant	Additional rental income to landlord.	Deductible as rent by tenant.
Payment of special assessments on property by tenant	Additional rental income to landlord.	Deductible by tenant over life of lease.
Payment of debt against property by tenant	Additional rental income to landlord.	Deductible as rent payment by tenant when paid.
Capital alterations to premises by tenant	If intended as rent, it is rental income to landlord when improvements are made.	Deductible by tenant as rent when improvements are made.
Alteration of premises by landlord for tenant	Landlord can take depreciation deductions for improvements. Cost is amortizable by landlord over life of lease if improvements are suitable only for tenant.	None.
Installation of trade fixtures by tenant	None.	Tenant may take depreciation deductions over useful life of trade fixtures.
Permanent improvements by tenant not intended as rent	Not income to landlord when improvements are made or when lease terminates.	Tenant may take depreciation deductions over useful life of improvements or over life of lease, whichever is shorter.
Restoration of premises by tenant at end of lease term	Landlord cannot deduct depreciation in improvements to leasehold unless agreement provides that tenant's duty to restore does not include restoration made necessary by ordinary wear and tear.	Cost is deductible by tenant when restoration is made.

* Subject to Special cases, as noted in the text.

Building Expenditures—Expensed and Capitalized

Whether an item is a repair or a capital improvement is of vital importance for tax purposes. Costs of repairs are deductible currently; capital improvement costs are recoverable over the life of the improvement via depreciation. Hence, taxpayers prefer to have their expenses deemed repairs.

The question whether a building expenditure will be regarded, for income tax purposes, as a fully deductible repair item or whether it must be treated as a capital investment subject to annual depreciation deductions spread over the useful life of the asset cuts across all classifications of real estate ownership and operation. There is no clear-cut rule of thumb that provides an infallible answer for every expenditure. The following table sets forth the general tax treatment of basic real estate building expenditure types.

Item	Expense	Capital	Item	Expense	Capital
Floors - patching	X		Conforming property to a taxpayer's different use		X
Floors - new		X			
Foundation - new		X	Casualties - repairs arising from	X	
Foundation - repair	X		Insulating		X
Fire escapes - new		X			
Fire escapes - rails replaced		X	Plumbing - defective replaced	X	
Stairway supports - new	X		Alteration -building		X
Roof - repair	X		Architect fee - building addition		X
Roof - reshingling		X			
Roof - replacement		X			
Ratproofing of building		X	Wells - cleaning out and repairing	X	
Plastering	X		Damaged property - restored to normal operating condition	X	
Papering	X				
Painting building	X				
Painting - inside	X				
Leaks - mending	X		Damaged property - restoration resulting in something different or better - deemed replacement		X
Electric wiring - new		X			
Electric wiring - defectives replaced	X				
Pipes - iron replaced by brass		X			
Office - layout temporarily changed	X		Maintenance of property - good housekeeping	X	
Heating - permanent conversion		X	Restoration of property purchased in rundown condition		X
Termite control	X				
Residence - converting upper floor for rental		X	Alterations conforming property to tax- payer's use		X
Front - new		X			
Furnace - relining		X	Repairs and improve- ments - part of general plan of betterment		X
Furnace - enameling	X		Assessments for local improvements		X
Commissions or fees paid for negotiating a lease or sale		X			

Comparison of Three Forms of Public Ownership of Real Estate*		
	Real Estate Investment Trust	Limited Partnership	Public Corporation

Organizational Features

	Real Estate Investment Trust	Limited Partnership	Public Corporation
Tax on Organization		None	
Number of investors required	Must have at least 100.	No set number required	
Form of organization	Trust form is okay; any other form of unincorporated association will probably not qualify.		
Investment and income requirements	75% of total assets must be real estate assets, cash and cash items; no more than 25% securities (and no more than 5% in one security). At least 75% of gross income must come from real estate and an additional 15% from real estate or other investment sources; not more than 30% can come from short-term capital gains from securities or real estate held less than 4 years.	No restrictions on investments or income; but, of course, major investment will be in real estate; no restriction on sale of property held less than 4 years.	No restrictions on types of investments or income, but here, too, emphasis will be put on real estate. If there is personal holding company possibility (see below), rent income will have to equal 50% of gross to avoid penalty. Property may have to be held three years to avoid collapsible corporation problem in some cases.
Rent income requirements	Rent income does not include profit sharing with the tenant. But fixed percentages of tenants' sales or receipts are okay.	There are no restrictions on the rental arrangements that can be made with tenants; rents can be based on income or profits as well as on gross sales or receipts.	

Promoter's Share

	Real Estate Investment Trust	Limited Partnership	Public Corporation
Promoters or organizers share in the syndicate	The promoters can own interests in the trust; but if 5 or fewer beneficiaries own more than 50% of the trust (directly or indirectly), the trust does not qualify under the tax law. Additional restrictions are noted below.	Promoters can be both general and limited partners. No restriction on portion of interests they own in the partnership — directly or indirectly.	Promoters can own stock in the corporation without restriction. If 5 or fewer own more than 50% of the stock (directly or indirectly), the corporation can be a personal holding company. But if 50% or more of the income comes from rents, the personal holding company penalty tax would not apply.

* Subject to changes noted in the text for the Tax Reform Act of 1976.

	Real Estate Investment Trust	Limited Partnership	Public Corporation

Comparison of Three Forms of Public Ownership of Real Estate (continued)

Promoter's Share

Promoter receives compensation for management

Trust cannot manage its own property but can have outside management do so. If promoter has beneficial interest in the trust, he cannot own, directly or indirectly, more than 35% of the management company or 35% of the trust.

Partnership or corporation can manage its own property. If it uses outside management, there are no restrictions or percentages of management company owned by any general or limited partners or corporate stockholders—although disclosures to investors of who management is, is probably required.

Promoter has interest in lessee of property owned by the syndicate

If he has a 10% or greater interest (directly or indirectly) and is also a beneficiary of the trust, trust will be deemed to own 10% of lessee and rents received will not qualify as rents for tax law purposes; this may cut the trust's income from rents below the required minimum.

Promoters can own interests in the lessees and benefit from their operations; disclosure to investors would probably be required.

Investor's Position

Double taxation

Trust is not taxed on the income it distributes if it distributes at least 90%. Thus, if all income is distributed, there is no double taxation at all.

Each partner picks up his share of the partnership income (whether or not distributed to him); the partnership pays no tax at all. So double taxation is avoided regardless of how much is actually distributed to each partner.

Corporation pays one tax on the income it earns, and stockholders pay another tax when distributed to them as dividends. Where capitalization is made up of both stock and bonds (or other evidences of debt), repayment of debt will not be taxed to stockholders if the debt is recognized as such and not deemed to be stock of "thin" corporation.

See Tax Reform Act of 1976

	Real Estate Investment Trust	Limited Partnership	Public Corporation
Investor's Position			
Passing through depreciation	Cash income can exceed taxable income because of depreciation deduction. If all cash income is distributed, only taxable income is taxable to beneficiaries; excess cash received reduces basis for their shares in the trust. After basis is recovered, excess cash is taxable as capital gain.	Partner is taxable on only his share of taxable income. Excess cash distributed to him reduces his basis for his partnership interest. After basis is recovered, excess cash is taxable as capital gain.	Corporate stockholder is taxable on dividend distributions only to extent they come from the current year's earnings and profits and accumulated earnings and profits of prior years. Distributions in excess of earnings and profits are treated as recovery of basis; after basis is recovered, excess over earnings and profits distributed is capital gain.
Passing through losses	Losses as such do not pass through to the beneficiaries. And the trust is not permitted to use its losses as carrybacks or carryovers to other taxable years. Where the trust has a net loss for the year but has cash to distribute, the beneficiaries would be taxable on those distributions only to the extent that past accumulated (i.e., undistributed) profits exceed the current loss. To the extent the cash distributed is not taxable, it reduces basis; after that distributions are capital gain.	Each partner picks up his share of the partnership's losses as his own. Losses picked up by a partner reduce his basis for his partnership interest. To the extent a partner's losses are not absorbed by other income, he can carry them back 3 years and forward 5 years to reduce income in those years.	Corporate losses belong to the corporation. They can be carried back 3 years and carried forward 5 years to reduce taxable income in those years and either get a tax refund or reduce or eliminate current taxes. Stockholders do not get direct benefits of the losses. Distributions in the current year are taxable as dividends to the stockholders to the extent they equal the current year's earnings plus accumulated surplus of prior years.

Comparison of Three Forms of Public Ownership of Real Estate (continued)*			
	Real Estate Investment Trust	Limited Partnership	Public Corporation
Investor's Position			
Passing through capital gains	If the trust distributes the long-term gains it realized during the same year, the beneficiaries pick up those distributions as long-term capital gains.	Each partner picks up as his own capital gains his share of the partnership's capital gains.	A corporation cannot pass through capital gains as such to its stockholders. Distributions would be ordinary dividends to the stockholders even though earned as capital gains by the corporation. (Subchapter S corporations can pass through capital gains; but a corporation with more than 20% of gross receipts coming from rents cannot qualify for Subchapter S; nor can a corporation. qualify if it has more than 10 stockholders.)

* Except as noted in the text for the Tax Reform Act of 1976.

BEFORE-TAX INCOME NEEDED FOR VARIOUS AMOUNTS OF AFTER-TAX INCOME
(WHAT TAX-EXEMPT INCOME IS WORTH)

Before-Tax Income Needed for Various Amounts of After-Tax Income

(What Tax-Exempt Income Is Worth)

This table serves a dual purpose. On the one hand, it tells us how much before-tax income people in different tax brackets need to net them a certain amount. Thus, if a married man with taxable income of $52,000 desires an additional $500 after taxes, he must earn an additional $1,065. This sum is obtained by multiplying $500 by 8.51 (the figure at the $52,000, 4% line) and dividing by 4. The table can also be used to calculate the true worth of tax-free income.

Married Persons Taxable Income		Tax-Exempt Yield						
Separate Return	Joint Return	4%	4.5%	5%	5.5%	6%	6.5%	7%
$ 10,000	$ 20,000	5.88	7.61	7.36	8.09	8.82	9.56	10.29
12,000	24,000	6.25	7.03	7.82	8.59	9.37	10.16	10.94
14,000	28,000	6.56	7.38	8.20	9.02	9.84	10.66	11.48
16,000	32,000	6.90	7.76	8.62	9.48	10.35	11.21	12.07
18,000	36,000	7.27	8.18	9.08	10.00	10.91	11.82	12.73
20,000	40,000	7.69	8.65	9.62	10.58	11.54	12.50	13.46
22,000	44,000	8.00	9.00	10.00	11.00	12.00	13.00	14.00
26,000	52,000	8.51	9.57	10.64	11.70	12.77	13.63	14.89
32,000	64,000	8.89	10.00	11.12	12.22	13.33	14.44	15.56
38,000	76,000	9.52	10.71	11.90	13.10	14.28	15.48	16.67
44,000	88,000	10.00	11.25	12.50	13.75	15.00	16.25	17.50
50,000	100,000	10.53	11.84	13.16	14.47	15.79	17.11	18.42
60,000	120,000	11.11	12.49	13.88	15.28	16.67	18.06	19.44
70,000	140,000	11.76	13.23	14.70	16.18	17.64	19.12	20.59
80,000	160,000	12.50	14.06	15.62	17.19	18.75	20.31	21.87
90,000	180,000	12.90	14.52	16.12	17.74	19.35	20.97	22.58
100,000	200,000	13.33	15.00	16.66	18.33	20.00	21.67	23.33

BEST TAX SALARY

The best *tax* salary (considering only the normal tax rates/rules) for the owner-employee of a corporation is the one that will cost the least in taxes when the tax cost to the owner-employee and corporation are combined. It is the salary that is at the point at which any increase will cost the employee more in taxes than the extra deduction will save the corporation, and any decrease will cost the corporation more than the owner-employee will save.

For example, suppose a corporation has earnings of $100,000 before the stockholder-employee's salary, and the sole shareholder will file a joint return. If his income from outside the corporation is just sufficient to offset his deductions and exemptions, his best salary (assuming the ''permanent'' corporate tax structure of 22% on the first $25,000 of income and 48% of the balance) is between $40,000 and $44,000. If he were paid more than $44,000 the corporation would save tax at a 48% rate, but sole stockholders would pay tax at a 50% rate. If he were paid less than $40,000, the corporation would pay tax at a 48% rate, but the sole stockholder would be saving tax at only a 45% rate.

If earnings left in the corporation will not be withdrawn in the near future either as a dividend or by liquidation, and assuming the owner-employee's other income equals his deductions and exemptions, there can be only one best tax salary. The following charts give the best salary levels for various corporate income levels. The first set of charts is based on the ''permanent'' corporate rate structure of 22% on the first $25,000 of corporate income and 48% of the balance. The second set of charts is based on the ''temporary'' corporate rate structure of 20% on the first $25,000, 22% on the second $25,000, and 48% on income in excess of $50,000. All apply the individual rates in effect as of January 1, 1977.

BEST TAX SALARY UNDER "PERMANENT" CORPORATE TAX RATES:

Single Return

Corporate Income	Best Salary
Up to $6,000	Full corporate income
$ 6,000-$31,000	$ 6,000
$31,000-$57,000	Corporate income less $25,000
over $57,000	$32,000

Married-Separate Return

Corporate Income	Best Salary
Up to $6,000	Full corporate income
$ 6,000-$31,000	$ 6,000
$31,000-$47,000	Corporate income less $25,000
over $47,000	$22,000

Married-Joint Return

Corporate Income	Best Salary
Up to $12,000	Full corporate income
$12,000-$37,000	$ 12,000
$37,000-$69,000	Corporate income less $25,000
over $69,000	$44,000

Head of Household

Corporate Income	Best Salary
Up to $ 8,000	Full corporate income
$ 8,000-$33,000	$ 8,000
$33,000-$68,000	Corporate income less $25,000
over $68,000	$38,000

BEST TAX SALARY UNDER "TEMPORARY" CORPORATE TAX RATES:

Single Return

Corporate Income	Best Salary
Up to $ 4,000	Full corporate income
$ 4,000-$29,000	$ 4,000
$29,000-$31,000	Corporate income less $25,000
$31,000-$56,000	$ 6,000
$56,000-$82,000	Corporate Income less $50,000
Over $82,000	$32,000

Married-Separate Return

Corporate Income	Best Salary
Up to $ 4,000	Full corporate income
$ 4,000-$29,000	$ 4,000
$29,000-$31,000	Corporate income less $25,000
$31,000-$56,000	$ 6,000
$56,000-$72,000	Corporate Income less $50,000
Over $72,000	$22,000

Married-Joint Return

Corporate Income Up to	Best Salary
	Full corporate income
$ 8,000-$33,000	$ 8,000
$33,000-$37,000	Corporate income less $25,000
$37,000-$62,000	$12,000
$62,000-$94,000	Corporate Income less $50,000
Over $94,000	$44,000

Head of Household

Corporate Income	Best Salary
Up to $ 6,000	Full corporate income
$ 6,000-$31,000	$ 6,000
$31,000-$33,000	Corporate income less $25,000
$33,000-$58,000	$ 8,000
$58,000-$88,000	Corporate Income less $50,000
Over $88,000	$38,000

Rate Schedule, Post-1976 Estates

If the amount with respect to which the tentative tax to be computed is:	The tentative tax is:
Not over $10,000	18 percent of such amount.
Over $10,000 but not over $20,000	$1,800, plus 20 percent of the excess of such amount over $10,000.
Over $20,000 but not over $40,000	$3,800, plus 22 percent of the excess of such amount over $20,000.
Over $40,000 but not over $60,000	$8,200, plus 24 percent of the excess of such amount over $40,000.
Over $60,000 but not over $80,000	$13,000, plus 26 percent of the excess of such amount over $60,000.
Over $80,000 but not over $100,000	$18,200, plus 28 percent of the excess of such amount over $80,000.
Over $100,000 but not over $150,000	$23,800, plus 30 percent of the excess of such amount over $100,000.
Over $150,000 but not over $250,000	$38,800, plus 32 percent of such amount over $150,000.
Over $250,000 but not over $500,000	$70,800, plus 34 percent of the excess of such amount over $250,000.
Over $500,000 but not over $750,000	$155,800, plus 37 percent of the excess of such amount over $500,000.
Over $750,000 but not over $1,000,000 ...	$248,300, plus 39 percent of the excess of such amount over $750,000.
Over $1,000,000 but not over $1,250,000..	$345,800, plus 41 percent of the excess of such amount over $1,000,000.
Over $1,250,000 but not over $1,500,000..	$448,300, plus 43 percent of the excess of such amount over $1,250,000.
Over $1,500,000 but not over $2,000,000..	$555,800, plus 45 percent of the excess of such amount over $1,500,000.
Over $2,000,000 but not over $2,500,000..	$780,800, plus 49 percent of the excess of such amount over $2,000,000.
Over $2,500,000 but not over $3,000,000..	$1,025,800, plus 53 percent of the excess of such amount over $2,500,000.
Over $3,000,000 but not over $3,500,000..	$1,290,800, plus 57 percent of the excess of such amount over $3,000,000.
Over $3,500,000 but not over $4,000,000..	$1,575,800, plus 61 percent of the excess of such amount over $3,500,000.
Over $4,000,000 but not over $4,500,000..	$1,880,800, plus 65 percent of the excess of such amount over $4,000,000.
Over $4,500,000 but not over $5,000,000..	$2,205,800, plus 69 percent of the excess of such amount over $4,500,000.
Over $5,000,000	$2,550,800, plus 70 percent of the excess of such amount over $5,000,000.

THE UNIFIED CREDIT

The rate schedules for pre-1977 estates and gifts have been unified into a single table that applies to the cumulative total of both taxable gifts made after 1976 and the taxable estates of decedents dying after 1976. The exemptions from the gift tax ($30,000) and estate tax ($60,000) have been replaced by a $47,000 unified credit that is available against the total transfer tax imposed upon post-1976 gifts and estates (Code §2010). The $47,000 credit is phased in as follows:

Year of Gift or Death	Amount of Credit	Exemption Equivalent
1977*	$30,000	$120,667
1978	34,000	134,000
1979	38,000	147,333
1980	42,500	161,563
1981 (and thereafter)	47,000	175,625

*For 1977 gifts, a credit of only $6,000 is allowed for transfers between January 1, and June 30, 1977. Beginning July 1, 1977, the full $30,000 credit is available.

SOCIAL SECURITY RATES

	Tax Rate		Salary Base		Maximum Withheld	
	Current	New	Current	New	Current	New
1978	6.05%	6.05%	$17,700	$17,700	$1,071	$1,071
1979	6.05	6.13	18,900	22,900	1,143	1,404
1980	6.05	6.13	20,400	25,900	1,234	1,588
1981	6.30	6.65	21,900	29,700	1,380	1,975
1982	6.30	6.70	23,400	31,800	1,474	2,131
1983	6.30	6,70	24,900	33,900	1,569	2,271
1984	6.30	6.70	26,400	36,000	1,663	2,412
1985	6.30	7.05	27,900	38,100	1,758	2,686
1986		7.15		40,200		2,874
1987		7.15		42,600		3,046

For self-employed persons, the tax rate would rise from 7.9% in 1977 to 8.1% in 1978, 9.3% in 1981, 9.35% in 1982, 9.9% in 1985, and to 10% in 1987. The taxable earnings base would remain the same for self-employed person as for employees.

1977 Tax Table A—SINGLE (Box 1)

(For single persons with tax table income of $20,000 or less who claim fewer than 4 exemptions)

To find your tax: Read down the left income column until you find your income as shown on line 34 of Form 1040. Read across to the column headed by the total number of exemptions claimed on line 7 of Form 1040. The amount shown at the point where the two lines meet is your tax. Enter on Form 1040, line 35.

The $2,200 zero bracket amount, your deduction for exemptions and the general tax credit have been taken into account in figuring the tax shown in this table. **Do not take a separate deduction for them.**

Caution: If you can be claimed as a dependent on your parent's return AND you have unearned income (interest, dividends, etc.) of $750 or more AND your earned income is less than $2,200, you must first use Schedule TC (Form 1040), Part II.

If line 34, Form 1040 is—		And the total number of exemptions claimed on line 7 is—			If line 34, Form 1040 is—		And the total number of exemptions claimed on line 7 is—			If line 34, Form 1040 is—		And the total number of exemptions claimed on line 7 is—		
Over	But not over	1	2	3	Over	But not over	1	2	3	Over	But not over	1	2	3
		Your tax is—					Your tax is—					Your tax is—		
If $3,200 or less your tax is 0					5,800	5,850	419	264	100	8,400	8,450	890	748	580
					5,850	5,900	427	273	108	8,450	8,500	900	757	590
3,200	3,250	4	0	0	5,900	5,950	436	283	116	8,500	8,550	909	767	601
3,250	3,300	11	0	0	5,950	6,000	444	292	124	8,550	8,600	919	776	611
3,300	3,350	18	0	0										
3,350	3,400	25	0	0	6,000	6,050	453	302	133	8,600	8,650	928	786	622
					6,050	6,100	461	311	141	8,650	8,700	938	795	632
3,400	3,450	32	0	0	6,100	6,150	470	321	150	8,700	8,750	947	805	643
3,450	3,500	39	0	0	6,150	6,200	478	330	158	8,750	8,800	957	814	653
3,500	3,550	46	0	0										
3,550	3,600	54	0	0	6,200	6,250	487	340	167	8,800	8,850	966	824	664
					6,250	6,300	495	349	175	8,850	8,900	976	833	674
3,600	3,650	61	0	0	6,300	6,350	504	359	184	8,900	8,950	985	843	685
3,650	3,700	69	0	0	6,350	6,400	512	368	192	8,950	9,000	996	852	695
3,700	3,750	76	0	0										
3,750	3,800	84	0	0	6,400	6,450	521	378	201	9,000	9,050	1,007	862	706
					6,450	6,500	529	387	210	9,050	9,100	1,018	871	716
3,800	3,850	91	0	0	6,500	6,550	538	397	219	9,100	9,150	1,029	881	727
3,850	3,900	99	0	0	6,550	6,600	546	406	229	9,150	9,200	1,040	890	737
3,900	3,950	106	0	0										
3,950	4,000	114	0	0	6,600	6,650	555	416	238	9,200	9,250	1,051	900	748
					6,650	6,700	563	425	248	9,250	9,300	1,062	909	758
4,000	4,050	122	0	0	6,700	6,750	572	435	257	9,300	9,350	1,073	919	769
4,050	4,100	130	0	0	6,750	6,800	580	444	267	9,350	9,400	1,084	928	779
4,100	4,150	138	0	0										
4,150	4,200	146	0	0	6,800	6,850	589	454	276	9,400	9,450	1,095	938	790
					6,850	6,900	597	463	286	9,450	9,500	1,106	947	800
4,200	4,250	154	4	0	6,900	6,950	606	473	295	9,500	9,550	1,117	957	811
4,250	4,300	162	11	0	6,950	7,000	615	482	305	9,550	9,600	1,128	966	821
4,300	4,350	170	19	0										
4,350	4,400	178	26	0	7,000	7,050	624	492	314	9,600	9,650	1,139	976	832
					7,050	7,100	634	501	324	9,650	9,700	1,150	985	842
4,400	4,450	186	34	0	7,100	7,150	643	511	333	9,700	9,750	1,161	996	852
4,450	4,500	194	41	0	7,150	7,200	653	520	343	9,750	9,800	1,172	1,007	862
4,500	4,550	203	49	0										
4,550	4,600	211	56	0	7,200	7,250	662	529	352	9,800	9,850	1,183	1,018	871
					7,250	7,300	672	538	362	9,850	9,900	1,194	1,029	881
4,600	4,650	220	64	0	7,300	7,350	681	546	371	9,900	9,950	1,205	1,040	890
4,650	4,700	228	71	0	7,350	7,400	691	555	381	9,950	10,000	1,216	1,051	900
4,700	4,750	236	79	0										
4,750	4,800	244	87	0	7,400	7,450	700	563	390	10,000	10,050	1,227	1,062	909
					7,450	7,500	710	572	400	10,050	10,100	1,238	1,073	919
4,800	4,850	251	95	0	7,500	7,550	719	580	409	10,100	10,150	1,249	1,084	928
4,850	4,900	259	103	0	7,550	7,600	729	589	419	10,150	10,200	1,260	1,095	938
4,900	4,950	266	111	0										
4,950	5,000	274	119	0	7,600	7,650	738	597	428	10,200	10,250	1,271	1,106	947
					7,650	7,700	748	606	438	10,250	10,300	1,282	1,117	957
5,000	5,050	283	127	0	7,700	7,750	757	615	447	10,300	10,350	1,293	1,128	966
5,050	5,100	291	135	0	7,750	7,800	767	624	457	10,350	10,400	1,304	1,139	976
5,100	5,150	300	143	0										
5,150	5,200	308	151	0	7,800	7,850	776	634	466	10,400	10,450	1,315	1,150	985
					7,850	7,900	786	643	476	10,450	10,500	1,326	1,161	996
5,200	5,250	317	159	6	7,900	7,950	795	653	485	10,500	10,550	1,337	1,172	1,007
5,250	5,300	325	168	14	7,950	8,000	805	662	495	10,550	10,600	1,348	1,183	1,018
5,300	5,350	334	176	21										
5,350	5,400	342	185	29	8,000	8,050	814	672	504	10,600	10,650	1,359	1,194	1,029
					8,050	8,100	824	681	514	10,650	10,700	1,370	1,205	1,040
5,400	5,450	351	193	36	8,100	8,150	833	691	523	10,700	10,750	1,381	1,216	1,051
5,450	5,500	359	202	44	8,150	8,200	843	700	533	10,750	10,800	1,392	1,227	1,062
5,500	5,550	368	210	52										
5,550	5,600	376	219	60	8,200	8,250	852	710	542	10,800	10,850	1,403	1,238	1,073
					8,250	8,300	862	719	552	10,850	10,900	1,414	1,249	1,084
5,600	5,650	385	227	68	8,300	8,350	871	729	561	10,900	10,950	1,425	1,260	1,095
5,650	5,700	393	236	76	8,350	8,400	881	738	571	10,950	11,000	1,436	1,271	1,106
5,700	5,750	402	245	84										
5,750	5,800	410	254	92										

Continued next column   Continued next column   Continued on next page

1977 Tax Table A—SINGLE (Box 1) *(Continued)*

(If your income or exemptions are not covered, use Schedule TC (Form 1040), Part I to figure your tax)

If line 34, Form 1040 is— Over	But not over	And the total number of exemptions claimed on line 7 is— 1	2	3	If line 34, Form 1040 is— Over	But not over	And the total number of exemptions claimed on line 7 is— 1	2	3	If line 34, Form 1040 is— Over	But not over	And the total number of exemptions claimed on line 7 is— 1	2	3
		Your tax is—					Your tax is—					Your tax is—		
11,000	11,050	1,447	1,282	1,117	14,000	14,050	2,200	1,998	1,804	17,000	17,050	3,053	2,834	2,617
11,050	11,100	1,459	1,293	1,128	14,050	14,100	2,214	2,011	1,816	17,050	17,100	3,069	2,849	2,631
11,100	11,150	1,470	1,304	1,139	14,100	14,150	2,227	2,025	1,829	17,100	17,150	3,084	2,863	2,646
11,150	11,200	1,482	1,315	1,150	14,150	14,200	2,241	2,038	1,841	17,150	17,200	3,100	2,878	2,660
11,200	11,250	1,493	1,326	1,161	14,200	14,250	2,254	2,052	1,854	17,200	17,250	3,115	2,892	2,675
11,250	11,300	1,505	1,337	1,172	14,250	14,300	2,268	2,065	1,866	17,250	17,300	3,131	2,907	2,689
11,300	11,350	1,516	1,348	1,183	14,300	14,350	2,281	2,079	1,879	17,300	17,350	3,146	2,921	2,704
11,350	11,400	1,528	1,359	1,194	14,350	14,400	2,295	2,092	1,891	17,350	17,400	3,162	2,936	2,718
11,400	11,450	1,539	1,370	1,205	14,400	14,450	2,308	2,106	1,904	17,400	17,450	3,177	2,950	2,733
11,450	11,500	1,551	1,381	1,216	14,450	14,500	2,322	2,119	1,917	17,450	17,500	3,193	2,965	2,747
11,500	11,550	1,562	1,392	1,227	14,500	14,550	2,335	2,133	1,930	17,500	17,550	3,208	2,979	2,762
11,550	11,600	1,574	1,403	1,238	14,550	14,600	2,349	2,146	1,944	17,550	17,600	3,224	2,994	2,776
11,600	11,650	1,585	1,414	1,249	14,600	14,650	2,362	2,160	1,957	17,600	17,650	3,239	3,008	2,791
11,650	11,700	1,597	1,425	1,260	14,650	14,700	2,376	2,173	1,971	17,650	17,700	3,255	3,023	2,805
11,700	11,750	1,608	1,436	1,271	14,700	14,750	2,389	2,187	1,984	17,700	17,750	3,270	3,038	2,820
11,750	11,800	1,620	1,447	1,282	14,750	14,800	2,403	2,200	1,998	17,750	17,800	3,286	3,053	2,834
11,800	11,850	1,631	1,459	1,293	14,800	14,850	2,416	2,214	2,011	17,800	17,850	3,301	3,069	2,849
11,850	11,900	1,643	1,470	1,304	14,850	14,900	2,430	2,227	2,025	17,850	17,900	3,317	3,084	2,863
11,900	11,950	1,654	1,482	1,315	14,900	14,950	2,443	2,241	2,038	17,900	17,950	3,332	3,100	2,878
11,950	12,000	1,666	1,493	1,326	14,950	15,000	2,457	2,254	2,052	17,950	18,000	3,348	3,115	2,892
12,000	12,050	1,679	1,505	1,337	15,000	15,050	2,472	2,268	2,065	18,000	18,050	3,363	3,131	2,907
12,050	12,100	1,691	1,516	1,348	15,050	15,100	2,486	2,281	2,079	18,050	18,100	3,379	3,146	2,921
12,100	12,150	1,704	1,528	1,359	15,100	15,150	2,501	2,295	2,092	18,100	18,150	3,394	3,162	2,936
12,150	12,200	1,716	1,539	1,370	15,150	15,200	2,515	2,308	2,106	18,150	18,200	3,410	3,177	2,950
12,200	12,250	1,729	1,551	1,381	15,200	15,250	2,530	2,322	2,119	18,200	18,250	3,425	3,193	2,965
12,250	12,300	1,741	1,562	1,392	15,250	15,300	2,544	2,335	2,133	18,250	18,300	3,441	3,208	2,979
12,300	12,350	1,754	1,574	1,403	15,300	15,350	2,559	2,349	2,146	18,300	18,350	3,456	3,224	2,994
12,350	12,400	1,766	1,585	1,414	15,350	15,400	2,573	2,362	2,160	18,350	18,400	3,472	3,239	3,008
12,400	12,450	1,779	1,597	1,425	15,400	15,450	2,588	2,376	2,173	18,400	18,450	3,487	3,255	3,023
12,450	12,500	1,791	1,608	1,436	15,450	15,500	2,602	2,389	2,187	18,450	18,500	3,503	3,270	3,038
12,500	12,550	1,804	1,620	1,447	15,500	15,550	2,617	2,403	2,200	18,500	18,550	3,518	3,286	3,053
12,550	12,600	1,816	1,631	1,459	15,550	15,600	2,631	2,416	2,214	18,550	18,600	3,534	3,301	3,069
12,600	12,650	1,829	1,643	1,470	15,600	15,650	2,646	2,430	2,227	18,600	18,650	3,549	3,317	3,084
12,650	12,700	1,841	1,654	1,482	15,650	15,700	2,660	2,443	2,241	18,650	18,700	3,565	3,332	3,100
12,700	12,750	1,854	1,666	1,493	15,700	15,750	2,675	2,457	2,254	18,700	18,750	3,580	3,348	3,115
12,750	12,800	1,866	1,679	1,505	15,750	15,800	2,689	2,472	2,268	18,750	18,800	3,596	3,363	3,131
12,800	12,850	1,879	1,691	1,516	15,800	15,850	2,704	2,486	2,281	18,800	18,850	3,611	3,379	3,146
12,850	12,900	1,891	1,704	1,528	15,850	15,900	2,718	2,501	2,295	18,850	18,900	3,627	3,394	3,162
12,900	12,950	1,904	1,716	1,539	15,900	15,950	2,733	2,515	2,308	18,900	18,950	3,642	3,410	3,177
12,950	13,000	1,917	1,729	1,551	15,950	16,000	2,747	2,530	2,322	18,950	19,000	3,659	3,425	3,193
13,000	13,050	1,930	1,741	1,562	16,000	16,050	2,762	2,544	2,335	19,000	19,050	3,676	3,441	3,208
13,050	13,100	1,944	1,754	1,574	16,050	16,100	2,776	2,559	2,349	19,050	19,100	3,693	3,456	3,224
13,100	13,150	1,957	1,766	1,585	16,100	16,150	2,791	2,573	2,362	19,100	19,150	3,710	3,472	3,239
13,150	13,200	1,971	1,779	1,597	16,150	16,200	2,805	2,588	2,376	19,150	19,200	3,727	3,487	3,255
13,200	13,250	1,984	1,791	1,608	16,200	16,250	2,820	2,602	2,389	19,200	19,250	3,744	3,503	3,270
13,250	13,300	1,998	1,804	1,620	16,250	16,300	2,834	2,617	2,403	19,250	19,300	3,761	3,518	3,286
13,300	13,350	2,011	1,816	1,631	16,300	16,350	2,849	2,631	2,416	19,300	19,350	3,778	3,534	3,301
13,350	13,400	2,025	1,829	1,643	16,350	16,400	2,863	2,646	2,430	19,350	19,400	3,795	3,549	3,317
13,400	13,450	2,038	1,841	1,654	16,400	16,450	2,878	2,660	2,443	19,400	19,450	3,812	3,565	3,332
13,450	13,500	2,052	1,854	1,666	16,450	16,500	2,892	2,675	2,457	19,450	19,500	3,829	3,580	3,348
13,500	13,550	2,065	1,866	1,679	16,500	16,550	2,907	2,689	2,472	19,500	19,550	3,846	3,596	3,363
13,550	13,600	2,079	1,879	1,691	16,550	16,600	2,921	2,704	2,486	19,550	19,600	3,863	3,611	3,379
13,600	13,650	2,092	1,891	1,704	16,600	16,650	2,936	2,718	2,501	19,600	19,650	3,880	3,627	3,394
13,650	13,700	2,106	1,904	1,716	16,650	16,700	2,950	2,733	2,515	19,650	19,700	3,897	3,642	3,410
13,700	13,750	2,119	1,917	1,729	16,700	16,750	2,965	2,747	2,530	19,700	19,750	3,914	3,659	3,425
13,750	13,800	2,133	1,930	1,741	16,750	16,800	2,979	2,762	2,544	19,750	19,800	3,931	3,676	3,441
13,800	13,850	2,146	1,944	1,754	16,800	16,850	2,994	2,776	2,559	19,800	19,850	3,948	3,693	3,456
13,850	13,900	2,160	1,957	1,766	16,850	16,900	3,008	2,791	2,573	19,850	19,900	3,965	3,710	3,472
13,900	13,950	2,173	1,971	1,779	16,900	16,950	3,023	2,805	2,588	19,900	19,950	3,982	3,727	3,487
13,950	14,000	2,187	1,984	1,791	16,950	17,000	3,038	2,820	2,602	19,950	20,000	3,999	3,744	3,503

Continued next column — Continued next column

1977 Tax Table B—MARRIED FILING JOINTLY (Box 2) and QUALIFYING WIDOW(ER)S (Box 5)

(For married persons filing joint returns or qualifying widow(er)s with tax table income of $40,000 or less who claim fewer than 10 exemptions)

To find your tax: Read down the left income column until you find your income as shown on line 34 of Form 1040. Read across to the column headed by the total number of exemptions claimed on line 7 of Form 1040. The amount shown at the point where the two lines meet is your tax. Enter on Form 1040, line 35.

The $3,200 zero bracket amount, your deduction for exemptions and the general tax credit have been taken into account in figuring the tax shown in this table. **Do not take a separate deduction for them.**

If line 34, Form 1040 is— Over	But not over	And the total number of exemptions claimed on line 7 is— 2	3	4	5	6	7	8	9
		Your tax is—							
If $5,200 or less your tax is 0									
5,200	5,250	4	0	0	0	0	0	0	0
5,250	5,300	11	0	0	0	0	0	0	0
5,300	5,350	18	0	0	0	0	0	0	0
5,350	5,400	25	0	0	0	0	0	0	0
5,400	5,450	32	0	0	0	0	0	0	0
5,450	5,500	39	0	0	0	0	0	0	0
5,500	5,550	46	0	0	0	0	0	0	0
5,550	5,600	53	0	0	0	0	0	0	0
5,600	5,650	60	0	0	0	0	0	0	0
5,650	5,700	67	0	0	0	0	0	0	0
5,700	5,750	74	0	0	0	0	0	0	0
5,750	5,800	81	0	0	0	0	0	0	0
5,800	5,850	89	0	0	0	0	0	0	0
5,850	5,900	96	0	0	0	0	0	0	0
5,900	5,950	104	0	0	0	0	0	0	0
5,950	6,000	111	0	0	0	0	0	0	0
6,000	6,050	119	0	0	0	0	0	0	0
6,050	6,100	126	0	0	0	0	0	0	0
6,100	6,150	134	0	0	0	0	0	0	0
6,150	6,200	141	0	0	0	0	0	0	0
6,200	6,250	149	4	0	0	0	0	0	0
6,250	6,300	156	11	0	0	0	0	0	0
6,300	6,350	164	18	0	0	0	0	0	0
6,350	6,400	171	25	0	0	0	0	0	0
6,400	6,450	179	32	0	0	0	0	0	0
6,450	6,500	186	39	0	0	0	0	0	0
6,500	6,550	194	46	0	0	0	0	0	0
6,550	6,600	201	54	0	0	0	0	0	0
6,600	6,650	209	61	0	0	0	0	0	0
6,650	6,700	216	69	0	0	0	0	0	0
6,700	6,750	224	76	0	0	0	0	0	0
6,750	6,800	232	84	0	0	0	0	0	0
6,800	6,850	240	91	0	0	0	0	0	0
6,850	6,900	248	99	0	0	0	0	0	0
6,900	6,950	256	106	0	0	0	0	0	0
6,950	7,000	264	114	0	0	0	0	0	0
7,000	7,050	272	121	0	0	0	0	0	0
7,050	7,100	280	129	0	0	0	0	0	0
7,100	7,150	288	136	0	0	0	0	0	0
7,150	7,200	296	144	0	0	0	0	0	0
7,200	7,250	304	151	4	0	0	0	0	0
7,250	7,300	312	159	11	0	0	0	0	0
7,300	7,350	320	166	19	0	0	0	0	0
7,350	7,400	328	174	26	0	0	0	0	0
7,400	7,450	336	181	34	0	0	0	0	0
7,450	7,500	344	189	41	0	0	0	0	0
7,500	7,550	352	197	49	0	0	0	0	0
7,550	7,600	360	205	56	0	0	0	0	0
7,600	7,650	368	213	64	0	0	0	0	0
7,650	7,700	376	221	71	0	0	0	0	0
7,700	7,750	384	229	79	0	0	0	0	0
7,750	7,800	393	237	86	0	0	0	0	0
7,800	7,850	401	245	94	0	0	0	0	0
7,850	7,900	410	253	101	0	0	0	0	0
7,900	7,950	418	261	109	0	0	0	0	0
7,950	8,000	427	269	116	0	0	0	0	0
8,000	8,050	435	277	124	0	0	0	0	0
8,050	8,100	444	285	131	0	0	0	0	0
8,100	8,150	452	293	139	0	0	0	0	0
8,150	8,200	461	301	146	0	0	0	0	0
8,200	8,250	469	309	154	6	0	0	0	0
8,250	8,300	476	317	162	14	0	0	0	0
8,300	8,350	484	325	170	21	0	0	0	0
8,350	8,400	491	333	178	29	0	0	0	0

Continued next column

If line 34, Form 1040 is— Over	But not over	And the total number of exemptions claimed on line 7 is— 2	3	4	5	6	7	8	9
		Your tax is—							
8,400	8,450	499	341	186	36	0	0	0	0
8,450	8,500	506	349	194	44	0	0	0	0
8,500	8,550	514	358	202	51	0	0	0	0
8,550	8,600	521	366	210	59	0	0	0	0
8,600	8,650	529	375	218	66	0	0	0	0
8,650	8,700	536	383	226	74	0	0	0	0
8,700	8,750	544	392	234	81	0	0	0	0
8,750	8,800	553	400	242	89	0	0	0	0
8,800	8,850	561	409	250	96	0	0	0	0
8,850	8,900	570	417	258	104	0	0	0	0
8,900	8,950	578	426	266	111	0	0	0	0
8,950	9,000	587	434	274	119	0	0	0	0
9,000	9,050	595	443	282	127	0	0	0	0
9,050	9,100	604	451	290	135	0	0	0	0
9,100	9,150	612	460	298	143	0	0	0	0
9,150	9,200	621	468	306	151	1	0	0	0
9,200	9,250	629	477	314	159	9	0	0	0
9,250	9,300	638	485	323	167	16	0	0	0
9,300	9,350	646	494	331	175	24	0	0	0
9,350	9,400	655	502	340	183	31	0	0	0
9,400	9,450	663	511	348	191	39	0	0	0
9,450	9,500	672	520	357	199	46	0	0	0
9,500	9,550	680	529	365	207	54	0	0	0
9,550	9,600	689	539	374	215	61	0	0	0
9,600	9,650	697	548	382	223	69	0	0	0
9,650	9,700	706	558	391	231	76	0	0	0
9,700	9,750	714	567	399	239	84	0	0	0
9,750	9,800	723	577	408	247	92	0	0	0
9,800	9,850	731	586	416	255	100	0	0	0
9,850	9,900	740	596	425	263	108	0	0	0
9,900	9,950	748	605	433	271	116	0	0	0
9,950	10,000	757	615	442	279	124	0	0	0
10,000	10,050	765	624	450	288	132	0	0	0
10,050	10,100	774	634	459	296	140	0	0	0
10,100	10,150	782	643	467	305	148	0	0	0
10,150	10,200	791	653	476	313	156	4	0	0
10,200	10,250	799	662	485	322	164	11	0	0
10,250	10,300	808	672	494	330	172	19	0	0
10,300	10,350	816	681	504	339	180	26	0	0
10,350	10,400	825	691	513	347	188	34	0	0
10,400	10,450	833	700	523	356	196	41	0	0
10,450	10,500	842	710	532	364	204	49	0	0
10,500	10,550	850	719	542	373	212	57	0	0
10,550	10,600	859	729	551	381	220	65	0	0
10,600	10,650	867	738	561	390	228	73	0	0
10,650	10,700	876	748	570	398	236	81	0	0
10,700	10,750	884	757	580	407	244	89	0	0
10,750	10,800	893	765	589	415	253	97	0	0
10,800	10,850	901	774	599	424	261	105	0	0
10,850	10,900	910	782	608	432	270	113	0	0
10,900	10,950	918	791	618	441	278	121	0	0
10,950	11,000	927	799	627	450	287	129	0	0
11,000	11,050	935	808	637	459	295	137	0	0
11,050	11,100	944	816	646	469	304	145	0	0
11,100	11,150	952	825	656	478	312	153	0	0
11,150	11,200	961	833	665	488	321	161	6	0
11,200	11,250	969	842	675	497	329	169	14	0
11,250	11,300	978	850	684	507	338	177	22	0
11,300	11,350	986	859	694	516	346	185	30	0
11,350	11,400	995	867	703	526	355	193	38	0
11,400	11,450	1,003	876	713	535	363	201	46	0
11,450	11,500	1,012	884	722	545	372	209	54	0
11,500	11,550	1,020	893	732	554	380	218	62	0
11,550	11,600	1,029	901	741	564	389	226	70	0

Continued on next page

1977 Tax Table B—MARRIED FILING JOINTLY (Box 2) and QUALIFYING WIDOW(ER)S (Box 5)
(Continued)

(If your income or exemptions are not covered, use Schedule TC (Form 1040), Part I to figure your tax)

If line 34, Over	But not over	2	3	4	5	6	7	8	9
11,600	11,650	1,037	910	751	573	397	235	78	0
11,650	11,700	1,046	918	760	583	406	243	86	0
11,700	11,750	1,054	927	770	592	415	252	94	0
11,750	11,800	1,063	935	779	602	424	260	102	0
11,800	11,850	1,071	944	789	611	434	269	110	0
11,850	11,900	1,080	952	798	621	443	277	118	0
11,900	11,950	1,088	961	808	630	453	286	126	0
11,950	12,000	1,097	969	817	640	462	294	134	0
12,000	12,050	1,105	978	827	649	472	303	142	0
12,050	12,100	1,114	986	836	659	481	311	150	0
12,100	12,150	1,122	995	846	668	491	320	158	3
12,150	12,200	1,131	1,003	855	678	500	328	166	11
12,200	12,250	1,139	1,012	865	687	510	337	174	19
12,250	12,300	1,148	1,020	874	697	519	345	183	27
12,300	12,350	1,156	1,029	884	706	529	354	191	35
12,350	12,400	1,165	1,037	893	716	538	362	200	43
12,400	12,450	1,173	1,046	903	725	548	371	208	51
12,450	12,500	1,182	1,054	912	735	557	380	217	59
12,500	12,550	1,190	1,063	922	744	567	389	225	67
12,550	12,600	1,199	1,071	931	754	576	399	234	75
12,600	12,650	1,207	1,080	941	763	586	408	242	83
12,650	12,700	1,216	1,088	950	773	595	418	251	91
12,700	12,750	1,225	1,097	960	782	605	427	259	99
12,750	12,800	1,235	1,105	969	792	614	437	268	107
12,800	12,850	1,245	1,114	979	801	624	446	276	115
12,850	12,900	1,255	1,122	988	811	633	456	285	123
12,900	12,950	1,265	1,131	998	820	643	465	293	131
12,950	13,000	1,275	1,139	1,007	830	652	475	302	139
13,000	13,050	1,285	1,148	1,017	839	662	484	310	148
13,050	13,100	1,295	1,156	1,026	849	671	494	319	156
13,100	13,150	1,305	1,165	1,036	858	681	503	327	165
13,150	13,200	1,315	1,173	1,045	868	690	513	336	173
13,200	13,250	1,325	1,182	1,054	877	700	522	345	182
13,250	13,300	1,335	1,190	1,063	887	709	532	354	190
13,300	13,350	1,345	1,199	1,071	896	719	541	364	199
13,350	13,400	1,355	1,207	1,080	906	728	551	373	207
13,400	13,450	1,365	1,216	1,088	915	738	560	383	216
13,450	13,500	1,375	1,225	1,097	925	747	570	392	224
13,500	13,550	1,385	1,235	1,105	934	757	579	402	233
13,550	13,600	1,395	1,245	1,114	944	766	589	411	241
13,600	13,650	1,405	1,255	1,122	953	776	598	421	250
13,650	13,700	1,415	1,265	1,131	963	785	608	430	258
13,700	13,750	1,426	1,275	1,139	972	795	617	440	267
13,750	13,800	1,437	1,285	1,148	982	804	627	449	275
13,800	13,850	1,448	1,295	1,156	991	814	636	459	284
13,850	13,900	1,459	1,305	1,165	1,001	823	646	468	292
13,900	13,950	1,470	1,315	1,173	1,010	833	655	478	301
13,950	14,000	1,481	1,325	1,182	1,020	842	665	487	310
14,000	14,050	1,492	1,335	1,190	1,029	852	674	497	319
14,050	14,100	1,503	1,345	1,199	1,039	861	684	506	329
14,100	14,150	1,514	1,355	1,207	1,048	871	693	516	338
14,150	14,200	1,525	1,365	1,216	1,058	880	703	525	348
14,200	14,250	1,536	1,375	1,225	1,067	890	712	535	357
14,250	14,300	1,547	1,385	1,235	1,077	899	722	544	367
14,300	14,350	1,558	1,395	1,245	1,086	909	731	554	376
14,350	14,400	1,569	1,405	1,255	1,096	918	741	563	386
14,400	14,450	1,580	1,415	1,265	1,105	928	750	573	395
14,450	14,500	1,591	1,426	1,275	1,115	937	760	582	405
14,500	14,550	1,602	1,437	1,285	1,124	947	769	592	414
14,550	14,600	1,613	1,448	1,295	1,134	956	779	601	424
14,600	14,650	1,624	1,459	1,305	1,143	966	788	611	433
14,650	14,700	1,635	1,470	1,315	1,153	975	798	620	443
14,700	14,750	1,646	1,481	1,325	1,162	985	807	630	452
14,750	14,800	1,657	1,492	1,335	1,172	994	817	639	462
14,800	14,850	1,668	1,503	1,345	1,181	1,004	826	649	471
14,850	14,900	1,679	1,514	1,355	1,191	1,013	836	658	481
14,900	14,950	1,690	1,525	1,365	1,200	1,023	845	668	490
14,950	15,000	1,701	1,536	1,375	1,211	1,032	855	677	500
15,000	15,050	1,712	1,547	1,385	1,222	1,042	864	687	509
15,050	15,100	1,723	1,558	1,395	1,233	1,051	874	696	519
15,100	15,150	1,734	1,569	1,405	1,244	1,061	883	706	528
15,150	15,200	1,745	1,580	1,415	1,255	1,070	893	715	538

Continued next column

If line 34, Over	But not over	2	3	4	5	6	7	8	9
15,200	15,250	1,756	1,591	1,426	1,266	1,080	902	725	547
15,250	15,300	1,767	1,602	1,437	1,277	1,089	912	734	557
15,300	15,350	1,778	1,613	1,448	1,288	1,099	921	744	566
15,350	15,400	1,789	1,624	1,459	1,299	1,108	931	753	576
15,400	15,450	1,800	1,635	1,470	1,310	1,118	940	763	585
15,450	15,500	1,811	1,646	1,481	1,321	1,127	950	772	595
15,500	15,550	1,822	1,657	1,492	1,332	1,137	959	782	604
15,550	15,600	1,833	1,668	1,503	1,343	1,146	969	791	614
15,600	15,650	1,844	1,679	1,514	1,354	1,156	978	801	623
15,650	15,700	1,855	1,690	1,525	1,365	1,165	988	810	633
15,700	15,750	1,866	1,701	1,536	1,375	1,176	997	820	642
15,750	15,800	1,877	1,712	1,547	1,385	1,187	1,007	829	652
15,800	15,850	1,888	1,723	1,558	1,395	1,198	1,016	839	661
15,850	15,900	1,899	1,734	1,569	1,405	1,209	1,026	848	671
15,900	15,950	1,910	1,745	1,580	1,415	1,220	1,035	858	680
15,950	16,000	1,921	1,756	1,591	1,426	1,231	1,045	867	690
16,000	16,050	1,932	1,767	1,602	1,437	1,242	1,054	877	699
16,050	16,100	1,943	1,778	1,613	1,448	1,253	1,064	886	709
16,100	16,150	1,954	1,789	1,624	1,459	1,264	1,073	896	718
16,150	16,200	1,965	1,800	1,635	1,470	1,275	1,083	905	728
16,200	16,250	1,976	1,811	1,646	1,481	1,286	1,092	915	737
16,250	16,300	1,987	1,822	1,657	1,492	1,297	1,102	924	747
16,300	16,350	1,998	1,833	1,668	1,503	1,308	1,111	934	756
16,350	16,400	2,009	1,844	1,679	1,514	1,319	1,121	943	766
16,400	16,450	2,020	1,855	1,690	1,525	1,330	1,130	953	775
16,450	16,500	2,031	1,866	1,701	1,536	1,341	1,141	962	785
16,500	16,550	2,042	1,877	1,712	1,547	1,352	1,152	972	794
16,550	16,600	2,053	1,888	1,723	1,558	1,363	1,163	981	804
16,600	16,650	2,064	1,899	1,734	1,569	1,374	1,174	991	813
16,650	16,700	2,075	1,910	1,745	1,580	1,385	1,185	1,000	823
16,700	16,750	2,086	1,921	1,756	1,591	1,396	1,196	1,010	832
16,750	16,800	2,099	1,932	1,767	1,602	1,407	1,207	1,019	842
16,800	16,850	2,111	1,943	1,778	1,613	1,418	1,218	1,029	851
16,850	16,900	2,124	1,954	1,789	1,624	1,429	1,229	1,038	861
16,900	16,950	2,136	1,965	1,800	1,635	1,440	1,240	1,048	870
16,950	17,000	2,149	1,976	1,811	1,646	1,451	1,251	1,057	880
17,000	17,050	2,161	1,987	1,822	1,657	1,462	1,262	1,067	889
17,050	17,100	2,174	1,998	1,833	1,668	1,473	1,273	1,076	899
17,100	17,150	2,186	2,009	1,844	1,679	1,484	1,284	1,086	908
17,150	17,200	2,199	2,020	1,855	1,690	1,495	1,295	1,095	918
17,200	17,250	2,211	2,031	1,866	1,701	1,506	1,306	1,106	927
17,250	17,300	2,224	2,042	1,877	1,712	1,517	1,317	1,117	937
17,300	17,350	2,236	2,053	1,888	1,723	1,528	1,328	1,128	946
17,350	17,400	2,249	2,064	1,899	1,734	1,539	1,339	1,139	956
17,400	17,450	2,261	2,075	1,910	1,745	1,550	1,350	1,150	965
17,450	17,500	2,274	2,086	1,921	1,756	1,561	1,361	1,161	975
17,500	17,550	2,286	2,099	1,932	1,767	1,572	1,372	1,172	984
17,550	17,600	2,299	2,111	1,943	1,778	1,583	1,383	1,183	994
17,600	17,650	2,311	2,124	1,954	1,789	1,594	1,394	1,194	1,003
17,650	17,700	2,324	2,136	1,965	1,800	1,605	1,405	1,205	1,013
17,700	17,750	2,336	2,149	1,976	1,811	1,616	1,416	1,216	1,022
17,750	17,800	2,349	2,161	1,987	1,822	1,627	1,427	1,227	1,032
17,800	17,850	2,361	2,174	1,998	1,833	1,638	1,438	1,238	1,041
17,850	17,900	2,374	2,186	2,009	1,844	1,649	1,449	1,249	1,051
17,900	17,950	2,386	2,199	2,020	1,855	1,660	1,460	1,260	1,060
17,950	18,000	2,399	2,211	2,031	1,866	1,671	1,471	1,271	1,071
18,000	18,050	2,411	2,224	2,042	1,877	1,682	1,482	1,282	1,082
18,050	18,100	2,424	2,236	2,053	1,888	1,693	1,493	1,293	1,093
18,100	18,150	2,436	2,249	2,064	1,899	1,704	1,504	1,304	1,104
18,150	18,200	2,449	2,261	2,075	1,910	1,715	1,515	1,315	1,115
18,200	18,250	2,461	2,274	2,086	1,921	1,726	1,526	1,326	1,126
18,250	18,300	2,474	2,286	2,099	1,932	1,737	1,537	1,337	1,137
18,300	18,350	2,486	2,299	2,111	1,943	1,748	1,548	1,348	1,148
18,350	18,400	2,499	2,311	2,124	1,954	1,759	1,559	1,359	1,159
18,400	18,450	2,511	2,324	2,136	1,965	1,770	1,570	1,370	1,170
18,450	18,500	2,524	2,336	2,149	1,976	1,781	1,581	1,381	1,181
18,500	18,550	2,536	2,349	2,161	1,987	1,792	1,592	1,392	1,192
18,550	18,600	2,549	2,361	2,174	1,998	1,803	1,603	1,403	1,203
18,600	18,650	2,561	2,374	2,186	2,009	1,814	1,614	1,414	1,214
18,650	18,700	2,574	2,386	2,199	2,020	1,825	1,625	1,425	1,225
18,700	18,750	2,586	2,399	2,211	2,031	1,836	1,636	1,436	1,236
18,750	18,800	2,599	2,411	2,224	2,042	1,847	1,647	1,447	1,247

Continued on next page

1977 Tax Table B—MARRIED FILING JOINTLY (Box 2) and QUALIFYING WIDOW(ER)S (Box 5)

(Continued)

(If your income or exemptions are not covered, use Schedule TC (Form 1040), Part I to figure your tax)

If line 34, Form 1040 is—		And the total number of exemptions claimed on line 7 is—							
Over	But not over	2	3	4	5	6	7	8	9
		Your tax is—							
18,800	18,850	2,611	2,424	2,236	2,053	1,858	1,658	1,458	1,258
18,850	18,900	2,624	2,436	2,249	2,064	1,869	1,669	1,469	1,269
18,900	18,950	2,636	2,449	2,261	2,075	1,880	1,680	1,480	1,280
18,950	19,000	2,649	2,461	2,274	2,086	1,891	1,691	1,491	1,291
19,000	19,050	2,661	2,474	2,286	2,099	1,902	1,702	1,502	1,302
19,050	19,100	2,674	2,486	2,299	2,111	1,913	1,713	1,513	1,313
19,100	19,150	2,686	2,499	2,311	2,124	1,924	1,724	1,524	1,324
19,150	19,200	2,699	2,511	2,324	2,136	1,935	1,735	1,535	1,335
19,200	19,250	2,711	2,524	2,336	2,149	1,946	1,746	1,546	1,346
19,250	19,300	2,724	2,536	2,349	2,161	1,957	1,757	1,557	1,357
19,300	19,350	2,736	2,549	2,361	2,174	1,968	1,768	1,568	1,368
19,350	19,400	2,749	2,561	2,374	2,186	1,979	1,779	1,579	1,379
19,400	19,450	2,761	2,574	2,386	2,199	1,990	1,790	1,590	1,390
19,450	19,500	2,774	2,586	2,399	2,211	2,001	1,801	1,601	1,401
19,500	19,550	2,786	2,599	2,411	2,224	2,012	1,812	1,612	1,412
19,550	19,600	2,799	2,611	2,424	2,236	2,023	1,823	1,623	1,423
19,600	19,650	2,811	2,624	2,436	2,249	2,034	1,834	1,634	1,434
19,650	19,700	2,824	2,636	2,449	2,261	2,045	1,845	1,645	1,445
19,700	19,750	2,836	2,649	2,461	2,274	2,056	1,856	1,656	1,456
19,750	19,800	2,849	2,661	2,474	2,286	2,069	1,867	1,667	1,467
19,800	19,850	2,861	2,674	2,486	2,299	2,081	1,878	1,678	1,478
19,850	19,900	2,874	2,686	2,499	2,311	2,094	1,889	1,689	1,489
19,900	19,950	2,886	2,699	2,511	2,324	2,106	1,900	1,700	1,500
19,950	20,000	2,899	2,711	2,524	2,336	2,119	1,911	1,711	1,511
20,000	20,050	2,911	2,724	2,536	2,349	2,131	1,922	1,722	1,522
20,050	20,100	2,924	2,736	2,549	2,361	2,144	1,933	1,733	1,533
20,100	20,150	2,936	2,749	2,561	2,374	2,156	1,944	1,744	1,544
20,150	20,200	2,949	2,761	2,574	2,386	2,169	1,955	1,755	1,555
20,200	20,250	2,961	2,774	2,586	2,399	2,181	1,966	1,766	1,566
20,250	20,300	2,974	2,786	2,599	2,411	2,194	1,977	1,777	1,577
20,300	20,350	2,986	2,799	2,611	2,424	2,206	1,988	1,788	1,588
20,350	20,400	2,999	2,811	2,624	2,436	2,219	1,999	1,799	1,599
20,400	20,450	3,011	2,824	2,636	2,449	2,231	2,010	1,810	1,610
20,450	20,500	3,024	2,836	2,649	2,461	2,244	2,021	1,821	1,621
20,500	20,550	3,036	2,849	2,661	2,474	2,256	2,034	1,832	1,632
20,550	20,600	3,049	2,861	2,674	2,486	2,269	2,046	1,843	1,643
20,600	20,650	3,061	2,874	2,686	2,499	2,281	2,059	1,854	1,654
20,650	20,700	3,074	2,886	2,699	2,511	2,294	2,071	1,865	1,665
20,700	20,750	3,087	2,899	2,711	2,524	2,306	2,084	1,876	1,676
20,750	20,800	3,101	2,911	2,724	2,536	2,319	2,096	1,887	1,687
20,800	20,850	3,115	2,924	2,736	2,549	2,331	2,109	1,898	1,698
20,850	20,900	3,129	2,936	2,749	2,561	2,344	2,121	1,909	1,709
20,900	20,950	3,143	2,949	2,761	2,574	2,356	2,134	1,920	1,720
20,950	21,000	3,157	2,961	2,774	2,586	2,369	2,146	1,931	1,731
21,000	21,050	3,171	2,974	2,786	2,599	2,381	2,159	1,942	1,742
21,050	21,100	3,185	2,986	2,799	2,611	2,394	2,171	1,953	1,753
21,100	21,150	3,199	2,999	2,811	2,624	2,406	2,184	1,964	1,764
21,150	21,200	3,213	3,011	2,824	2,636	2,419	2,196	1,975	1,775
21,200	21,250	3,227	3,024	2,836	2,649	2,431	2,209	1,986	1,786
21,250	21,300	3,241	3,036	2,849	2,661	2,444	2,221	1,999	1,797
21,300	21,350	3,255	3,049	2,861	2,674	2,456	2,234	2,011	1,808
21,350	21,400	3,269	3,061	2,874	2,686	2,469	2,246	2,024	1,819
21,400	21,450	3,283	3,074	2,886	2,699	2,481	2,259	2,036	1,830
21,450	21,500	3,297	3,087	2,899	2,711	2,494	2,271	2,049	1,841
21,500	21,550	3,311	3,101	2,911	2,724	2,506	2,284	2,061	1,852
21,550	21,600	3,325	3,115	2,924	2,736	2,519	2,296	2,074	1,863
21,600	21,650	3,339	3,129	2,936	2,749	2,531	2,309	2,086	1,874
21,650	21,700	3,353	3,143	2,949	2,761	2,544	2,321	2,099	1,885
21,700	21,750	3,367	3,157	2,961	2,774	2,556	2,334	2,111	1,896
21,750	21,800	3,381	3,171	2,974	2,786	2,569	2,346	2,124	1,907
21,800	21,850	3,395	3,185	2,986	2,799	2,581	2,359	2,136	1,918
21,850	21,900	3,409	3,199	2,999	2,811	2,594	2,371	2,149	1,929
21,900	21,950	3,423	3,213	3,011	2,824	2,606	2,384	2,161	1,940
21,950	22,000	3,437	3,227	3,024	2,836	2,619	2,396	2,174	1,951
22,000	22,050	3,451	3,241	3,036	2,849	2,631	2,409	2,186	1,964
22,050	22,100	3,465	3,255	3,049	2,861	2,644	2,421	2,199	1,976
22,100	22,150	3,479	3,269	3,061	2,874	2,656	2,434	2,211	1,989
22,150	22,200	3,493	3,283	3,074	2,886	2,669	2,446	2,224	2,001
22,200	22,250	3,507	3,297	3,087	2,899	2,681	2,459	2,236	2,014
22,250	22,300	3,521	3,311	3,101	2,911	2,694	2,471	2,249	2,026
22,300	22,350	3,535	3,325	3,115	2,924	2,706	2,484	2,261	2,039
22,350	22,400	3,549	3,339	3,129	2,936	2,719	2,496	2,274	2,051

Continued next column

If line 34, Form 1040 is—		And the total number of exemptions claimed on line 7 is—							
Over	But not over	2	3	4	5	6	7	8	9
		Your tax is—							
22,400	22,450	3,563	3,353	3,143	2,949	2,731	2,509	2,286	2,064
22,450	22,500	3,577	3,367	3,157	2,961	2,744	2,521	2,299	2,076
22,500	22,550	3,591	3,381	3,171	2,974	2,756	2,534	2,311	2,089
22,550	22,600	3,605	3,395	3,185	2,986	2,769	2,546	2,324	2,101
22,600	22,650	3,619	3,409	3,199	2,999	2,781	2,559	2,336	2,114
22,650	22,700	3,633	3,423	3,213	3,011	2,794	2,571	2,349	2,126
22,700	22,750	3,647	3,437	3,227	3,024	2,806	2,584	2,361	2,139
22,750	22,800	3,661	3,451	3,241	3,036	2,819	2,596	2,374	2,151
22,800	22,850	3,675	3,465	3,255	3,049	2,831	2,609	2,386	2,164
22,850	22,900	3,689	3,479	3,269	3,061	2,844	2,621	2,399	2,176
22,900	22,950	3,703	3,493	3,283	3,074	2,856	2,634	2,411	2,189
22,950	23,000	3,717	3,507	3,297	3,087	2,869	2,646	2,424	2,201
23,000	23,050	3,731	3,521	3,311	3,101	2,881	2,659	2,436	2,214
23,050	23,100	3,745	3,535	3,325	3,115	2,894	2,671	2,449	2,226
23,100	23,150	3,759	3,549	3,339	3,129	2,906	2,684	2,461	2,239
23,150	23,200	3,773	3,563	3,353	3,143	2,919	2,696	2,474	2,251
23,200	23,250	3,787	3,577	3,367	3,157	2,931	2,709	2,486	2,264
23,250	23,300	3,801	3,591	3,381	3,171	2,944	2,721	2,499	2,276
23,300	23,350	3,815	3,605	3,395	3,185	2,956	2,734	2,511	2,289
23,350	23,400	3,829	3,619	3,409	3,199	2,969	2,746	2,524	2,301
23,400	23,450	3,843	3,633	3,423	3,213	2,981	2,759	2,536	2,314
23,450	23,500	3,857	3,647	3,437	3,227	2,994	2,771	2,549	2,326
23,500	23,550	3,871	3,661	3,451	3,241	3,006	2,784	2,561	2,339
23,550	23,600	3,885	3,675	3,465	3,255	3,019	2,796	2,574	2,351
23,600	23,650	3,899	3,689	3,479	3,269	3,031	2,809	2,586	2,364
23,650	23,700	3,913	3,703	3,493	3,283	3,044	2,821	2,599	2,376
23,700	23,750	3,927	3,717	3,507	3,297	3,057	2,834	2,611	2,389
23,750	23,800	3,941	3,731	3,521	3,311	3,071	2,846	2,624	2,401
23,800	23,850	3,955	3,745	3,535	3,325	3,085	2,859	2,636	2,414
23,850	23,900	3,969	3,759	3,549	3,339	3,099	2,871	2,649	2,426
23,900	23,950	3,983	3,773	3,563	3,353	3,113	2,884	2,661	2,439
23,950	24,000	3,997	3,787	3,577	3,367	3,127	2,896	2,674	2,451
24,000	24,050	4,011	3,801	3,591	3,381	3,141	2,909	2,686	2,464
24,050	24,100	4,025	3,815	3,605	3,395	3,155	2,921	2,699	2,476
24,100	24,150	4,039	3,829	3,619	3,409	3,169	2,934	2,711	2,489
24,150	24,200	4,053	3,843	3,633	3,423	3,183	2,946	2,724	2,501
24,200	24,250	4,067	3,857	3,647	3,437	3,197	2,959	2,736	2,514
24,250	24,300	4,081	3,871	3,661	3,451	3,211	2,971	2,749	2,526
24,300	24,350	4,095	3,885	3,675	3,465	3,225	2,984	2,761	2,539
24,350	24,400	4,109	3,899	3,689	3,479	3,239	2,996	2,774	2,551
24,400	24,450	4,123	3,913	3,703	3,493	3,253	3,009	2,786	2,564
24,450	24,500	4,137	3,927	3,717	3,507	3,267	3,022	2,799	2,576
24,500	24,550	4,151	3,941	3,731	3,521	3,281	3,036	2,811	2,589
24,550	24,600	4,165	3,955	3,745	3,535	3,295	3,050	2,824	2,601
24,600	24,650	4,179	3,969	3,759	3,549	3,309	3,064	2,836	2,614
24,650	24,700	4,193	3,983	3,773	3,563	3,323	3,078	2,849	2,626
24,700	24,750	4,208	3,997	3,787	3,577	3,337	3,092	2,861	2,639
24,750	24,800	4,224	4,011	3,801	3,591	3,351	3,106	2,874	2,651
24,800	24,850	4,240	4,025	3,815	3,605	3,365	3,120	2,886	2,664
24,850	24,900	4,256	4,039	3,829	3,619	3,379	3,134	2,899	2,676
24,900	24,950	4,272	4,053	3,843	3,633	3,393	3,148	2,911	2,689
24,950	25,000	4,288	4,067	3,857	3,647	3,407	3,162	2,924	2,701
25,000	25,050	4,304	4,081	3,871	3,661	3,421	3,176	2,936	2,714
25,050	25,100	4,320	4,095	3,885	3,675	3,435	3,190	2,949	2,726
25,100	25,150	4,336	4,109	3,899	3,689	3,449	3,204	2,961	2,739
25,150	25,200	4,352	4,123	3,913	3,703	3,463	3,218	2,974	2,751
25,200	25,250	4,368	4,137	3,927	3,717	3,477	3,232	2,987	2,764
25,250	25,300	4,384	4,151	3,941	3,731	3,491	3,246	3,001	2,776
25,300	25,350	4,400	4,165	3,955	3,745	3,505	3,260	3,015	2,789
25,350	25,400	4,416	4,179	3,969	3,759	3,519	3,274	3,029	2,801
25,400	25,450	4,432	4,193	3,983	3,773	3,533	3,288	3,043	2,814
25,450	25,500	4,448	4,208	3,997	3,787	3,547	3,302	3,057	2,826
25,500	25,550	4,464	4,224	4,011	3,801	3,561	3,316	3,071	2,839
25,550	25,600	4,480	4,240	4,025	3,815	3,575	3,330	3,085	2,851
25,600	25,650	4,496	4,256	4,039	3,829	3,589	3,344	3,099	2,864
25,650	25,700	4,512	4,272	4,053	3,843	3,603	3,358	3,113	2,876
25,700	25,750	4,528	4,288	4,067	3,857	3,617	3,372	3,127	2,889
25,750	25,800	4,544	4,304	4,081	3,871	3,631	3,386	3,141	2,901
25,800	25,850	4,560	4,320	4,095	3,885	3,645	3,400	3,155	2,914
25,850	25,900	4,576	4,336	4,109	3,899	3,659	3,414	3,169	2,926
25,900	25,950	4,592	4,352	4,123	3,913	3,673	3,428	3,183	2,939
25,950	26,000	4,608	4,368	4,137	3,927	3,687	3,442	3,197	2,952

Continued on next page

1977 Tax Table B—MARRIED FILING JOINTLY (Box 2) and QUALIFYING WIDOW(ER)S (Box 5)

(Continued)

(If your income or exemptions are not covered, use Schedule TC (Form 1040), Part I to figure your tax)

If line 34, Form 1040 is—		And the total number of exemptions claimed on line 7 is—							
Over	But not over	2	3	4	5	6	7	8	9
		Your tax is—							
26,000	26,050	4,624	4,384	4,151	3,941	3,701	3,456	3,211	2,966
26,050	26,100	4,640	4,400	4,165	3,955	3,715	3,470	3,225	2,980
26,100	26,150	4,656	4,416	4,179	3,969	3,729	3,484	3,239	2,994
26,150	26,200	4,672	4,432	4,193	3,983	3,743	3,498	3,253	3,008
26,200	26,250	4,688	4,448	4,208	3,997	3,757	3,512	3,267	3,022
26,250	26,300	4,704	4,464	4,224	4,011	3,771	3,526	3,281	3,036
26,300	26,350	4,720	4,480	4,240	4,025	3,785	3,540	3,295	3,050
26,350	26,400	4,736	4,496	4,256	4,039	3,799	3,554	3,309	3,064
26,400	26,450	4,752	4,512	4,272	4,053	3,813	3,568	3,323	3,078
26,450	26,500	4,768	4,528	4,288	4,067	3,827	3,582	3,337	3,092
26,500	26,550	4,784	4,544	4,304	4,081	3,841	3,596	3,351	3,106
26,550	26,600	4,800	4,560	4,320	4,095	3,855	3,610	3,365	3,120
26,600	26,650	4,816	4,576	4,336	4,109	3,869	3,624	3,379	3,134
26,650	26,700	4,832	4,592	4,352	4,123	3,883	3,638	3,393	3,148
26,700	26,750	4,848	4,608	4,368	4,137	3,897	3,652	3,407	3,162
26,750	26,800	4,864	4,624	4,384	4,151	3,911	3,666	3,421	3,176
26,800	26,850	4,880	4,640	4,400	4,165	3,925	3,680	3,435	3,190
26,850	26,900	4,896	4,656	4,416	4,179	3,939	3,694	3,449	3,204
26,900	26,950	4,912	4,672	4,432	4,193	3,953	3,708	3,463	3,218
26,950	27,000	4,928	4,688	4,448	4,208	3,967	3,722	3,477	3,232
27,000	27,050	4,944	4,704	4,464	4,224	3,981	3,736	3,491	3,246
27,050	27,100	4,960	4,720	4,480	4,240	3,995	3,750	3,505	3,260
27,100	27,150	4,976	4,736	4,496	4,256	4,009	3,764	3,519	3,274
27,150	27,200	4,992	4,752	4,512	4,272	4,023	3,778	3,533	3,288
27,200	27,250	5,008	4,768	4,528	4,288	4,037	3,792	3,547	3,302
27,250	27,300	5,024	4,784	4,544	4,304	4,051	3,806	3,561	3,316
27,300	27,350	5,040	4,800	4,560	4,320	4,065	3,820	3,575	3,330
27,350	27,400	5,056	4,816	4,576	4,336	4,079	3,834	3,589	3,344
27,400	27,450	5,072	4,832	4,592	4,352	4,093	3,848	3,603	3,358
27,450	27,500	5,088	4,848	4,608	4,368	4,107	3,862	3,617	3,372
27,500	27,550	5,104	4,864	4,624	4,384	4,121	3,876	3,631	3,386
27,550	27,600	5,120	4,880	4,640	4,400	4,135	3,890	3,645	3,400
27,600	27,650	5,136	4,896	4,656	4,416	4,149	3,904	3,659	3,414
27,650	27,700	5,152	4,912	4,672	4,432	4,163	3,918	8,673	3,428
27,700	27,750	5,168	4,928	4,688	4,448	4,178	3,932	3,687	3,442
27,750	27,800	5,184	4,944	4,704	4,464	4,194	3,946	3,701	3,456
27,800	27,850	5,200	4,960	4,720	4,480	4,210	3,960	3,715	3,470
27,850	27,900	5,216	4,976	4,736	4,496	4,226	3,974	3,729	3,484
27,900	27,950	5,232	4,992	4,752	4,512	4,242	3,988	3,743	3,498
27,950	28,000	5,248	5,008	4,768	4,528	4,258	4,002	3,757	3,512
28,000	28,050	5,264	5,024	4,784	4,544	4,274	4,016	3,771	3,526
28,050	28,100	5,280	5,040	4,800	4,560	4,290	4,030	3,785	3,540
28,100	28,150	5,296	5,056	4,816	4,576	4,306	4,044	3,799	3,554
28,150	28,200	5,312	5,072	4,832	4,592	4,322	4,058	3,813	3,568
28,200	28,250	5,328	5,088	4,848	4,608	4,338	4,072	3,827	3,582
28,250	28,300	5,344	5,104	4,864	4,624	4,354	4,086	3,841	3,596
28,300	28,350	5,360	5,120	4,880	4,640	4,370	4,100	3,855	3,610
28,350	28,400	5,376	5,136	4,896	4,656	4,386	4,114	3,869	3,624
28,400	28,450	5,392	5,152	4,912	4,672	4,402	4,128	3,883	3,638
28,450	28,500	5,408	5,168	4,928	4,688	4,418	4,143	3,897	3,652
28,500	28,550	5,424	5,184	4,944	4,704	4,434	4,159	3,911	3,666
28,550	28,600	5,440	5,200	4,960	4,720	4,450	4,175	3,925	3,680
28,600	28,650	5,456	5,216	4,976	4,736	4,466	4,191	3,939	3,694
28,650	28,700	5,472	5,232	4,992	4,752	4,482	4,207	3,953	3,708
28,700	28,750	5,489	5,248	5,008	4,768	4,498	4,223	3,967	3,722
28,750	28,800	5,507	5,264	5,024	4,784	4,514	4,239	3,981	3,736
28,800	28,850	5,525	5,280	5,040	4,800	4,530	4,255	3,995	3,750
28,850	28,900	5,543	5,296	5,056	4,816	4,546	4,271	4,009	3,764
28,900	28,950	5,561	5,312	5,072	4,832	4,562	4,287	4,023	3,778
28,950	29,000	5,579	5,328	5,088	4,848	4,578	4,303	4,037	3,792
29,000	29,050	5,597	5,344	5,104	4,864	4,594	4,319	4,051	3,806
29,050	29,100	5,615	5,360	5,120	4,880	4,610	4,335	4,065	3,820
29,100	29,150	5,633	5,376	5,136	4,896	4,626	4,351	4,079	3,834
29,150	29,200	5,651	5,392	5,152	4,912	4,642	4,367	4,093	3,848
29,200	29,250	5,669	5,408	5,168	4,928	4,658	4,383	4,108	3,862
29,250	29,300	5,687	5,424	5,184	4,944	4,674	4,399	4,124	3,876
29,300	29,350	5,705	5,440	5,200	4,960	4,690	4,415	4,140	3,890
29,350	29,400	5,723	5,456	5,216	4,976	4,706	4,431	4,156	3,904
29,400	29,450	5,741	5,472	5,232	4,992	4,722	4,447	4,172	3,918
29,450	29,500	5,759	5,489	5,248	5,008	4,738	4,463	4,188	3,932
29,500	29,550	5,777	5,507	5,264	5,024	4,754	4,479	4,204	3,946
29,550	29,600	5,795	5,525	5,280	5,040	4,770	4,495	4,220	3,960
29,600	29,650	5,813	5,543	5,296	5,056	4,786	4,511	4,236	3,974
29,650	29,700	5,831	5,561	5,312	5,072	4,802	4,527	4,252	3,988
29,700	29,750	5,849	5,579	5,328	5,088	4,818	4,543	4,268	4,002
29,750	29,800	5,867	5,597	5,344	5,104	4,834	4,559	4,284	4,016
29,800	29,850	5,885	5,615	5,360	5,120	4,850	4,575	4,300	4,030
29,850	29,900	5,903	5,633	5,376	5,136	4,866	4,591	4,316	4,044
29,900	29,950	5,921	5,651	5,392	5,152	4,882	4,607	4,332	4,058
29,950	30,000	5,939	5,669	5,408	5,168	4,898	4,623	4,348	4,073
30,000	30,050	5,957	5,687	5,424	5,184	4,914	4,639	4,364	4,089
30,050	30,100	5,975	5,705	5,440	5,200	4,930	4,655	4,380	4,105
30,100	30,150	5,993	5,723	5,456	5,216	4,946	4,671	4,396	4,121
30,150	30,200	6,011	5,741	5,472	5,232	4,962	4,687	4,412	4,137
30,200	30,250	6,029	5,759	5,489	5,248	4,978	4,703	4,428	4,153
30,250	30,300	6,047	5,777	5,507	5,264	4,994	4,719	4,444	4,169
30,300	30,350	6,065	5,795	5,525	5,280	5,010	4,735	4,460	4,185
30,350	30,400	6,083	5,813	5,543	5,296	5,026	4,751	4,476	4,201
30,400	30,450	6,101	5,831	5,561	5,312	5,042	4,767	4,492	4,217
30,450	30,500	6,119	5,849	5,579	5,328	5,058	4,783	4,508	4,233
30,500	30,550	6,137	5,867	5,597	5,344	5,074	4,799	4,524	4,249
30,550	30,600	6,155	5,885	5,615	5,360	5,090	4,815	4,540	4,265
30,600	30,650	6,173	5,903	5,633	5,376	5,106	4,831	4,556	4,281
30,650	30,700	6,191	5,921	5,651	5,392	5,122	4,847	4,572	4,297
30,700	30,750	6,209	5,939	5,669	5,408	5,138	4,863	4,588	4,313
30,750	30,800	6,227	5,957	5,687	5,424	5,154	4,879	4,604	4,329
30,800	30,850	6,245	5,975	5,705	5,440	5,170	4,895	4,620	4,345
30,850	30,900	6,263	5,993	5,723	5,456	5,186	4,911	4,636	4,361
30,900	30,950	6,281	6,011	5,741	5,472	5,202	4,927	4,652	4,377
30,950	31,000	6,299	6,029	5,759	5,489	5,218	4,943	4,668	4,393
31,000	31,050	6,317	6,047	5,777	5,507	5,234	4,959	4,684	4,409
31,050	31,100	6,335	6,065	5,795	5,525	5,250	4,975	4,700	4,425
31,100	31,150	6,353	6,083	5,813	5,543	5,266	4,991	4,716	4,441
31,150	31,200	6,371	6,101	5,831	5,561	5,282	5,007	4,732	4,457
31,200	31,250	6,389	6,119	5,849	5,579	5,298	5,023	4,748	4,473
31,250	31,300	6,407	6,137	5,867	5,597	5,314	5,039	4,764	4,489
31,300	31,350	6,425	6,155	5,885	5,615	5,330	5,055	4,780	4,505
31,350	31,400	6,443	6,173	5,903	5,633	5,346	5,071	4,796	4,521
31,400	31,450	6,461	6,191	5,921	5,651	5,362	5,087	4,812	4,537
31,450	31,500	6,479	6,209	5,939	5,669	5,378	5,103	4,828	4,553
31,500	31,550	6,497	6,227	5,957	5,687	5,394	5,119	4,844	4,569
31,550	31,600	6,515	6,245	5,975	5,705	5,410	5,135	4,860	4,585
31,600	31,650	6,533	6,263	5,993	5,723	5,426	5,151	4,876	4,601
31,650	31,700	6,551	6,281	6,011	5,741	5,442	5,167	4,892	4,617
31,700	31,750	6,569	6,299	6,029	5,759	5,459	5,183	4,908	4,633
31,750	31,800	6,587	6,317	6,047	5,777	5,477	5,199	4,924	4,649
31,800	31,850	6,605	6,335	6,065	5,795	5,495	5,215	4,940	4,665
31,850	31,900	6,623	6,353	6,083	5,813	5,513	5,231	4,956	4,681
31,900	31,950	6,641	6,371	6,101	5,831	5,531	5,247	4,972	4,697
31,950	32,000	6,659	6,389	6,119	5,849	5,549	5,263	4,988	4,713
32,000	32,050	6,677	6,407	6,137	5,867	5,567	5,279	5,004	4,729
32,050	32,100	6,695	6,425	6,155	5,885	5,585	5,295	5,020	4,745
32,100	32,150	6,713	6,443	6,173	5,903	5,603	5,311	5,036	4,761
32,150	32,200	6,731	6,461	6,191	5,921	5,621	5,327	5,052	4,777
32,200	32,250	6,749	6,479	6,209	5,939	5,639	5,343	5,068	4,793
32,250	32,300	6,767	6,497	6,227	5,957	5,657	5,359	5,084	4,809
32,300	32,350	6,785	6,515	6,245	5,975	5,675	5,375	5,100	4,825
32,350	32,400	6,803	6,533	6,263	5,993	5,693	5,391	5,116	4,841
32,400	32,450	6,821	6,551	6,281	6,011	5,711	5,407	5,132	4,857
32,450	32,500	6,839	6,569	6,299	6,029	5,729	5,424	5,148	4,873
32,500	32,550	6,857	6,587	6,317	6,047	5,747	5,442	5,164	4,889
32,550	32,600	6,875	6,605	6,335	6,065	5,765	5,460	5,180	4,905
32,600	32,650	6,893	6,623	6,353	6,083	5,783	5,478	5,196	4,921
32,650	32,700	6,911	6,641	6,371	6,101	5,801	5,496	5,212	4,937
32,700	32,750	6,930	6,659	6,389	6,119	5,819	5,514	5,228	4,953
32,750	32,800	6,949	6,677	6,407	6,137	5,837	5,532	5,244	4,969
32,800	32,850	6,969	6,695	6,425	6,155	5,855	5,550	5,260	4,985
32,850	32,900	6,988	6,713	6,443	6,173	5,873	5,568	5,276	5,001
32,900	32,950	7,008	6,731	6,461	6,191	5,891	5,586	5,292	5,017
32,950	33,000	7,027	6,749	6,479	6,209	5,909	5,604	5,308	5,033
33,000	33,050	7,047	6,767	6,497	6,227	5,927	5,622	5,324	5,049
33,050	33,100	7,066	6,785	6,515	6,245	5,945	5,640	5,340	5,065
33,100	33,150	7,086	6,803	6,533	6,263	5,963	5,658	5,356	5,081
33,150	33,200	7,105	6,821	6,551	6,281	5,981	5,676	5,372	5,097

Continued next column

Continued on next page

(If your income or exemptions are not covered, use Schedule TC (Form 1040), Part I to figure your tax)

If line 34, Form 1040 is— Over	But not over	2	3	4	5	6	7	8	9
					Your tax is—				
33,200	33,250	7,125	6,839	6,569	6,299	5,999	5,694	5,389	5,113
33,250	33,300	7,144	6,857	6,587	6,317	6,017	5,712	5,407	5,129
33,300	33,350	7,164	6,875	6,605	6,335	6,035	5,730	5,425	5,145
33,350	33,400	7,183	6,893	6,623	6,353	6,053	5,748	5,443	5,161
33,400	33,450	7,203	6,911	6,641	6,371	6,071	5,766	5,461	5,177
33,450	33,500	7,222	6,930	6,659	6,389	6,089	5,784	5,479	5,193
33,500	33,550	7,242	6,949	6,677	6,407	6,107	5,802	5,497	5,209
33,550	33,600	7,261	6,969	6,695	6,425	6,125	5,820	5,515	5,225
33,600	33,650	7,281	6,988	6,713	6,443	6,143	5,838	5,533	5,241
33,650	33,700	7,300	7,008	6,731	6,461	6,161	5,856	5,551	5,257
33,700	33,750	7,320	7,027	6,749	6,479	6,179	5,874	5,569	5,273
33,750	33,800	7,339	7,047	6,767	6,497	6,197	5,892	5,587	5,289
33,800	33,850	7,359	7,066	6,785	6,515	6,215	5,910	5,605	5,305
33,850	33,900	7,378	7,086	6,803	6,533	6,233	5,928	5,623	5,321
33,900	33,950	7,398	7,105	6,821	6,551	6,251	5,946	5,641	5,337
33,950	34,000	7,417	7,125	6,839	6,569	6,269	5,964	5,659	5,354
34,000	34,050	7,437	7,144	6,857	6,587	6,287	5,982	5,677	5,372
34,050	34,100	7,456	7,164	6,875	6,605	6,305	6,000	5,695	5,390
34,100	34,150	7,476	7,183	6,893	6,623	6,323	6,018	5,713	5,408
34,150	34,200	7,495	7,203	6,911	6,641	6,341	6,036	5,731	5,426
34,200	34,250	7,515	7,222	6,930	6,659	6,359	6,054	5,749	5,444
34,250	34,300	7,534	7,242	6,949	6,677	6,377	6,072	5,767	5,462
34,300	34,350	7,554	7,261	6,969	6,695	6,395	6,090	5,785	5,480
34,350	34,400	7,573	7,281	6,988	6,713	6,413	6,108	5,803	5,498
34,400	34,450	7,593	7,300	7,008	6,731	6,431	6,126	5,821	5,516
34,450	34,500	7,612	7,320	7,027	6,749	6,449	6,144	5,839	5,534
34,500	34,550	7,632	7,339	7,047	6,767	6,467	6,162	5,857	5,552
34,550	34,600	7,651	7,359	7,066	6,785	6,485	6,180	5,875	5,570
34,600	34,650	7,671	7,378	7,086	6,803	6,503	6,198	5,893	5,588
34,650	34,700	7,690	7,398	7,105	6,821	6,521	6,216	5,911	5,606
34,700	34,750	7,710	7,417	7,125	6,839	6,539	6,234	5,929	5,624
34,750	34,800	7,729	7,437	7,144	6,857	6,557	6,252	5,947	5,642
34,800	34,850	7,749	7,456	7,164	6,875	6,575	6,270	5,965	5,660
34,850	34,900	7,768	7,476	7,183	6,893	6,593	6,288	5,983	5,678
34,900	34,950	7,788	7,495	7,203	6,911	6,611	6,306	6,001	5,696
34,950	35,000	7,807	7,515	7,222	6,930	6,629	6,324	6,019	5,714
35,000	35,050	7,827	7,534	7,242	6,949	6,647	6,342	6,037	5,732
35,050	35,100	7,846	7,554	7,261	6,969	6,665	6,360	6,055	5,750
35,100	35,150	7,866	7,573	7,281	6,988	6,683	6,378	6,073	5,768
35,150	35,200	7,885	7,593	7,300	7,008	6,701	6,396	6,091	5,786
35,200	35,250	7,905	7,612	7,320	7,027	6,719	6,414	6,109	5,804
35,250	35,300	7,924	7,632	7,339	7,047	6,737	6,432	6,127	5,822
35,300	35,350	7,944	7,651	7,359	7,066	6,755	6,450	6,145	5,840
35,350	35,400	7,963	7,671	7,378	7,086	6,773	6,468	6,163	5,858
35,400	35,450	7,983	7,690	7,398	7,105	6,791	6,486	6,181	5,876
35,450	35,500	8,002	7,710	7,417	7,125	6,809	6,504	6,199	5,894
35,500	35,550	8,022	7,729	7,437	7,144	6,827	6,522	6,217	5,912
35,550	35,600	8,041	7,749	7,456	7,164	6,845	6,540	6,235	5,930
35,600	35,650	8,061	7,768	7,476	7,183	6,863	6,558	6,253	5,948
35,650	35,700	8,080	7,788	7,495	7,203	6,881	6,576	6,271	5,966
35,700	35,750	8,100	7,807	7,515	7,222	6,900	6,594	6,289	5,984
35,750	35,800	8,119	7,827	7,534	7,242	6,919	6,612	6,307	6,002
35,800	35,850	8,139	7,846	7,554	7,261	6,939	6,630	6,325	6,020
35,850	35,900	8,158	7,866	7,573	7,281	6,958	6,648	6,343	6,038
35,900	35,950	8,178	7,885	7,593	7,300	6,978	6,666	6,361	6,056
35,950	36,000	8,197	7,905	7,612	7,320	6,997	6,684	6,379	6,074
36,000	36,050	8,217	7,924	7,632	7,339	7,017	6,702	6,397	6,092
36,050	36,100	8,236	7,944	7,651	7,359	7,036	6,720	6,415	6,110
36,100	36,150	8,256	7,963	7,671	7,378	7,056	6,738	6,433	6,128
36,150	36,200	8,275	7,983	7,690	7,398	7,075	6,756	6,451	6,146
36,200	36,250	8,295	8,002	7,710	7,417	7,095	6,774	6,469	6,164
36,250	36,300	8,314	8,022	7,729	7,437	7,114	6,792	6,487	6,182
36,300	36,350	8,334	8,041	7,749	7,456	7,134	6,810	6,505	6,200
36,350	36,400	8,353	8,061	7,768	7,476	7,153	6,828	6,523	6,218
36,400	36,450	8,373	8,080	7,788	7,495	7,173	6,846	6,541	6,236
36,450	36,500	8,392	8,100	7,807	7,515	7,192	6,865	6,559	6,254
36,500	36,550	8,412	8,119	7,827	7,534	7,212	6,884	6,577	6,272
36,550	36,600	8,431	8,139	7,846	7,554	7,231	6,904	6,595	6,290

If line 34, Form 1040 is— Over	But not over	2	3	4	5	6	7	8	9
					Your tax is—				
36,600	36,650	8,451	8,158	7,866	7,573	7,251	6,923	6,613	6,308
36,650	36,700	8,470	8,178	7,885	7,593	7,270	6,943	6,631	6,326
36,700	36,750	8,491	8,197	7,905	7,612	7,290	6,962	6,649	6,344
36,750	36,800	8,512	8,217	7,924	7,632	7,309	6,982	6,667	6,362
36,800	36,850	8,533	8,236	7,944	7,651	7,329	7,001	6,685	6,380
36,850	36,900	8,554	8,256	7,963	7,671	7,348	7,021	6,703	6,398
36,900	36,950	8,575	8,275	7,983	7,690	7,368	7,040	6,721	6,416
36,950	37,000	8,596	8,295	8,002	7,710	7,387	7,060	6,739	6,434
37,000	37,050	8,617	8,314	8,022	7,729	7,407	7,079	6,757	6,452
37,050	37,100	8,638	8,334	8,041	7,749	7,426	7,099	6,775	6,470
37,100	37,150	8,659	8,353	8,061	7,768	7,446	7,118	6,793	6,488
37,150	37,200	8,680	8,373	8,080	7,788	7,465	7,138	6,811	6,506
37,200	37,250	8,701	8,392	8,100	7,807	7,485	7,157	6,830	6,524
37,250	37,300	8,722	8,412	8,119	7,827	7,504	7,177	6,849	6,542
37,300	37,350	8,743	8,431	8,139	7,846	7,524	7,196	6,869	6,560
37,350	37,400	8,764	8,451	8,158	7,866	7,543	7,216	6,888	6,578
37,400	37,450	8,785	8,470	8,178	7,885	7,563	7,235	6,908	6,596
37,450	37,500	8,806	8,491	8,197	7,905	7,582	7,255	6,927	6,614
37,500	37,550	8,827	8,512	8,217	7,924	7,602	7,274	6,947	6,632
37,550	37,600	8,848	8,533	8,236	7,944	7,621	7,294	6,966	6,650
37,600	37,650	8,869	8,554	8,256	7,963	7,641	7,313	6,986	6,668
37,650	37,700	8,890	8,575	8,275	7,983	7,660	7,333	7,005	6,686
37,700	37,750	8,911	8,596	8,295	8,002	7,680	7,352	7,025	6,704
37,750	37,800	8,932	8,617	8,314	8,022	7,699	7,372	7,044	6,722
37,800	37,850	8,953	8,638	8,334	8,041	7,719	7,391	7,064	6,740
37,850	37,900	8,974	8,659	8,353	8,061	7,738	7,411	7,083	6,758
37,900	37,950	8,995	8,680	8,373	8,080	7,758	7,430	7,103	6,776
37,950	38,000	9,016	8,701	8,392	8,100	7,777	7,450	7,122	6,795
38,000	38,050	9,037	8,722	8,412	8,119	7,797	7,469	7,142	6,814
38,050	38,100	9,058	8,743	8,431	8,139	7,816	7,489	7,161	6,834
38,100	38,150	9,079	8,764	8,451	8,158	7,836	7,508	7,181	6,853
38,150	38,200	9,100	8,785	8,470	8,178	7,855	7,528	7,200	6,873
38,200	38,250	9,121	8,806	8,491	8,197	7,875	7,547	7,220	6,892
38,250	38,300	9,142	8,827	8,512	8,217	7,894	7,567	7,239	6,912
38,300	38,350	9,163	8,848	8,533	8,236	7,914	7,586	7,259	6,931
38,350	38,400	9,184	8,869	8,554	8,256	7,933	7,606	7,278	6,951
38,400	38,450	9,205	8,890	8,575	8,275	7,953	7,625	7,298	6,970
38,450	38,500	9,226	8,911	8,596	8,295	7,972	7,645	7,317	6,990
38,500	38,550	9,247	8,932	8,617	8,314	7,992	7,664	7,337	7,009
38,550	38,600	9,268	8,953	8,638	8,334	8,011	7,684	7,356	7,029
38,600	38,650	9,289	8,974	8,659	8,353	8,031	7,703	7,376	7,048
38,650	38,700	9,310	8,995	8,680	8,373	8,050	7,723	7,395	7,068
38,700	38,750	9,331	9,016	8,701	8,392	8,070	7,742	7,415	7,087
38,750	38,800	9,352	9,037	8,722	8,412	8,089	7,762	7,434	7,107
38,800	38,850	9,373	9,058	8,743	8,431	8,109	7,781	7,454	7,126
38,850	38,900	9,394	9,079	8,764	8,451	8,128	7,801	7,473	7,146
38,900	38,950	9,415	9,100	8,785	8,470	8,148	7,820	7,493	7,165
38,950	39,000	9,436	9,121	8,806	8,491	8,167	7,840	7,512	7,185
39,000	39,050	9,457	9,142	8,827	8,512	8,187	7,859	7,532	7,204
39,050	39,100	9,478	9,163	8,848	8,533	8,206	7,879	7,551	7,224
39,100	39,150	9,499	9,184	8,869	8,554	8,226	7,898	7,571	7,243
39,150	39,200	9,520	9,205	8,890	8,575	8,245	7,918	7,590	7,263
39,200	39,250	9,541	9,226	8,911	8,596	8,265	7,937	7,610	7,282
39,250	39,300	9,562	9,247	8,932	8,617	8,284	7,957	7,629	7,302
39,300	39,350	9,583	9,268	8,953	8,638	8,304	7,976	7,649	7,321
39,350	39,400	9,604	9,289	8,974	8,659	8,323	7,996	7,668	7,341
39,400	39,450	9,625	9,310	8,995	8,680	8,343	8,015	7,688	7,360
39,450	39,500	9,646	9,331	9,016	8,701	8,362	8,035	7,707	7,380
39,500	39,550	9,667	9,352	9,037	8,722	8,382	8,054	7,727	7,399
39,550	39,600	9,688	9,373	9,058	8,743	8,401	8,074	7,746	7,419
39,600	39,650	9,709	9,394	9,079	8,764	8,421	8,093	7,766	7,438
39,650	39,700	9,730	9,415	9,100	8,785	8,440	8,113	7,785	7,458
39,700	39,750	9,751	9,436	9,121	8,806	8,461	8,132	7,805	7,477
39,750	39,800	9,772	9,457	9,142	8,827	8,482	8,152	7,824	7,497
39,800	39,850	9,793	9,478	9,163	8,848	8,503	8,171	7,844	7,516
39,850	39,900	9,814	9,499	9,184	8,869	8,524	8,191	7,863	7,536
39,900	39,950	9,835	9,520	9,205	8,890	8,545	8,210	7,883	7,555
39,950	40,000	9,856	9,541	9,226	8,911	8,566	8,230	7,902	7,575

Continued next column

411

1977 Tax Table C—MARRIED FILING SEPARATELY (Box 3)

(For married persons filing separate returns with tax table income of $20,000 or less who claim fewer than 4 exemptions)

To find your tax: Read down the left income column until you find your income as shown on line 34 of Form 1040. Read across to the column headed by the total number of exemptions claimed on line 7 of Form 1040. The amount shown at the point where the two lines meet is your tax. Enter on Form 1040, line 35.

The $1,600 zero bracket amount, your deduction for exemptions and the general tax credit have been taken into account in figuring the tax shown in this table. **Do not take a separate deduction for them.**

Caution: *If you or your spouse itemize deductions, or if you can be claimed as a dependent on your parent's return AND you have unearned income (interests, dividends, etc.) of $750 or more AND your earned income is less than $1,600 you must first use Schedule TC (Form 1040), Part II.*

If line 34, Form 1040 is— Over	But not over	1	2	3	If line 34, Form 1040 is— Over	But not over	1	2	3	If line 34, Form 1040 is— Over	But not over	1	2	3
		Your tax is—					Your tax is—					Your tax is—		
If $2,600 or less your tax is 0					5,000	5,050	403	227	68	7,800	7,850	980	780	580
					5,050	5,100	413	236	76	7,850	7,900	991	791	591
2,600	2,625	2	0	0	5,100	5,150	422	245	84	7,900	7,950	1,002	802	602
2,625	2,650	5	0	0	5,150	5,200	432	254	92	7,950	8,000	1,013	813	613
2,650	2,675	9	0	0	5,200	5,250	441	264	100	8,000	8,050	1,024	824	624
2,675	2,700	12	0	0	5,250	5,300	451	273	108	8,050	8,100	1,035	835	635
2,700	2,725	16	0	0	5,300	5,350	460	283	116	8,100	8,150	1,046	846	646
2,725	2,750	19	0	0	5,350	5,400	470	292	124	8,150	8,200	1,057	857	657
2,750	2,775	23	0	0	5,400	5,450	479	302	133	8,200	8,250	1,068	868	668
2,775	2,800	26	0	0	5,450	5,500	489	311	141	8,250	8,300	1,079	879	679
2,800	2,825	30	0	0	5,500	5,550	498	321	150	8,300	8,350	1,090	890	690
2,825	2,850	33	0	0	5,550	5,600	508	330	158	8,350	8,400	1,101	901	701
2,850	2,875	37	0	0	5,600	5,650	517	340	167	8,400	8,450	1,114	912	712
2,875	2,900	41	0	0	5,650	5,700	527	349	175	8,450	8,500	1,126	923	723
2,900	2,925	44	0	0	5,700	5,750	536	359	184	8,500	8,550	1,139	934	734
2,925	2,950	48	0	0	5,750	5,800	546	368	192	8,550	8,600	1,151	945	745
2,950	2,975	52	0	0	5,800	5,850	555	378	201	8,600	8,650	1,164	956	756
2,975	3,000	56	0	0	5,850	5,900	565	387	210	8,650	8,700	1,176	967	767
3,000	3,050	61	0	0	5,900	5,950	574	397	219	8,700	8,750	1,189	978	778
3,050	3,100	69	0	0	5,950	6,000	584	406	229	8,750	8,800	1,201	989	789
3,100	3,150	76	0	0	6,000	6,050	593	416	238	8,800	8,850	1,214	1,000	800
3,150	3,200	84	0	0	6,050	6,100	603	425	248	8,850	8,900	1,226	1,011	811
3,200	3,250	91	0	0	6,100	6,150	612	435	257	8,900	8,950	1,239	1,022	822
3,250	3,300	99	0	0	6,150	6,200	622	444	267	8,950	9,000	1,251	1,033	833
3,300	3,350	106	0	0	6,200	6,250	631	454	276	9,000	9,050	1,264	1,044	844
3,350	3,400	114	0	0	6,250	6,300	641	463	286	9,050	9,100	1,276	1,055	855
3,400	3,450	122	0	0	6,300	6,350	650	473	295	9,100	9,150	1,289	1,066	866
3,450	3,500	130	0	0	6,350	6,400	661	482	305	9,150	9,200	1,301	1,079	877
3,500	3,550	138	0	0	6,400	6,450	672	492	314	9,200	9,250	1,314	1,091	888
3,550	3,600	146	0	0	6,450	6,500	683	501	324	9,250	9,300	1,326	1,104	899
3,600	3,650	154	4	0	6,500	6,550	694	511	333	9,300	9,350	1,339	1,116	910
3,650	3,700	162	11	0	6,550	6,600	705	520	343	9,350	9,400	1,351	1,129	921
3,700	3,750	170	19	0	6,600	6,650	716	530	352	9,400	9,450	1,364	1,141	932
3,750	3,800	178	26	0	6,650	6,700	727	539	362	9,450	9,500	1,376	1,154	943
3,800	3,850	186	34	0	6,700	6,750	738	549	371	9,500	9,550	1,389	1,166	954
3,850	3,900	194	41	0	6,750	6,800	749	558	381	9,550	9,600	1,401	1,179	965
3,900	3,950	203	49	0	6,800	6,850	760	568	390	9,600	9,650	1,414	1,191	976
3,950	4,000	211	56	0	6,850	6,900	771	577	400	9,650	9,700	1,426	1,204	987
4,000	4,050	220	64	0	6,900	6,950	782	587	409	9,700	9,750	1,439	1,216	998
4,050	4,100	228	71	0	6,950	7,000	793	596	419	9,750	9,800	1,451	1,229	1,009
4,100	4,150	237	79	0	7,000	7,050	804	606	428	9,800	9,850	1,464	1,241	1,020
4,150	4,200	245	87	0	7,050	7,100	815	615	438	9,850	9,900	1,476	1,254	1,031
4,200	4,250	254	95	0	7,100	7,150	826	626	447	9,900	9,950	1,489	1,266	1,044
4,250	4,300	262	103	0	7,150	7,200	837	637	457	9,950	10,000	1,501	1,279	1,056
4,300	4,350	271	111	0	7,200	7,250	848	648	466	10,000	10,050	1,514	1,291	1,069
4,350	4,400	280	119	0	7,250	7,300	859	659	476	10,050	10,100	1,526	1,304	1,081
4,400	4,450	289	127	0	7,300	7,350	870	670	485	10,100	10,150	1,539	1,316	1,094
4,450	4,500	299	135	0	7,350	7,400	881	681	495	10,150	10,200	1,551	1,329	1,106
4,500	4,550	308	143	0	7,400	7,450	892	692	504	10,200	10,250	1,564	1,341	1,119
4,550	4,600	318	151	0	7,450	7,500	903	703	514	10,250	10,300	1,576	1,354	1,131
4,600	4,650	327	159	6	7,500	7,550	914	714	523	10,300	10,350	1,589	1,366	1,144
4,650	4,700	337	168	14	7,550	7,600	925	725	533	10,350	10,400	1,602	1,379	1,156
4,700	4,750	346	176	21	7,600	7,650	936	736	542	10,400	10,450	1,616	1,391	1,169
4,750	4,800	356	185	29	7,650	7,700	947	747	552	10,450	10,500	1,630	1,404	1,181
4,800	4,850	365	193	36	7,700	7,750	958	758	561	10,500	10,550	1,644	1,416	1,194
4,850	4,900	375	202	44	7,750	7,800	969	769	571	10,550	10,600	1,658	1,429	1,206
4,900	4,950	384	210	52										
4,950	5,000	394	219	60										

Continued next column   Continued next column   Continued on next page

If line 34, Form 1040 is—		And the total number of exemptions claimed on line 7 is—			If line 34, Form 1040 is—		And the total number of exemptions claimed on line 7 is—			If line 34, Form 1040 is—		And the total number of exemptions claimed on line 7 is—		
		1	2	3			1	2	3			1	2	3
Over	But not over	Your tax is—			Over	But not over	Your tax is—			Over	But not over	Your tax is—		
10,600	10,650	1,672	1,441	1,219	13,800	13,850	2,627	2,352	2,078	17,000	17,050	3,778	3,453	3,148
10,650	10,700	1,686	1,454	1,231	13,850	13,900	2,643	2,368	2,093	17,050	17,100	3,798	3,471	3,166
10,700	10,750	1,700	1,466	1,244	13,900	13,950	2,659	2,384	2,109	17,100	17,150	3,817	3,490	3,184
10,750	10,800	1,714	1,479	1,256	13,950	14,000	2,675	2,400	2,125	17,150	17,200	3,837	3,509	3,202
10,800	10,850	1,728	1,491	1,269	14,000	14,050	2,691	2,416	2,141	17,200	17,250	3,856	3,529	3,220
10,850	10,900	1,742	1,504	1,281	14,050	14,100	2,707	2,432	2,157	17,250	17,300	3,876	3,548	3,238
10,900	10,950	1,756	1,516	1,294	14,100	14,150	2,723	2,448	2,173	17,300	17,350	3,895	3,568	3,256
10,950	11,000	1,770	1,529	1,306	14,150	14,200	2,739	2,464	2,189	17,350	17,400	3,915	3,587	3,274
11,000	11,050	1,784	1,541	1,319	14,200	14,250	2,755	2,480	2,205	17,400	17,450	3,934	3,607	3,292
11,050	11,100	1,798	1,554	1,331	14,250	14,300	2,771	2,496	2,221	17,450	17,500	3,954	3,626	3,310
11,100	11,150	1,812	1,567	1,344	14,300	14,350	2,787	2,512	2,237	17,500	17,550	3,973	3,646	3,328
11,150	11,200	1,826	1,581	1,356	14,350	14,400	2,804	2,528	2,253	17,550	17,600	3,993	3,665	3,346
11,200	11,250	1,840	1,595	1,369	14,400	14,450	2,822	2,544	2,269	17,600	17,650	4,012	3,685	3,364
11,250	11,300	1,854	1,609	1,381	14,450	14,500	2,840	2,560	2,285	17,650	17,700	4,032	3,704	3,382
11,300	11,350	1,868	1,623	1,394	14,500	14,550	2,858	2,576	2,301	17,700	17,750	4,051	3,724	3,400
11,350	11,400	1,882	1,637	1,406	14,550	14,600	2,876	2,592	2,317	17,750	17,800	4,071	3,743	3,418
11,400	11,450	1,896	1,651	1,419	14,600	14,650	2,894	2,608	2,333	17,800	17,850	4,090	3,763	3,436
11,450	11,500	1,910	1,665	1,431	14,650	14,700	2,912	2,624	2,349	17,850	17,900	4,110	3,782	3,455
11,500	11,550	1,924	1,679	1,444	14,700	14,750	2,930	2,640	2,365	17,900	17,950	4,129	3,802	3,474
11,550	11,600	1,938	1,693	1,456	14,750	14,800	2,948	2,656	2,381	17,950	18,000	4,149	3,821	3,494
11,600	11,650	1,952	1,707	1,469	14,800	14,850	2,966	2,672	2,397	18,000	18,050	4,168	3,841	3,513
11,650	11,700	1,966	1,721	1,481	14,850	14,900	2,984	2,688	2,413	18,050	18,100	4,188	3,860	3,533
11,700	11,750	1,980	1,735	1,494	14,900	14,950	3,002	2,704	2,429	18,100	18,150	4,207	3,880	3,552
11,750	11,800	1,994	1,749	1,506	14,950	15,000	3,020	2,720	2,445	18,150	18,200	4,227	3,899	3,572
11,800	11,850	2,008	1,763	1,519	15,000	15,050	3,038	2,736	2,461	18,200	18,250	4,246	3,919	3,591
11,850	11,900	2,022	1,777	1,532	15,050	15,100	3,056	2,752	2,477	18,250	18,300	4,266	3,938	3,611
11,900	11,950	2,036	1,791	1,546	15,100	15,150	3,074	2,769	2,493	18,300	18,350	4,285	3,958	3,630
11,950	12,000	2,050	1,805	1,560	15,150	15,200	3,092	2,787	2,509	18,350	18,400	4,306	3,977	3,650
12,000	12,050	2,064	1,819	1,574	15,200	15,250	3,110	2,805	2,525	18,400	18,450	4,327	3,997	3,669
12,050	12,100	2,078	1,833	1,588	15,250	15,300	3,128	2,823	2,541	18,450	18,500	4,348	4,016	3,689
12,100	12,150	2,092	1,847	1,602	15,300	15,350	3,146	2,841	2,557	18,500	18,550	4,369	4,036	3,708
12,150	12,200	2,106	1,861	1,616	15,350	15,400	3,164	2,859	2,573	18,550	18,600	4,390	4,055	3,728
12,200	12,250	2,120	1,875	1,630	15,400	15,450	3,182	2,877	2,589	18,600	18,650	4,411	4,075	3,747
12,250	12,300	2,134	1,889	1,644	15,450	15,500	3,200	2,895	2,605	18,650	18,700	4,432	4,094	3,767
12,300	12,350	2,148	1,903	1,658	15,500	15,550	3,218	2,913	2,621	18,700	18,750	4,453	4,114	3,786
12,350	12,400	2,163	1,917	1,672	15,550	15,600	3,236	2,931	2,637	18,750	18,800	4,474	4,133	3,806
12,400	12,450	2,179	1,931	1,686	15,600	15,650	3,254	2,949	2,653	18,800	18,850	4,495	4,153	3,825
12,450	12,500	2,195	1,945	1,700	15,650	15,700	3,272	2,967	2,669	18,850	18,900	4,516	4,172	3,845
12,500	12,550	2,211	1,959	1,714	15,700	15,750	3,290	2,985	2,685	18,900	18,950	4,537	4,192	3,864
12,550	12,600	2,227	1,973	1,728	15,750	15,800	3,308	3,003	2,701	18,950	19,000	4,558	4,211	3,884
12,600	12,650	2,243	1,987	1,742	15,800	15,850	3,326	3,021	2,717	19,000	19,050	4,579	4,231	3,903
12,650	12,700	2,259	2,001	1,756	15,850	15,900	3,344	3,039	2,734	19,050	19,100	4,600	4,250	3,923
12,700	12,750	2,275	2,015	1,770	15,900	15,950	3,362	3,057	2,752	19,100	19,150	4,621	4,271	3,942
12,750	12,800	2,291	2,029	1,784	15,950	16,000	3,380	3,075	2,770	19,150	19,200	4,642	4,292	3,962
12,800	12,850	2,307	2,043	1,798	16,000	16,050	3,398	3,093	2,788	19,200	19,250	4,663	4,313	3,981
12,850	12,900	2,323	2,057	1,812	16,050	16,100	3,416	3,111	2,806	19,250	19,300	4,684	4,334	4,001
12,900	12,950	2,339	2,071	1,826	16,100	16,150	3,434	3,129	2,824	19,300	19,350	4,705	4,355	4,020
12,950	13,000	2,355	2,085	1,840	16,150	16,200	3,452	3,147	2,842	19,350	19,400	4,726	4,376	4,040
13,000	13,050	2,371	2,099	1,854	16,200	16,250	3,470	3,165	2,860	19,400	19,450	4,747	4,397	4,059
13,050	13,100	2,387	2,113	1,868	16,250	16,300	3,488	3,183	2,878	19,450	19,500	4,768	4,418	4,079
13,100	13,150	2,403	2,128	1,882	16,300	16,350	3,506	3,201	2,896	19,500	19,550	4,789	4,439	4,098
13,150	13,200	2,419	2,144	1,896	16,350	16,400	3,525	3,219	2,914	19,550	19,600	4,810	4,460	4,118
13,200	13,250	2,435	2,160	1,910	16,400	16,450	3,544	3,237	2,932	19,600	19,650	4,831	4,481	4,137
13,250	13,300	2,451	2,176	1,924	16,450	16,500	3,564	3,255	2,950	19,650	19,700	4,852	4,502	4,157
13,300	13,350	2,467	2,192	1,938	16,500	16,550	3,583	3,273	2,968	19,700	19,750	4,873	4,523	4,176
13,350	13,400	2,483	2,208	1,952	16,550	16,600	3,603	3,291	2,986	19,750	19,800	4,894	4,544	4,196
13,400	13,450	2,499	2,224	1,966	16,600	16,650	3,622	3,309	3,004	19,800	19,850	4,915	4,565	4,215
13,450	13,500	2,515	2,240	1,980	16,650	16,700	3,642	3,327	3,022	19,850	19,900	4,936	4,586	4,236
13,500	13,550	2,531	2,256	1,994	16,700	16,750	3,661	3,345	3,040	19,900	19,950	4,957	4,607	4,257
13,550	13,600	2,547	2,272	2,008	16,750	16,800	3,681	3,363	3,058	19,950	20,000	4,978	4,628	4,278
13,600	13,650	2,563	2,288	2,022	16,800	16,850	3,700	3,381	3,076					
13,650	13,700	2,579	2,304	2,036	16,850	16,900	3,720	3,399	3,094					
13,700	13,750	2,595	2,320	2,050	16,900	16,950	3,739	3,417	3,112					
13,750	13,800	2,611	2,336	2,064	16,950	17,000	3,759	3,435	3,130					

Continued next column   Continued next column

1977 Tax Table D—HEAD OF HOUSEHOLD (Box 4)

(For unmarried (including certain married persons living apart) or legally separated persons who qualify as heads of household with tax table income of $20,000 or less who claim fewer than 9 exemptions)

To find your tax: Read down the left income column until you find your income as shown on line 34 of Form 1040. Read across to the column headed by the total number of exemptions claimed on line 7 of Form 1040. The amount shown at the point where the two lines meet is your tax. Enter on Form 1040, line 35.

The $2,200 zero bracket amount, your deduction for exemptions and the general tax credit have been taken into account in figuring the tax shown in this table. **Do not take a separate deduction for them.**

If line 34, Form 1040 is— Over	But not over	And the total number of exemptions claimed on line 7 is— 1	2	3	4	5	6	7	8	If line 34, Form 1040 is— Over	But not over	And the total number of exemptions claimed on line 7 is— 1	2	3	4	5	6	7	8
		Your tax is—										Your tax is—							
If $3,200 or less your tax is 0										6,000	6,050	432	289	127	0	0	0	0	0
										6,050	6,100	440	298	135	0	0	0	0	0
3,200	3,250	4	0	0	0	0	0	0	0	6,100	6,150	448	307	143	0	0	0	0	0
3,250	3,300	11	0	0	0	0	0	0	0	6,150	6,200	456	316	151	0	0	0	0	0
3,300	3,350	18	0	0	0	0	0	0	0	6,200	6,250	464	325	159	4	0	0	0	0
3,350	3,400	25	0	0	0	0	0	0	0	6,250	6,300	472	334	167	12	0	0	0	0
3,400	3,450	32	0	0	0	0	0	0	0	6,300	6,350	480	343	175	20	0	0	0	0
3,450	3,500	39	0	0	0	0	0	0	0	6,350	6,400	488	352	183	28	0	0	0	0
3,500	3,550	46	0	0	0	0	0	0	0	6,400	6,450	496	361	191	36	0	0	0	0
3,550	3,600	53	0	0	0	0	0	0	0	6,450	6,500	504	370	200	44	0	0	0	0
3,600	3,650	60	0	0	0	0	0	0	0	6,500	6,550	512	379	209	52	0	0	0	0
3,650	3,700	67	0	0	0	0	0	0	0	6,550	6,600	520	388	218	60	0	0	0	0
3,700	3,750	74	0	0	0	0	0	0	0	6,600	6,650	528	397	227	68	0	0	0	0
3,750	3,800	81	0	0	0	0	0	0	0	6,650	6,700	536	406	236	76	0	0	0	0
3,800	3,850	88	0	0	0	0	0	0	0	6,700	6,750	544	415	245	84	0	0	0	0
3,850	3,900	95	0	0	0	0	0	0	0	6,750	6,800	552	424	254	92	0	0	0	0
3,900	3,950	102	0	0	0	0	0	0	0	6,800	6,850	560	433	263	100	0	0	0	0
3,950	4,000	109	0	0	0	0	0	0	0	6,850	6,900	568	442	272	108	0	0	0	0
4,000	4,050	117	0	0	0	0	0	0	0	6,900	6,950	576	451	281	116	0	0	0	0
4,050	4,100	125	0	0	0	0	0	0	0	6,950	7,000	584	460	290	124	0	0	0	0
4,100	4,150	133	0	0	0	0	0	0	0	7,000	7,050	593	469	299	132	0	0	0	0
4,150	4,200	141	0	0	0	0	0	0	0	7,050	7,100	601	478	308	140	0	0	0	0
4,200	4,250	149	4	0	0	0	0	0	0	7,100	7,150	610	487	317	148	0	0	0	0
4,250	4,300	157	11	0	0	0	0	0	0	7,150	7,200	618	496	326	156	1	0	0	0
4,300	4,350	165	18	0	0	0	0	0	0	7,200	7,250	627	504	335	165	9	0	0	0
4,350	4,400	173	25	0	0	0	0	0	0	7,250	7,300	635	512	344	174	17	0	0	0
4,400	4,450	181	32	0	0	0	0	0	0	7,300	7,350	644	520	353	183	25	0	0	0
4,450	4,500	189	39	0	0	0	0	0	0	7,350	7,400	652	528	362	192	33	0	0	0
4,500	4,550	197	46	0	0	0	0	0	0	7,400	7,450	661	536	371	201	41	0	0	0
4,550	4,600	205	53	0	0	0	0	0	0	7,450	7,500	669	544	380	210	49	0	0	0
4,600	4,650	213	60	0	0	0	0	0	0	7,500	7,550	678	552	389	219	57	0	0	0
4,650	4,700	221	67	0	0	0	0	0	0	7,550	7,600	686	560	398	228	65	0	0	0
4,700	4,750	229	74	0	0	0	0	0	0	7,600	7,650	695	568	407	237	73	0	0	0
4,750	4,800	236	82	0	0	0	0	0	0	7,650	7,700	703	576	416	246	81	0	0	0
4,800	4,850	243	90	0	0	0	0	0	0	7,700	7,750	712	584	425	255	89	0	0	0
4,850	4,900	250	98	0	0	0	0	0	0	7,750	7,800	720	593	434	264	97	0	0	0
4,900	4,950	257	106	0	0	0	0	0	0	7,800	7,850	729	601	443	273	105	0	0	0
4,950	5,000	264	114	0	0	0	0	0	0	7,850	7,900	737	610	452	282	113	0	0	0
5,000	5,050	272	122	0	0	0	0	0	0	7,900	7,950	746	618	461	291	121	0	0	0
5,050	5,100	280	130	0	0	0	0	0	0	7,950	8,000	754	627	470	300	130	0	0	0
5,100	5,150	288	138	0	0	0	0	0	0	8,000	8,050	763	635	479	309	139	0	0	0
5,150	5,200	296	146	0	0	0	0	0	0	8,050	8,100	771	644	488	318	148	0	0	0
5,200	5,250	304	154	4	0	0	0	0	0	8,100	8,150	780	652	497	327	157	0	0	0
5,250	5,300	312	162	11	0	0	0	0	0	8,150	8,200	788	661	506	336	166	6	0	0
5,300	5,350	320	170	18	0	0	0	0	0	8,200	8,250	797	669	515	345	175	14	0	0
5,350	5,400	328	178	25	0	0	0	0	0	8,250	8,300	805	678	524	354	184	22	0	0
5,400	5,450	336	186	32	0	0	0	0	0	8,300	8,350	814	686	533	363	193	30	0	0
5,450	5,500	344	194	39	0	0	0	0	0	8,350	8,400	822	695	542	372	202	38	0	0
5,500	5,550	352	202	47	0	0	0	0	0	8,400	8,450	831	703	551	381	211	46	0	0
5,550	5,600	360	210	55	0	0	0	0	0	8,450	8,500	839	712	560	390	220	54	0	0
5,600	5,650	368	218	63	0	0	0	0	0	8,500	8,550	848	720	569	399	229	62	0	0
5,650	5,700	376	226	71	0	0	0	0	0	8,550	8,600	856	729	579	408	238	70	0	0
5,700	5,750	384	235	79	0	0	0	0	0	8,600	8,650	865	737	588	417	247	78	0	0
5,750	5,800	392	244	87	0	0	0	0	0	8,650	8,700	873	746	598	426	256	86	0	0
5,800	5,850	400	253	95	0	0	0	0	0	8,700	8,750	882	754	607	435	265	95	0	0
5,850	5,900	408	262	103	0	0	0	0	0	8,750	8,800	890	763	617	444	274	104	0	0
5,900	5,950	416	271	111	0	0	0	0	0										
5,950	6,000	424	280	119	0	0	0	0	0										

Continued next column

Continued on next page

1977 Tax Table D—HEAD OF HOUSEHOLD (Box 4)

(Continued)

(If your income or exemptions are not covered, use Schedule TC (Form 1040), Part I to figure your tax)

If line 34, Form 1040 is— Over	But not over	1	2	3	4	5	6	7	8
		Your tax is—							
8,800	8,850	899	771	626	453	283	113	0	0
8,850	8,900	907	780	636	462	292	122	0	0
8,900	8,950	916	788	645	471	301	131	0	0
8,950	9,000	925	797	655	480	310	140	0	0
9,000	9,050	935	805	664	489	319	149	0	0
9,050	9,100	945	814	674	498	328	158	0	0
9,100	9,150	955	822	683	507	337	167	3	0
9,150	9,200	965	831	693	516	346	176	11	0
9,200	9,250	975	839	702	525	355	185	19	0
9,250	9,300	985	848	712	534	364	194	27	0
9,300	9,350	995	856	721	544	373	203	35	0
9,350	9,400	1,005	865	731	553	382	212	43	0
9,400	9,450	1,015	873	740	563	391	221	51	0
9,450	9,500	1,025	882	750	572	400	230	60	0
9,500	9,550	1,035	890	759	582	409	239	69	0
9,550	9,600	1,045	899	769	591	418	248	78	0
9,600	9,650	1,055	907	778	601	427	257	87	0
9,650	9,700	1,065	916	788	610	436	266	96	0
9,700	9,750	1,075	925	797	620	445	275	105	0
9,750	9,800	1,085	935	805	629	454	284	114	0
9,800	9,850	1,095	945	814	639	463	293	123	0
9,850	9,900	1,105	955	822	648	472	302	132	0
9,900	9,950	1,115	965	831	658	481	311	141	0
9,950	10,000	1,125	975	839	667	490	320	150	0
10,000	10,050	1,135	985	848	677	499	329	159	0
10,050	10,100	1,145	995	856	686	509	338	168	0
10,100	10,150	1,155	1,005	865	696	518	347	177	8
10,150	10,200	1,165	1,015	873	705	528	356	186	16
10,200	10,250	1,175	1,025	882	715	537	365	195	25
10,250	10,300	1,185	1,035	890	724	547	374	204	34
10,300	10,350	1,195	1,045	899	734	556	383	213	43
10,350	10,400	1,205	1,055	907	743	566	392	222	52
10,400	10,450	1,215	1,065	916	753	575	401	231	61
10,450	10,500	1,225	1,075	925	762	585	410	240	70
10,500	10,550	1,235	1,085	935	772	594	419	249	79
10,550	10,600	1,245	1,095	945	781	604	428	258	88
10,600	10,650	1,255	1,105	955	791	613	437	267	97
10,650	10,700	1,265	1,115	965	800	623	446	276	106
10,700	10,750	1,275	1,125	975	810	632	455	285	115
10,750	10,800	1,285	1,135	985	819	642	464	294	124
10,800	10,850	1,295	1,145	995	829	651	474	303	133
10,850	10,900	1,305	1,155	1,005	838	661	483	312	142
10,900	10,950	1,315	1,165	1,015	848	670	493	321	151
10,950	11,000	1,325	1,175	1,025	857	680	502	330	160
11,000	11,050	1,336	1,185	1,035	867	689	512	339	169
11,050	11,100	1,346	1,195	1,045	876	699	521	348	178
11,100	11,150	1,357	1,205	1,055	886	708	531	357	187
11,150	11,200	1,367	1,215	1,065	895	718	540	366	196
11,200	11,250	1,378	1,225	1,075	906	727	550	375	205
11,250	11,300	1,388	1,235	1,085	917	737	559	384	214
11,300	11,350	1,399	1,245	1,095	928	746	569	393	223
11,350	11,400	1,409	1,255	1,105	939	756	578	402	232
11,400	11,450	1,420	1,265	1,115	950	765	588	411	241
11,450	11,500	1,430	1,275	1,125	961	775	597	420	250
11,500	11,550	1,441	1,285	1,135	972	784	607	429	259
11,550	11,600	1,451	1,295	1,145	983	794	616	439	268

Continued next column

If line 34, Form 1040 is— Over	But not over	1	2	3	4	5	6	7	8
		Your tax is—							
11,600	11,650	1,462	1,305	1,155	994	803	626	448	277
11,650	11,700	1,472	1,315	1,165	1,005	813	635	458	286
11,700	11,750	1,483	1,325	1,175	1,016	822	645	467	295
11,750	11,800	1,493	1,336	1,185	1,027	832	654	477	304
11,800	11,850	1,504	1,346	1,195	1,038	841	664	486	313
11,850	11,900	1,514	1,357	1,205	1,049	851	673	496	322
11,900	11,950	1,525	1,367	1,215	1,060	860	683	505	331
11,950	12,000	1,536	1,378	1,225	1,071	871	692	515	340
12,000	12,050	1,547	1,388	1,235	1,082	882	702	524	349
12,050	12,100	1,559	1,399	1,245	1,093	893	711	534	358
12,100	12,150	1,570	1,409	1,255	1,104	904	721	543	367
12,150	12,200	1,582	1,420	1,265	1,115	915	730	553	376
12,200	12,250	1,593	1,430	1,275	1,125	926	740	562	385
12,250	12,300	1,605	1,441	1,285	1,135	937	749	572	394
12,300	12,350	1,616	1,451	1,295	1,145	948	759	581	404
12,350	12,400	1,628	1,462	1,305	1,155	959	768	591	413
12,400	12,450	1,639	1,472	1,315	1,165	970	778	600	423
12,450	12,500	1,651	1,483	1,325	1,175	981	787	610	432
12,500	12,550	1,662	1,493	1,336	1,185	992	797	619	442
12,550	12,600	1,674	1,504	1,346	1,195	1,003	806	629	451
12,600	12,650	1,685	1,514	1,357	1,205	1,014	816	638	461
12,650	12,700	1,697	1,525	1,367	1,215	1,025	825	648	470
12,700	12,750	1,708	1,536	1,378	1,225	1,036	836	657	480
12,750	12,800	1,720	1,547	1,388	1,235	1,047	847	667	489
12,800	12,850	1,731	1,559	1,399	1,245	1,058	858	676	499
12,850	12,900	1,743	1,570	1,409	1,255	1,069	869	686	508
12,900	12,950	1,754	1,582	1,420	1,265	1,080	880	695	518
12,950	13,000	1,766	1,593	1,430	1,275	1,091	891	705	527
13,000	13,050	1,779	1,605	1,441	1,285	1,102	902	714	537
13,050	13,100	1,791	1,616	1,451	1,295	1,113	913	724	546
13,100	13,150	1,804	1,628	1,462	1,305	1,124	924	733	556
13,150	13,200	1,816	1,639	1,472	1,315	1,135	935	743	565
13,200	13,250	1,829	1,651	1,483	1,325	1,146	946	752	575
13,250	13,300	1,841	1,662	1,493	1,336	1,157	957	762	584
13,300	13,350	1,854	1,674	1,504	1,346	1,168	968	771	594
13,350	13,400	1,866	1,685	1,514	1,357	1,179	979	781	603
13,400	13,450	1,879	1,697	1,525	1,367	1,190	990	790	613
13,450	13,500	1,891	1,708	1,536	1,378	1,201	1,001	801	622
13,500	13,550	1,904	1,720	1,547	1,388	1,212	1,012	812	632
13,550	13,600	1,916	1,731	1,559	1,399	1,223	1,023	823	641
13,600	13,650	1,929	1,743	1,570	1,409	1,234	1,034	834	651
13,650	13,700	1,941	1,754	1,582	1,420	1,245	1,045	845	660
13,700	13,750	1,954	1,766	1,593	1,430	1,256	1,056	856	670
13,750	13,800	1,966	1,779	1,605	1,441	1,267	1,067	867	679
13,800	13,850	1,979	1,791	1,616	1,451	1,278	1,078	878	689
13,850	13,900	1,991	1,804	1,628	1,462	1,289	1,089	889	698
13,900	13,950	2,004	1,816	1,639	1,472	1,300	1,100	900	708
13,950	14,000	2,016	1,829	1,651	1,483	1,311	1,111	911	717
14,000	14,050	2,029	1,841	1,662	1,493	1,322	1,122	922	727
14,050	14,100	2,041	1,854	1,674	1,504	1,334	1,133	933	736
14,100	14,150	2,054	1,866	1,685	1,514	1,345	1,144	944	746
14,150	14,200	2,066	1,879	1,697	1,525	1,357	1,155	955	755
14,200	14,250	2,079	1,891	1,708	1,536	1,368	1,166	966	766
14,250	14,300	2,091	1,904	1,720	1,547	1,380	1,177	977	777
14,300	14,350	2,104	1,916	1,731	1,559	1,391	1,188	988	788
14,350	14,400	2,116	1,929	1,743	1,570	1,403	1,199	999	799

Continued on next page

1977 Tax Table D—HEAD OF HOUSEHOLD (Box 4)
(Continued)

(If your income or exemptions are not covered, use Schedule TC (Form 1040), Part I to figure your tax)

If line 34, Form 1040 is— Over	But not over	1	2	3	4	5	6	7	8
14,400	14,450	2,129	1,941	1,754	1,582	1,414	1,210	1,010	810
14,450	14,500	2,141	1,954	1,766	1,593	1,426	1,221	1,021	821
14,500	14,550	2,154	1,966	1,779	1,605	1,437	1,232	1,032	832
14,550	14,600	2,166	1,979	1,791	1,616	1,449	1,243	1,043	843
14,600	14,650	2,179	1,991	1,804	1,628	1,460	1,254	1,054	854
14,650	14,700	2,191	2,004	1,816	1,639	1,472	1,265	1,065	865
14,700	14,750	2,204	2,016	1,829	1,651	1,483	1,276	1,076	876
14,750	14,800	2,216	2,029	1,841	1,662	1,493	1,287	1,087	887
14,800	14,850	2,229	2,041	1,854	1,674	1,504	1,299	1,098	898
14,850	14,900	2,241	2,054	1,866	1,685	1,514	1,310	1,109	909
14,900	14,950	2,254	2,066	1,879	1,697	1,525	1,322	1,120	920
14,950	15,000	2,267	2,079	1,891	1,708	1,536	1,333	1,131	931
15,000	15,050	2,280	2,091	1,904	1,720	1,547	1,345	1,142	942
15,050	15,100	2,294	2,104	1,916	1,731	1,559	1,356	1,153	953
15,100	15,150	2,307	2,116	1,929	1,743	1,570	1,368	1,164	964
15,150	15,200	2,321	2,129	1,941	1,754	1,582	1,379	1,175	975
15,200	15,250	2,334	2,141	1,954	1,766	1,593	1,391	1,186	986
15,250	15,300	2,348	2,154	1,966	1,779	1,605	1,402	1,197	997
15,300	15,350	2,361	2,166	1,979	1,791	1,616	1,414	1,208	1,008
15,350	15,400	2,375	2,179	1,991	1,804	1,628	1,425	1,219	1,019
15,400	15,450	2,388	2,191	2,004	1,816	1,639	1,437	1,230	1,030
15,450	15,500	2,402	2,204	2,016	1,829	1,651	1,448	1,241	1,041
15,500	15,550	2,415	2,216	2,029	1,841	1,662	1,460	1,252	1,052
15,550	15,600	2,429	2,229	2,041	1,854	1,674	1,471	1,264	1,063
15,600	15,650	2,442	2,241	2,054	1,866	1,685	1,483	1,275	1,074
15,650	15,700	2,456	2,254	2,066	1,879	1,697	1,494	1,287	1,085
15,700	15,750	2,469	2,267	2,079	1,891	1,708	1,506	1,298	1,096
15,750	15,800	2,483	2,280	2,091	1,904	1,720	1,517	1,310	1,107
15,800	15,850	2,496	2,294	2,104	1,916	1,731	1,529	1,321	1,118
15,850	15,900	2,510	2,307	2,116	1,929	1,743	1,540	1,333	1,129
15,900	15,950	2,523	2,321	2,129	1,941	1,754	1,552	1,344	1,140
15,950	16,000	2,537	2,334	2,141	1,954	1,766	1,563	1,356	1,151
16,000	16,050	2,550	2,348	2,154	1,966	1,779	1,575	1,367	1,162
16,050	16,100	2,564	2,361	2,166	1,979	1,791	1,586	1,379	1,173
16,100	16,150	2,577	2,375	2,179	1,991	1,804	1,598	1,390	1,184
16,150	16,200	2,591	2,388	2,191	2,004	1,816	1,609	1,402	1,195
16,200	16,250	2,604	2,402	2,204	2,016	1,829	1,621	1,413	1,206
16,250	16,300	2,618	2,415	2,216	2,029	1,841	1,632	1,425	1,217
16,300	16,350	2,631	2,429	2,229	2,041	1,854	1,644	1,436	1,229
16,350	16,400	2,645	2,442	2,241	2,054	1,866	1,655	1,448	1,240
16,400	16,450	2,658	2,456	2,254	2,066	1,879	1,667	1,459	1,252
16,450	16,500	2,672	2,469	2,267	2,079	1,891	1,678	1,471	1,263
16,500	16,550	2,685	2,483	2,280	2,091	1,904	1,690	1,482	1,275
16,550	16,600	2,699	2,496	2,294	2,104	1,916	1,701	1,494	1,286
16,600	16,650	2,712	2,510	2,307	2,116	1,929	1,713	1,505	1,298
16,650	16,700	2,726	2,523	2,321	2,129	1,941	1,724	1,517	1,309
16,700	16,750	2,739	2,537	2,334	2,141	1,954	1,736	1,528	1,321
16,750	16,800	2,753	2,550	2,348	2,154	1,966	1,749	1,540	1,332
16,800	16,850	2,766	2,564	2,361	2,168	1,979	1,761	1,551	1,344
16,850	16,900	2,780	2,577	2,375	2,179	1,991	1,774	1,563	1,355
16,900	16,950	2,793	2,591	2,388	2,191	2,004	1,786	1,574	1,367
16,950	17,000	2,807	2,604	2,402	2,204	2,016	1,799	1,586	1,378
17,000	17,050	2,821	2,618	2,415	2,216	2,029	1,811	1,597	1,390
17,050	17,100	2,835	2,631	2,429	2,229	2,041	1,824	1,609	1,401
17,100	17,150	2,849	2,645	2,442	2,241	2,054	1,836	1,620	1,413
17,150	17,200	2,863	2,658	2,456	2,254	2,066	1,849	1,632	1,424

If line 34, Form 1040 is— Over	But not over	1	2	3	4	5	6	7	8
17,200	17,250	2,877	2,672	2,469	2,267	2,079	1,861	1,643	1,436
17,250	17,300	2,891	2,685	2,483	2,280	2,091	1,874	1,655	1,447
17,300	17,350	2,905	2,699	2,496	2,294	2,104	1,886	1,666	1,459
17,350	17,400	2,919	2,712	2,510	2,307	2,116	1,899	1,678	1,470
17,400	17,450	2,933	2,726	2,523	2,321	2,129	1,911	1,689	1,482
17,450	17,500	2,947	2,739	2,537	2,334	2,141	1,924	1,701	1,493
17,500	17,550	2,961	2,753	2,550	2,348	2,154	1,936	1,714	1,505
17,550	17,600	2,975	2,766	2,564	2,361	2,166	1,949	1,726	1,516
17,600	17,650	2,989	2,780	2,577	2,375	2,179	1,961	1,739	1,528
17,650	17,700	3,003	2,793	2,591	2,388	2,191	1,974	1,751	1,539
17,700	17,750	3,017	2,807	2,604	2,402	2,204	1,986	1,764	1,551
17,750	17,800	3,031	2,821	2,618	2,415	2,216	1,999	1,776	1,562
17,800	17,850	3,045	2,835	2,631	2,429	2,229	2,011	1,789	1,574
17,850	17,900	3,059	2,849	2,645	2,442	2,241	2,024	1,801	1,585
17,900	17,950	3,073	2,863	2,658	2,456	2,254	2,036	1,814	1,597
17,950	18,000	3,087	2,877	2,672	2,469	2,267	2,049	1,826	1,608
18,000	18,050	3,101	2,891	2,685	2,483	2,280	2,061	1,839	1,620
18,050	18,100	3,115	2,905	2,699	2,496	2,294	2,074	1,851	1,631
18,100	18,150	3,129	2,919	2,712	2,510	2,307	2,086	1,864	1,643
18,150	18,200	3,143	2,933	2,726	2,523	2,321	2,099	1,876	1,654
18,200	18,250	3,157	2,947	2,739	2,537	2,334	2,111	1,889	1,666
18,250	18,300	3,171	2,961	2,753	2,550	2,348	2,124	1,901	1,679
18,300	18,350	3,185	2,975	2,766	2,564	2,361	2,136	1,914	1,691
18,350	18,400	3,199	2,989	2,780	2,577	2,375	2,149	1,926	1,704
18,400	18,450	3,213	3,003	2,793	2,591	2,388	2,161	1,939	1,716
18,450	18,500	3,227	3,017	2,807	2,604	2,402	2,174	1,951	1,729
18,500	18,550	3,241	3,031	2,821	2,618	2,415	2,186	1,964	1,741
18,550	18,600	3,255	3,045	2,835	2,631	2,429	2,199	1,976	1,754
18,600	18,650	3,269	3,059	2,849	2,645	2,442	2,211	1,989	1,766
18,650	18,700	3,283	3,073	2,863	2,658	2,456	2,224	2,001	1,779
18,700	18,750	3,297	3,087	2,877	2,672	2,469	2,237	2,014	1,791
18,750	18,800	3,311	3,101	2,891	2,685	2,483	2,250	2,026	1,804
18,800	18,850	3,325	3,115	2,905	2,699	2,496	2,264	2,039	1,816
18,850	18,900	3,339	3,129	2,919	2,712	2,510	2,277	2,051	1,829
18,900	18,950	3,353	3,143	2,933	2,726	2,523	2,291	2,064	1,841
18,950	19,000	3,368	3,157	2,947	2,739	2,537	2,304	2,076	1,854
19,000	19,050	3,383	3,171	2,961	2,753	2,550	2,318	2,089	1,866
19,050	19,100	3,399	3,185	2,975	2,766	2,564	2,331	2,101	1,879
19,100	19,150	3,414	3,199	2,989	2,780	2,577	2,345	2,114	1,891
19,150	19,200	3,430	3,213	3,003	2,793	2,591	2,358	2,126	1,904
19,200	19,250	3,445	3,227	3,017	2,807	2,604	2,372	2,139	1,916
19,250	19,300	3,461	3,241	3,031	2,821	2,618	2,385	2,151	1,929
19,300	19,350	3,476	3,255	3,045	2,835	2,631	2,399	2,164	1,941
19,350	19,400	3,492	3,269	3,059	2,849	2,645	2,412	2,176	1,954
19,400	19,450	3,507	3,283	3,073	2,863	2,658	2,426	2,189	1,966
19,450	19,500	3,523	3,297	3,087	2,877	2,672	2,439	2,202	1,979
19,500	19,550	3,538	3,311	3,101	2,891	2,685	2,453	2,215	1,991
19,550	19,600	3,554	3,325	3,115	2,905	2,699	2,466	2,229	2,004
19,600	19,650	3,569	3,339	3,129	2,919	2,712	2,480	2,242	2,016
19,650	19,700	3,585	3,353	3,143	2,933	2,726	2,493	2,256	2,029
19,700	19,750	3,600	3,368	3,157	2,947	2,739	2,507	2,269	2,041
19,750	19,800	3,616	3,383	3,171	2,961	2,753	2,520	2,283	2,054
19,800	19,850	3,631	3,399	3,185	2,975	2,766	2,534	2,296	2,066
19,850	19,900	3,647	3,414	3,199	2,989	2,780	2,547	2,310	2,079
19,900	19,950	3,662	3,430	3,213	3,003	2,793	2,561	2,323	2,091
19,950	20,000	3,678	3,445	3,227	3,017	2,807	2,574	2,337	2,104

Continued next column

Index

Index

Index

Index

Property "(cont.)"
  mortgaging out, 302-304 (*see also* Mortgaging out)
  mortgagor abandonment, 295
  new, finding basis, 149
  new residential rental, 55
  nondepreciable, 60-61
  purchase of other, 117
  qualifying for credit, 122-123
  "real estate" into personal, 71-73
  recapture (*see also* Depreciation recapture)
  rental, 117
  replacement, 131-133
  residential, 113
  residential rental, 89
  satisfaction for indebtedness, 103
  tangible personal, 63
  tax reasons for exchange, 150
  trade, 112-113, 113-114
  unimproved, 230-231
  use, 116
  used, reselection, 126
  used in part as principal residence, 33
  used v. new, 123-124
Purchase, property acquired by, 101

R

Reacquisition of mortgaged property, 299
Real estate investment trust:
  advantages to investors, 219-220
  at least 100 beneficial owners, 217
  corporation, 218
  distribution of income, 218
  election, 218
  how income is taxed, 220
  late dividends, 220
  management by trustees, 218
  no active business enterprise, 218
  organizing, 217-219
  personal holding company, 218
  Tax Reform Act of 1976, 220-222
  transferable shares, 217
  unincorporated trust or association, 217
Real estate paper, 313
Real property taxes, 8-9
"Reasonable certainty" test, 268
Recapture:
  depreciation (*see* Depreciation recapture)
  farms, 338
  investment credit, 124-126
  sale-leaseback, 288-289
Recovery of cost method, 313
Reduction of mortgage, 296-298
Refinancing, 86
Refund, 142-143
Rehabilitation expenditures, 66-71
Related taxpayers, 79-80
Relational values, 152
Rental property, 117
Rentals:
  advance, 265-266
  bargain, 266
Rent-free apartments, 266
Rents:
  assignment, 308
  capital gains tax rates, 119
  deductions, 4
Reorganizations, 92
Repairs, 4
Replacement cost, 268
Replacement property, 131-133
Repossession, 104
Reselection of used property, 126

Residential realty, 113
Residential rental properties, 89
Resort/vacation homes, 43-46
Retiring partner, 179-180
Retroactive allocations, 189
"Reverse-interest" deal, 317

S

Salaries, 234
Sale:
  corporate stock, 237-238
  depreciable property, 242
  home, 5, 21, 23, 31-33, 41
Sale-leaseback:
  avoid treatment as loan, 282-284
  building, 279-280
  building alterations, 284
  build-leasebacks, 286
  buyer-lessor, 280-281
    advantages, 280
    disadvantages, 281
  casualty, 284
  condemnation of property, 284
  deductible loss, 286-287
  destruction of property, 284
  developers, 289-290
  farmers, 289-290
  insurance coverage, 284
  new construction, 285
  obligation for rent, 284
  pension trusts, 285
  problems, 284
  recapture provision, 288-289
  repair covenants, 284
  restoration of property, 284
  security against loss, 284
  seller-lessee, 281-282
    advantages, 281-282
    disadvantages, 282
  split financing, 285
  stockholders, 287-288
    80 percent or more, 288
    more than 50 percent, 288
    unexpected dividends, 287-288
  subleasing, 284
  tax advantages, 4
  use of family, 286
  use of insurance recovery, 284
Sale price, 105
Sales, real estate:
  acquisition costs, 106
  allocation of basis, 105
  basic tax planning, 100
  basis, 101-105
  depreciation and amortization, 106-107
  figuring the tax, 107-108
  gain or loss, 105-106
  maximum tax, 111
  minimum tax, 109-111
  sale price, 105
  selling expenses, 105-106
  tax rules, 100
  timing, 106
Sales and purchases, farm, 338-339
Sales prices, 5-7
Salvage value, 57-58
"Same general class" texts, 135
Scenic easement, 322
Scheduled income, 151
Security deposit, 4, 265
Self-employed individuals, 41-42
Selling expenses, 105